D1271726

THE BEDFORD HISTORICAL SERIES: XV

KING JAMES VI AND I

THE BEDFORD HISTORICAL SERIES

KING JAMES VI AND I

THE BEDFORD HISTORICAL SERIES

KING JAMES VI AND I

by

DAVID HARRIS WILLSON

JONATHAN CAPE
THIRTY BEDFORD SQUARE
LONDON

FIRST PUBLISHED, JANUARY 1956
SECOND IMPRESSION, MAY 1956

FIRST PUBLISHED IN
THE BEDFORD HISTORICAL SERIES
1959
REPRINTED 1962

PRINTED IN GREAT BRITAIN IN THE CITY OF OXFORD
AT THE ALDEN PRESS
BOUND BY A. W. BAIN & CO. LTD, LONDON

CONTENTS

CONTENTS

ILLUSTRATIONS

ACKNOWLEDGMENT

I AM happy to acknowledge my indebtedness to the John Simon Guggenheim Memorial Foundation for granting me fellowships upon two occasions; and to the Graduate School of the University of Minnesota for financing a summer of research. To the libraries in which I have done the bulk of my work — the libraries of the University of Minnesota and of Harvard University, the Henry E. Huntington Library, the British Museum, the Public Record Office, the Institute of Historical Research, the Register House and the National Library of Scotland — I must return thanks for many courtesies. I should mention also the kindness of Mr. R. L. Atkinson, Secretary of the Historical Manuscripts Commission. My thanks are due to the National Portrait Gallery and to the Scottish National Portrait Gallery for allowing me to illustrate my book from their collections; as also to the *Huntington Library Quarterly* for permission to use material from an article of mine published there. I am grateful to my colleague, Dr. H. D. Lamb, for helping me diagnose the illnesses of King James. Two of my friends, Professor Wallace Notestein and Professor J. E. Neale, have read my book in manuscript, to my great advantage, and I owe them many thanks. Finally, I am grateful to my wife, Lillian Malone Willson, not only for her assistance but for her patience while I have followed the fortunes of the British Solomon.

DAVID HARRIS WILLSON

St. Paul, Minnesota

KING JAMES VI AND I

CHAPTER I

A PRINCELY PARAGON

BETWEEN nine and ten o'clock on the morning of Wednesday, June 19th, 1566, in a tiny retiring room in Edinburgh Castle, Mary Queen of Scots gave birth to her only son. The guns of the castle boomed forth their cheerful message. Nobility and common folk gathered for a service of thanksgiving at the Great Kirk. Couriers were dispatched to France, England and Savoy. Bonfires flaring that night from a hundred hills carried the news throughout the country; and patriotic Scots, whatever their religion or politics, rejoiced at the birth of a Prince, heir not only to their own ancient kingdom but more distantly to a greater kingdom to the south.

About two in the afternoon Lord Darnley, Mary's husband, came to her apartment and asked to see the child. 'My Lord,' said Mary, 'God has given you and me a son, begotten by none but you.' Darnley blushed and kissed the infant. The Queen took the child in her arms, drew back the coverlet to show its face, and said once more: 'My Lord, here I protest to God, as I shall answer to Him at the great day of judgment, this is your son and no other man's son!' She then spoke to Sir William Stanley, Darnley's English attendant. 'This', she said, 'is the son whom I hope shall first unite the two kingdoms of Scotland and England.' 'Why, Madam,' answered Sir William, 'shall he succeed before your Majesty and his father?' 'Because', said Mary, 'his father has broken to me.'[1]

The scene was an epitome of things past and an omen of things to come. It pointed at the suspicion of illegitimacy which clouded the birth of the Prince; it showed how the child embodied the Scottish hope that the house of Stuart would follow the house of Tudor upon the English throne; and it contained tragic evidence that the marriage of Mary and Darnley, rash and ill-advised from the beginning, was now in utter shipwreck.

The young mother must have felt her triumph, for she was lighter of a fair son and had provided Scotland with an heir while Elizabeth in England was but a barren stock. But the clouds were gathering fast around Mary, and the birth of her son was one of few events during her troubled years in Scotland which she could regard as fortunate. Her chances of ruling that wild and lawless kingdom with any success had been small at best, and her character and conduct reduced such chances to zero. Her beauty, her charms and graces, her love of pleasure, her high spirits and reckless daring, her fondness for war and manly sports, her soaring ambition, and the burning passion of her loves and hates — these things, together with her tragic death, have fascinated posterity and given her a higher place in legend and literature than either her political importance or her natural intelligence deserves. Had she been the consort of a strong and wealthy monarch who could have controlled and protected her, she might have charmed the world. But as a ruler in her own right she was beneath contempt. Frivolous, extravagant, careless, emotional, utterly self-centred, lacking in judgment and temper, unmindful of the interests of her country, she looked upon the world largely as it advanced or retarded her personal aspirations. Her diplomacy and plottings, though daring and clever, were brittle and unrealistic, for her preoccupation with personal interests blinded her to the gulf between hope and hard reality. To her son she transmitted her extravagance, her carelessness, her highly emotional nature easily finding relief in tears, her fondness for pleasure, her capacity for love and hate. Her beauty and her courage she did not. On the other hand, James was far more intelligent than his mother.

Mary had returned to Scotland in 1561, a young widow of nineteen, after an absence of thirteen years in France, where she had been trained for the lofty place of Queen Consort, only to see her hopes destroyed by the early death of her husband, Francis II, and by the animosity of her mother-in-law, Catherine de Medici.

Those thirteen years had been perhaps the most momentous in all the annals of Scotland. They had seen the overthrow of the Roman Church, not by an autocratic ruler as in England, but by a revolution that rendered the change more uncompromising and more complete. Events in 1560 had enabled the Scottish Protestants to sever connections with Rome and to establish a new system of dogma, though the organization of the reformed Kirk was left for the future. The tone of the Scottish Reformation was set by John Knox, that thundering Scots Elijah, who called upon the people to forsake the false prophets of Baal and filled his followers with a holy horror of all things Roman. Knox declared one Mass more awful than the landing of ten thousand foreign foes. He blasted Mary as an idolatrous Jezebel because she was true to the older faith. But though the Scottish Reformation drew its strength from the people of the towns and from the gentry, it had been possible only through the support of the Protestant nobles. At the time of Mary's return to Scotland, its politics were controlled by these nobles in close alliance with the ministers of the Kirk.

There was at first a period of mutual forbearance between Mary and the Protestant nobility, though Knox held aloof. The nobles were to govern Scotland as before and Mary's religion was to be her own affair. Had she been able to satisfy her ambitions by a brilliant marriage or by recognition from England of her claim to succeed Elizabeth, her senior by a decade, she might have remained content. But Elizabeth, for reasons of sound policy, blocked Mary's moves towards marriage and refused recognition of her title to the English succession. Hence Mary chafed at her position in Scotland. In rash revolt she carried through in 1565 the marriage with her cousin, Henry Stewart, Lord Darnley, despite the angry protests of Elizabeth and of the Scottish Protestant lords. Darnley, like Mary, was a descendant of Margaret Tudor, the sister of Henry VIII, though by a second marriage. He was thus close to the Scottish throne and a possible heir to that of England. Born in England, he there attended the Anglican Church, but his background was Catholic; and the marriage established Mary as the leader of the Catholic factions in both kingdoms. For a moment she was successful. The Protestant lords were driven into exile south of the Border in an exciting raid in which Mary rode in armour with her troops. But the price was heavy. She was now openly hostile towards Elizabeth and the Scottish Protestants; she must rule Scotland under impossible conditions; and Darnley proved a vicious fool.

When he first came to Scotland Mary had liked him well. She thought him 'the lustiest and best proportioned long man that she had seen, for he was of high stature, slender, straight and shapely; well instructed from his youth in all honest and comely exercises'.[2] He was only nineteen, with pleasant boyish face and yellow hair, and with the outward graces of the courtier. But his true character soon became apparent. He was not only stupid, but vain, insolent, treacherous and debauched. Without maturity or self-control, he was a raw boy dragged to his ruin by evil courses before he ever became a man. He drank heavily, consorted with loose women, and behaved with great brutality to the Queen. The court was filled with quarrels; and Mary, infatuated at first with her husband's physical beauty and high animal spirits, soon regarded him with a kind of nausea. She turned for counsel and consolation to her Italian secretary, David Rizzio, 'not without grief to many that see their sovereign guided chiefly by such a fellow', and to a much more dangerous companion, the wicked, dare-devil Earl of Bothwell.

The horrible murder of Rizzio occurred on March 9th, 1566, less than nine months after Mary's marriage. She was six months gone with child. Angry at his exclusion from power and jealous of Rizzio's intimacy with his wife, Darnley had plotted with the exiled Protestant lords and with their friends in Scotland. The conspirators, Darnley among them, entered Mary's apartments at Holyrood while she sat at supper with Rizzio, dragged him shrieking from her presence, and stabbed him to death at the entrance to her chamber. There are hints that the plotters hoped the shock would prove fatal to Mary and her child. According to one account, Lord Ruthven gave the Queen a push in the direction of Darnley, bidding him care for his wife while the deed was done; and another of the murderers pressed a pistol to her breast. In later years gossip attributed to this night James's physical peculiarities and his horror of pistols and cold steel. Such tales may be discounted. But the next day Mary feared a miscarriage; and the child was again in mortal danger two nights later. Though feeding her heart with thoughts of revenge, Mary persuaded Dranley to desert his fellow conspirators and to flee with her to Dunbar. Escaping their guards by a ruse, they slipped from the palace. 'At midnight they took horse. The King took only Sir William Stanley. The Queen rode behind Sir Arthur Erskine, her master stabler. The captain of the guard took one of the Queen's maids behind him; and one Sebastian Broune rode single. These were all the train.' Mary cried out in anguish and swore she could go no farther. But Darnley urged her on, and the next morning found them safe at Dunbar, twenty-five miles from Holyrood. Then, by one of those sudden shifts so common in Scottish history, Mary found herself again in power. Her friends rallied about her and the conspirators fled once more to England. But she now hated her husband to the death; for Rizzio's murder 'made such an impression in the Queen's heart, because the King [Darnley] assisted thereunto, and she being then great with child, that the fruits thereof made an tragic end'.

Nevertheless, at the time of James's birth, the court was quiet. We have several glimpses of the little Prince during these early days. Sir Henry Killigrew, in Scotland on a mission for Elizabeth, saw James when he was five days old. Killigrew wrote that he 'was brought to the young Prince, sucking of his nurse, and afterwards saw him as good as naked, I mean his head, feet, and hands, all to my judgment well proportioned and like to prove a goodly Prince'. There is a charming story of James's first contact with the Kirk. On the day following his birth the General Assembly sent congratulations to Mary with a request that the child be baptized according to Protestant rites. The messenger was John Spottiswoode, the elderly superintendent of Lothian, father of the Archbishop and historian. To the message itself Mary made no answer. But both she and Spottiswoode were in a friendly mood. She had the child brought from his nursery and placed in the minister's arms. Spottiswoode fell upon his knees, uttered a short prayer, then playfully asked the infant to say amen. James made some sound which the minister construed to the proper sense, and thenceforth both Mary and her son called Spottiswoode their 'Amen'. In later years King James was not to follow so readily the requests of his Scottish clergy!

The Prince was baptized in the chapel at Stirling Castle in December 1566, when he was six months old. The occasion was one of pomp and festivity. The Count de Brienne represented France, the Earl of Bedford, England, and M. du Croc, Savoy. Bedford brought a handsome font of gold, the gift of Elizabeth. The Prince was carried from his chamber to the chapel by the French ambassador who walked between two rows of barons and gentlemen and was followed by a number of Scottish nobles, all Catholics, one bearing the great cierge, another the salt, another the rood, another the basin and laver. At the entry to the chapel the Prince was received by the Archbishop of St. Andrews, attended by other Catholic prelates. 'The Countess of Argyll by commission from the Queen of England did hold up the Prince at the font, where the Archbishop did administer the baptism with all the ceremonies accustomed in the Roman Church, the spittle excepted, which the Queen did inhibit.' Bedford and the Scottish lords who were Protestant stood outside the chapel during the ceremony. Lyon King of Arms then proclaimed the Prince's names and titles: Charles James, Prince and Stewart of Scotland, Duke of Rothesay, Earl of Carrick, Lord of the Isles, and Baron of Renfrew. But in all the festivities and pastime Darnley made no appearance although he was in Stirling, 'neither was he required nor permitted to come openly'.

The second half of the year 1566 had seen strange things. Mary's loathing for her husband had increased and her interest in the Earl of Bothwell had become the controlling passion of her life. This reckless Earl, 'a man high in his own conceit, proud, vicious, and vainglorious above measure, one who would attempt anything out of ambition', had first won Mary's trust and had now gained her love. Her ruin followed with appalling rapidity. Two months after the baptism Darnley was murdered at Kirk o' Field, just beyond the walls of Edinburgh.

> Although the loon was weill away,
> the deid was foully done.

That Bothwell was the murderer no one can doubt; and that Mary was his accomplice seems equally certain. An uprising of the Protestant lords was inevitable; and, on the advice of her friends, Mary placed her son in the custody of the Earl of Mar at Stirling Castle, for 'Mar was esteemed a trusty man, whose predecessors had oft been trusted with the tuition of the kings in their infancy'. James was taken to Stirling in March 1567. A month later, as Mary returned to Edinburgh from Stirling where she had gone to see the Prince, she was abducted by Bothwell, doubtless by pre-arrangement, and was taken to Dunbar. In May she and Bothwell were married. She never saw her son again.

By her marriage to Bothwell Mary not only abandoned James but placed his life in dire peril. Bothwell sought at once to gain possession of the Prince, and Mary was ready to yield. 'She intends', wrote a Scots lord, 'to take the Prince out of Mar's hands and put him in Bothwell's keeping, who murdered his father.' The Protestant lords, gathering their forces at Stirling, entered a bond to punish Bothwell, to separate him from Mary, and to 'preserve the young Prince, lest Bothwell getting him in custody should make him away, as no one doubted he would, as well to advance his own succession, as to cut off the innocent child, who in all probability would one day revenge his father's death'. In the strange and unnatural relations of Mary and her son, it was Mary who committed the first great wrong.[2]

Mary's forces and those of the Protestant lords met at Carberry Hill in June. There was no battle, but Bothwell fled the country and Mary was brought captive to Edinburgh amid the curses of the people and the execrations of the clergy. She was confined to Lochleven Castle. About a month later she signed, under duress, an abdication conveying the Crown to her son and appointing her half-brother, the Earl of Moray, as Regent. On July 29th, 1567, in the parish kirk at Stirling on the hillside rising to the castle, the Prince was crowned King of Scots. Knox preached a coronation sermon; and two of the great lords took oaths on James's behalf that he would defend the Protestant faith. Thus James was a King at the age of thirteen months, and could not in later life remember a time when he had not borne that title. Formal provisions were now made for his household at Stirling. Mar was confirmed as guardian, and his wife was to care for the physical wants of the little King. Provision was made for the King's wet-nurse and her servants, for four young ladies described as 'rockers', for two others to keep the King's clothes, and for three Gentlemen of the Bedchamber. Cunningham of Drum-whassel, Moray's cousin, was appointed Master of the Household, which included two musicians, Thomas and Robert Hudson, of whom we will hear again. Ample provision was made for food and drink, with an allowance for the 'King's own mouth daily' of two and a half loaves of bread, three pints of ale, and two capons. Most of Mary's furniture lay idle at Holyrood, but three tapes-tries were brought to Stirling. The King slept in a gloomy bed of black damask, the ruff, head-piece, and pillows being fringed with black. A little picture of his grandfather, James V, hung on the wall. These arrangements surrounded the child for several years.

Before he had reached his fourth birthday the government appointed two scholars to supervise his education: George Buchanan, poet, humanist and historian, and Peter Young, a much younger man fresh from studies at Geneva. Two connec-tions of the Earl of Mar, David and Adam Erskine, lay Abbots of Cambuskenneth and Dryburgh, were named to train the King in riding and in manly sports. A few years later, upon Mar's death in 1572, his brother, Sir Alexander Erskine, became the King's guardian; while Lady Mar, widow of the late Earl, continued her care for her young charge.

Alexander Erskine, says the diplomat Sir James Melville, was 'a nobleman of a true, gentle nature, well loved and liked of every man for his good qualities and great discretion, in no wise factious nor envious', who desired to see men of good conversation about the King. Cunningham of Drumwhassel, on the other hand, Melville considered ambitious and greedy. 'My Lady Mar was wise and sharp and held the King in great awe, and so did Master George Buchanan. Master Peter Young was gentler, and was loath to offend the King at any time and used himself warily, as a man that had mind of his own weal by keeping of his Majesty's favour. But Master George Buchanan was a stoic philosopher and looked not far before the hand; a man of notable qualities for his learning and knowledge in Latin poesy, much made account of in other nations, pleasant in company, rehearsing on all occasions moralities short and forceful. He was also of good religion for a poet, but he was easily abused and so facile that he was led with any company that he haunted for the time, which made him factious in his old days. He was extremely vengeable against any man that had offended him which was his greatest fault.'

A learned and a gifted man, Buchanan had long experience as an educator, but was not fitted to deal with a child scarcely out of the nursery. His age, for he was sixty years the senior of his small charge, his constant ill health, and his preoccupation with his own studies rendered him morose and irascible. He proved a harsh and unsympathetic master. A bitter enemy of Mary, whose character he blackened on all occasions, he did not conceal from the son his hatred of the mother. A story is told of a boyish tussle between James and his playmate, the young Earl of Mar, over the possession of a sparrow. In the course of the argument the sparrow met its end. Buchanan, hearing of the matter, flew into a rage, gave the King a box on the ear, and told him he was a true bird of the bloody nest from which he sprang. On another occasion James and Mar were somewhat noisy at their play while Buchanan was at his books. Buchanan threatened punishment. The King had been writing a theme on the conspiracy of Archibald Bell-the-Cat against James III; the episode flashed into the boy's mind and he remarked with impudence that he would be glad to see who would now bell the cat. At this Buchanan thrashed him soundly and answered Lady Mar with gross vulgarity when she sought to intervene. It is small wonder that James regarded his tutor with great fear and with cordial dislike. Many years later the King told one of his officials 'that he trembled at his approach, it minded him so of his pedagogue'. Nor is it surprising that James, as soon as freedom was within his grasp, hastened to escape from the dour tyranny of his tutor and repudiated many of the lessons that Buchanan had sought to instil. This was the natural reaction of a self-willed though timid lad against an early despotism.

Nevertheless he boasted in later years of his training under a famous master. He told the Venetian ambassador in England in 1603 how his tutor had instructed him in the excellence of the Venetian constitution. When an English scholar praised the King's ability to speak Latin, James answered: 'All the world knows that my master, Mr. George Buchanan, was a great master in that faculty. I follow his pronunciation both of the Latin and Greek, and am sorry that my people of England do not the like; for certainly their pronunciation utterly spoils the grace of these two learned languages.' And though James said hard things of Buchanan's politics, he once remarked: 'Buchanan I reckon and rank among poets, not among divines. If the man hath burst out here and there into excess or speech of bad temper, that must be imputed to the violence of his humour and heat of his spirit, not in any wise to the rules of true religion rightly by him conceived.' In his youthful pursuit of the muses, the King found his literary models partly in the Latin poems of Buchanan.[4]

His other tutor, Peter Young, handled the King with greater sympathy and understanding, praising his pupil and teaching him to think of himself as a very clever and accomplished boy. This method was far more successful than Buchanan's severity. Not only did James respond to Young's gentleness and approbation, but displayed affection for his tutor to whom in later years he gave substantial tokens of esteem and confidence. Young must have been a tactful person, for he was able to please the King without forfeiting the regard of Buchanan who spoke of his colleague in the highest terms.

Both tutors, Young especially, made every effort to build a

library for the King's use; and while James was still a schoolboy
he had at his disposal some six hundred volumes, probably the
largest collection in Scotland at the time. Young appealed to the
Council for funds with which to purchase books, an appeal not
without effect, for the Justice Clerk noted on one of Young's
letters: 'Si faut que le Roy dresse une Bibliothèque peu à peu.'
The Greek and Latin classics were purchased in large numbers,
both in the original tongues and in French, Italian and English
translations, along with grammars and works on pronunciation.
Collections of maxims and moral tales such as the apophthegms
of Plutarch, the distiches of Cato, and the fables of Aesop and
Phaedrus were to form the first source for the King's store of wise
saws and aphorisms. His tutors also bought histories of most of
the countries of Europe, lives of the emperors and of the popes, the
Magdeburg Centuries, and treatises on government and on the
education of princes including the works of Cordier and Ascham,
Castiglione's *Il Cortegiano*, and Sir Thomas Elyot's *Booke Named the
Gouernor*. There were many books of theology, both medieval and
modern, the writings of the Protestant reformers, the *Augsburg
Confession* and those of the French and Swiss churches. Works on
geography, cosmography, natural history and mathematics, as
well as on logic and dialectics were included. The majority of
these books were written in Latin, many were in French, some in
Greek, Spanish and Italian, surprisingly few in English.

From Mary's library at Holyrood, of which about a hundred
and fifty volumes remained undisturbed though others had been
scattered, Young recovered what books he could. They consisted
largely of medieval romances and of French and Italian poetry,
adding lightness to the ponderous tomes bought by Young and
Buchanan and forming in the field of French poetry an excellent
collection. When the young King in his late teens turned royal
rhymester he found his models in the classics and in French rather
than in English verse, to which he had little access. A number of
books were presented to him during his infancy, and these gifts
tended to increase as his precocity and 'great towardness in learning' became generally known. They included large numbers of
the classics, Bibles, Psalters and books of devotion, history, science,
magic, hunting, courtly deportment, military science, and many
other subjects. Thus was the King surrounded by many books in
his much be-tutored boyhood.

KING JAMES, AT THE AGE OF EIGHT

Buchanan and Young were determined to make their small pupil a royal paragon of scholarly attainments — a king, said Buchanan, should be the most learned man in his dominions — and they found that James was highly intelligent, that he learned with admirable ease and possessed an excellent memory. They pushed him very hard. Young has left a picture of the King's daily routine of study. 'First in the morning he sought guidance in prayer, since God Almighty bestows favour and success upon all studies. Being cleansed through prayer and having propitiated the Deity, he devoted himself to Greek, reading either from the New Testament, or Isocrates, or from the apophthegms of Plutarch, with practice in the rules of grammar. After breakfast he read Latin, either from Livy, Justin, Cicero, or from Scottish or foreign history. After dinner he gave some time to composition; and during the rest of the afternoon, if time permitted, he studied arithmetic or cosmography, which included geography and astronomy, or dialectics or rhetoric. But these subjects were taken up in turn, not followed all at the same time.'[5] A stiff agenda for a youngster!

Rarely, indeed, has a small boy been propelled on a more extended *tour de force* through the many provinces of knowledge, and rarely has more information been pumped prematurely into a youthful mind. 'At this early age,' Buchanan told the King when he was sixteen, 'you have pursued the history of almost every nation and have committed many of them to memory.' Training in Latin was a prime objective of James's tutors. The little King, with a flash of penetrating protest, scribbled in one of his copy-books: 'They gar me speik Latin ar I could speik Scotis.' But he learned his Latin well, writing and speaking it with ease. The minister James Melville tells in his autobiography how he and his uncle Andrew visited Stirling in 1574 when James was eight years of age. He saw 'the King, the sweetest sight in Europe that day for strange and extraordinary gifts of wit, judgment, memory and language. I heard him discourse, walking up and down in the old Lady Mar's hand, of knowledge and ignorance, to my great marvel and astonishment'. Sir Henry Killigrew, Elizabeth's emissary, saw him during the same year. 'The King seemed to be very glad to hear from her Majesty,' Killigrew reported, 'and could use pretty speeches, as how much he was bound unto her Majesty, yea, more than to his own mother. At my departure he prayed me to thank her Majesty for the good remembrance she had of him; and further desired me to make his hearty commendations unto her Majesty. His Grace is well grown, both in body and spirit, since I was last here. He speaketh the French tongue marvellous well; and that which seems strange to me, he was able *extempore* (which he did before me) to read a chapter of the Bible out of Latin into French, and out of French after into English, so well, as few men could have added anything to his translation. His schoolmasters, Mr. George Buchanan and Mr. Peter Young, rare men, caused me to appoint what chapter I would; and so did I, whereby I perceived it was not studied for. They also made his Highness dance before me, which he likewise did with a very good grace; a Prince sure of great hope, if God give him life.'

From Young, who had studied at Geneva under Theodore Beza, a man close to Calvin, James received a thorough grounding in theology, especially in Calvinistic theology, and a fondness for the argumentative solution of high theological questions. He was strongly influenced by Calvinistic methods of reasoning. Quick to appropriate to himself the data and methods of other minds, he took readily to the logic and completeness of Calvin's system which, starting from an infallible premise, arrived through logical argument at absolute truth. This narrow, rigid and dialectic method, with its hard and crude approach to divinity, leaving no room for mysticism, appealed strongly to him, for though he was trained in the spirit of the Renaissance, he inclined to syllogisms and to disputation in the manner of the medieval schoolmen. Having so argued on any matter, theological or secular, he felt supreme confidence in the rectitude of his conclusions.

At the same time he imbibed from his tutors a deep aversion to the Catholic Church. In 1577 he was shown a book by Archibald Hamilton, a Catholic controversialist who had originally been a Protestant. The King 'marvelled that such a book should be put forth by a Scotsman. One said, "What recks, Sir, it is a Hamilton's work." His Grace answered saying, "I love him not so evil because he is a Hamilton as that I do because he is an apostate." ' So sententious had the King become at the age of eleven!

He was taught to know the Bible thoroughly, and it was his custom to have a chapter of the Scriptures read and discussed at every meal. James Gordon, a Jesuit with whom he disputed in

1588, declared that the King 'is naturally eloquent, has a keen intelligence, and a very powerful memory, for he knows a great part of the Bible by heart. He cites not only chapters, but even the verses in a perfectly marvellous way'.[6]

On the other hand, James's tutors failed signally to instil their political ideas into the young King's mind. Buchanan taught a lofty conception of kingship. A king, he said, should be a lover of piety, his life a pattern for every citizen, his countenance the terror of evil doers and the delight of all good men. He should exist for his subjects and not for himself, for he was the father of his people. These ideals James readily accepted. But Buchanan went much further, declaring that kings had been chosen originally by the people and were continued in office through their will, that kings could not override the law, and that those who broke it could justly be called to account and in the last resort put to death. Upon principles such as these Buchanan justified the deposition of Mary. Whatever James may have thought of them as a child, he cast them aside with detestation as soon as he was free from Buchanan's control.

The little King bending over his books presents a rather pitiful picture. The long hours, the difficult material, the severe discipline, the absence of love and tenderness so important for a child, were alike misguided and unfortunate. He was a nervous, excitable, overstrung boy, and the hothouse character of his education may well have increased these tendencies. Admirable as his training was in many ways, there was something artificial and pedantic about it. The same may be said of his scholarship in later life, extensive and even profound as that scholarship was. Studies, wrote Bacon, serve for delight, for ornament, and for ability. In the case of King James, they served truly for delight for the King always loved his books; they also served for ornament, though marred by pedantry and conceit; for ability and for the disposition of business they scarcely served at all.

The inclination of a child to find diversion in the materials of his lessons may be seen in the King's youthful witticisms, carefully preserved by the admiring Young. A few are apt and clever, especially those citing Biblical texts. But on the whole they are not remarkable, contrasting strangely with the weighty tomes through which the King was ploughing. They show his homely wit, the queer turns and twists of his humour, his fondness for puns and jocular translations, and his sententious love of weighty saws and grandiose pronouncements. The word *tyran*, said James, was derived from *tir ane*, to strip one of his property. Durstus, a wicked King of Scotland to be found in Buchanan's *History*, though unknown to modern scholars, should have been named Curstus 'because he was cursed and had accursed us'. It was impossible to do nothing because *faire* was an active verb. There were puns upon *naevus* and *knaevus*, upon *verge* and *vierge*, upon *chaste* and *chased*. A *prestre* was so called 'pour ce qu'il est prest à mal faire'. In speaking of the papal claim to the keys of heaven and hell, James quoted St. Luke (xi. 52): 'Woe unto you lawyers: for ye have taken away the key of knowledge; ye enter not in yourselves, and them that are entering ye hindered.' When Young punished a small fault by forbidding the King to read the lesson for the day, which was the 119th Psalm, James quoted the Psalm very aptly: 'Wherewith shall a young man cleanse his way?' He also found relief from the drudgery of his studies in a somewhat abnormal interest in the supernatural, in the horrible and awful, in magic, in witchcraft, and in the freaks and monstrosities of nature.

He was a good-natured boy, but had fits of temper. A playfellow having told him a long wearisome tale in French, the King exploded in the same language: 'I have not understood a single word that you have said, and what the Lord Regent has said of you seems to be true, that your French is nothing and your Scots little better.' When Young told him he should never be angry, he retorted: 'Then I should not wear the lion in my arms but rather a sheep.'

Of companionship and diversion his boyhood was not wholly devoid. His constant playmate was the young Earl of Mar, a few years his senior, whom the King nicknamed 'Jockie o' the sclaitiss', a reference to Mar's ability in mathematics. At times there were other boys receiving instruction at Stirling: Sir William Murray of Abercairnie, a nephew of Lady Mar, Sir Walter Stewart, later Lord Blantyre and Treasurer of Scotland, and Lord Inverhyle. The King's chief pastime was riding, and he was often on horseback with Sir Alexander Erskine and the two lay Abbots. For dogs, horses, and hunting he developed a passion that remained with him always. The many bows and arrows presented to him would indicate an interest in archery, and other gifts included a beautiful glove to be used in hawking and two golf clubs. James recommended golf to his son, though we have no evidence that he played himself.

He was given little if any training in gentlemanly manners or in the courtly graces becoming a prince. Doutbtless Buchanan regarded such things as unimportant and even reprobate. Dour democrat that he was, he told the King that flattery was a loathsome vice and that titles — majesties, lordships and excellencies — were positively nauseous. This lack of training in good manners was highly to be deplored, for James was an awkward lad with spindly legs and staring eyes, and his narrow jaws made it difficult for him to eat and drink with becoming dignity. He grew up slovenly and careless about his dress and table manners, of which his notion, as set forth in his writings, was one of honest but crude simplicity. He cautioned his son against affectation and excess, but had little to say about refinement of manners or the amenities of a royal court.

James as a boy saw little of young ladies. Certainly he received no training in the politeness due to them. Young mentions a game of *trou-madame*, in which the King made a small wager with several young ladies, lost the game, and rudely displayed his irritation at having to pay the forfeit. As he grew into a youth he showed no interest in young women and held them in contempt. Indeed, through all his life he entertained most lofty views of the superiority of the male, views first inculcated by the boorish Buchanan, a bachelor, who thought that women did nothing but cause trouble and make cuckolds of their husbands.[7]

Thus the young King was an interesting and intelligent boy, precocious and learned beyond his years, very much of a prig though sincerely attached to his books, thoroughly convinced of his own piety, delighting in puns, fond of weighty pronouncements, amiable for the most part though capable of tempers, with bad manners and a high opinion of himself. The future was to uncover other traits, on the whole less pleasant than these.

CHAPTER II

REVOLT FROM THE TEACHINGS OF
BUCHANAN

THE upheavals of Queen Mary's reign, which had awakened old feuds and created new ones among the fierce and warlike nobles, caused her flight to England in 1568 to be followed not by peace but by five years of civil war. Her supporters refused to recognize her deposition or the legality of the King's government, while Moray and other Regents who followed in rapid succession stood for the King's authority, for the Protestant settlement, and for alliance with England.

These wars left the young King untouched, though in August 1571, he was brought for a moment into contact with them. His grandfather, the Earl of Lennox, then Regent, had summoned his adherents to a convention at Stirling, and the little King opened the assembly with a short speech calling upon those present 'to do as ye will answer to God and to me hereafter'. James, we are told, spoke without abashment. Even at five he took readily to speechifying. As he sat among the lords he espied a hole in the cloth that covered the table and, asking the name of the house in which they were assembled and being told it was the Parliament house, he said gravely: 'This Parliament has a hole in it.' His remark was remembered a few days later when the Marian lords made a sudden raid upon the town of Stirling. They were driven out, but not before Lennox was fatally wounded. Years later the King was to remember how his grandfather was borne into the castle and died the same day.[1]

The Earl of Morton, selected as Regent in 1572, had long been the strong man of the King's party. Stark and wrathful, feeling neither pity nor remorse, he was a stern and extortionate ruler; yet possessed a wonderful courage and fortitude and a statesman's grasp of the problems confronting the nation. If he proved a tyrant, it was only by tyranny that Scotland could be governed. His major role in dethroning Mary left him no other course but opposition to Catholicism and reliance upon Elizabeth, with whom he skilfully maintained good relations without becoming

the tool of her policy. In Scotland he ended the civil war, enforcing with a heavy hand an order and tranquillity unknown for
years. His enemy Sir James Melville, though regarding him as
proud and avaricious and much too fond of the English, admitted
that he 'held the country under great obedience in an established
estate'. Statecraft and avarice dictated his policy towards the
Kirk. In opposing the growing pretensions of the ministers he
acted wisely, yet he so robbed them of their revenues that he gave
legitimate grounds for the violence of their opposition to him. His
aim, in a word, was absolutism in Church and State, and he
pointed the way that the King was later to follow.

James regarded him with mingled fear and approbation. The
fierce old noble would certainly inspire any boy with considerable
awe, and the King learned early that he must simulate approval
of those in power over him. 'Owing to the terrorism under which
he has been brought up,' wrote the Frenchman Fontenay a few
years later, 'he is timid with the great lords, seldom venturing to
contradict them.' Yet he appears not only to have grasped but
to have approved the aims of Morton's policy. When the Earl
complained that he was growing old, James answered: 'Would to
God that you were as young as the Earl of Angus [Morton's
nephew] and yet were as wise as you are.' And again the King
remarked that 'no nobleman's service in Scotland was to be
compared to Morton's'.[2]

The quiet routine of the schoolroom was rudely interrupted in
the spring of 1578. A formidable coalition had been forming
against the harsh rule of the Regent. Its leaders, the two Highland
Earls of Atholl and Argyll, had friends about the King, for Morton
had been niggardly in providing the royal household with cash;
and when he discovered his error and sent money, those who had
spoken against him 'durst not alter their language because of the
King's wit and good memory' who quickly noted that money
brought altered opinions. On March 4th, 1578, Atholl and
Argyll appeared at Stirling and were admitted to the castle.
Innocently they explained to James that, having quarrelled with
Morton, they wished the King to summon the nobility to judge
between them and the Regent. To a boy of eleven, alarmed at
the sudden appearance of these fierce Highland strangers, whose
friends were gathering quickly, their request may have sounded
plausible. But it was grossly illegal: it meant that the Earls were

striking at Morton by seizing the person of the King. From Edinburgh Morton sent proof of the evil conduct of the rebels, declaring he must either punish them or resign his place as Regent. At this last suggestion the lords at Stirling quickly grasped. They persuaded James that in order to pacify the dispute he should accept Morton's proffered resignation and assume the administration himself. 'The King liking best the persuasions that were given him to reign (a thing natural to princes), resolution was taken to discharge the Regent of authority and to publish the King's acceptance of the government.' A helpless child, as James was, in the hands of his villainous subjects, he was never the victim of his own modesty, and the lamb was doubtless confident it could pacify the wolves. His assumption of the government at such a tender age made small difference in practice, for he could not hope to rule. Yet it was to increase his difficulties as a youth and to expose him to the designs of dishonest adventurers.

Then came a counter-revolution. James's playfellow, the young Earl of Mar, eight years his senior, became convinced at a timely moment that the guardianship of the King belonged to him and not to his uncle, Alexander Erskine, the friend of the rebels. Early on the morning of April 26th, Mar sought out Erskine, charged him with fraud, and demanded the keys of the castle. There followed what the Scots gently called a ruffle, in which several men were slain and Mar obtained possession of the castle. This violence, almost in James's presence, filled him with wild excitement and terror, shattering for the moment his timid nature. 'He was in great fear,' wrote Bowes, the English ambassador, 'and teared his hair, saying that the Master [Erskine] was slain; and (as I am informed) his Grace by night hath been by this means so discouraged as in his sleep he is thereby greatly disquieted.' Morton appeared and was admitted to the castle. With the King in his possession, he became once more the great man of the kingdom in control of the government, while Argyll and Atholl, seeing their strength diminish, accepted an empty compromise. The young King settled back into the schoolroom for another year.

These events had been followed closely by Queen Mary and her friends. In France the Duke of Guise hoped to invade Scotland in her behalf, while Philip of Spain, though careless of Mary's fate, saw possibilities of troubling Elizabeth by intrigues with Scottish Catholics. That Atholl and other Scots were devoted to her, Mary was convinced. She begged them to send James to the Guises in France, where he would be safe from capture by Elizabeth, would become Catholic, and be taught to be his mother's champion, to wreak vengeance upon her enemies and restore her to her rights. Of her son's worldly prospects she appears to have thought little, nor is it surprising that as James became aware of her intrigues, his suspicion grew apace. But Atholl and Argyll, though they wished well to Mary, were not inclined to follow her wild courses, and fell from power before they could construct a policy.[3]

After the King reached his thirteenth birthday in June 1579, he was permitted some freedom from the routine of his studies. There were short excursions from Stirling during the summer, and in September came an exciting journey to Holyrood. Escorted by members of the nobility with followers of two thousand horse, the King rode from Stirling, passed north of Edinburgh, and so came to Holyrood as cannon thundered from the castle.

On October 17th he made a formal entry into the capital. Provost, bailies and councillors, riding with foot mantles, and three hundred citizens clad in silks and velvet met him at the West Port, where a pageant presented King Solomon judging between the two mothers contending over a child. An oration of welcome was read in Latin. At the port of the Strait Bow hung a great globe from which a boy descended to present the King with the keys to the city, all of massive silver. Musicians sang and played upon viols. At the Tolbooth the standards of the craft guilds were displayed; and four maidens, each representing a cardinal virtue, delivered orations. Dame Religion then desired the King's presence at a sermon in St. Giles. As James emerged from the Kirk after the sermon, he found Bacchus at the Mercat Cross, seated upon a huge puncheon of wine, who welcomed him with jollity to his own town. The genealogy of the Scottish Kings and the conjunction of the planets at James's nativity were portrayed in other pageants, while all along the way from the West Port to the Nether Bow, whence the King rode down the Canongate to Holyrood, the fronts of the tall houses were draped with handsome tapestries.

In later years James chafed under such triumphs, but a boy of thirteen, not over-modest, who knew himself to be the hero of the occasion, doubtless found them very wonderful, and must have sensed the sincerity of his welcome, for he was 'a great delight to the beholders'. He opened Parliament in October, was entertained by Morton at Dalkeith, and did not return to Stirling until February 1580. A progress through Fife and Angus occupied the summer of that year. The young King delighted in a crossbow, which he carried wherever he went, and in a pied horse, a gift from the Earl of Leicester in England. At Dundee he 'ran for the golden ring on the pied horse, and ran right bravely'. He was back at Stirling in August.[4]

A new figure, fascinating but sinister, now appeared upon the Scottish scene. This was Esmé Stuart, Seigneur d'Aubigny, who arrived from France in September 1579. He was the son of John Stuart, brother of James's grandfather, the Earl of Lennox, and was thus first cousin to Darnley, James's father. Catholic in religion, French in training and manners, he came as the secret agent of the Guises to win the friendship of the young King of Scots and to promote the cause of France, of Catholicism, and of Mary Stuart. Yet he possessed such genius for intrigue and deception that contemporaries and posterity alike have been baffled as to his true intentions. In Scotland he declared himself a convert to Protestantism and was soon playing an astonishing game of intrigue, not only with Guise, Mary and the Catholic powers, but with Elizabeth and the Scottish Kirk as well. Ambition explains much of his conduct. His close connection with the Scottish royal house offered such hope of wealth and power that his coming may be accounted inevitable. Once established, though not unmindful of his original mission, he discovered he had more to gain from the favour of the King than from France or Spain or from the forlorn hopes of Mary.

James found him fascinating. He was a man of great charm and affability, of easy conversation and courtly manners, 'of comely proportion, civil behaviour, red-bearded, honest in conversation, well liked by the King and a part of his nobility at the first'. Into the dour surroundings of the young King he brought colour, amusement, gaiety, the grace and lightness of France, as well as a knowledge of life and the discovery that humanism had aspects other than the study of Greek and Latin and of the writings of bellicose divines. Above all, he brought love. Deeply affectionate by nature, the King delighted all his life in the love of intimate companions. Of this he had been starved. Now he found a person whom he could truly love, and he loved him with a passion and abandon scarcely normal in a boy. He was too young to know that d'Aubigny's charms were tawdry and superficial, that the depraved court of France had made him no fit companion, that love for such a man had many pitfalls. Nor did he understand that his favourite's French and Catholic connections were certain to produce violent repercussions in Presbyterian Scotland; and that d'Aubigny lacked the stamina to face the perils of Scottish politics.

The two formed a striking contrast; the elegant French courtier and the awkward and ungainly lad. James did not learn good manners from d'Aubigny, whose influence was rather upon his character, his morals, his political philosophy. And without exception that influence was malignant.

D'Aubigny's rise to power was instantaneous. The King gave him the rich Abbey of Arbroath, created him Earl and later Duke of Lennox, admitted him to the Council, and placed in his hands the custody of Dumbarton Castle, the key to western Scotland. 'Lennox's greatness is greatly increased,' wrote Bowes, 'and the King so much affected to him that he delights only in his company, and thereby Lennox carries the sway.' Morton's position was threatened. His enemies, led by his old foe Argyll, quickly gathered around Lennox with whom they made bonds of friendship, while Morton, regarding the favourite with proud contempt, though contempt tinged with alarm, frequently absented himself from court and sulked in his own castles, gathering his friends about him.

Plots and rumours of plots to seize the King and to redistribute the great offices of state followed one another in rapid succession. Argyll whispered to James that Morton planned to kidnap him, carry him to Dalkeith, and thence to England; at which the King, greatly alarmed, abandoned his hunting and kept close in Stirling Castle. A month later Lennox persuaded him to ride as far as Doune, but there, catching sight of armed men among Lennox's attendants, James suddenly wheeled his horse about and galloped back to Stirling. With boyish pride at having eluded capture, he boasted to Bowes that he could easily frustrate such attempts in the future. 'And into whose hands soever he should fall,' he continued, 'they should note in him such inconstancy, perjury and falsehood,' that they would shortly regret their action. But plotting continued, despite a strange scene in the Scottish Council in which one noble followed another in hot protestations of innocence, while James begged them all to live in mutual love and concord. 'The young King is in heavy case,' wrote Bowes, 'and much amazed with these troubles, and more by reason of his great affection towards d'Aubigny whom he perceives to be the mark they shoot at.'

Poverty augmented James's danger. An armed guard he could not afford. His councillors paid their own charges while they remained at court and hence their attendance was irregular. Arrington, an English diplomat, bringing a letter from Elizabeth to James, found only one councillor with the King, and though James read the letter carefully, as his tutor Peter Young instructed him, Arrington was informed he must await an answer until other councillors assembled.

The star of Lennox continued to rise while that of Morton sank, 'for he was loved by none and envied and hated by many, so that they all looked through their fingers to see his fall'. The Kirk and Queen Elizabeth should have been his allies. But the Kirk, remembering its many grievances, held aloof, while Elizabeth, unwilling to intervene in force, relied upon diplomacy and intrigue. Bowes spoke to the King with great severity, threatening the loss of England's friendship should he prefer 'any Earl of Lennox before a Queen of England'. Appalled and troubled, James promised again and again to please Elizabeth in every way he could. But part with Lennox he would not.

On December 31st, 1580, as the King sat in Council, Captain James Stewart, a bold adventurer whose fortune was rising at court, suddenly accused Morton of a part in Darnley's murder. Morton replied in bitter terms; the two men all but came to blows and were removed, but rushed back into the Council chamber. Morton was arrested.

James was now completely in Lennox's hands. Against his old councillor he took an active part, talking privately with the nobles against him. Thomas Randolph, the veteran diplomat sent by Elizabeth to Scotland, found the situation impossible. His warnings to the King were parried skilfully. 'Though he be young,' wrote Randolph, 'he wants neither words nor answers to anything said to him.' Morton's friends melted away; Randolph, after a pistol was fired through his window, fled to Berwick. In June 1581, Morton was tried and executed. The old warrior met his death with pride and courage and with a pious certainty of eternal bliss for which his manner of life would seem to have offered but slender foundation. The night before he died he wrote letters to James defending his conduct, 'but the King would not look upon them, nor take heed what they said; but ranged up and down the floor of his chamber, clanking with his finger and thumb'. [5]

At Morton's death the King was fifteen years of age and was to remain under Lennox's influence for about a year longer. He was growing from a child into a youth, prematurely old and sophisticated in certain ways, simple and naive in others. Baffling contradictions were appearing in his character.

He took great delight in the pleasures that opened before him in the freedom and gaiety of Lennox's regime. Unattracted by music or dancing, he spent his time in sports, especially in riding and hunting. Six pairs of fine horses, a gift from the Duke of Guise, filled him with joy. There was in Lennox's train a certain M. Momberneau, 'a merry fellow, very able in body, most meet in all respects for bewitching the youth of a prince'. This young gallant was a skilful horseman. 'Tuesday last', wrote Randolph early in 1581, 'the King ran at the ring, and, for a child, did very well. Momberneau challenged all comers. The whole afternoon and great part of the night were passed with many pleasures and great delights. The next day the King came to Edinburgh to the preaching. That afternoon he spent in like pastimes as he had done the day before.' At Leith, where he dined a few days later, a castle, built on boats and called in derision the Pope's palace, was bravely assaulted and set on fire. There was horseracing on the sands and a ludicrous joust between courtiers in small boats.

The young King's sports were normal and innocent enough, but he was surrounded by evil companions. Lennox and the courtiers he brought from France were licentious and filthy-tongued. Captain James Stewart, rewarded for his part in Morton's ruin with the stolen title of Earl of Arran, was grasping and immoral; and his wife, a daughter of the Catholic Atholl, now the chief lady at court, was no fit person to be near the King. She had been married to his uncle, the Earl of March, whom she had divorced on the ground of impotency though she was pregnant at the time, having been seduced by Arran.

James was falling into bad habits of various kinds. He acquired a taste for oaths and bawdy jests that remained with him through life. Swearing he severely condemned in his writings, naively finding it the more inexcusable because it was a sin 'clothed with no delight or gain', yet his conversation was filled with oaths, for which he found ingenious palliation in the plea that swearing sprang from sudden anger when conscience was asleep and was thus less heinous than premeditated sin. More cogently he might have argued that thoughts and words about God came easily to him so that he sometimes appeared blasphemous when in truth he was but over-homely with the Deity. His conscience did not trouble him greatly; when admonished by the clergy 'to forbear his often swearing and taking the name of God in vain', he replied, 'I thank you', with a little laughter. More offensive to moderns was his fondness for filthy jests. The age was not over-nice in such matters, but James achieved a florescence of obscenity that contrasted painfully with his interest in holy things.

His love for Lennox contained a sexual element. In later life he was notorious for his interest in beautiful young men, and this taste was first awakened by Lennox. 'His Majesty,' wrote the chronicler Moysie, 'having conceived an inward affection to the Lord d'Aubigny, entered in great familiarity and quiet purposes with him', a phrase bearing a special connotation in the Scots idiom of the time. The clergyman John Hacket, writing many years later in England, supplied a delicate hint: 'I pray the reader to consider the sweetness of this King's nature, that from the time he was fourteen years old and no more, that is, when the Lord d'Aubigny came into Scotland, even then he began, and with that noble personage, to clasp some one Gratioso in the embraces of his great love, above all others.' More bluntly the Scottish clergy declared 'that the Duke of Lennox went about to draw the King to carnal lust', fostering him in his bawdy talk and provoking him to dissolute manners. Ever louder grew the denunciations of the ministers until they went far beyond the truth.

But James did not spend all his time in vanities. Surrounded as he was by temptations, he did not throw away his books. His interest in letters took a new turn, for we will find him gathering a little circle of poets and poetasters with whose assistance he began his boyish excursions into original composition. The ministers complained that he indulged in pastimes on the Sabbath, was remiss in attending the Kirk, no longer called for preachings after dinner and supper, and disliked to hear his shortcomings reproved from the pulpit. But in these matters he was quite exemplary. A chapter of the Bible continued to be read at every meal, sermons were attended with commendable regularity, the royal interest in theology did not flag.

Nor were there grounds for the terror gnawing at the hearts of the clergy that the King might become a Catholic. It was Lennox, not James, who changed his religion. Met on his arrival in Scotland by 'vehement presumptions' regarding his Catholicism and by the 'loud and timeous warnings' of the clergy, he was persuaded by the King to come to Edinburgh in April 1580, 'to be instructed by the ministers who mean to labour on him till the first of June'. Strenuous treatment! James, the youthful theologian, employed his powers upon his reprobate of a cousin, gave him copies of the Scriptures in French, and besought him to accept Protestantism. The result was gratifying. In June, doubtless according to schedule, Lennox professed himself a convert, writing an astounding letter to the General Assembly in which he declared that God in His infinite goodness had called him to a knowledge of his salvation![6]

But though the King remained constant in religion, his political ideas were changing profoundly. He revolted from the democratic teachings of Buchanan. Convictions that a king should be absolute, that he ruled by divine right, and should be master of the Church as well as of the State, were taking root in his mind. They sprang from his egotism, from the counsel of those about him, from the counter-claims of the Kirk. Lennox taught him to admire the absolutism of France and to think of the Scottish clergy in the way French Catholics thought of the Huguenots, as seditious disturbers of the peace. James came to regard the Scottish Reformation as an anti-monarchical revolt against constituted authority. In that time of confusion, he wrote, 'some fiery-spirited men in the ministry got such a guiding of the people as finding the gust of government sweet they began to fancy to themselves a democratic form of government. They settled themselves so fast upon that imagined democracy as they fed themselves with the hope to become *tribuni plebis*; and so in a popular government by leading the people by the nose to bear the sway of all the rule.'

It was a pity, wrote the minister James Melville sadly, to see so well brought up a Prince thus miserably corrupted, both with a false interpretation of the events of his childhood and with evil and dangerous principles of government in Kirk and commonwealth. He was made to think evil, continued Melville, of those who had served him best and to regard the Reformation as 'done by a privy faction turbulently'. Among others, Arran 'put the opinion of absolute power in his Majesty's head'; and Patrick Adamson, the worldly Archbishop of St. Andrews, taught him he should have bishops under him to hold the Kirk in order.[7]

Meanwhile very different theories had developed in the Kirk. John Knox had held that the laws of God, needing no confirmation from king or parliament, were to rule the State. Kings who fought against God, that is, kings who opposed the Kirk, should be brushed aside. Under the stress of practical politics, however, Andrew Melville, who led the Kirk in James's reign, moulded the theocracy of Knox into the famous doctrine of the two kingdoms. He made a distinction between the civil power of the ruler, to be exercised in temporal affairs, and the spiritual power of the Kirk, to have jurisdiction in matters of religion. The first was the power of the sword, the second of the keys. The spiritual power, contended Melville, flowed from God the Father through Jesus Christ the Mediator directly to His Kirk, by-passing entirely both king and State, for the Kirk had 'no temporal head on earth, but only Christ, the only spiritual king and governor of His Kirk'. Thus the ministers ruled the Kirk by divine right of the most direct and immediate kind. In the Kirk the king had no higher place than any private person and must obey the clergy in all matters of the spirit.

The Second Book of Discipline, set forth in 1581, went further than this, for while the independence of the Kirk was inviolable the independence of the State was less secure. God spoke through His clergy, and to God's word the king should listen. 'The ministers exercise not the civil jurisdiction, but they teach the magistrate how it should be exercised; and all godly princes and magistrates ought to hear and obey.' Had the ministers had their way, they would have dictated to the State on all occasions. Any ruler was certain to resist such claims if he wished to preserve his authority.

Much of the quarrel centred on the question of bishops. Presbyterianism asserted the equality of all pastors and called for church government through disciplinary courts, that is, through presbyteries, synods and General Assemblies. Episcopacy in any form was debarred and, to the Presbyterians, bishops — symbols alike of Roman error and of royal tyranny — were anathema. But to James they seemed the only possible antidote to the Hildebrandine authoritarianism of the clergy and the only safeguard of royal prerogative in matters ecclesiastical. 'No bishop, no king' held as true in Scotland as in England.

Another aspect of government was also unfolding before the King. Of the details of Lennox's intrigues with the Catholic world he was ignorant, but he stood on the periphery of them, understanding their general drift, and was introduced to the subtle courses of a double diplomacy. He was taught to give Elizabeth protestations of friendship but at the same time to practise secretly with Catholic States. He soon acquired an unpleasant reputation for deceit. 'The King's fair speeches and promises', wrote an English noble, 'will fall out to be plain dissimulation, wherein he is in his tender years better practised than others forty years older than he is.' He 'is holden among the Scots for the greatest dissembler that ever was heard of for his years'. And Elizabeth, speaking of his part in Morton's ruin, is said to have exclaimed, 'That false Scotch urchin! What can be expected from the double dealing of such an urchin as this?'[8]

The most interesting part of the King's new diplomacy concerned his relations with his mother. When as a boy he had listened to Buchanan's scurrilous attacks upon her, his reaction had been one of resentment, and he had displayed a sentimental interest in her story. He now turned with violence against Buchanan's views. The Regent Moray became 'that bastard who unnaturally rebelled and procured the ruin of his own sovereign and sister'. Savagely the King denounced the clergy for their part in Mary's deposition. Well fed upon the ruin first of his grandmother and then of his mother, he wrote, the ministers now found fault with him as part of one continuous campaign to undermine all royal authority. He obtained from Parliament in 1584 a condemnation of Buchanan's writings; and years later counselled his son to read history but not 'such infamous invectives as Buchanan's and Knox's chronicles'. Persons, he continued, who retained in their possession the works of those arch-inciters of rebellion should be severely punished. Nor should his son tolerate malicious words against his predecessors, for those who attack a king 'seek craftily to stain the race and to steal the affection of the people from their posterity'. He had found his most loyal servants, he added, among those who had been loyal to his mother. Thus the filial piety incumbent upon a religious prince was buttressed by hatred for the ministers and by notions of the divine right of kings.

Under Lennox's tutelage he began to correspond with Mary. He wrote her loving little letters assuring her that he held her in high honour and would act in all things as her most obedient son.

The sincerity of these sentiments was shortly tested when Mary in 1581 proposed a plan that came to be known as the Association. She could not recognize the legality of her abdication in Scotland or the transfer of sovereignty to her son. Hence she proposed to associate James with herself in the Scottish Crown, to allow him the title of King, and to appoint him to rule the country in their joint names. But her terms were high. Not only should her abdication be formally annulled, James crowned anew, and her old friends pardoned, but her authority in Scotland should be so great that no important decision could be made without her approval. She asked that Catholics have liberty of worship and expressed the hope that her son would be reconciled to Rome. Her bribe was that only through the Association could James be recognized as King of Scotland by Catholic States and her implication that only through Catholic aid could he hope to secure the English Crown.

James answered that he would joyfully accept the Association. But alas! If he had a tender love for his mother, he had a love for himself more tender still. He was shrewd enough to see the harm her proposals would inflict upon him, and in his heart he opposed the Association. Luckily Lennox opposed it also, while the horror in Scotland, among Catholics and Protestants alike, when Mary's proposal became known, was very great. Hence it came to nothing, though she was to revive it later.

Her intrigues continued. Hope of aid from the King of France was now gone, she was uncertain of Guise and suspicious of Lennox, and hence she turned to Spain, telling Philip that she placed herself, her son and her kingdom in his hands. James was to be sent to Spain. But Philip, though gladly accepting her overtures, had his own policy regarding Scotland. His aim was a Catholic

King of Scots who would become his ally against Elizabeth when the great day of decision should arrive. He urged upon Mary the necessity of her son's conversion; and in the summer of 1581 his ambassador in London, Mendoza, acting with Mary, dispatched two Jesuits to Scotland. They obtained a secret interview with the King who received them cordially, assuring them that, though he deemed it advisable to appear pro-French in public, his heart was inclined to Spain. But obviously he had no thought of altering his religion, for early in 1582 the Jesuits reported a plot by a group of Catholic nobles to obtain his conversion by force.

Events then took a different turn. Another Jesuit, William Crichton, also commissioned to convert the King, arrived in Scotland from Rome and joined forces with the Jesuits from England. In their over-zealous hands the cautious plan of Philip to convert the King of Scots mushroomed suddenly into a grandiose scheme for an immediate assault upon England. The enterprise was to be led by Lennox whose terms, though insanely high, were accepted by the Jesuits on their own responsibility. Mendoza and Mary were dismayed and angered, Philip withdrew in disgust, and the plot collapsed. The King of Scots was fortunate.[9]

It is probable that Lennox, in demanding high terms from the Jesuits, was intent upon bringing Spanish troops and money to Scotland in order to strengthen his position. For things were not going well with him. He was hated by all but his own faction, and his nerves were growing frayed. His terror at feeling himself at constant struggle and daily in the presence of death, wrote Mendoza, was reducing him to a deplorable condition.

He was engaged in a furious conflict with the Kirk, having persuaded James to appoint Robert Montgomery, a minister at Stirling, as Archbishop of Glasgow under terms that left the revenues of the see in the favourite's hands. A vile bargain it was, wrote the church historian Spottiswoode. Angry deputations of ministers, waiting upon the King, threatened to excommunicate Montgomery. 'We will not suffer you', said James. 'We must obey God rather than men,' retorted the small but fiery John Durie, whom Lennox called *le petit diable*, 'and we pray God to remove evil company from about you. The welfare of the Kirk is your welfare; the more sharply vice is rebuked the better for you.' Smarting and angry, the King was close to tears. Shortly thereafter Andrew Melville preached a famous sermon in which 'he inveighed against the bloody gully [knife] of absolute authority, whereby men intended to pull the crown off Christ's head and to wring the sceptre out of His hand'. The wrath of the clergy was fanned to white heat by the arrival in Scotland of an emissary, one Seigneur Paul, from the Duke of Guise. John Durie, hastening to the King, ran full into the envoy but pulled his bonnet over his eyes that they might not be polluted with sight of the Devil's ambassador. He then berated James to his face in unmeasured terms, charging him to adhere to his religion, to refuse a Catholic marriage, and to keep his body unpolluted. Overawed by the violence of the minister, James answered quietly that his body was pure and that he would have no Catholic for a wife.

The King, to allay the strife, requested the ministers to present their grievances in writing, which Andrew Melville and other clergymen hastened to do. As the grievances were read before the King, Arran began to storm: who dared, he asked, to subscribe these treasonable articles? 'We dare and will subscribe them', retorted Melville, and seizing the pen from the hand of the clerk he subscribed and called upon his brethren to do the same. Arran and Lennox were taken aback, for they saw that the ministers must have a faction behind them.

A conspiracy was indeed forming against the favourite, its leaders the former adherents of Morton: his nephew Angus; Gowrie who had been his Lord Treasurer; Mar, the King's old playfellow; and Lindsay, a rough soldier but a good Protestant. Many other nobles joined the plot.

Suddenly in August 1582, the conspirators — their plans but half-formed — learned that Lennox was about to strike first. It happened that the King was hunting near Perth, an area in which Gowrie, Lindsay and Glamis were powerful and in which stood Ruthven Castle, a seat of Gowrie's. Here was a perfect opportunity to seize the King. Lured into Ruthven Castle, he suspected that something was afoot, 'yet dissembled the matter, thinking to free himself the next day when he went abroad to his sports. But as he was about to go, the Master of Glamis stept to the door of the parlour and told him he must stay. When the King saw it to be so, and found his liberty restrained, he grew into a passion, and after some threatening speeches burst forth into tears. The Master, seeing him weep, said: "It is no matter of his tears, better that bairns should weep than bearded men." Which words entered so deeply into the King's heart, as he did never forget them'.[10]

He was a prisoner, separated from Lennox who was ordered to leave the country; though Lennox did not go at once, James never saw him again.

PROGRESS IN KINGCRAFT

To the young King, who held that his subjects should fear and obey him as God's lieutenant on earth, his capture by the Ruthven lords was a bitter humiliation. 'His Majesty', wrote Sir James Melville, 'took the matter further to heart than any man would have believed, lamenting his hard estate and mishandling by his own subjects, and how he was thought but a beast by other princes for suffering so many indignities.' Lennox he defended with passionate earnestness. During an audience granted to a messenger from his favourite, James cried out suddenly that he was a prisoner and called upon Lennox to free him from his captors. The triumph of the Kirk deepened his sense of degradation, for the ministers proclaimed their victory with joyous exultation; they blessed the new regime and spoke to the King with harshness and brutality. One of their number, John Craig, rebuked him so sharply from the pulpit that he wept and said he might have been told privately; to which Craig retorted that the truth had often been told him privately but to no purpose. It was only with great difficulty that the Ruthven lords obtained the King's consent to a proclamation acknowledging the freedom of the Kirk. 'He spared not to say', wrote Calderwood, 'that the ministers were but a pack of knaves, that he had rather lose his kingdom than not be avenged upon them, that the professors of France [the Huguenots] were but seditious traitors, rebels, and perturbers of commonwealths.'[1]

Thus bitterly did James speak of his Protestant nobles and clergy. Individual lords he could in time forgive, though he was determined to be their master. The rebel ministers he could not; throughout his long reign he hated them with the venom of a Scots blood feud.

In an amusing passage in the *Basilikon Doron*, which the King wrote in 1598, he commanded his son to tell the truth, yet if 'some unhappy mutiny or sudden rebellion were blazed up', it might in lawful policy be met with fair general speeches. 'To do otherwise,' he added with unconscious humour, 'it were no magnanimity, but rash tempting of God.' He began to treat the Ruthven lords more graciously, hoping to reconcile them to Lennox. In this he was disappointed. Throughout the autumn Lennox lingered at Dumbarton, but showed himself 'so far appalled and cast down as there appeared in him little courage or resolution', and after the failure of a wild plot to seize the King, which goaded the Ruthven lords into threatening James with death if Lennox did not leave the country, the favourite sadly began his journey through England to France where he died shortly after.

James also gave good words to Elizabeth. He was ready, he said, to follow the counsel of his dearest sister in all decisions of importance; he recognized how deeply he was indebted to her and he regarded ingratitude as the vilest of vices. The Ruthven lords, most anxious for English support without which they could not hope to remain in power, sent an embassy to London in April 1583. In return for a close alliance, Elizabeth was asked to grant the King the English estates of his grandfather, the Earl of Lennox, to send him £10,000 for his immediate needs, and to supply an annual pension of half that sum. But Elizabeth, considering the terms exorbitant, offered only a small annual pension of £2500, which was ruefully declined.

Her decision was influenced by other negotiations between herself and the Scottish King. She assumed that he was sincerely devoted to his mother's interests, and she saw, or pretended to see, the possibility — if an alliance could be made with Scotland — of releasing Mary, provided that her good behaviour was guaranteed by James and by the King of France. Negotiations with Mary were begun to that end. But when they were laid before James the result was enlightening to Elizabeth and perhaps to James also. Annoyed to find his mother edging her way into negotiations for an alliance between Scotland and England, he complained that she did so solely to advance her own interests. He gave Bowes his version of the history of the Association. The plan had been suggested to him by his mother, he said, under guise of a friendly offer to strengthen his position, but he had shortly discovered that she claimed precedence over him in Scottish affairs. The Association was 'tickle to his Crown', and he had therefore told his mother that her terms were unacceptable. Her entanglements with Catholic powers, he continued with more wisdom than filial piety, rendered her unfit to rule either Scotland or England.

He, on the other hand, had none of her incapacities but gave promise of becoming the kind of ruler sought by both kingdoms. It may well be that the prospect of Mary's release, which he looked upon with dread, made him see more clearly that the true path to the English succession was friendship with England's Queen. There was no necessity for Elizabeth to give credence to all that he said. Her negotiations with Mary ended, and the need to pension James in order to draw him from the side of his mother disappeared.[2]

But if the King was slowly evolving a sounder policy towards England, his immediate object was escape from the Ruthven lords. Hopefully he intrigued with two French ambassadors who came to Scotland shortly after the Ruthven Raid, and he was soon telling them 'that though he had two eyes, two ears, and two hands, yet he had but one heart, which was French'. The arrival of the ambassadors filled him with joy. He was pleased to observe that their presence irritated the Kirk, he was happy that the French thus recognized him as King of Scots despite the failure of the Association, and he knew that the ambassadors would foster a counter-revolutionary party among Lennox's former adherents.

A plot devised in June 1583, to liberate the King and to overthrow the Ruthven lords succeeded admirably, though there were anxious moments. James was to obtain permission to hunt in the vicinity of Falkland and to make a progress through Fife, then slip away to the castle at St. Andrews, held by Archbishop Adamson, where members of the old Lennox faction would be summoned, the Ruthven lords excluded, and a new government formed. With courage and resolution and with surprising powers of deception the King played his part. The young cock, Bowes confessed later, outwitted him completely. So eager was James to be free, that he left Falkland several days before the rendezvous at St. Andrews. 'His Majesty', wrote Sir James Melville, who by his own account was very close to the King at this time, 'thought himself at liberty, with great joy and exultation, like a bird flown out of a cage, and passed his time in hawking by the way, thinking himself then far enough. Albeit I thought his estate far surer when he was in Falkland.' Arriving at St. Andrews, he did not enter the castle but lodged carelessly in an inn. Some of the Ruthven lords were still in his company, and Melville, losing all patience, gave him some very plain advice and hustled him into the castle. Even then there was danger. But the conspirators soon arrived in strength, and the King by his own volition was once more in the hands of Lennox's faction.

Bowes found him surrounded by nobles most of whom were Catholic, some old adherents of Mary, some in touch with Guise. It appeared likely that the policies of Lennox's supremacy would be resumed. James, indeed, had his own notions. He would put his high conception of kingship into practice, 'draw his nobility to unity and concord, and be known as a universal king, impartial to them all'. Secret, constant and counsellable, he would forgive past offences, surround himself with wise and virtuous advisers, listen to every man's opinion, then declare his princely judgment. Such hopes, of course, were quite impractical. And in point of fact the new regime quickly took its tone from the return of Arran to power. He had been a prisoner while the Ruthven lords controlled the government, but now made his way to court, quickly gained ascendancy over the King, drew to himself the management of affairs, and within a year became Lord Chancellor. This was not done without bitter strife. Arran quarrelled and bullied until the court was convulsed by disputes, and James found himself in a hornets' nest of feuds and hatreds, not only disobeyed but often treated with scornful contumely. The supremacy of such an audacious and unprincipled man as Arran, fitter, said Calderwood, to serve a Nero than a Christian prince, could only result in a regime of fierce and brutal terrorism.

James's admiration for Arran differed completely from the love he had borne to Lennox. The King was dazzled by Arran's magnificent presence. There was an imperious boldness about him, a gift for leadership and an air of splendid mastery to which James's weaker nature paid homage. What youth of seventeen would not have admired Arran? The King's surrender was far more normal and healthy than his perverted love for Lennox. Arran, moreover, was no mere cutthroat, though he did not shrink from throat-cutting. A younger son of Lord Ochiltree, he had received a good education. He was polished, accomplished and able, an excellent talker, 'quick, penetrating, subtle, desirous of goods and greatness, arrogant, confident and capable of many things'. But both he and his wife were avaricious to an inordinate degree.

He made his profit from a new trait that was appearing in the

King. For though James was more wilful and headstrong, so that
'he could hardly be withdrawn from the thing that he desired',
more determined to be master and to direct policy, yet the daily
routine of government was repugnant to him. The Frenchman
Fontenay, who came to Scotland a year later, considered him 'too
lazy and thoughtless about business, too devoted to his pleasures,
especially to hunting, leaving all his affairs to be managed by the
Earl of Arran'. Fontenay expostulated with him, pointing to the
fainéant kings of France and their mayors of the palace. But James
had many answers. In spite of appearances, he said, nothing of
importance took place without his knowledge, for he had spies at
the chamber doors of his councillors and was told everything that
they said; and though he spent much time in hunting, he could,
when he applied himself, do more business in an hour than other
men did in a day. He watched, listened and spoke simultaneously
and sometimes did five things at once. It was true, he added, that
like a Spanish gennet he lacked endurance, and constant application made him ill; but when he worked he accomplished more
than six men together. He had, moreover, another safeguard:
had he promoted earls he could not have controlled them, but he
had advanced only simple soldiers and gentlemen whom he could
easily ruin if he wished. This reliance upon petty tricks and low
devices, upon maxims of government that might be sound in
theory but were doubtful in practice, and upon his superiority over
ordinary mortals was characteristic of James. But the funda-
mentals of good government were neglected.

Ever more violent and lawless grew Arran's rule. The Ruthven
lords were treated with great severity. In April 1584, they
attempted a counter-revolution but their plans miscarried, and
they fled to England where a colony of exiled Scots, constantly
recruited by fresh arrivals, formed a standing menace to the
government at home. Gowrie, who had fallen into Arran's hands,
was tricked into a confession of treason and executed; and his
widow was treated with savage brutality when she attempted to
approach the King. Men were ruined not only because they had
aided the exiled lords but because they were worth ruining.
'These cruel and rigorous proceedings caused such a general
fear, as all familiar society and intercourse of humanity was in a
manner lost, no man knowing to whom he might safely speak or
open his mind.'[3]

The King and Arran turned with equal vehemence against the
Kirk. James's first interview with the ministers after his escape
from the Ruthven lords augured ill, though it had a touch of
comedy. When a deputation of the clergy waited upon him at
Falkland, he glared at them in silence for a quarter of an hour,
then rose and walked from the room. Relenting, he called them
into his cabinet. To their complaints of alterations at court, he
first denied there had been any, then said that no king in Europe
would have suffered the things he had suffered. 'I am Catholic
King of Scotland,' he declared roundly, 'and may choose any that
I like best to be in company with me; and I like them best that are
with me for the present.' The word Catholic was misunderstood
and the ministers began to storm, but David Ferguson explained
the King's meaning. 'No, brethren,' he said, 'he is universal
King and may make choice of his company, as David did in the
110th Psalm.' This was adroit, for James had recently para-
phrased the Psalm in English verse. But other ministers spoke
very sharply: 'We will look no more to your words,' they told him,
'but to your deeds and behaviour; and if they agree not, which
God forbid, we must damn sin in whatsoever person. Neither is
that face upon flesh that we may or will spare in case we find
rebellion to our God, whose message we carry.' The King smiled
wilfully.

More serious was a collision when John Durie and Andrew
Melville, called before the Council to answer for their sermons,
refused its jurisdiction. The King, cried Melville, perverted the
laws of God and man, and councillors possessed no power over the
messengers of a King and Council far greater than they. Taking
a Hebrew Bible from his belt, 'he clanked it down on the board
before the King and Chancellor. There, says he, are my instructions and warrant'. Let them judge him by that. He was ordered
into confinement at Blackness Castle, but fled to England where
he was joined by other ministers.

The King and Arran determined upon the overthrow of Presbyterianism, in which they were assisted by Patrick Adamson,
Archbishop of St. Andrews. He has been so vilified by Presbyterian writers that it is difficult to reconstruct his character, though
even his enemies admitted his ability, learning and eloquence.
Probably he was more the man of action than the divine, the
enemy of Presbyterianism on political grounds. The assemblies of

the Kirk, he wrote, were not only repugnant to Scripture but were hotbeds of sedition; and to maintain his power the King must rule the Church and have bishops under him. Adamson looked to the assimilation of the Scottish to the English Church, both in government and liturgy, as a step towards political union. On a visit to London in 1583 he studied the Church in England and found opportunity to confer with some of the English bishops.

A Parliament summoned in May 1584, ended temporarily the Presbyterian system in Scotland. The King was declared the head of the Church; he and his Council were given jurisdiction over ecclesiastical cases; the courts and assemblies of the Kirk were dissolved and were not to reconvene without royal permission; the institution of bishops was confirmed; and affairs of State were not to be dealt with in the pulpit. To those ministers who dared to object Arran replied fiercely that they were too pert, that he would shave their heads, pare their nails, and make them examples for all who rebelled against the King. A number of the clergy fled to England.

Although these Acts—the black Acts, as the Presbyterians called them — must have brought the King great satisfaction, he was disturbed by the flight of so many of the ministers and by the scurrilous things they said about him in England. Their strident assertions that he was devoid of religion and ready to abandon the Protestant faith would, he lamented, impair the reputation he justly enjoyed abroad as a pious and God-fearing Prince whose greatest care was the preservation of the Kirk. In their malice, he added, the ministers spread suspicion that he was illegitimate, not Darnley's son but Rizzio's, an accusation shattering to his pride and injurious to his worldly prospects. We catch a glimpse of him weeping in mortification as he bemoaned that invidious slander.[4]

The course of events in Scotland caused anger and exasperation in London. The King and Arran, as a matter of fact, were to prove more friendly to England than Elizabeth anticipated, but of this she was unaware, and her first move was to send her Secretary, Walsingham — whose importance was a measure of her concern — on a special mission to Scotland. Puritan in sympathy, he came in no pleasant mood. Perhaps it would be best, he wrote, to leave this ingrate of a King, this dissembler with God and man, to run his short course to ruin. He read James a sharp lecture on his errors, especially his change of councillors without

Elizabeth's approval. James in reply first protested his friendship
for England, then tried to brazen out a defence. He fell, wrote
Walsingham, 'into some kind of distemperature and did with a
kind of jollity say that he was an absolute King', praying that
Elizabeth would allow him to select his councillors freely, as he
allowed her to select hers. Walsingham answered with heat and
brutality. He told James that his power was insignificant, that he
was too young to judge affairs of State, that he should rejoice in
such a friend as Elizabeth, and that young kings who sought to be
absolute were apt to lose their thrones. He left James smarting
and indignant and returned to England with most uncomplimentary phrases about the King of Scots. It is small wonder that
James spoke of him as a very Machiavelli.

Estranged from Elizabeth, menaced by the exiled lords and
ministers, and aware of discontent in Scotland, James and Arran
renewed the foreign intrigues of Lennox's regime. Shortly after
his escape from the Ruthven raiders the King received a letter
from the Duke of Guise to whom he hastened to reply, thanking
him warmly for his friendship and for his offers of protection. He
praised Guise as the first soldier of the age. He was convinced, he
added, that his own virtues and rare qualities, with which God
had been pleased to endow him, must be attributed to his descent
from the house of Lorraine. Here Philip of Spain, who obtained
a copy of the letter, noted in the margin: 'He is quite ready to
confess them himself.' James was prepared, he continued, to ally
with Guise in an enterprise for his mother's release and for vengeance against Elizabeth. Less complaisant and more urgent in
its appeal for help was a second letter in February 1584. His
present difficulties arose, James wrote, from his repudiation of the
English faction in Scotland and from his support of his dearest
mother; but the strength of his enemies was growing daily and
without assistance he would be crushed. To the Pope he wrote in
a similar strain. 'I trust', he concluded, 'to be able to satisfy your
Holiness on all other points, especially if I am aided in my great
need by your Holiness.' Here was a hint, though not a promise,
that assistance might smooth the way to conversion. Appeals for
help were addressed also to the Kings of France and Spain.[5]

It was evident that James and Arran believed themselves in such
desperate straits that in order to obtain assistance they were ready
to acquiesce in an attack upon England. No doubt they believed,

as Lennox had done, that foreign troops in Scotland would at least secure their position. But they knew quite well that they were playing with fire, and their fears were underscored by the appearance in Scotland of a new figure, Patrick, Master of Gray. This beautiful, polished, and perfidious young man, who rose quickly in James's favour, had been one of Mary's agents in France and knew her secret plans. He was still in her service, or at least she thought he was. But he had become convinced that her cause was hopeless and had lost faith in the Catholic enterprise against England. Philip, he believed, was hesitant, the Pope niggardly, Guise preoccupied with politics at home. Plans for the grand assault on England, slipping from Guise's hands, were now becoming a purely Spanish undertaking and, should Philip be victorious, he would hardly bestow the English Crown upon the Protestant King of Scots. That there was little to be gained and much to be feared from Spanish imperial ambition James clearly understood. The lesson was driven home once more that the path to the English succession lay through alliance with Elizabeth. Agreement with her, said Gray, was a necessity, for James could not hope to resist so rich and so redoubtable a Princess.

Hence the King's policy was to disregard his mother's interests and to reach an accord with Elizabeth. Even while he sought aid from Catholic powers he strove tenaciously to improve his relations with England. Elizabeth was faced with a choice of policy. Should she aid the exiled Scottish lords in a push across the Border to drive Arran from power, or should she make exploratory trial of the friendship offered by James and Arran in the hope of winning them to the English interest? The latter course seemed worth a test. An opportunity arose in the summer of 1584 when Elizabeth reopened negotiations for a treaty that would provide for Mary's release upon guarantee of her good conduct by James and by the King of France.

Mary, who assumed that her son would treat in her behalf, proposed once more their Association in the Crown of Scotland, and sent to Edinburgh M. Fontenay, the brother of her French secretary. But though James received the envoy cordially, he was determined to refuse the Association, and Fontenay found him very slippery. He protested loudly he would never abandon his mother. On one occasion he summoned Arran and made him take an oath in Fontenay's presence that Scottish policy would support Mary's cause, an astonishing bit of acting. But Fontenay knew that his mission was a failure.

He has left an admirable picture of the young King whom he considered 'for his years the most remarkable Prince that ever lived. Three qualities of the mind he possesses in perfection: he understands clearly, judges wisely, and has a retentive memory. His questions are keen and penetrating and his replies are sound. In any argument, whatever it is about, he maintains the view that appears to him most just, and I have heard him support Catholic against Protestant opinions. He is well instructed in languages, science, and affairs of state, better, I dare say, than anyone else in his kingdom. In short, he has a remarkable intelligence, as well as lofty and virtuous ideals and a high opinion of himself'. He is timid, continues Fontenay, yet has a great desire to be thought courageous; there is nothing he will not attempt for the sake of virtue. Having heard that a Scottish laird passed two days and two nights without sleep, the King passed three. But if he finds himself surpassed in such labours, he abhors them for ever after. 'He dislikes dancing and music, and the little affectations of courtly life such as amorous discourse or curiosities of dress, and has a special aversion for ear-rings. In speaking and eating, in his dress and in his sports, in his conversation in the presence of women, his manners are crude and uncivil and display a lack of proper instruction. He is never still in one place but walks constantly up and down, though his gait is erratic and wandering, and he tramps about even in his own chamber. His voice is loud and his words grave and sententious. He loves the chase above all other pleasures and will hunt for six hours without interruption, galloping over hill and dale with loosened bridle. His body is feeble and yet he is not delicate. In a word, he is an old young man.

'I have remarked in him three defects that may prove injurious to his estate and government: he does not estimate correctly his poverty and insignificance but is over-confident of his strength and scornful of other princes; his love for favourites is indiscreet and wilful and takes no account of the wishes of his people; he is too lazy and indifferent about affairs, too given to pleasure, allowing all business to be conducted by others. Such things are excusable at his age, yet I fear they may become habitual.' James's carelessness about money and the shiftless poverty of the Scottish court

Fontenay found shocking. 'The King is extremely penurious. To his domestic servants — of whom he has but a fraction of the number that served his mother — he owes more than 20,000 marks for wages and for the food and goods they have provided. He lives only by borrowing.' Yet he gave courtiers the lands and revenues confiscated from the Ruthven lords and foolishly presented Gray with 6000 crowns sent him by the Duke of Guise. When Fontenay asked him about money, he first declared that his finances were in good condition, then confessed they were not and promised to be less liberal, though, he said, his youth and nature were great impediments. Fontenay told Mary not to send money to her son. James's religion, said Fontenay, though not Catholic, was far from orthodox Calvinism. The Pope he hated, but he also hated the Presbyterian clergy. An able priest could probably convert him, though if he became head of the Scottish Church and master of its wealth, he might prove obdurate.[6]

In August 1584, James sent Gray to London to represent him in negotiations between Elizabeth and Mary and to improve Scottish relations with England. The choice of Gray as ambassador had significance. If James and Arran wished to prove the sincerity of their proffered friendship, Elizabeth had hinted, they should do so by revealing the secrets they had learned of Catholic plots. No one in Scotland was so well versed in such matters as was Gray, and hence his selection as ambassador meant that the King was ready to abandon his mother, to reveal her secrets, and to reach an understanding with Elizabeth in which Mary had no part. Gray got on well in London. He did not make startling revelations, but he showed Elizabeth that James was most eager for an English alliance and that an enmity existed between Gray and Arran of which she might make her profit.

When Mary discovered that Gray was negotiating, not for her release but for an Anglo-Scottish alliance that left her in captivity, she was aghast and terrified. In March 1585, after Gray had returned to Scotland, she knew the worst. James now denied that he had ever promised to accept the Association. Coldly he wrote to his mother that he could not be expected to join in a treaty with her while she remained a prisoner. Beside herself with rage, she threatened him with a mother's malediction, declaring she would disinherit him as an unnatural and perfidious son. But, loud as were her imprecations, she did not carry out her threats. According to James's own statement, he never wrote to his mother again.[7]

Perfidious his conduct was. Yet it is only fair to add that cruel circumstance had utterly distorted the normal relations of mother and son. Ample proof he had that Mary thought only of herself. To remain loyal to such a mother a son must needs have been angelic in his selflessness, and James was no angel. Politically his conduct was eminently wise. The way stood open for a league with England, and the path to the English succession had been cleared of one great barrier. The exiled lords and ministers, still hated by James, and Arran, still suspect in London, barred cordial relations with Elizabeth, but it was growing clearer that these obstacles were not insuperable.

The abuses of Arran's intolerable government were moving at last towards their just retribution. He was the most hated man in Scotland. To the long list of his former enemies he had now added the Catholic nobles, alienated by the negotiations with Elizabeth. His insolence and that of his wife were beginning to irritate the King. Davison, the English ambassador, 'observed the strangeness of their behaviour towards the poor young Prince, who is so distracted and worried with their endless importunities as it pitied me to see, and, if I be not abused, groweth full of their fashions and behaviours, which he will sometimes discourse of in broad language, showing he is not ignorant of how they use him'. After Gray's return from England the enmity between him and Arran became so bitter that each feared assassination at the hands of the other, and the court sank into such a state of confusion, uproar, and threatened violence that Arran's heart of triple bronze began to fail him. He went about armed to the teeth, brought armour and victuals into Edinburgh Castle, and strengthened his chamber at Holyrood. Returning one night through Edinburgh to the castle, he left his wife to pass up the High Street, while he, with torches extinguished and a strange cloak about his shoulders, stole by a secret way accompanied by one servant only.

Elizabeth was now willing to negotiate a league with Scotland, and in May 1585, she sent north Sir Edward Wotton, an accomplished scholar and a fine sportsman who soon acquired great influence with the King. He brought a present of horses from Elizabeth with which James was overjoyed, not, as he said, because of the horses — though he preferred that kind of visitation to any other he could think of — but because of his love for the sender. Wotton offered him a gift of £4000 and an annual pension of the same amount. The ambassador feared the sum was too small, having been reduced from £5000 by the frugal Elizabeth, but James was delighted. When he saw the English articles upon which a treaty might be based, he declared they could not have suited him better had they been drawn at his command. He was ready to accept them at once without consulting his Council. 'The King is so eager in the matter of the amity,' wrote Wotton, 'that I fear nothing, if her Majesty is pleased to take hold of it, as is hoped here.'

Suddenly a cloud appeared. Sir Francis Russell, son of the Earl of Bedford, was slain in a Border scuffle by an ally of Arran; and Elizabeth and Wotton, hoping the affair could be used for Arran's ruin, protested loudly that it broke the amity promised by Scotland. James was in great distress. Pension, treaty, the succession itself appeared to be slipping away. 'He shed tears over it like a newly beaten child,' wrote Wotton, 'protesting by his honour and crown that he was ignorant of this practice, desiring her Majesty not to condemn him for other men's faults.' Wotton found him alone and melancholy in his chamber, his eyes swollen from weeping. Elizabeth, he lamented, would consider him a dissembler. He would rather lose all the kingdoms of the world, provided he had them, than be found false in the least word he had spoken. For twenty-four hours he neither ate, drank, nor slept. Arran was imprisoned at St. Andrews, and Wotton hoped he might be sent to England for punishment.

Yet within a few weeks the King's indulgence towards Arran reappeared. James acted with great vacillation, at one time defending him, at another promising to do as Elizabeth wished, and 'was so restless and passionate that he seemed rather a man beside himself than otherwise'. He permitted Arran to go to his own house at Kinneil, carelessly ignoring the danger that Arran might murder his enemies at court, seize the King, and perhaps take him from the country.

Affairs in Scotland having come to this desperate pass, Elizabeth reversed her policy and let slip the exiled lords. With astonishing swiftness they crossed the Border, dispersed to gather their forces, and reassembled at Falkirk with eight thousand men. Arran rushed to the King at Stirling, charged Gray with treachery in a furious exchange of imprecations, threatening to murder him.

But at the appearance of strong hostile forces before Stirling, Arran's courage failed him and he fled. In nervous terror the King attempted to follow through a postern gate, but Gray had locked the postern. The exiled lords entered the castle, knelt before the King, and begged for favour and forgiveness. Accounts of James's behaviour differ. Spottiswoode puts in his mouth a noble oration of kingly pardon. Sir James Melville declares the King spoke pertly and boastfully as though he were victorious over the exiles, yet said he would remit their faults. According to Calderwood, James met the lords with the sardonic remark that there was no need of words, weapons had spoken loud enough and procured them audience. He thanked God that they had returned with so little bloodshed and welcomed them, 'with cheerfulness as it seemed'.[8] Arran spent the rest of his life in political obscurity.

CHAPTER IV

THE HARP OF DAVID

I T is pleasant to turn from James the sly young politician to James the youthful poet; for although his earliest verses, composed while he was still in his teens, are crude, immature and amusingly ambitious, the work of a clever schoolboy, they illustrate the amiable and good-natured aspects of his character and place him in a pleasing and attractive light.

As he had emerged from the schoolroom into the happy freedom of life at Holyrood during Lennox's regime, he had begun to enjoy the genial company of a little group of versifiers, drawn chiefly from his domestics at court, with whom he lived on terms of convivial and easy goodfellowship. Alexander Montgomerie, a partisan of Lennox, Thomas and Robert Hudson, musicians in James's household since his childhood, William Fowler, a man of letters and business and uncle of the poet William Drummond of Hawthornden, and Sir Patrick Home of Polworth, Master of the Household, belonged to this group, of which Montgomerie was easily the most distinguished. He was James's 'master poet', 'the prince of poets in our land', 'beloved Sanders, master of our art'. He appears as a somewhat rakish individual, frequently in trouble of one kind or another, over-fond of drink, temperamental, but jovial and spirited and with much keenness of wit. He could turn with surprising ease from verse of an obscene and rollicking character, such as the *Flyting with Polwart*, to poetry of a highly religious nature. James had a taste for both; and though in his own verse he showed a preference for sacred themes, he delighted in the coarse jests and boisterous humour of the *Flyting* (tumbling verse, as he called it), in which one poet assailed another with salvoes of witty invective. Montgomerie refers to James's glee:

> Vhose Highnes laughed som tym for to look
> Hou I chaist Polwart from the chimney nook.

In another of these encounters, however, Montgomerie found himself worsted and was further humbled by a poem from the royal pen, *An admonition to the Master poet to be warr of great bragging hereafter, lest he not onlie slander him selfe bot also the whole professours of the art.* The poem describes Montgomerie's discomfiture and adds:

> When all was done ye hade so evill a grace
> Ye stoll awaye and durst no more be seene.

There is a hint in the final stanza that wine as well as good-fellowship supplied inspiration for James's jovial little band. 'With pen and drink', says the King, he began the composition of the poem early in the evening and had it finished before dawn,

> Such pith hade Bacchus ou'r me God of wine.

And a sonnet to Bacchus by the King, written at a later time and implying Montgomerie's final surrender to the ruddy God, suggests an epitaph for the poet's tomb:

> Here lyes whome Bacchus by his wyne
> Hath trapped first, and made him render sine. (*surrender thereafter*)

In these convivial gatherings the discussions to which the King was accustomed at his meals could easily be turned from sacred to literary themes. There was talk of the respective merits of ancient and modern languages as vehicles for literary expression, of the introduction into Scotland of new literary forms, of appropriate themes for poems, translations, and paraphrases. James set a number of his companions at literary labours which he deemed suitable for their talents. It was at the King's command that Thomas Hudson translated *La Judith* by the French poet Sallust du Bartas. Hudson explains in his dedication that James, as he was discoursing at table, had expressed the opinion that not only the Greek of Homer and the Latin of Virgil but also the lofty French of du Bartas were inimitable in English. Hudson had ventured to differ. 'Whereupon it pleased your Majesty to assign me *The Historie of Judith* as an agreeable subject to your Highness to be turned by me into English verse.' Hudson adds that when his work was complete it was 'corrected by your Majesty's own hand'.[1] James also suggested to William Fowler that he translate the *Triumphs* of Petrarch, and though the translation was never printed, there is a sonnet by the King in its praise. Every age, James says, had produced its poets:

So loftie Petrarch his renoume did blaze
In toungue Italique in a sugred stile
And to the circled skies his name did raise
For he by poems that he did compile
  In triumphe ledde love, chastness, deathe, and fame
  Bot thou [Fowler] triumphes ouer Petrarch's propre
          name.

The writers in this little circle admired each other's work in verses of extravagant praise, of which the lion's share was naturally accorded to royalty.

James's juvenile poems are found in two slender volumes: *Essayes of a Prentise in the Divine Art of Poesie* and *His Majesties Poeticall Exercises at Vacant Houres.* The first appeared in 1584 when he was eighteen and the second in 1591 when he was twenty-five. All these verses, however, were probably written while he was in his teens, for in a preface to the second volume he excuses faults by saying that he 'composed these things in his very young and tender years wherein nature (except she were a monster) can admit no perfection' and that now when his age is riper his affairs give him no time to revise his rough and unpolished work. 'Scarcely but at stolen moments have I the leisure to blink upon any paper, and yet not that with free and unvexed spirit.' We know, however, that some revision was made at the time of publication. The juvenilia in these little volumes are supplemented by two modern collections of his poems.[2]

The *Essayes of a Prentise* includes a short study in prose upon the technique of writing verse, *Ane Schort Treatise, Conteining some Reulis and Cautelis to be observit and eschewit in Scottis Poesie.* It is a schoolboy's essay, expounding with amusing gravity the most obvious matters. Faulty rhymes and weak endings should be avoided 'except necessity compel you', accented and unaccented syllables should fall in proper cadence, of which 'your ear must be the only judge'. The words of a poem should follow each other naturally and be appropriate to the theme. Alliteration, similes and proverbs are admired as ornaments to verse, but trite expressions are to be shunned. Thus a poet in describing his beloved should not dwell upon her shape and fairness — for this has been rather overdone — but touch upon them lightly, saying they pass his powers of description and leaving the reader to judge whether the lady be not a match for Venus. A poet should select his themes with originality but should avoid topics, such as philosophy or affairs of State, too lofty for him to meddle with.

Right valiantly James strove to follow his own rules. Thus in the fragment of a masque he attempts to make his characters speak in language appropriate to their callings. But the effect is heavy, and the one bright touch is unconscious. A number of rivals are seeking the hand of a certain lady and each explains his qualifications at some length when suddenly the lady interrupts the argument to ask coyly whether this rivalry can possibly have anything to do with her.

Thus armed with mechanical rules and fortified by Montgomerie's assistance, the King took his 'painful pen' in hand and produced the *Essayes of a Prentise*. The volume opens with a number of laudatory sonnets by members of James's literary entourage who assure him that he possesses every virtue known to earth or heaven.

> O Macedon, adorned with heavenly grace,
> O Roman stout, adorned with learned skill,
> The Monarchs all to thee shall quit their place.
> Thy endless fame shall all the world fulfill.

Then follows a sequence of twelve sonnets by the King invoking the aid of a whole galaxy of Greek and Roman gods and of the nine muses as well.

> Of all that may the perfyte Poems make,
> I pray you let my verses have no lake.

The longest poem in the volume is a translation from the French of Sallust du Bartas's *Uranie*, to which we will turn presently.

Another poem of some length, *Ane Metaphoricall Invention of a Tragedie called Phoenix*, is a lament for the death of Lennox. After an invocation to the grisly ghosts that live with Pluto grim, James tells the story of the Phoenix, a beautiful bird that makes its way from Arabia to Scotland, where it is tamed and beloved by the King. But other birds grow envious of the Phoenix and attack it. It seeks the protection of James, who defends it until he drips with blood, but eventually the Phoenix flies away and dies in a foreign land. This poem, though puerile, possesses more feeling than does the empty jumble of the King's introductory sonnets. There follows a paraphrase of a passage from the Roman poet Lucan, and here, contrary to his rules, James touches a political theme. Should all the streams of the world cease to flow into the ocean, he contends, the ocean would be unaffected, and in the same way if the subjects of a king foolishly rebel against him, the king remains unharmed. A few oddments conclude the volume: a poetical rendering of the 104th Psalm, a poem on time in which the King laments sloth in others though not in himself, a sonnet declaring that great things may spring from small beginnings, a glossary of classical names drawn doubtless from some copy-book. A few vacant pages remain. 'I have inserted for the filling out of these vacant pages', the King remarks with unusual economy, 'the very words of Plinius upon the Phoenix. I helped myself also in my tragedy thereof with the Phoenix of Lactantius Firmianus, with Gesnerus de Avibus, and divers others, but I have only inserted these foresaid words of Plinius because I follow him most in my tragedy. Farewell.'

That Montgomerie supplied the King with models, ideas, and very material aid in composition is evident throughout the volume. James began to write, as he began to rule, at such an early age — he is said to have composed his first verses at fifteen[3] — that he could not hope to surmount the difficulties before him without assistance, and his boyish dependence upon Montgomerie is perfectly understandable. But he was learning some unfortunate lessons. There was, for instance, a very close similarity between his essay on the technique of writing verse and a book on that subject by the English poet George Gascoigne; and though the age was one of carelessness in acknowledging authorities, it is clear that the King did not shrink from petty plagiarism.

Both volumes of his youthful verse contained translations of poems by Sallust du Bartas: his *Uranie*, his *Furies* and fragments of some of his other writings. Thus opened another phase of the King's poetic endeavours. Du Bartas, a Huguenot, represented a school of Christian poetry which had arisen in opposition to the secular and pagan literature of the Renaissance. This Christian verse was devoted to divine and holy themes, to the praise and glory of God, in contrast to the bawdy ballads of secular poets, those 'madrigal fellows, whose only business in verse is to rhyme a poor sixpenny soul a suburb sinner into hell'. The Christian poet sang of God, as David did upon his harp, eschewing ditties of wars and princely amours. He besought heaven for that inspiration which had animated Moses and David and other penmen of the Holy Ghost. In 1574 du Bartas introduced a Christian muse, Urania, the classical goddess of astronomy, who came to be identified in divine poetry with the Holy Spirit and was the heavenly muse invoked by Milton in the opening lines of *Paradise Lost*. She appeared before du Bartas, the poet explains, and begged him to turn to Christian poetry. The inspiration to compose celestial verse, she said, was a gift from heaven, a divine fury which descended upon the poet, lifting him above his earthly limitations and bestowing upon him a heavenly elevation of thought and expression. And eternal fame awaited those who sang of things eternal.[4]

The writings of du Bartas had a profound influence upon the young King. James was in his own opinion a deeply religious Prince, well versed in the Scriptures and in theology, with a pardonable ambition to make these qualities more generally known. He had at the same time a youthful urge to write and to emulate the authors he admired. For a merging of these aspirations du Bartas opened the way, and James quickly assumed the role of Christian poet. He was, he believed, the elect of heaven, chosen not only to rule the State and to be a nursing father of the Church, but also to publish, to elucidate and to defend the Scriptures. Even as David and Solomon had written of the works of God, so the young King of Scots, their sixteenth-century equivalent, would write in his own day. This conception, merging with his vanity, became deeply embedded in his character and remained with him through life. He was to fancy himself a David as he rewrote the Psalms in doggerel English verse; a Solomon as he set forth golden sentences and pious precepts in the *Basilikon Doron*. He was to think of himself as St. Paul as he composed 'An Epistle to the Whole Church Militant in whatever part of the Earth'; and as one of the early Fathers as he defended the Church of England against the errors of Rome and the heresies of the Dutch Arminians. Nor should we condemn too quickly these celestial identifications, for without them the King James Version might never have been written.

The King's dedication to the cult of Christian verse appears in an invocation prefacing his translation of du Bartas's *Furies*. He thus addresses the Deity:

O Thou that mightilie does toone
My warbling holie Harpe, . . .
Inspires my sacred Muse to sing
Unto the Lord of Lords,
O now inflame my furious Spirit,
That furiously I may
These Furies (mankinds plagues allace!)
With furious Pen display.

Again, beginning another poem, the King prays to God

To make thy holy Spirit my Muse
And eik my pen inflame,
Above my skill to write this worke
To magnify thy name.

James began his career as a Christian poet in a modest way by translating portions of du Bartas into English verse and thus bringing him to the attention of Scottish and English readers. The King explained his purpose in a prose introduction. He had, he declared, read and reread the works of the divine du Bartas and was moved with a restless and lofty desire to attain to the like virtue. But since, alas, God had denied him du Bartas's wit and skill, he determined to set forth the poet's praise by publishing a translation of some of his writings. Even this, he feared, was beyond his powers. Yet he had ventured to translate the shortest and easiest of du Bartas's poems, *Uranie*. He admitted that he had done it poorly and only hoped that some quicker spirit would be moved to translate it 'well and best where I have both evil and worst broiled it'.

Broiled it he had. The kindest of critics could only pronounce the translation atrocious. It is written in lines of fourteen syllables which fall into a sing-song pattern that is most unpoetic. The technicalities of rhyme and rhythm are not impossible, but the King resorts to the most tortured syntax and sentence structure and fills out the feet with *eik*, *als* and *alway* past all endurance, while his slavish adherence to the letter of du Bartas's French causes all kinds of trouble. He himself is apologetic. 'I must desire you to bear with it,' he begs the reader, 'albeit it be replete with innumerable and intolerable faults that are forbidden in my own treatise of the art of poesy.' His translation of the *Furies* is no

THE HIGHE AND MIGHTIE PRINCE, Iames THE SIXT, BY THE GRACE OF GOD KINGE OF SCOTLANDE. R.E. *fecit.*

KING JAMES, AS A YOUTH

better, and the theme is worse, for it is nothing more than a catalogue of the plagues that have beset mankind as a result of the fall of Adam and Eve. Ample scope is offered to the King's interest in the horrible and ghastly. He recounts with gruesome detail and evident enjoyment the terrors of earthquakes, of tempests, and of wild beasts (with special attention to gorgons, hydras and pythons), of famine, of war and of pestilence, listing enough diseases to fill a text-book on medicine. We have reached the nadir of James's verse.

His one attempt to write celestial poetry of an original kind is his *Lepanto*, a poem of some thousand lines describing the naval victory of Christian Europe over the Turks in 1571. The battle is treated as a triumph of God over Satan, and thus the poem is given its divine character. It opens with a scene in heaven in which God accuses Satan of inciting the Turks to attack the Christians. Satan replies that the Turks have been given to him to do with as he pleases, but God, declaring that Christendom will resist the infidel, dispatches the Angel Gabriel to 'Venice town' to stir the people to a war of revenge. There follows a ludicrous description of Venice in which the city appears prostrate at the thought of war. Men die, women swoon, babies weep, and the children are dressed in black. James becomes fearful

> Lest trickling tears do fill my pen
> That it will write no more.

However, the Venetians take heart, a league is formed with other Christian States, and a great fleet assembles and sets forth.

> This cloud of Gallies thus began
> On Neptune's back to row
> And in the Shippes the marriners
> Did skip from toe to toe.

Rumour, described in obvious imitation of Virgil, informs the Turks of the approach of the Christians. The Turks receive the news with contempt but decide to send forth their fleet. The scene shifts once more to heaven where God, weighing Christians and Turks in the balance, finds the Turks to be wanting. The conflict is described with becoming fury. The cannon belch forth bullets, razors, chains and nails, the fish in the sea are astonished, the wounded shriek in pain.

My pen for pity cannot write
My hair for horror stands
To think how many Christians there
Were killed by pagan hands.
O Lord, throughout this labrynth
Make me the way to view
And let Thy holy three-fold spirit
Be my conducting clew.

The ships of the two leaders grapple, a Macedonian warrior decapitates the Turkish chieftain, the Christians win the day. A chorus of victory is sung by the ladies of Venice. The poet grows weary, his leaden pen slips from his hand, his eyelids close for lack of rest. But as he lies in repose he hears an angel chorus proclaiming that God will strengthen Christians against their foes.

The King suffered the fate of many better writers and discovered that his poem was misinterpreted. He was accused of celebrating a Catholic triumph and of writing, like a professional scribbler, in praise of the Catholic commander, Don John of Austria. Indignantly he denied these charges, pointing out the celestial nature of his poem and explaining that his purpose was to show that just as God defended the Christians against the Turks so He would defend Protestants against Catholics. The explanation was ingenious but would hardly convince the Presbyterian clergy.

These base murmurs of disapproval, however, were drowned by a chorus of commendation. A King who befriended poets, who wrote celestial verse, and who welcomed flattery provided ample scope for those who wished to praise him. The English poet, Henry Constable, wrote:

Where others hooded with blind love do flie
Low on the ground with buzzard Cupids wings,
A heavenlie love, from love of love thee brings,
And makes thy muse to mount above the skie.

A Scottish writer urged the King to 'use his gifts divine'. Du Bartas showered him with flowery compliments, translated his *Lepanto* into French verse, and presented it to the public in France as the work of 'the Apollo of our time', whose verses appeared to emerge from the lips of Homer.

James's poetry was known and praised in England, where Sir Philip Sidney was interested in the cult of Christian verse and referred to the King as one of its patrons. Sidney's friend, Gabriel Harvey, noted that Homer had been an inspiration to many princes, and then added: 'I cannot forget the worthy Prince that is a Homer to himself, a golden spur to nobility, a sceptre to virtue, a verdure to the spring, a sun to the day; and hath not only translated two divine poems of Sallustius du Bartas, his heavenly *Uranie* and his hellish *Furies*, but hath read a most valorous martial lecture to himself in his own victorious *Lepanto*, a short heroical work in metre, but royal metre, fit for a David's harp.'[5]

Such bombast is ludicrous enough. It is only fair to repeat, however, that we are dealing with the poems of a clever boy, an avowed apprentice. A group of verses written by the King under the romantic impulse of his marriage at the age of twenty-three shows some improvement, and a few of his later sonnets achieve dignity and decorum. His maturing conception of poetry is evident in his advice to his son: 'If ye write in verse, remember that it is not the principal part of a poem to rhyme right and flow with many pretty words. But the chief commendation of a poem is that when the verse shall be shaken apart into prose it shall be found so rich in quick inventions and poetic flowers and in fair and pertinent comparisons as it shall retain the lustre of a poem although in prose.'

None the less, James's poetry suffered at all times from preoccupation with the mechanical technique of writing verse. The composition of a poem was little more than an exercise in placing words in a neat and clever pattern, a tendency accentuated by his preference for the sonnet. The lines of a poem, he held, must flow smoothly, and he disliked the rougher verses of some of the poets he was to meet in England. His sonnet addressed to his friend, Sir William Alexander, upon *Alexander's Harshe Verses after the Engliche Fasone*, was a complaint that the muses were being treated too roughly.

> Hould, hould your hand, hould, mercy, mercy spare
> Those sacred nine that nurst you many a yeare. . . .
> Our songs are fil'd with smoothly flowing fire.

Gracefully Alexander replied in praise of a King who

numbrous notes with measured fury frames,
Each accent weighed, no jarr in sense or sound.

James's mechanical approach to poetry and his lack of true poetic feeling were doubtless the reasons why he gradually abandoned verse — although he continued to write occasional poems all his life — and turned to prose. His choice was well advised, for his prose was often racy, pungent and picturesque. Perhaps he recognized his limitations as a poet. 'If nature be not the chief worker in this art,' he had written as a boy, 'rules will be but a band to nature and will make you within short space weary of the whole art.'

CHAPTER V

THE SPANISH POLYPHEMUS

WHEN Arran fled before the exiled Scottish lords advancing from England in November 1585, the King once more saw his government overthrown and his person made prisoner. Months later he was smarting still at the dishonour to which he had been subjected. But he soon discovered that his position was far better than after the Ruthven Raid and that in fact he was more his own master than he had ever been before.

A number of factors produced this happy result. The victorious lords were not a compact party but a coalition drawn from discordant elements, united only by common hatred of Arran. Angus, Mar and Glamis — the former Ruthven lords — had headed the revolution which now restored them to power. But the returning exiles included Lord John Hamilton, an old adherent of Mary though a Protestant, Lord Claud, his younger brother, a Catholic, and the Catholic Maxwell, a Border chieftain; while other Catholic lords were admitted to the Council. Moreover, some members of the former government — Gray, Sir John Maitland and Sir Lewis Bellenden — having abetted the fall of Arran, were continued in office. They formed the group in the new administration most pleasing to James and were employed by the other lords to place policy before him. There was thus for a time a balance of forces at court which gave the King an unexpected independence. Most of the lords, moreover, were intent upon restoring their private fortunes, which could be done most easily through royal favour, and hence they used the King gently. To humour him they yielded precedence to his young favourite, Ludovick Stuart, the son of Lennox and the only Duke in Scotland, whom James had recently brought over from France. They placed no guard about the King and allowed him to hunt as he pleased. Even in graver matters they hesitated to cross him.

From the ministers returning joyfully to Scotland such moderation was not to be expected. They assumed that the Acts of 1584 would be swept aside, that Presbyterianism would be fully established, and that the lords, more pious and docile in exile, would now work mightily for the Kirk. The lords, however, found the King very difficult. 'He set himself despitefully against the Kirk', and especially against the ministers who had been in exile, calling them loons, contemptible fellows and seditious knaves. The lords were unwilling to force upon him a settlement of the Church against his will. They must first be firmly seated in their own places, they told the ministers, and then they would work wonders. The ministers pleaded with them, then threatened, denounced and cursed them. But for the moment no action was taken, and the future status of the Kirk remained in doubt.

The ministers, at James's request, set down in writing their objections to the Acts of 1584. To their surprise the King retired to his cabinet and within the space of twenty-four hours produced a vigorous and remarkable reply. Shrewdly he took his stand on Andrew Melville's doctrine of the two kingdoms. He denied all intention of making himself head of the Kirk or of interfering in ecclesiastical affairs, but he denounced the intrusion of the clergy in matters of State, especially their treasonable and seditious sermons. Bishops he warmly defended as sanctioned both by the Scriptures and by the practice of the primitive church. Stoutly he maintained his right to summon or to refuse to summon the General Assemblies of the Kirk, he denied the request of the clergy to be represented in Parliament by their own commissioners, and he prayed that God would purge them of the indecent affections peculiar to their calling. He wrote with the lofty assurance of a king who ruled by divine right.

The clergy answered with great heat, telling James that his fate would be that of King Jeroboam who was rooted out with all his issue for seducing Israel to idolatry. A certain James Gibson was especially offensive. He had thought, he said, that Arran and his Lady Jezebel had been the persecutors of the Kirk but now he saw it was the King. Gibson was summoned before the Council. 'What,' cried James, 'call ye me a persecutor?' 'Yes, Sir. So long as ye maintain the wicked Acts against God and the liberty of His Kirk, ye are a persecutor. Whosoever will intrude any tyranny upon the Kirk and maintain the same against the Word of God he is a persecutor.' 'What is that I maintain against the Word of God?' 'The tyranny of bishops and absolute power.' Gibson added with some insolence that he had often preached before

James in the past and had not been reproved. 'I give not a turd for thy preaching', howled the King, and Gibson was sent to prison. Meanwhile a clash at St. Andrews between the Melvilles and Archbishop Adamson increased the furore.

But both the King and the ministers knew that neither episcopacy nor Presbyterianism could for the moment be imposed in its entirety. Before Arran's regime had ended, there had developed in the Kirk a moderate party that refused the leadership of the Melvilles and had subscribed to the Acts of 1584, though with certain reservations. This moderate group was led by the elderly John Craig who now scoffed at the Melvilles as the 'peregrine ministers', and preached that obedience to kings was a religious duty. Thus the Kirk was divided, and at a General Assembly in May 1586, a compromise was arranged that continued episcopacy though in attenuated form. On the other hand, the erection of presbyteries was to go on apace, synods and General Assemblies were to meet with regularity, and their jurisdiction was extended to all ecclesiastical causes. Yet James had saved the existence of bishops. 'In this Assembly', wrote Calderwood, 'was first perceived what fear and flattery of court could work among weak and inconsiderate ministers. The bishops retained some piece of preeminence by reason of the King's great importunity.'[1]

Elizabeth's first letter to James after the raid at Stirling expressed her astonishment that the exiled lords, to whom she had given permission to go to Germany, should have converged so strangely on Scotland; and the King answered that he wished to deal as honestly with Elizabeth as she had dealt with him and therefore called God to witness that he had never practised with any foreign country against her. By this felicitous exchange the way was opened for renewed negotiations for a league. In March 1586, Elizabeth sent to Edinburgh Thomas Randolph who easily persuaded the King to sign articles providing for an alliance in defence of true religion and for mutual assistance in case of invasion from abroad. James asked in return for recognition of his claim to the succession, for a pension of £5000, and for some honour and dignity in England.

Despite the great issues at stake, he also pleaded earnestly for a gift of horses and fallow deer. The horses were refused but the deer were sent. James met them at Musselburgh and carefully supervised their embarkation as they were taken across the water to Falkland. Thither he followed them. 'The King has been at Falkland with his bucks,' wrote Randolph, 'whom he entertained honourably with bran, oats and hay, and they are now in a fair park left to shift for themselves. The King still follows his hunting, riding and writing in metre.'

Sir John Maitland, the Secretary, believed that the English articles had been signed too soon, and his forebodings were shortly justified. The King had hoped for a pension of £5000. 'Marry, he looks to receive the pension she hath promised, else no bargain,' wrote Thomas Miles, a Scot in the English service, 'for they are as bare as beggars.' But Elizabeth reduced the figure to £4000. Moreover, James had drawn up a statement regarding the succession, but Elizabeth rejected it and sent him a stinging letter at which he changed colour, swearing, by God, he would not have signed so soon had he known how he was to be treated. Yet so eager was he for the alliance that he 'digested all'. In May he was offered £4000 in cash and found the money irresistible. Elizabeth sent him a revised statement concerning the succession. She gave him her 'firm promise in the word of a Queen that she would never directly or indirectly do or suffer to be done anything that she could withstand to the diminution or derogation of any right or title that might be due to him in any time present or future, unless by manifest ingratitude she should be justly moved and provoked to the contrary'. This was not what he had hoped for, but it was far more solid than the offers of dubious friends on the continent. The treaty was formally signed in July.[2]

Randolph was pleased with James and has left a favourable picture of him. In religion Randolph thought him perfectly sound. Sermons he attended almost daily, on Sunday both morning and afternoon, on Wednesday and Friday in the morning. If he was to be absent, which was seldom, he informed the minister in advance. He did not hear sermons in private but came to the Great Kirk, displaying much patience in hearing himself reproved by the preachers there, 'though they speak home and with much liberty'. If he sometimes talked to his attendants during the preaching, he spoke of points raised by the minister; he constantly professed his love of true religion and his detestation of Popery; and by the testimony of the clergy themselves he was as ready in the Scriptures as any man in the kingdom. His conversation, though marred by profanity, was excellent; he was of staid deportment, very chaste yet desirous of marriage, not without modesty as was seen by an occasional blush. He disliked the discipline of the Kirk and the power of the nobles because they lessened the King's authority, 'which he thinketh little enough in Scotland as it is'. Ready to end all quarrels, he was willing to compose matters that troubled his peace, though with some disadvantage. His great delights were hunting and writing poetry, in which he spent most of his time, and he loved to retire from public view 'to places of more solitude and repast with very small retinue'.[3]

His character was now to be tested in a fundamental way. Just as English and Scottish commissioners were signing the league, Walsingham was gathering evidence of Mary's complicity in the Babington Plot; on August 3rd she was arrested, her papers seized, her servants questioned; the final act of her sad drama was about to begin. James did not understand at first that his mother's life was in danger but assumed that henceforth she would be more closely confined. That prospect did not disturb him. He remarked that Mary should drink the ale she had brewed, that in future she should meddle with nothing beyond prayer and serving God. Her religion was contrary to his and he could not agree with her. When a courtier reminded him that Mary was faithful to her religion as he was to his, the King replied that he knew his religion to be the true one though he had grown up among knavish ministers whose doctrines he never approved. His mother bore him no good will, she had threatened to disinherit him, and he must protect his interests. Hence when Walsingham sounded him as to Mary's punishment, he answered that though he could not agree to her death he cared not how strictly she was imprisoned. Let her 'be put in the Tower or some other firm manse and kept from intelligence', let her old knavish servants be hanged, and let Elizabeth appoint new attendants. 'The only thing he craves is her life,' wrote Roger Aston, an Englishman in the Scottish service, 'all other things to be just as her Majesty pleases.'[4]

In September, however, he received a startling letter from Archibald Douglas, the corrupt lawyer who represented him in London. Douglas foresaw the distinct possibility of Mary's execution, an event which James could only regard as a shattering blow to his honour and a source of deep resentment among the Scots. Douglas, moreover, advised him not to intercede for his mother because in so doing he might injure his claim to the succession. In 1584 the English Parliament had passed an Act by which persons found guilty of plotting against Elizabeth should, *ipso facto*, forfeit any claim they might have to the throne; and their descendants, being in any way assenting or privy to their plots, were also debarred. Mary's trial, said Douglas, had done nothing to prejudice James's title, but if he should intercede with vehemence he might easily give the impression that he was a party to her plottings. Thus the King learned that he might have to choose between his mother's life and his hopes of the English throne.

Meanwhile he was under severe pressure from those about him. That Elizabeth should lay violent hands upon a Scottish queen appeared intolerable to the Scots who assumed that Mary's death would bring war with England and alliance with England's enemies. Bothwell, a wild young Earl, told James that if he permitted Elizabeth to kill his mother he deserved to be hanged next day, at which the King laughed and said he would provide for that. Lord Claud Hamilton swore he would burn the country as far as Newcastle if Mary was injured, and even Angus, Mary's enemy, asserted that no one could blame her if she cut Elizabeth's throat. The King was indeed in trouble. 'All men', wrote Gray, 'drive at him.'

James now instructed Douglas in peremptory terms to work for Mary's life, and he dispatched to England a special messenger, Sir William Keith, a young member of his household. Douglas and Keith were to do two things: 'the one to deal very earnestly both with the Queen and her councillors for our sovereign mother's life, the other that our title to that Crown be not prejudged'. Thus closely did James couple these two questions; and it became apparent at once that his tremulous anxiety concerning his title greatly weakened his plea for his mother's life. The English, sensing the elements of a bargain, went out of their way to convince him that his title was untouched. Elizabeth offered a formal statement to that effect. But at the same time Douglas reported that Mary's life was in extreme peril.

Thoroughly alarmed, James hinted that he might break the league with England. 'The King nor no man ever believed the matter would have gone so far', Gray wrote to Douglas on November 23rd. 'If her life be touched or her blood meddled

with, he can no longer remain on good terms with the Queen or
estate of that realm. He will find it hard to keep the peace if her
life be touched. I never saw all the people so willing to concur in
anything as in this. They that hated most her prosperity regret
her adversity.' Here was a threat, but would it be driven
home?

A few days later James wrote to Keith and Douglas that he was
sending an honourable embassy and begged that Mary's life be
spared until it arrived. Part of his letter was in strong terms. He
was sorry that Elizabeth had so dishonoured him and injured her
own fame as to allow subjects to pass judgment upon a sovereign
Prince. Though Henry VIII had besmirched his reputation by
beheading his bedfellows, that tragedy was far inferior to what
Elizabeth appeared to contemplate. But the King's letter ended
on a plaintive note. If Elizabeth could see his heart she would
discover a jewel of honest meaning locked in a coffer of perplexity.
'Guess ye in what strait my honour will be in, this disaster being
perfected, since before God I already dare scarce go abroad, for
crying out of the whole people. And what is spoken by them of the
Queen of England it grieves me to hear, yet I dare not find fault
with it except I would dethrone myself, so is the whole of Scotland
incensed with this matter.' He appeared to measure his dishonour
by his inconvenience. When Elizabeth saw his letter, which
Douglas treacherously showed her, she staged a scene of high
wrath and indignation. She 'took such a chafe as ye would
wonder'. She was trying to discover whether James would break
the league.

On the day that James's letter arrived in London Douglas had
a talk with Leicester in his carriage. Leicester offered to support
James's title and pointed out that Mary's death would be greatly
to her son's advantage. He then asked Douglas pointedly whether
James would break the league if Mary were executed. Douglas
replied in the negative. The league, he said, was the King's
policy, he would not break it unless the English forced his hand,
a proviso understood by Leicester to refer to the succession.
Douglas thus conveyed the impression that James would digest his
mother's death.

News of the Queen's tartness and of Douglas's conversation
with Leicester reached Scotland together, December 14th. The
time for decision had arrived. James knew that, unless he cor-

rected the impression left by Douglas, Mary would die; and the only way to correct it was to threaten openly to end the league and to ally with England's enemies. But what a prospect! To break with England was to alienate Elizabeth, her councillors and her people, to set aside all hope of the English succession. What could he anticipate from Spanish victory? At best, dependence upon Philip; at worst, complete ruin. The temptation to be rid of Mary was very great. If she survived Elizabeth, the English would probably ignore her claim and thus debar her son. Hence if he threatened to break the league and if that threat saved Mary's life — as Mr. Rait and Miss Cameron, the authorities on this episode, believe it would have done — he would merely have succeeded at great risk in doing himself much harm. All his instincts and traits of character, all his training and experience, cried out against allowing the great prize to slip away. To look through his fingers as Elizabeth put Mary to death, to retain England's friendship and strengthen his own chances, offered a course of action which he found irresistible.

He wrote two letters, one to Elizabeth, merely saying he was dispatching an embassy, the other to Leicester. To Leicester he denied that he had been in touch with Mary. 'This far shortly may I say, I am honest, no changer of course, altogether in all things as I profess to be, and whosoever will affirm that I had ever intelligence with my mother since the Master of Gray's being in England [in 1584-85], or ever thought to prefer her to myself in the title, or ever dealt in any other foreign course, they lie falsely and dishonestly of me. But specially how fond and inconstant I were if I should prefer my mother to the title let all men judge.' The literal meaning of this sentence, derived from its context, was that James had never placed Mary's title to the English throne before his own title to that throne and that he would be fond and inconstant so to do. But the words were ambiguous. To one seeking the writer's thoughts, they could easily carry the meaning that the King was prepared to sacrifice his mother if forced to choose between her and the English succession. There was no threat in the letter. The impression left by Douglas was confirmed. Elizabeth and Leicester were convinced that James would not break with them, that the wound to his honour would heal, and that he could with impunity be left in his difficulties.

His ambassadors, Gray and Sir Robert Melville, carried a strongly worded letter to Elizabeth. James spoke of his honour and of the divinity of kings, whose sacred diadems were not to be profaned nor their lives disposed of at the appetite of subjects. He argued that his mother's death would be a sad return for the friendship he had shown Elizabeth. He begged her to be clement and to avoid the revenge of Mary's friends. Let Mary be sent to a foreign country, presumably France, under guarantees of good behaviour. Or let her sign a bond that if she plotted again she would endure a traitor's death. James's plea, however, was belied by his employment of Gray as ambassador, for Gray had betrayed Mary on a former mission and his position in Scotland rested upon the King's desertion of his mother.

The ambassadors found they had no credit in England. They believed that Douglas was playing them false. Sir Alexander Stewart, a Scot who came with them, declared he had instructions superior to theirs and that the King would digest his mother's death. This was the settled conviction of the English and the ambassadors could not shake it. Their interviews with Elizabeth were stormy. When Gray suggested that Mary, in return for her life, make over her claims to her son, Elizabeth burst out: 'By God's passion, that were to cut my own throat, and, for a duchy or an earldom to yourself, you or such as you would cause some of your desperate knaves kill me. No, by God, he shall never be in that place. Tell your King what good I have done for him in holding the Crown on his head since he was born, and that I mind to keep the league that now stands between us, and if he break, it shall be a double fault.' The ambassadors begged for delay. 'Not for an hour', replied the Queen.

The embassy had failed. Yet at the last moment Elizabeth hesitated and James learned of her hesitation. Knowing that a strong statement might still avail, he wrote a final letter. If Elizabeth knew of his grief and of his difficulties in Scotland, she would have mercy on him. He returned to the argument that princes were not subject to earthly censure. He spoke of the 'almost' universal hatred the deed would evoke in other rulers. Sir Alexander Stewart he repudiated and begged for a comfortable answer. Twice in the letter there was an approach to a threat, but it was never made. Indeed there was a hint that while all other princes would turn against Elizabeth, there might be one exception. The letter contained nothing calculated to move Elizabeth. Mary was executed on February 9th, 1587.

Thus James made clear to Elizabeth that while he would deeply resent his mother's death he was not prepared to avenge it; and to ensure that the English received the impression he wished to convey, he may have gone further than we know. He was aware of the treacherous conduct of Douglas, yet continued for some time to employ him in London. Hearing of the words of Sir Alexander Stewart, he 'was in marvellous choler and sware and protested before God that if Stewart came back to Scotland he would hang him before he put off his boots'. Yet Stewart returned with impunity. It is not impossible that he had been given secret instructions.

Of the King's deportment at the news of his mother's death, there are conflicting accounts. Calderwood asserts that he shammed a false sorrow but could not conceal his joy and remarked to those about him: 'I am now sole King'; while Maitland ordered courtiers from the room, so ashamed was he of his master's conduct. An eyewitness declares that 'the King moved never his countenance at the rehearsal of his mother's execution, nor leaves not his pastime and hunting more than of before'. But other accounts indicate that James was deeply moved. Moysie reports that he 'was in great displeasure and went to bed without supper', and rode to Dalkeith next morning 'desiring to be solitaire'. The King, says an English spy, took the news 'very grievously and offensively and gave out in secret speeches that he would not digest the same or leave it unavenged'. When, a few weeks later, he was given a vivid and touching description of his mother's death by one of her ladies-in-waiting, he 'was very sad and pensive all that day and would not sup that night'.[5]

In the year and a half between the death of Mary and the coming of the Spanish Armada James followed a complicated and tortuous policy. He was furious with Elizabeth, yet tried to obtain compensation for the wrong he had endured; he resented the insubordination that flared in Scotland, yet hoped to turn it to his advantage; he supported England when the crisis came, yet temporized with Spanish agents.

His sense of humiliation and outraged dignity found compensation in some foolish talk. He said in private that he would have little courage if he allowed himself to be intimidated by Elizabeth, an old woman, unloved by her subjects, who were weary of her rule. She was, he added, in perpetual fear of her own servants and fled at the approach of strangers. 'He protesteth, though he be a mean King with small ability, he would not change fortune with her; choosing rather to live securely among his subjects than to seek after the blood of his people of contrary religion as she does.'

He rejected her lame excuse that a 'miserable accident' had caused Mary's death. 'Whereas ye purge yourself of yon unhappy fact,' he wrote, 'I dare not wrong you so far as not to judge honourably of your unspotted part therein, so I wish that your honourable behaviour in all times hereafter may fully persuade the whole world of the same. I look that ye will give me at this time such a full satisfaction in all respects as shall be a means to strengthen and unite this isle, establish and maintain true religion, and oblige me to be, as of before I was, your most loving James R.'

With combined shrewdness and naivety he wrote Elizabeth as though she could prove her innocence and heal his wounded honour by some material recompense. He asked to be recognized as her lawful and nearest successor to the Crown. To remove all suspicion of evil after the infernal proceedings against his dearest mother, he thought that Elizabeth should give him lands in northern England with the title of duke. He was soon suggesting through Douglas in London that he was in a position to exact revenge, that he had large offers from Catholic States, and that his thirst for vengeance was held in leash only by moral considerations. 'But ye may be sure,' so ran instructions for Douglas, 'he cannot be long restrained.' Elizabeth, however, was undismayed by this sudden apparition of a bloodthirsty King of Scots and was cold to his requests for worldly advantage. A jibe by a Spanish diplomat was much to the point. The King, he said, held that the wound to his honour could only be healed by a declaration that he was heir to the English throne, 'to which the English replied that this was rather a point of profit than of honour and that he had no right to raise it'.

Meanwhile James had to deal with a surge of Scottish hatred against England. Bothwell scoffed at the purple weeds worn by the King as mourning for his mother. The best suit of mourning would be a suit of mail. At a Parliament in July 1587, Maitland made an impassioned plea that Mary's death be avenged; and all the nobles present swore upon their knees to assist the King in such a venture. This ardour James held in leash. But he did little to restrain the wild Border raids that now swept into England. He consented to the ruin of Gray who was thought to have betrayed his trust in his recent embassy to England. Further to appease the Scottish nobles, he wrote to Henry III of France, to Catherine de Medici, and to the Duke of Guise asking for aid to avenge his mother's death. Replies came slowly and offered small encouragement, doubtless to his satisfaction. His correspondence with Henry III did not prevent his cultivating the friendship of Henry of Navarre. He had promised Henry III, with a flourish regarding the iniquity of rebellion, that no Scot would serve in the armies of Navarre, yet the promise was broken at once; and it was at this time that the poet, du Bartas, a follower of Navarre, delighted the King by a visit to Scotland. James's wish for revenge was less than half-hearted. [6]

Preparations in Spain for the great attempt, now overshadowing all other events, revived his dread of Spanish victory. An English envoy once reminded him that if Philip conquered England Scotland could expect a similar fate, to whom James answered wittily 'that he looked for no other benefit of the Spanish in that case than that which Polyphemus promised to Ulysses, namely, to devour him after all his fellows were devoured'. Such fears were fully justified. The claims of Mary had been a problem in Madrid where her death was considered fortunate, while the possibility of her son's conversion was viewed with alarm. Philip told the Pope that the King of Scots, a hopeless heretic, should not be converted but dethroned. To a mission of William Chisholm, the exiled Bishop of Dunblane, who came to Scotland in hope of converting the King, the Spanish were hostile; and Philip asserted that Chisholm, after talking with James, was quite disillusioned, though another account implies that James temporized with the Bishop and gave a pledge of assistance against Elizabeth. Meanwhile Philip made the happy discovery that he himself was heir to the English throne through his descent from John of Gaunt. He also set forth a story that Mary had made a will in which she disinherited her son and ceded her claims to Spain. It is true that she had threatened to do so, but the will has never been found, probably because it never existed. To the moment of her death Mary cherished hope of her son's conversion. When on the scaffold she said she had done nothing to his prejudice she may have been telling the truth. But Philip used the story of her will for his own purposes, while Elizabeth, to frighten James, was not unwilling that the tale should be told.[7]

A further cause for apprehension lay in the plottings of the Scottish Catholic nobility. These nobles, led in the north by Huntly, head of the great clan of Gordon, and by his adherents, Crawford and Montrose, and in the south Maxwell and Lord Claud Hamilton, had grown to considerable strength. In the months before the Armada they plotted to bring a Spanish army to Scotland and to force the conversion of the King. Philip, how-ever, was not interested, and the lords, turning to more normal enterprises, attempted a revolution by assembling their forces at Dunfermline and Linlithgow. But Edinburgh was strengthened and the danger passed. A few weeks later the King was induced by Huntly to attend a banquet at Dunfermline, but James, in sudden alarm, arose next morning before dawn and galloped from the town with greater haste than dignity. These plottings were the more dangerous because conditions at court had altered. Maitland, now Chancellor, was the King's principal adviser, but he stood alone, opposed and resented by both Protestant and Catholic lords, a target for violence and revolution.

James did not curb the Catholic lords, for they enhanced his bargaining power with Elizabeth, formed a counterpoise to the Kirk, and offered hope of survival in case of Spanish victory. With their agents he temporized. Robert Bruce, a spy in their employ, reported that the King, whom he had seen on three occasions, was willing to negotiate with Philip. A Spanish agent from the Netherlands, one Colonel Semple, said the same. And Semple was permitted to move about Scotland, plotting as he would.

Despite these shufflings the King was resolved to stand by England. Yet, until the moment of crisis was at hand, his pre-parations took a most singular form. He felt impelled, as a pen-man of heaven, to come to the aid of Protestantism by interpreting the Scripture in the light of current events, and he turned to the Book of Revelation which had at all times a strange fascination for him. Its symbolism called for elucidation, its theme of the rise and fall of empires formed a fit subject for a kingly pen, and its horrible descriptive passages were much to his taste. Early in 1588 he published a short meditation on selected verses of the Book,[8] and at the same time prepared a much longer work, not published until 1616, *A Paraphrase upon the Revelation of the Apostle S. John.* In this paraphrase the King enlarged the text to perhaps five times its original length, explaining and interpolating as he went along and buttressing his views by references to other portions of the Scripture. The language has some flow and dignity, borrowed from the text, but is not free from the peculiar twists of the royal mind. Thus heresies have long hair, says James, because a woman's hair is a great part of her alluring beauty.

His interpretation is the same in both the shorter and the longer work. The imprisonment of Satan foretold in the Revelation is said to represent the first centuries of the Christian era when the Church flourished in blessed purity. Then Satan was loosed, and with him arose a horrible Antichrist, symbolized by the pale horse of the Apocalypse, by the king of the locusts, by the beast rising from the sea, and by the woman in scarlet sitting upon the waters. This Antichrist James identifies with the Pope. Throughout Europe, says the King, Antichrist is preparing to attack the faithful who must gird themselves for battle. But the destruction of Antichrist is at hand, and gleefully James proceeds to the lurid punishments that await Antichrist and his hosts. Dead bodies float upon seas of blood, the followers of Satan gnaw their tongues for dolour. Finally the King arrives at the rejoicings of the elect who alone are to be saved. This identification of Antichrist with the Pope is found in many Protestant writings of the time, but James sets it forth with great confidence as though it were quite original.

A further proof of his Protestant zeal was his challenge to the Jesuit James Gordon, uncle of the Earl of Huntly, to a public disputation at court. For five hours King and Jesuit debated together. James spoke modestly, saying he bore no malice to those who disagreed with him, while Gordon, praising him highly, was more than conciliatory. Thus the affair went well, the King was triumphant, the courtiers greatly edified. One of them boasted that the most learned Papist in Europe could not trip the King of Scots. 'I hear,' wrote Mendoza, the former Spanish Ambassador in England, 'that after the disputation the King said in his chamber that Gordon did not understand the Scripture, which is a fairly bold thing to say, only that the King has the assurance to translate Revelation and to write upon the subject as if he were Amadis de Gaul himself.'[9]

As the hour of the Armada drew near, James's relations with Elizabeth improved. She offered to drink a large draught of the river of Lethe and called God to witness that she was innocent of Mary's blood, while a gift of £2000 buttressed her plea that he seal his ears with the wax of Ulysses against siren offers from the continent. Her ambassador in Scotland, Sir William Asheby, terrified lest the King waver, exceeded his instructions and made James handsome offers: a dukedom and its revenue, a pension of £5000, money to support a guard and to pacify the Borders. But alas! When Elizabeth discovered what her nervous ambassador had done, these happy visions faded.

But while they retained their magic and as the crisis deepened, James offered Elizabeth 'his forces, his person, and all that he commanded against yon strangers'. He would be her son and compatriot, not a foreign prince. His assistance was negative, but it was something. His defences he prepared as best he could, the Catholics he kept quiet, in Ireland and on the Borders he caused no difficulty. He could write that the Spanish fleet 'never entered within any road or haven within his dominion, nor never came within a kenning near to any of his coasts'. The danger from the Spanish Polyphemus passed away.[10]

The King's rejoicings took the novel form of *Ane Meditation upon the 25, 26, 27, 28, and 29 Verses of the 15 Chapter of the First Buke of the Chronicles of the Kings*. This passage tells how King David, having triumphed over the Philistines, danced before the Ark of the Lord, and how Michal, daughter of Saul, saw David dancing and despised him in her heart. James's interpretation is confused and meandering. Now that the victory promised in his former meditation has been won, he wishes to teach his people what yet remains to be achieved. He wishes also that his writings may testify to his upright and honest meaning. David, he explains, praises God for making him a king and for giving him victory. Elders, captains, priests and Levites accompany David, showing that a godly king will obtain support from his estates. One must not frown upon David's music and dancing, for they are indifferent things, good or bad as they are used, but Michal is a godless hypocrite who sees nothing but wantonness in David's dancing. The victory over Spain, James continues, is far greater than David's victory over the Philistines, and the duty of the present generation is to bring in the Ark of Christ, the New Testament. In conclusion, a triumphant sonnet declares that the nations had banded against the Lord, but He had hurled them to destruction beneath the waves.

One small accompaniment of these rejoicings deserves mention. It concerns the Spanish agent, Colonel Semple. The King allowed him full liberty until the defeat of the Armada, then with great Protestant zeal threw him into prison. Shortly after, however, perhaps fearing that Semple might talk too loudly upon examination, or wishing perhaps to have a story for Spain as well as for England, James looked the other way while Semple bribed his way to freedom.[11]

CHAPTER VI

ANNE OF DENMARK

KING JAMES's marriage to Anne of Denmark in 1589, the one romantic episode of his life, forms a human and pleasant interlude in the turmoil and self-seeking of his reign in Scotland. He was at first but a cold wooer. The King, wrote an English intelligencer, 'never regards the company of any woman, not so much as in any dalliance', and his mind was directed to marriage by the promptings of his councillors rather than by any great urge of his own. Piously he told his people on the eve of his marriage: 'God is my witness, I could have abstained longer than the weal of my country could have permitted, [had not] my long delay bred in the breasts of many a great jealousy of my inability, as if I were a barren stock.' He had, he said, awaited the occasion offered by God, had heeded the behests of his subjects, and was about to marry prudently with all worldly circumspection.

During his boyhood one hears of many proposals for his marriage, but when he came of age the choice quickly narrowed to two ladies, the Princess Catherine de Bourbon, sister of Henry of Navarre, and the Princess Anne, younger daughter of Frederick II of Denmark. A tall tale of Sir James Melville relates that the King, finding decision difficult, armed himself with portraits of the two Princesses and retired to a fortnight of prayer for divine guidance. On the fifteenth day, says Melville, he emerged and announced his decision in favour of Denmark.[1] But the matter was not quite so simple, for negotiations extended over a number of years with some indecision to the last.

The French marriage was supported by Lord Chancellor Maitland, by most of the nobility, and in France by a group in Henry's entourage including the poet du Bartas who urged the match unofficially during his visit to Scotland in 1587. Returning to France, he wrote flattering letters to his 'Scottish Apollo' and counselled Henry to ally with a Protestant Prince, handsome, brave, eloquent, active, and wise, the very image of Henry himself. The walls of Rome would tremble at such an alliance. Cordial letters passed between James and Henry; and James addressed a note of conventional flattery to Madame Catherine, who replied in kind, modestly attributing his attentions to his affection for her brother. The foundation of material advantage, however, was lacking in the French match. James wanted a substantial dowry, but Henry was quite penurious and, though he might become King of France, that eminence was unobtainable without hard fighting in which the King of Scots had no wish to take part. Henry on his side looked for military assistance which was not forthcoming from Scotland. Hence the marriage did not prosper. James brought negotiations to an end in 1589, begging Henry to remain his friend and excusing his silence to Catherine on the ground that he lacked leisure to write a dainty letter.[2]

More advantageous was the Danish match. A prosperous, orderly, and well established kingdom, Denmark was Protestant but aloof from the religious wars of Europe, a bridge for Scottish alliance with the Protestant Princes of north Germany. The Scottish towns, especially Edinburgh, strongly favoured the Danish match, 'having their most necessary trade with the Easterlings'. Anne, moreover, had the advantage in age and beauty. In 1589 she was not quite fifteen, while Catherine was thirty-one, James twenty-three. Advocates of the French marriage pictured Catherine as prudent and virtuous, a mature woman who could give the King good counsel, while Anne was only a child. But the friends of Denmark whispered that 'the sister of Navarre was old and crooked and something worse if all were known', and they painted Anne's allurements in such fetching colours that the King 'conceived a liking in imagination'.

Negotiations had begun with Denmark in 1585, though it was not until two years later that James dispatched his old tutor, Peter Young, and a wealthy merchant, Sir Patrick Vaus, to make formal request for a Danish bride. At this time the King was thinking of Frederick's elder daughter, the Princess Elizabeth, not of Anne, the younger, who was but twelve years old. Before the ambassadors departed they asked instructions to cover various contingencies. Suppose, they said, they should find the Princess Elizabeth already betrothed. 'Forfend the omen,' answered James the pious opportunist, 'but if it happen, ask for the other.' The ambassadors were received rather coldly in Denmark and at length were told that the elder Princess was already promised to the Duke of Brunswick, 'but for the second, Anna, if the King did like her he should have her'. The ambassadors replied with dignity that Kings of Scotland were accustomed to marry the eldest daughters of other sovereigns, to which the Danes answered that there was little to choose between the two sisters, 'and howbeit Madame Elizabeth was the more beautiful', the Princess Anne was far from unlovely and for her age was taller and more fully developed than her sister.

Negotiations continued. But the French marriage had not yet been abandoned. A crisis arose in May 1589, when the Earl Marischal, a wealthy and accomplished nobleman, about to sail for Denmark to complete negotiations, was ordered to stay his departure. This caused a riot in Edinburgh. Provost, bailies and many citizens entered Maitland's chambers, threatening to kill him if the Danish marriage was broken off. Hastily James summoned his Council, then announced his solemn intention to proceed with the Danish match. For the moment he was little more than a prisoner in the city and, though he was not unwilling to yield, the affair seemed astonishing to Thomas Fowler, an English intelligencer. 'Here is a strange country', he wrote, 'I should say a most vile people.'

The Earl Marischal, who sailed in June, was instructed to ask for high terms: a dowry of £1,000,000 Scots, concessions to Scottish merchants, naval and military assistance against invasion or in case the King had to fight for a foreign title due to him through just inheritance. Denmark was asked to abandon an ancient claim to the Orkneys and to form with Scotland an anti-Catholic league to which other Protestant States should be invited to adhere. James offered in return to settle a handsome property upon his bride, though the ambassador was cautiously instructed to give no figures. The Danes, astonished and angered at these demands, refused to give more than a small sum of money left to his second daughter by Frederick, who had died in 1588.

The marriage was salvaged but not by the diplomats. The Queen Mother, Sophia, having embarked upon the joyous labour of providing her daughter's trousseau, was not to be denied, and preparations in Denmark went on apace. Reports reached Scotland of rich provision of apparel, jewels and furnishings. Five hundred Danish tailors and embroiderers were said to have been at work for three months. Anne's coach contained no iron, for all its metallic parts were made of silver. Meanwhile the young King of Scots, in boyish and romantic fashion, became more and more enamoured of his bride-to-be. 'The King grows in affection for the gentlewoman and talks much of her virtues.' Persuaded that her affection was growing in proportion to his, he feared that to break the marriage would bring death to his beloved. He dropped his request for a large dowry, saying he would not be a merchant for his bride. There would be no stay on his part if the Danes would send the Princess. In the end he obtained little beyond the advantage of the Danish connection.

Rumours of great preparations in Denmark contrasted painfully with a great lack of them in Scotland. Fowler wrote that the King 'has neither plate nor stuff to furnish one of his little half-built houses, which are in great decay and ruin. His plate is not worth £100, he has only two or three rich jewels, his saddles are of plain cloth. He is served with six or seven dishes of meat but eats but of two; no bread but of oats, and cares not of what apparel'. 'Surely Scotland was never in worse state to receive a Queen than at present,' commented Asheby, the English ambassador, 'for there is not a house in repair.' It was feared that the bride might arrive before the King's wedding garments were prepared. Already spent was a tax of £10,000 Scots granted by Parliament for the marriage, and James turned in desperation to England. Never had his poverty pinched him so cruelly and never did he beg so abjectly for funds. Elizabeth sent £1000 in cash and advanced £2000 to purchase plate in England.

The marriage was celebrated by proxy in Copenhagen on August 20th, 1589. About ten days later Anne set sail for Scotland, but storms and strong west winds rendered the passage impossible, and after three attempts the Danish admiral turned back to Copenhagen. Anne, however, was taken to Oslo, a concession to the Scottish envoys who were most reluctant that the bride return to Denmark. Meanwhile the foul weather that prevented her arrival in Scotland prevented also the arrival of news concerning her. James knew only of her departure. As the days lengthened into weeks he became deeply alarmed, commanded public prayers, and retired to Craigmillar near Edinburgh, where like a true lover he spent his time in sighing, thinking every day a year as he waited for his bride's arrival. Late in September he sent out a small fleet to bring what news it could. With it he dis-

patched a tender little note to Anne expressing his deep anxiety
for the safety of his 'seul amour'.[3]

During these weary weeks he found some solace in writing
amatory verse. In a short sonnet sequence he laments his sad
state and complains of the stormy weather, though the sincerity
of his emotion is hidden beneath a mass of awkward phrases and
classical allusions. Simpler but more pleasing is a song which he
appears to have written at this time:

> What mortall man may live but hart
> (without heart)
> As I doe now suche is my cace,
> For now the whole is from the part
> Devided eache in divers place.
> The seas are now the barr
> Which make us distance farr
> That we may soone winn narr
> God graunte us grace.
>
> Full manie causes suire I have
> Which does augment my woe and caire
> But one more speciall nor the leave (than the rest)
> When I doe think what joye was thaire
> What gladnes and what greeting
> At our long wished meeting
> I can not well unwitting   (without wetting)
> My checkis declare.

Another song in the same metre compares the plight of James and
Anne to that of Hero and Leander.[4]

Finally on October 10th a ship arrived from Norway telling of
Anne's exile at Oslo; and it was then that James secretly resolved
to sail in person to fetch home his bride, 'to commit himself and
his hopes Leander-like to the waves of the ocean, all for his beloved Hero's sake'. On October 22nd he embarked at Leith,
taking with him the Chancellor, whom he had cleverly hood-
winked, a few other councillors, and a retinue of about three
hundred persons. Of three documents which he left behind, one,
an explanation of his action, was written in his own hand with a
quaint self-revelation that makes it unique among State papers. It
was a youthful declaration of independence. His marriage had

been long delayed, he began, because he was alone, without father or mother, brother or sister; 'and this my nakedness made me to be weak and my enemies strong, and the want of succession bred disdain'. He then discovered, he continued, that the Queen, his bedfellow, was stayed by contrary winds, and he determined instantly to make the voyage, not one of his councillors being present. He kept his resolution secret in part to shield Maitland from the accusation of having proposed it, for Maitland already bore great envy 'for leading me by the nose, as it were, to all his appetites, as if I were an unreasonable creature or a bairn that could do nothing of myself'. Moreover, it was unfitting that subjects should give princes advice in such matters. He had also come to his resolution alone in order to demonstrate that he could make his own decisions and that he was no 'irresolute ass who could do nothing of himself'. The voyage, he argued, would be brief and secure, and he begged his subjects not to condemn his conduct but to live peaceful lives during his absence.

Two other documents provided for the government of the country until his return. The Duke of Lennox, a youth of fifteen years, was to be President of the Council, with the Earl of Bothwell as an advisory associate. Bothwell's wild and unstable temper made him appear a strange choice, and it was said that the King had left the geese in the fox's keeping; but other important councillors were to remain in constant session, reinforced by groups of nobles who should attend in rotation. Military authority was vested in Lord John Hamilton who was placed in charge of the Borders with a Council of his own. The two Councils might merge in any crisis. Finally, though this was not mentioned in the documents, considerable authority was given to Robert Bruce, an eminent clergyman of Edinburgh. These arrangements worked more smoothly than might have been anticipated.[5]

A fair wind carried James to the southern coast of Norway in five days. 'All in good health,' reported one of the party, 'the King's Majesty was never sick.' The voyage along Norway's southern shore, however, was slow, and it was not until November 11th that James landed at Tönsberg, whence he travelled overland to Oslo. A Scottish account relates in homely fashion that the King made his way at once to the old Bishop's Palace where Anne was lodged, 'passed quietly with boots and all to her Highness', and offered to kiss her after the Scots fashion. Anne demurred. 'Marry, after a few words privately spoken betwixt his Majesty and her, there passed familiarity and kisses.' A good story, but one unhappily belied by a Danish narrative of the King's sojourn in Scandinavia. According to this account, he entered Oslo in some state, preceded by heralds, and accompanied by Danish and Norwegian nobles who met the Scots outside the city. He is described as a tall, thin gentleman, with deep-set eyes, dressed in a red velvet coat ornamented with gold and in a black velvet cloak lined with sable fur. He and Anne spent half an hour together, and he then was escorted to his lodgings in another house where the Bishop of Oslo welcomed him in a Latin oration to which he listened with the utmost attention. Next morning, dressed in blue velvet bespangled with gold and escorted as before by the local nobility, he visited Anne once more and spent the day in her company. [6]

The marriage was celebrated on November 23rd in the hall of the old Bishop's Palace with such splendour as time and place allowed. Tapestries decorated the walls, and upon a large red cloth in the middle of the hall were placed two handsome chairs with red velvet cushions and a red damask canopy. In solemn procession the King was escorted from his lodgings to the palace where trumpets proclaimed his arrival. The bride and groom entered the hall together, and the King then advanced and stood upon the red cloth where Anne took her place by his side. The marriage ceremony, performed in French by David Lindsay, minister at Leith, included a sermon by the Bishop of Oslo upon the significance of Christian marriage. At the close of the service, which had lasted about an hour, Anne left the hall alone, while James remained to receive the congratulations of the company to whom he replied in Latin.

He was deeply in love with his young bride. She was very blonde, with lovely white skin and golden hair, slender, graceful and of a good height, 'a Princess', wrote David Lindsay, 'both godly and beautiful, as appeareth by all that know her. I trust she shall bring a blessing to the country, like as she giveth great contentment to his Majesty'. The Bishop of Oslo was kept waiting an hour for a promised audience while the King dallied in the Queen's chamber.

A month of festivities followed the wedding, by which time the winter was so far advanced that James rejected an immediate

return to Scotland and accepted an invitation from his new relatives to visit Copenhagen. Leaving Oslo on December 22nd to
begin the long journey overland by sledge, the royal party
travelled through Bohuslän and arrived, on New Year's Day
1590, at Bohus Castle near the Swedish frontier. There the King
attended divine worship, and though it was thought that he and
his courtiers entered the church in some disorder, it was noted also
that he gave close attention to the service. A great banquet followed, with innumerable toasts, each accompanied by a volley of
artillery, and with dancing and festivities until a late hour. The
travellers then passed, royally attended, through a small portion
of Sweden near present-day Gothenburg and came to Varberg
Castle in Halland. On January 21st they crossed the Sound to
Elsinore where they were welcomed by the Danish royal family
and took their places in a stately procession to Kronborg Castle
while cannon thundered for half an hour.

The King remained in Denmark until late April 1590, enjoying
a whirl of sports and pleasures in which deep drinking played no
inconsiderable part. A letter to his favourite, Alexander Lindsay,
later Lord Spynie, is written 'from the castle of Kronborg where
we are drinking and driving over in the old manner', and another
of his letters speaks of Denmark as a very drunken country. But
he found time for other things. At the royal academy in Copenhagen he listened to lectures on theology and medicine, and was
complimented on his learning by Dr. Paulus, Superintendent of
Sealand, to whom he answered in Latin: 'From my most tender
years I have been given to books and letters, which even today I
willingly acknowledge.' At Roskilde he was the guest of the
theologian Nils Hemmingsen, with whom he disputed long in
Latin on the nature of predestination; and it was said (in Scotland)
that the King persuaded many Danes of their errors in theology.
He visited Tycho Brahe at his observatory on the island of Hveen,
spending a day in learned discourse upon the Copernican theory.
Meanwhile there began at court a new round of festivities with
the arrival of Duke Henry of Brunswick who was married on
Easter Day to the Princess Elizabeth, Anne's elder sister.

James was not free from worry. There were quarrels among the
Scots who had come with him — a reminder of what was probably
taking place at home. Preparations in Scotland for his home-
coming were, he feared, inadequate, nor could he predict the

exact moment of his arrival. In a medley of Biblical texts he warned the clergyman, Robert Bruce, that he might return like a thief in the night; 'and whose lamp I find burning, provided with oil, these will I give thanks to and bring into the banquet house with me, but those that lack their burning lamps will be barred at the door. For God's sake,' he added, coming to earth with a thud, 'take all the pains ye can to tune our folks well now against our homecoming lest we be all shamed before strangers. Thus recommending me and my new rib to your daily prayers, I commit you to the only All-sufficient'.

On May 1st the King and Queen landed at Leith where they were welcomed by nobles and citizens, and after a stay of six days proceeded to Holyrood, King and nobles on horseback, the Queen in a Danish coach richly adorned with cloth of gold and purple velvet and drawn by eight horses. On May 17th she was crowned in the Abbey Kirk in a ceremony lasting for seven hours. A solemn procession was followed by sermons in Latin, French and English. Anne retired to a cabinet and returned clothed in her royal robe, the crown was placed upon her head, her robe was loosed to expose part of her right arm and breast upon which Robert Bruce poured 'a bonny quantity of oil', the sceptre and sword were presented to her. Trumpets sounded, drums beat, artillery thundered from the castle. Two days later the Queen made a formal entry into Edinburgh, and shortly thereafter the Danes who had come with her to Scotland took their leave.

The King doubtless breathed a sigh of relief, for he had been under heavy strain. At this return to Scotland, a host of matters, the accumulation of the last six months, all demanded immediate attention, and to them were added negotiations concerning Anne's jointure and arrangements for her coronation and entry into Edinburgh. The ministers had made themselves unpleasant by denouncing anointment as a pagan and Jewish custom, and by objecting to Anne's entry upon the Sabbath; and when this point was arranged to their satisfaction, the citizens found their preparations disturbed. The pressure of business was so great that the King had scarcely three hours sleep a night, 'was much disquieted in mind and body', and had a painful swelling in his hand. His complaints that close application to business quickly undermined his health contained some truth.[7]

He remained infatuated with his bride, whose praises he sang in sonnets and in other verse. Her beauty, he wrote, has caused his love, long smouldering as fire hidden among coals, to burst into sudden blaze. She inspires his verse, and her approbation spurs him to persevere, though government brings stormy cares. But she is a sweet physician who can soothe and cure his ills.

> How oft you see me have an heavie hart,
> Remember then, sweete doctour, on your art.

He imagines that three goddesses joined hands at her birth to bestow their graces upon her.

> That blessed houre when first was brought to light
> Our earthlie Juno and our gratious Queene,
> Three Goddesses how soone they hade her seene
> Contended who protect her shoulde by right.
> But being as Goddesses of equall might
> And as of female sexe like stiffe in will
> It was agreed by sacred Phoebus skill
> To joyne there powers to blesse that blessed wight.
> Then, happie Monarch sprung of Ferguse race,
> (that is, James)
> That talkes with wise Minerve when pleaseth thee
> And when thou list some Princlie sports to see
> Thy chaste Diana rides with thee in chase
> Then when to bed thou gladlie does repaire
> Clasps in thine arms thy Cytherea faire.

It was natural for James to speak of his bride as Cytherea, and even as Diana, since she sometimes hunted with him, but to compare her to Minerva was to take great poetic licence. For she was incurably frivolous and empty-headed. She possessed high spirits and a playful sprightliness, but these qualities were shallow and vacuous, and they must have easily palled. Her love for gaiety and dancing, for games, masques and pageants, was childish rather than courtly. The ministers quickly condemned her 'want of godly and virtuous exercise among her maids', her absence from the Kirk, her 'night-waking and balling'. There was skipping at court, as Knox had said in Mary's reign, not very comely for honest women. But, though Anne's tastes were innocent enough, they were foolish and expensive. The King soon discovered that her household was costing more than his, and that

in obtaining money she possessed a shrewdness remarkable in one
so childish.[8]

The Scottish court with its feuds and intrigues was a dangerous
place for one so young and so naive. Courtiers did not scruple to
draw her into the plottings of Scottish politics nor to set her
against the King in the rivalries of the moment. She had a quick
temper, high words came easily, and in her childish tantrums she
could be violent, spiteful, indiscreet and quite ingenious in her
efforts to annoy. Hence the early years of the King's married life
were far from tranquil. Some time in the 1590s Anne became a
Roman Catholic. A Lutheran in Denmark, she did not take
kindly to Presbyterianism nor to the freedom of the Scottish
ministers in instructing royalty. Very likely she adopted Catholicism in the half-trifling way in which idle persons sometimes occupy
themselves with a new faith. Her conversion did not make her
serious or devout, nor did it strengthen her character.

Generally speaking, the King treated his wife with restraint and
patience. In their early married life he showed her tenderness and
affection. As his first ardour abated, which it did rather quickly,
love was succeeded by a casual camaraderie not without its tender
side. Later, in England, the two drifted apart and did not live
together. Anne had little influence over her husband. She could
not share his intellectual interests, and she confirmed the foolish
contempt with which he regarded women. Alas! The King had
married a stupid wife.

CHAPTER VII

THE CATHOLIC EARLS
AND THE DEVIL OF NORTH BERWICK

IN May 1587, more than two years before the King's marriage, he celebrated his majority with a Parliament and with other solemnities for which most of the Scottish nobles assembled in Edinburgh. It was then that he held his famous love-feast. Gathering the nobles at Holyrood, he besought them with youthful earnestness to enter upon a general pacification of their feuds and hatreds. He then gave them a banquet, after which he caused them to walk in solemn and picturesque procession, two by two, each holding his enemy by the hand — which must have caused some grim glances — from Holyrood up to the Mercat Cross. There he drank to them and they drank to each other, while cannon roared from the castle and the people sang for mirth. But alas! The turbulence of the nobles, their feuds, plottings and defiance of royal authority were to form the central theme of Scottish politics for some years to come.

The revolutions that punctuated James's minority, together with his theory of divine right, rendered him keenly aware of the problem of the nobles. It was a problem that would have perplexed the wisest of men. The nobles did not think of the King as a sovereign lord, commanding universal obedience, but rather as a feudal suzerain, against whom rebellion was no great crime. They were themselves small kings in their own districts, combining the authority of feudal chieftains, landlords, magistrates and heads of clans, and hence they could force the lower classes into their service and summon the whole countryside to arms. Since they were bound in duty to defend their followers against all the world, they were at constant feud with each other, and then, as the King wrote, 'they bang it out bravely, he and all his kin against him and all his'. The enforcement of the law, James rightly believed, was the heart of the problem. Great crimes were rife in Scotland, he said, because men set themselves to defend their kindred and their friends against the course of justice. His aim was to teach the nobles that they must obey the law as precisely as the meanest of the lieges, to train the gentry to appeal to the Crown and not to the great lords, to enforce laws against guns and pistols, and to reduce where possible the heritable magistracies which exalted the noble and oppressed the poor. But these things could only come slowly.[1]

Meanwhile there were a number of reasons why the problem of the nobles became suddenly acute. One was the pre-eminent position of Sir John Maitland, the King's principal adviser. This remarkable man, reversing the career of his brother, William Maitland of Lethington, had been at first an adherent of Queen Mary and later had entered the King's service when the friends of Mary were welcome during Lennox's regime. Thenceforth he grew steadily in the King's confidence, becoming Secretary in 1584, Vice-Chancellor in 1586, and Chancellor a year later, an office he retained until his death in 1595. He 'was a man of rare parts,' wrote Spottiswoode, 'of a deep wit, learned, full of courage, and most faithful to his King and master. No man ever carried himself in his place more wisely nor sustained it more courageously against his enemies than he did'. In addition to the solid qualities of the statesman, he possessed literary tastes that commended him to the King. He wrote both English and Latin verse, had a sharp Scots tongue, loved raillery and sarcasm, and mingled grave matters of State with jests and facetiousness, to James's great amusement. His politics grew with the years. Despite his indifference to the religious disputes of the age he urged upon the King the necessity of better relations with the ministers, and though he bitterly resented Mary's death he saw clearly that moderate friendship with England was essential to Scottish interests.

Maitland stood for modernization and reform throughout the whole fabric of government, for vigorous administration, for firm assertion of royal authority. And the King, inspired by his councillor, resolved to grapple more strenuously with the problems of the State. His majority in 1587 was made the occasion for new measures against lawlessness and crime. When he returned from Denmark 'like a new Jason to his languishing people', he hoped to inaugurate sweeping reforms. With Maitland's assistance he would play a great role in European affairs. At home he would reform his chamber and household, not only to curtail expense but to live with more kingly dignity; and an attempt was made, not very successfully, to tighten the lax rules governing access to the royal presence. But he and Maitland hoped for much more.

They wished to secure the wisest of councils, to purify the Court of Session, to strengthen royal finance, as well as to improve relations with the Kirk, provide for the defence of the kingdom, and pacify the Borders, Highlands, and Western Isles. Thus Maitland represented a bold and ambitious effort towards firm and efficient government, with the King playing an important part in the advance.[2]

But Maitland's preponderance and the reforms he advocated were regarded by the nobles as a direct challenge to aristocratic rule. He was not a noble by birth, but a mere 'paddock-stool [toadstool] of a night', as Bothwell sneered, in contrast to the cedars of the ancient nobility. The lords suspected that his reforms would undermine their position, robbing them of free access to the King and of their vote in Council. They begged James to govern 'with his nobility in wonted manner, not by private persons hated, nor by order of Denmark'. Maitland was surrounded by a ring of foes. Bothwell, drawing other Stewarts after him, became the arch-enemy of the Chancellor, ready to go to any length to drive him from office. Other Protestant lords were jealous of him, the Catholic Earls hated him, and the Queen, remembering his hostility to the Danish marriage, foolishly joined the opposition. Supported only by the King, Maitland saw his reforms vanish away and the turbulence of the nobles increase deplorably.

There were, moreover, other conditions which rendered the nobles unusually dangerous. The Catholic Earls of the north formed a strong party. They were led by Huntly, by the two young Earls of Errol and Angus, and by Crawford, older, but luxurious and lawless. Some of these men, as we know, had plotted with Spain before the coming of the Armada; and now, failing to grasp the finality of Spain's defeat, they continued to plot with that country for a renewed assault upon England. In traitorous fashion they offered Philip their allegiance if he would send men and money to Scotland. Thus an important segment of the peerage was drawn into treason and rebellion, intensifying the clash of religions in Scotland and posing terrible problems for the government.

The Catholic Earls were to be feared the more because their leader, Huntly, was a royal favourite whom the King loved dearly. Young, handsome, gay and attractive, Huntly in 1588 had married Lady Henrietta Stuart, a sister of the young Duke of Lennox, and was thereby admitted to the innermost circle of those on whom the King lavished affection. Thenceforth he was almost a member of the royal family. James laboured to convert him to Protestantism, and when Huntly, with utter hypocrisy, agreed to attend the Kirk, the King was overjoyed, made him captain of the guard, and lodged him in his own chamber. James thought of him merely as a joyous companion, too thoughtless to bother with matters of State and too incompetent to lead great enterprises. But Huntly's character was not as simple as this. He was both treacherous and cruel. Despite the hocus-pocus of his conversion he remained ardently Catholic, he plotted and rebelled, relying on James's indulgence to moderate chastisement. Though a man of no great ability, he developed into a competent military leader. Away from court and on his native heath he could be as barbarous as the most savage of his clansmen. He butchered the Earl of Moray in a foul murder, captured two cooks from an enemy clan and roasted them alive, and adorned the turrets of his castle of Strathbogie with the severed limbs of his foes.

Protestant Scotland, supported by Queen Elizabeth, insisted that the Catholic Earls be punished with the utmost severity. But the King was inclined to be lenient. Loving Huntly as he did, he was loath to believe him a traitor, and maintained for years a secret understanding with him. 'It is thought', wrote Fowler, 'that this King is too much carried by young men that lie in his chamber and are his minions.' But James had sounder reasons. The Catholic Earls he regarded as a counterpoise to the Kirk and as a means of contact with the Catholic world. To punish them too harshly he said, would lay the ground for everlasting feuds. He knew they had many friends at court. Huntly and his wife were beloved by Lennox and had a friend in the Queen. The Catholic Errol and the Protestant Glamis — Lord Treasurer — had married sisters. Alexander Lindsay, Lord Spynie, Vice-Chamberlain and a great favourite, whom the King called 'Sandie', was a brother of the Earl of Crawford. 'He is the King's best loved minion,' wrote Fowler, 'a proper man and Huntly's wholly. There is not one in the chamber or of the stable, which two sorts of persons are nearest attending on the King's person, but are Huntly's. These men have the King's ear and work great effect for Huntly, and the Chancellor cannot mend it, for the King will not change his servants, he loves them so well.'³ Finally, James was lenient because the Earls offered protection against Bothwell, whom the King feared and hated above all other living men.

The career and character of Francis Stewart Hepburn, Earl of Bothwell, reflected the influence of two famous uncles. His father, John Stewart, was a brother of the Regent Moray, both natural sons of James V. From his uncle, the Regent, Bothwell derived a traditional alliance with the Kirk and with its ministers, whose interests he undertook to represent at court and with whom he maintained an understanding long after he had grown disreputable. But the alliance was always grotesque. His mother, Jane Hepburn, was a sister of the Bothwell who had been Queen Mary's lover; and it was this uncle, not the good Regent, whom the younger Bothwell resembled in conduct and character. He was fierce, profligate and lawless, spending his time in carousals, feuds and rebellions. There was little reason or logic in his actions. Slowly reduced to the status of an outlaw, he appeared to believe he could restore his fortunes if only he secured possession of the person of the King; and his wild and quixotic pranks to that end rendered James's life miserable for many years. But he never could have caused the trouble he did, had he not become a symbol of aristocratic hatred for Maitland and of Protestant loathing for the Catholic Earls. He was handsome, dashing and loquacious. 'This nobleman hath a wonderful wit', wrote the Dean of Durham upon whom he once forced his presence, 'and as wonderful a volubility of tongue as agility of body on horse and foot; competently learned in the Latin; well languaged in the French and Italian; much delighted in poetry; and of a very resolute disposition both to do and to suffer; nothing dainty to discover his humour or any good quality he hath.' 'There is more wickedness, more valour, and more good parts in him', wrote Fowler, 'than in any three of the other noblemen.'

In the early 1580s, when he first became prominent at court, he had been a royal favourite. James hung about his neck and embraced him tenderly. But affection changed gradually to anger at his perpetual misconduct; and anger deepened into hate as the King came to believe that Bothwell, having formed a connection with certain witches and sorcerers, possessed supernatural power for mischief. The outlaw, James suspected, planned to build his alliance with the Kirk, as the Regent Moray had done, until he controlled the State and could grasp perhaps at the Crown itself.[4]

Thus menaced on one side by the treasons of the Catholic Earls and on the other by Bothwell's unpredictable enterprises, the timid, bookish and negligent young King was not far from despair. 'He hath oft told me the wickedness of his nobility and their evil natures,' wrote Fowler in 1589, 'declaring himself weary of his life among them.' Yet in the turmoil of these years he acted rather well. More admirable in adversity than in better fortune, he faced dangers and difficulties with energy and courage, and dealt in the end such heavy blows to the nobility that when he left Scotland in 1603 the problem was close to solution.

In February 1589, when Huntly, Errol and Crawford were present at court, a sudden dispatch from Elizabeth brought letters that she had intercepted on their way from Scotland to Spain. They were written to Philip by Huntly, Errol and other Scottish Catholics, lamenting the failure of the Armada, hoping for a new attempt in the near future, and promising, if Philip sent assistance, to invade England within a few weeks. 'Good Lord!' wrote Elizabeth: 'Methinks I do but dream! No King a week would bear this!' Clap up the Earls, advised the Queen, and teach them how a King deals with treason. James was in great perplexity. He removed Huntly from the captaincy of the guard and imprisoned him in Edinburgh Castle, but dined with him next day, treating him with great affection, 'yea, kissing him at times to the amazement of many; and the next day was with him again and hath given his wife, servants and friends free access to him'. He wrote him a letter pathetic in its distress. 'Are these', he asked sadly, 'the fruits of your new conversion?' To the English ambassador he promised that Huntly would be punished, yet within a few days the Earl was released and restored to the captaincy of the guard. At this Maitland rebelled, telling the King he would leave his service if the guard remained in Huntly's control. James yielded, dismissed Huntly once more, and ordered him to his own lands in the north.

The King soon had further proof of Huntly's treason. Before the Earl left Edinburgh, James foolishly went hunting in his company and as a result narrowly escaped capture. A few weeks later, as he spent the night in the country near Edinburgh, he received sudden intelligence that Huntly, Errol and Crawford were marching down from the north, while Bothwell, who had joined their enterprise in hope of ruining Maitland, was advancing from the Border. At midnight the King took horse, and by three o'clock in the morning was safe in Maitland's house in Edinburgh. Bothwell then retired to Dalkeith and the Catholic Earls to Perth.

Strong measures were now a necessity. James had no money, and the English ambassador described his position as pitiful, with every insolent earl ready to beard him. Yet with great vigour he assembled his Protestant nobles, summoned the lieges of southern Scotland, secured a force from Edinburgh, and marched north so rapidly that within two weeks he was approaching Aberdeen where, at the Bridge of Dee, the Catholic Earls prepared for battle. The King's forces feared a night attack. 'That night we watched in arms,' wrote a member of the expedition, 'and his Majesty would not so much as lie down on his bed, but went about like a good captain encouraging us.' Fowler also praised James's efforts. 'This people', he wrote, 'must have free access to the King's presence. If there were no more but the continual disquiet of such a throng from morning to night and their enter- tainment, it were too much toil for any prince; but he must visit their watches nightly, he must comfort them, be pleased with them passing from place to place, that day or night the good King has little quiet and less rest. He hath watched two nights and never put off his clothes.'

A battle at the Bridge of Dee seemed certain. But Huntly's followers, learning that the King was in the field against them, lost heart and began to melt away into the hills. Huntly followed them, and James entered Aberdeen without a battle. But his difficulties were great: the country denuded of victuals, the weather bad, his men weary from forced marches and eager to be home. If he left Aberdeen while Huntly was still at large, his expedition would have failed. Huntly was therefore informed in some secret way that if he placed himself in the King's mercy he would not be harshly punished. Thereupon he surrendered, as did Crawford and Bothwell, and James was able to return trium- phantly to Edinburgh with the principal culprits in custody. Tried for treason and found guilty, they were merely placed in easy confinement from which within a few months they were released, to the exasperation of the Kirk and of Queen Elizabeth. Yet James had acted well. He had pursued an independent policy, had chastised the Catholic lords without crushing them, and had added to his authority and to that of his Chancellor.[5]

His difficulties during the next two years were not caused by the Catholic lords but by the gradual degeneration of the Earl of Bothwell. He had been greatly incensed by Bothwell's participation in the recent revolt, yet readmitted him to a kind of probationary favour, telling him that 'as he had resolved to be a reformed King, so he would have him to be a reformed lord'. But Bothwell would not reform. His Border district of Liddesdale was lawless and disorderly, causing serious friction with England; his companions were thieves and murderers. In January 1591, during the trial of one of his disreputable adherents, he abducted a witness from the Tolbooth in Edinburgh, though the King himself was in an adjoining chamber; and that same night James rode to Kelso to prevent a brawl in which he knew Bothwell would take part. Next day he summoned the Earl and reproached him bitterly. He had loved and advanced him, he said, only to receive indignities in return. He vowed to God that unless Bothwell mended his ways, the law would be enforced with all vigour.

Then in April came revelations that turned the King's anger into loathing and undying hate. Throughout the winter of 1590-1591 there had been in the Lothians a number of witch trials, and in them, partly because of his taste for the abnormal, James had taken a fascinated interest. A poor fellow, said to be bewitched, capered and shrieked before the King 'to the great admiration of his Majesty'. A witch named Jely Duncan, who confessed to have danced and played upon a trumpet before other witches in the kirkyard at North Berwick, was brought before James to repeat her antics; and another witch, Agnes Sampson, whispered to him things he had said to his Queen on their wedding night, at which he 'swore by the living God that he believed all the devils in hell could not have discovered the same'. 'In respect of the strangeness of these matters the King took great delight to be present at their examinations.'

He was interested also because he regarded witchcraft as a branch of theology. Witches and sorcerers, he believed, were persons of abandoned morals who had been lured by Satan to repudiate God and to yield themselves wholly to the guidance of the Devil, happy to execute his evil commands. Baptism was replaced by a lick of the Devil's tongue which left a mark insensible to pain upon some secret part of the witch's body. In blasphemous parody of Christian rites, witches met in congregations to worship the Devil, who appeared before them and preached from a pulpit, teaching them the mischief they were to do and making them kiss his hinder parts as an act of adoration. James's little treatise, *Daemonologie*, reflecting the belief of the time, describes these meetings in some detail. Witches could come to them, it says, either in natural ways or carried on great winds, though for some unexplained reason they could fly through the air only so long as they could hold their breath. The Devil supplied them with enchanted stones, powders, poisons, and waxen figures, and, thus equipped, they could raise storms, induce insanity, impotency, or exaggerated sexual desire, could perhaps cause death, and could raise spirits to plague mankind. There were more witches than sorcerers, says the King, because women are more frail than men, and because the Devil, having seduced Eve in the beginning, has been 'the homlier with that sex' ever since. Indeed, to the modern reader, perhaps the strongest impression left by James's book is its vivid portrayal of the intense reality of Satan. He is as actual as God, and his habits, personality and powers are known in astonishing detail.

These beliefs were possible because the witch cult in Scotland was derived in part from ancient heathen practice in which devotees worshipped an incarnate god that appeared before them and in which the ritual consisted largely of fertility rites. The witches of Lothian confessed that they met in a congregation at North Berwick where the Devil came to them in the likeness of a man with a blackened or masked face or wearing the skin of an animal. They also confessed that there was dancing, singing and drinking at their meetings and that the Devil used them carnally.

Then suddenly James made the terrifying discovery that it was against himself and his life that the witches had been employing their devilish arts, and that they had done so at Bothwell's instigation. Happily their methods had not been efficacious, but their intentions had been murderous. By casting cats bound to the severed joints of dead bodies into the sea, they had sought to raise storms while the King was on his voyage to Denmark. Poisons had been concocted 'for his Highness' destruction'; and a waxen image of the King had been passed from hand to hand with the words, 'This is King James the Sixth, ordained to be consumed at the instance of a nobleman, Francis, Earl of Bothwell.' Some of the confessions, moreover, implied that Bothwell was himself the leader of the witches, the Devil who appeared before them at North Berwick and urged them to strike at the King. The King was to be destroyed, said a witch, 'that another might rule in his Majesty's place and the government might go to the Devil'. Another confession declared that the Devil asked the witches whether their magic was proving effective, 'and because a poor old silly ploughman named Grey Meill chanced to say that nothing ailed the King yet, God be thanked, the Devil gave him a great blow'. The witches in turn asked the Devil why their enchantments had failed, and he answered in frustration: 'Il est un homme de Dieu.' James's faith had saved him!

Thenceforth he followed the trials with bated breath: he questioned the witches, acquiring in his own opinion great skill in cross-examination; he tried desperately for confessions, for a witch who confessed lost her power for evil; he permitted gross indignities and horrible torture. He has been accused of sadistic pleasure in inflicting pain, but this is unjust. Fear is a potent cause of cruelty, and James was in great terror. Moreover, when he hated, he hated with vindictive intensity, and he regarded witchcraft, with its repudiation of God, as the vilest of sins, 'the highest point of idolatry, wherein no exception is admitted by the law of God'. The magistrate who was lenient not only committed a heinous offence but exposed himself to the machinations of the witches. His zeal was his only protection, for God defended His own, promising to shield the honest official who fought the power of Satan; but God did not defend the hesitant. Despite his fears, James was gratified to think of himself as a pious Prince doing his godly duty though it involved some danger, and with sanctimonious conceit he contrasted himself with the witches: he was the child and servant of God, they of the Devil, he was the Lord's anointed, they the opposite. Inevitably accelerating the pace of the persecution, he freely admitted his responsibility. 'For these witches,' he said, 'whatsoever hath been gotten from them hath been done by me myself, not because I was more wise than others, but because I believed that such a vice did reign and ought to be suppressed.' Later in England his views became more moderate, bordering on scepticism, and he mitigated the ferocity of the

English trials. He did not do so in Scotland, and his one defence must be that he was in great terror and was utterly sincere. [6]

The very name of Bothwell was now odious to him, and he determined that punishment should be harsh. But Bothwell was a difficult man to punish. Imprisoned upon the accusations of the witches, his fierce temper would not await a trial, and he escaped from Edinburgh Castle to his fastnesses along the Border. The Council proclaimed him a traitor, but no one dared to assume his vacant offices or to accept his forfeited estates. Indeed, there was general sympathy for him. His crimes were condoned and minimized by the Kirk as youthful exuberances, the foam from new-pressed wine. The nobles, regarding measures against him as a new attack on their order, and approving his hostility to Maitland, supported him secretly; while the mass of the people contrasted the King's severity towards him with the gentle punishment of the Catholic Earls. Though Bothwell lived the life of an outlaw, spending some nights in the woods, he had friends everywhere. He was seen at Dalkeith, at Crichton and at Leith. Emboldened by potations with his friends, he came to the Canongate and issued a taunting challenge to the Chancellor. Thus he roamed about, keeping the King in a state of superstitious dread and of constant fear of capture.

On December 27th he made a daring raid upon Holyroodhouse, in which he pursued Maitland to his chamber and the King to a remote tower, set fires at their doors and tried to break through with hammers. Word, however, was smuggled to the provost of Edinburgh, the townspeople came flocking to the palace, and Bothwell withdrew. Yet the King found little support or sympathy. When next day he attended service at St. Giles and attempted to thank the people, the clergyman rebuked him and half justified the raid. He heard that Bothwell was lurking near Haddington and made a dash to that town, but, far from capturing the outlaw, he was nearly drowned when his horse fell into the waters of Tyne. Holyrood was abandoned, and James took up his residence in Edinburgh. His condition was pitiful. Both he and the Queen were unpopular, Maitland was widely disliked, the poverty of the Crown was so pressing that the royal table 'was like to have been unserved for want'.

Then in February 1592, came a deed that shook his feeble throne to its foundations. This was Huntly's barbarous murder of the Earl of Moray, a handsome and spirited noble, beloved by the Kirk and the people as the heir and son-in-law of the good Regent. Huntly had taken advantage of the distracted state of the kingdom to pursue an old feud against Moray and other Stewarts until much of northern Scotland was aflame. At the time of the murder he was at court, while Moray was nearby at his mother's castle of Donibristle on the northern bank of the Firth of Forth. Why Moray had come south is not certain. His enemies said he had come to assist Bothwell who was his cousin and with whom he had more than casual dealings. His friends asserted he had been lured southward by the hope that the King would end the feud between him and Huntly. On February 7th Huntly, breaking an engagement with the King, suddenly crossed the water, besieged Donibristle and set it on fire. Moray made a desperate sally, broke through his enemies, and fled to the shore where he was followed and savagely butchered in a cave.

The outcry against this evil deed was deep and terrible. Men felt it insufferable that the brave Protestant Earl should be thus slaughtered by the cruel Catholic potentate of the north. Rumours and suspicions were commemorated in the ballad:

> Ye Highlands and ye Lawlands,
>   Oh! where have you been?
> They hae slain the Earl o' Murray,
>   And laid him on the green.
>
> 'Now wae be to you, Huntly!
>   And wherefore did ye sae?
> I bade you bring him wi' you,
>   But forbade you him to slay.'
>
> He was a braw callant,
>   And he rade at the ring;
> And the bonnie Earl o' Murray,
>   Oh! he micht ha' been a king.
>
> He was a braw callant,
>   And he rade at the glove;
> And the bonnie Earl o' Murray,
>   Oh! he was the Queen's luve.

The crime was more than an isolated occurrence in a personal feud. Maitland, it is clear, had so bent before the storm of his Protestant enemies as to enter a murder band with Huntly that had wide ramifications. James's part is not clear. It is true that he hated Moray as the defender of Bothwell and as the heir of the Regent's influence; he shielded Huntly as far as he could, never calling him to account in a serious way for what he had done. 'Always', he wrote to him, 'I shall remain constant.' Thus it may be that Huntly acted with the King's knowledge and approbation. And yet for James to plan murder in cold blood would not be in keeping with his character. Perhaps he merely allowed Huntly, whom he still loved, to betray him into seeming acquiescence. Nor was Anne's foolish praise of Moray, in order to irritate her husband and to embarrass the Chancellor, likely to goad the King into crime.

The murder was followed by chaos. King and Chancellor fled from Edinburgh, Maitland seeking refuge in his own house at Lethington, the King wandering about in aimless fashion under pretence of an expedition for Bothwell's capture.[7]

Months later, hoping to retrieve their lost position, they summoned a Parliament in May 1592, and allowed it to pass legislation very favourable to the Kirk. The Parliament, however, was not a surrender to the ministers but rather a culmination, prudently timed, of Maitland's efforts to achieve a better understanding between Church and State.

That his endeavours had already met with some success there is much evidence. Councillors and clergymen had been able to co-operate during the King's absence in Denmark. At his return to Scotland James gave the Kirk a solemn pledge that he would rule in a way to win its approval; and shortly after, coming to the General Assembly, he thanked God he had been born into a Kirk like that of Scotland, the sincerest Kirk in the world. 'As for our neighbour Kirk in England,' he added, 'it is an evil said Mass in English, wanting nothing but the liftings.' The Assembly was so rejoiced that nothing was heard for a quarter of an hour but praising of God and praying for the King. His jibe at England was shrewd, for there had been a bitter exchange between the Churches of the two kingdoms. In February 1589, the English cleric Richard Bancroft, in a famous sermon, had made an abusive and violent attack upon Scottish Presbyterianism, declaring it subversive of all order and government; and James Melville in reply had denounced 'these Amaziahs, the bell-god bishops in England', who sought, he declared, the advancement of episcopacy in Scotland.

In another matter also James showed his wish to conciliate the Kirk. At this time Puritanism was under severe persecution in England. Hence the Kirk instructed its ministers to offer prayers for their English brethren; and three English Puritans — Udall, Penry and Waldegrave — fleeing the wrath at home, sought asylum in Scotland. Elizabeth protested with more than usual vigour. 'There is risen both in your realm and mine', she wrote to James, 'a sect of perilous consequence, such as would have no kings but a presbytery and take our place while they enjoy our privilege. Yea, look we well unto them. I pray you stop the mouths or make shorter the tongues of such ministers as dare presume to make orisons in their pulpits for the persecuted in England for the Gospel.' Penry, she insisted, should be expelled from Scotland. But though the King must have breathed a heartfelt amen as he read her letter, he acted, surprisingly, half in alliance with the Kirk. Prayers for the English Puritans were forbidden and Penry expelled, yet James moved slowly and with obvious reluctance, retained Waldegrave as his printer, and interceded with Elizabeth in 1591 on behalf of Udall, Cartwright and other English Puritans.

Legislation passed by the Parliament of 1592 established, fully and clearly, ecclesiastical government by presbyteries, synods and General Assemblies, while an Act of 1584 which confirmed the status of bishops was rescinded. However, another Act of the same year, which asserted the royal supremacy, was retained with slight modifications. Thus it was clear that Maitland and the King, though they might for the moment substitute presbyter for bishop as ruler of the Kirk, had no intention of increasing clerical influence in temporal government. Indeed, James requested from Parliament an Act to punish attacks upon him from the pulpit, and 'chafed and railed against the ministers' when the Act was denied.[8]

As a device to quiet the resentment aroused by Moray's slaughter, the Parliament was no great success. New intrigues disrupted the court, and Bothwell gained such sympathy that he attempted a fresh assault upon the King. A little before midnight on June 27th he came to Falkland with three hundred men, surrounded the palace, and tried to beat down the gate with a battering-ram. He was repulsed, but continued till morning to besiege a tower in which the King had been locked for safety. The raid was followed by investigations that showed how completely James was surrounded by treachery. As courtiers whom he had trusted were found to have been involved and as they in turn accused others, making suspicion widespread and punishment impossible, the King was deeply dejected, 'lamenting his estate and accounting his fortune to be worse than any prince living'. His difficulties led to a short quarrel with Queen Anne. He had arrested a Gentleman of his Bedchamber, John Wemyss, the young laird of Logie, for dealings with Bothwell; but Logie's sweetheart, a Danish serving-woman of the Queen, led her lover through the royal sleeping-apartment at Holyrood in the dead of night and 'conveyed him out at a window in a pair of sheets'. James spoke so sharply to Anne about the conduct of her servant that both he and the Queen were soon in tears. He swore he was destined to die in himself, that is, to be betrayed by those nearest to him. Throughout the summer and autumn he fled from place to place in nervous dread of Bothwell, and was weakened further in August when Maitland, deciding that the opposition to him at court was so great as to render him useless, retired temporarily to his house at Lethington.⁹

A new Catholic conspiracy, an episode known as the Spanish Blanks, broke upon the country in the winter of 1592-93. A Scottish Catholic, George Ker, arrested as he was about to sail for Spain, was found to have in his possession some mysterious sheets of blank paper signed at the bottom by Huntly, Errol, Angus and Sir Patrick Gordon of Auchindoun. A taste of the torture known as the boot brought from Ker a ready confession. The plot, he said, had begun with Father William Crichton, a Scottish Jesuit in Spain, who believed that Philip would send an army to Scotland if assured of Scottish support; and the Earls, glad to promise aid, were taking the precaution of sending blanks to be filled in later by Ker and Crichton.

The Presbyterian ministers, who demanded instant action not only against the Earls but against the whole body of Scottish Catholics, talked as though James was himself a party to the plot. And among the papers in Ker's chest there was, indeed, a document drawn up by the King. It was not a letter but a private memorandum setting forth the pros and cons, from the standpoint of his interests, of a Scottish invasion of England in the summer of 1592. Very wisely he concluded that such an invasion was impossible. Scotland, he argued, was in such disorder that he could not conquer it for some time, much less conquer it and another kingdom simultaneously. And if the nobles acted as they did while he was in Scotland, what would they do in his absence? Perhaps he could invade England in the future with a little aid from abroad, the less the better. But not now. 'In the meantime', he continued, 'I will deal with the Queen of England fair and pleasantly for my title to the Crown of England after her decease, which thing, if she grant to (as it is not impossible, howbeit unlikely), we have attained our design without stroke of sword. If by the contrary, then delay makes me to settle my country in the meantime and, when I like hereafter, I may in a month or two (forewarning of the King of Spain) attain to our purpose, she not suspecting such a thing as she does now, which, if it were so done, would be a far greater honour to him and me both.' The argument is a strange amalgam of shrewdness, naivety and sublime self-confidence. It makes clear that James, though committed to the Protestant cause, might have accepted help from Spain had he believed he could do so with real advantage; and also that he toyed occasionally with the fatuous notion of enforcing his claim to the English throne by armed invasion. The document, moreover, is a clue to the thinking of the Catholic Earls. Their enemy was the Queen of England, not the King of Scots, who might well profit from their plottings, a point which James fully appreciated.

His policy, as before, was to give some satisfaction to the Kirk and to the people, to check the Earls but not to destroy them, and not to embark upon an anti-Catholic crusade. He was determined, however, that the Earls be taught a lesson, and therefore, gathering what forces he could, he marched north to Aberdeen in February 1593. But the conspirators fled to the wilds of Caithness where pursuit was impossible. The King took bonds of good behaviour from towns and gentry, left garrisons at strategic points, and seized the estates of the rebels, though their principal houses were placed in the custody of their friends. Lord Burgh, the English ambassador, wrote in disgust that James merely 'dissembled a confiscation'. And a Parliament summoned in July, presumably to pass sentence of forfeiture upon the culprits, was dissolved without taking that action.[10]

Such leniency brought upon James the furious wrath of the Kirk and the exasperated displeasure of Elizabeth. Both turned to Bothwell. He was a sanctified plague, said the minister John Davidson, sent by the Lord to turn the King from evil; and Elizabeth, reversing her policy, began a series of rather discreditable dealings with the outlaw, hoping to construct a party in Scotland that would crush the Catholic Earls. James resented her intrigues intensely. 'Touching that vile man,' he said bluntly to Burgh, 'as his foul affronts towards me are unpardonable and most to be abhorred by all sovereign princes, so we most earnestly pray the Queen to deliver him in case he have refuge within her dominions, praying you to inform her plainly that if he be reset or comforted in any part of her country, I can no longer keep amity with her, but will be forced to join in friendship with her greatest enemies for my own safety.' He wrote Elizabeth he would rather be a slave in the Turk's galleys than show leniency to one who had dishonoured him in such barbarous fashion. Nor did he believe she could think him so ignorant of a prince's honour, unless she imagined he had been bewitched by Bothwell's magic from a King into a senseless ass. His passionate language astonished Elizabeth, who wrote him a conciliatory letter.

But she did not alter her policy. On the morning of July 24th, 1593, as the King awoke and was about to dress, he heard a strange commotion in the adjoining chamber. Rushing from his bedroom in a very dishevelled state, he was horrified to behold Bothwell on his knees with a drawn sword lying before him. By this symbolism the outlaw intended to convey the meaning that he was in possession of Holyroodhouse and had the King in his power yet would do no harm to the royal person. Naturally enough, however, James was more impressed by the sword than by Bothwell's suppliant position. Shouting 'Treason', he made for the Queen's bedchamber but found it bolted. He then faced his enemy with a courage born of desperation. Bothwell might take his life, he screamed, but should not, like Satan dealing with a witch, obtain his immortal soul. He was a sovereign King, twenty-seven years of age, and he would die rather than live in shame and captivity. In dramatic fashion Bothwell offered him the sword, telling him to strike. But the tension of the melodrama was now relieved by the appearance of Lennox and other friends of the outlaw, and the King began to recognize a familiar pattern of Scots persuasiveness. He agreed to a parley. With rare presence of mind he pretended to be touched by Bothwell's show of contrition, questioned him sharply about his dealings with Elizabeth, and agreed to a compromise by which the rebel should withdraw from court until he stood trial for his old offence of witchcraft. After the trial, which all parties assumed would end in acquittal, Bothwell should be pardoned for all his other offences but should retire once more from court at the discretion of the King. Meanwhile a crowd of armed citizens had gathered round the palace. But James, not wishing to be the centre of attraction in a struggle for the possession of royalty, leaned out of the window and assured the people in homely and unkingly fashion that all was well.

He appeared to have reached the nadir of his fortunes. Yet it was now, when the clouds seemed darkest, that matters began to mend. Bothwell's insolence and presumption in his hour of victory drove home the lesson that he could not be left in control of the State. Moreover, he made a grave error in agreeing to retire from court after his seizure of the King, for he thus offered James the opportunity of achieving what he had long sought, the construction of a middle party willing to protect him against both the outlaw and the Catholic Earls. The basis of this party was a reconciliation of Maitland with some of his former adversaries — with Glamis, the Treasurer, who was followed by many Stewarts and Douglases, with Lord John Hamilton, one of the greatest of the nobles, and with the Catholic Homes and Maxwell with whom Bothwell was at feud along the Border. Such an alliance could not last, but it brought Maitland back to court and it served James's turn for the moment. In September he was strong enough to declare himself a free King, and Bothwell was informed that unless he went into exile his agreement with James would not be honoured.

Thenceforth Bothwell's fortunes slowly declined. He was able, it is true, to lead a final raid against the King in April 1594. Appearing with a small force near Leith, he manoeuvred about Arthur's Seat and drove some of the King's horse back upon Edinburgh. Calderwood comments maliciously that James 'came riding into the city at the full gallop with little honour'. But Bothwell could not follow up his success, his raid was a failure, and thenceforth Elizabeth deserted him as useless. Though no one at first had dared to accept his forfeited estates, they now passed gradually into other hands. A beggarly fugitive, Bothwell as a last resource joined forces with the Catholic Earls, but this cost him the support of the Kirk. In April 1595, he left Scotland never to return.

Not only did he ruin himself, he helped to bring ruin upon the Catholic Earls. Throughout the year 1593 the King had continued to deal with the Earls in very lenient fashion. Huntly, Errol and Angus, he said to Bowes, were three of the most potent noblemen in his kingdom, and 'if he should again pursue them and toot them with the horn he should little prevail'. In November he secured from a slim convention of nobles in Edinburgh an Act of Oblivion by which the Earls were forgiven their recent conspiracy of the Spanish Blanks provided they fulfilled certain conditions (which, as a matter of fact, they never did). To obtain this Act, it was said, the King manipulated the convention and even tampered with the text. The clergy raved, and the Synod of Fife excommunicated the earls without consulting the King. Elizabeth wrote him a stinging letter in which she lamented the sight of a seduced King, an abusing Council, and wry-governed kingdom.[11]

Yet James would probably have held to his course had it not been for Bothwell. Hard pressed at the time of Bothwell's raid at Leith, he came to St. Giles and besought the people to aid him. 'If ye will assist me against Bothwell at this time,' he pleaded, 'I promise to prosecute the excommunicated lords so that they shall not be suffered to remain in any part of Scotland.' So solemn and so public a pledge could not easily be repudiated. James, moreover, discovered that the Earls were deep in new plots with Spain, and he therefore prepared for a punitive expedition, drawing his strength, as before, not from the nobility, but from the lairds and burghs, and also from the Kirk. When the ministers were first asked for assistance they displayed suspicion and told James that they would pray for him; but they could not refuse their aid after Bothwell joined the Catholic Earls. In September 1594, the King was ready to march. On October 3rd, the young Earl of Argyll, who had been permitted to advance before the main body of the King's army, was roughly handled by Huntly's forces at the battle of Glenlivet. But the Earls, with no stomach for a second encounter, fled to the wilds of Caithness, and to satisfy the Kirk James burned their houses to the ground. Within a few months he obtained an agreement by which Huntly and Errol promised to go abroad, which they did in March 1595. Angus lurked among his friends in the Highlands but was powerless to do harm.

The King had won a victory which could not fail to impress the nobility as a whole and, though faction was to plague him still, no noble dared henceforth to defy him as Bothwell and the Catholic Earls had done. He had really been very fortunate. Bothwell had ruined himself by his own evil courses; the Catholic Earls had become odious to all Protestant Scotland; the ferocity of the nobles had burned itself out before government was completely destroyed. But there were deeper causes for the King's success. In one crisis after another he had drawn his support, not from the nobility nor from England, but from the Scottish middle classes, from the lairds, the burghs and the Kirk. As these classes emerged as a power in Scotland, the ancient preponderance of the feudal nobles passed slowly away. Moreover, Bothwell had demonstrated the futility of the vicious old practice of kidnapping the King, a practice now happily going out of fashion. More was to be gained, as the nobles were learning, in wealth, in power, and certainly in permanence, by co-operation with the Crown and by the favour of the monarch. Though James had no money, he could and did enrich the nobles by erecting temporal lordships upon the lands once held by the ancient Church. Thus the problem posed by the grim and bloody barons of sixteenth-century Scotland was moving towards a solution.

CHAPTER VIII

KING AND SOVEREIGN LORD

WITH the departure from Scotland of Bothwell and the Catholic Earls early in 1595 the condition of the country became less tempestuous, and the King was able to turn to problems other than that of mere survival. In foreign affairs his attention was absorbed by the question of the English succession which will be dealt with in a separate chapter. At home he pressed forward eagerly to a consolidation and increase of royal authority. Here, favoured by circumstances, he achieved results that would have appeared quite impossible a few years earlier. As partial success came to him, his grim determination to be master of his kingdom grew steadily greater. In his speeches, writings and actions he shrewdly made the most of every opportunity to instruct his subjects in their duty towards an absolute sovereign and to bring the theory of divine right and the facts of government into closer approximation.

The birth of an heir strengthened his position. On February 19th, 1594, while the future of his dynasty was still beclouded by Bothwell and the Catholic Earls, his first child, a son, was born at Stirling Castle. There followed a burst of joy and loyalty among the people whom a contemporary described as appearing to be 'daft for mirth'. In memory of his two grandfathers the Prince was named Henry Frederick, though without doubt James was thinking also of Henry VII, to whom as the founder of the Anglo-Scottish marriage alliance his mind frequently reverted. He determined that the baptism of his son should be a great event. Sending invitations somewhat rashly to many foreign courts, he scraped together money in Scotland and busied himself in devising sports and pageants. One of the interludes written for the occasion came from the royal pen. During the festivities, which took place towards the end of August, James appeared in a masque as a Christian Knight of Malta; the Border lord, Buccleuch, and other nobles donned women's clothes, doubtless after some persuasion, to represent Amazons; and chariots, mimic ships, deities, Moors and windmills added to the splendour.

These celebrations, however, not only were planned on such an ambitious scale that many details went awry, but came at a time when Bothwell was still in Scotland and when preparations were in progress for James's final expedition against the Catholic Earls. The arrangement of a host of matters fell upon the King, who increased his trials by attempting grandiose negotiations with his foreign guests. So sadly was he harassed by business, anxieties and intrigues that, according to a malicious writer, a foul suspicion grew in his mind that the Duke of Lennox was father of the Prince.

A year later, in the summer of 1595, he had a serious quarrel with the Queen over the Prince's custody. Following the precedent of his own childhood, he had placed his son in Stirling Castle under the protection of the Earl of Mar, his old playfellow, who after various vicissitudes was now high in royal favour. But Anne wanted her son with her at Holyrood. She vented her anger in a most unreasonable hostility to Mar, healing her old quarrel with Maitland and intriguing with other nobles because they were Mar's enemies. There was thus good reason to keep the Prince out of her hands. James was keenly aware of the evil that might ensue if a group of nobles obtained possession of his son. They might be tempted, he feared, to overthrow him as they had overthrown his mother, in order to control the kingdom during a long minority. Hence he was adamant, swearing that if he were about to die he would with his last breath command Mar to retain possession of the Prince.

Finding her importunities useless, Anne fell ill. She begged the King who was at Falkland to come to her at Holyrood, but James was suspicious even of Maitland and feared that if he came he might find himself a prisoner of the Queen's faction. To such a pass had her folly brought them. Then, discovering that she was truly ill, James came to Holyrood in spite of danger. But the quarrel continued. 'My heart,' said the King, 'I am sorry you should be persuaded to move me to that which will be the destruction of me and my blood.' Anne replied merely with tears. Next day, in an angry interview with Maitland, the King declared that 'if any think I am further subject to my wife than I ought to be, they are but traitors and such as seek to dishonour me'. Happily the atmosphere soon cleared. Some of the nobles of the Queen's faction departed for their homes, James was able to make peace with his wife, and they returned to Falkland very lovingly together. He had shown both firmness and restraint, but Anne had been folly incarnate.[1]

The death of Chancellor Maitland in October 1595, offered the King an opportunity to assert his preponderance in the government and to assume a more direct control of affairs. He was most ungenerous to Maitland's memory. It is true that he wrote an epitaph in the form of a lumbering sonnet praising his late Chancellor. But far from acknowledging the great services which Maitland had rendered, the King complained that he found many things otherwise than he had looked for, and blamed his old servant for all that was awry in the State. 'His Majesty', courtiers noted, 'took little care for the loss of the Chancellor.' The truth was that James, now in his thirtieth year, had grown restless under Maitland's tutelage and welcomed his death as an opportunity to rule alone as a king should do. He determined that in future there should be no great official at court pre-eminent above all others to rival the person of the sovereign. For more than three years the Chancellorship remained unfilled. If he appointed a noble, James said, the new Chancellor would shortly 'be better attended upon than the King himself'; if he appointed a meaner man, the Chancellor would build a faction to enhance his strength and thus fill the court with intrigue. He discovered, moreover, that there was great rivalry for the office and that any appointment would leave sore hearts. These patterns of thought and action — his ingratitude, his periodic resolves to achieve his ideals of kingship, his tendency to leave offices unfilled when appointments became difficult — were to be repeated many times in the years to come.

Building upon the foundations which Maitland had laid, though refusing to acknowledge that he did so, James threw himself with great energy into the tasks of government. He issued a kingly proclamation warning all men to obey the law. 'As he is their King and Sovereign Lord', the proclamation asserts, so he lets them know 'that he will be obeyed and reverenced as a king, and will execute his power and authority against whatsoever persons' — his nobles, councillors, domestic servants, or any others — who shall 'contemn his Highness, his authority or laws.' The registers of the Council are filled with rules and orders against criminals, outlaws and those who carried dags and pistols. Men at deadly feud were summoned before the King and Council. 'At his own pain and travail', James sought by mingled force and persuasion to reconcile enmities, while those who disregarded his summons or awards were punishable by imprisonment. These measures accomplished some good, though the nature of the country could only be altered slowly.

He turned also to the wilder portions of his kingdom. 'As for the Highlands,' he wrote, 'I shortly comprehend them all in two sorts of people: the one that dwelleth in our mainland, that are barbarous for the most part and yet mixed with some show of civility; the other that dwelleth in the Isles and are all utterly barbarous without any sort or show of civility.' On two occasions he announced his intention of visiting the Isles and Western Highlands, but lack of provisions in the west compelled him to abandon his first expedition and in the second he went no further than Glasgow and Dumbarton. He summoned the western chiefs to appear in Edinburgh and show the titles to their lands, but few of them came. With the inhabitants of the Western Isles, of whom he spoke scornfully as wolves and wild boars, he hoped to deal by planting colonies among them of responsible Lowlanders 'that within short time may root them out and plant civility in their rooms'. An Act of 1597 provided for the planting of three burghs, one in Kintyre, one in Lochaber and one on the island of Lewis. A group of gentlemen-adventurers, most of them from Fife, began a settlement in Lewis on the present site of Stornaway, but everything went wrong and the town was abandoned, while an attempt to revive the venture in 1605 was also a failure. For the moment James accomplished almost nothing in the Western Isles, though his policy is of interest as foreshadowing the plantation of Ulster.

On the Borders, whose lawlessness not only challenged his authority but caused serious friction with England, he met with better success. With great bitterness he denounced the barbarity of Scottish raids across the Border, swearing he would not approve them against his most deadly foes, much less against the subjects of Elizabeth. But his authority was limited. In the spring of 1596, moreover, the Borders were thrown into confusion by the affair of Kinmont Willie, a notorious Scottish freebooter, who was seized by the English on a day of truce and carried to Carlisle. Scottish protests bringing no result, Buccleuch, the keeper of

Liddesdale, determined to take the law into his own hands. In the popular ballad he exclaims:

> And have they ta'en him, Kinmont Willie,
> Against the truce of the Border tide,
> And forgotten that the bauld Buccleuch
> Is keeper on the Scottish side?

On a dark and murky night in April Buccleuch led a daring raid against Carlisle, surprised the castle, rescued the prisoner, and brought him back to Scotland. The Scots were jubilant. But Elizabeth was naturally furious and demanded that Buccleuch be delivered to her for punishment. James would gladly have complied, but dared not face the wrath of his subjects, and could do no more than imprison Buccleuch for a short time at St. Andrews. So alarmed was he at Elizabeth's anger that in a strange scene in the Scottish Council he produced and formally entered in the register the letter she had written him years before promising not to oppose his lawful right of succession. When his second child, a daughter, was born at Dunfermline in August, he determined upon the name of Elizabeth in deference to Elizabeth of England.

The affair of Kinmont Willie was followed by great lawlessness along the Border. In the year following, however, the two governments appointed a joint commission to try notorious offenders and to prepare a treaty providing for better justice. Despite much friction and bitterness this treaty did great good and was also of significance because henceforth both countries abandoned Border raids as an instrument of policy. James visited the Borders frequently, hanged many thieves, and strengthened his authority.

His new concern with the details of government included an inquiry into his finances which he found in a condition rather worse than their normal state of dilapidation. Indeed, except for one brief period, his poverty during the 1590s was excruciating. He was reduced to the most miserable shifts. His household was frequently maintained from the private means of his officers who were asked to supply his needs from the rents of their places, and later, in 1599, there was the astounding spectacle of a Minister of State absconding in order to avoid the financial ruin that service of the Crown entailed. In debt to moneylenders as well as to his own servants, James anticipated revenue, obtained money for one purpose and spent it for another, debased the coinage and robbed the mint. This inability to handle money — an inability so patent that he recognized it himself — led to a curious episode in 1596.

As the King looked into his finances after Maitland's death, he came to believe that the officers of the Exchequer were making considerable profits at the expense of the Crown. At the same time, Queen Anne's councillors, who had been handling her finances with marked success, offered to administer the King's revenues also and promised him sufficient funds to maintain his estate. The offer was reinforced by an amusing episode on New Year's Day, 1596. Anne's Council had presented her with a purse containing a thousand pounds in gold. She came to James, playfully shook the purse in his face, dutifully gave him half her little treasure, and asked him when his Council would give him as much. The King decided to act. With evil words he dismissed Glamis, the Treasurer, and other Exchequer officials, and appointed Anne's councillors as a board to control his finances. These councillors, eight in number — whence they were known as the Octavians — included some very able men who were to make their mark in the years to come. Walter Stewart, Prior of Blantyre, educated as a boy at Stirling along with the King, was later Lord Treasurer. Alexander Seton, Lord Urquhart, President of the Court of Session, became Chancellor and Earl of Dunfermline in 1605. John Lindsay, Parson of Menmuir, praised by Spottiswoode as a man of 'exquisite learning and a sound judgment', might have had a brilliant career had he not died prematurely. James Elphinstone, later Lord Balmerino, was an able Secretary, while Thomas Hamilton, Tam o' the Cowgate, as James called him from his residence in that street, has been described as the most successful Scot of his generation and was to acquire a great position in the administration of the country. But though he possessed much shrewdness and versatility, he lacked the common honesty essential for an unblemished reputation, and at his death a wit offered the epitaph:

> Here lies a lord who while he stood
> Had matchless been had he been [good].

They were given great power. The King, who enjoyed drawing up directives, prepared a document in which he allowed them virtual control of all royal revenue and bound himself not to override their decisions. By this self-denying ordinance he erected a shield against his own carelessness and also, rather shrewdly, against the odium which the Octavians were certain to incur. No longer would he employ a Chancellor or other great man, he said in jest, but would use persons whom he could hang if he wished. New order and stability were brought into public finance by the Octavians, but unfortunately within the year they fell from power in a new clash of Church and State.[2]

This clash arose partly, perhaps, because Maitland's moderating influence was gone, but more fundamentally because the ministers dreaded a renewed assault from Spain and a resurgence of Catholicism in Scotland. News of preparations in Spanish dockyards caused apprehensions scarcely less fearful than in 1588, and at the same time the ministers were maddened to observe a trend towards Catholicism in the King's government. Catholic in sympathy some of his councillors were known to be. The Princess Elizabeth and another Princess, Margaret, who was born in 1598 but died in infancy, and also Prince Charles, born in 1600, were entrusted to guardians suspected of Catholicism;[3] while Lady Huntly's presence at court where she enjoyed 'the plurality of her Majesty's kisses' was rightly thought to presage Huntly's return from exile. He and Errol, in fact, came back to Scotland in the summer of 1596. Without a doubt it was James's hope of the English succession that provided his policy. Catholic hostility he regarded as the greatest bar to his ambition, and hence Catholic factions in England and Scotland and Catholic rulers on the Continent must, he believed, be carefully cultivated. 'Papists', he told the ministers, 'might be honest folks and good friends to him, for his mother was a Catholic and yet he behoved to say she was an honest woman.' As for the Catholic Earls, he could not hope to drive them abroad once more without facing a rebellion that would terminate his efforts to improve his government. In August 1596, therefore, he obtained from a convention of the estates at Falkland a decision that if the Earls satisfied both King and Kirk they should be permitted to remain in Scotland.

Against this action the high Presbyterians flung themselves in passionate protest. Andrew Melville, who appeared at the convention at Falkland although the King told him to be gone, accused the entire assembly of treason against Christ for tolerating the return of the Catholic Earls. A month later Melville and other ministers came again to James at Falkland. Scarcely had the conference begun when Melville 'broke out upon the King in so zealous, powerful and irresistible a manner, that howbeit the King used his authority in most crabbed and choleric manner, yet Mr. Andrew bore him down, calling the King but God's silly vassal; and, taking him by the sleeve, says this in effect: Sir, you are brought in extreme danger both of your life and Crown, and with you the country and Kirk of Christ is like to wreck. And, therefore, Sir, I must tell you, there are two Kings and two Kingdoms in Scotland. There is Christ Jesus the King, and His Kingdom the Kirk; whose subject King James the Sixth is, and of whose Kingdom not a King, nor a lord, nor a head, but a member!' With astonishing self-control James listened, dismissed the ministers pleasantly, and promised that the Catholic Earls should obtain no grace from him until they had satisfied the Kirk.

New fuel was added to the fire by a monstrous sermon of David Black, minister at St. Andrews, whose efforts in the pulpit Calderwood describes as copious, powerful, piercing and pertinent. A year earlier Black had been in trouble because of a tirade against Queen Mary. Now, throwing discretion to the winds, he denounced Elizabeth as an atheist, declared that religion in England was an empty show, and warned that the English bishops had persuaded James to introduce episcopal government in Scotland. The King, he said, had known from the first that the Catholic Earls were coming home. But what could be expected when Satan ruled in the court and in the Council, when judges and councillors were cormorants and men of no religion, when the Queen of Scotland was a woman for whom, for fashion's sake, the clergy might pray but from whom no good could be hoped. Were not all kings Devil's bairns?

So offensive the sermon was and so contrary to all that the King had asked of the clergy that he had every right to intervene. Black was called before the Council but refused its jurisdiction, declaring he could be tried only in an ecclesiastical court, and his refusal, penned in extravagant terms, was sent by the Kirk to every presbytery in the country. This was provocative action indeed. Determined that Black should be punished, James stood his ground, though the barrage against him from the pulpits of Edinburgh 'pressed forward and sounded mightily'.

By these quarrels both the court and the city were thrown into a state of nervous tension which was increased by a group of courtiers who hoped thereby to drive the Octavians from power. With malicious intent these courtiers whispered to the ministers of Edinburgh that the Octavians sought their ruin. Next day, December 17th, there were violent sermons at St. Giles, one of them dealing with the story of Mordecai and Haman, the king's proud servant; and, as the congregation grew more and more excited, a sudden shout arose, doubtless begun by a courtier, 'Save yourselves! Armour, armour! Bills and axes!' Rushing from the church, the people seized arms and ran in all directions, scarcely knowing what they were about. Some hastened to defend their ministers, some ran to the King who was in the Tolbooth with his lords of session. Weapons clashed on the doors. There were cries of 'Bring forth the wicked Haman!' But the crowd was beaten back, the provost calmed the people, and the riot subsided as quickly as it arose. Accompanied by the provost and by loyal craftsmen, the King hastened down the Canongate to Holyrood-house. He saw that a powerful weapon had been placed in his hands, and he determined to punish Edinburgh severely for the sins of the ministers and thus turn the citizens against them. Next day the King and the entire court removed to Linlithgow, the Council declared that the riot had been treason, while the alarm and dismay of Edinburgh were further enhanced when James returned to the city with a great troop of Border ruffians. Gladly did the citizens make their peace at a cost of 20,000 marks. Meanwhile the ministers took flight and James's triumph was complete. But the Octavians suffered, for the King now asked them to resign as his financial advisers.

The riot in Edinburgh proved to be a turning point in the history of the Kirk and in its relations with the King. For the zealots were now driven from power. In the Kirk itself, where there had long been a more moderate party, a strong current began to run against them, while the nobles and many of the people were ready to support the King. James, moreover, was learning to manipulate the General Assemblies. He summoned them to meet in Perth or Dundee, where many of the southern ministers were replaced by those from the north who disliked the 'Popery of Edinburgh'. The most combative of the clergy were successfully excluded, royal agents were set to work among the ministers, clergymen were called into the King's cabinet and dealt with earnestly. James took a prominent part in the debates. 'Sir,' warned a minister, 'ye are to remember that ye sit not here as *Imperator*, but as a Christian; *ades ut intersis, non ut praesis.*' By cajolery and persuasion, by hints of larger stipends, by threats, by downright dishonesty, the King managed to have his way. 'Alas,' wrote James Melville, whose account of these years is pathetic in its sincere and manly grief, 'where Christ guided before, the court began then to govern all.'

From a General Assembly at Perth in February 1597, and from another at Dundee in May, the King secured important concessions. Ministers were to be more circumspect in their sermons, to avoid political themes, and to refrain from attacks upon the King until after his shortcomings had been told him in private. To ecclesiastical affairs must presbyteries confine themselves. Commissioners, appointed to deal with the Catholic Earls, received them into the Kirk at Aberdeen. Other commissioners were to remain in constant session as an advisory body for the King, though the high Presbyterians regarded them with great suspicion. 'They were the King's led horse,' wrote James Melville, 'and usurped boldly the power of the General Assemblies. They were as a wedge taken out of the Kirk to rend her with her own forces, and the very needle which drew in the thread of the bishops.'

That the King should employ his new-found power to impose bishops upon the Kirk was all but inevitable, and it is surprising to find that he first considered an alternate plan of ecclesiastical reorganization set forth by Lord Menmuir, his able Secretary. This plan proposed a reform of the first estate in Parliament in order to give the ministers what they had long demanded, an adequate voice in that body. The first estate was indeed a scandal, since it was composed for the most part not of clergymen but of lay lords who held ecclesiastical titles and who voted in the name of the Kirk though they had no official connection with it. Menmuir suggested, therefore, that the presbyteries be allowed to send representatives to Parliament to sit with the lay prelates; and that, as the latter died off, these representatives should constitute the whole of the first estate. This wise and statesmanlike plan was at first supported by the King. 'I mind not', he said, 'to bring in papistical or Anglican bishoping; but only to have the best and the wisest of the ministers to have place and counsel in Parliament.'

If he spoke sincerely, he shortly changed his mind. He found that Menmuir's plan was suspect to the ministers, who clogged it with many reservations and caveats. It was opposed also by the nobles. In its place they passed an Act declaring that those ministers appointed by the King as bishops or other prelates should have a vote in Parliament, that such appointments be given only to bona-fide clergymen, and that their position in the Kirk be determined by the King and General Assembly. An aristocratic first estate appointed by the King was thus proposed by the nobles; and this became James's policy. The first indication of his design is found in his book, *Basilikon Doron*, written in the summer or autumn of 1598. In the midst of a furious passage denouncing the zealots in the Kirk[4] he declares that one of their weapons is the parity of all ministers, 'whereby the ignorants are emboldened' to cry down their betters. The remedy is to 'advance the godly, learned and modest men of the ministry to bishoprics and bene-fices [and thus] not only banish their conceited parity but also re-establish the old institution of three estates, which can no otherwise be done'. The *Basilikon Doron* was written in secret, but Andrew Melville saw a manuscript copy, took notes of its 'Anglo-pisco-papistical conclusions', and tried in vain to raise a storm against the King. A year later, in October 1600, James named three diocesan bishops to the sees of Caithness, Ross and Aberdeen, and in a General Assembly at Montrose in 1602 secured approval for what he had done; but since the new bishops, though they sat and voted in Parliament, had no defined functions in the govern-ment of the Kirk, they formed but an alien and extraneous addition to a system that remained thoroughly Presbyterian.[5]

Meanwhile the King was involved in that strange mystery known as the Gowrie Plot. Over many episodes in his life James drew a veil of judicious uncertainty, but the Gowrie Plot was his masterpiece, for here the mystery remains inscrutable to the pre-sent day. We are certain only of the salient facts: that on the morning of August 5th, 1600, the King was hunting near Falk-land; that after the kill he rode to Gowrie House at Perth with Alexander, the Master of Ruthven, younger brother of the Earl of Gowrie; that after dinner, James and the Master being with-drawn from the rest of the company, the Master assaulted the King; that James in terror shrieked for help; and that his attendants rushing to his assistance slaughtered both the Master of Ruthven and the Earl his brother.

Gowrie was a handsome and accomplished young noble, only about twenty-two years old, just returned from six years of travel and study on the Continent. That there would be ill will between him and the King was certain. His grandfather had been Mary's enemy and Rizzio's assassin; his father a leader in the Ruthven Raid, beheaded for treason while Arran was in power. Gowrie, moreover, before he went abroad, had been an ally of the ministers and had probably had dealings with Bothwell. On his way home he was cordially received in London, so that James taunted him, half in jest but half in earnest, with his popularity at Elizabeth's court. His triumphal entry into Edinburgh also angered the King. There had been a larger crowd, James sneered, with Gowrie's father at the scaffold; and on another occasion the King referred with scorn to the part the Earl's grandfather had played in Rizzio's slaughter. Hence Gowrie, finding attendance at court unpleasant, shortly retired to his estates, though he came to a Parliament in June when he further angered the King by opposing his policy. To all of these causes of ill will it must be added that James owed the Earl a large sum of money and knew that Gowrie, while studying abroad, had dabbled in magic and astrology. On the other hand, the Earl's younger brother, the Master of Ruthven, a handsome lad of nineteen, was a favourite of the King, and his sister, Beatrix, was one of Anne's ladies-in-waiting.

Shortly after the tragedy at Gowrie House the King issued an official account of what had taken place. As the hunt was about to begin, so ran this account, the young Master of Ruthven, his eyes fixed strangely upon the ground, drew the King aside, told him he had discovered a stranger in Perth carrying a pot of gold, and begged the King to come and investigate. James refused. But the Master's story kept running in his mind, and later in the day he rode to Perth accompanied by sixteen attendants, all very lightly armed. Gowrie, informed by his brother of the King's approach, met him outside the city and brought him to Gowrie House, though James noted an uneasiness and lack of cordiality in the Earl's deportment. After he had dined James left the company and went with the Master to investigate the stranger and the pot of gold. The Master led him through a number of chambers, carefully locking each door behind them, and brought him at length to a small apartment in a tower where, to the King's horror, there was no pot of gold but a man in armour with a dagger in his belt. Ruthven seized the dagger, accused James of murdering his father, and declared that the King must die. The man in armour stood still, amazed and trembling. With the dagger thus held to his breast, James entered upon a long discourse, telling Ruthven the wickedness of shedding innocent blood. By these words Ruthven was touched, declared that no harm would befall the King if he remained quiet, and left the room, saying he must consult his brother. Thereupon James turned the weapon of his eloquence upon the man in armour whom he persuaded to open a window. Meanwhile Gowrie and his guests arose from table, a servant announced that the King had departed, and the company left the house to go out to their horses. They were still in the courtyard when Ruthven returned to the King and told him once more that he must die. The two men grappled. James, by his own account, had the better of the struggle, dragged Ruthven to the window, and shouted for help. His attendants rushed back into the house, and one of his pages, young John Ramsey, made his way to the tower where the King and Ruthven were struggling. Ruthven was on his knees before the King, his head under James's arm, his hand raised over the King's face as though to stifle outcry. Ramsey struck him from behind, wounding him severely. Meanwhile Gowrie in wild excitement seized a sword and rushed up the stairs, but was thrust through by Ramsay and others. Both the Ruthvens were dead.

The King's story was inconsistent, much of it highly improbable, some of it palpably false. And there are writers who have asserted that Gowrie was not plotting against the King but the King against Gowrie, that James came to Perth with the intention of picking a quarrel and of murdering the Earl and his brother. There is, however, a strong argument against such an hypothesis, for to believe that James would quarrel with Gowrie in his own house and hazard the royal person in a deadly brawl is to credit him with greater daring than he had at his command. He used this argument himself. 'I see, Mr. Robert,' he said to the Edinburgh minister who refused to believe his story, 'that ye would make me a murderer. It is known very well that I was never bloodthirsty. If I would have taken their lives, I had causes enough; I needed not to hazard myself so.'

If, on the other hand, Gowrie plotted to kidnap or even to kill the King, his blunders and lack of precautions bordered on insanity. Vital matters were left wholly to chance. There is no evidence of an understanding with other nobles. In 1608 a broken Scots attorney, George Sprot, who was promptly executed, confessed that he had letters proving that Gowrie intended to take the King to Fast Castle, a fortress on a sea-cliff near Berwick; but the letters are now known to be forgeries and this evidence falls to the ground. It is difficult to believe that Gowrie plotted against the King.

There remains the possibility of a sudden and accidental quarrel in which the King in panic called upon his attendants to strike. This was the explanation accepted by Sir William Bowes, the English ambassador. Bowes believed that the King, being alone with Ruthven, 'a learned, sweet and artless young gentleman', angrily called Ruthven's father a traitor; 'whereat the youth showing a grieved and expostulatory countenance, the King, seeing himself alone and without weapon, cried Treason! Treason! The Master, abashed to see the King to apprehend it so . . . put his hand to stay the King's showing his countenance in that mood, immediately falling upon his knees to entreat the King . . . Ramsey ran the poor gentleman through'. Bowes thought that though the matter began accidentally, the King, 'to give it an honourable cloak, pursued it with odious treasons'.[6] James had to explain the fact that he had called on Ramsey to strike. 'Strike him high,' he is said to have cried, 'because he has a chain doublet upon him.'

Whatever the truth may be, James turned the Gowrie Plot to his own advantage with astonishing speed and success. Before he returned to Edinburgh he commanded the five ministers of the capital to summon their congregations, to relate his story of the events at Gowrie House, and to return thanks for his deliverance from mortal danger. When the ministers, deeply suspicious in their hearts, refused to proclaim facts of which they were uncertain, they were summoned before the Council and were asked by the King, each in turn, whether they believed his account. They avowed distrust and doubt, upon which they were banished from the city. So instantaneous and so sharp was James's resentment that he was clearly determined to make belief in his story a test of clerical loyalty and a new weapon against the ministers. He succeeded fully. Clergymen to fill the places of the Edinburgh recalcitrants were easily found. An order that ministers throughout the country proclaim a solemn thanksgiving was universally obeyed. When four of the Edinburgh ministers capitulated, they were compelled to journey to various parts of the kingdom, humbly repeating their submission in many public places. One only of their number, Robert Bruce, stood firm. Though a leader of the Kirk, a man of great dignity and eminence, and a former confidant of the King, he was banished from Scotland on pain of death. Moreover, James obtained approval for what he had done from a convention of the clergy.

Upon Gowrie and the Master of Ruthven, he inflicted the utmost punishment due to traitors. Their bodies were gibbeted, quartered and exposed throughout the country, their estates and honours forfeited, the very name of Ruthven abolished.[7] The fifth of August was made a day of solemn thanksgiving for all time to come.

Though the country as a whole supported the King, there were more sceptics than the ministers of Edinburgh. Some of the courtiers were highly suspicious. Angry at the banishment of Beatrix Ruthven, Anne sulked in her rooms and refused to be dressed, saying she required the assistance of her former lady-in-waiting, and she told the King to beware how he treated her for she was not an Earl of Gowrie. James wooed her by spending considerable sums upon a tight-rope dancer in whom she delighted. Incredulity met the King's story in both England and France. Elizabeth, congratulating him on his escape, remarked that since Gowrie had so many familiar spirits she supposed there were none now left in hell. In France the King's account was received with such ridicule that his ambassador had it suppressed.[8]

A final point remains. When the tragedy at Gowrie House was complete and the two poor lads lay dead, James fell upon his knees and thanked God for his deliverance. Let us hope that his soul was white as driven snow, for, if it was not, his hypocrisy stinks to heaven.

The King's determination to be master of his kingdom and of all classes within it appears vividly in his writings during his last years in Scotland. Ideas of divine right, maturing in his mind for many years, were now set forth in *The Trew Law of Free Monarchies*:

Or The Reciprock and Mutuall Dutie Betwixt a Free King and his Naturall Subjects, published in September 1598. This is no academic treatise on government. James's purpose is the highly practical one of teaching the people the nature of their duty to their king, the religious obligation of obedience, and the wickedness of revolt. The language of the *Trew Law* is studiously simple. The exposition is lucid, vivid, succinct and forceful. There is not an ambiguity in the entire pamphlet. Nor is there elaborate rebuttal of those who justify rebellion, though, as James says, his opponents will find 'most of their great guns paid home again ... My purpose is to instruct and not irritate'.

The position and duties of a king, James asserts, are clearly set forth in the Scriptures. 'Kings are called gods by the prophetical King David because they sit upon God His throne in earth and have the count of their administration to give unto Him.' Their office is to minister justice, to advance good men and to punish evil ones, to establish and enforce good laws, to procure peace, and as a good pastor to go in and out before the people. The king is thus judge and avenger, lawgiver, peacemaker and priest. He is a loving father to his subjects, cherishing their welfare, tempering chastisement with pity, and remembering that he is ordained for them, not they for him.

Turning to the duty of the people to their king, James declares that kingship was begun by God's own ordinance. When the Israelites begged God to send them a king, God commanded Samuel to warn them that a king would bring many burdens. The warning of Samuel, says James, was to prepare the people's hearts for the obedience they must yield to a king. Once they had a king they must obey him and retain him for ever. Only God could make a king and God alone could unmake him. None the less the Israelites continued to beg for a king until God sent them one. How, then, can broiling spirits revolt against their rulers when God's chosen people were forbidden to resist? God's ordinance is that the people must obey their king, fearing him as their judge, loving him as their father, praying for him as their protector. To their king they can offer no resistance save by tears and sobs to God.

James employs an historical justification for the absolute power of kings. His ancestor, King Fergus, coming out of Ireland, conquered Scotland in ancient times; in the same way William of

Normandy conquered England; and Scottish and English kings, by conquest and by uninterrupted use and possession from time immemorial, obtained rights in their kingdoms that amounted to absolute ownership. Thus the rights of a feudal lord over his fief are transferred, in James's argument, to the king as the lord of the entire realm. Absolute ownership brings absolute power. As the king is the overlord of the whole land, 'so is he master over every person that inhabiteth the same, having power over the life and death of every one of them'. Kings arose 'before any estates or ranks of men, before any parliaments were holden, or laws made, and by them was the land distributed, which at first was wholly theirs. And so it follows of necessity that the kings were the authors and makers of the laws, and not the laws of the kings'.

It has been argued, James continues, that men should remove a tyrannical king. But evil kings as well as good ones come from God, and men may not remove the curse that God has placed upon them. Again it has been said that a king by his oath at coronation enters a compact with his people for their mutual benefit and that if he breaks the agreement by ruling wickedly the people are freed from their allegiance. James denies that any compact has been made. And if a king should break his promise, who is to be his judge? No one but God. Let no man think, however, that evil kings escape chastisement. They will be punished far above other men, 'for the highest bench is sliddriest to sit upon'. But all must be left to God.

The theory of divine right must not be regarded as a mere oddity of James's quixotic nature. It is true that it pandered to his vanity and brought him close to heaven, a worthy successor of David and Solomon. But it had other uses. The age demanded religious sanctions for temporal things. James must of necessity claim the support of heaven if he hoped to combat the pretensions of the Kirk, the doctrines of Rome, and the arrogance of the nobles. He must have a religious sanction for his demand that all classes obey and reverence their king. And finally, his hereditary claim to the throne of England was rendered indefeasible by divine right. Small wonder, then, that he grasped at the theory with all the intense tenacity of his nature. It was his justification and his hope, a touchstone of all thought and action.

The *Basilikon Doron*,[9] the best prose James ever wrote, is concerned with another aspect of kingship. The origin of the book lay in a dream from which the King awoke with a presentiment that his life would be short. He resolved, therefore, to write a book of instruction for Prince Henry, then four years old, on the duties of a king and 'timeously to provide for his training up in all the points of a king's office'. The tone of the *Basilikon Doron* is moral and didactic. Stressing the patriarchal nature of kingship, James sets forth a host of sanctimonious precepts for his son's guidance. Henry is told he must possess every virtue, eschew every vice, and stand before his people as a model of self-restraint, wisdom and godliness.

In writing upon the education of a prince the King could turn to many models, for the theme was a favourite one among Renaissance authors. He used their books, probably turning back to many volumes he had studied as a boy, though he does not mention them. It was not the fashion to do so, and his only acknowledgments are to the Bible and to the classics. From the Bible he drew heavily, building whole passages around quotations from the Scriptures. His references to the classics, however, do not appear until the second edition and form an obvious after-thought added to lend an air of learning to his work. Some of the classical references are extremely vague, and the King's habit of quoting from memory introduces many errors. Perhaps he lifted references from some compilation of quotations from the classics. Yet he knew at first hand the authors whom he cited, and his errors are due to carelessness rather than to lack of erudition.

Despite these artificialities the style of the *Basilikon Doron* is fresh, natural and spontaneous, abounding in quaint and racy phrases, in picturesque and salty passages that are both enter-taining and quotable. James writes from his own experience, from his hatreds, hopes and frustrations, and does so with vividness and force. A contemporary speaks of the 'energy of the words and the pithiness of the phrases wherein it is written'. Much of the King's advice to his son is sensible, pertinent and wise. His weakness lies in the ease with which shrewd comment and sage advice shade away into sententious moralizing which could be of small avail to Henry in a work-a-day world and which gives the book a tone of sanctimonious pretence. The *Basilikon Doron* paints a remarkable picture of contemporary Scotland and of its King. James's com-bination of shrewdness and naivety, his pious satisfaction at abstinence from vices which did not attract him, his capacity for

combining lofty ideals with sordid practice, his astonishing vanity
— all are revealed in the *Basilikon Doron*.

The work opens with a well-known sonnet:[10]

> God giues not Kings the stile of Gods in vaine,
> For on his throne his Scepter doe they sway:
> And as their subiects ought them to obey,
> So Kings should feare and serue their God againe.
> If then ye would enioy a happie raigne
> Obserue the statutes of your heauenlie King,
> And from his Lawe, make all your Lawes to spring,
> Since his Lieuetenant heere ye should remaine.
> Reward the iust, be stedfast, true, and plaine
> Represse the proude, maintayning aye the right,
> Walke alwaies so, as euer in his sight,
> Who guardes the godlie, plaguing the prophane
> And so ye shall in Princelie vertues shine
> Resembling right your mightie King Diuine.

There follows a prose epistle to Prince Henry who is commanded
to receive the book as a faithful preceptor and to keep it always
with him as Alexander did the *Iliad* of Homer. 'It will not come
uncalled, neither speak unspeered at'; yet Henry, conferring with
it in private, will never be alone.

Of the three books into which the work is divided, the first
concerns the duty of a king towards God. Henry must attain to
a knowledge and fear of God by study of the Scriptures, by prayer,
by preservation of a sensitive conscience, by distinction of funda-
mentals from things indifferent. 'As for the particular points of
religion, I need not to delate them; I am no hypocrite, follow my
footsteps and your own present education therein.'

The second book deals with the duty of a king in his office.
Much of James's advice is hackneyed and conventional, and perhaps the most interesting portion of the book is that in which he
analyses the faults of various classes in Scotland — the ministers,
the nobles, the merchants and craftsmen. As to marriage, Henry
will hope for beauty, wealth and position in his bride; but these
things are secondary to virtue. Here the King preaches a little
sermon upon fornication and adultery, pointing with pride to his
own spotless chastity. Henry is told to rule with moderation,
avoiding on the one hand the pride of a Nebuchadnezzar and on

the other 'the preposterous humility of the proud Puritans, claiming to their parity and crying "We are all but vile worms", and yet will judge and give law to their King but will be judged nor controlled by none. Surely there is more pride under such a one's black bonnet than under Alexander the Great his diadem'.

The third book concerns the behaviour of a king in things indifferent: in food and clothing, in language, in writing, in gesture, in sports and pastimes, and in the selection of companions. Henry is not to be uncivil in eating like a gross cynic nor fastidious like a dainty dame, but to eat 'in a manly, round and honest fashion'. He should not dispatch business nor be sad and pensive during meals but should be cheerful, having pleasant histories read to him or engaging in honest conversation. He is to dress with moderation, not artificially decked like a courtesan nor sluggishly clothed like a country clown, not lightly dressed like a candy soldier nor over-gravely like a minister. But his garments should be proper, clean, comely, honest and suitable for the occasion. Thus armour should be worn when he goes to war, unless he wishes to be light 'for away running'. Effeminate things, such as perfume and long hair or nails, must be avoided. In his language Henry is told to be plain, honest, natural, short and sententious, eschewing both rustic crudeness and 'book language and pen and ink-horn terms'. The King recommends sports and hunting, he does not forbid cards, but finds chess 'over fond and philosophic a folly'. As to the selection of companions his advice is excellent, though he never followed it himself, except when he warned Henry to avoid the idle company of dames 'which are no other thing else but *irritamenta libidinis*'.

The *Basilikon Doron* was printed first in 1599 in a secret edition of seven copies which the King distributed among his trustiest servants. At a later time he explained that since he had written the book for the exercise of his own wit and for the instruction of his heir, he had seen no reason to publish it to the world. But also, without a doubt, he had wished to keep it from the knowledge of the clergy. The first public edition, in 1603, represented a thorough revision, in part for improvement of literary style,[11] in part for reasons of State. He feared that passages from the secret edition, having reached England in garbled form, might cause suspicion in that country. The English Puritans might well resent his bitter words against the Scottish ministers; and his references to his mother might perhaps be construed as a wish to avenge her death. He added, therefore, a lengthy preface explaining with less truth than ingenuity that by the word Puritan he meant only the vile sect of the Anabaptists known as the Family of Love. Nor had his remarks about Mary implied the slightest hostility towards England. He begged his readers not to expect perfection in his work. And yet, he added, the world could judge from his book what was to be looked for in him.

The *Basilikon Doron* was an immense success. By a lucky chance it was on sale in London within a few days of Elizabeth's death. Englishmen and foreigners, anxious to learn of the new King, bought his book eagerly, ambassadors sent it to their governments, and it was soon translated into most of the languages of western Europe. It continued to be popular for many years. Its pious maxims were highly regarded and reappeared constantly in the courtesy books written for the education of young men of the upper classes. In the many collections of King James's table talk and apophthegms which were published during the seventeenth century, quotations from the *Basilikon Doron* played an important part. And though much of the praise accorded to James's book was flattery of a King, there can be no doubt that it was sincerely admired.[12]

The *Basilikon Doron* is a reminder that though James was grimly determined to augment his power and was learning how that aim might be achieved, he remained also the man of letters, witty, familiar and amusingly whimsical. This combination of qualities appears in a description of him by Sir Henry Wotton, the English diplomat and poet, who visited Scotland in 1601. 'This King,' says Wotton, 'though born in 1566, does not appear to be more than twenty-eight years old. He is of medium stature and of robust constitution; his shoulders are broad but the rest of his person from the shoulders downward is rather slender. In his eyes and in his outward appearance there is a natural kindliness bordering on modesty. He is fond of literary discourse, especially of theology, and is a great lover of witty conceits. His speech is learned and even eloquent. In imitation of his grandfather, James V, he wears his hair cut short. About food and clothing he is quite indifferent. He is patient in the work of government, makes no decision without obtaining good counsel, and is said to be one of the most secret princes of the world. On occasion he has shown bitter hatred, especially against the Earl of Gowrie, and he reduced to obedience the ferocious spirit of Bothwell whom he banished. Yet by his lavish creations of marquises, earls and barons, he does not appear jealous of the great lords. Such creations, far more numerous than in England, he uses to bind his followers to him since he lacks the means to reward them in other ways. An admirable quality is his chastity which he has preserved without blemish, unlike his predecessors who disturbed the kingdom by leaving many bastards.

'His court is governed more in the French than in the English fashion. Anyone may enter the King's presence while he is at dinner, and as he eats he converses with those about him. The domestics who wait upon him wear caps on their heads. Dinner finished, he remains at table for a time before he retires, listening to banter and to merry jests in which he takes great delight. With his domestics and with the gentlemen of his chamber he is extremely familiar, but with the great lords he is grave. He has no guard, either because he cannot afford one or because he relies upon the love of his people which he calls the true guardian of princes. Though the kingdom is small, his court is composed of a large number of gentlemen, who, either from curiosity or from zeal to protect their Prince, accost newcomers at once and ask them what they want.'[13]

CHAPTER IX

A PRIZE MUCH COVETED

'SAINT GEORGE surely rides upon a towardly riding horse,' James once wrote wistfully, 'where I am daily bursten in daunting a wild, unruly colt.' With all his soul he yearned for the English succession. He was ready to accept it, said a disillusioned Jesuit, from the Devil himself. Resenting Elizabeth's longevity as a personal affront, he asked with petulance whether she meant to thwart him by lasting as long as the sun and the moon. After 1595, when Scotland was less tumultuous and Elizabeth was ageing, he approached the problem with new intensity. Irresponsible, dishonest, sometimes ridiculous, he most certainly was, and his palpitating eagerness led him into strange paths, for he convinced himself that the world was willing to assist him and saw an ally behind every bush. Yet he followed his purpose with rare pertinacity and with considerable shrewdness.

The succession came to him in the end so naturally and so easily that one is apt to forget the alarms and difficulties that beset him for so long. His claim was far superior to any other. Yet he was, in the first place, an alien; and the common law allowed no alien to inherit land in England. This made him fearful of the claim of his first cousin Arabella Stuart, also descended from Margaret Tudor, though by a second marriage, but born and bred in England. It was because he dreaded exclusion as an alien that he pressed Elizabeth so constantly to grant him the English estates of his grandparents, the Earl and Countess of Lennox. When these were refused he tried to insinuate that his English pension had been given him in compensation. The will of Henry VIII was also a bar to his title. This will passed over Margaret Tudor and vested the succession, should Henry's children die without issue, in the line of his younger sister, Mary, who had married Charles Brandon, Duke of Suffolk. But Edward Seymour, Lord Beauchamp, the representative of the Suffolk line in the reign of Elizabeth, was all but debarred by the dubious legality of his parents' marriage and in any case was not thought fit to rule.

James also regarded as dangerous an Act passed by the English Parliament in 1584. This Act, which had terrified him at the time of Mary's execution, declared that persons guilty of plotting against the life of Elizabeth should forfeit any claim they might have to the throne; and though this Act did not touch him directly, since he had not been privy to Mary's plottings, it formed one reason why he was most sensitive to his mother's reputation. There was, moreover, a deeper reason closely related to the succession. He venerated Mary's memory in order to defend himself against the accusation of bastardy. He secured from the Scottish Parliament in 1596 an Act making it treasonable to slander the King's parents or progenitors, an Act under which at least two persons were hanged in Edinburgh. In the same year he took offence at certain passages in Spenser's *Faerie Queen* which reflected on Mary; and demanded at once from Elizabeth that Spenser be tried and punished.

The Act debarring plotters accounts for James's vehemence in the minor affair of Valentine Thomas. Thomas was an English Catholic, a villainous ruffian, to whom the King had unwisely granted an audience in Scotland. Arrested later in England, Thomas hinted that James had whispered to him that he should assassinate Elizabeth. The story was absurd and Elizabeth wrote to James that she did not believe it; and though she obtained from Thomas a confession that might be useful in her Scottish diplomacy, she kept him quietly in prison without trial, for a trial could not have been held without mention of the King of Scots. Far from being grateful, James demanded that she erase his name from all records connected with Thomas and issue a declaration of his innocence. When she refused, he whipped himself into a fury. Thomas, he declared, had been suborned to make a false confession; the charges were exactly those that had been brought against his mother; there was nothing he would not do to vindicate his innocence. Friendships at home and abroad, his place, his Crown, his life — all should be sacrificed. He would issue a public challenge to do battle with any accuser. He would print the letter in which Elizabeth had expressed her disbelief in Thomas's story and send it from prince to prince. Elizabeth was not to be moved. Thomas remained in prison until the Queen's death when he was promptly tried and executed at James's command.[1]

In refusing to name a successor Elizabeth was adamant. She

would have no rising sun to eclipse her glory and increase the divisions in her kingdom. In 1586 she had promised James she would do nothing to injure any right or title that might be due him, unless his ingratitude provoked her to the contrary; and beyond these words, with their threatening reservation, she would not go. Undoubtedly as she grew older she regarded his accession as inevitable; she met his petulance with moderation and attempted to give him some timely instruction in kingly behaviour. But her lessons were harshly administered. She assumed the right to interfere and to censure, and the tone of her letters was imperial, caustic and humiliating. But though his resentment was deep and burning, he was baffled, torn between a dislike that bordered on hatred and the stark necessity of avoiding an open break. Against the Cecils he was also bitter, which divided him from the dominant faction in London and drew him to Essex, a far less desirable ally.

A foreign claim to the English throne also caused James anxiety. It was set forth in a book in 1594 by Robert Parsons, the famous English Jesuit, who declared that the vital matter of the succession in monarchies could not be based solely on hereditary right.[2] The religion of the heir, he asserted, was of far greater importance, for should a people accept a prince of a contrary or wrong religion, they acted in a way that was both wicked and dangerous. He then examined with a clever pretence at impartiality the claims and qualifications of all possible heirs to the English throne. But he found objections to every candidate, and to James in particular, until he came to consider the absurd pretensions of Philip of Spain and of his daughter, the Infanta Isabella Clara Eugenia, descendants of John of Gaunt. In Parsons's skilful hands, the claims of Philip and of the Infanta became impeccable and the object of the book grew clear. It was Spanish propaganda and very effective. At James it was a double thrust; it denied the principle of hereditary right and disabled his personal qualifications, leaving him outraged and aghast.

Terrified lest the great prize slip away, he embarked upon many activities of which one was literary. In both the *Trew Law* and the *Basilikon Doron* he answered Parsons by stressing the hereditary nature of kingship. Hereditary right, he asserted, was God's method of selecting kings; the right of the lawful heir was inalienable and indefeasible; and to him the people were bound as fully as to the ruling sovereign. They could no more reject the one than depose the other. The throne was never vacant, 'for at the very moment of the expiring of the king reigning, the nearest and lawful heir entereth in his place'. This — James's great argument — he repeated over and over again.

He talked rather freely to those about him, and soon a little literature, half surreptitious, half comical, much of it never printed, began to make its appearance. Verses, books and pamphlets, anagrams and prophecies, set forth his claim and foretold the good fortune that was to be his. An Irish poet, Walter Quin, coming to Edinburgh in 1595, found royal favour by verses such as the following:

> A worthie peerles Prince claymes Arthur's seat,
> Borne to the same by heavinlie providence.
> No force, no sleight, no vayne clame or pretence
> This woorthie wight can of his right defeat. . . .
> Ceas lets, Arthur I am, of Bretain King,
> Come by good right to clayme my seat, and throne,
> My kingdomes severed to rejoyne in one,
> To mend quhat is amiss in everie thing.

Both Quin and Alexander Dickson, an English schoolmaster, wrote Latin answers to Parsons — the King providing some of the material — but these works remained in manuscript because the King's printer, Robert Waldegrave, a Puritan who had fled from England, declared he dared not print them. More substantial was a tract on the succession by the Englishman Peter Wentworth, published in Edinburgh in 1598, and a similar pamphlet, probably also from an English pen, printed a year later. A powerful book by Sir Thomas Craig, *Concerning the Right of Succession to the Kingdom of England*, though not published, was written and dedicated to the King before 1603. But the strangest of these writings was the *Palinod* of John Colville. This renegade parson, an old ally of Bothwell, was now in exile. Hoping to obtain James's favour, he adopted the quaint course of claiming falsely that he had written against the King's title and that now, overcome by remorse, he was writing a recantation. He deserved, he said, to be hanged and proposed to return to Scotland to take his merited place on the gibbet. Meanwhile to the English he commended James as their future king. Much pleased, James promptly published the work,

but said in private that he thought Mr. John had gone mad. Nor
did he restore him to favour.[3]

Propaganda had uses but also limitations, and the King turned
to diplomacy. In broad terms his policy was to pose in Britain
and in northern Europe as the Protestant heir to England, but at
the same time to commend himself secretly to Catholic powers, to
win their neutrality if not their support, at least to blunt their
opposition. Such a policy was tortuous, secretive and dishonest.
Yet it contained some elements of statesmanship that cannot fairly
be ignored.

Confident of friendship in Denmark, in Holland, and among the
north German Protestant Princes, James's problem was to translate good wishes into something more substantial. This might be
done, he thought, through a league of Protestant States. Of such a
league he had spoken as early as 1585, had urged it at the time of
his marriage, and had tried to revive it when foreign envoys came
to Scotland to attend Prince Henry's christening. But he met with
opposition from Elizabeth, who had no liking for his pushing
diplomacy with her allies. Berating him for his moans to foreign
States, she snubbed him in 1596 by excluding him from negotiations for a new alliance with France and Holland. However, he
was not to be deterred. In 1598, despite his poverty, he dispatched
an embassy to Denmark and to the north German Princes. His
ambassadors spoke first of their master's grief at recent inroads by
the Turks, then set forth his title to the English throne and asked
what help he could hope for if he had to fight for his inheritance.
They suggested that since Elizabeth was growing old — a point
which did not please her when she heard of it — a league might
well be formed to induce her to name the King of Scots as her heir.
But though the Danes and the German Princes wished James well,
their commitments were few, and they sought refuge in the lofty
tone of his dispatches, commending him to the protection of the
Almighty by whose will kingdoms were disposed.[4]

More subtle were his dealings with Catholic States and with the
Papacy. He could not send formal embassies to Elizabeth's foes,
nor risk exposure as a trafficker with Rome. He could not incur
the slightest suspicion that he aimed at shortening Elizabeth's life.
Hence he had to approach Catholic rulers through secret and
unofficial agents whose credentials were inadequate and whose
actions could be easily disavowed. English intelligencers, he knew,

were keen and ubiquitous, while his own were very inadequate. He was at the mercy of his emissaries if they proved dishonest or if they exceeded their instructions, and he was well aware that some of them lacked judgment, for he employed the most unlikely persons, whose very unfitness lulled suspicion. None the less he developed a definite procedure in approaching Catholic powers. First he sent an agent, with only the vaguest commission, to present compliments and to spy out the land. If his agent was well received, he then dispatched a second emissary with fuller instructions, though they were verbal at first and only committed to writing when he was sure of his ground. He asked for recognition as Elizabeth's successor, he angled for loans, he offered to grant toleration to English Catholics if he became their King, he hinted that his conversion to Catholicism was not to be despaired of. In the divisions between Spain and other Catholic States lay his chief hope of success, for Spanish ambition and arrogance were feared and hated in many quarters. France and Spain were at war; the Pope was surrounded by anti-Spanish sentiment; Venice and Florence were hostile to Madrid. Though the Jesuits were normally Spanish in sympathy, the secular priesthood outside of Spain was apt to be anti-Spanish, while similar divisions existed among the English Catholic exiles on the Continent.

From Spain James knew that he had much to fear. But he had practised with Spanish agents in the past and would certainly have welcomed an understanding now if he could have obtained it. His eagerness to explore every path makes it likely that he had some connection with the strange diplomacy of John Ogilvy of Poury.

Ogilvy, a Scottish Catholic, began in 1595 a journey which took him to Flanders, to Rome and to other Italian cities, and finally to Spain. He claimed to be James's accredited agent in highly important and secret negotiations. But everywhere he played an astonishing double game, negotiating with anti-Spanish elements and with the Pope in one way, and with the Spaniards in quite another. In Rome he asked for money, for papal recognition of the King's title, for the excommunication of English Catholics who refused to accept it. But in Spain he declared that James planned to become a Catholic and wished to ally with Spain in a war of revenge against Elizabeth. Philip was asked not only to renounce his claim to the English succession and to recognize that of James, but also to send to Scotland an army and great sums of money with which to begin the war. Suspicious of such wild proposals, the Spanish cast the adventurous Ogilvy into prison and brought his negotiations to an inglorious end.

His mission had a curious sequel. The Spanish had set a spy upon him, one John Cecil, an English priest, who denounced not only Ogilvy but Ogilvy's master. The King of Scots had not the slightest wish to be reconciled to Rome, asserted Cecil; he hated, banished and slaughtered Catholics, and had done his utmost to bring about his mother's execution. This diatribe was answered by William Crichton, a Jesuit famous for many plottings, but a true Scot and a forward man for his King. In an amusing panegyric he defended James as wise, learned, moderate and honest, no obstinate heretic but a friend of Catholics, a valiant and warlike Prince who had crushed the wild Earl of Bothwell and who thirsted for vengeance against Elizabeth. Cecil rushed into an ill-advised reply, thus widening the gulf between Spanish and anti-Spanish Catholics.

How far the King was responsible for Ogilvy's mission it is impossible to say, but if he gave him secret instructions, as is more than likely, Ogilvy went far beyond them, for his reckless diplomacy does not square with James's normal caution in approaching Catholic States. Three years later, after the death of Philip in 1598, James sent another agent, Lord Robert Semple, to Madrid to ask again for recognition of his title. But Semple's credentials were inadequate, he was asked some direct and awkward questions regarding his master's religion, and the mission came to nothing. The approach to Spain was hopeless.

There was greater hope of support from France where Henry IV — at war with Spain — could not tolerate a Spanish king in England. Henry, moreover, having accepted Catholicism, enjoyed great prestige at Rome and might well be able to open for the King of Scots some secret avenue of approach to the Papacy. James therefore wooed him with gifts and embassies, declared with a flourish that the entire resources of Scotland should be placed at his disposal, and urged that the old Franco-Scottish alliance be brought to life once more. But here Elizabeth, whom Henry dared not offend, imposed her veto. And, in truth, the two Kings did not like each other. James piously contrasted his own steadfastness in religion with the apostasy of Henry, while Henry's caustic wit poked fun at the wisest fool in Christendom, a great King who wrote little books, a charlatan who practised with everybody but who was true to none. Well might James be called Solomon, said Henry. Was he not the son of David? None the less Henry came to the conclusion that in the hard choice between James and a Spanish candidate for the English throne, he must support the former, and in 1601 he wrote his ambassador at Rome that the King of Scots was the rightful heir to England.

An amusing incident occurred in 1596, when a Gascon poet, one M. de la Jessé, appeared in Scotland, and James conceived the idea of sending him to Paris and to other Catholic courts to seek amity and assistance in obtaining the succession. M. de la Jessé, however, was an impossible ambassador, a conceited coxcomb who had the effrontery to compose a set of his own letters of introduction, filling them with bombastic praises of his virtues. Secretary Menmuir brought James to earth by ridicule of Jessé's preposterous antics, and the mission ended before it began. But one can see what the King was thinking. He hoped to win Henry IV, to publicize his title, and possibly to build a league of Catholic powers that would aid him in his quest. The story of M. de la Jessé makes it more likely that James had commissioned John Ogilvy.[5]

The King also made an approach to Pope Clement VIII, the most daring and fateful of his many moves. That such an approach could possibly bring him advantage might well appear fantastic, yet there were in fact circumstances that gave it some chance of success. What Clement desired was a Catholic king in England who would be independent of both France and Spain, but no suitable candidate was available, and Clement was thus in the same dilemma as Henry IV. There was, however, a difference. It was James's religion which offended the Pope; and if the King of Scots, following the example of the King of Navarre, was ready to embrace Catholicism, the papal objection would be removed. There were those about the Pope who counselled patience and moderation in dealing with King James. Thus if James could create the impression that his conversion was imminent he might obtain the inestimable advantage of the Pope's neutrality or even his support.

The story begins with a famous but mysterious letter from the King to Clement in 1599. The text was innocuous, a request that

William Chisholm, Bishop of Vaison in France, be advanced to the rank of Cardinal; but the salutations — 'Beatissime Pater' and 'Obedientissimus Filius' — were those of a person contemplating conversion. The implication of the letter was crystal-clear.

Almost a decade later, in 1608, a Catholic writer obtained access to this letter and published it gleefully in an attack upon the King. It happened that Elphinstone, James's Scottish Secretary, was in London at the time. Called upon for an explanation and placed under severe pressure, he confessed that he and other Catholics at the Scottish court had written the letter without James's knowledge and had obtained his signature by placing the letter among others which the King signed hurriedly as he was about to go hunting. It is impossible, however, to accept this confession as true. James was highly sensitive in 1599 to the implications of his Italian correspondence and would not have signed letters to that country in so careless a fashion. When a reply came back from Rome he was quick to take advantage of the deception that had been practised. And it is incredible that he could have recalled in 1608, as he claimed to do, that nine years earlier he had inadvertently signed a certain letter as he hurried to the chase. One must therefore believe that if his advisers secured his signature by a subterfuge, which is not unlikely, they did so with his knowledge and approval. It is true that he shrank from addressing the Pope in terms that implied a recognition of papal supremacy. He had never written to the Pope, he declared in 1598, because in good conscience he could address him by no other title than that of Bishop Rome, which, he feared, might give offence. Yet such was his eagerness to negotiate with Clement in 1599 that in all probability he laid aside his scruples.

Clement replied in April 1600, saying little about Chisholm, but imploring the King to consider conversion, and other letters may have come in 1601. Clement was answered not by the King but by Queen Anne. We do not have her letter to the Pope, though we know she wrote one, but we have a letter to Cardinal Borghese in which she excused her husband's silence and declared she was writing in his name as well as in her own. She spoke of her conversion, using the words 'we' and 'our' with an ambiguity that was doubtless intentional. Her letter offered hope that James was about to be reconciled to Rome. Clement in reply sent affectionate greetings, expressed joy at Anne's conversion, urged the King to follow her example, and begged that Prince Henry be educated as a Catholic. James did not answer, but he drafted instructions for Sir James Lindsay, the Pope's messenger, who was to return to Italy. He would never, he said, dissemble his religious convictions nor would he allow self-pride to blind him to what he believed was sound and reasonable. Lindsay, however, delayed by illness and by other causes, did not reach Rome until 1605 when the great crisis had passed. The result of this correspondence was all that the King could have hoped, for Clement's hostility was softened, and though he did not recognize James's title, he did not denounce it. [6]

Other Italian States were also approached by the King. In Venice he asked for money and for an anti-Spanish alliance, though both were politely refused. With Ferdinand I, Grand Duke of Tuscany, his dealings were more extended and more interesting. Ferdinand was the most wealthy of the Italian Princes, his wife was James's kinswoman through the house of Lorraine, and it had been through his mediation that Henry IV had made his peace with the Papacy. Thus attracted to Tuscany for many reasons, the King in 1598 dispatched to Florence Sir Michael Balfour of Burley, a rather unlikely envoy, a lawless little knight, who had been the friend of Bothwell and was always in trouble with the Kirk. The principal result of his mission was a kindly letter of advice from Ferdinand. James, said the Duke, must seek friends everywhere, though with great secrecy; he must cultivate Henry IV; he must be reconciled to Rome, and here Ferdinand offered his good offices; he must augment his military strength, build a party in England, and seize the country the moment that Elizabeth died, though avoiding a battle. He must win Essex, the idol of the English soldiery; yet Essex was a man to be feared. That James pondered this letter deeply there can be no doubt. Some years later, in 1601, Burley returned to Florence to propose a marriage between Prince Henry and a daughter of Duke Ferdinand. James asked for a large sum of money as an advanced instalment of the dowry, while Elphinstone sent Burley a code in which 'buying of arms' meant 'negotiation with the Pope'. But nothing came of these overtures. The Duke would not part so easily with his money, and James, absorbed in developments elsewhere, became less eager for the Florentine alliance. [7]

Although for years the King thus busied himself in playing the mendicant across the Continent, his efforts for the most part were clearly barren of result. Something he accomplished by increasing the divisions among his opponents and by his deception of the Papacy, though that deception was to cast a shadow over his entire reign in England. Yet the absence of a strong Catholic candidate in whose interest the Catholic world could unite stood him in far better stead than did all his diplomacy, and had he been forced to rely upon aid from continental powers at the time of Elizabeth's death, his difficulties would have been great indeed. Nor did he enhance his personal prestige, for he was considered a kind of irrepressible and erratic bounder whose bizarre diplomacy was crass and uncivilized and whose words and actions offered no basis of confidence. 'He practises in Rome, in Spain, and everywhere else, as he does with me,' wrote Henry IV, 'without attaching himself to any one, and is easily carried away by the hopes of those about him without regard for truth or merit. Hence I foresee he will allow himself to be surprised on all occasions.'[8]

Meanwhile he found opportunity for intrigue in Ireland where the rebellion of the Earl of Tyrone was causing Elizabeth great difficulty. As her ally, James's conduct appeared to be perfectly correct. He issued proclamations which forbade the clansmen of the Western Isles to aid Tyrone and prohibited trade between Scotland and the Irish rebels, and he offered aid to Elizabeth when Spanish troops landed at Kinsale. But seeing in Tyrone a person who might be a power at the moment of Elizabeth's death, he corresponded with him secretly, gladly accepted his offers of service, and looked the other way as the royal proclamations were disobeyed. When Elizabeth protested, he asserted his innocence and issued new proclamations.

He also set out to cultivate the English Catholics. They knew he was extending a secret hand to the Catholic world and, though they do not appear to have hoped for his conversion, they believed he would grant them toleration in religion. These hopes he did all in his power to foster. To English Catholics who came to Scotland he granted ready access and offered full assurance that toleration could be anticipated. He corresponded with the Earl of Northumberland, a leading Catholic noble. 'It were pity', wrote Northumberland, 'to lose so good a kingdom for not tolerating a Mass in a corner'; and James answered: 'As for the Catholics, I will neither persecute any that will be quiet and give but an outward obedience to the law, neither will I spare to advance any of them that will by good service worthily deserve it.' These words, as he hoped, became known to many. And hence the majority of the English Catholics supported him as Elizabeth's successor, while only a few fanatics held out for the Infanta.

Was he utterly insincere? Was his policy summed up in a phrase attributed to him after his succession and which can be rendered only in Scots: 'Na, na, gud faiyth, we's not need the papists noo.' Some Catholics thought so. The King's language consists of blasphemy and heresy, wrote a Jesuit in 1601, his only object is to attain the English Crown, he hates all Catholics except those he can use to further his great design, and though his ambition might impel him to a hypocritical conversion only a miracle could make him a good Catholic.[9] But this judgment is unfair. His offer of toleration to the English Catholics was sincere, though he had in mind a restricted toleration on his own terms. Along many lines he was prepared to meet the Catholic world half way. Yet his promises gave the impression that he would do more as King of England than he actually did, and he was at the same time making pledges of a very different nature to the English Protestants.

His agent in London, James Hamilton, was instructed in 1600 to assure all honest men that the King would 'not only maintain and continue the profession of the Gospel there, but withal not suffer or permit any other religion to be professed and avowed within the bounds of that kingdom'. Here was a solemn pledge to Protestants that there would be no toleration of Catholicism. It was a pledge given in words that would appeal to the English Puritans, and Calderwood mistakenly asserts that it was sent to one of their number. That James cultivated the Puritans where he could is certain, and that he had an understanding with them and that Presbyterians in both kingdoms were working for his accession is highly probable.[10]

Meanwhile the prospect opened before him of intrigue with the Earl of Essex, Elizabeth's brilliant but unstable favourite, whose rivalry with Cecil was dividing the English court. If Cecil was growing odious and Elizabeth was losing her grasp, if Essex was as strong and popular as he appeared to be, if he was as devoted to the King of Scots as he professed, and if by some coup he became dominant in England, then he and James together might force

from Elizabeth a recognition of the King's title whether she would
or no. Here were alluring vistas, but they were highly dangerous,
as James knew full well. Fortunately he was both weak and cautious. His caution saved him from open and irreversible support
of Essex, while his weakness convinced him that he could not
employ force but must wait upon events. A number of things
drew the two men together. They were both hostile to Cecil,
who managed Elizabeth's Scottish policy and was cordially disliked in Scotland not only by the King but by those who advised
him on English affairs. James hoped, moreover, that through
Essex he might strengthen his contacts with the Puritan party in
England. 'He desires the continuation of Essex's affection,' wrote
one of James's confidants, 'and promises to reward it in a proper
time and place. I cannot represent in writing his affection. He
will show it himself one day.' Essex, on his side, employed the
problem of the succession to lend an appearance of statesmanship
to his wild ambitions and to win the King of Scots. He wrote
James in an undated letter: 'The affections of my heart breathe
only after the prosperous success of a King of so much worth,
whose servant I was born by nature. Such as I am, I consecrate
unto your royal throne. Neither do I doubt that the minds of all
my countrymen will jointly unite their hopes in your Majesty's
noble person.'

But Essex's unruly spirit was leading him into trouble. With
Elizabeth he had a serious quarrel in 1598. Early in the following
year he was sent to Ireland to command the Queen's forces against
Tyrone, but, though he went with great strength, he wasted time
and energy and finally concluded a truce on shameful terms.
Elizabeth's letters grew bitter. In anger and chagrin he contemplated rebellion, then suddenly shifted his plans, abandoned his
Irish command contrary to instructions, and returned to England
in September 1599. He met the wrath of Elizabeth, temporary
imprisonment, and political eclipse. Two of his followers later
confessed that he had intrigued with Scotland during the Irish
campaign, and one of them added that he spoke many times of
protestations of love made to him by the King of Scots. Moreover,
his intimate friend, Lord Mountjoy, sent an agent, one Henry
Leigh, to Scotland. Leigh assured the King that Essex had no
thought of the English throne for himself and that he would
tolerate no successor but the Scottish King, who would do well

to demand from Elizabeth a public recognition of his right. Cautiously James replied that he 'would think of it and put himself in a readiness to take any good occasion'.

For some years he had been doing what he could to increase his military strength and his efforts were now redoubled. Hoping at first to throw the burden on the people, he commanded them to supply themselves with arms and ordered a grand muster or 'waponschowing' on a national scale for May 1st, 1599. But if the muster was held, it proved a disappointment; and a few months later the King commissioned Sir Michael Balfour of Burley, his envoy to Florence, to buy arms in the Netherlands and bring them to Scotland to be purchased by the people. Again he was disappointed, for the people would not buy the arms, and the plan collapsed. He then turned to taxation. In December 1599, and in June of the year following, he summoned conventions of the estates and sought by many means, honest and otherwise, to obtain funds. Important persons were dealt with before the estates assembled, a rumour was spread that Elizabeth was ill, and the conventions were harangued by the King, who cajoled and persuaded in the very sittings of the assemblies. He was met by stubborn opposition. There were members bold enough to scoff at the notion that Scotland could increase her military power to a point where she could threaten England, 'at which the King raged'. But though he dismissed the estates with bitter words, he had no funds and his hope of arming Scotland was ended.

Meanwhile, in February 1600, Leigh came once more to Scotland, now with a definite plan. Mountjoy, about to go to Ireland as Essex's successor, would bring back troops from that country, join Essex, and effect a coup at court, while the King's part was to gather an army on the Border and send an ambassador to London to demand recognition of his title. As to James's reply there is doubt. Two of the confessions at Essex's trial, from which comes our information, imply that his answer was dilatory and amounted to a refusal. But Southampton, a noble close to Essex, declared that the King 'liked the course well and prepared himself for it'. In all probability he was discreetly vague. Mountjoy departed for Ireland where he began a brilliant campaign against Tyrone; and when, in the spring of 1600, Essex called upon him to bring troops to England, he refused. Distance had brought him cooler thoughts, and the intrigue ended.

Essex's fortunes soon reached their brief and tragic climax. Goaded by passionate hatred of his foes and by the evil counsel of his friends, he summoned his followers to London in December 1600, planning to obtain access to Elizabeth by force, to drive his enemies from office, and to summon a Parliament that would confirm his actions and recognize James as Elizabeth's successor. From neither Mountjoy nor the King of Scots did he expect military assistance. He asked Mountjoy for a letter of countenance to be shown to Elizabeth, and in the same way he asked James only to send a qualified ambassador to London by February 1st. 'You shall', he promised, 'be declared and acknowledged the certain and undoubted successor to this Crown and shall command the services and lives of as many of us as undertake this great work.' He sent a cypher, to be returned as a token of the King's acceptance. For James the moment of decision had arrived. He believed that discontent in England was widespread and that the strength and ability of Essex were greater than they actually were. A large portion of England's fighting strength was in Ireland, where Tyrone was not his enemy. And yet to break with Elizabeth and to join in rebellion against her! From this step he wisely shrank. He returned the cypher, but did not send his ambassadors at the appointed time, and to that extent he played Essex false. Before the ambassadors left Edinburgh he knew that Essex's rising had failed, that the situation had altered completely, and that his policy must alter with it.[11]

On February 9th, 1601, Essex made his insane raid into London, failed to rally the citizens, was arrested in his own house, and within three weeks was tried and executed.

Rumours of the debacle reached Edinburgh quickly, but the King, though 'in the dumps', remained incredulous until a letter commanding belief arrived from Cecil to George Nicolson, the English ambassador in Scotland. James questioned the ambassador sharply about its contents, as though they could not be true. But he was shaken, and Nicolson wrote, 'I do see this matter is of rare moment.' For the Scottish ambassadors who were about to depart for London, the King hastily prepared revised instructions 'anent this accident'. It is clear that he did not fully comprehend what had taken place in England but continued to believe that a general rising was still a possibility. If revolt was imminent and likely to prove successful, he wrote, and if his friends in England lacked only a leader, he was ready to step into Essex's place. If, on the other hand, all hope was gone, his ambassadors must begin the task of rebuilding a party in his interest, for he could not remain so long inactive that discontented spirits should go suing to other saints. To gauge the imminence of rebellion was thus the ambassadors' first duty, and meanwhile they should 'dally with the present guiders of the court' and walk warily 'betwixt these two precipices of the Queen and the people who now appear to be in so contrary terms'.

The ambassadors were further instructed to demand from Elizabeth a statement that the King had had no part in the Essex rising. So preposterous a request was proof of James's nervousness. Again and again he asked Nicolson whether his name was being mentioned in the trials that were taking place in England, and was greatly relieved to learn that it was not.[12] With rare moderation Elizabeth suppressed all reference to the King of Scots. She could not brand him as a conspirator unless she was prepared to exclude him as her heir and, had she permitted his name to figure in the trials, the whole problem of the succession would have been aired in a way highly displeasing to her. James's ambassadors, so soon as they arrived in London, realized the folly of his demand and quietly dropped it.

They had been told by the King to deal with Elizabeth with all due reverence but to take a high tone with Cecil. If Cecil would not assist him now, said James, he must expect no favours in the future, 'but all the Queen's hard usage of me to be hereafter craven at his hands'.

Though the King was wont to remark that the age of miracles was past, an event now occurred which he might well have placed in that category. His ambassadors were deeply discouraged by their reception in England. Cold and resentful was Elizabeth, and she wrote the King a sharp letter in which she showed clearly that she knew much more than she had allowed to be made public. Then the miracle took place. Summoning the Scottish ambassadors to the most secret of interviews, Cecil offered, under stringent conditions, to correspond with the King and to promote his interests in England. The joy of the ambassadors may be imagined, for here was the true path to the English throne.

Thus began a remarkable correspondence. In a first guarded letter the King expressed his hearty pleasure that Cecil had been 'so honourably plain', suggested Henry Howard, an English Catholic, as intermediary, brushed aside Essex's memory with cold-blooded brevity, and promised Cecil great future rewards in return for present service. Cecil in a masterly answer declared his gratitude and in the same breath laid down his conditions with admirable lucidity and succinctness. The King must expect nothing from him that could cause the slightest harm to Queen Elizabeth; not a word, not a thought, should touch his dear and precious sovereign. He insisted upon absolute secrecy. 'The subject itself is so perilous to touch amongst us as it setteth a mark upon his head forever that hatcheth such a bird.' Frequently he would be forced to act in ways that the King might think suspicious, and he thanked James for the assurance that when the King's feast could be lawfully proclaimed, Cecil should not be forgotten though he lacked a wedding garment. He explained his reasons for opening the correspondence. He was alarmed, he said, lest false rumours that he favoured the Infanta, together with James's unfounded belief that Elizabeth opposed his title, might drive the King to action which would compromise his future. Right joyfully did James accept these terms. And Cecil, the erstwhile object of his hearty execration, was now his dearest friend, whose 'happy and honest concurrence for my weal doth force me, out of the abundance of a thankful mind, to write in a loving, plain and familiar style'. 'My dearest and trusty Cecil,' wrote the King, 'my pen is not able to express how happy I think myself for having chanced upon so worthy, so wise, and so provident a friend.' Cecil in return spoke with joy and admiration. His motives, though selfish, were prompted by the instinct of the statesman, for the succession was a problem which demanded solution, but the King's unbounded and dancing delight was that of the self-centred opportunist.

With consummate skill Cecil instructed James in the proper behaviour towards Elizabeth; and the King, appropriating Cecil's wisdom as his own, hastened to comply. He should not, said Cecil, press the matter of the succession upon the Queen but should merely treat her with all kindness and consideration. By clear and temperate courses he should 'secure the heart of the highest, to whose sex and quality nothing is so improper as either needless expostulations or over much curiosity in her own actions, the first showing unquietness in yourself, the second challenging some untimely interest in hers; both which are best forborne'. Nor should he seek to win popularity in England, to be busy, and to prepare the vulgar beforehand. He must trust to those already in power, by whose management his 'ship shall be steered into the right harbour, without cross of wave or tide that shall be able to turn over a cockboat'.

The transformation wrought in the King by these precepts was instantaneous, complete and amusing. In place of the petulant and jibing letters he had been writing to Elizabeth, his communications now breathed a beautiful spirit of love and affection. Her letters, he told her, filled his heart with more contentment than pen or tongue could express. They made him more happy than if he had won the Golden Fleece. He protested to God she should ever be his oracle. And with unaccustomed sincerity he concluded his letters by committing her, 'richt excellent, richt heich and michtie princesse, our dearest sister and cousine', to the protection of the Almighty. She was doubtless surprised, but was pleased by his new kindness. 'My dear brother,' she wrote, 'never was there any prince nor meaner wight to whose grateful turns I did not correspond. So trust I that you will not doubt but that your last letters are so acceptably taken as my thanks cannot be lacking for the same, but yield them you in grateful sort.'

The thought of disturbing such sweet concord was now highly offensive to him. What a blot on his honour it would be, he wrote, to break, for an untimely ambition, his friendship with Elizabeth, a friendship won by his long years of honest behaviour towards her. God, who had clothed him with an undoubted right to the Crown, would also in due time give him peaceful possession, nor would he be so lacking in religion as to thwart God's will by unlawful anticipation. 'It were very small wisdom by climbing of ditches and hedges for pulling of unripe fruit to hazard the breaking of my neck, when by a little patience and by abiding the season I may with far more ease and safety enter at the gate of the garden and enjoy the fruits at my pleasure in the time of their greatest maturity.' Thus he rambled on in all virtuous innocence. Northumberland, to whom he was writing, must have wondered at his trust in the unerring justice of divine providence. From any notion of employing force against Elizabeth he now shrank with pious horror. A Scottish laird, thinking to please him, drank to the speedy union of the Crowns, saying he had forty muskets ready for the King's use. But James reproved him. He swore he had no thought of haste, he would obtain England by right and not by conquest, and he called upon God to deprive him of England and Scotland alike if in the secrets of his heart he had ever thought otherwise. His intrigues with continental States diminished though they did not end entirely, and he informed Elizabeth of most, though not all, of his dealings with foreign powers. That Cecil had greatly improved Anglo-Scottish relations, easing the declining years of his great mistress, there can be no doubt.

The number of persons who shared the secret was very small: the Earl of Mar and his cousin, Sir Thomas Erskine; Edward Bruce, lay Abbot of Kinloss; and the diplomat David Foulis in Scotland; at first only Henry Howard in England. Two other Englishmen of uncertain identity were later told of the correspondence. Of them one was probably Charles Howard, Earl of Nottingham, and Thomas Howard, Baron Howard de Walden, may possibly have been the other.

Of great importance in the secret correspondence was Lord Henry Howard. His relations with the King were to be close, prolonged and discreditable, but we do not know their origin. He was a Catholic who, like his elder brother, the Duke of Norfolk, had had mysterious dealings with Mary Queen of Scots upon which he could build in commending himself to her son. A man of dark counsels and creeping schemes, learned but bombastic, and a most fulsome flatterer, he had never found favour with Elizabeth; but he met better fortune with James, who spoke of him when the correspondence opened as 'his long approved and trusty Howard'. His lengthy and complicated letters, to which the King referred as ample, Asiatic and endless, breathed a spirit of unctuous adulation. He kisses the sacred hand ordained by heaven to carry sceptres heavier than those it now holds; he thinks of the King, the base of all beatitude, as he thinks of God; when he hears that James has fallen from his horse but has escaped injury, he returns thanks to heaven for not extinguishing the light of Israel.

He was employed by Cecil to stress the need for secrecy and to handle the less creditable portions of the correspondence. Of detection both men lived in constant dread. Cecil dismissed a secretary whose daily attendance might discover the secret; he was suspicious of Nicolson and fearful of Queen Anne. Howard was assigned the delicate task of warning James against her. With deep and cringing apologies he wrote to the King that though Anne possessed every virtue, yet the sweetest and most innocent creatures might be deceived and the fairest stars besmirched. Eve was beguiled by the serpent; sirens might sing and crocodiles lament; and the pure Anne might be led astray. The King, with a closer knowledge of his consort and quite aware that she was prying and meddlesome, took the admonition in good part. Against his rival, Sir Walter Ralegh, and against Ralegh's friends Lord Cobham and the Earl of Northumberland, Cecil also instructed Howard to warn the King; and Howard, showing himself for what he was, performed his task with a pen that dripped hate and venom. Ralegh, Cobham and Northumberland, he wrote, were James's sworn enemies, who would rather see him buried than crowned, a diabolical triplicity of wicked plotters, hatching treasons from the cockatrice eggs 'that are daily and nightly sitten on'. Without a doubt the King came to England poisoned against them.

A number of persons in both countries, eager to assist the King as his fortunes rose, had to be kept in the dark, or led astray by false scents, or held inactive in their longings to serve. The Master of Gray whispered to James that he would gladly use his influence with Cecil to open a secret correspondence, but was silenced when Cecil pretended a violent hostility against the King of Scots. 'Never,' wrote Howard gleefully, 'was jackdaw so well cozened in his own school-points and quiddities.' Lennox, in London in 1601, thought to please his master by winning friends, but the King wrote him piously that he would never seek support from the subjects of another Prince. None the less there were moments when he questioned the wisdom of relying wholly upon Cecil and of ignoring so completely the proffered friendship of other Englishmen. Since they never heard from him, he said, he feared they might wonder at his long flat silence and think that he held them in contempt. He considered a resident ambassador in London, but Cecil imposed his veto.

The King's anxiety was needless, for in the last years of Elizabeth's life there was a general acceptance of the Scottish title. Protestant States on the Continent approved, the Pope and Henry IV were ready to acquiesce, Spain knew her impotence. In England the trend was quite clear. 'They think your Majesty their young lord', wrote a Scottish traveller. Elizabeth's policy would indicate that she agreed, and there is a story, perhaps apocryphal, that on her death-bed she gave a sign that James should be her successor.

The days of her last illness in March 1603, were days of tremendous excitement in Scotland. Rumours from England came thick and fast. Kinloss begged Howard for frequent news. 'Care never how short you be to King James,' he wrote, doubtless thinking of Howard's interminable letters, 'so you give him any sense of your meaning, for now he goes not abroad and longs every hour for news from you.' Kinloss advised that in case of Elizabeth's death Howard should temper the King's 'too great haste in removing hence, for now he burns to be gone'. Meanwhile in England Cecil was making quiet preparations. He spoke of the succession in the Council and asked the King for a warrant that present councillors retain their places until his arrival. Warning was sent to strategic fortresses, London was placed under guard, malcontents were rounded up. Cecil sent the King a draft of a proclamation announcing his succession and asked for corrections. But James had none. He found it 'music that sounded so sweetly in his ears that he could alter no note in so agreeable an harmony'.[13]

Early in the morning of Thursday, March 24th, the great Queen passed away, and within eight hours of her death James was proclaimed King in London.

CHAPTER X

THE PROMISED LAND

OFFICIAL word from the English Council did not reach Edinburgh until five days later, but the King already had the news. Sir Robert Carey, son of Lord Hunsdon, having laid careful plans to be the first bearer of glad tidings, was riding hard for the north within a few hours after the Queen's death. Despite an ugly fall from his horse, he knocked at the gate of Holyroodhouse on the Saturday night, was quickly brought to James's chamber, knelt before him, and saluted him as King of England. Eagerly James asked many questions until far into the night. He assured Carey he had won a master who knew how to reward service; and with much shrewdness Carey asked to be made a Gentleman of the Bedchamber, which was readily granted, though later in England, through the ill will of the English Council, he lost the post and must have reflected sadly that the race is not always to the swift.

The King's thoughts were conflicting ones. With jovial good nature he saluted George Nicolson next morning as his first servant. But the letter he wrote Cecil that day was sober enough and not without anxiety. He had heard from Carey, he began, that the Queen was dead and that he had been proclaimed her successor, for which he returned thanks to God, praying he might prove equal to the high place to which he was now called. He gave thanks also for the wisdom and providence of his dearest friends whose care and devotion were thus translating a monarchy. They would see him strive to the utmost to fulfil their expectations, so that no prince would surpass him in justice and piety. And in his own hand he added: 'How happy I think myself by the conquest of so faithful and so wise a counsellor I reserve it to be expressed out of my own mouth unto you.' The truth was that he had meditated so long upon the difficulties of the succession that he could scarcely credit the ease with which it appeared to be taking place. That very day he sent the Abbot of Holyrood to take possession of Berwick — the gateway to the south. Berwick received the

Abbot with all joy and submission, and the King breathed more easily.

The letter from the English Council, when it arrived, was all that he could wish. Grief for the Queen's death, it declared, was mitigated by hope of the King's heroic virtue, joy filled all English hearts; councillors offered the King their obedience and besought him — quite unnecessarily — to come to them with all speed. He hastened to comply. Convening those nobles who were accessible, he placed the government in the hands of the Scottish Council and confirmed the custody of his children to those already entrusted with them. The Queen, being pregnant, was to follow the King at leisure, but she arrived in England with a speed that was scarcely deemed possible.

On Sunday, April 3rd, James attended divine service in St. Giles. After the sermon — a friendly admonition to good behaviour — he rose and bade farewell to the people. Their mood had changed. Joy and pride at the accession of a Scottish King to the throne of England now gave way to the sad reflection that they were losing a resident sovereign, that Edinburgh must suffer in dignity and profit, that pomp and power were moving to the south. James promptly interpreted his people's sorrow as a personal tribute to himself. Deeply moved by their grief, which he could well understand, he begged them not to take his departure too sorely to heart. They would continue, he declared, to enjoy the benefits of his rule though he was far away. New greatness would not lessen his love. Every third year he would visit them, and at those happy moments the meanest amongst them should have ready access. Two days later he set forth from Edinburgh amid the tears of his people. His parting from Anne, which took place in public, was tender and edifying, though the moment he was gone she renewed her old quarrel with the family of Mar over the custody of Prince Henry, a quarrel that brought embarrassment to her husband and danger to herself. Failing to obtain possession of her son, she became so furious that she contracted a fever and suffered a miscarriage. James wrote her a letter admirable both in its firmness and gentleness, reproving her for her ill-timed hostility to Mar and for the 'froward womanly apprehensions' with which she accused the King of preferring Mar to his wife. Tenderly the letter concludes: 'I have herein omitted praying God, my heart, to preserve you and all the bairns, and send me a blithe

meeting with you, and a couple of them. Your own James.'
The King had not found time to visit Prince Henry, but he wrote
him a letter of sage and sonorous advice. Good fortune, he
warned, must not make Henry proud; 'a King's son and heir was
ye before, and no more are ye yet'. With the letter James sent a
copy of the *Basilikon Doron*, newly printed. 'Study and profit in it
as ye would deserve my blessing. Be diligent and earnest in your
studies that at your meeting with me I may praise you for your
progress in learning. Farewell.'[1]

Before the King left Edinburgh a number of persons had
arrived from England, and the stream of officials, nobles, courtiers
and place-hunters swelled constantly as he travelled south. Some
came on official business. Sir Thomas Lake, Cecil's secretary, was
sent north to report the King's first thoughts as he became
acquainted with English affairs. The Dean of Canterbury was
hastily dispatched by Archbishop Whitgift to discover James's
intentions towards the Church of England. But most men came
for their own ends. 'There is much posting that way,' wrote
Chamberlain — the keen retailer of public and private gossip —
'and many run thither of their own errand, as if it were nothing
else but first come first served, or that preferment were a goal to be
got by footmanship.' The King was besieged by suitors before he
left his native land. Perhaps still dreading some mischance, he
was lavish with rewards and promises and, as he reached the
joyous conviction that the great prize was truly his, his rash be-
stowal of favours increased from sheer exultation. More than
three hundred persons, commended by his English hosts or by his
Scottish favourites, he knighted on his way to London. The Scots
made a good thing of their influence, and it was said that the English had the blows and the Scots the crowns. These early days
might have taught the King that he was certain to be the target of
constant, shameless and violent importunity. Unfortunately it
was the courtiers who learned the easy indulgence of their
master.[2]

His progress south might well have dazzled a stronger mind
than his, for it was one long succession of welcomes, rejoicings and
entertainments, each more lavish than the last. He entered Berwick with some pomp, attended by many Border chieftains. The
people shouted 'Welcome' and 'God save King James', till they
were (in a manner) entreated to be silent; the Recorder presented

a purse of gold; great ordnance roared until the earth trembled and smoke beclouded the town. Next day the King, having attended church, inspected the fortifications and touched off a cannon with such boldness that the gunners were filled with admiration. He was most pleasant and gracious to all. A sudden rainstorm broke, but quickly he interpreted the omen. The sun before the rain represented his happy departure, the rain the grief of Scotland, the succeeding fair weather the joy of England at his approach. Thus ever more sublime and exalted became his frame of mind. Welcomed into Northumberland by the high sheriff and by a large train of gentlemen, he set forth for Widdrington Castle, the house of Sir Robert Carey. But such was his longing to enter upon his inheritance that he 'departed upon the spur, scarce any of his train being able to keep him company', and rode near forty miles in less than four hours. Yet when he arrived and saw fat deer in the park, he went forth at once and slew two of them. Over Sunday he rested at Newcastle, and heard a sermon by Tobias Matthew, Bishop of Durham, with whom he joked and jested in high good humour.

He entered York with solemnity and magnificence, being now supplied from London with jewels and regalia, coaches, heralds, trumpeters and men-at-arms. It had been the opinion of the English Council that these trappings of royalty need not be sent farther north than Burghley in Northamptonshire, but the King insisted that York was 'our second city' and that the county contained peers and gentlemen of the best sort. In this there was wisdom, though doubtless his longing to show himself in glory was an argument of equal strength. At York he wished to be attended by some of his English councillors. Earlier he had written to them that they might meet him at Burghley, but was now irritated to find they had taken him at his word. Surely, he thought, the younger councillors might have come as far as York. Thither he summoned Cecil, having things to discuss with him, he said, that could not be entrusted to paper; and Cecil journeyed up from London, full of cares and perplexities, already worried by lack of money. He knew that complaints from Ireland had reached the King and feared that his first audience might be marred by unpleasantness.

These early conferences of the King and his chief minister were chaotic and disordered, wedged between banquets and journeyings. James was intent, not upon learning the thoughts and problems of his new kingdom, but upon his entry into his personal inheritance. He discussed with Cecil the details of his progress (for if he continued his present speed he would reach London at the moment of Elizabeth's funeral), he discussed the coronation, which was not to take place until Anne's arrival. His letters to the Council breathe the same spirit of absorption in his personal affairs. His first request was for money, for he had scarcely had enough of his own to take him to Berwick. He wrote for jewels and ladies-in-waiting for the Queen. New coins were to be minted, one side of which should join the arms of Scotland to those of his other kingdoms, adding the sublime legend, *Exsurgat Deus Dissipentur Inimici*; while the other should depict 'our head crowned'. Problems which concerned England rather than her King must await their turn. Yet Cecil wrote that James's 'virtues were so eminent as by my six days' kneeling at his feet I have made so sufficient a discovery of his royal perfections, as I contemplate greater felicity to this isle than ever it enjoyed'.

Meanwhile the King journeyed to Doncaster where he stayed at the Bear Inn and gave the host a valuable reversion to a manor house; thence to Worksop and Belvoir Castle to be royally entertained by the Earls of Shrewsbury and Rutland. He hunted as he went, live hares being brought in baskets, and the gentry sending their best hounds to follow the game. At Newark-upon-Trent a cutpurse was hanged without trial by royal order. Upon his arrival at Burghley House, the seat of Cecil's elder brother, the King was 'received with great magnificence, the house seeming so rich as if it had been furnished at the charges of an emperor'. James fell from his horse near Burghley, to the consternation of his train; but he made light of it, though he rode in a coach next day, being in considerable pain, and his physician, Mayerne, afterwards declared he had broken his collarbone. Continuing his progress, he was entertained by Sir Anthony Mildmay, by Sir Oliver Cromwell, and by Sir Henry Cock, and finally by Cecil at Theobalds some twelve miles north of London. The sheriff with 'three score men in fair livery cloaks' met him at the border of Middlesex, and later the Lord Mayor and Aldermen, accompanied by five hundred citizens, all well mounted, and clad in velvet cloaks and chains of gold. The press of people was becoming insupportable. An observer tried to count them at Theobalds but could not do so, declaring that each blade of grass had changed into a man. 'The multitude of people in highways, fields, meadows, closes and on trees were such that they covered the beauty of the fields; and so greedy were they to behold the countenance of the King that with much unruliness they injured and hurt one another', following the King with shouts and cries and casting up of hats. James made his way to the Charterhouse over the fields, avoiding the road; and having been entertained there for three days by Lord Thomas Howard and having invested a hundred and thirty persons with the dignity of knighthood, he came down Aldergate to the Thames and took a barge to the Tower.[3]

Despite his long journey, he entered at once upon a joyous inspection of his new-found treasures. From the Tower he went unofficially by coach and water to see London and to view the palace at Whitehall where he feasted his eyes upon the jewels of the Crown. During the summer and autumn he travelled from one to another of the royal houses within easy reach of London, 'and therein took high delight, especially to see such store of deer and game in his parks for hunting, which is the sport he preferreth above all worldly delights and pastime'. Many aspects of his reign were to spring from the fact that these rural parks and palaces so won his heart. To business he gave small attention. 'Sometimes he comes to Council,' wrote Thomas Wilson, an author whom Cecil had been employing as foreign intelligencer, 'but most time he spends in fields and parks and chases, chasing away idleness by violent exercise and early rising.' Though he travelled privately, his councillors followed him and so did a vast throng of peers and gentry who clogged the roads and fought for lodgings. Cecil wrote from Woodstock that 'only the King and Queen with the Privy Chamber ladies and some three or four of the Scottish Council are lodged in the house, and neither Lord Chamberlain nor one English councillor have a room'. A more sinister cause for travel soon appeared as the plague settled upon southern England, 'which drives us up and down so round', said Cecil, 'as I think we shall come to York'. Festivities continued none the less, and the King was entertained by the great men of the localities through which he passed.

The approach of Anne from Scotland had caused a new rush to the north. Lady Anne Clifford, the remarkable daughter of the Earl of Cumberland, tells how she and her mother killed three horses in their haste to greet the Queen and how, when James met Anne near Windsor, 'there was such an infinite number of lords and ladies and so great a court as I think I shall never see the like again'. The King was in high good humour, as well he might be. In jovial and homely fashion he asked a courtier 'if he did not think his Annie looked passing well; and my little Bessy too', he added, taking his daughter up in his arms and kissing her, 'is not an ill-faurd wench and may outshine her mother one of these days'. The little Princess, then seven years old, expressed her joy at seeing her father again in so endearing a fashion that James was more than delighted. A great banquet at Windsor honoured Prince Henry, who was invested with the Garter.[4]

The coronation on July 25th was shorn of its normal splendour by the plague, but the opening of Parliament and an entry into London in March 1604 were occasions of great pomp. The King was 'as royally attended as if the gods had summoned a parliament and were all in their steps of triumph to Jove's high court'. City and suburbs formed one great pageant, triumphal arches adorned the way, and at each there were orations, songs and entertainments, though for fear of wearying his Majesty many songs went unsung and orations undelivered.[5]

The truth was that James had long since tired of playing the gracious sovereign. Large crowds, the normal precursors of trouble in Scotland, alarmed him, and he chafed at the petty tyranny of public ceremonies. One of the first whispers of criticism against him sprang from his inability to charm the multitude as Elizabeth had done. The people, wrote Thomas Wilson, desired more of that gracious affability which the good old Queen did afford them; but the King 'naturally did not love to be looked on, and the formalities of State were but so many burdens to him'. At his entry into London he 'sucked in their gilded oratory, though never so nauseous, but afterwards in his public appearances, especially in his sports, the access of the people made him so impatient that he often dispersed them with frowns, that we may not say with curses'. More bluntly wrote a gentleman from the Isle of Wight, Sir John Oglander: the King, he says, would swear with passion, asking his attendants what the people would have. He was told they came of love to see him. 'Then he would cry out in Scottish, "God's wounds! I will pull down my breeches and they shall also see my arse."'[6]

Anne was more affable than her husband. At the entry into London an observer wrote that 'our gracious Queen, mild and courteous, placed in a chariot of exceeding beauty, did all the way so humbly and with mildness salute her subjects, never leaving to bend her body this way and that, that men and women wept with joy'.

But if the people found King James lacking in courtesy, they rejoiced none the less in his accession. Their apprehensions of what might ensue upon Elizabeth's death had been great, and when they found 'the just fear of forty years, for want of a known successor, dissolved in a minute', their contentment and relief were boundless. Beloved as Elizabeth had been, there was satisfaction in a masculine ruler, especially in one with children. A pamphlet of the day constantly repeats the words 'We have a King!' James's books were eagerly purchased, and the lucky publication of the *Basilikon Doron* at the very moment of his accession greatly enhanced his reputation. 'This book,' wrote Bacon, 'falling into every man's hand, filled the whole realm as with a good perfume or incense before the King's coming in, for being excellently written and having nothing of affectation', it offered great hope of the King's good disposition. 'What applause had it in the world,' cried the courtly Bishop Montagu, 'how did it enflame men's minds to a love and admiration of his Majesty beyond measure!' Thus at first their new King pleased the English. 'Nothing was talked of but the religion, virtue, wisdom, learning, justice and many other most noble and worthy praises of King James.' The House of Commons told him in 1604, already with a touch of disillusionment, that a general hope had risen in the minds of all his subjects that under him religion and virtue might reign again and flourish.

Upon English officials the King made a favourable first impression. They noted the casual simplicity of his audiences, his familiar and homely manner, his loquacity, good nature and apparent virtue, the ease and rapidity with which he comprehended business and came to his resolve. 'He is very facile,' wrote Lake, 'using no great majesty nor solemnities in his accesses, but witty to conceive, and very ready of speech.' Bacon found him the opposite of vainglorious, more like a prince of ancient than of modern times. 'His speech is swift and cursory, and in the full dialect of his country; and in point of business short; in point of discourse large. He is thought somewhat general in his favours, and his virtue of access is rather because he is much abroad and in press than that he giveth easy audience about serious things. Methought his Majesty rather asked counsel of the time past than of the time to come.' 'The King', wrote Roger Wilbraham, an eminent lawyer and Master of Requests, 'is of sharpest wit and invention, ready and pithy speech, and exceeding good memory; of the sweetest, pleasantest and best nature that ever I knew; desiring nor affecting anything but true honour.' Wilbraham prayed that the King's noble qualities and heroic mind would not be corrupted by the wealth and peace of England or by the painted flattery of the court.

These impressions were echoed by foreign ambassadors. 'The King of England', wrote the Venetian envoy, 'is very prudent, able in negotiation, capable of dissimulating his feelings. He is said to be personally timid and averse from war. I hear on all sides that he is a man of letters and business, fond of the chase and of riding, sometimes indulging in play. These qualities attract men to him and render him acceptable to the aristocracy. Besides English, he speaks Latin and French perfectly and understands Italian quite well. He is capable of governing, being a Prince of culture and intelligence above the common.' In describing his first audience at Greenwich in May 1603, the ambassador gave no hint of any lack of dignity in the King's demeanour. Escorted by guards who could scarcely force a passage through the tremendous press of people, the ambassador at length arrived in James's presence. 'I found all the Council about his chair, and an infinity of other lords almost in an attitude of adoration. His Majesty rose and took six steps towards the middle of the room, and then drew back one, after making me a sign of welcome with his hand. He then remained standing up while he listened to me attentively. He was dressed in grey silver satin, quite plain, with a cloak of black tabinet reaching below his knees and lined with crimson, he had his arm in a white sling, the result of a fall from his horse; from his dress he would have been taken for the meanest among his courtiers, a modesty he affects, had it not been for a chain of diamonds around his neck and a great diamond in his hat.'

James's physical appearance was also found attractive. 'The King's countenance is handsome, noble and jovial,' wrote an

Italian observer, 'his colour blond, his hair somewhat the same, his beard square and lengthy, his mouth small, his eyes blue, his nose curved and clear-cut, a man happily formed, neither fat nor thin, of full vitality, neither too large nor too small.' 'His stature was of the middle size,' wrote Arthur Wilson, an historian of the reign, 'rather tall than low, well set and somewhat plump, of a ruddy complexion; his hair, of a light brown in his full perfection, had at last a tincture of white. His beard was scattering on his chin and very thin; and though his clothes were seldom fashioned to the vulgar garb, yet in the whole man he was not uncomely.'[7] Thus it would appear that despite some physical and mental oddities the King was admired in his prime as a man of intelligence, of dignity, and of pleasing appearance. He was not the buffoon in purple or the impossible pedant that the scandal-mongers of the court would have us believe. It was, alas, his character that contained shocking defects, of which one of the worst was vanity.

He passed abruptly from the rude outspokenness of the Scottish lieges to the obsequious flattery of a highly sophisticated court. Cecil addressed him in terms of deep humility and deference, while a courtier like Henry Howard descended to fawning and grovelling adoration. In an audience granted to Sir Thomas Smith, who was about to sail around the North Cape to Russia, the King remarked, 'It seems that Sir Thomas goes from the sun'; and Howard standing by replied at once, 'He must needs go from the sun departing from your resplendent Majesty.' James smiled and allowed Sir Thomas to kiss his hand. Courtiers discovered that no adulation was too gross, no praise too strained or fulsome for the taste of their new monarch. Eventually, it was said, he ignored words spoken to him unless they were prefaced by titles such as most sacred, pleaseful, wise, or learned. A courtier, instructing his friend in the proper manner of addressing the King, gave this advice: 'Do not of yourself say, "This is good or bad"; but "If it were your Majesty's good opinion, I myself should think so and so"; ask no more questions than what may serve to know the Prince's thought.' The King's high opinion of himself, now so sweetly confirmed, was revealed in the legend on a medal struck in his honour, *Caesar Caesarum*. Ceremonies that fostered the pride and self-complacency of the monarch, some initiated by Henry VIII but unused by Elizabeth, now appeared once more.

'They are introducing the ancient splendours of the English court', wrote the Venetian ambassador, 'and almost adoring his Majesty, who day by day adopts the practices suitable to his greatness. On Sunday last he dined in state, as it is called, waited upon by the greatest lords of the realm; it was a splendid and unwonted sight.' These majestic dinners, when the nobility served the King on bended knee, became common, for James loved to preen himself in glory, especially before the wondering eyes of the Scots. [8]

'The very poets with their idle pamphlets', wrote Chamberlain, 'promise themselves great part in his favour', and the flattery of the court was repeated in a flood of eulogistic verse. Henry Petowe described

> A King whose virtues make the Muses labour
> Striving which most and best may sing his praise,
> Begging no pension but the world's kind favour,
> For singing James in their celestial layes.
> James, England's King, defender of the faith,
> Long may he be so, so his England prai'th.

The poets turned naturally to the King's literary achievements. Samuel Rowlands wrote:

> Descend you Muses from Parnassus hill:
> Bring Art in libyrall handes, and now bestow it:
> Let every one present a flowing Quill,
> In honour of our famous kingly Poet:
> And as the chearefull Lark doth mounting sing,
> So elevate the honour of the King.

The red and white roses, continued Rowlands, having come originally from paradise, had now joined together to produce a beautiful flower which, on examination, was revealed to be King James. May he never want a bud!

> Graunt that his dayes may be like Salomon,
> A mirrur unto all the world beside,
> That those which heare his fame farre of to ring,
> Like Sabaes Queene, may all admire our King.

Anthony Nixon sang of

> A King endued with such royall parts,
> Both of his body and his princely mind,
> Of manhood, prowesse, learning, wit, and arts,
> As though Queene Vertue had a place assign'd
> Within the Centre of his learned brest,
> For her and all her sacred gifts to rest. [9]

A greater than these swelled the chorus. Shakespeare prophesied that Elizabeth should leave her blessedness to one

> Who, from the sacred ashes of her honour,
> Shall star-like rise, as great in fame as she was,
> And so stand fix'd: peace, plenty, love, truth, terror,
> That were the servants to this chosen infant,
> Shall then be his, and like a vine grow to him:
> Wherever the bright sun of heaven shall shine,
> His honour and the greatness of his name
> Shall be, and make new nations.

The clergy, however, surpassed both courtiers and poets in their adulation of the King. They cast a halo of holiness about him and discovered his celestial proximity to the Deity. Astounded by his knowledge and grasp of theology, they declared that he spoke through the inspiration of the Holy Spirit and that God had bestowed upon him far more than upon ordinary mortals the power to interpret Scripture. He was constantly compared to David, the sweet singer of Israel, and to Solomon, the wisest of kings. 'God hath given us a Solomon,' cried Bishop Montagu, 'and God above all things gave Solomon wisdom; wisdom brought him peace; peace brought him riches; riches gave him glory.' Indeed the King surpassed Solomon, the Bishop continued, for he had been steadfast in religion throughout a longer span of years than Solomon had reigned, nor had he been drawn into unchastity by an immoderate excess of women. And another Bishop found him uniting the laws of England and Scotland as David had done those of Judah and Israel. [10]

How intoxicating for a man like James! In place of the suspicion and difficulties he had anticipated in England, he was greeted by the joy of the people, a joy sincere and spontaneous that would have warmed the heart of any monarch. To James it came as a wonderful surprise. In his first speech to Parliament he recalled how, as he came down from Scotland, 'the people of all sorts rid and ran, nay rather flew to meet him, their eyes flaming nothing but sparkles of affection, their mouths and tongues uttering nothing but sounds of joy, their hands, feet and all the rest of their members in their gestures discovering a passionate longing and earnestness to meet and embrace their new sovereign'. In this, with his inflated ego, he saw nothing beyond a personal tribute, a splendid recognition of his high qualities, a dutiful devotion to his sacred person. There followed the flattery of courtiers, poets and churchmen which he accepted at its face value. At last he was truly appreciated! And what a contrast to rugged, insolent and rebellious Scotland! He commented on the happy change as he opened the Hampton Court Conference in 1604. He found little to alter, he said, in the state of England, 'which state, as it seemed, so affected his royal heart that it pleased him to enter into a gratulation to Almighty God (at which words he put off his hat) for bringing him into the promised land, where religion was purely professed, where he sat among grave, learned and reverend men, not, as before, elsewhere, a King without state, without honour, without order, where beardless boys would brave him to his face'.

Above all, he had arrived. Honest Roger Aston, sent ahead to England at Elizabeth's death, was asked by the English Council how his master felt concerning his good fortune. 'Even, my lords,' came the spontaneous reply, 'like a poor man wandering about forty years in a wilderness and barren soil and now arrived at the land of promise.' The great prize on which he had set his heart was now his. The strife was o'er, the battle done, the victory of life was won; and there seemed little left for the British Solomon save to sing perpetual hallelujahs.

The complacency of the King had many bad results. As a youth in Scotland, as we know, he had often fancied himself the successor of the prophets and kings of the Old Testament, and now in England these celestial identifications were greatly strengthened. He was close to heaven not only because he had been called to rule three kingdoms. There was proximity also in the peace he brought to England and in the union of England and Scotland. There was proximity in his title of Defender of the Faith. God and the King would act in closest harmony, and opposition to the one would be opposition to the other.

Sometimes the results of such thoughts were ludicrous rather than harmful. A story was told that once when playing cards James lost set after set and cried at length: 'Am I not as good a King as King David? as holy a King as King David? as just a King as King David? and why should I then be crossed?' The anniversary of the Gowrie Plot, the fifth of August, he set aside for England as well as for Scotland as a holy day of feasting and thanksgiving, and a church service written for that day alone was set forth by royal authority. Extolling the King in extravagant terms, it called down vengeance upon his enemies with most unchristian ferocity. One of the collects returned thanks to God for preserving His servant, King James, 'from the wicked designments of those bloodthirsty wretches, the Earl of Gowrie and his brother'; and the Almighty was implored to 'smite the King's enemies upon the cheek bone, break their teeth, frustrate their counsels and bring to naught all their devices'. This service, which disappeared in the Civil Wars, was performed at court with regularity as long as James lived, though the day's celebrations placed more emphasis upon feasting than upon devout return of thanks. It was a function, wrote the Venetian ambassador, that consisted chiefly of unlimited drinking. The King could speak of it with a touch of humour. Having celebrated the feast in 1608 at the house of Lord St. John at Bletsoe, he wrote: 'Here hath been kept the feast of King James's delivery at Saint Johnston [Perth] in Saint John's house.' Because the Gowrie Plot had fallen on a Tuesday, the fifth of August, that day of the week and month invariably caught the King's attention, especially after the Gunpowder Plot which was planned for Tuesday, November 5th. Tuesday sermons became a normal part of the court calendar, and James attempted, though in vain, to force them upon the universities.

These devotions the scandalmongers regarded with cynicism. 'By the King's frequenting sermons he appeared religious,' sneered Anthony Weldon, 'yet his Tuesday sermons, if you will believe his own countrymen, were dedicated for a strange piece of devotion.' Pamphleteers writing to please the Puritans after the Civil Wars spoke of the King's devotions on the fifth of August as sheer blasphemy. But it was the vanity of the man that was astounding.

His common sense did not entirely desert him. When he first came to England he declared that neither he nor any other king possessed the power to heal the scrofula, or King's Evil, by touching the afflicted parts. The age of miracles, he said, was past. He feared that the ritual, of which the royal act of healing was a part, savoured of Roman superstition, and he shrank from placing his hands upon the ulcerous sores of the persons brought before him. Yet he continued the practice, in part to humour the people, more largely because he would not discontinue a custom which emphasized the divine nature of royalty. He was willing for the people to believe the ceremony

> A most miraculous work in this good King.
> ... How he solicits heaven,
> Himself best knows: but strangely-visited people,
> All swoln and ulcerous, pitiful to the eye,
> The mere despair of surgery, he cures;
> Hanging a golden stamp about their necks,
> Put on with holy prayers.

There were, however, many proofs of his scepticism. He did not make the sign of the cross upon the afflicted parts, as the rubric of the Elizabethan service prescribed, nor did he follow that service by touching the sores, but gently passed his hands over them without physical contact. The inscription on the angel, or gold coin, hung about the neck of each sufferer, was altered to a form expressing disbelief that a miracle had taken place. 'He was a King in understanding,' wrote Arthur Wilson, 'and was content to have his subjects ignorant in many things, as in curing the King's Evil, which he knew a device to aggrandize the virtue of kings when miracles were in fashion. But he let the world believe it, though he smiled at it in his own reason, finding the strength of the imagination a more powerful agent in the cure than the plasters his chirurgeons prescribed for the sore.' On one occasion he burlesqued the ceremony. A foreign ambassador whose son was afflicted with scrofula begged the King to effect a cure, 'whereat his Majesty laughed heartily and as the young fellow came near him he stroked him with his hand, first on one side and then on the other, marry without Pistle or Gospel'.

There is no doubt none the less that James permitted the glorious sunshine of his entry to blind his judgment in many ways. He was inclined to think that England was exactly as it should be, with little need of reform. Not unnaturally he exaggerated the power at his disposal, conjuring into the Tudor period an absolutism more complete than the reality. Parliaments, judges, Puritans, nobles, all must give way before him. 'For he was born a King and never underwent crosses and afflictions' — so wrote an Englishman who must have known little Scottish history — 'inasmuch as he imagined heaven and earth must give way to his will.' Two of his first appointments might have taught him caution. He named Lord Kinloss as Master of the Rolls, but such an outcry arose from the lawyers that no other Scot was given high judicial office; and his appointment of his old tutor, Peter Young, as Dean of Lichfield had to be withdrawn because the place was not in the royal gift. There was, moreover, a notable decline in his drive and energy. 'As the King is by nature of a mild disposition and has never really been happy in Scotland,' wrote the Venetian ambassador, 'he wishes now to enjoy the Papacy, as we say, and so desires to have no bother with other people's affairs and little with his own. He would like to dedicate himself to his books and to the chase and to encourage the opinion that he was the real arbiter of peace.' To the problems of his new kingdom he gave no serious study. No doubt in any case he would have lacked the patience and humility to do so, but in his present exalted state of mind application became superfluous. Hence he arrived at his decisions far too quickly and in too offhand a manner. They were based upon preconceived ideas and principles forged in the mêlée of Scottish politics and now applied uncritically to England. They were founded upon emotion and self-interest. His approach to government was personal, and much of his policy was a mere projection of plans for his own advantage. He did not love England though he professed to do so. He loved himself, and England must minister to that self-love.[11]

CHAPTER XI

A SYLVAN PRINCE

WHILE the King was still in Scotland he had written to Cecil that as a first token of his gratitude he would retain all of Elizabeth's councillors. They were fourteen in number, of whom the most important were Archbishop Whitgift; Egerton, the cautious Lord Keeper, who now became Chancellor and Baron Ellesmere; Sackville, Lord Treasurer, made Earl of Dorset; Nottingham, the elderly Lord Admiral; the courtier Earls of Shrewsbury and Worcester; and Cecil, the central figure of the government. These were men of ability and experience whom the King was wise in retaining, but his additions to the Council, twelve in number, were more doubtful. He admitted Henry Howard, now Earl of Northampton, and Thomas Howard, whom he made Lord Chamberlain and Earl of Suffolk. There were other newcomers: Northumberland, to whom the King gave credit for the good behaviour of the English Catholics; Cumberland, courtier and buccaneer; Mountjoy, Essex's friend, who returned from Ireland to become Earl of Devonshire; Zouch and Burghley, presidents respectively of the Council in Wales and in the North. Five Scots were added to the English Council: Lennox, Mar, Sir George Home, soon to be Earl of Dunbar, Elphinstone, and Edward Bruce, who became Lord Kinloss and whom the King abetted in his prompt quest for a rich English wife. By these appointments James paid some of his debts, honoured men who had made their mark in Elizabeth's reign, and added to the Council representatives of royal authority in the outlying portions of his dominions.

He declared on a number of occasions that he would not appoint Scots to high office in England and, though he was not entirely true to his word, it cannot be said that the Scots played a great part in English affairs. Lennox was of some consequence in foreign affairs but for the most part was concerned with the ceremonial of the court; Mar and Elphinstone resided in Scotland; Kinloss did not long survive his good fortune. More important was Dunbar. He is described as omniprevalent with James, a prime favourite, his Majesty's very breath and spirit. He was the King's chief adviser for Scottish affairs, but was also for a time Chancellor of the Exchequer and Master of the Wardrobe in England, and his advice was taken on the appointment of an Archbishop of Canterbury.

Yet if few of the Scots who came to England received high office, they did very well none the less. Money, pensions and grants they easily obtained. They were given the coveted places in the Bedchamber and in the Privy Chamber which brought them into daily contact with the King, and they obtained similar posts in the households of the Queen and Prince. The marked deference paid by the greatest men in England to Sir John Murray, Groom of the Bedchamber, indicates what it meant to be a Scottish favourite of the King. Some Scots, such as Hay, Ramsey and Thomas Erskine profited enormously, while a host of lesser Scotsmen made a good thing of their master's new eminence. Their spirit of plunder, which was not unshared by the King, and their influence and success aroused the bitter jealousy of English courtiers. Sir John Stanhope, the Vice-Chamberlain, for example, a privy councillor and a member of the Commons, seldom came to court after James told him to his face that 'he could not be quiet' till he had conferred his office upon a certain Scot. 'Many such like wrestlings there are with the old servants, tho' most of them carry a certain show of contentment and conformity to the King's pleasure.'

Within the Council, now almost doubled in size, an inner circle of four rapidly took shape: Cecil, Northampton, Suffolk and Worcester. Sir George Home wrote to Cecil early in 1604: 'My Lord, since you are come to a good point with his Majesty, let a secret course be kept with him in his weightiest affairs by you four; and let his general errands be done by his whole Council; so shall you be most able both to serve him and to secure your own estates.'

Cecil, soon to be Earl of Salisbury, was of course pre-eminent. As Principal Secretary, Master of the Wards and later Lord Treasurer, he remained until his death the pivot about which the entire machinery of government revolved. 'More than a president, he was alpha and omega in Council. He solely managed all foreign affairs, especially Ireland; he directed Parliament; he managed all the revenues and great affairs of King, Queen and Duke of

York.' No living king, James told him, 'shall more confidently and constantly rely upon the advice of a councillor and trusty servant than I shall ever do upon yours. Before God I count you the best servant that ever I had, albeit you be but a beagle'. Seldom has one man more completely governed England.

Historians have underrated Salisbury, dismissing him as an industrious mediocrity whose single object was to maintain the *status quo*. It is true he was not a man to change with changing times. But none the less in James's reign he flowered into greatness. His caution, prudence and sagacity maintained affairs on an even keel at a time when chaos threatened; nor did he, amid endless routine, lose sight of larger ends. He was a man of wit and liveliness, a spirited writer and speaker, a cultured gentleman, who could be genial, warm and generous in friendship. Courteous and patient under great provocation, his self-control was marvellous, and it was only towards the end of his life, when his health was failing and his responsibilities were becoming intolerable, that his equanimity deserted him. 'Of bounty in all expenses, magnanimous courage, infinite in wit and policy, admirable to all men in eloquence upon the sudden, deep secret and prudent in Council', he was a servant far nobler and more able than James deserved. The failures of the reign should not be attributed to him, for he did not have freedom of action, and was never more than the first servant of a royal master who soon treated him with callous indifference and in the end with shameless ingratitude. Salisbury was keenly aware that his pre-eminent position depended upon the continued favour of the King, and he therefore played upon James's vanity, encouraged him to trust to his 'little beagle' for money, frowned upon possible rivals, and, when necessary, bent to the royal will against his better judgment. In 1612 Sir Walter Cope reminded the King that Salisbury had learned two lessons under him, as well to obey as to command; and to conclude with Seneca, '*Sapiens non se mutat sed aptat.*'

Salisbury was greatly overworked. Few pictures offer a more vivid contrast than that of the little hunchbacked Secretary bending over his papers at midnight and that of the King lolling at ease or galloping over hill and dale after a rabbit. Well founded was Shrewsbury's friendly warning that Salisbury would blear out his eyes and quite overthrow his body. As month after month of confusion and uncertainty followed the change in dynasty, it is

little wonder that Salisbury felt the strain. Writing to his friend
Sir John Harington, he contrasted his present situation with his
former place under Elizabeth. 'I wish I waited now in her
Presence Chamber,' he wrote, 'with ease at my food and rest in
my bed. I am pushed from the shore of comfort and know not
where the winds and waves of a court will bear me. I know it
bringeth little comfort on earth; and he is, I reckon, no wise man
that looketh this way to heaven. In trouble, hurrying, feigning,
suing and such-like matters, I now rest, your true friend, R.
Cecil.'[1]

The importance of Henry Howard, Earl of Northampton, in the
secret correspondence before 1603 assured him royal favour; but
it is strange that James did not see through his pompous learning
and emetic flattery, as Elizabeth had done, and judge the man for
what he was, a worthless, self-seeking and crafty courtier. His
pride of family amounted to a vice. His ambition and jealousy
caused him to hate colleagues as well as rivals. His venom against
Cobham and Ralegh is understandable; but he hated Salisbury
also, and his letters after Salisbury's death are filled with jibes and
sneers at his late colleague. Though he attended the Church of
England, his Catholicism was only half-concealed and he stood
constantly for leniency to Catholics, severity to Puritans, alliance
with Spain, and an end of Parliaments. Of the other two men in
the inner circle of the Council, Thomas Howard, Earl of Suffolk,
was dignified, moderate and easy-going, doubtless an excellent
Lord Chamberlain; but, though a brave sailor and a loyal subject,
he possessed small strength of character. Worcester, the perfect
courtier, had been a favourite of Elizabeth who had declared that
he achieved the impossible, for he combined utter loyalty with
devout Catholicism. He quickly won James's favour and, since
the King often took him into the country, he was not infrequently
the one councillor in attendance. With the exception of Salisbury, these men were Catholic in sympathy.

Councillors soon discovered that the transaction of business was
rendered difficult by the peculiar habits of the King, and especially
by his fondness for country life. It was quite natural that during
his first months in England he should visit his country houses and
see something of his new kingdom. But the nervous and perpetual
wanderings of this peripatetic Prince never ceased; year in and
year out, for weeks and months on end, he loitered in the country

or journeyed from one hunting-seat to the next though business demanded his presence in London. We cannot follow these wanderings, but we may sample them. Late in November 1604, he was at Royston, a favourite residence throughout his reign. What for the pleasure I take of my recreation here,' he wrote, 'and what for the fear I stand in to offend the Puritans [by celebrating Christmas], I mind not to return to London till after that profane Christ's tide.' Of this he thought better and came to Whitehall for Christmas, which became his invariable custom. But by the middle of January 1605, the disorderly revels at Whitehall having ended, he was again at Royston, then at Huntingdon and Hinchinbrook. He came to London early in February but soon returned to Royston, travelled thence to Ware, Newmarket and Thetford, then back to Newmarket and Royston, then to London about the middle of March. For some four months he remained in the vicinity of the capital, moving between Greenwich, Richmond, Windsor and Oatlands, hunting as he went. A progress in July and August took him towards Oxford. Thence he came to Windsor and to Hampton Court for part of September. In October he was again at Royston, Huntingdon, Hinchinbrook and Ware, and though he came to London to open Parliament in November, he returned to Royston for most of the remainder of the year.

Thus he was constantly on the move, coming to London only for a few days at a time. He spoke of one visit as 'a flash of lightning, both in going, stay there and returning'. The Duke of Frias, Constable of Castile, in England in August 1604, to sign a peace which James had very much at heart, was told that the King's sojourn in the capital would be brief. And brief it was. Having sworn to observe the treaty, the King arranged at once for his departure. When that time arrived the Constable was ill, but James, without waiting for his recovery, came to his lodgings, made adieux, and left the city, so eager was he to return to his paradise of pleasure.[2]

Of many reasons for the King's love of country life, the chief was his passion for the chase. He had always loved it dearly, but had been hampered in Scotland by poverty and other factors. In England it became his great joy, a major preoccupation of his life, on which he lavished time, energy and treasure, to the astonishment of observers. 'He seems to have forgotten that he is a King,' wrote the Venetian ambassador, 'except in his kingly pursuit of stags, to which he is quite foolishly devoted.' Interruption of his sports filled him with fury. An ambassador daring to intrude in 1609, the King asked Salisbury to deal with 'this pantaloon' and to prevent further disturbance of the royal hunting. Countless are the stories of James's bursts of temper when mischance crossed his sports. At one time he is out of humour with the sky for not raining, thereby weakening the scent for his dogs. Again he is angry because the rain comes down in torrents. Calling for a chair, he plants himself wrathfully at the door of his hunting-lodge to see whether God will keep His promise never to drown the world again, 'fearfully swearing that if the rain so continued three days it would be a greater flood than ever Noah's was. And he did a thousand such like as this in his impatient humour when he was crossed: he was so passionate that a fly chancing into his eye, he asked of it whether there was not room enough in his three kingdoms but that of malice it must fly into his eye'. Hunting needed no defence. The Constable of Castile hoped to please him by coupling hunting with a love of letters, but the King answered tartly that if all kings and all men of letters were mustered together, only one huntsman would be found in the first group and none in the second.

James's hunting in his prime was a dangerous and violent sport. 'Running hounds', as he called them, were set upon the scent of a stag, and the hunters followed at a wild gallop across the countryside. Upon reaching the game, already brought down and killed by the dogs, the King dismounted, cut the stag's throat, and opened its belly. He thrust his hands (and sometimes his feet) into the stag's entrails, sating the dogs with its blood and daubing the faces of his courtiers, a token of their sportsmanship and of their sovereign's high esteem. The 'running hound' was a hunting dog known as a limer, something between a harrier and a greyhound, very swift and with the keenest sense of smell. These hounds rarely lost the scent though the stag hid deep in the woods or mingled with other deer. The King followed them at a fast pace, his daring on horseback contrasting with his normal timidity, although his jealousy of the great French hunter, De Vitry, who followed the hounds at their very heels, would indicate that James did not do so. The speed of stag and hounds could be lessened artificially, but the King preferred to hunt without a handicap.

Hunting with hounds, he wrote, 'is the most honourable and noblest sort thereof; and greyhound hunting [of hares] is not so martial a game'. He was contemptuous of the tamer sport of shooting with bow and arrow from a bower in a tree as the deer were driven past, though occasionally he hunted in this fashion when ladies were in the party.

A secretary of the Duke of Saxe-Weimar, whom the King entertained at Theobalds in 1613, has left a description of a hunt. The King, he says, was dressed in green satin and a grey hat. He wore black boots with the ribbon of the Garter above the left boot and he and his guests rode to the hunting-grounds in a carriage. 'The hunt generally takes place in this way: the game-keepers are ready with twenty or thirty dogs at the place where the game is to be found. If the King fancies a particular stag among the herd he signifies his pleasure to the keepers who mark the spot where the animal stood. Thither they lead the dogs which are trained to follow one animal only. Away they run straight upon its trail. Should there be fifty or sixty deer together, the dogs do not touch them, but follow only the one and never stop until they have overtaken and brought it down. Meanwhile the King hurries incessantly after the dogs until they have caught the game. There is therefore no particular enjoyment in this sport.' James's hunting bored his foreign guests and disgusted some of his own subjects. There was much that was repulsive about it — his vindictive fury in pursuing and slaughtering the game, his dabbling in its blood, his rage when it escaped, his low company and bad manners at the chase.

Volatile in temper, the King was elated or depressed by the good or bad fortune of the day's sport. Having killed a great stag, he 'was very well and very merry', swearing that a visit from Salisbury had brought him luck and sending venison to his councillors who, he vowed, were honest men. At another time, having toiled all day after a stag only to lose it, and having no better luck when he tried another, his dogs being weary, he became sad and disconsolate. A number of letters from London required answers but he left them till morning; he supped in his with-drawing-chamber, was not amused by the efforts of his companions to make him merry, and soon retired for the night. Next day he relaxed but did some business in the afternoon. The morning after he was at his hunting once again. It was his claim that hunt-

ing preserved his health and thus the health of the kingdom; but
in truth he hunted in so violent a fashion that he overtaxed his
strength and was inclined to lie abed the next morning. Listless
and drowsy when he arose, he amused himself with cards or some
other indolent pastime. 'He is now fallen into a great humour of
catching larks,' wrote Chamberlain in 1605, 'and takes as much
delight in it or more than in hunting.'

'As for hawking,' James wrote, 'I condemn it not but I must
praise it more sparingly.' It did not, like hunting, harden a man
or make him a skilful rider, and was subject to so many mischances
that it caused frustration and anger. The King hawked a good
deal none the less and kept cormorants to dive for fish. He was
fond of other sports: cockfighting and bull- and bear-baiting.
Lady Anne Clifford noted in her diary that 'cocking' at court
brought her husband 'into great grace and favour with the King',
though the sport was expensive and kept her husband away from
home, where she sat like an owl in the desert. The bear-garden
at Southwark, known as Paris Garden, which housed not only
bears, bulls and savage mastiffs, but also lynxes and tigers, was
owned by James who attended its shows. He tried to bait lions at
the Tower where he constructed a lion-baiting pit, but he discovered that the king of beasts was not a true fighter. An attempt
to bait a bear with lion proved a ludicrous fiasco, for the lion,
upon seeing his adversary, put his tail between his legs and withdrew. The King had planned that the lion inflict punishment
upon the bear, which had killed a child; and, the executioner
having failed in his duty, it was ordered that the bear be baited
to death. There were other instances in which James punished
animals as though they were humans. It is more pleasant to note
that he patronized horse-racing, making it a royal sport at the
beginning of its modern development; he built several race-tracks,
the most important at Newmarket, and introduced some Arab
blood into England.

His love of sports merged with his keen interest in animals. In
addition to the beasts at the Tower and at Paris Garden, his
zoological oddments included crocodiles, red deer and antelope
from India, and a flying squirrel from Virginia. The Prince of
Orange sent him a tiger; the Duke of Savoy a tiger, a lioness and
a lynx, though they died on the way. In 1623 Philip of Spain
gave him five camels and an elephant. Londoners could see the

camels grazing in St. James's Park until stables were constructed
for them at Theobalds, but for some reason the elephant was kept
from public view. Its captivity was enlivened by a gallon of wine
daily from September to April, a period during which its keepers
declared it could drink no water.[3]

Country life had allurements in addition to hunting. London
James heartily disliked, much preferring the retired privacy and
careless ease of the country. He wished to escape from business,
from perplexing diversity of counsel, from the merciless importunity of suitors. An official wrote in 1610 that the King was 'so
distracted with variety of opinions from a number about him,
especially Scots, that though he would, he cannot resolve that
which he desires; which is the reason that as often as he can he
absents himself from the town, yet is quickly fetched again on
every occasion which much troubles him'. The chaos of Whitehall
was increased as James did away with much of Elizabeth's formal
etiquette and decorum. Having done so, he fled. In the privacy
of a distant hunting-lodge, he could be at ease with a few jovial
companions, with Hay or Ramsey, or with Philip Herbert, 'the
wanton Earl of Montgomery', whose comely person, skill in
hunting, and fondness for dogs and horses, says Clarendon, made
him 'the first who drew the King's eyes towards him with affection'. His accomplishments revived the lines:

> The Herberts every cockpit day
> Do carry away
> The gold and glory of the day.

Restraints of speech, of ceremony, of morals could be thrown
aside; and the King could be jovial, intimate, careless, idle and
debauched. Having sent Montgomery to Salisbury on business
in 1605, James wrote: 'Haste him back I pray you for our match
again Sunday at night, for he is secretary of our corporation that
is of fools, horses and dogs.' Should Montgomery's wife resent
his speedy return, 'tell her I shall make her satisfaction with a
tribute of kisses, but this must be kept counsel both from the
bearer and my wife'. 'We fear', he wrote again, 'ye shall think us
all turned Puritans for such a feasting night as was made upon
Friday last. I assure you it chanced well that the Act of Parliament
against drunkenness is not yet passed.'

In thus indulging his love of country life, he wasted a vast amount of time and spent a prodigious amount of money. His principal country palaces at his accession were Windsor and Hampton Court, but he developed many others and acquired new ones. We have figures of the sums spent on his country houses up to Michaelmas 1611: £13,567 at Greenwich, for which Anne was doubtless responsible; £4966 at Eltham; £9246 at Richmond; £6434 at Hampton Court; £3406 at Nonsuch; £8272 at Theobalds; £2618 at Enfield; £3802 at Royston; £1342 at Newmarket; £1002 at Thetford, with lesser sums at Hinchinbrook, Ware and Woking. Expenses mounted through duplication of stables, kennels, deer parks, offices and living-quarters. An excessive number of houses were kept in a state of preparedness for the King's use, for he flew into a rage if all things were not prepared for his arrival. To the number of his country residences he added constantly, at least in his mind's eye, but as his finances grew more difficult he abandoned many of his plans and fixed his affections upon three: Royston, bought in 1604; Theobalds, acquired from Salisbury in 1607 in exchange for Hatfield; and Newmarket. These he visited constantly, maintained a private road to them from London, and journeyed from one to the other with a regularity that became routine. They grew more sumptuous as government accommodated itself to the King's habits. In 1613 the Duke of Saxe-Weimar was entertained at Theobalds with a splendour that showed how the pomp and ceremony of Whitehall had made its way into the country.

The King's presence imposed a heavy burden upon the farmers of the locality. For food he depended upon his right of purveyance, allowing its abuse by minor officers, and his hunting-parties trampled the grain in the fields. While hunting at Royston in 1604 he suddenly missed one of his hounds named Jowler, at which he was much put out. Next day Jowler reappeared in the pack with a letter round his neck. 'Good Mr. Jowler,' it read, 'we pray you speak to the King (for he hears you every day, and so doth he not us) that it will please his Majesty to go back to London, for else the country will be undone; all our provision is spent already and we are not able to entertain him longer.' But James treated the matter as a jest and remained at Royston a fortnight longer. Late in the reign a long prayer in verse addressed to the King contained the lines:

Then let him hear, good God, the sounds
And cries of men as well as hounds.[4]

This sylvan existence caused many difficulties in government. It is true that James found an occasional defender. The clergyman John Hacket, biographer of Bishop Williams, declared that the court at Royston and Newmarket was large and well attended both for business and recreation and that 'the principal secretaries there protested they were held to it closer and sat up later in those retirements to make dispatches than at London. The King was not out with the hounds above three days a week and hunting was soon over. Much of the time his Majesty spent in State contrivances and at his book. Surely, then, whatsoever any capperwitted man may observe, neither was the King's chastity stained, nor his wisdom lull'd asleep, nor his care of government slackened by lodging in those courts remote from London, where he was freer from disturbances. He had the dexterity to purchase less labour with much ease, and to shift the toil of a king sometimes into the pleasure of a scholar's studies'. But other writers tell a different story.

Government was conducted largely by correspondence. Packets of letters from the councillors in London came down into the country by daily post. Having read them, often at odd moments, or having been told of their contents, James instructed his secretaries how to reply; and Lake, who was in constant attendance, became very skilful in setting down the thoughts, instructions and often the exact words of the King. But almost anyone who happened to be present — Aston, Fenton, Dunbar, Stanhope, Worcester — might be pressed into service to answer the dispatches from London. Salisbury at times sent down officials to talk with the King and to report his wishes.

Loud were the complaints of officials who had to hunt with the King by day and write dispatches late at night, or who had to catch him as he went to his horse in the morning or to chapel on Sundays and Tuesdays, or read letters to him at supper or in his bedchamber when he was weary from a long day's sport. 'This tumultuary and uncertain attendance upon the King's sports', said an official, 'affords me little time to write.' 'We are all become wild men wandering in a forest from the morning till the evening', wailed Dunbar; and Worcester wrote that 'since my

departure from London I think I have not had two hours of
twenty-four of rest but Sundays, for in the morning we are on
horse-back by eight and so continue in full career from the death
of one hare to another until four at night; then for the most part
we are five miles from home; by that time I find at my lodging
sometimes one, most commonly two packets of letters, all which
must be answered before I sleep, for here is none of the Council
but myself, no, not a clerk of the Council nor Privy Signet'. [5] The
greatest burden fell upon Salisbury, who wrote innumerable letters
to the King. They are marvels of judgment and lucidity. Business
is spiced with quips and quiddity, for James demanded amusement as well as information. Affairs of State are mingled with
flattery. That, too, was a necessity. Salisbury begs the King to
send him copies of his writings, as though the poor Secretary had
not reading matter a plenty; or he writes that a kind word from
James has cured a recent illness. His letters breathe always that
devotion to duty and that complete loyalty which formed the
bed-rock of his character.

The King's letters to Salisbury, the famous 'little beagle letters',
are of great interest. They illustrate James's shrewdness and
ability, his capacity to grasp a situation swiftly and to reach a
prompt decision, traits without which government by correspondence would have broken down at once. His sublime self-confidence and preoccupation with his own advantage, together with his
set principles of government, tended to make decision easy; yet
he reached conclusions without knowledge of detail, signed proclamations without reading them, and was caught in those mis-
understandings that correspondence necessarily involves.

The predominant tone of his letters is one of care-free and happy
ease. He addresses Salisbury with playful intimacy and bantering
good humour, with superficial affection though with no true
sympathy. Salisbury is the little beagle 'that lies at home by the
fire when all the good hounds are daily running on the fields'. He
is 'the King's best beagle if he hunt well in the hard ways'. James
wishes 'that my little beagle had been stolen here in the likeness
of a mouse, as he is not much bigger, to have been partaker of the
sport which I had this day at hawking', or he writes that he is
sending a kennel of little beagles on a diplomatic mission to
France and would know 'if ye mind to be of that number, for that
King would be a fine huntsman for you except that ye could never

trust his hallow'. Salisbury did not relish his nickname. 'I see nothing that I can do', he complains to Lake, 'can procure me so much favour as to be sure one whole day what title I shall have another. For from Essendon to Cranborne, from Cranborne to Salisbury, from Salisbury to Beagle, from Beagle to Thom Derry, from Thom Derry to Parrot, which I hate most, I have been walked as I think by that I come to Theobalds I shall be called Tare or Sophie.'

There was a bullying quality about James's playfulness. The beagle, he says, 'hath cause to complain of my being a peripatetic, for I will oft times walk so fast round about and above with him that he will be like to fall down dead upon the floor'. About to visit Greenwich in 1605, the King writes a challenge to a trinity of knaves, Salisbury, Suffolk and Northampton. 'If I find not at my coming to Greenwich that the big Chamberlain [Suffolk] have ordered well all my lodging, that the little saucy Constable [Salisbury] have made the house sweet and built a cockpit, and that the fast-walking keeper of the park [Northampton] have the park in good order and the does all with fawn, although he has never been a good breeder himself, then shall I make the fat Chamberlain to puff, the little cankered beagle to whine, and the tall black and cat-faced keeper to glower. If my wife shall not produce a fair young lion at this time [Anne was pregnant] the Constable shall bear the blame; if I have not good fortune at the beginning of my hunting then the keeper shall have the shame and never be thought a good huntsman after; and if I get not good rest all night the big Chamberlain's fat back shall bear the burthen of all.' The letter ends with conceits about the miracle of Balaam's ass, about the Scots proverb that many a man courts the child for love of the nurse (which is grossened to imply an attempt upon the nurse's chastity), and about the bearer of the letter 'who swears he will venture all the hairs of his beard in my quarrel'. Thus the King wrote to his gravest councillors.

He pretends to be suspicious of their relations with Queen Anne during his absence. 'I know Suffolk is married; but for your part, master 10 [Salisbury],[6] who is wanton and wifeless, I cannot but be jealous of your greatness with my wife; but most of all am I suspicious of 3 [Northampton], who is so lately fallen into acquaintance with my wife; for besides that the very number of three is well liked of by women, his face is so amiable as it is able to

entice, and his fortune hath ever been to be great with she-saints;
but his part is foul in this, that never having taken a wife to himself in his youth, he cannot now be content with his grey hairs to
forbear another man's wife. But for expiation of this sin, I hope
that ye have all three with the rest of your society taken this day a
eucharistic cup of thankfulness for the occasion [anniversary of the
Gowrie Plot] which fell out at a time when ye durst not avow me.'

References to hunting, theology, witches, animals, pregnancy,
portents and wonders are jumbled ludicrously with affairs of State.
'Busy with hunting of witches, prophets, Puritans, dead cats and
hares', he pretends to be over-worked, declaring he has written a
letter for every hare he has killed. He apes the formal style of a
secretary, and asks whether he is not prettily exercised in that
office. His councillors, he asserts, are idle. 'Ye sit at your ease and
direct all; the King's own resolutions depend upon your posting
dispatches, and when ye list, ye can (sitting on your bed-sides)
with one call or whistling in your fist make him to post night and
day till he come to your presence.' He commands Montgomery to
escort certain witches to London, but countermands the order
because Montgomery 'rides post and witches never ride post but
to the Devil; and he hath conjured all the devils here with his
Welsh tongue, for the Devil himself, I trow, dare not speak
Welsh'. A lioness whelps in the Tower and the King is all interest.
Irritated at a warning that the cubs may die, he sends a description of a nipple to be attached to the mouth of a bottle in order to
feed them. 'I pray God your lordship can understand my description of a new engine to give a beast suck,' Montgomery wrote to
Salisbury, 'but you must be content to take it as it was delivered
unto me.'

James's humour was a tumbling wit that turned things upside
down and heaped together incongruous thoughts and images in a
hurly-burly jumble, as when he prayed the Pope to permit him
the hawking of the stream in purgatory. His mind passed easily
from topic to topic, and he applied the vocabulary of one set of
ideas to things entirely different, throwing discordant images into
grotesque juxtaposition. His wit was the rollicking foolery of the
court jester, enriched by his extensive knowledge. Much of it
consisted of puns, conceits and plays on words. Much of it was
mere bawdry, and so easily did the words of the Scriptures come to
his lips that his wit acquired a blasphemous tone which is offensive

to modern ears. He liked to mimic the grave and the sententious, as in his humorous interpretation of an eclipse, and he loved a tone of intimate banter and of calculated impudence. A part of his humour was the homely bluntness of the Scot who spoke the truth with amusing directness. For piquant phrases he never lacked. His was a true wit, he loved a jest for its own sake, and he told it well. 'He was very witty,' wrote Weldon, 'and had as many ready jests as any man living, at which he would not smile himself but deliver them in a grave and serious manner.' His humour was perfectly natural, and its saltiness lay in its revelation of the strange and unpredictable gymnastics of the royal mind.

There were moments when the King was troubled in conscience. 'My little beagle,' he wrote, 'although I be now in the midst of my paradise of pleasure, yet will I not be forgetful of you and your fellows that are frying in the pains of purgatory for my service.' But perhaps God had willed it so. 'Your zeal and diligence are so great as I will cheer myself in your faithfulness and assure myself that God hath ordained to make me happy in sending me so good servants, and the beagle in special.' He was full of praise for councillors who watched while he slept and who snipped and trimmed the house against his return. For all his great turns, he had never been so free from care. He asked Salisbury to thank councillors, to tell them there was no king in the world so proud of his Council as he was, and to assure them that he would not be absent a longer time (for the necessary maintenance of his health) than other kings consumed upon their physical diet and in going to their whores.

His praise, however, did not prevent him from turning upon councillors when things went awry, and his tantrums at any cross vented themselves upon Salisbury as well as upon lesser folk. He did not like Salisbury's draft of a document, or he thought him too tender with the Puritans or too soft with Parliament. An important conference took place between Lords and Commons but Salisbury did not send him a full account. He fell from his horse yet Salisbury neglected to inquire about his health. His praise was a fair-weather praise that ceased abruptly when the smallest cloud appeared. He could not, of course, free himself entirely from annoyance. Some amusing letters to Salisbury concern Lady Dorset who, after her husband's death, importuned the King with implacable fury, following him into the country and knocking on the very door of his bedchamber to which he had fled for sanctuary.[7]

The problems of government that arose from the King's fondness for the country life were merely exchanged for others when he returned to the capital. The court at Whitehall was a large community of some fifteen hundred persons, and was at once the centre of government and of fashion, the symbol of royalty and the place to which all men looked who hoped for a career in the service of the State. To guide and to control the court was no mean task. The ruler must maintain its splendour and high spirits to attract men to it, to keep the nobles amused lest they find more dangerous employment, and to impress the envoys of foreign lands. If he hoped for a successful reign he must win the devotion of his courtiers, since from them he selected not only his household officials but his great ministers of State. He must still the quarrels of haughty nobles and of jealous bureaucrats and must restrain his many servants within the bounds of decency and decorum. And all this must be done at a reasonable charge. The task required both strength and patience, which the King sadly lacked, nor could it be accomplished without a resident sovereign. Under James's loose hand, the court quickly increased in lavishness and cost while it degenerated in order and sobriety.

It became more and more elaborate. An army of attendants waited upon the King from the moment he arose in the morning until he retired at night. The number of Gentlemen of the Bedchamber, of Gentlemen, Ushers and Grooms of the Privy Chamber and of the Presence Chamber, of carvers, cup-bearers and sewers, of clerks of the closet and esquires of the body, of harbingers, yeomen, pages and messengers increased beyond all bounds. The gentlemen of the Privy Chamber rose from eighteen to forty-eight, each with a fee of £50 a year, and soon there were two hundred gentlemen extraordinary. As early as 1604 a commission was appointed to curtail the expenses of the household. Never a man was allowed to eat at court, it reported, but he cost the King £60 a year, and if he was given a private table for himself and for his personal servants he might cost £300; while the charge for every laundress and seamstress was £86. 'The confusion is great, the redress hard, and the envy insupportable without the King's special countenance and Salisbury's assistance.' Economy was difficult not only because of the carelessness of the King but because the tone of society was lavish and extravagant. 'The drain on private purses is enormous', wrote the Venetian ambassador. Even the lesser nobles and councillors, he added, appear in public with forty or fifty horsemen and sometimes with two or three hundred. 'No one can say that this is the realm of avarice.'

James's tastes were less extravagant than those of many of his courtiers, but his wish to appear wealthy and magnificent expressed itself in a fondness for wearing jewels, on which he spent large sums of money. At a banquet to honour the French ambassador in 1603 'his Majesty made a vast display of plate and on his person a wealth of jewels'. Yet his grandeur was accompanied by a personal uncleanliness that offended his new subjects, themselves not dainty in matters of soap and water. 'We all saw a great change between the fashion of the court as it is now and of that in the Queen's time,' wrote Lady Anne Clifford, 'for we were all lousy by sitting in the chamber of Sir Thomas Erskine.' And there were comments upon the filth of James's personal habits that pass far beyond the possibilities of bowdlerized exposition.[8]

Festivities were numerous, extravagant and disorderly. Queen Anne delighted in masques; and these entertainments, with their costly floats, costumes and scenery, their songs and dances, became the fashion. The court, wrote Arthur Wilson, was 'a continued masquerado, where the Queen and her ladies, like so many sea-nymphs, or Nereids, appeared often in various dresses to the ravishment of the beholders, the King himself being not a little delighted with such fluent elegancies as made the night more glorious than the day'. It is true that James enjoyed the atmosphere of revelry; he was more interested in the ladies than is often supposed and found their immodesty attractive. But the masques often bored him. He was not musical, and his taste in drama ran to clever satire and to low comedy. There is little indication that he was interested in serious drama or that he detected the genius of Shakespeare. Feasts and banquets, on the other hand, he enjoyed thoroughly, not for the food but for the elevation of spirit that came with wine and good company. Warming to the occasion, he loved to pledge his guests in countless bumpers, to address the assembly, to embrace the gentlemen and to kiss the ladies.

His first Christmas in England was celebrated at Hampton Court where there were feasts in honour of the ambassadors from France, Spain and Poland, many plays and 'dances with swords', and a number of masques in one of which the Queen and eleven of her ladies appeared as goddesses bringing gifts to the King. The costumes in each masque, thought Roger Wilbraham, must have cost from two to three thousand pounds, and the jewels twenty thousand, while those worn by the Queen he judged to be worth a hundred thousand. After Christmas there was running at the ring, a sport in which the King took part, though he was annoyed to find that other riders were more skilful than he was, 'and then they all feasted together privately'. Sir Dudley Carleton, the courtier and future diplomat, described the revels at Whitehall a year later when the court donned its finest bravery to celebrate the marriage of the King's favourite, the Earl of Montgomery, to Lady Susan Vere. Prince Henry and the Duke of Holstein, Queen Anne's brother, led the bride to church; the King gave her, swearing that if he were unmarried he would keep her for himself. 'No ceremony was omitted of bride-cakes, points, garters and gloves; and at night there was sewing into the sheet, casting off the bride's left hose, with many other pretty sorceries.' A feast in the great chamber was followed by a masque. 'There was no small loss that night of chains and jewels, and many great ladies were made shorter by the skirts.' Bride and groom were lodged in the Council chamber where the King in his shirt and nightgown paid them an early visit next morning before they were up 'and spent a good time in or upon the bed, choose which you will believe'. There was gaming at court for high stakes; little Prince Charles, then four years old, was created Duke of York; and an elaborate masque was given by the Queen and her ladies. Upon a great float, containing figures of sea-horses and other large fish ridden by Moors, Anne and three other ladies were seated in a shell. Carleton thought that their apparel, though rich, was too light and courtesan-like for such great personages. Their faces and arms, he added, were painted black, which 'became them nothing so well as their red and white, and you cannot imagine a more ugly sight than a troop of lean-cheeked Moors. The night's work was concluded with a banquet in the great chamber which was so furiously assaulted that down went table and trusses before one bit was touched'.

A visit of Christian IV of Denmark in the summer of 1606 was the occasion of astonishing licence. Delighted at the thought of entertaining a King, James set himself to please his royal guest, but in truth entertainment was a simple matter, for Christian's conception of happiness began and ended in the bottle. God forbid, wrote Salisbury, that this Dane should think the English did anything but drink. Sir John Harington, a wit of Elizabeth's court, has left a well-known picture of the revels at Theobalds where Salisbury played the host to both sovereigns. 'The sports began each day in such manner as persuaded me of Mahomet's paradise. We had women and indeed wine too of such plenty as would have astonished each sober beholder. Our feasts were magnificent, and the two royal guests did most lovingly embrace each other at table; I think the Dane hath strangely wrought on our good English nobles, for those whom I never could get to taste good liquor now follow the fashion and wallow in beastly delights. The ladies abandon their sobriety and roll about in intoxication. There hath been no lack of good living: shows, sights and banquetings from morn to eve. One day a great feast was held, and after dinner the representation of Solomon his Temple and the coming of the Queen of Sheba was made before their Majesties. The lady who did play the Queen's part did carry most precious gifts to both their Majesties; but forgetting the steps arising to the canopy overset her caskets into his Danish Majesty's lap and fell at his feet, though I rather think it was in his face. Much was the hurry and confusion; cloths and napkins were at hand to make all clean. His Majesty then got up and would dance with the Queen of Sheba; but he fell down and humbled himself before her and was carried to an inner chamber and laid on a bed of state, which was not a little defiled with the presents of the Queen which had been bestowed on his garments, such as wine, cream, jelly, beverage, cakes, spices and other good matters. The entertainment went forward and most of the pre-senters went backward or fell down, wine did so occupy their upper chambers. Now did appear Hope, Faith and Charity. Hope did assay to speak but wine rendered her endeavours so feeble that she withdrew and hoped the King would excuse her brevity. Faith was then all alone for I am certain she was not joined with good works, but left the court in a staggering condition. Charity came to the King's feet and seemed to cover the multitude of sins her sisters had committed. In some sort she made obeisance and brought gifts, but said she would return home again as there was no gift which heaven had not already given his Majesty. She then returned to Hope and Faith who were both sick and spewing in the lower hall. Next came Victory in bright armour and presented a rich sword to the King who did not accept it but put it by with his hand; but Victory did not triumph long, for after much lamentable utterance she was led away like a silly captive and laid to sleep on the outer steps of the ante-chamber. Now did Peace make entry and strive to get foremost to the King; but I grieve to tell how great wrath she did discover unto her attendants and much contrary to her semblance most rudely made war with her olive branch and laid on the pates of those who did oppose her coming. I did never see such lack of good order, discretion and sobriety as I have now done.' It is small wonder that Lady Anne Clifford wrote that the ladies about the court had gotten ill names and that the Queen herself had fallen from her former reputation.[9]

Although the King drank a good deal, it would be unfair to call him a drunkard. He drank small quantities of wine and ale at frequent intervals throughout the day, and on festive occasions he drank to excess. But in his prime he had a hard head and was seldom intoxicated, though in later life he was not infrequently drunk at Buckingham's jovial suppers. Weldon, no friendly critic, remarked that the King 'was not intemperate in his drink-ing. It is true he drank very often, which was rather out of a custom than any delight, and his drinks were of that strength that had he not had a very strong brain, he might have daily been overtaken, although he seldom drank at any one time above four spoonfuls, many times not above one or two'. Rumour asserted that the King's liquor was of unusual potency, and Roger Coke writing at the end of the century tells how his grand-father, attending James while hunting, ventured to sample the wine reserved for royalty and was quite disordered by its strength. But Mayerne, the King's physician, is the best witness. In drink-ing, he says, his Majesty 'errs as to quality, quantity, frequency, time and order. He promiscuously drinks beer, ale, Spanish wine, sweet French wine, white wine (his normal drink), Muscatelle and sometimes Alicant wine. He does not care whether the wine be strong or not so it is sweet'. Thus the King hovered on the peri-phery of that seductive vice, allowing it to grow upon him and leaning heavily upon the mental and physical stimulus which alcohol provides.[10]

The distractions at court rendered it difficult for the King to attend properly to affairs of State during the short periods he spent at Whitehall. Always a rush of business demanded immediate attention. Ambassadors pressed for audience, councillors for decision, and suitors, excluded from the King's rustic haunts, crowded about him when he came to London. The result was feverish haste and confusion. Wilbraham noted in 1603 that when Salisbury presented patents for eight barons and two earls, 'the King signed them all at one time confusedly, not respecting who should have antiquity'. His disorder in creating knights was notorious and became the subject of many jests. On one occasion, in knighting a Scot, he did not catch the long Celtic name and exclaimed, 'Prithee, rise up, and call thyself Sir What Thou Wilt.'[11]

There was great irregularity in obtaining access, and suitors 'swarmed about his Majesty at every back gate and privy door, to his great offence'. Charles decreed at his accession that suitors 'must never approach him by indirect means, by back stairs or private doors leading to his apartments, nor by means of retainers or grooms of the chambers, as was done in the lifetime of his father'. James thus subjected himself to constant irritation, and it is strange that a man who loved privacy as he did could not have handled matters better. Yet at the end of his reign the situation had not altered. 'The King is much disgusted with it,' wrote a courtier in 1623, 'but knows not how to help it; and I am told that he said to somebody the other day, "You will never let me alone. I would to God you had first my doublet and then my shirt and when I were naked I think you would give me leave to be quiet." '

It is true that if he was determined to resist a suitor he could do so with some skill, for he loved an argument and never lacked for words. On one occasion, as he wrote boastfully to Salisbury, he refused the suit of an impecunious noble, overwhelming him with remarkable volubility and telling him he was bound to be no man's banker. But such firmness was rare. He had a Scottish weakness for liking to please people. He seemed to think that no man was sincerely bound to him unless he was bound by a gift, and indeed he was rather contemptuous of those few modest souls who did not ask for favours. The granting of one suit appeared to justify the granting of others; and we find him telling Salisbury that since he had been so prodigal in rewarding persons who had no claim upon him he could not justly deny those who had.

Inevitably the English began to revise their early estimate of their new sovereign. The first fond hope that the King would prove a paragon of learning, wisdom and virtue faded away in sad disillusionment. 'The English', wrote Beaumont, the French ambassador, 'are for the most part little edified with the person or with the conduct of the King and declare openly enough that they were deceived in the opinion they were led to entertain of him.' One source of criticism contained poetic justice. James's attitude towards women, as we know, had never been chivalrous or gentlemanly. 'He piques himself', continued the ambassador, 'on great contempt for women. They are obliged to kneel before him when they are presented, he exhorts them openly to virtue, and scoffs with great levity at men who pay them honour. You may easily conceive that the English ladies do not spare him but hold him in abhorrence and tear him to pieces with their tongues, each according to her humour.'[12]

CHAPTER XII

THE ENFORCEMENT OF CONFORMITY

A CHRISTIAN monarch, said James, must begin with religion for even among pagans the affairs of Jove came first; and it was fitting that so theological a King should commence his reign with an ecclesiastical settlement. What was that settlement to be? As Englishmen looked to the north in 1603 they could not be certain. The King presented contradictions, he had beclouded his purpose, he had offered encouragement to Anglican, to Catholic and to Puritan alike. 'The formalists, the Papists, the sincere professors,' wrote Calderwood, 'had all their hopes.' There was a moment of breathless uncertainty. But the fear of Anglican divines that a Scottish mist might over-spread the kingdom passed quickly away. James took the Church of England to his heart in a long rapturous embrace that lasted the rest of his life.

He found it exactly to his taste. The ranks of the upper clergy included some remarkable men, worldly and often arrogant, but learned, able and strong, scholars, administrators and statesmen. Yet they displayed a deference and submissiveness towards the King that delighted him beyond measure. Whitgift, the Archbishop, and Bancroft, Bishop of London, who became the Primate in 1604, were austere men whom the King perhaps valued rather than liked. But there were others, and the number steadily increased, who were his personal friends, of whom he was sincerely fond and with whom he loved to converse. He kept them in constant attendance. There was no more familiar sight at court than that of the King at dinner discussing theology with three or four of his churchmen — bishops, deans and royal chaplains — who stood deferentially behind the royal chair. He employed their talents in his writings against the Papacy. He admitted them to his private devotions. Sometimes in later life, as he sat in his retiring-room in the evening or lay in bed and recalled sins he had committed during the day, he would summon one of the divines with whom he was intimate, and together they would pray for the forgiveness of the royal transgressions. Sermons he attended with great regularity on Sundays and Tuesdays, on all major feasts and communion days, wherever he happened to be. He selected clergymen to preach at court, provided them with texts and other material, and listened with close attention and with embarrassing signs of approval or dissent.

Of the courtly divines whom he gathered about him, Lancelot Andrewes, successively Bishop of Chichester, Ely and Winchester, was probably his favourite. Famous alike as scholar, teacher and preacher, Andrewes was both learned and witty, both pious and adroit, combining a good life with the ready tongue of the courtier. On one occasion only, though that a vital one — when he gave his vote for the divorce of Lady Frances Howard — did worldliness prove stronger than conscience. James admired him greatly, spoke of his sermons as a voice from heaven, and once asked him for his notes to lay beneath the royal pillow. In Andrewes's presence the raucous and bawdy mirth of the King was hushed. There were other clergymen favoured at court: Barlow, the pushing Dean of Chester, Bilson, the learned Bishop of Winchester, King, whom James called the king of preachers, Williams, the chatty politician, Donne, the mordant wit; and the King with his love of intimacy liked the Church better because he liked its clergy.[1]

The Church of England he probably knew better than any other part of his new kingdom. He was well versed in a movement that was to affect his reign profoundly, a movement known today as Anglo-Catholicism, though described in his time as anti-Calvinist, anti-predestination, Arminian. Refusing to consider the Church as a political compromise, a convenient half way house between Rome and Geneva, the Anglo-Catholics sought a broader and more convincing foundation. They turned to the primitive Church during the first five centuries after Christ before the Bishop of Rome developed into the Pope. They studied early creeds and councils and the writings of the early Fathers; and they reached the conclusion that the Church of England, as reformed in the sixteenth century, was the true descendant of primitive Christianity. They thought of the Church of Rome as part of the visible Church (like those of Jerusalem, Antioch and Alexandria), but one that had fallen into error, becoming unsound in doctrine and corrupt in manners. None the less it had served as a conduit-pipe to convey to modern times those primitive truths and godly ceremonies which it had superstitiously defiled. Thus the Anglo-Catholics accepted the whole Christian heritage, while the Puritans refused to look beyond the Scriptures and could see nothing but evil in the medieval Church. Anglo-Catholicism was a conservative reaction against Calvinist rigidity. Its outlook was broader, more humane, more moderate, more latitudinarian. It regarded the doctrine of predestination as harsh and terrible; and it saw a means of grace in ritual and ceremony.

Shortly after his arrival in England, according to Isaak Walton, the King inquired for Richard Hooker whose book, *Ecclesiastical Politie*, was a corner-stone of Anglo-Catholicism; and hearing that Hooker was dead he expressed sorrow that he could not talk with one from whose books he had derived such satisfaction. He observed in Hooker, he said, gravity, comprehension and reason, backed by the Scriptures, by the Fathers, by the schoolmen, and by law both sacred and civil. The words are Walton's but the thoughts could well be James's.[2]

There was, however, another party in the Church, a party labelled Calvinist, Puritan, anti-Arminian. It stood for implacable hostility to Rome, for a Puritan code of morals, for orthodoxy in the Church of England, and for unity with the Protestant Churches on the Continent. It was represented by George Abbot, who became Archbishop in 1611, by his brother Robert, Bishop of Salisbury, and by George Carleton, Bishop of Chichester. James could understand this party as well as the other; and certain things, we shall find, drew him to the anti-Arminians. In appointments and policy he balanced one group against the other, he straddled the doctrinal points at issue, and thereby created divided counsels in the Church as well as in the State.

The English bishops of both schools were Erastian, accepting the supremacy of the State in ecclesiastical affairs. This filled James with delight. It was a joy to find the bishops in England firmly in control of the Church yet ready to accept the divine right of kings with enthusiasm and completeness. A close, abiding and fateful alliance of Church and Crown was formed at once. The Church exalted the power of the King and sanctified his person, denounced criticism of the monarch as blasphemous, and preached the religious duty of passive obedience. The King was quick to defend the Church; and attacks upon it were punished as offences against the Crown.

James also took kindly to the ritual of the English Church. In Scotland ritual had not concerned him greatly. He had appeared content with the forms prescribed by the Book of Common Order. He had complained that the Scottish clergy were too familiar with the Deity and had warned his son not to be over-homely with God in prayer 'like the vain proud Puritans that think they rule Him upon their fingers'. But he had declared with apparent sincerity that he did not dislike a minister who preferred the simple Scottish forms to the ceremonies of the Church of England or who smelt papal error in surplice and cornered cap.' 'No,' he wrote, 'I am so far from being contentious in these things (which for my own part I ever esteemed as indifferent), as I do equally love and honour the learned and grave men of either of these opinions. We all (God be praised) do agree in the grounds, and the bitterness of men upon such questions doth but trouble the peace of the Church and gives advantage and entry to the Papists by our division.' This was written with an eye to England but it was more than propaganda. The King's indifference to ritual enabled him to pass easily into the English Church. He liked its ceremonies, doubtless for their own sake, but also because they exalted the monarch and increased the divinity that hedged the King. In 1605 Chamberlain noted with amusement that John Gordon, a Scot whom James had made Dean of Salisbury, had 'come so far about the matter of ceremonies' that he found authority in Scripture for cross, cap and surplice as he preached before the King. James needed no such proof. In things indifferent the King could do as he pleased, and ritual now pleased the King.

This belief that ritual was a matter of choice enabled him to tolerate Roman Catholics more readily; but it did not help him in dealing with the Puritans. If he could detect no veil in bowing at the name of Jesus, why should they? If kneeling at Communion was a matter of indifference, who but an obstinate fool would make objection? Especially was he exasperated by Puritan rejection of ceremonies on the ground that they had been used when England was Roman Catholic. Shoes had been worn in the time of Popery, he shouted at the Hampton Court Conference; why therefore did not the Puritans go barefoot? There was another consideration. If a ceremony became a symbol of submission to royal authority, the King's indifference disappeared and he was ready to enforce it with every weapon in his armoury. 'In things that are against the Word of God,' he declared, 'I will with as great humility as any slave fall upon my knees or face. But in things indifferent, they are seditious which obey not the magistrate. There is no man half so dangerous as he that repugns against order.'[3]

The Puritans, though conforming members of Elizabeth's Church, were dissatisfied with it; and in the first half of her reign they had loudly demanded reform. After 1588, however, they had grown more quiescent. Their most influential advocates at court had passed away. Their spirit was not in accord with the exuberant nationalism that followed Spain's defeat. An Act of 1593 had borne heavily upon them, and 'the seasonable execution of some principal sticklers', as a malicious Anglican observed, had produced a great calm in Church and State.[4] But the advent of a new ruler, especially one who had offered them hope, naturally led them to seek an improvement in their position.

As the King was journeying down from Edinburgh the Puritan clergy presented him with the famous Millenary Petition. It was an able and well-timed document, studiously moderate and respectful in tone. The petitioners trusted to the Christian judgment of their dread sovereign to lighten their burdens. They were not, they said, factious men like the Presbyterians, nor schismatics like the Brownists, but loyal subjects of the King. They asked modification first in ritual: discontinuance of the use of the sign of the cross in baptism, of the ring in marriage, and of the terms 'priest' and 'absolution'. They wished the rite of confirmation abolished, the wearing of the surplice made optional, the length of the service abridged, and church music moderated to better edification. The ministry should be recruited from more able and learned men, non-residence and pluralities should be abolished, the church courts reformed, and the Sabbath observed more strictly.

The King received the petition with a graciousness that rejoiced the Puritans and dismayed the English bishops. Still on the threshold of his new kingdom, he did not as yet identify the English Puritan with the Scottish Presbyterian. When, as he left Edinburgh, a group of Scottish ministers had begged him to relieve 'the good brethren of the ministry of England', he had answered 'that he would show favour to honest men, but not to Anabaptists'. Might not the Millenary Petition come from honest men? Its suggestion of a conference between Puritans and Anglicans pleased him. He would be Solomon to whom the tribes could come for judgment. He did not understand that a conference, whatever its outcome, would give the Puritans a recognition they had never been granted by Elizabeth, and yet was certain to raise hopes that must end in bitter frustration.

But the King's first careless moment of sympathy passed rapidly away. The Puritans, elated by their initial success, began a campaign to secure large numbers of minor petitions. Opportunity was thus given to more radical elements to ask for things tending to Presbyterianism, and in Sussex the campaign for petitions caused local disturbance of the peace. Both Oxford and Cambridge answered the Millenary Petition. Oxford's reply, long, scolding and contemptuous, branded the Puritans as treasonous and seditious persons and identified them with the Presbyterian ministers in Scotland. Their aim was 'the utter overthrow of the present church government and instead thereof the setting up of a presbytery in every parish'. Equally hostile and contemptuous was the tone of the court. The King, moreover, now in contact with the English bishops, held long and earnest conferences with them in the summer of 1603. In July he visited Bancroft, that arch-enemy of Puritans, at his palace in Fulham.

As a result the King began to identify the English Puritan with the Scottish Presbyterian. If English Puritanism was like its Scottish counterpart, he would have none of it. Its preciseness over ritual reminded him, he said, of those brainsick and heady preachers in Scotland who made as great commotion over the smallest point of ecclesiastical policy as if the doctrine of the Trinity had been called in question; and rather than yield they would defy authority and would let King, people and law all be trodden under foot. 'I will tell you,' James said to the bishops at the Hampton Court Conference, 'I have lived among this sort of men ever since I was ten years old, but I may say of myself, as Christ did of Himself, though I lived amongst them, yet since I had ability to judge, I was never of them.'

In thus equating the English Puritan with the Scottish Presbyterian James made a gross, cardinal and most unhappy error. For Puritanism in England in 1603 was mild in tone and diffuse in essence. It lacked the ferocity of Scotland. There were Presbyterian elements within it; and some English Puritans saw a model for their Church as they looked northward. But English Puritanism was much broader than this. It included many who wished to purify the Church without setting up the presbytery. Even this is too confining. There were Puritans who accepted ritual and there were certainly many who disliked fanatics. Puritanism defies exact definition. In its broadest sense it was an awakening of conscience, a striving after godliness, a will to oppose evil wherever evil was found, in State, in Church, or in the world at large.

James began to stress his resolve to keep the Church essentially as it was. A proclamation of October 1603, prohibited the practice of soliciting signatures to petitions concerning religion, for the reform of the Church belonged to the King; and asserted further that the constitution and doctrine of the Church of England were agreeable to God's Word and close to the condition of primitive Christianity. The bishops, James remarked, could advise him as well as others whose zeal ran faster than their discretion. He wrote to Whitgift that clergymen who used unauthorized forms should be punished severely and that all men must 'conform to that which we have by our open declaration published'.

The outlook for the conference was not happy. But the Puritans heard rumours that gave them hope. When Bishop Bilson counselled James against a conference, the King replied: 'Content yourself, my Lord, we know better than you what belongeth to these matters.' It was also rumoured that the King at table had declared his intention of introducing a more learned ministry. [5]

On the first day of the conference, January 14th, 1604, the King admitted to his presence only bishops, deans and privy councillors. Opening the conference with a lengthy speech, he reviewed the Church's history under the Tudors, declaring himself happier than they, because they had been forced to make alterations while he found more cause to confirm than to innovate. Yet corruption entered the fairest houses. He had heard many complaints which, like a good physician, he proposed to examine. If they proved frivolous, he would at least have cast a sop into Cerberus's mouth so that he could never bark again. He wished first to consult the bishops alone, so that some things could be done quickly and quietly, and he raised a number of points suggested by the Millenary Petition: confirmation, absolution, private baptism, excommunication. Whitgift, falling upon his knees, thanked God for bringing England a King so wise, learned and judicious. With the aid of other bishops he explained the Church's stand on the points that James had raised. The King took a lively and delighted part in the discussion, calling for the Bible or for the Book of Common Prayer to read pertinent passages aloud. Most of the doctrine of the Church he found apostolic and very good. He grew angry in denouncing baptism by women or by laymen, though he thought baptism might be performed in private places. When a bishop claimed that the Church did not permit baptism by laymen, James cited the Prayer Book to prove the bishop wrong. This was a point, he thought, upon which the primitive church need not be followed. He told a story of a pert minister in Scotland who asked him whether a child, dying unbaptized, would be damned. 'I answered him, no,' said the King, 'but if you, being called to baptize the child, though privately, should refuse to come, I think you should be damned.' Thus pleasantly James and the bishops agreed upon minor changes.

The Puritans later spoke of this part of the conference as a struggle between the Puritan sympathies of the King and the popish notions of the bishops. 'For five hours', it was said, 'his Majesty did wonderfully play the Puritan,' accusing the Church of corruptions and the prelates of evil deeds. But the Puritans were wrong, for there was no struggle at all. The King was conservative and the bishops yielding; they were filled with wonder, 'so admirably, both for understanding, speech and judgment, did his Majesty handle all those points, sending us away, not with contentment only, but astonishment, and, which is pitiful, you will say, with shame to us all, that a King, brought up among Puritans, not the learnedest men in the world, and schooled by them, swaying a kingdom full of business and troubles, naturally given to much exercise and repast, should in points of divinity show himself so expedite and perfect, as the greatest scholars and most industrious students there present might not outstrip him'. The King was in his element and enjoyed himself hugely.

To the second day's debate the Puritans were admitted. In Barlow's account of the conference, which was undoubtedly written at the King's command,[6] they are made to appear rather stupid and their arguments inconsequential. Yet their chief spokesman was Dr. John Rainolds, professor of divinity and master of Corpus Christi College, Oxford, a stern Puritan but an able man; other Puritan spokesmen were from Cambridge. Either the

Puritans were so bullied by the King, whose language grew coarse and abusive, that they presented their case badly, or else Barlow did not do them justice.

Repeating his speech of the day before, which he doubtless considered too good for the Puritans to miss, the King invited them to present their grievances. Dr. Rainolds said they would divide their subject into four heads: doctrine, a learned ministry, the Prayer Book, and the government of the Church. Under the first of these headings he asked that predestination be more clearly acknowledged, that laymen be prohibited from administering the sacraments, that confirmation be re-examined. Suddenly Bishop Bancroft, throwing himself upon his knees and begging leave to speak, poured forth a torrent of bitter and insolent invective against the Puritans. Their aim, he said, was not the reform but the overthrow of the Church; they were demanding the full Presbyterian doctrine of predestination; they disliked the rite of confirmation because they themselves could not confirm. Against this truculence the King had the fairness to protest; he excused Bancroft's passion, but declared that both sides must be heard without chopping. He then spoke at some length on predestination, although it was a subject on which he could never quite make up his mind, and asked that it be handled very tenderly.[7] There followed a discussion of the points that Rainolds had raised, but the King's decisions were against him.

Continuing the list of Puritan complaints, Rainolds asked that the clergy be allowed to administer the Communion though they did not believe all the teaching of the Church concerning it. This the King refused. He told a story of a Scottish minister who so filled his sermons with things that he detested, renounced and abhorred that the poor simple people fell back into Popery. Rainolds asked for one catechism instead of two, which James approved, provided that the new one be short, simple and easily understood, for complications must be avoided in the instruction of the people. To Rainolds's request that the Sabbath be kept holy there was no objection. With his request for a new translation of the Bible Bancroft took issue, but the King approved, with highly important results.

'And surely, said his Majesty, if these be the greatest matters you be grieved with, I need not have been troubled with such importunities as have been made unto me, and looking upon the lords he shook his head, smiling.' At other points raised by Rainolds the King and the bishops laughed heartily, and a jest was whispered among them that a Puritan was a Protestant frayed out of his wits.

The Puritans then asked for a more learned ministry. To this the King answered that a learned ministry was the desire of all men but that for the present it was impossible. The Church would do what it could, the rest must be tolerated. The point did not pass without further interruption by Bancroft, who defended a ministry which emphasized the prayers in the Prayer Book as opposed to one which placed greater value upon preaching. The King denounced those clergymen who found praying too much trouble, but said none the less, reflecting his background, that a preaching ministry was best where it could be had.

Turning to the Prayer Book, the Puritans opposed its command to read the Apocrypha in church. When the Book of Ecclesiasticus was mentioned, the King called for the Bible and, arguing like a divine, discoursed upon the book, its authorship, analysis and interpretation, to the amazement of the company. To the lords he said pleasantly, 'What trow ye, makes these men so angry with Ecclesiasticus? By my soul, I think he was a bishop.'

Dr. Knewstubs, a Puritan with a knack of saying the wrong thing, argued against the sign of the cross in baptism by asserting that it offended the weaker, that is, the more precise, of the clergy. James caught him up. How long would they be weak? Was not forty-five years sufficient time to gain strength? Ministers were not supposed to be fed with milk, but to feed others; and some deemed themselves strong enough to teach the King and the whole bench of bishops. Again Knewstubs offended by saying that the Christian liberty of the clergy must not be infringed. He thus raised the question of obedience. The King answered hotly that he would not argue the point but would merely refuse it, for it smelt rankly of Anabaptism. He recalled a Scottish minister, a mere beardless boy, who offered to obey in matters of doctrine but declared that in ceremonies he must do as the light of God's spirit directed. 'Even till they go mad, quoth the King, with their own light. But I will have none of that; I will have one doctrine and one discipline, one religion in substance and ceremony, and therefore I charge you never to speak more to that point (how far ye are to obey), when the Church hath ordained.'

The hour growing late, James suggested another session on the day following; and the Puritans would have been wise to have agreed, for the King was weary and irritable. But they decided to present the final division of their subject, that of church government. It was here that Rainolds used the unlucky word 'presbytery' which like a flash of lightning brought conviction to the King that the Puritans were mere Presbyterians. His patience came abruptly to an end and he broke out in wild native fury, 'thinking that they aimed at a Scottish presbytery, which, sayeth he, as well agreeth with a monarchy as God and the Devil. Then Tom and Dick shall meet and at their pleasure censure me and my Council and all our proceedings. Then Will shall stand up and say, "It must be thus"; then Dick shall reply and say, "Nay marry but we will have it thus." Stay, I pray you, for one seven years before you demand that of me; and if you find me pursy and fat and my windpipes stuffed I will perhaps hearken unto you. For let that government be once up I am sure I shall be kept in breath. Then shall we all of us have work enough, both our hands full. But, Dr. Rainolds, till you find that I grow lazy, let that alone. How they used that poor lady my mother is not unknown, and how they dealt with me in my minority you all know.' Were the bishops once out of power and the Puritans in, cried James, 'I know what would become of my supremacy. No bishop, no King. When I mean to live under a presbytery I will go into Scotland again, but while I am in England I will have bishops to govern the Church.' Turning to the Puritans he said in fury, 'If this is all they have to say, I will make them conform themselves or I will harry them out of this land or else do worse.'

On the third day, before the Puritans were admitted to a short final session, Bancroft presented the articles of faith to which they objected. The King declared warmly that conformity was essential in every well-governed Church and that, if a clergyman would not be quiet and obey, the Church was better without him and he deserved to be hanged. The Puritans were then admitted and informed of the royal pleasure. To their request for leniency, the King replied that no clergyman would be removed from his place before he had been fully admonished. But James grew angry at a remark of the blundering Knewstubs who said that the credit of the ministers would be damaged if they were forced to conform. Knewstubs, said the King, preferred the credit of a few men to the peace of the Church. His method was that of the Scottish ministers who obeyed only after they had flouted authority. 'I will have none of that. Let them conform themselves and that shortly or they shall hear of it.'

Bishops and councillors were again astounded at the learning and readiness of the King. Bancroft thanked God for such a sovereign 'as since Christ His time the like he thought had not been; whereunto the lords with one voice did yield a very affectionate acclamation'. But there were other opinions. 'The King', wrote Sir John Harington, 'talked much Latin and disputed with Dr. Rainolds at Hampton, but he rather used upbraidings than arguments; and told the petitioners that they wanted to strip Christ again and bid them away with their snivelling. Moreover he wished those who would take away the surplice might want linen for their own breeches. The bishops seemed much pleased and said his Majesty spoke by the power of inspiration; I wist not what they meant, but the spirit was rather foul-mouthed.' This we may well believe. Barlow draws a decent veil over royal filthiness of language, and the bishops were less certain of the divinity of James's phrases when, shortly after, he told Parliament that the Devil, sparing neither labour nor pains, was a busy bishop. Bancroft thought his Majesty might have chosen another name.

James was greatly pleased with his part at the conference. 'We have kept such a revel with the Puritans here these two days,' he wrote Northampton, 'as was never heard the like, where I peppered them soundly. It were no reason that those that will refuse the airy sign of the cross after baptism should have their purses stuffed with any more solid and substantial crosses. They fled me so from argument to argument without ever answering me directly, *ut est eorum moris*, as I was forced at last to say unto them that if any of them had been in a college disputing with their scholars, if any of their disciples had answered them in that sort, they would have fetched him up in place of a reply, and so should the rod have plied upon the poor boy's buttocks.'[8] But in truth the King had done great harm. He was the controversialist, thirsting for wordy victory, not the statesman who might find Puritan notions unacceptable but who would seek to avoid dissension and bitterness. He had first encouraged the Puritans, then called them to argue a case already decided against them and treated them with scorn and contumely. Conformity was to be more rigidly enforced; and the Church was headed not towards greater comprehension but towards a hard and narrow exclusiveness. In this fateful decision the King's will was a vital factor.

Convocation now passed new canons enforcing conformity upon the clergy on pain of the loss of their livings. Hoping that persuasion would do much, the King instructed the bishops to speak mildly and discreetly with their Puritan clergy; yet they were to distinguish between those ministers who seemed to offer promise of reform and those whose lofty and turbulent natures fitted them only for punishment. The time allowed the clergy for reaching a decision was extended from July to November, and for this leniency the King assumed great credit. When this period of probation elapsed, however, the bishops were instructed to take action and ejections began. The Puritans claimed that some three hundred ministers were deprived or suspended, while the Church placed those deprived at fifty. Recent research has raised that estimate to about ninety.

Blaming the bishops rather than the King, the Puritans petitioned for leniency; but petitions merely hardened James's heart. When one was presented while he was hunting near Royston in November, he sent the petitioners to the Council and wrote savagely to Salisbury: 'I have daily more and more cause to hate and abhor all that sect, enemies to all kings, and to me only because I am a King.' A more serious matter was a petition from certain knights and gentlemen of Northamptonshire. This petition enraged the King because it argued that if ministers were deprived thousands of the people would be discontented, which James regarded as a threat. 'Next day he sat eight hours in Council with the lords and most bitterly inveighed against the Puritans, saying that the revolt in the Low Countries, which had lasted ever since he was born and whereof he never expected to see an end, began first by a petition for matter of religion, and so did all the troubles in Scotland; that his mother and he from their cradles had been haunted with a Puritan devil which he feared would not leave him to his grave; and that he would hazard his crown but he would suppress those malicious spirits.' Thus his irritation against the Puritans hardened into hate. He was glad to hear that the Council was taking vigorous action. 'I am wonderfully well satisfied with the Council's proceedings anent the

Puritans', he wrote to Salisbury. Councillors, he continued, 'have used justice upon the obstinate, showing grace to the penitent, and enlarged them that seemed to be a little schooled by the rod of affliction. According to the one hundred and first Psalm they have sung both of mercy and judgment, and therefore thank them in my name for their pains and uniform concurrence in my service'.

Some of the bishops, finding their best clergy among the obstinate, wished to draw back from the policy of the King. 'The bishops themselves', wrote Chamberlain, 'are loath to proceed too rigorously in casting out and depriving so many well reputed of for life and learning. Only the King is constant to have all come to conformity.' Even Montagu, a worldling and high churchman, thought the King was going too fast. Montagu urged that turbulent ministers should be called out little by little 'rather than all without difference be cut down at once', for he feared that the clergy who lost their places would gain more by pity than they could by their piety. This was exactly what happened. 'The poor Puritan ministers, ferreted out in all corners', stood forth as martyrs to a cause, as a symbol of resistance, as a reproach to clergymen who conformed for worldly considerations. Good and able ministers, it was said, were replaced by idle drones and dumb images, a point which worried the King considerably. The discontent of the Puritans found only too much to feed upon as the reign wore on. A deep fissure was appearing in the Church; and while the bishops turned to the King, the Puritans turned to Parliament.[9]

James wanted to be good to the Church. Fully aware that many of its problems arose from its poverty, he refused to deepen that poverty by alienations of church property. Nor was he guilty of simony, though it existed at his court. He rejected with scorn a project to reassess the evaluation of benefices so as to obtain larger sums in first fruits; and he would not translate bishops merely for that purpose. He supported the Church in its highly unpopular efforts to obtain enhanced revenues from tithes.

The sight of a cathedral fabric falling into decay caused him genuine concern. He complained in 1608 to the Bishop of London that St. Paul's was in a disgraceful condition and asked how repairs could be financed, though he offered no money himself. He attempted in 1620 to stimulate contributions by a royal visit to the cathedral. Coming in great state on a Sunday afternoon, accompanied by bishops, peers and courtiers, he supplied the Bishop of London with a text and protested he would fast on bread and water until repairs were complete. Yet he permitted his visit to degenerate into an absurd glorification of his kingly piety, while a purse of 1000 marks, presented to him as he entered the city, was not devoted to the repair of Paul's. Some curious old prints commemorate this occasion. On one of them appears the inscription: 'Blessed be the Lord God of our Fathers which putteth such things as these into the heart of our good King, to beautify the House of the Lord. Amen'; while angels hovering about the spire (which was destroyed in Elizabeth's reign) sound verses from their trumpets:

> This goodly King shall reign and rule in peace,
> Because by him the Gospel doth increase.

In 1617 he named Laud as Dean of Gloucester partly because the Puritan Bishop, Miles Smith, had tolerated dilapidation in the cathedral fabric.[10]

The King supported the ecclesiastical courts in their struggle with the courts of common law; he defended the bishops when they were under fire in Parliament; he resented criticism of the Church in whatever form it came.

Yet his allies invariably suffered from their connection with him, and the Church was no exception. When Parliament refused him funds, he forgot the Church's poverty and called upon the clergy for loans and benevolences. Constantly were the bishops asked to finance projects which the King wished to advance but could not pay for. What was much worse, he assumed that the patronage of the Church was at his disposal. The number of Scots who obtained places in the English Church is rather startling. Bishop King of London complained bitterly of the many letters he received from great men who were permitted to use the name of the King in requesting livings for Scots and for other persons. So frequently did James interfere, and so unmindful was he of the rights of others, that the Church, submissive as it was, occasionally rebelled. There was a quarrel between the King and the cathedral chapter at Canterbury over Bancroft's election, the chapter thinking its rights had been ignored. The northern bishops were offended at the appointment of one Francis Browne, an unworthy man, as registrar of the province of York. James made the appointment, then asked the bishops to approve, saying that if the office was not in his gift he would refrain from appointing anyone to it in the future. The famous case of *Commendams* in 1615 began in part because the King exercised a doubtful right of advowson.

There was no consistent policy in his appointment of bishops, and men were elevated for diverse and contradictory reasons. That James's personal preference played a great part may be seen in the number of royal chaplains who rose to be bishops. A book that pleased the King was an easy road to advancement. He remarked to Robert Abbot: 'Abbot, I have had much to do to make thee a bishop; but I know no reason for it, unless it were because thou hast written a book against a popish prelate.' Montagu became Bishop of Bath and Wells after helping James write a pamphlet against Rome, and Bishop of Winchester after editing the King's collected works. But these were the more creditable causes of elevation, for bishoprics were sought and obtained at court like any other preferment. 'The manner of carrying bishoprics', wrote the clergyman George Carleton who, it must be admitted, was long a disappointed candidate, 'is now come to such a pass that I am much ashamed to write.'

In the most important appointment of the reign, that of an Archbishop of Canterbury in 1611, the King's selection bordered on the eccentric. And a favourite played no unimportant part. Passing over Lancelot Andrewes, to the astonishment of the clergy, James's choice fell upon George Abbot, a university man who had but small experience in the administration of the Church and whose theological views were distinctly Calvinistic. The appointment was made against the wishes of the Council, 'to whom the King used some sharp words, declaring it to be his will in order to oblige one of his servants'. That servant was Dunbar who, strange to say, was dead. The King told Abbot that his advancement did not spring from his learning, wisdom, or sincerity (though he did not doubt that Abbot possessed those qualities) but from 'the recommendation of his faithful servant, Dunbar, that is dead, whose suit he cannot forget nor will suffer to lose his intention'. Serving as Dunbar's chaplain, Abbot had visited Scotland where he had met with some success in furthering the King's ecclesiastical policy; and it has been suggested by a modern historian of the Church that James first used Abbot in anglicizing the Scots and now thought to use him in scotticizing the English. Perhaps the King felt that Andrewes's conception of the episcopat almost too lofty, and preferred an archbishop who would regard his appointment as the gift of an earthly rather than of a heavenly king. There was an element of compromise in James's decision. Abbot's elevation would please the Puritans, yet he was too weak a man to do the King much harm. His appointment added to the discord in the Church and was not a happy one.[11]

James harmed the Church in other ways. He dragged the bishops through the filth of Lady Frances Howard's divorce. He was determined to tune the pulpit to the royal pleasure, and the bishops were expected to play their part in controlling the sermons of the clergy. Yet it should not be forgotten that the bishops, making a deliberate choice, threw in their lot with divine right just as that theory was beginning to be questioned.

Bad as the King's record was, he achieved one notable success. The Authorized Version of the Bible, first suggested by Dr. Rainolds at the Hampton Court Conference, owed much to James's interest and support; and here his passion for sketching programmes and directives bore noble fruit. A new translation was needed because, while the Bishops' Bible was the official Bible of the Church, the Geneva Bible was the one most commonly used by the people. The King wanted one uniform version. He had never seen, he said, a well-translated English Bible and he considered the Geneva Bible worst of all. He objected to the anti-monarchical tone of its marginal notes which he pronounced 'very partial, untrue, seditious and savouring too much of dangerous and traitorous conceits'. He spoke as though he had never heard of the Geneva Bible until he came to England, when, he said, an English lady brought it to his attention, but it was the Bible he had known best from childhood. In an eloquent speech, though one perhaps designed to display the royal knowledge of the Scriptures, he had urged a new translation before the General Assembly of the Kirk in 1601. At the Hampton Court Conference, he at once suggested a procedure which was, in broad outline, the one adopted. The translation, he said, should be made by the most learned linguists in the two universities; it should be reviewed by the bishops and by other learned churchmen, then presented to the Privy Council, and finally ratified by royal authority.

In the months following the conference, the new translation

received the warm and vigorous support of the King. As early as June 1604, translators had been selected; James had approved the choice and had set down elaborate instructions for their guidance. Fifty-four translators were divided into six groups or companies, two at Westminster under the direction of Lancelot Andrewes, two at Oxford under John Harding and two at Cambridge under Edward Lively, both professors of Hebrew. Every translator worked by himself and then conferred with other members of his company on what he had done; as each chapter of the Bible was thus completed it was subjected to the scrutiny of other companies. 'His Majesty was very careful in this point.' Criticisms and differences of opinion were then sent back to the first translators, and in each case a decision was made at a meeting of the 'chief persons of each company'. Learned men, both in the Church and at the universities, though they had not been named as translators, were encouraged to submit their judgment on difficult and doubtful points. Six men, two selected from each centre, met at London to review the work as a whole, and finally Bishop Bilson and Miles Smith, who was rewarded by the bishopric of Gloucester, gave a last revision to the completed text.

There were many other points of interest in the instructions sent by the King to the translators. He commanded that the Bishops' Bible be followed as far as possible, with old ecclesiastical words retained (thus *church* should not be rendered *congregation*), and that where words had several meanings the writings of the early Fathers should serve as a guide. The translators were also instructed to employ those proper names already known to the people; they were not to insert marginal notes except to explain the meaning of words or to cite parallel passages in other parts of the Scriptures. It is evident that though the King desired the new Bible to be Anglican in tone, which was but natural, he also wished it to be written in language that the people could easily comprehend. Declarations of religious belief, he always insisted, should be set forth in clear, simple and understandable English without intricate or esoteric phrasing. The application of this principle to the translation of the Scriptures undoubtedly assisted in making the Authorized Version the marvellous achievement that it became.

Although the men with whom the King conferred as he planned the undertaking were all high Anglicans — Bancroft, Andrewes and Barlow, Dean of Chester — the sound practice was followed that translators be selected for their skill in languages and not for their religious views. One Puritan, Hugh Broughton, was excluded because of the violence of his opinions; but Dr. Rainolds, the Puritan spokesman at the conference, was included in the Oxford group, in which he shortly overshadowed John Harding, the nominal leader. And there were other Puritan translators. This wise and impartial search for talent was first suggested by the King and may well have been adhered to in deference to his wishes. Only partially successful were his efforts to finance the undertaking. A suggestion that the bishops contribute funds brought only a meagre response, but he also asked them to remember the translators when livings fell vacant, promising to do the same with livings in his gift; and there were a number of translators who received preferment in reward for their labours. Charges have been made that the King imposed his own rendering of certain passages in the Scriptures, but such accusations can neither be proved nor disproved. And on the whole, though he scarcely deserves the fulsome praise of the dedication, he merits perhaps a reference (omitted in modern Bibles) to 'his constancy for the survey of the English translations'.[12]

When he had urged a new translation of the Scriptures before the General Assembly of the Kirk in 1601, he had at the same time proposed a new metrical version of the Psalms to be sung in churches and in private worship. This was a project he had long held dear. As a schoolboy he had translated at least one Psalm from Latin into English verse; in 1591 he wrote that he had completed a number of others and hoped to translate the rest. Many years later in England he took up the task once more. He 'set the most learned divines of that Church a-work for the translation of the Bible', wrote Spottiswoode, but 'the revising of the Psalms he made his own labour, and at such hours as he might spare from the public cares went through a number of them, commending the rest to a faithful and learned servant, who hath herein answered his Majesty's expectation'. This servant was the poet and colonizer Sir William Alexander, James's friend and literary crony. Alexander's letters to William Drummond of Hawthornden show that they both aided the King in this undertaking and that Alexander was rather annoyed by James's preference for his own renderings above those of his collaborators. 'I received your last letter,' he wrote Drummond in 1620, 'with the Psalm you sent, which I think very well done. I had done the same long before it came; but he prefers his own to all else, though, perchance, when you see it, you will think it the worst of the three. No man must meddle with that subject, and therefore I advise you to take no more pains therein.' Alexander implies that the project had ended, but the King was still talking of it when, as Bishop Williams remarked, God called him to sing Psalms with the angels.

James's translation of the Psalms, however, met a melancholy fate. At the time of his death he had finished about thirty of them; and Alexander, looking about for cash, hit upon the plan of completing the royal work and of issuing it under the name of his late master. From King Charles he obtained not only the sole right to publish *The Psalms of King David Translated by King James*, which appeared in 1631, but also a royal command to the Church to adopt the new translation. The bishops, however, knowing full well, as a modern writer has observed, that 'the proportion of James to Alexander was as Falstaff's bread to his sack', would have nothing to do with it. Alexander then turned to the Scottish Presbyterians, but they, too, rejected his Psalms with impolite curtness. They suspected a translation by a courtier-poet who referred to the moon as 'the pale lady of the night'. Alexander prepared a new edition, with obnoxious phrases expunged, and this edition appeared in 1636. But it was associated in the popular mind with the Scottish Prayer Book of 1637, and neither of these works served to enhance the attractiveness of the other. The Prayer Book occasioned a famous riot and was condemned by the Scots in solemn terms. *The Psalms of King David Translated by King James* was passed by in contemptuous silence.[13]

CHAPTER XIII

THE DEFENDER OF THE FAITH

KING JAMES was more enlightened and more tolerant in dealing with the English Roman Catholics than with the English Puritans. Roman priests he regarded with deep suspicion and Jesuits with abhorrence and terror, but he distinguished sharply between them and the Roman Catholic laity for whom he had much sympathy and to whom he was prepared to grant a restricted toleration. In the early years of his reign, moreover, despite his hatred of papal supremacy, he offered Rome a compromise, visionary, but friendly and sincere; and if ideals could have brought success he might have allayed the cruel hatreds that divided Christendom. Yet in practice his policy was a failure. It contained so many inconsistencies, due to his fears and to his petulance, that it brought him neither the loyalty of the English Catholics nor the friendship of the Pope. He was caught in the commitments he had made before he became King of England, for the Catholics expected great things of him and he could no longer feed them with fair promises. If they believed themselves duped he was sure to face their vengeance; yet if he was lenient to them he was certain to enrage his Protestant subjects. The truth was that Protestant England, with its long tradition of hostility to Rome, was not ready for the toleration he proposed. His leniency to English Catholics stiffened the Protestant hatred of Catholicism, postponed the day of true toleration, and alienated the people far more than did the harshness meted out to the Puritan clergy.

Before he left Scotland he had written to Salisbury that he would seek a golden mean in dealing with English Roman Catholics. He was, he said, strongly averse to persecution, and would never allow in his conscience that the blood of any man should be shed for diversity of opinions in religion. On the other hand, he could not permit Catholics to engage in rebellion nor to increase in numbers until they became masters, 'able to practise their old principles upon us'. To attain this middle ground between persecution and a tolerance so full as to be dangerous, he asked two things of the English Roman Catholics. In the first place, they must be loyal. Most Catholic laymen, he held, did not accept the treasonous doctrines of the Jesuits, and he saw no reason why they could not be good subjects. Even those Catholics who had succumbed to Jesuit influence should not be entirely condemned, for he believed that the Roman faith in a peculiar fashion exposed the laity to deception by the priesthood. He asked the English Catholics, in the second place, to yield an outward conformity to the law by attending the services of the Church of England. Such forced and reluctant conformity is apt to appear to modern eyes as a worthless sham and an invitation to hypocrisy. Yet it had been asked by Elizabeth in England and by James in Scotland. Conformity was a token of loyalty and submission, the first step towards conversion. A conforming Catholic, said the King, was a tame duck that might attract the wild ones; and conformity would be a deterrence to that multiplication of Catholics which he dreaded. Nor did he desire to persecute the secular priests. He did not wish, he said, to separate their heads from their bodies, but rather to separate both their heads and bodies from Britain by transporting them beyond the seas where they might freely glut themselves upon their imagined gods. Hence his constant though futile reliance upon a policy of banishing priests from England. But the Jesuits, those envenomed wasps and firebrands of sedition, who made merchandise of the blood and crowns of princes — they were intolerable.

Although his approach to Catholicism was far from intransigent, and although he had every intention of treating the Catholics well, he permitted the fines payable by Catholics under the Elizabethan code to be collected in May of 1603. Already pressed for money, he was doubtless told by his advisers that these substantial sums could not be spared. Resentment among the Catholics, naturally intense, found expression in the foolish plot of a secular priest, William Watson, who had visited the King in Scotland and had obtained what he believed was a promise of toleration. Bitterly disillusioned by the collection of the fines, Watson and a few others conceived the childish notion of seizing the King and of holding him prisoner until he did their will. The plot came to nothing, for the Jesuits, getting wind of it and being at daggers' points with the secular priests, sought to ingratiate themselves with the King by exposing their co-religionists. James was not only grateful, but vastly impressed. Acting rather impulsively, he declared that the fines would no longer be collected; and for about a year and a half, until February 1605, the Catholics were relieved of these payments. Thus the King took a long step towards toleration.

At the same time he offered Rome a compromise which had been maturing in his mind for some years. We meet it first in England when, in a conversation between Kinloss and the Venetian ambassador in 1603, Kinloss remarked that the King was grateful to Clement VIII for withholding excommunication and that the English Catholics would not be persecuted. The ambassador replied that the Catholic world expected more than this; it hoped that James would restore England to the Roman Church. Kinloss answered that that was impossible. The King's bow, which in the past had had two strings, would henceforth have only one. But if Clement would summon an Oecumenical Council, superior to all doctrines, churches and princes, to end the distractions of Christendom, the King would support it warmly and would gladly abide by its decrees.

Of all the visions that floated in James's imagination, the most Olympian was that of uniting Catholics and Protestants in one universal Church. The ideal of Christian unity was far from dead in his time, and his proposals had some reason in them, at least in theory. He saw the political divisions among Protestants, with zealots like Andrew Melville threatening the crowns of conservative monarchs like himself. He saw the division between the Jesuits (who, he said, were nothing but Puritan-Papists) and the more moderate type of Catholic such as Clement VIII. Did not he and Clement have more in common with each other than either of them had with the extremists of their faiths? Was it not possible that the Pope, renouncing temporal sovereignty and the political methods of the Jesuits, and the King, renouncing the Puritans (oh happy renunciation!), might meet upon some middle ground of Christian compromise?

That compromise might be religious as well as political. James's views become clear when we remember the growth of Anglo-Catholicism and when we turn to a confession of faith which he wrote in 1609. He was, he said, a member of the Ancient, Catholic and Apostolic Church, a Catholic Christian, who took his stand upon the primitive Church before the year 500. Now the Anglicans used the year 500 as a rough dividing line between the era of primitive Christianity and the emergence of the Bishop of Rome as Pope; and hence the King's invitation to Rome was that the two Churches, assembling in a general council, should seek to reach some compromise in dogma and ritual by an examination of the Church in pre-papal times. 'We have always wished', he wrote, 'that some good course might be taken by a general council, lawfully called, whereby it might once for all be made manifest which is the doctrine of antiquity nearest succeeding to the primitive Church.' If Catholics and Protestants could agree upon that doctrine of antiquity, he would yield a happy conformity to it. But his hope of compromise was based upon the supposition that the Roman Church would willingly abandon a host of practices that had arisen since the year 500 and would model itself in some measure upon a church without a Papacy — which was most unlikely.

He was willing to accord the Pope a high place in a united Church. For were there not patriarchs above the bishops in primitive times? 'I would with all my heart give my consent that the Bishop of Rome should have the first seat. And for his temporal principality over the seigniory of Rome, I do not quarrel it neither; let him in God's name be *Primus Episcopus inter omnes Episcopos*, and *Princeps Episcoporum*; so it be no otherwise but as Peter was *Princeps Apostolorum*.' If the Pope would but 'quit his godhead and usurping over kings', James would acknowledge him as universal bishop with jurisdiction in spiritual affairs. But that the Popes should be temporal rulers of the Church, Christ's vicars, triple-crowned kings of heaven, earth and hell, judges of all the world, superiors of all emperors and kings, yea, supreme vice-gods, James utterly denied.

If a great church council was assembled, he declared that the Roman Church would not find him obstinate. He reverenced the works of St. Augustine and of St. Bernard more highly than he did those of Luther and Calvin. 'I acknowledge', he said, 'the Roman Church to be our mother church. I could wish from my heart that it would please God to make me one of the members of such a general Christian union in religion as laying wilfulness aside on both hands we might meet in the middest which is the centre and perfection of all things.'

He seems to have contemplated a Hampton Court Conference on a continental scale, and he did not doubt that he could supply the magic formula which would pave the way to concord. Who would preside over such an assembly? A pamphlet of the time, *The Triumphs of King James*, suggests an answer: 'We have a Constantine among us capable to preside as the other did in the Nicene Assemblies, the presence of whom is able to dispose of differences, to soften the sharpest, to restore and place peace and concord among all good Fathers, and to make them happily to finish such a design.' Who could this be but the British Solomon?[1]

Clement, however, was thinking along totally different lines, for James's secret negotiations with him before 1603 had led him to believe that the King's conversion was possible. He had wept for joy as Parsons read him passages from the *Basilikon Doron* in praise of virtue; and though closer perusal lowered his opinion of that work, he did not place it on the Index.[2] His hopes of James's conversion reached their height in 1605. Three years earlier, it will be remembered, he had sent letters to Scotland by Sir James Lindsay to whom the King had given instructions for a verbal answer calculated to continue the hopes that were entertained in Rome. But Lindsay's return was delayed by illness, and after Elizabeth's death he followed the court to England, thinking his instructions would be altered. Very strangely, however, the King told him to follow the instructions he already had. Perhaps James was careless; or perhaps he thought that his cloaked insinuations would now be construed as empty phrases of politeness. Arriving in Rome early in 1605 and doubtless exceeding his instructions, Lindsay gave Clement the impression that the King's conversion was imminent. The Pope rejoiced greatly, appointed a congregation of Cardinals to watch events in England, and offered prayers for the return of that country and its ruler to the Catholic fold.

The embarrassment and annoyance of the King were increased by the actions of his wife, whose Catholicism, an asset in Scotland, was proving to be awkward in England. Despite his entreaties she refused to partake of the Anglican Communion at her coronation, a refusal visible to all. Catholic lords and ladies besought her assistance in the campaign for toleration. She urged a Catholic marriage for Prince Henry, and sought to obtain office for her co-religionists, though the councillors turned gradually against her and refused suits brought in her name. With great indiscretion she corresponded with the Spanish Infanta, whom she asked to send two friars to Jerusalem, there to pray for the King and for herself. Sir Anthony Standen, James's ambassador in Italy, she employed as her private agent at Rome; but when he brought her sacred objects from the Pope, the King returned them to Clement, imprisoned Standen, and warned Anne's Chamberlain, Lord Sidney, to exercise great care in the selection of her household.

James, moreover, was meeting with other annoyances in his Catholic policy. He found that Clement, though wishing the English Catholics to remain quiet, would take few practical steps to lessen the threat of Catholic plots. There were suspicions that Ralegh and his follower, Lord Cobham, had conspired with the Count of Aremberg, ambassador from the Spanish Netherlands, to depose the King and to place Arabella Stuart upon the throne. The evidence against Ralegh was absurdly weak, but the King, who considered him dangerous, malcontent and warlike, a kind of English Bothwell, could strike with ruthless fury at the slightest danger to his dynasty. Hence Ralegh and Cobham were sentenced to death, a sentence commuted to imprisonment, though in James's peculiar fashion. Having great faith in confessions made at the point of death, he permitted Cobham and other conspirators to be brought upon the scaffold in expectation of instant execution; but just as the axe was about to fall, a messenger rushed from the crowd with a warrant in the King's own hand ordering that execution be stayed. It is pleasant to record that his scurvy trick brought him no new information. Ralegh, whose execution had been set for another date, was also reprieved.

After peace was made with Spain in 1604 there was talk of a marriage between Henry and a Spanish Princess, but James discovered to his astonishment that Spain was demanding the conversion of the Prince.

Above all, the English Catholics increased in numbers and boldness. 'It is hardly credible', runs a letter of the time, 'in what jollity they now live. They make no question to obtain at least a toleration if not an alteration of religion; in hope whereof many who before did dutifully frequent the Church are of late become recusants.' As a result of the King's excessive clemency, said Salisbury, priests went openly about the country, and the English clergy were in an uproar; while Archbishop Hutton complained that severity to Puritans was accompanied by leniency to Catholics who 'have grown mightily in number, favour and influence'.

The King found himself opposed by his councillors, by his bishops, and by his judges who enforced the anti-Catholic laws where they could.

As a result of these pin-pricks and irritations, he turned back to the Elizabethan code. At a meeting of the Council in February 1605, he inveighed against both Puritans and Roman Catholics. As to the latter, he declared, he was so far from favouring their superstitious religion that if he thought his son would tolerate it after his death, he would wish him buried before his eyes; and he commanded a rigorous execution of the laws against 'both the said extremes'. His first move towards toleration had ended in defeat.[3]

The Gunpowder Plot, which burst upon the country in November 1605, sprang directly from his broken promises to Roman Catholics. It was not the result of his latest pronouncement, however, for it appears to have originated in the mind of Robert Catesby as early as 1603. Catesby was a Catholic gentleman of much strength of character who had been active in many Catholic enterprises. His hopes of James were quickly shattered, as were those of his friend, Thomas Percy, who told him in great bitterness in 1603 that he planned to kill the King. Catesby asked Percy to save himself for a grander enterprise. By May 1604, Catesby had confided his plan to four men: his cousin, Thomas Winter; his intimate friend, John Wright; Percy; and Guy Fawkes, a soldier of great toughness of character brought over from the Netherlands. The plot was to place barrels of gunpowder under the Parliament house and, during the opening ceremonies of a new session, to blow up the King, the Queen, and Prince Henry, bishops, nobles, councillors, judges, knights and burgesses, all at one thunderclap and in one horrible and diabolical Doomsday. In May 1604, the conspirators set to work. They rented a house abutting upon the Parliament building and began digging a subterranean passage to a point directly under the chamber of the House of Lords. The digging, however, proved extremely difficult. Then in March 1605, the plotters discovered that the house next to theirs contained a cellar which ran directly under the Parliament building. This house they were able to rent. Breaching the wall on which the two houses rested, Guy Fawkes carried some twenty barrels of gunpowder into the cellar under the Parliament, placed iron bars upon them to increase the impact of the explosion, and laid over all a covering of faggots.

Meanwhile, the number of conspirators had been dangerously enlarged. This was made necessary by lack of funds, by the grinding physical labour, and by the wider plans of the enterprise. If advantage was to be taken of the confusion resulting from the explosion, a body of Catholics must be available to aid the plotters in seizing power. Accordingly it was decided to hold a great hunting-party at Dunchurch in Warwickshire at the time of the opening of Parliament. To this hunting-party the Catholic gentry of the midlands would be invited. The Princess Elizabeth, who was living nearby at Combe Abbey, could easily be made prisoner. Prince Charles was to be seized by Percy; while Prince Henry would be attending Parliament and would thus be destroyed. To facilitate these plans the number of conspirators was increased to thirteen, among them Francis Tresham, who had recently inherited a very considerable property.

Tresham betrayed the plot. The conspirators had been distressed to think that the Catholic peers attending Parliament would most certainly perish; and Tresham determined to warn his brother-in-law, Lord Monteagle. The manner in which the warning was given would indicate that Tresham told Monteagle of the plot and that their wish was to prevent it while allowing the conspirators an opportunity to escape. On October 26th, eleven days before the opening of Parliament, Monteagle, while at supper, was handed a note which had been given to one of his servants. 'They shall receive a terrible blow this Parliament,' so ran the message, 'and yet they shall not see who hurts them. The danger is past as soon as you have burned the letter.' Monteagle instructed his servant, Ward, to read the letter aloud, surely with the intent that Ward should warn the plotters, as he did, that the secret was out. Monteagle then took the letter to Salisbury, who was dining with Suffolk, Northampton, Nottingham and Worcester. They studied the letter and guessed it might refer to an explosion by gunpowder. But they were incredulous. They decided to postpone a search until the last possible moment, partly in fear of ridicule, partly in hope that the plot, if plot there was, could develop and be exposed more fully.

The King, away at his usual hunting, was not shown the letter until two days before Parliament opened. He agreed with his ministers that it might refer to a plot to blow up the Parliament house. He remembered, he said, that his father had died by gunpowder; and he ordered Suffolk to search the cellars and other parts of the building.

Once the plot was discovered, he assumed full credit for having solved it single-handed.

> And though the letter seemed most obscure,
> Like great Apollo's Delphian mystery,
> Our King a Joseph — Daniel — was most sure
> T'untwine the twist of its obscurity.

Early in 1606 a short tract appeared, *A Discourse of the Maner of the Discovery of this Late Intended Treason*, in which the King employed someone about the court to set down the royal version of what had taken place. According to this tract, James himself, with God's aid, discovered the plot and was thus the saviour first of his own sacred person and secondly of the whole realm besides. The tract slurs over the suspicions of Salisbury and Suffolk, merely saying that they referred the matter to the King since they knew 'his fortunate judgment in clearing and solving of obscure riddles and doubtful mysteries'. It states that the letter was handed to James without comment, that Salisbury discounted its importance, but that the King 'apprehended it deeplier', surmised that the blow was to come by gunpowder, and ordered the search under the Parliament house. Salisbury, the tract continues, was astonished at the royal perspicacity. He knew, of course, that the King was completely indifferent to peril, 'whereby he had drawn himself into many desperate dangers', and that his vigilance sprang from his care for the State and not for the safety of his own person. The author of this tract tells us clearly that he was an official; but the King, having supplied the material, adopted the tract as his own and placed it in his collected works without troubling to remove the preface that shows it was written by someone else.

Not until the afternoon of November 4th, the day before the opening of Parliament, did Suffolk carry out his search. In the cellar under the Parliament house he found the pile of faggots with Guy Fawkes standing guard. He asked to whom the faggots belonged. Fawkes answered Thomas Percy. The Catholic name of Percy struck Suffolk with alarm; and the King, on being informed, commanded a stricter search. At about eleven o'clock that night the powder was discovered and Fawkes arrested. The King had retired but was awakened and told at once. He praised God for

his deliverance, ordered that watch be kept, and gave instruction
that Fawkes be guarded with great care lest he attempt suicide.

In the trials and executions that followed, he took a fascinated
interest. He framed questions to be asked of the prisoners, commanded that torture be employed to extract information, and
pestered Sir Edward Coke, the government's prosecutor, with
instructions. At one time he thought he would like to interview
the prisoners, but the idea rather appalled him and he did not
carry it out.

The plot made a profound impression upon him, bringing many
reflections, some of them bright and triumphant, others dark and
terrible. His speech to Parliament on November 9th was an
astonishing exhibition of vanity and egotism. The principal
reason, it appeared, why all should rejoice was that he himself had
not been destroyed. After reminding Parliament that kings were
gods, adorned and furnished with some sparkles of divinity, he
compared his escape to that of Noah from the flood. Kings, like
the tallest trees, were exposed to the greatest dangers. Of the two
great perils of his life, the first had been the plot of Gowrie, a
baptism of blood, when his destruction would have brought ruin
to Scotland and, through future interest, to England as well. The
second was the Powder Plot, a roaring, a thundering sin of fire and
brimstone, from which God as by a miracle had delivered him,
and them, and the whole body of his estate. With triumphant
pride he spoke of the part he supposed himself to have played in
its discovery. Having seen the letter to Monteagle, he 'did upon
the instant interpret and apprehend some dark phrases therein'
to mean an explosion by gunpowder. Had he interpreted the
letter otherwise, the destruction of all of them would certainly
have followed. Yet he thanked God that if he had died by the
powder treason, he would not have passed away in an ale-house
or a stew, or in some such filthy place, but in good and honourable
company and in the performance of kingly functions.

He then touched upon a theme more worthy of a ruler. The
plot, he said, was the work of a few fanatics, not of the English
Catholics as a whole. It was true that no sect of the heathen,
though they worshipped the very Devil, preached, as did some
Catholics, that kings should be murdered and governments overthrown. Yet many Catholics were good men and loyal subjects,
and only the guilty should be punished.

But though he preened himself before the Lords and Commons in triumphant glory, the plot led to dark reflections. In his mind it was primarily an attempt to kill the King. When would the lightning strike again? His dread of assassination at Catholic hands, always with him in some degree, deepened and increased until it became a part of his very being. When we look back at the Powder Plot after three and a half centuries we are apt to forget the horror it inspired. 'The King is in terror,' wrote the Venetian ambassador, 'he does not appear nor does he take his meals in public as usual. He lives in the innermost rooms with only Scotsmen about him. The lords of the Council also are alarmed and confused by the plot itself and by the King's suspicions.' We catch a glimpse of the frightful anxiety of Lord Harington in whose custody the Princess Elizabeth was living at Combe Abbey. Nero and Caligula, he wrote, were but fly-killers compared to these horrible plotters; 'this poor lady hath not yet recovered the surprise and is very ill and troubled'. And the King, seeing the young Prince Charles, cried impulsively that he had been saved by his child's innocence.

The Catholic problem troubled him greatly. 'His Majesty on Sunday last,' wrote the Venetian ambassador early in 1606, 'while at chapel and afterwards at dinner, appeared very subdued and melancholy; he did not speak at all, though those in attendance gave him occasion. This is unlike his usual manner. After dinner, however, he broke out with great violence, "I have dispatches from Rome informing me that the Pope intends to excommunicate me; the Catholics threaten to dethrone me and to take my life unless I grant them liberty of conscience. I shall most certainly be obliged to stain my hands with their blood, though sorely against my will. But they shall not think they can frighten me, for they shall taste of the agony first. I do not know upon what they found this cursed doctrine that they are permitted to plot against the lives of princes. Sometimes I am amazed when I see that the Princes of Christendom are so blinded that they do not perceive the great injury inflicted on them by so false a doctrine." He continued for a whole hour to talk in a similar strain, and those in attendance praised and approved.'[4]

Yet he did not abandon his ideal of toleration for the Roman Catholic laity. When Parliament passed severer laws against Catholics, as was inevitable, those laws contained a device known as the oath of allegiance by which he hoped to salvage something of his former programme. A recusant might now be asked to take an oath, not only acknowledging James as lawful King and denying the power of the Pope to depose him, but swearing also that the doctrine that an excommunicated king might be lawfully deposed or murdered was an impious, heretical and damnable doctrine. Loyal Catholics, it was thought, would take the oath, while disloyal and incorrigible ones, those thoroughly Jesuited, would not; and in practice the oath made this distinction rather neatly. Relying upon its efficacy, the King soon drifted into a policy of banishment for priests and Jesuits and of leniency to Catholic laymen who would take the oath of allegiance.

This oath produced some unexpected results, for it involved the King in his famous pamphlet war against the Papacy. He claimed that the oath was a civil affair of the allegiance of his subjects to their prince. But it was viewed at Rome as a spiritual matter, a device to impose denial of the doctrine of papal supremacy and to create heresy and schism. And since the oath denounced as heretical a doctrine held by most Catholics, there was much justice in the Roman point of view. To take the oath, wrote Cardinal Bellarmine, was not so much to swear allegiance to the King as to abjure allegiance to the Vicar of Christ. Two briefs by Paul V, who had succeeded Clement in 1605 and was far less inclined to moderation, denounced the oath and forbade the English Catholics to take it. From this quarrel grew a great battle of print which penetrated every corner of Europe and produced scores of books and pamphlets on both sides. It dealt with every aspect of the relations of the Pope with temporal sovereigns. But it centred upon the pretensions of the Papacy in dealing with heretical princes: the power to depose them, to free their subjects from allegiance, to foster rebellion, invasion, even assassination as sanctions against rulers who had left the fold.[5]

The background of this pamphlet war is found not only in the oath of allegiance but in the King's fondness for theological discussion. He had surrounded himself with a group of Anglo-Catholic divines whose talk was of the primitive Church, of the early councils, and of patristic writings, and he loved to gather round him at table his favourite churchmen and a few selected laymen whose learning and dispositions were such as he could appreciate.

His learned repasts are well known. 'It was the custom of King

James', so wrote an observer of the court, 'to discourse during meals with the chaplain that said grace or other divines concerning some point of controversy in philosophy.' 'That King's table was a trial of wits', wrote Hacket. 'The reading of some books before him was very frequent while he was at his repast. Otherwise he collected knowledge by variety of questions which he carved out to the capacity of those about him. He was ever in chase after some disputable doubts which he would wind and turn about with the most stabbing objections that ever I heard, and was as pleasant and fellow-like in all those discourses as with his huntsmen in the field. Those who were ripe and weighty in their answers were ever designed for some place of credit or profit.' Again Hacket wrote: 'I have stood at his table often and have heard learned pieces read before him at his dinners.' On these occasions, to be sure, James sat enjoying his meal, while those who attended him stood reverently, and dinnerless, behind his chair. His knowledge was often paraded. His preoccupation was not with scholarship or letters in general but with the lore of the Anglo-Catholic proving the historicity of his Church. His method was contentious and polemical, for he argued by marshalling citations from the Scriptures and from theologians of all ages in support of his views. Yet while his learning lacked the spirit of impartial inquiry, it was far more worthy of praise than the ribald foolery of his normal conversation.

These learned discussions had an intimate bearing upon his writings in the Catholic controversy. His churchmen provided an audience to which he could expound his views. They supplied the flattering encouragement and sympathy he required, for he had to be intimate and familiar with those about him whether they were the keepers of his dogs or of his dioceses. From them he obtained the assistance of new ideas and approaches, of apt illustrations and pertinent material of all kinds. He selected those who pleased him to help him with his writing, to collect material and run down references, to ease the drudgery of composition, to criticize and polish his work. Such assistance could easily be rewarded and need not be acknowledged publicly. Not that he merely picked the brains of his divines. He did not lack for matter, and he devoted much time to his writing. But he did not possess the patience of the true scholar, and hence he accepted more assistance than is compatible with normal standards of authorship, appropriating the labour of others with untroubled ease and publishing books of which the thoughts were his but which he had not written. His accounts of how his works came into being are not to be trusted. Finally, as a result of these gatherings, a good many people were set to work writing books of their own, supplementing or defending the writings of the King.

In this wordy controversy James became ever more deeply engaged. He was always the passionate advocate of the cause of monarchy; and as the disputant eager to cross swords with distinguished opponents and the Defender of the Faith who valued that title — or so he said — more highly than the title of King, he felt impelled to engage in the quarrel. He told a favourite that 'the state of religion through all Christendom, almost wholly, under God, rests now upon my shoulders'. He drew the bishops after him and they in turn urged him to battle, while the shafts of his Catholic adversaries provoked him to angry replies. 'The King,' wrote the scholar, Isaac Casaubon, 'great and learned as he is, is now so entirely taken up with one sort of book that he keeps his own mind and the minds of all about him occupied exclusively on the one topic. Hardly a day passes on which some new pamphlet is not brought him, mostly written by Jesuits, on the martyrdom of Saint Garnet, the sufferings of the English Catholics, or matters of that description. All these things I have to read and give my opinion upon. Neither his private affairs nor public business interest his Majesty so deeply as do affairs of religion.' The King of England was becoming a doctor of divinity.

Casaubon's story is an illustration of what was taking place. While James was still living in Scotland he was impressed by the writings of this great continental scholar and invited him to visit Edinburgh, telling him that 'besides the care of the Church, it was his fixed resolve to encourage letters and learned men, as he considered them the strength, as well as the ornament, of kingdoms'. This invitation came to nothing at the time, but the death of Henry IV rendered Casaubon's position in France highly precarious, and the idea of visiting England began to take shape in his mind. When he arrived, James was delighted with him. He was admitted at once to the favoured circle about the King, and it became a rule that he stand behind the royal chair at dinner every Sunday. His opinion of James was high. 'I enjoy the favour of this excellent monarch, who is really more instructed than people give him credit for. He is a lover of learning to a degree beyond belief; his judgment of books, old and new, is such as would become a professed scholar, rather than a mighty prince.' But if Casaubon hoped that his kind reception in England and the modest income provided for him arose from James's love of learning and a desire to endow a famous scholar, he was speedily undeceived. Casaubon was to be enjoyed, though his attendance on the King dragged him from his books to some hunting-seat far away. Also he was to be used. He was a former Calvinist who, by his study of the primitive Church, found himself reaching essentially the same opinions as those held by the English King and bishops; and he came to England an Anglican ready made. There was much for him to do. He was asked to read Roman Catholic tracts and give his opinion on them; he was asked to criticize the writings of the bishops and to find Latin for the thoughts of the King; he was set writing himself. 'All my old studies have entirely ceased', he laments. Thus James did not endow a great scholar but degraded him from the pursuit of knowledge to the writing of tracts in the constant bickerings of the pamphlet war.

Four works of the King are concerned with this controversy; for brevity we may call them the *Apology*, the *Premonition*, *A Declaration Concerning Vorstius*, and *A Remonstrance for the Right of Kings*.[6]

As soon as Paul V denounced the English oath and Cardinal Bellarmine attacked it, James decided to reply, and the result was his *Apology*. His story of how the *Apology* was written is found in the preface to his collected works edited by Bishop Montagu. According to this tale he planned to sketch brief notes of a reply but to assign the task of answering, on the basis of these notes, to Bishop Bilson. Once embarked upon his notes of instruction, however, he became so absorbed that he continued writing until he had finished a book of a hundred and twelve printed pages. 'I know not how it came to pass,' explained Montagu, 'but the King's pen ran so fast that in the compass of six days his Majesty had accomplished that which he now calleth his *Apology*; which when my lord of Canterbury that then was [Bancroft], and my lord of Ely [Andrewes] had perused, being indeed delivered by his Majesty but as brief notes, and in the nature of a minute to be explicated by the Bishop in a larger volume; yet they thought it so sufficient an answer both to the Pope and Cardinal, as there needed no other; whereupon his Majesty was persuaded to give way to the coming of it forth.' And Montagu calls upon the reader to judge whether or not a divine hand had guided that of his Majesty.

This story is incredible. The *Apology* might possibly have been composed in six days, but the material could not have been prepared in that time. It appeared about the middle of February 1608; and it is important to note, first, that the Roman Catholic attacks which the *Apology* answered probably came to James's hands late in the autumn of 1607, and, secondly, that both the French and Venetian ambassadors reported that during December the King was leading a most secluded life in the country, appearing only for meals, and spending his time with his books. Boderie, the French ambassador, wrote that James 'was neither seen nor helped during this solitude except by the Master of the Chapel [James Montagu] and by a minister whom he called specially from the city to furnish him with memory and material'. The Venetian ambassador tells the same story. The King, he says, was living in almost complete retirement in the company of one man, a dean, very learned. At this time Montagu was master of Sidney Sussex College, Dean of Worcester, and Master of the Chapel. He was a logical person for James to summon to his aid. Hacket records that during the King's visits in the country at Royston and Newmarket, Montagu read to him the four tomes of Cardinal Bellarmine's controversies, and that James, while enjoying the fresh country air, 'weighed the objections and answers of that subtle author and sent often to the libraries in Cambridge for books to examine his quotations'. The true story of the *Apology* seems to be that the King shut himself up for some time, perhaps a month, with Montagu and another divine, whose identity is obscure, and that together they produced the *Apology*. James probably did most of the writing but had data assembled for him. Thus a list of errors to be found in Bellarmine's earlier books and a compilation of his slurring references to kingship are introduced irrelevantly as though supplied by someone other than the author.

The *Apology* is a dreary composition, save for a few clever hits. The King is not answering Bellarmine, he asserts, from vanity in disputing with a learned man, but because of his desire to save the innocent from the smooth Circe's charms and gilded pills of Bellarmine's sophistries. He contrasts the horror of the Powder

Plot with his early clemency to the English Roman Catholics. His magnanimity could not have been disturbed more maliciously by the Devil himself than by the Pope's denunciation of the oath of allegiance. He reiterates again and again that the oath is a matter of civil obedience to a temporal prince, that it touches no article of faith or point of salvation, that it names no saint or apostle (save in James's signature). The Scriptures, the councils, the early Fathers, all advocate subjection to temporal authority, and here the old round of Scriptural references to the divine right of kings is rehearsed once more. He turns to Bellarmine's jibe that no ruler but the King of England feared assassination at papal hands. He has, he declares, good reason to fear the Papacy. He shows how medieval emperors were 'tossed and turmoiled', how one stood barefoot in the snow, and how another 'was driven to lie on his belly and suffer the Pope to tread upon his neck'. The murder of the French King Henry III and the plots against Elizabeth are cited; yet he is in no panic. He has merely devised an oath to distinguish between loyal subjects and those fire-brands of hell, the powder plotters. Bellarmine had accused him of inserting hidden phrases in the oath to delude his Catholic subjects into heresy, as Julian the Apostate had placed idols in the pictures of the Emperor to be worshipped by the people. This James repudiates with scorn. He contrasts himself with Julian in a very puerile way, but concludes rather neatly that his oath was not to seduce the people to idolatry but to save them from it. His tone has become violent and passionate. Bellarmine is a liar and a madman.

A rumour persisted at court that James was writing a book against the Jesuit Parsons, and the King may perhaps have had this in mind. But no such book appeared. 'As for the book of Robert Parsons,' Boderie wrote in March 1608, 'to which I told you that the King was still replying, I believe that he will refrain; at least I know that his two principal councillors, the Earls of Northampton and Salisbury, have begged him to do so. They would have wished that he had not printed the other or at least not acknowledged it as his own.' Obviously the note of triumph at the English court as each new broadside was fired at the Papacy — one would think, wrote Boderie, that they were snatching the Pope from his throne — was not shared by those who had to conduct relations with foreign States. James might boast that he had given Bellarmine a sound thrashing, and Montagu might declare that while the King's adversaries were secure from bleeding by his Majesty's sword, they could not escape the blasting breath of his Majesty's books. Salisbury's point of view was very different, and we find Lake complaining bitterly in 1609 that the churchmen had persuaded the King to take up his pen once more.

Having issued five editions of the *Apology*, two English, two Latin, and one French, James awaited the result on tiptoe, and at the same time collected material in anticipation of the replies he expected to be made to his book. 'It is indeed true that the book will attract many replies,' wrote Boderie, 'but that will only put the author in his element, for this is the science of which he knows the most and in which he most delights.' He was not kept waiting long. He was attacked at once by both Bellarmine and Parsons with a wealth of learning, a keenness of argument, and a salvo of biting personalities that shocked him into the utmost irritation and anger. He was like a man who, expecting perhaps a scratch while pruning his roses, is suddenly stung by a scorpion. James was, in fact, a thin-skinned person, infinitely sensitive to what was said of him, and he was deeply wounded.

His first act was to ruin his Scottish Secretary, Elphinstone, Lord Balmerino, in the hope of shielding himself. In 1599, as we know, a letter implying the possibility of his conversion had been sent to Clement VIII, and this letter was now printed by Cardinal Bellarmine, who made great play of it as a revelation of the King's duplicity. Much dismayed at this blow to his reputation for honesty, James was filled with moral indignation. He summoned Balmerino to Royston, concealed witnesses where they could overhear what was said, and demanded an explanation. That he had written the letter Balmerino admitted, but declared that the King had known what was being done. Then at a second interview he confessed that he had drawn up the letter without the King's knowledge. 'We have drawn from him a confession', James wrote to the Council, 'that the said letters were written by him or by his privity, but how our hand was gotten to them, it is not yet clearly discovered.'

The King asked his councillors to examine Balmerino, begging them most earnestly, as they valued the good repute of their sovereign, to discover the truth and advise him how best to clear his name before the world. 'Though ye were born strangers to the country where this was done, yet are ye no strangers to the King thereof, and ye know if the King of Scotland prove a knave the King of England can never be an honest man; work therefore in this as having interest in your King's reputation.' Sending a list of questions to be asked of Balmerino, he wrote an angry letter to Salisbury who did not at first understand what was expected of him. There was nothing he would not do, James declared, to prove his innocence. 'I pray you to think that never thing in this world touched me nearlier than this doth. God knows I am and ever was upright and innocent. But how the world may know it I look to hear your advice after his examination.' The Council questioned Balmerino narrowly; and he confessed that the letter was presented to the King along with others as he was in haste to be away at his hunting and that he signed unsuspectingly. Balmerino swore before God and the angels that this was true.

Overjoyed to hear how councillors had vied with each other in defence of his innocence, the King thanked them effusively. God had blessed their endeavours through the confession of the culprit. 'For my part I may justly say that the name given me of James included a prophetical mystery of my fortune, for as a Jacob I wrestled with my arms upon the 5 of August for my life [the Gowrie Plot] and overcame; on the 5 of November I wrestled and overcame with my wit [the Gunpowder Plot], and now in a case ten times dear to me than my life, I mean my reputation, I have wrestled and overcome with my memory.' His meaning was that by a prodigious feat of memory he now recalled how on a certain morning nine years before, when in great haste to go hunting, he had signed the letter without knowing what he was doing. Balmerino was sent north for trial in a Scottish court where, upon secret promise of leniency, he repeated his confession. He was condemned to death but the sentence was not carried out; he lived in retirement until he died shortly after.[7]

It has been argued that the King was honest in this affair and that in truth he had been victimized by the zeal of his Catholic advisers in Scotland. But this is most unlikely, and it is all but certain that in Scotland he knew all about the letter, though he may have left himself some loophole for equivocal denial, and that in England he suggested to Balmerino what it would be expedient to confess.

Meanwhile he prohibited the sale of Bellarmine's book until his answer was ready, and to that he applied himself with great diligence. Believing that a crisis had arisen that called for prompt and drastic action, he summoned his bishops to his aid. Thus began a series of consultations lasting some nine months as he and the bishops planned their campaign, divided their labours, criticized each other's work, recast, corrected and polished the results. The reply to Bellarmine was a co-operative enterprise of King and bishops. James may have had in mind the procedure employed in translating the Authorized Version, and doubtless felt that the two undertakings were of commensurate significance. Four books were planned and produced within a year, the precursors of many to follow. Andrewes was commissioned to reply to Bellarmine;[8] Barlow to answer Parsons; John Barclay, a young poet trying to make his way in the world, to prepare an edition of his father's book, *De Potestate Papae*, the work of a Roman Catholic who argued that the Pope should abandon all pretensions to temporal power. The King's own part, the keystone of the arch, took a double form. He decided in the first place to re-issue the *Apology*. This was done, his opponents claimed, in order to remove the many inaccuracies they had pointed out; but James declared that he did nothing more than correct printers' errors, and the alterations in the re-issued *Apology* do not appear to be significant. Secondly, he added a *Monitory Preface* or *Premonition*, longer and more elaborate than the *Apology* itself. It was, indeed, the most ambitious work he ever attempted. Addressed to all the rulers of Christendom, it warned them in solemn terms of the dangers to their crowns and persons arising from the claims of the Papacy to temporal power.

Though he laboured valiantly on the *Premonition*, writing, as Lake reported, from morning till night, it is clear that he obtained a good deal of assistance. In the margin of his manuscript copy he jotted down the phrase, 'remember to speak with Barclay', who, as we have seen, was working on a closely related theme. Late in November 1608, the Venetian ambassador reported that the King had completed his book and had handed it to Andrewes to refute certain of Bellarmine's citations. Now a large portion of the *Premonition* was devoted to refutation, and hence Andrewes's assistance was probably great. Though James remained in the country he sent frequently to the bishops asking for data and, when some of them came to him on other business, he held a long conference with them on his reply to Rome. There was thus constant application to the clergy for aid as the work progressed.

Yet he had great difficulties with the final stages of the *Premonition*. It went to press early in 1609 but was held back in the printer's hands for many weeks while the King corrected and revised. 'This Prince continues always to write; yet he labours in undoing that which he has written.' Even so, when the book first appeared about April 1st, he was horrified to discover that it contained many errors. Quotations from the Fathers were found in many places to be inaccurate. A proclamation on April 7th declared that, owing to the rashness of the printer and the errors of the examiner, the book was 'uncorrected of some faults varying from the original copy which do not a little pervert the sense'. Copies already abroad were declared adulterate, and persons possessing them were ordered to return them to the King's printer from whom in due course they would receive new copies corrected to the truth. 'As soon as the book appeared,' wrote Boderie, 'many faults were discovered. The author, learning of these defects, became very angry and thought indeed of having the printer punished. His anger is now moderated, however, and his only thought is to correct what he judges at fault and to augment rather than diminish the work.' He returned the book to the bishops for correction. 'As four bishops are working on it,' wrote the Venetian ambassador, 'it should not be long ere it is reprinted', and then the court, delayed in London by the King's literary labours, could begin its annual progress. But James was not to be moved till corrections were complete. 'I hear', wrote Chamberlain, 'he is so wholly possessed and overcareful about his book that till that be finished to his liking he can brook no other sport or business.'

The book was being translated into Latin and French and this also caused delay, as the King wished the editions to appear together as far as possible. 'There is a little congregation of learned men', wrote Boderie with a touch of scorn, 'who assemble every day before the King to correct the translations that have been made. Before long it will appear in four languages.' Of translations James had learned some caution from his experience with his *Apology* which he had had translated into Latin and published before he discovered that the Latin was 'a little gross'. There were five Latin translators of the *Premonition*: Sir Henry Savile, the

learned though worldly warden of Merton College; Andrew
Downes, professor of Greek at Cambridge; Lionel Sharp, an
ambitious divine who had won the patronage of Northampton
and preached fawning sermons before the King; Thomas Wilson
and John Barclay. The *Premonition* finally appeared in May.
There were London editions in English, Latin and French; a
Latin edition was published in Amsterdam and a Dutch translation at Leyden. The Venetian ambassador spoke of an Italian
edition, but there does not appear to have been one.

Copies of the *Premonition*, sumptuously bound in velvet with arms
and corner-pieces of gold, stamped with the rose, the thistle, the
lion and the lilies, were presented to the Princes of Europe. But
alas! Their reception of the work was disappointingly cool. From
Protestant rulers the King had perfunctory thanks and a few words
of faint praise. But he had allowed the tone of his book to become
so violent and had included so many passages highly offensive to
Catholic Princes that Boderie thought they might recall their ambassadors from England; and their reception of the work was most
dubious. The King of Spain, the Archduke in the Netherlands,
and the Emperor curtly declined the copies presented to them.
James found himself engaged in ridiculous efforts to soften their
intransigence. Nor did his Catholic allies give him any great
satisfaction. Henry IV accepted the book but expressed ironical
doubt that it would achieve the desired results. In Venice, though
its circulation was banned, the Doge and Senate agreed reluctantly
to receive the copy sent to them from England; but upon its
presentation it was at once deposited unopened in the most secret
archives of the State where it has remained unmolested to the
present day.

There was unpleasantness of another kind in store for the author
of the *Premonition*. In its pages he had unwisely shown the world
that despite his arrogance and self-righteous vanity he was highly
sensitive to personal abuse. With great naivety he had compiled
from the works of his adversaries a list of the uncomplimentary
things they had said about him and was aghast that such affronts
should be offered to a king. Clearly he was wounded. Of this
weakness the German controversialist G. Scioppius (Schoppe)
now took full advantage, and his writings heaped malicious and
outrageous ridicule upon the King of England. His *Corona Regia*
(1615), cast in the form of a mock panegyric and amusingly

ascribed to Casaubon, was as scurrilous a book as ever found its way into print. How the King must have writhed! Suspecting that Erycius Puteanus, professor at Louvain, was the author, he demanded that Puteanus be punished, and when the Archduke demurred he threatened to sever diplomatic relations with the Netherlands. Finally persuaded that Puteanus had not written the *Corona Regia*, James allowed one of his ambassadors to attempt to kidnap Puteanus's printer and bring him to England in the hope of obtaining further information.[9]

Thus the controversy continued, its grave and far-reaching issues given tragic poignancy by the assassination of Henry IV in 1610. James used his position to reward and encourage those who came to his assistance, and not infrequently they took up their pens at his suggestion. The number of persons who were set writing in England — churchmen, professors, moderate or renegade Catholics, miscellaneous authors of many sorts — is indeed astonishing. One of the most interesting figures among them was Marcus Antonius de Dominis, Archbishop of Spalatro. James's dealings with this corpulent and avaricious prelate contain matter for high comedy; de Dominis left the Catholic Church, embraced Anglicanism, and received constant and lucrative favours from the King, only to horrify his patron in the end by returning to his earlier faith.

In 1609 the Dean of Exeter, Matthew Sutcliffe, suggested to the King that a college be built in Chelsea where Anglican writers should devote themselves to the refutation of Catholic polemics. Approving highly, James granted a charter of incorporation under the name of King James's College in Chelsea, laid the first stone, provided timber from Windsor Forest, and named a provost, seventeen fellows and two historians. But though building was begun and though Sutcliffe and the King made valiant efforts to raise funds, scarcely an eighth of the structure was ever completed. Even that portion erected soon fell into decay and the project ended in failure.[10]

One aspect of the controversy that touched James nearly was the accusation of Catholic writers that he was a heretic and no member of the true church; hence a series of attempts on his part, often half-comic, but at one point tragic enough, to vindicate his orthodoxy. In the first place he included, as we know, in the *Premonition* a confession of faith, and this he expanded in 1612 in a long open letter from Casaubon to the Cardinal du Perron in France. Du Perron had spoken of him in flattering terms but had declined to allow him his cherished title of 'Catholic'. James instructed Casaubon to reply, providing him with material in long conversations. 'The King', wrote Casaubon, 'is making use of my services as secretary, but the piece is his Majesty's. He has thought out this his response in a very exact way.'

A further vindication of royal orthodoxy was James's tract against Conradus Vorstius. Here the King was in alliance, not with the Anglo-Catholic clergy, but with Abbot, the Calvinist Archbishop. Vorstius was a follower of the Dutch theologian Arminius both in his professorship of divinity at Leyden and in his religious views, which, reacting against the doctrine of predestination, asserted man's free will and tended to limit the range of God's unconditional decrees. Vorstius raised questions of the eternity, the omnipotence and the essence of God; and there is no doubt that James was deeply shocked. Fancying himself a nursing father of the Church, he sprang to its defence against such heresy and schism, his anger brought to white heat by Vorstius's rash assertion that his views conformed to the doctrine of the Church of England. Upon Vorstius he turned with vindictive fury. Such a viper was worthy of the faggot, for he had entered the sacred cabinet of God and inquired into His inmost parts, flippantly treating of holy things as of a tale of Toby's dog. The King began to bombard the Dutch with demands that Vorstius be dismissed from his post, and eventually he had his way. But the Dutch acted slowly, and in 1612 James gave the world a proof of his noble rage by publishing his recent correspondence with Holland. Obtaining documents from Salisbury, and employing George Calvert, an able clerk of the Council, to arrange them for publication, the King supplied a running commentary and a flood of gross invective. With astonishing and blasphemous conceit he dedicated his tract 'To the Honour of Our Lord and Saviour Jesus Christ'.

On one occasion his defence of his orthodoxy assumed a more horrible form. While the dispute over Vorstius was raging, two men, Edward Wightman and Bartholomew Legate, were convicted of heresy in the church courts. With Legate the King held several conferences and, thinking to surprise him into an acknowledgment of Christ's divinity, suddenly asked him whether he did not pray. Legate answered that he had not prayed for seven years. 'The King in choler spurned at him with his foot. "Away, base fellow!" said he, "It shall never be said that one stayed in my presence that hath never prayed to our Saviour for seven whole years together." ' Abetted by Andrewes and other bishops, James determined that these men should die. The two wretches were burned at the stake, the last persons to be executed for heresy in England.[11]

A final work, *A Remonstrance for the Right of Kings*, published in 1615, completes the dreary catalogue of James's writings against Rome. It was an answer to the French Cardinal du Perron. The third estate in France in its meeting of 1614-15 had proposed an oath, to be taken by all churchmen and officials, which was very similar to the English oath of allegiance and was obviously inspired by it. The French clergy, however, successfully opposed its adoption. They selected Cardinal du Perron to set forth their views. His oration before the nobles and the third estate was printed; and James, seeing so open a challenge from such a distinguished source, decided to reply. He was here addressing the whole body of the French Catholic clergy, and he sought the assistance of the French Protestant, Pierre du Moulin, who was brought to England for some three months in 1615. A man of learning and high spirit, du Moulin was a voluminous author who had written a defence of the King in 1610 against the attacks of the Dominican Nicolas Coeffeteau. It is highly probable that James inspired this book, for du Moulin later remarked that he was well rewarded for his labour.

In the Paris edition of the *Remonstrance* du Moulin states clearly, repeating his assertion twice over, that the King had written the work in French and had requested him to polish its style. Du Moulin's autobiography, however, tells a different story. He was invited to come to England, he says, and had many audiences with the King as he stood behind the royal chair at dinner. His Majesty asked him to reply to the Cardinal du Perron. 'This', says du Moulin, 'I did. I presented the King with my response which is printed under his name.' Du Moulin then lists, with obvious satisfaction, the net profits of his expedition: a D.D. at Cambridge, a chain of gold for his brother, a prebend at Canterbury worth £200 a year 'avec une belle maison', a benefice in Wales worth an equal amount. Such rewards would not be given for polishing French style. It seems clear that James, after giving du Moulin instructions which were doubtless quite detailed, left him to do the writing and calmly appropriated the result which appeared in French, Latin and English and was later included in the King's collected works.

Although James loved theological controversy, he was not a good controversialist. He entered the lists to attack his opponents but expected them to treat him with the deference due to a King. His tantrums in print are as puerile as his tantrums in daily life, his disregard for the rights of others is just as complete, his vanity is worse.

Behind the dust clouds of these combats, the English Catholics fared far better than might have been anticipated. The anti-Catholic laws, though occasionally enforced with much injustice, remained for the most part in abeyance. But English hatred of Catholicism grew apace.

CHAPTER XIV

THE ROYAL PREROGATIVE

'THE state of monarchy', James told the House of Commons, 'is the supremest thing upon earth. For kings are not only God's lieutenants upon earth and sit upon God's throne, but even by God Himself they are called gods.' Like God 'they make and unmake their subjects. They have power of raising and casting down, of life and of death, judges over all, and yet accountable to none but God only. They have the power to exalt low things and abase high things and make of their subjects like men at the chess, a pawn to take a bishop or a knight, for to emperors or kings their subjects' bodies and goods are due for their defence and maintenance'. With passages such as this, often quoted from memory from the *Trew Law of Free Monarchies*, the King sought to enlighten the English House of Commons.

His only notion of Parliament came from the Parliament of Scotland, at this time, for all its age, a weak, primitive and feudal body. 'Their Parliaments hold but three days,' wrote Weldon, that caustic critic of the Scots, 'their statutes are but three lines.' In the *Trew Law* James had called Parliament the head court of the king and his vassals, and in England he declared, 'it is nothing else but the king's great council', assembled for changing old laws or making new, for punishing notorious offenders or for rewarding public virtue. This was the Parliament of Scotland, not of England, yet James presented it to the English Commons as a model. It contained, he said, none of their rash desire for liberty. About twenty days before it met, he continued, members were told that any laws they had in mind must be submitted to the King, and only such as he approved were offered to the Parliament. Should any member ask for other legislation, he was informed by the Chancellor that no such bill was allowed by the King, nor could he speak at all without the Chancellor's permission. Laws passed by Parliament, James added, became statutes only upon his ratification, 'and if there be anything that I dislike, they raise it out before'.

Parliament, then, was a court and an advisory council which

could debate nothing but what the King propounded to it. It was not a place 'for every rash and hair-brained fellow to propose new laws of his own invention'. A man wishing a new law, said James, should come with a halter round his neck, and if the law proved unacceptable the propounder should be hanged forthwith. The King would have no novelties, no laws to drive a wedge between prince and people, or to gratify private ends or personal grudges. Nor was Parliament a place for members to display their wit, to scoff at their prince, or to crack jests over each other's heads. Let them do so in an ale-house but not in the King's Council. 'Hold no Parliaments', James told his son, 'but for necessity of new laws, which would be but seldom.'[1]

How abysmal was his ignorance of the English House of Commons! It was, he discovered, a formidable body that challenged his prerogative; but he never fathomed the sources of its strength, the growing effectiveness of its procedure and leadership, or the inevitability of its advance to power.

Under the Tudors the House of Commons had grown from strength to strength. The reign of Henry VIII, who had taken the Commons into partnership and had broken with Rome through parliamentary action, had been a time of training in the art of legislation and a period of growing self-confidence. Manipulation of Parliament there had been, some of it very crude. But Henry had shown the Commons that they were worth manipulating and had paid them an outward respect that added to their self-esteem. In the reign of Elizabeth they were far more aggressive and independent. They assumed that theirs was a recognized place in the counsels of the nation, they were making their privileges realities, they were developing parliamentary procedures, they were more in the public eye. Against royal management they chafed, while Puritanism brought bold determination to follow conscience with small regard for the wishes of earthly kings. There was not one session in Elizabeth's long reign in which some dispute did not arise between her and the Commons. By 1603 they were ready, though they would have been the first to deny it, to make a successful bid for sovereignty in the decades ahead.

Elizabeth followed her father's lead, combining outward respect with quiet manipulation of the Commons. By her able and flattering speeches, her regal bearing and tactful management, her love-tricks with her Parliaments, she was able to obtain most of what she wanted without sacrificing points on which she knew she must stand firm. There was an essential harmony between her and the Commons. But she was forced to make concessions, to combine her gracious affability with tart reproof, to leave constitutional issues unsettled because she dared not bring them to the test. She played a part that no one else could play, and won temporary advantage at the cost of embarrassing her successor.

The rise of the Commons is inseparable from the rise of the country gentlemen, who as a class were becoming the most powerful and wealthy in the kingdom. Having acquired land from the dissolution of the monasteries, they continued to increase their possessions at the expense of both the nobles and the Crown, and, engaging in a hundred local activities, controlled the administration of rural England as justices of the peace. They were the great men of the countryside, accustomed to power, authority and respect. They found a seat in Parliament highly attractive, as a badge both of local distinction and of participation in national affairs, and as they crowded into the House of Commons they added greatly to its wealth, its talent and its social standing. It was said in 1628 that the Commons could buy out the Lords thrice over. Thus James had to deal with men who were not to be insulted or pushed about with impunity. Nor could such a body, so formidable, so aggressive, so self-confident, so loquacious, so sophisticated, be long excluded from a larger part in shaping the national destiny.

Small wonder that James found himself opposed in Parliament. Yet he was always puzzled. In 1604 he told the Commons he was sure they did not mean to be seditious, but they were rash, curious and over-busy. They appeared (God forgive them!) to be suspicious of him. 'In my government bypast in Scotland (where I ruled among men not of the best temper) I was heard not only as a King but, suppose I say it, as a counsellor. Contrary, here nothing but curiosity from morning to evening to find fault with my propositions. There all things warranted that came from me. Here all things suspected.' As time went by his anger grew, but he was still perplexed. 'We are sorry of our ill fortune in this country', he wrote bitterly in 1610. 'We came out of Scotland with an unsullied reputation and without any grudge in the people's hearts but for want of us. Wherein we have misbehaved ourself here we know not, nor we can never yet learn. Yet our fame and actions have been tossed like tennis balls amongst them, and all that spite and malice might do to disgrace and infame us hath been used. To be short, this Lower House by their behaviour have perilled and annoyed our health, wounded our reputation, emboldened all ill-natured people, encroached upon many of our privileges and plagued our purse with their delays.' Without a doubt he meant what he said.[2]

The fissure between King and Commons may be seen in their divergent approach to grievances. James's government brought abuses which the Commons were not slow to point out, and redress of grievances became their constant theme. But grievances meant more than new abuses. Things that had been suffered under Elizabeth now appeared outmoded and intolerable, and the time seemed ripe for their reform. Often they involved a diminution of royal authority or revenue, and thus grievances merged with a demand for fundamental change, change that would shift power from Crown to Parliament.

To James the demand for redress of grievances was highly irritating. He was a pious King, the father of his people, willing to take great pains in hearing cases and in redressing wrongs. How could a kingdom with a King like James be such an un-weeded garden? Hence he considered the furore about grievances as a personal affront, not to be attributed to flaws in government or in himself, but to the busy and turbulent nature of the Commons. In seeking redress, he informed them in 1610, they must not tell him how to govern, for that was his craft, and to meddle with that would be to lessen him. He had ruled in Scotland, he said, for thirty-six years and in England for seven more; he was an old King who must not be taught his office. Nor should the rights and powers he had received from his forebears be made into grievances. 'All novelties are dangerous, and therefore I would be loath to be quarrelled in my ancient rights and possessions, for that were to judge me unworthy of that which my predecessors left me.' The Commons' demand for redress of grievances, more-over, should not widen into attacks upon institutions established by law, such as the Court of High Commission, or, most repre-hensible of all, upon the prerogative itself, for, as it was blasphemy to dispute what God might do, so it was sedition in subjects to debate what a king might do in the height of his power. The redress of grievances must be left wholly to the ruler. It angered

James to find that the Commons asked for the same things over and over, though they had been denied already and were certain to be refused once more.

Yet upon himself he placed no restraint. He interfered constantly in the work of the Commons, sending them commands and instructions and making them far too many speeches. As a result he not only irritated them greatly but disturbed those avenues of influence that were still open to the Crown. It was Salisbury who had managed the government's business in Parliament during the last years of Elizabeth and who continued to do so in the reign of James, though his peerage removed him from the House of Commons. Versed in tactics and methods of influence, he was a skilful parliamentarian; but he was frustrated by the inept meddling of the King, by his tantrums and complaints, and by his misguided instructions, detailed and disturbing.

When James's first Parliament assembled in March 1604, a dispute arose at once between King and Commons. This was the famous case of Goodwin v. Fortescue and, though it was not so violent a clash as is often supposed, it augured ill for the future, for James at once broke every rule that caution should have dictated.

In the proclamation summoning Parliament the King had commanded that all returns should be sent to Chancery where, if irregularities were discovered, a return should be rejected and a new writ issued for a second election. This function of the Chancery was not an innovation, but the Commons, eager to obtain control of election disputes, had protested against it in 1586 and were all but certain to resist it now. A test case speedily arose in the election for Buckinghamshire where the rival candidates were Sir Francis Goodwin and Sir John Fortescue. Goodwin secured the larger number of voices and was returned. But Fortescue, a councillor, had the backing of the government. Chancery found a technical flaw in Goodwin's election, a new writ was issued, and Fortescue returned. The Commons, however, ignored this action, found Goodwin duly elected, and instructed him to take his seat. Thus the issue was clearly drawn.

James interfered at once. He told the Commons that the case touched his honour and asked them to confer with the House of Lords. But the Commons had already declined conference with the Lords, and the King's interference, so sudden and unexpected, placed them in a quandary. They asked for an audience and explained their case. The King, somewhat startled, compared their complaints to the murmuring of the people of Israel and said he would be loath to alter his tune to grief and contestation. He was sure they did not mean to offend; but since they derived their privileges from him, he expected that privilege should not be used against him. Nor did he like their precedents which were drawn, he said, from the reigns of minors, tyrants, women and foolish kings. He asked them to confer with the judges and then report their decision to the Privy Council. There was a touch of contempt in his words and a total ignorance of parliamentary procedure.

To his annoyance the Commons did not follow his suggestion but debated the origin of privilege and sent him a long document justifying their position. In reply he declared by the faith he bore to God that no prince was ever more desirous than he to maintain their privileges; but he was now distracted by many arguments and he therefore commanded as an absolute ruler that the conference with the judges take place in the presence of the King and Council. As this message was read, there was amazement and silence in the Commons. At length a member declared: 'The Prince's command is like a thunderbolt, his command upon our allegiance like the roaring of a lion. To his command there is no contradiction.' Thus James obtained a conference but only by the use of heavy artillery.

The conference went well. The King presided, surrounded by his judges and councillors. Bacon, representing the Commons, spoke with tact and humility. He found James's voice the voice of God in man (he would not say the voice of God because he was no flatterer). The Commons, he declared, were ready to reconsider their decision, a thing they had done for no former ruler. The King replied he would not press his prerogative against his subjects but would allow free rein to his sweet and kindly nature by confirming their privileges. He suggested a compromise: that the election of both Goodwin and Fortescue be voided and a new writ issued. This the Commons accepted after some hesitation; and James remarked that though the Devil had cast in this bone of contention, God had turned it to good, for he had seen the loyalty of his people and they had seen his grace and bounty. Thus the dispute was ended amicably, and both Salisbury and the King were delighted with the royal graciousness and wisdom. But the Commons had won, for henceforth they settled election disputes without challenge. James had lost much and gained nothing.

The Commons turned to grievances — purveyance, wardship, the cause of the Puritan ministers — and at the end of the session they drew up a famous Apology. It was a bold declaration of right, a lecture to a foreign king upon the constitution of his new kingdom. It asserted that parliamentary privileges were sacred, that they had been grossly invaded, that they were the rights and inheritance of the Commons — no less than their lands and goods — and did not spring from royal grace. Surveying the events of the session, the Commons justified their actions at every turn. They asked that the Puritan ministers be reinstated and added a ringing declaration that the King could not alter religious laws without the consent of Parliament.

James answered in a long scolding speech. He would not give thanks, he said, where no thanks were due. He was sure there were many dutiful subjects in Parliament, but the pertness and boldness of some idle heads had cried down honest men. There were common babblers with an itch to be ever talking, ready to burn the temple of Ephesus for a little notoriety. There were those of a new religion who wished to build Jerusalem over-night and would not wait till Doomsday. 'I can not enough wonder that in three days after the beginning of the Parliament, men should go contrary to their oaths of supremacy. I did not think the Puritans had been so great, so proud, or so dominant in your House. You have done many things rashly. I say not you meant disloyally. Only I wish you had kept a better form. I like form as well as matter. It shows respect and I expect it, being a King as well born (suppose I say it) as any of my progenitors. I wish you would use your liberty with more modesty in time to come.' Concluding with a more gracious word, he asked them to believe that he loved his people and had a care to ease their burdens; and so the session ended.[3]

James's great objective in his first Parliament, apart from obtaining funds, was to promote a closer union between England and Scotland. To hope and plan for a union of the Crowns he had been taught from childhood; he had meditated long upon what such a union might mean, and had attempted to prepare Scotland for it. Ideals and ambitions went hand in hand, for unity as an abstract principle appealed to him strongly. He went out of his way to remind the English Commons that Henry VII had united the houses of York and Lancaster and that he, as Henry's descendant, perpetuated that union. Of Henry he spoke often as a symbol of union between England and Scotland, for Henry had arranged the Scottish marriage upon which Stuart claims to England rested. Henry had believed himself a descendant of King Arthur, proclaimed by legend the ruler of all Britain; he had given the name of Arthur to his son. James also, before 1603, had called himself a new Arthur about to unite the kingdoms. He named his son Henry, he appropriated Henry's Chapel in the Abbey as a burial place for Stuart royalty, and he himself was laid to rest in the tomb of Henry of Lancaster and Elizabeth of York.[4]

Now that the union of the Crowns was so happily consummated, he would establish a larger union, complete, inseparable and lasting. There should be one king, one faith, one language; one law, one parliament, one people alike in manners and allegiance. The names of England and Scotland should disappear in the name of Britain, the Borders should be erased and become the middle shires. English and Scot should 'join and coalesce together in a sincere and perfect union, as two twins bred in one belly, to love one another as no more two but one estate'. And the King would be alike to both in utter impartiality. But that he also entertained less lofty motives is clear from a letter to the Scottish Council. Union, he wrote, would augment the grandeur and strength of his estate, it would solidify the allegiance owed by his subjects to him and to his posterity for ever, it would increase his fame and reputation throughout the world. Only as an afterthought did he consider the benefits — the strength, peace and security — that would accrue to his people.

He considered himself the instrument through which God was promoting the union of the two kingdoms. To the English Parliament he declared that union with Scotland was a blessing 'which God hath in my person bestowed upon you. Hath He not made us all in one island, compassed with one sea and of itself by nature indivisible? And now in the end and fullness of time He hath united the right and title of both kingdoms in my person, alike lineally descended of both the Crowns, whereby it is now become like a little world within itself, being intrenched and fortified round about with a natural and yet admirable strong pond or ditch. What God hath conjoined let no man separate. I am the husband and all the whole isle is my lawful wife; I am the head and it is my body; I am the shepherd and it is my flock. I hope therefore that no man will think that I, a Christian King under the Gospel, should be a polygamist and husband to two wives; that I being the head should have a divided or monstrous body or that being the shepherd to so fair a flock should have my flock parted in two. And as God hath made Scotland the one half of this isle to enjoy my birth and the first and most unperfect half of my life and you here to enjoy the perfect and last half thereof, so can I not think that any would cut asunder the one half of me from the other'.

Upon those who opposed the union James turned with a kind of fury. Such persons were disloyal to the King and wicked in the sight of God. They were either fools or knaves, who deserved to be buried in the bottom of the sea. He painted the choice before the Commons in a vivid passage: 'Let not yourselves be transported with the curiosity of a few giddy heads, for it is in you now to make the choice, either by embracing that which God hath cast in your mouths, to procure the prosperity and increase of greatness to me and mine, you and yours, and by the taking away of that partition wall which already by God's providence in my blood is rent asunder, to establish my throne and your body politic in a perpetual and flourishing peace; or else, contemning God's benefit, to spit and blaspheme in His face by preferring war to peace, trouble to quietness, hatred to love, weakness to strength, and division to union, to sow the seed of discord to all our posterities, to dishonour your King, and to make both you and me a proverb of reproach in the mouths of all strangers and all enemies to this nation.'

He assumed at first that, since union was already established in his person, Parliament need only recognize an accomplished fact; and he wrote to the Scottish Council as though union could be completed in a few days' time, although he understood, he added, that in England Parliaments lasted for a month at the least. But he realized shortly that union would be a more protracted matter. In April 1604, he asked the Commons to take two preliminary steps, first to allow him to assume the title of King of Great Britain, and secondly to appoint commissioners to treat with commissioners from Scotland in preparing other measures. But the Commons refused to alter the name of England, that old and famous name under which they had prospered. To cross the rose with the thistle might well produce a monster. The ancient Britons came in for abuse as savages and worshippers of devils, and James's cause was not aided by a whimsical member, Sir William Maurice, who urged repeatedly that the King assume the title of emperor. The Commons feared that an alteration in the name of the kingdom might abrogate the laws and necessitate their re-enactment, an argument in which the judges concurred despite great pressure from the King. Nor would the laws passed in the future by the English Parliament be binding on all Britain. The Commons therefore resolved that the change in name should wait until the union had been perfected. James appeared to accept this defeat, announced that he would not alter his style, and asked merely for commissioners. But again there was hesitation, and the commissioners were voted only with obvious reluctance. At the end of the session the King berated the Commons soundly. Despite opposition, he told them, he would sing no palinode. 'I am not ashamed of my project, neither have I deferred it (I be to deal plainly) out of a liking of the judges' reasons or yours.'

In announcing his determination to further the union with Scotland he was very much in earnest. In October 1604, despite his pledge to the Commons, he assumed by proclamation the title of King of Great Britain. It was the name, he said, that God had given to the island. One of the State papers, reflecting very likely the opinion of the Council, dissuaded this step as provocative and injudicious, a mere shadow without substance. But James was not to be moved. He was determined, wrote the Venetian ambassador, 'to call himself King of Great Britain and like that famous and ancient King Arthur to embrace under one name the whole circuit' of the island. In assuming the title by proclamation rather than by statute he was following the advice of Bacon who argued that the new style could thus be used in letters, treaties, proclamations, dedications and coinage, though not in 'any legal proceeding, instrument or assurance'. In this way the King obtained what he wanted, or part of it, though at the cost of offending the Commons and of jeopardizing the union itself. The new name was far from popular. A 'cruel pasquil' predicting

James's destruction for assuming the 'name of Britain' appeared in 1605. The King thought it might have been written by Guy Fawkes, though surely Guy Fawkes had other matters on his mind. In Scotland the new style was even less popular than in England, for, while the English Parliament continued to employ the old style, the Scots Parliament was forced to use the new. As in many other matters, England resisted James's will and half escaped it, but Scotland which could not resist felt the full impact of his despotism.

During the next few years he advanced the union in various ways without seeking Parliament's approval. He thought of making Bancroft primate of Great Britain. Councillors were asked to consider the feasibility of reducing the laws of the two kingdoms to a single system, and to weigh the impact that might be expected from free trade. Progress was made towards a common coinage; the College of Arms devised a new flag by imposing the cross of St. George upon that of St. Andrew; the pacification of the Borders went on apace.[5]

When the King was intent upon some objective, a little literature was apt to spring into existence espousing his views. Sermons, pamphlets and poems now sang the praises of union, reflecting with much accuracy the royal mood of triumphant achievement. One of the first compositions of this kind was by John Gordon, a learned Scot long resident in France and once the servant of Mary Stuart. He was now summoned to England, given lands in Scotland, and made Dean of Sarum, whereupon he hastily took holy orders at the age of fifty-eight. In a florid sermon preached upon the occasion of James's assumption of his new title, Gordon returned thanks to God for the union of the realms, compared the King to Solomon, and besought him to end the diversities of religion within his dominions. And many other writers, seeing the rich harvest obtained by Gordon, caught up the theme.[6] The poet Samuel Daniel thus addressed his country:

> Now thou are all Great Britain, and no more,
> No Scot, nor English, nor no debates;
> No Borders but the Ocean and the Shore,
> No wall of Adrian serves to separate
> Our mutual Love, nor our obedience,
> All subjects now to one imperial Prince.

The Scotsman Robert Pont praised union in Latin verse, though somewhat damaging the effect of his latinity by concluding with a painful English pun:

> Sith God hath made all under one,
> Let Albion now all-be-one.

The King had intended to preside when the English and Scottish commissioners assembled in London in October 1604, and though hunting intervened he kept in close touch with the debates. About a month earlier he had set down the points on which discussion was to focus: the union of the kingdoms in a single monarchy, inseparable and for ever, and the reduction of the two Parliaments to one. Perhaps Salisbury convinced him that such measures were too heroic. At least they do not appear in the deliberations of the commissioners who from the first debated four things: repeal of hostile laws, that is, laws of each nation aimed at the other; mutual naturalization; free trade between the kingdoms; and improvement of Border justice, chiefly by extradition of criminals. These points became the government programme and were offered to the Commons as a basis for legislation in 1606 and 1607.

In the Commons the hostile laws were easily repealed, but the rest of the programme met with much opposition. Free trade was completely refused. The English merchants, fearing the competition of the Scots and their admission to English trading companies, protested violently, as did also English shipowners who declared that a Scots sailor could live on oysters while an English sailor demanded beer and roast beef. The recommendations of the government concerning Border trials were whittled down to nothing. The Commons believed, no doubt correctly, that an Englishman extradited for trial in Scotland would be given short shrift by a Scots jury, and extradition was refused.

The debates on the naturalization of the Scots as English citizens were more extended and more interesting. The commissioners, following the English judges, had made a distinction between persons born before James's accession to the English throne (the ante-nati) and those born afterwards (the post-nati). The Scottish ante-nati, of course, were aliens in England and the commissioners recommended that they be naturalized by statute. But the Scottish post-nati, since they were born in the King's allegiance, were held to be naturalized already by common law throughout all his dominions. Hence they were capable of holding office in England, a right which the commissioners denied to the ante-nati. But James here raised an objection. He was willing to debar the ante-nati from office and offered a solemn pledge that he would give them no appointments, yet demanded that this self-denying ordinance be accompanied by a clause reserving his prerogative to do as he pleased, a clause that made bad reading in the House of Commons.

As the Commons debated the naturalization of the Scots they found themselves differing from the commissioners in two important respects. They refused to accept the ruling that the post-nati were naturalized by common law. The precedents of the judges, it was thought, were drawn from ancient times when allegiance was strong and nationalism weak. 'Unions of kingdoms are not made by law,' said Sir Edwin Sandys, a great man in the Commons, 'but by act express', and naturalization should not be conferred so easily by the chance results of royal marriages. Nor would the Commons accept the view that the post-nati were capable of holding all offices in England. Hard things were said of the Scots. England was pictured as a rich pasture about to be overrun by herds of lean and hungry cattle; and Sir Christopher Pigott, almost with impunity, despite royal rage, poured forth a torrent of abuse: the Scots were proud, beggarly, quarrelsome and untrustworthy.

Hence the Commons came to the conclusion that no distinction should be made between ante- and post-nati; neither were naturalized as things stood and neither should have the full rights of English citizens. But what should be allowed and what withheld? How could the prerogative be bound where Parliament imposed restrictions? The difficulties of these questions were endless. And how could the Scots, having received benefits in England, be held to the payment of English taxes and to the fulfilment of English service? There was but one way — to make them subject to English law. This could be done only by uniting the kingdoms in one legal system, and that in turn could not be permanent unless there was one Parliament. One Parliament was necessary to prevent the laws from diverging, and one Chancellor and one Great Seal to keep them equally enforced. Thus the Commons came to believe in what they called a perfect union, one law and one Parliament for both countries. The Scots would then be subject to all the duties of Englishmen and could share in all their benefits. In these debates on the perfect union the Commons were not unstatesmanlike and they were not ungenerous. But the government was now committed to the lesser course, to the imperfect and partial union of the commissioners; and the King now argued that the perfect union was a work of time, that courtship must precede marriage, and that the two parties must not be put to bed on such short acquaintance. Angrily he told the Commons that those who advocated the perfect union did so only with their lips and not in their hearts. The Commons, however, were implacable. A deadlock ensued and Parliament concluded nothing, to the King's great annoyance.

Instead of accepting this rebuff and waiting for better times, as he should have done, he fell back upon the prerogative and upon the law. He was particularly incensed at the Commons' refusal to permit the extradition of criminals in trials along the Borders, for, from the moment of his accession, he had sought means to pacify those peccant parts of his kingdoms. Five Scottish and five English commissioners had been appointed to punish Border crimes and had been given a small force of mounted police. Ruthless their methods had been — one hears of a poor lad, Tom Armstrong, hanged on mere suspicion of stealing a nag, though the owner testified to Tom's innocence — but conditions had been improved. In 1607 James boasted that the Borders, once desolate, lawless and bloody, 'are now become the navel or umbilic of both kingdoms, planted and peopled with civility and riches. Their churches begin to be planted, their doors stand now open, they fear neither robbery nor spoiling. They now live every man peacefully under his own fig-tree'. For a continuance of this happy state the King believed that extradition was essential. In 1610 he obtained from the English Parliament an Act by which the practice was permitted, but the Act was conditional upon other legislation that was never passed; and hence in 1612 he attempted to employ extradition by prerogative. Salisbury pointed out that such action would be illegal. Of that, James answered tartly, he was fully aware, 'but the necessity of his service required it'. His use of high prerogative, he added, might be questioned when employed in a noisome or oppressive design, but not when his object was the welfare of his people. His had been the honour to reduce those barbarous parts to some civility and his efforts would not relax. It was Salisbury's duty to find a solution, for extradition 'must be'. Yet it does not seem to have been used, and in unhappy fact there was some degeneration in the state of the Borders during the latter years of the reign.[7]

To obtain the naturalization of the Scots in England, which the Commons had refused, James turned to the English judges who had held that the post-nati were naturalized by common law throughout his dominions. A collusive suit involving an infant, Robert Colvill, born in Edinburgh in 1605, was made to turn upon whether the child was an alien or a citizen of England; and the judges found Colvill a natural subject of the English King. Thus James had his way.

But he was discovering, to his anger and astonishment, that the judges were not always on his side and that a judge had arisen who challenged his prerogative in a fundamental way. This was Sir Edward Coke, Chief Justice of the Common Pleas since 1605. Coke loved the common law and became its champion, not only against the prerogative courts, with which the Common Law courts had long been at feud, but against a King whose views clashed so often with its basic principles. In defence of the common law Coke was the most obstinate, opinionated and difficult of men. He might fall upon his knees before the wrath of the King but even in that position he clung tenaciously to his opinions.

To the common law James was a stranger. His ideas of law came from his theory of divine right, from the kingly judges of the Old Testament, and from the Roman law of Scotland. Kings made the law; and a king, having made the law, could unmake it or alter it at his pleasure. A law was an expression of the king's will. Hence the king was the supreme interpreter of the law, the great judge from whom inferior judges drew their authority and competence. 'Kings are properly judges, and judgment properly belongs to them from God; for kings sit in the throne of God and thence all judgment is derived.' Other judges were but the deputies of the king, drawing their power from him as he drew his from God. And the king could if he pleased sit and judge in any court and call its judgments in question.

The power and position of the judges were distinctly limited. They were not to usurp the king's function of making law. They were not to encroach upon the prerogative but to defend it. They should not deal with it without first consulting the king, and they should silence pert lawyers who touched upon it in argument. 'That which concerns the mystery of the king's power is not lawful to be disputed; for that is to wade into the weakness of princes and to take away the mystical reverence that belongs unto them that sit in the throne of God. It is atheism and blasphemy to dispute what God can do, so it is presumption in a subject to dispute what a king can do, or say that a king cannot do this or that.' Above all, the judges should obey the king. When in 1608 they reminded James that they had an oath of office to fulfil, he answered hotly that 'the King is their judge and it is his part to interpret their oaths, and not they, for in disobeying his commandment they deserved to be hanged'. He pretended to believe that the common law gave ample scope for his prerogative. A king of England who despised the common law, he told Parliament, was neglecting his own Crown, for no law was more favourable for a king or extended his prerogative further; but he must have been speaking either in ignorance or with insincerity.[8]

His first quarrel with Coke concerned a dispute between the Common Law courts and the courts of the Church. There was an ancient writ, the writ of prohibition, by which the judges of the common law exercised considerable control over the ecclesiastical courts, for the writ halted proceedings in any court of the Church until the judges were satisfied that the matter in dispute fell within the jurisdiction of that court. Hoping to free the church courts from this control, Archbishop Bancroft appealed to the King in 1605. He argued that all judicial authority began in the Crown and flowed thence in two great streams, the temporal jurisdiction to the Common Law courts, the spiritual to the courts of the Church. Hence if a dispute arose between the two jurisdictions, the king might intervene, a view which James heartily endorsed. But Coke replied that the writ of prohibition was part of the common law and as such could not be altered by the king, for only Parliament could change the law. Thus Bancroft appealed to the King and Coke appealed to Parliament.

The question of prohibitions arose again in 1607. In that year a Puritan lawyer, Nicholas Fuller, already in the King's ill graces, sought writs of prohibition against the Court of High Commission. His language denouncing the court was so intemperate that the High Commission cited him to appear before it. James boiled with rage. He swore that if Fuller escaped punishment by the High Commission he would summon him before the Council and censure him in person. 'I pray you,' he wrote to Salisbury, 'forget not Fuller's matter that the ecclesiastical commission may not be suffered to sink, besides the evil deserts of the villain. For this I dare prophesy unto you, that whensoever the ecclesiastical dignity shall be turned in contempt and begin to evanish in this kingdom, the kings thereof shall not long prosper in their government and the monarchy shall fall in ruin, which I pray God I may not live to see.' The judges, though inclined at first to defend Fuller by a writ of prohibition, decided on technical grounds to leave him to the mercy of the High Commission. Yet the King was suspicious. The judges, he said with an oath, had acted wisely, 'for he was resolved if they had done otherwise he would have committed them'. And he added that he would curb their liberty to issue prohibitions at will. [9]

Yet the flow of prohibitions continued, some against the Council of Wales, at which James was greatly angered. Here was a brazen attempt to rob him and the Prince of their prerogative. In 1608 and 1609, therefore, he summoned a series of conferences in which the whole matter was argued at length. He sat in his chair of state, flanked by his councillors and bishops, while the judges stood deferentially before him. He seems to have hoped, as at Hampton Court, to reach a quick decision, but the conferences dragged on until he grew weary of legal wrangling. In a session in November 1608, the royal wrath exploded. Coke had said brusquely that the arguments of the churchmen counted for nothing, that the law remained the law, and that only the judges could expound it. James answered that this was quite wrong; the supreme judge was the King and it was for him to decide between rival jurisdictions; yet he would defend the common law. On the contrary, said Coke, the common law defended the King. James trembled with anger. Coke's words, he shouted, were those of a traitor. The King protected the law, not the law the King, for the King was protected by none save God. 'His Majesty fell into that high indignation as the like was never known in him, looking and speaking fiercely with bended fist, offering to strike him, which the Lord Coke perceiving fell flat on all fours, humbly beseeching his Majesty to take compassion on him and to pardon him if he through zeal had gone beyond his duty and allegiance.'

There were other clashes between Coke and the King. And Coke, throwing several scenes into one narrative, described them in words which have become famous. It was alleged, he wrote, that the King could decide cases in person. 'To which it was answered by me that the King in his own person cannot adjudge any case, but this ought to be determined and adjudged in some court of justice. Then the King said he thought the law was founded upon reason, and that he and others had reason as well as the judges.' Coke answered that though the King had great endowments of nature, yet he was not learned in the laws of England. 'Causes are not to be decided by natural reason but by the artificial reason and judgment of law, which law is an act that requires long study and experience; and that the law was the golden metwand and measure to try the causes of the subjects and which protected his Majesty in safety and peace. With which the King was greatly offended and said that then he should be under the law, which was treason to affirm; to which I said that Bracton saith that the king should not be under man but under God and the law.' These were brave words and Coke was the man to speak them. Yet he probably did not emerge as triumphantly as his own account would imply.

No royal pronouncement followed these conferences, and prohibitions continued. We find James complaining bitterly in 1609. A recent prohibition, he said, if he understood it correctly, displayed an insolence and a dishonesty which he would not tolerate. He vowed with many oaths 'that he would make those judges know he was their sovereign and feel what his power was. He could be served with as honest men and as well learned as they, who should better understand how to demean themselves towards him'. Coke in this instance was able to satisfy the King, but he offended again shortly after, at which James wrote an angry letter to Salisbury. In recent months, he said, he had suffered a long series of insolences in various parts of the kingdom: the students at Cambridge had insulted him, his officers did not clear idle people from the fields when he went hunting, the justices of the peace neglected to repair the roads. But he did not wonder at disobedience among the people when his judges gloried in displeasing him; and he hinted that he might dismiss Coke from his place so as to be vexed no longer by his perverse spirit.[10]

A book appeared in 1607 which underscored the prerogative in another way. This was *The Interpreter*, a law dictionary, by John Cowell, who was professor of civil law at Cambridge, master of Trinity Hall, and a protégé of Bancroft. His object was to vindicate the civil law, now fallen into disrepute, and to reconcile the civilian and the common lawyer. But his definitions exalted the prerogative beyond all measure. The King, he says, is absolute and is above the law. 'Of these two, one must needs be true, that either the King is above the Parliament, that is, the positive laws of the kingdom, or else that he is not an absolute king.' Such a book was certain to cause trouble in the House of Commons.

The royal prerogative was closely connected with royal finance, for the lavish expenditures of James's first years in England soon threatened his government with ruin and tempted him to employ the prerogative for the purpose of augmenting his revenues. It is true that the financial difficulties in which he found himself were not entirely of his own making. Prices were higher than in Elizabeth's reign and old sources of revenue were diminishing in value. Nor had Parliament learned the unpleasant lesson that the cost of government was certain to increase and must be paid for by heavier taxation. Yet James made matters far worse than a more prudent sovereign would have done. He had no financial sense. Any money that came into his hands he considered a happy windfall, to be squandered at once; he could not resist the temptation of extravagance; and he allowed himself to be cheated on every hand. Of Elizabeth's constant scrutiny of the whole fabric of public finance, he was utterly incapable.

The Earl of Dorset, his first Lord Treasurer, though not an astute financier, was able to increase the non-parliamentary revenues of the crown from £247,000 in 1603 to £366,000 in 1608. In this he was aided by a rise in the Customs that came with peace. It was no fault of his that in 1608 expenditure soared to £544,000, leaving a deficit of £178,000. Nor did he sell Crown lands recklessly. But he had to find money, and he fell into the error of borrowing heavily, normally at 10 per cent, until the debt threatened bankruptcy. The truth was that in these early years James was living partly on credit; the sums he gave away so easily were not his to give. At Michaelmas 1606, the debt stood at £550,331; and, when Dorset died in 1608, at £597,337.

At once the King named Salisbury Treasurer. Thus this indefatigable servant, in addition to his duties as Secretary, and to a host of others, undertook the task of filling an exchequer which the lavishness of the King and the cruel facts of economic change had made into a bottomless pit. He set about his task with great determination, but he found it a desperate business. The royal expenditure he could not diminish; he could only increase revenue, which he did very substantially. He paid off the major portion of the debt, though in order to do so he sold Crown lands to the value of £426,151, a sad reduction of royal capital. It is small wonder that he turned to a new source of income that opened before him in 1607.

Occasionally in the Tudor period the Crown had levied Customs duties known as impositions, which were payments over and above the normal schedule of rates authorized by Parliament. This had been done to regulate foreign commerce and not to raise revenue. Dorset, however, had levied a few impositions for income. The merchants demurred, and a test case arose in 1606 when John Bate, a merchant importing currants from the Levant, refused to pay. The result was a famous decision in the Court of the Exchequer declaring that since foreign commerce was regulated by prerogative and since impositions formed part of that regulation, the King could, without recourse to Parliament, levy such duties. On the strength of this decision Salisbury placed new impositions upon commerce in 1608, which he estimated would produce about £60,000 a year.

Government finance was approaching a crisis in 1610. By that year Salisbury had reduced the debt to £160,000 and had raised the revenue to an estimated £460,000 per annum, surely an admirable showing. But the deficit was running at something like £130,000, and James's expenditure for the year was likely to be close to £600,000. Salisbury, having played all his cards without solving the financial problem, advised the King that recourse must now be had to Parliament.[11]

In matters of finance James was of no assistance to his Treasurers. Sometimes he worried and often he promised reform. In 1604 he had written: 'I cannot but be sensible of that needless and unreasonable profusion of expenses whereof ye wrote me in your last. When I consider the extremity of my state my only hap and hope that upholds me is in my good servants that will sweat and labour for my relief. Otherwise I could rather have wished with Job never to have been born than that the glorious sun of my entry should be so soon overcast with the dark clouds of irreparable misery. I have promised and I will perform it that there shall be no default in me; for my apprehension of this strait (howsoever I disguise it outwardly) hath done me more harm already than ye would be glad of.' The one disease he feared was the eating canker of want, from which, if he could be free, he would be as happy as any king since the birth of Christ. Councillors, he wrote again, were the physicians; he was the patient; he promised to keep a strait diet and to apply their remedies, on which, as he knew, they were breaking their brains. Urging them to redouble their efforts, he suggested ways in which economies might be effected, which surely required a monstrous conceit. At these promises of royal parsimony councillors expressed becoming joy, for James expected them to do so. But he was a man of many moods. Sometimes he appeared to be jealous of the Council, as though he feared it would gain credit for denying suitors while he was left with the opprobrium. Sometimes he was angry. Salisbury remarked in a moment of despair that the King would never be rich; and James took him sharply to task. Again he wrote in a bantering tone: Salisbury was the spendthrift and James the niggard. If we are to believe that dubious scandalmonger, Anthony Weldon, the King could jest with his intimates about his finances. Certain Scots, says Weldon, complained to James that the English called them beggars. 'Content yourselves,' came the answer, 'I will shortly make the English as beggarly as you and so end that controversy.' Doubtless only a tall tale. But it was evident that any reform must come from the Council. James would not alter his ways, and action disappeared in much speaking.[12]

Thus many threads wove themselves together in the parliamentary sessions of 1610. The new impositions, the clash with Coke, Cowell's *Interpreter*, all pointed to the prerogative and raised the basic question of how far it was to go. On the other hand, the state of James's finances gave power to the Commons. Small wonder that they used it to survey the years since his accession and to place before him, fully, deliberately, implacably, the many things in Church and State to which they took exception.

On March 21st, some time after Parliament opened, the King addressed the two Houses in a lengthy speech. Members wondered, he said, whether he planned to govern by the ancient forms or by absolute power, whether he would continue the common law or substitute the civil law he had known in Scotland. He would hide his faith neither from man nor angel, and therefore he must tell them that kings were gods who could do what they pleased with their subjects. But a good king was willing to be bound by the laws he had made; and fortunately he was a good King, of which, God be thanked, he had given ample proof. His piety was thus a happy bridge between divine right and the precepts of the common law. He was not an enemy of prohibitions, but he had seen them swelling and overflowing in numbers and used by one court to steal cases from another. Hence he had asked the judges to use them with restraint. The need for restraint made him think of the Commons, to whom he read a lecture upon the manner in which grievances should be selected, pruned and presented. He then turned to finance. It was true that he had spent a great deal of money, but a large number of his charges could not have been avoided. He was now placing his wants before his people, a thing few kings would do; he asked merely that the Commons do their duty and begged them to act quickly. His conclusion — a request for new game laws — might appear an anticlimax but was probably the one part of his speech that was well received. He had talked for two hours and had offended many of his audience by his frequent and casual use of the name of God and by his lofty exaltation of the royal prerogative.

Within a few days a proclamation appeared condemning Cowell's book, a proclamation that has brought the charge of hypocrisy. But James may have thought that Cowell had dealt with transcendent matters, and there is a hint that he did not like some of Cowell's conclusions. More than once was that author called before the King and Council to 'answer some other passages of his book, which do as well pinch upon the authority of the King, as the other points were derogatory to the liberty of the subject'.[13]

Laying the King's wants before the Commons, Salisbury asked them to consider not only an ordinary grant but also some means by which a permanent revenue could come to the Crown. The King, he added, was ready to redress certain grievances, and hence perhaps a bargain might be arranged. In July he reached a tentative agreement with the Commons, known as the Great Contract, by which the King, in return for a permanent annual revenue of £200,000, would abandon purveyance, wardship and other feudal rights, would protect purchasers of Crown lands against loss through technical flaws in their titles, and would exempt English shires from the jurisdiction of the Council of Wales. Salisbury was indefatigable 'in bringing all the great hounds to a perfect tune' and, had the contract succeeded, the achievement would have been his. James accepted the tentative agreement of July in a jovial mood. He said that he had not liked the Commons' first offer of nine-score-thousand pounds because nine was the number of the muses or poets who were always beggars. He preferred twelve score because twelve was the number of the apostles. But he was well content with ten, for there were ten commandments. A rather novel basis for finance.

Meanwhile difficulties had developed as the Commons began their long accumulation of grievances, including many things which the King was certain to resent: the Council of Wales, the frequency of proclamations, the silenced ministers, the courts of the Church, and above all, impositions. To debate impositions was to debate the King's prerogative to levy them, a dangerous point. On May 21st James addressed the Commons once more. He would permit them, he said, to discuss abuses in the collection of impositions, but not his power to exact them. He suggested a compromise: that he retain the impositions then in force but that he levy no more in the future without Parliament's consent. Yet the Commons would have to rely upon his word, for he would bind neither his own prerogative nor that of his posterity. Warming to his theme, he declared that the kings of other countries collected impositions without recourse to Parliament, and concluded with an imperious command that the prerogative should not be called in question.

These words, with their challenge to free speech, were deeply resented in the Commons. The King's speech, wrote Chamberlain, 'bred generally much discontent to see our monarchical power and royal prerogative strained so high and made so transcendent every way'. Members declared that their goods could not be taken from them except by Act of Parliament; they drew up a petition of right, asserting their privilege of free debate. In doing so, they said, they had no intention of restricting the prerogative but they must know its limitations, for otherwise their ancient liberties were gone, and they asked permission to continue their debate on impositions. At this the King drew back, attempted to minimize what he had said, and told the Commons to debate impositions as they pleased. The result was a famous discussion lasting four days, in which the Commons so convinced themselves that impositions were illegal without consent of Parliament that the government dared not bring the matter to a vote.

In July the Commons presented their grievances in a lengthy document. So long was it, said James, that he thought he might use it as a tapestry. His answer came piecemeal. On certain points he yielded, but on the prerogative and on the Church he was adamant.

When the autumn session began in October, both King and Commons were dissatisfied with the Great Contract; both raised their terms, and to Salisbury's infinite sadness the contract came to an end. He continued to seek supply in the ordinary way. But the King, who had retired to Royston, grew more and more angry at every report of the doings of the Commons. 'His Highness', Lake wrote to Salisbury, 'wisheth your lordship to call to mind that he hath now had patience with this assembly these seven years, and from them received more disgraces, censures and ignominies than ever prince did endure. He followeth your lordship's advices in having patience, hoping for better issue. He cannot have asinine patience, he is not made of that metal that is ever to be held in suspense and to receive nothing but stripes, neither doth he conceive that your lordships are so insensible of those indignities that you can advise any longer endurance.' A few days later the King wrote more savagely that no house save the house of hell could have treated him as the Commons had been doing.

Meanwhile Salisbury struggled to obtain some equitable compromise from the Commons, to moderate the rash and headstrong anger of the King, above all to compose the bitterness on both sides and to prevent a rupture. When a forlorn hope arose of agreement on one portion of the contract, proposals were sent post-haste to the King. But he received them coldly. He must deal warily, he said, with a multitude from whom he had obtained so little comfort. He set his price very high, suggested a peremptory message to inform the Commons they were about to be dissolved, and wished that the question of supply be forced to a vote whether or not there was hope of success. These highly impolitic suggestions Salisbury managed to evade, but James then ordered a prorogation that ended hope of compromise and looked towards a dissolution.

In the last week of November, when the issue hung in the balance, Salisbury begged the King earnestly to come to London for consultation on parliamentary affairs. But James saw no necessity. If he could be assured of some hope he would come; otherwise a meeting with his Council would merely cause him vexation and unpleasant travel. He saw nothing to decide beyond the form that dissolution was to take and the punishment of audacious members who had compared him to King Joram, the evil King of the Jews. Elizabeth, he said, had punished members, why could not he? Salisbury counselled patience and had his way. But he discovered an evil influence behind James's anger, for the young Scots favourite, Sir Robert Carr, alarmed at anti-Scottish feeling in the Commons, was urging the King to dissolve. Carr, we know, had agents in the Commons and may well have employed them to act in a way that would irritate the King and thus help to break the Parliament. And Carr was poisoning James against Salisbury. About the middle of January 1611, the King dissolved his first Parliament.

It is difficult to forgive him for loitering in the country at a time when parliamentary affairs had become so delicate and complicated, and for listening to the advice of Carr, a raw Scots youth, rather than to that of Salisbury. It is impossible to forgive his unfair and heartless ingratitude to Salisbury after the Parliament was over. The King turned sharply upon him as though the failure of the Parliament was his. 'Your greatest error', James wrote, 'hath been that ye ever expected to draw honey out of gall, being a little blinded with the self-love of your own counsel in holding together of this Parliament, whereof all men were despaired, as I have oft told you, but yourself alone.' Goaded beyond endurance, Salisbury answered as though he had lost the King's favour and ended with a dignified reproach: 'You will please so to dispose of me or suffer me to be treated as you shall think may best agree with your service; for when I resolved to serve your Majesty as I have done (in a time of want, of practice, and in a place of envy) I searched my heart and found it well resolved to suffer for such a master all the incidents to such a condition.' The King softened his asperity. He wondered, he said, that Salisbury could find in his letters any diminution of royal favour, for all who knew him were aware that he never altered his affections for any man unless the cause was printed on his forehead. Yet 'ye have broken forth in more passionate and strange discourses these last two sessions of Parliament than ever ye were wont to do; wherein for pity of your great burden I forbear to admonish you'.[14]

After the dissolution of the Parliament the relations of the King and his principal minister appeared upon the surface to be following their former course. James returned to his rural delights, and Salisbury received the old flow of instructions, admonitions and criticism, as the King read his letters and replied through Lake, or Fenton, or John Murray, or, more often now, Robert Carr, soon to be Viscount Rochester. Many of James's letters dealt with trivialities. He was irritated by the felling of trees in the Forest of Dean which disturbed the hawks; or he set down the names of the courtiers he wished to have with him in the country; or he sent instructions for the care of an albino hind. He wrote also of more serious matters: the middle shires, the Queen's illness in 1611, foreign affairs, the oath of allegiance and fines from those who refused it. He heard that deprived ministers still preached in the vicinity of Peterborough, and Salisbury must admonish the Bishop. Or he objected to Salisbury's draft of a commission because it might limit the prerogative.

But none the less he was angry with Salisbury, blaming him for the failure of the Parliament, and quietly dropped him as his principal adviser. There were no more 'little beagle' letters, the old jocularity disappeared, and the royal communications were formal and businesslike. 'It is certain', wrote Bishop Goodman in his memoirs of the reign, 'that the King did not love him.' Despite his high office and former pre-eminence, Salisbury found himself relegated to matters of routine while James took counsel with Rochester, with Northampton or Suffolk, or with Worcester and Shrewsbury. Pitiable were Salisbury's last years. He had fought well to make the Parliament a success but he had failed. 'I have seen this Parliament at an end,' he wrote sadly, 'whereof the many vexations have so overtaken one another as I know not to what to resemble them so well as to the plagues of Job.' He knew that his enemies were watching, that Rochester intrigued against him, that Northampton hated him. His struggle to replenish the exchequer continued, but it had grown grim and deadly. The King's extravagance was incorrigible, and we find Salisbury falling into a great passion over the lack of money and refusing the legitimate requests of ambassadors. Above all, he had lost the good will of a monarch to whom, as he must have reflected bitterly, he had all but given a throne.

In December 1611, and again in the following February, Salisbury was seriously ill. James expressed a mild concern. He was, as a friend wrote to Salisbury, 'careful exceedingly of your lordship's health', the more so because Salisbury, though in pain, had not forgotten instructions about a royal paddock. When Salisbury fell ill a second time, the King came to see him, and there is a pathetic letter of thanks from the stricken statesman. James's visit, he wrote, had made him well save for some dregs of pain in his arm. 'This royal voice of visitation (like *visitatio beatifica*) has given new life to those spirits which are ready to expire for your service.' Yet within a few days James wrote a complaining letter. He did not like the manner in which Salisbury had dealt with a problem in London where many Englishmen were attending Mass in the chapels of ambassadors from Roman Catholic States. James declared roundly that if he had been present the matter would have been handled better.

In April Salisbury abandoned his work and journeyed painfully to Bath in hope that the waters would bring him some relief. But he was tormented in mind and body and decided to return; and on his weary way he died, May 12th. At the last he regained his equanimity. 'His making ready to die was the greatest blessing of his life unto him, for he never went to bed without cares till then, but had alarms everywhere to wake him, save in his conscience. When death came to be his business, he was in peace; and so he died.'

He was grossly maligned after his death. 'I never knew so great a man so soon and so generally censured,' wrote Chamberlain, 'for men's tongues walk very liberally and freely, but how truly I cannot judge.' Northampton, unable to conceal his malicious satisfaction, spoke of 'the death of the little man for which so many rejoice and so few do so much as seem to be sorry'. A scurrilous epitaph circulated at court:

Here lies thrown, for the worms to eat,
Little bossive Robin that was so great.

James was indifferent. When the news of his noble servant's
death was brought to him at Whitehall, he delayed his intended
departure for the country only until after dinner.[15]

CHAPTER XV

THE PEACEMAKER

'**P**EACE be to you in the land of peace under the King of peace.' So begins a tract of 1619, *The Peace-Maker, or Great Brittaines Blessing*, of which the King probably wrote small portions and Lancelot Andrewes the rest. 'Peace hath conceived and smiling Isaac hath left us Jacob, a new Israel, a Prince of God, a man that hath prevailed with God to plant His peace among us.' Peace, the tract continues, was born with the King in Scotland where he nursed it for many years and brought it with him to England. He has now lived a full half-century in peace. 'O blessed jubilee! Let it be celebrated with all joy and cheerfulness, and all sing *Beati Pacifici*! Let England (the seat of our Solomon) rejoice in her happy government, yea, her government of governments; and she that can set peace with others, let her enjoy it herself. We live in Beth-salem, the house of peace, then let us sing this song of peace, *Beati Pacifici*.'

Poets echoed the sentiments of the King and his clergy. Robert Aylett wrote of

> That great peacemaker, Britain's peaceful King,
> Who through the Christian world doth peace maintain;
> God grant, for peace on earth, thou heavenly peace mayest gain.

While a French *Himne de la Paix* saluted

> Le plus sage des Roys et le Roy des plus Sages,
> De qui les saincts discours sont oracles de Paix,
> Et les escripts divins des Miracles parfaicts.

Thus peace had come to England with King James, inherent in some mystic fashion in his royal presence. When, in addressing his first English Parliament, he counted 'the blessings which God hath in my person bestowed upon you', the first of these blessings was peace. 'I have ever, I praise God, kept peace and amity with all, which hath been so far tied to my person, as at my coming here you are witnesses I found the State embarked in a great and tedious war, and only my arrival here, and by the peace in my person, is now amity kept where war was before.' Proud was the King of his peaceful attributes. 'I know not', he wrote, 'by what fortune the dicton of *Pacificus* was added to my title at my coming to England, that of the lion, expressing true fortitude, having been my dicton before. But I am not ashamed of this addition. For King Solomon was a figure of Christ in that he was a king of peace. The greatest gift that our Saviour gave his apostles immediately before His ascension was that he left His peace with them.' And Christ was born under Augustus Caesar, also a king of peace.

Flowing from James's dominions, peace was to become universal. He spoke as though he could bestow it where he would, boasting in 1617 that he had established a settled repose in all neighbouring lands. Nations who quarrelled should bring their disputes before him for settlement. 'Come they not hither', asks the *Peace-Maker*, 'as to the fountain from whence peace springs? Here sits Solomon and hither come the tribes for judgment. O happy moderator, blessed Father, not Father of thy country alone, but Father of all thy neighbour countries about thee.'[1]

But alas! The King's dream of universal peace was the most impossible of all his dreams. If he had maintained peace with foreign countries while he lived in Scotland, it was due in no small measure to the remoteness and insignificance of his kingdom; and if he exalted his burlesque diplomacy prior to 1603 into a sustained effort at universal concord, he was deceiving himself. Nevertheless he brought some things from Scotland and found some things in England that were conducive to the pacification of Europe. He was now the ruler of the most powerful of Protestant States, strengthened by union with Scotland. His prestige was high in Scandinavia and in northern Germany. He had been friendly with the Dutch and was the inheritor of Elizabeth's great influence in that country. Kinloss was repeating the royal thoughts when he told the Venetian ambassador that Denmark, Sweden, Norway, Holland and the free cities of the Empire all depended upon the King 'as though upon an emperor'. James was also on good terms with the Catholic States opposed to Spain. To English friendship with France he could add the old tradition of Franco-Scottish alliance. He had cultivated Tuscany and Venice. He was thus a leader of Protestant and anti-Spanish Europe. Towards mighty Spain and towards the nexus of her satellites his policy in the past had been dominated by fear and suspicion. But though the suspicion remained, the fear was now mitigated and a new approach seemed possible. James thought himself sufficiently great and powerful to extend the hand of friendship to Spain and thus make universal the orbit of his amity. Friendly with all nations, allied with Protestant States, on peaceful terms with Spanish lands, he saw a vision of imposing peace and concord on a continental scale.

Yet in sad reality his foreign policy proved the most shameful failure of his reign, bringing disgrace upon England and ruin upon her allies. The reasons are clear enough. James's cardinal error was his belief that he could be a champion of Protestantism and at the same time a friend of Spain. This basic contradiction enmeshed him in endless difficulties. In Scotland he had practised promiscuously with all powers, but he could not do so in England. His policy met with some success during the first decade of his reign, but thereafter its difficulties increased, and after 1618 it became impossible. He could not combine friendship with Protestant and with Catholic powers when the two had gone to war. Yet he tried to do so, clinging with obstinate and foolish blindness to his dream of universal peace after all hope had vanished.

His policy, moreover, was a personal policy, not shared or understood by his people, to whom he gave no explanation of what he was trying to do. Hence his actions were misunderstood, he was thought to be more friendly with Spain than he actually was, and in disgust his Parliaments left him without funds. His diplomacy, lacking the foundations of national support and of military power, became a paper diplomacy, ridiculed by the realists on the Continent. Unable to fulfil his commitments or to make good his threats, he became a defender who could defend no one, a champion who could do nothing but talk, while his failures, palpable to all, tempted Parliament to make for the first time a serious demand for a voice in shaping foreign policy.

He was hampered also by his personal timidity, and by his distaste for soldiers and for all things military. A story was told that when a soldier offered to kiss his hand, the King drew it quickly back, saying he feared it might be bitten; and when an old warrior came to court wearing a brace of pistols, James wittily expressed his displeasure by telling the man that if he were only well victualled he would be impregnable. In the navy he took but a superficial interest and allowed it to decay with shocking rapidity. 'King James was the most cowardly man that ever I knew,' wrote the country gentleman, Sir John Oglander. 'He could not endure a soldier or to see men drilled, to hear of war was death to him, and how he tormented himself with fear of some sudden mischief may be proved by his great quilted doublets, pistol-proof, as also his strange eyeing of strangers with a continual fearful observation.' His fear of assassination played no small part in his foreign policy.[2]

But quite apart from his blunders and inconsistencies, the times were against his hopes of peace. In the combustible atmosphere of the Counter-reformation German Catholics and German Protestants were dividing into two armed camps. France was too aggressive under Henry IV and Spain became too aggressive as a result of Henry's death, while the hard-headed Dutch, ready to push economic advantage against every competitor, hated Spain with an implacable hatred. Thus the peacemaker of Britain was faced with well-nigh impossible odds.

His first moves were wise and sound enough. As evidence of his own inclination and of his desire for peace with Spain, he recalled the letters-of-marque of the English privateers who preyed upon Spanish commerce, and despite the cursing along the coast he saw to it that his orders were enforced. This had an unexpected result, for it drove the wilder spirits into piracy. If ever a king hated pirates it was King James. When the Venetian ambassador in 1603 complained of English pirates in the Mediterranean, accusing Lord Admiral Nottingham of sharing in the loot, James listened 'with extreme impatience, twisting his body, striking his hands together, and tapping with his feet. "By God," he said in a loud voice, "I'll hang the pirates with my own hands and my Lord Admiral as well".' It is not surprising that Nottingham escaped the rope, but there is proof in a long series of proclamations that the King detested piracy. Nineteen pirates might have been seen hanging in a row at Wapping in 1608, and some years later the King was willing to send a fleet against the Barbary pirates, 'those enemies of God and man, who deter all on the seas'.[3]

Events moved quickly towards the peace with Spain signed in August 1604. James resisted the pressure of those in England who wished to continue the war and who argued that Spain was now so weak that one determined blow might crush her for ever. To the enticements of Henry IV, eager to lure him into schemes against Spain and Austria, he turned a deaf ear. And he resisted also the angry protests of the Dutch who saw themselves left to fight Spain alone, for though he had no thought of abandoning them, he let them know that they could not stand in the way of English peace with Spain.

He had been friendly with the Dutch before 1603, but his attitude towards them now became lofty and condescending. An explanation can be found only in the fact that they owed him large sums of money advanced by Elizabeth, for which he held the Cautionary Towns of Flushing, Brille and Rammekens as pledges of repayment. The position of creditor was to James a novel and exhilarating thing, and he looked upon the Dutch as his poor struggling clients. He was not alarmed as yet by their growing power at sea. He believed, said the Venetian ambassador, 'that at a single nod of his the Dutch would yield him all the dominion that they had gained'. But he bethought himself of the fact that they were rebels and talked foolishly of their revolt from Spain as though it were a crime. When he was told that Ostend might fall to Spain if English aid was withheld, he answered: 'What of it? Was not Ostend originally the King of Spain's and therefore now the Archduke's?' Rather strangely, he asked the clergy in Convocation whether a Christian ruler might justly assist a people in revolt against their sovereign. Convocation replied in the affirmative, but blundered in asserting that the Dutch, like all other subjects, owed allegiance to their *de facto* rulers, irrespective of hereditary right. The answer displeased the King who sent a stinging reply. When the Dutch dispatched Barnevelt, Pensionary of Holland, to plead their cause, he was unable to obtain audience in the ordinary way but had to have himself smuggled into a gallery where the King was about to walk. He swore that by every law, divine and human, the Dutch were justified in fighting Spain. James then asked him whether he would defend his country's position in a public debate before the ambassadors of Spain and the Archduke, a new departure in diplomatic procedure.

The peace with Spain was no surrender. Believing rightly that Spain was in greater need of peace than England, James stood his ground on all points. He was annoyed at Spanish manœuvres to hold the negotiations in Brussels and forced the Spanish envoys to come to London. The Dutch lost none of the aid they were receiving, for though the King promised not to assist them directly, he left them free to raise money and volunteers in England, while a similar concession to Spain meant little. A Spanish demand for possession of the Cautionary Towns was met by an empty phrase that left things as they were. Nor would James admit the illegality of English trade in the new world. He held the Elizabethan view that only effective occupation of territories overseas conferred exclusive rights upon a European power, and he rejected the Spanish claim that prior discovery gave perpetual monopoly over vast unoccupied areas. Hence he was ready to prohibit English trade in regions under Spanish control but not throughout the Indies. In the end the treaty said nothing whatever on this point. English traders continued to enter the Spanish Indies at their own risk. The treaty, moreover, opened Spain and the Netherlands to English commerce, and English merchants were not to be subject to the Inquisition so long as they behaved discreetly in Spanish ports.

The King was undoubtedly right in making peace with Spain. If Elizabeth could not deliver a knockout blow, her successor was wise not to make the attempt. The peace with Spain, based as it was upon suspicion and mistrust, brought advantage to the stronger party, and for a decade this was England. England and Scotland could benefit from peace and could trade with Spain and the Netherlands; Ireland could be pacified without danger of Spanish intervention. On the other hand, Spain remained at war with the Dutch, while the hostility of Henry IV hung like a suspended dagger over her head. Spanish proposals of a marriage alliance with England, put forward largely to drive a wedge between James and the Dutch, were not unattractive in the terms they offered. It was only after 1613, when the balance began to shift, that the Spanish raised their price.

Yet the peace was an uneasy one, and the King soon found himself drifting away from Spain towards closer alliance with his old friends. His quarrels with the Spanish were incessant. Spain complained at once that she was denied facilities to raise volunteers in England, while the Dutch were encouraged to do so. After the Gunpowder Plot, with its threat of invasion by English

Catholic troops serving in Flanders, James prohibited Spanish recruiting despite the treaty. To Spanish protests he answered hotly that persons cognizant of the Powder treason found sanctuary in the Netherlands, which violated the treaty far more. And English merchants in Spain were loud in complaint of the treatment they received.

In the year following the Gunpowder Plot a confused and nebulous affair known as the Franceschi Plot again appeared to threaten the King with assassination. Ramifications of both plots led to Spanish territories though not to Spanish governments. The Venetian ambassador reported James as saying: 'I do not believe that the King of Spain or the Archduke have any hand in such execrable designs; I do not see what they could gain by my death, for it is thanks to me that they enjoy the peace they so greatly desire. Still it is a remarkable fact that every plot against myself and my kingdom has had its roots in Spain or in Flanders.' There followed the oath of allegiance and the pamphlet war with Rome, both deeply resented in Spain; and in 1606 a dispute which threatened war arose between Venice and the Papacy over somewhat similar issues. The King was quite swept off his feet by enthusiasm for a Catholic State that dared defy the Pope. In an audience granted to the Venetian ambassador James launched into a long and violent tirade against the temporal powers claimed by Rome, speaking with such force of reason, such wealth of citation from Holy Writ, and such a flow of eloquence that the ambassador was amazed. The King derived the greatest satisfaction from his performance, and those present declared they had never seen him more content and delighted. When the ambassador told him that the clergy in Venice remained loyal to the Republic, he exclaimed: 'Oh, this will very soon completely confound the Pope.' And when he was told that Venice had expelled the Jesuits he could not conceal his joy. 'O blessed and wise Republic,' he cried, 'how well she knows the way to preserve her liberty; for the Jesuits are the worst and most seditious fellows in the world.' He made large promises of assistance, though Salisbury's prudence added a more cautious tone to the correspondence. That he would have honoured his pledges is highly doubtful. Fortunately both France, supporting Venice, and Spain, supporting Rome, desired peace and a compromise was arranged. The episode left England and Spain farther apart than before, for

Philip was convinced that James had stiffened the Venetians.[4]

In two matters of much greater import James threw his weight against Spain. One was the long negotiation (1607 to 1609) for a peace between Spain and Holland. Continuance of the war was so obviously to England's advantage that James put aside the role of peacemaker. English agents in Holland were instructed not to oppose peace openly, but to encourage the Dutch in secret to continue the war if they showed any inclination to do so. Peace would strengthen both Spain and Holland; and James was beginning to realize that the Dutch would emerge from the war a great and notable power with strong forces on land and sea and with a commerce that could rival England's. Yet if he did not support the Dutch they were sure to turn to France.

The Dutch wished for a guarantee of assistance from England and France in case the peace, once made, should be broken by Spain. The King at first demurred. Such a guarantee, especially in unison with France, might easily bring war with Spain. He thought that the Dutch were asking for a great deal and he found them very annoying. He vented his irritation in a letter to Salisbury. Why should be ruin himself to maintain the Dutch? If they could not exist without his help, perhaps he should leave them to Spain or divide them between himself and France. 'Otherwise the King of Spain will be sure to consume us, making us waste ourselves to sustain his enemies.' It was well for James that he had a minister like Salisbury to show him where his true interests lay. Discovering that France gave the Dutch the guarantee they asked, he pledged himself in 1608, if Spain broke the peace, to send Holland 6000 foot, 600 horse, and a fleet of 20 ships. English, French and Dutch diplomats, now working together, obtained from Spain, not peace, but the Twelve Years' Truce, to run from 1609 to 1621. The truce was a deep humiliation for Spain. She was forced to make a settlement implying, though not formally admitting, the independence of the Dutch, and though she was adamant in refusing to legalize Dutch trade in the West Indies (which, of course, continued), she jettisoned the interests of Portugal by permitting the merchants of Holland to trade in the east. Her discomfiture was due in part to England.

Meanwhile a crisis developed on the Lower Rhine where John William, the Catholic Duke of Cleves, Julich and Berg, died without children in 1609. To his dominions, highly valuable both in themselves and in their strategic position as a gateway to Germany, there were two principal claimants, John Sigismund, Elector of Brandenburg, and Wolfgang Wilhelm, son of the Count of Neuburg, both Protestant. But the Emperor, Rudolph II, on very flimsy pretexts, sent his brother, the Archduke Leopold, to occupy the Duchies pending a settlement. Leopold seized Julich but could go no further. Against this imperial threat to Cleves and Julich, Henry IV, the Dutch and the newly formed Union of south German Protestant States formed a strong coalition; and Henry was maturing wider plans against both Spain and Austria.

Rather surprisingly, James joined this warlike coalition in 1610 by promising 4000 troops, not from England, but from the English and Scottish forces serving with the Dutch. He wished to keep the Duchies in Protestant hands, he was well disposed to the Elector of Brandenburg, he did not want Henry to have all the glory. He knew that he had strong allies and doubtless thought there would be little fighting. He was not risking much.

Then, like a stroke of lightning, came the assassination of Henry IV. A shout of exultation arose from Spanish States and the rest of Europe was stunned. James, refusing at first to believe the news, was profoundly moved, not from love of the French King, for he had none, but from fear and horror of assassination, a horror increased a hundredfold because the victim was a king. Hurried consultations were held at Whitehall; and precautions were taken at once to guard James more carefully, especially while hunting. A few days later, as he rode through London, the people saw their King surrounded by an armed guard. But if James looked beyond his personal alarms and jealousies, he must have known that he and England had suffered a grievous blow, for Henry's death removed the greatest obstacle in Europe to the advance of Hapsburg power.

James had no mind to pursue a warlike policy in the clash over Cleves and Julich. 'I only wish', he wrote, 'that I may handsomely wind myself out of this quarrel, wherein the principal parties do so little for themselves.' But English and Scottish troops under Sir Edward Cecil, acting with the French and Dutch, soon drove the Archduke Leopold from Julich. Though James failed to achieve a settlement and though the Duchies were to trouble him again, he had helped to place the disputed territories in

Protestant hands. He had drawn closer to the Dutch and to the German Protestants in opposition to Spain and Austria.

He remained on good terms with France. 'The King', wrote the Venetian ambassador, 'displays a growing affection towards France as it becomes evident that her rivalry and power are waning and that, on account of the tender age of the new King, she will require support rather than restraint. He omits no mark of regard and has ordered the court to go into full mourning.'[5]

James's diplomacy in 1611 and 1612 centred in marriage proposals for Prince Henry and Princess Elizabeth. The trends of his policy became clearer than ever. A Protestant husband, Frederick V of the Palatinate, was provided for Elizabeth; and this marriage, increasing James's influence in Germany, made him in truth the great champion of Protestantism. On the other hand, attempts to strengthen friendship with Spain by a marriage between Henry and a Spanish princess proved abortive and left the two countries farther apart than before. When James sought other brides, all of them Catholic, for his son, he looked to Catholic lands that were, or had been, anti-Spanish.

Prince Henry, wrote his tutor, Sir Charles Cornwallis, 'was of a comely, middle stature, about five feet and eight inches high, of a strong, straight, well-made body (as if nature in him had showed all her cunning), with somewhat broad shoulders and a small waist, of an amiable majestic countenance, with hair of an auburn colour, long-faced and broad forehead, a piercing grave eye, a most gracious smile, with a terrible frown, courteous, loving and affable'. His forehead bore marks of severity, wrote Bacon, his mouth a touch of pride; yet once beyond these outworks one found him gentle and easy to deal with. He delighted in martial sports, tossing the pike, shooting with the bow or pistols, leaping and vaulting, tilting and riding at the ring. He was said to spend five or six hours a day in armour. He trained himself to endure the privations of the soldier, and was fascinated by all the strategy and tactics of military and naval operations. In the navy he took an especial interest, often visiting the shipyards at Chatham, where he was intimate with Phineas Pett, James's master shipwright. Ralegh he greatly admired, and remarked that only his father would keep such a bird in a cage. Never, indeed, did as peaceful a mother hen as King James hatch out such a fighting cock as the Prince.

He was a grave young man, decorous, resolute and ambitious beyond his years. He was not fond of books, and though he honoured learning he did not spend much time upon it. Yet Bacon found him strong in understanding though slow in speech, patient in listening, capable of great concentration. He was reserved and reticent, 'being of a close disposition, not easy to be known, or pried into; of a fearless, noble, heroic and undaunted courage, thinking nothing impossible that ever was done by any'. He was careful of religious observance and governed his household strictly. There was something of the prig about this correct and determined young man. A story was told that once when he was hunting, the game escaped through a mischance and a courtier remarked that had King James been so served he would have sworn most horribly. 'Away,' cried the Prince, 'all the pleasure in the world is not worth an oath.'

There was a lack of sympathy between Henry and his father, though rumours of hostility were wide of the mark. It was difficult for the King to appreciate a young man whose thoughts were so preoccupied with war, while Henry, eager to take part in public affairs, was critical of much that he observed. 'The Prince did sometimes pry in the King's actions,' wrote Goodman, 'and a little dislike them. Truly I think he was a little self-willed. I have heard that he did sometimes abuse the King's servants, which the King took ill.' Carr, the King's beloved, Henry regarded with contempt. Nor did the Prince's immense popularity endear him to his father who remarked peevishly, as he saw courtiers flocking to St. James's, 'Will he bury me alive?' Henry's indifference to the chase wounded the King at a tender point, and a story was told that on one occasion James became so angry at his son's behaviour during a hunt that he rode at him with upraised whip. Henry galloped away, and reconciliation came with dinner. Yet he was a dutiful and obedient son of whom the King should have been proud, for he had the makings of a man.[6]

The charm of Princess Elizabeth's personality, her high rank, and her sad misfortunes tempted contemporaries to be over-lavish in her praise. But if she was not 'th' eclipse and glory of her kind', as the courtly Sir Henry Wotton would have us believe, she was as a girl a most attractive and endearing creature. Graceful, athletic and playful, spontaneous and high-spirited, prettily impulsive, generous and affectionate, she possessed a most engaging charm.

Her face was oval and somewhat long, her hair dark and rich, her nose rather large like her father's, her eyes large, again like his. Her portraits in womanhood bear a strong resemblance to him, while Henry resembled his mother. James provided for her education with rare good judgment by placing her, away from court, in the care of Lord Harington at Combe Abbey near Coventry. Perhaps remembering his own childhood, he told Harington not to make her a Greek and Latin scholar (for where learning did good to one woman it did harm to twenty), but to instruct her in religion, history and general science. Harington was the perfect guardian, and Elizabeth profited greatly. Boderie found her 'full of virtue and merit, handsome, engaging, very well-read, able to speak French exceedingly well, much better than her brother'. Coming to live at court in 1608, though still under Harington's supervision, she greatly enjoyed the pageantry of Whitehall and delighted in picnics and hunting parties with her brother Henry. The attachment between them was a tender and endearing thing. The darker side of the court seems to have left untouched this natural, gay and innocent child.

She had many suitors, but negotiations for her marriage were comparatively simple because James followed a consistent course, favouring from the first young Frederick, the Elector of the Palatinate. It was disappointing that Frederick was not a king, but there were compensations. The Palatinate was wealthy, the dowry need not be large, the marriage would be pleasing to Protestants and would bring alliance with Protestant Germany. In May 1612, the marriage articles were signed, and when Frederick came to England in October the King was highly pleased with the son-in-law he had selected and received him with jovial cordiality. Frederick was the same age as Elizabeth (they were both sixteen), straight and well grown for his years, with a kindly and attractive face, brown complexion, and curly hair. He had been carefully educated, with almost as much Latin and theology as the King, but with more attention to good manners. His lack of judgment and his fatal proclivity for rash adventure were as yet concealed.[7]

More complicated and more prolonged were negotiations for Henry's marriage. There had been suggestions of a Spanish match but they had come to nothing. The first move in this direction was made by Queen Anne who told the Spanish Constable, in England in 1604 to sign the peace, that she would welcome a marriage between Henry and the Infanta Anne, then heiress of Philip III. James approved his wife's action, but soon discovered that Spain would negotiate only on the basis that Henry should become a Roman Catholic and should be educated in Spain; and thus the King might have learned an early and salutary lesson in Spanish intransigence regarding religion. Negotiations came to an end. They were reopened by Spain in 1605 and again in 1607 in the hope that James would bring pressure upon the Dutch to make peace on Spanish terms. Generous were the offers made by Spain to England, but religion proved again to be an insuperable barrier.

In 1611 the Spanish opened negotiations once more and the King received them cordially. Then Digby, his ambassador in Spain, discovered that the eldest Infanta was designed for the King of France and that Philip was offering England a younger daughter, a mere child. James was very angry. For some time he refused an audience to the Spanish ambassador in England, and when he granted one it proved to be brief and unpleasant. 'The King continues in great displeasure, so does the Queen and Prince, and there is no one who dares say a word about the second Infanta.' Salisbury feigned anger also, though he was well content to have the negotiations come to an end. 'Our brave Prince', he said, 'may find roses elsewhere instead of this olive.' Alarmed at the irritation in London, Philip sent a special ambassador, Pedro de Zuñiga, to minimize the Franco-Spanish marriage and to hint, if the omens appeared propitious, at a marriage between Elizabeth and King Philip, now a widower. Anne caught at the suggestion and whispered that her daughter might alter her religion. But James would have none of it. In a meeting of the Council he gave vent to his ill humour, swearing that his daughter should never marry a Papist and heaping abuse upon Zuñiga. He hoped that the ambassador would make a formal proposal so that he might reject it sharply, but Zuñiga, finding his reception so chilly, said nothing, which made James more angry than ever. For some years the Spanish match dropped out of sight.[8]

Quickly making other plans, he was soon holding what has been aptly called an auction at which Tuscany, Savoy and France offered brides dowered respectively with wealth, with beauty and with power.

While James was still in Scotland he had looked on one occasion to Tuscany for a marriage alliance, and in 1611 he reopened negotiations, proposing a match between Henry and the Infanta Caterina, sister of Duke Cosmo II. Cosmo's wealth was the great attraction. Salisbury hinted that in return for a generous dowry the bride should enjoy free exercise of her religion and that concessions to English Catholics might easily follow. But though Cosmo was well pleased, he reckoned without Paul V, whose consent he regarded as necessary. With implacable sternness Paul imposed the conditions that Henry become a Roman Catholic and that English Catholics be allowed full liberty of worship. As the Florentines pleaded, argued and threatened, the Pope merely hardened his heart. James was paying for his blasts at Rome. The Tuscan match then waned, though negotiations were not abandoned.

At the same time the King received offers from Savoy whose Duke, the restless and high-spirited Charles Emmanuel, proposed a match between his daughter and Prince Henry. The Duke was in a difficult position. Chafing under Spanish tutelage he had thrown in his lot with Henry IV, only to have the assassin's knife disrupt his calculations and expose him to Spanish vengeance. In the winter of 1611 Sir Henry Wotton, passing through Savoy on his way to England, was allowed to observe the rare beauty of the Infanta. She rode masked in a sledge in frosty weather, but as her sledge passed that of Wotton her mask required adjustment and was removed, exposing her face, flushed with exercise and appearing to great advantage. Wotton left Savoy an ardent advocate of the match. Savoyard overtures were not at first received with any warmth in England, where the Duke's poverty and turbulence counted against him. Then the King thought better of his coldness and sent Wotton back to Savoy with costly gifts. The ambassador was feasted in every town until upon reaching Turin his digestion went completely awry and he was too ill to see the Duke. James now regarded the marriage favourably, the Queen approved, and so for a moment did Henry, attracted by the beauty of the Infanta and the warlike character of her father.

Overtures came also from France, where Marie de Medici, the widow of Henry IV, had reversed his anti-Spanish policy and had arranged a double marriage for two of her children with those of Philip III. But she had a large family and many Huguenot subjects. She therefore sent the Protestant Duke of Bouillon to England with proposals of marriage between Henry and the little French Princess Christina. The ambassador, an eminent leader of the Calvinists in France, got on famously with James, who swore he would live in harmony with the French if the French would do the like with him. The Princess was only six; but if she came to England there was hope of her conversion, the offered dowry was liberal, there were no conditions regarding religion. Henry, consulted by his father, was non-committal. 'My part,' he said, 'which is to be in love with any of them, is not yet at hand.'[9]

But while James balanced the offers at his auction, the poor young Prince was dying. All through the autumn of 1612 he was far from well, and on November 6th he died of typhoid fever. His death was a heartbreaking tragedy. The nation was prostrate with grief. He had a gallant spirit. Whether he would have attained to wisdom or whether, valiant but unschooled, he would have plunged England into needless wars, we cannot know. His nature was left obscure, as Bacon said, and could only be revealed by time, which was not allowed him. But those points that appeared were excellent; which is enough for fame.

The Prince died about eight in the evening. Some hours earlier the King, 'apprehending the worst and not enduring to be so near the place, removed very privately to Theobalds' where he was ill for three days. In a paroxysm of grief and melancholy he suffered one of the violent digestive disturbances which now occasionally came upon him as the result of strain. He then went to Kensington, 'not brooking well the sight of any of his own houses'. He has been censured, justly, for leaving his son in his last hours, but there can be no doubt of the depth and sincerity of his grief, much greater than those about him anticipated. His message to Frederick saying that Frederick must fill the place in his heart left vacant by Henry's death carries a touch of sentimental cheapness, but it is not out of keeping with his emotional nature. Perhaps the truest mourner was the Princess Elizabeth whom Henry loved so well. 'Where is my dear sister?' were his last words as he sank into delirium.[10]

The marriage of Elizabeth and Frederick took place as soon as decency allowed, for there were strong reasons to speed it. Frederick's presence at court imposed a heavy financial burden; and those in England who had opposed the marriage, Northampton among them, were now working for its indefinite postponement. In November, therefore, the pair were betrothed, and on February 14th, 1613, they were married. 'The next morning the King went to visit these young turtles that were coupled on St. Valentine's day'; with shocking pruriency he questioned Frederick minutely about what had happened during the night. There followed a week of festivities which were elaborate, tedious, poorly managed and grossly extravagant. Why the King, knowing as he did of the empty exchequer, permitted such lavish, vulgar and senseless waste is difficult to understand. Chamberlain, coming to Whitehall to see what he could, was quite dazzled by the excess of bravery, for the bride wore a coronet valued at a million marks and the nobles were dressed with exotic richness and coarse display. There was a great lack of good order. The congestion at court was such that the players in a masque could not make their way through the crowd, and the ladies were forbidden to wear farthingales. A sham battle on the Thames, said to cost £9000, proved so realistic with shooting and potting of guns that men were maimed, to the horror and disgust of the spectators, and the show was discontinued. A masque by a group of lords proved rich, long and wearisome; while another, which was to have been given by Gray's Inn and the Inner Temple, had to be postponed because the King after two sleepless nights refused to attend. In great chagrin Bacon told him that such a disgrace would bury the players quick, but James answered that the alternative was to bury him quick. A few days later he invited the Inns to a banquet where he did his best to please.

On April 25th the young couple sailed from England. Their ship, the *Royal Prince*, had been built under Henry's eye and was captained fittingly by Phineas Pett. James rode with them to Rochester where in tears he begged Frederick to give his wife precedence, as the daughter of a king, over all the Princes of Germany, including her husband, a request that could hardly be refused at such a moment but was to cause much trouble in the future. With many tears and embraces James parted from his daughter, never to see her again.[11]

He was now closely allied with the Protestant Union of south German Princes with whom he concluded a treaty of mutual assistance that made him, in effect, a member of the Union, and within a few months he persuaded the Dutch to enter a similar agreement. Thus his position as Protestant champion was greatly enhanced, while his relations with Spain had gradually worsened until many of his subjects thought, and hoped, that war would break out between the two countries.

Two of James's other relatives claimed his attention about this time. His cousin, Arabella Stuart, had continued to live at court after his accession and had been treated kindly. Early in 1610, however, the King was alarmed to hear that she had fallen in love with William Seymour, a younger son of Lord Beauchamp. Their marriage would unite the claim of Arabella to the throne with that of the Suffolk line — a threat to James's dynasty not to be tolerated — and he commanded the lovers to put away all thought of marriage. It must be confessed that Arabella's choice of a husband was singularly injudicious and that the King had reason for displeasure. When he discovered some months later that the couple had married secretly despite his prohibition, he acted with the harshest severity. Seymour was sent to the Tower and Arabella into custody at Lambeth. They escaped, hoping to fly to France, but their plans miscarried; and though Seymour reached the Continent Arabella was captured at sea and brought back to England. She was imprisoned in the Tower, lost her reason, and died a miserable death in 1615. James could be brutal on occasion.

In October 1612, the body of Mary Queen of Scots was exhumed from Peterborough Cathedral and brought to the Chapel of Henry VII in the Abbey where a magnificent tomb had been prepared. Standing in juxtaposition to that of Queen Elizabeth, this tomb was of the same general design, but was larger, more elaborate and more costly. To the King, Northampton wrote an account of the burial. He spoke of Mary as the most worthy Queen in the world, he noted the piety of her priceless son, and scoffed at Walsingham and the Cecils. One wonders what thoughts were in James's mind as he thus did honour to his mother.[12]

CHAPTER XVI

THE GREAT SCHOOLMASTER OF THE REALM: ENGLAND

IR JOHN HARINGTON, the wit and saucy poet of Eliza-beth's court, had wooed James's favour by a tract on the succession and by the gift of a curious lantern which bore the legend: 'Lord, remember me when thou comest into thy kingdom.' In 1607 Harington was accorded the honour of a private audience. He was led by a servant, he tells us, 'to a small room where was good order of paper, ink and pens, put on a board for the Prince's use'. The King entered almost at once. He inquired much of my learning, says Harington, 'and showed me his own in such sort as made me remember my examiner at Cambridge'. James quoted learnedly from Aristotle and from other philo-sophers, then asked Harington to read from Ariosto. He asked him what he thought 'pure wit was made of, and whom it did best become? Whether a king should not be the best clerk in his own country, and if this land did not entertain good opinion of his learning and wisdom?' James then discoursed on witchcraft and asked with great gravity why the Devil did work more with ancient women than with others. To Harington's embarrassment, he spoke of his mother's execution, which, he said, had been foretold by soothsayers in Scotland who had seen a bloody head dancing before them in the air. He mentioned a number of books from which he had sought to discover a way of foretelling the future, but advised Harington not to read them lest they lead him into evil consultation. The King touched upon tobacco, then upon religion, and said finally: 'Now, Sir, you have seen my wisdom in some sort, and I have pried into yours. I pray you, do me justice in your report, and in good season I will not fail to add to your understanding in such points as I find you lack amendment.'[1] Harington's description, with its undertone of sarcasm, does not do justice to the King, whose approach to learning was kindly and whose desire to instruct was most sincere.

James derived great pleasure from his visits to the English universities. These wealthy and influential societies, now combining some luxury with learning, courted his favour assiduously and made great occasions of his visits. In August 1605, he came in state to Oxford. Dignitaries, students and townspeople met him outside the city near Aristotle's Well, where he was welcomed with Greek and Latin orations and a speech in English from the mayor. Within the city he was received by three boys dressed as nymphs who emerged from an ivory tower to speak prettily in Latin; the undergraduates shouted a welcome; and the King was escorted to supper at Christ Church. In the evening he saw a Latin comedy which was no great success, for he was weary and took little trouble to conceal it.

There followed two crowded days of lively disputations on divinity, philosophy, law and science to which James listened with keen interest. A lighter touch was introduced by a debate upon the effects of tobacco, in which Dr. William Paddy, 'a great drinker of tobacco', argued convincingly that its use was most harmful. One disputant produced a tobacco pipe, explaining that in the Indies physicians became drunk with tobacco before visiting their patients, 'whereat the King laughing heartily said our physicians should go to the Indians to be drunk that so they might minister physic'. There were many other jests, and the King was jovial and merry. He attended a great feast given by Dorset, the university's Chancellor, who also sent venison and wine to every college, so that the students 'did thankfully frolic it' and ate and drank much more than was good for them. But James hurried from the feast to attend more disputations, one concerning the question whether gold could be produced by art or magic. He listened intently, interrupted often, and broke at length into a discourse in Latin so eloquent and learned that his listeners fancied, with such a King, they lived in Plato's commonwealth. 'Apollo, if his Tripos had been up again, would have pronounced him his Socrates.' The disputations ended, the King returned thanks. He could not, he said, make a learned speech, for he lacked time to be learned, but he promised to be a Maecenas to learning and a friend to Oxford. He warned his hearers to teach the true word of God, eschewing both Roman superstition and Puritan novelty, and ever translating contemplation into practice. That night he attended another comedy, but he was weary, fell asleep, and awoke in no pleasant humour.

Next morning he visited the Bodleian Library. He had seen

the fruits of the university, he said, and he was happy to visit the garden from which they sprang. A bust of the founder prompted a feeble pun: the name should be Godly, not Bodley. The King examined manuscripts and rare texts of the Bible. Picking up Gaguinus's *De Puritate Conceptionis Virg. Mar.*, he denounced it roundly, saying such books should be burned, and he likewise denounced a recent book by a Puritan at Cambridge. In a burst of spacious generosity he offered the Bodleian any books it cared to take from the royal libraries, though later his liberality relaxed or was circumvented. If he were not a King, said James, he would be a university man; and if he were a captive he would wish to be imprisoned in the Bodleian, chained with its chains, to spend his days in enviable captivity. The librarian, coached to make his oration short, sweet and full of stuff, and to imitate the King's pronunciation of Latin, performed his part to perfection. That afternoon James departed from Oxford, leaving a tradition of royal learning among the dons and of royal drunkenness among the undergraduates.[2]

Though the King was frequently in the neighbourhood of Cambridge and borrowed books from the library, he did not visit that university until 1615. His first associations with Cambridge were not without friction. He disliked the Puritanism of some colleges; and he was offended by an occurrence in 1612 when one faction at the university nominated Northampton as Chancellor, while another, disliking Northampton's Catholicism, named Prince Charles as a rival candidate. The King was highly annoyed to find his son set in balance against a subject, and Cambridge fell under a cloud of royal displeasure, darkened by Northampton's irritation at the awkward position in which he found himself. Cambridge sent to court a suave divine, John Williams, who had preached a sermon that the King had liked and who had then received, as he said, a great deal of court holy water. Williams appeased both James and Northampton, and the latter, after a fresh nomination, accepted the proffered Chancellorship. But Cambridge offended again a year later when it entertained the Elector Palatine with a disputation as to whether succession to kingdoms should be by heredity or election. Queen Elizabeth had listened to a similar debate with equanimity, but James was furious.

Great were the preparations, therefore, when it was learned in

1615 that the King would visit Cambridge. Puritanism caused some difficulties. Emmanuel College, fearing that the royal visit would repeat the drunkenness at Oxford, refused to deck itself out for the occasion.

> The pure House of Emmanuel
> Would not be like proud Jezebel,
> Nor show herself before the King
> An hypocrite or painted thing.
> But that the ways might prove all fair,
> Conceived a tedious mile of prayer.

And some students scrupled to appear in the comedies prepared for James's enjoyment.

The visit, however, was a great success. The King was pleased with the disputations and was much amused by one in a jocular vein that dealt with the question whether dogs could make syllogisms. The major proposition, it was argued, formed itself in the dog's mind thus: the hare has gone either this way or that way, and hence a syllogism was erected. But it was answered that dogs might have sagacity but not sapience; they might be *nasutuli* but not *logici*. At this point the Moderator, fearing for the dignity of the debate, intervened, but James caught him up, recalled an incident in hunting in which a dog displayed great intelligence, and told the Moderator to think better of dogs and less of himself. A disputant came to the Moderator's rescue by saying that the King's dogs were exceptions to all rules, since they hunted, not by common law, but by prerogative.

The great triumph of the visit was George Ruggle's comedy *Ignoramus*. This clever but obscene comedy, with its ribald humour and raucous horse-play, delighted James beyond measure. Its hits at the expense of the common lawyers were most apt, for the King was quarrelling again with Sir Edward Coke. *Ignoramus* put James in high good humour. He visited almost all the colleges and commended them above Oxford. After his departure he invited the players to repeat their performance in London; and, this proving impractical, he revisited Cambridge within two months to see the comedy once more. Oxford might sneer that the King was not as amused as he appeared and that such comedies, performed by divinity students, were degrading. Cambridge could reply

You cannot say
The King did go from you in March
And came again in May.

James visited Cambridge once more in 1623 and saw more comedies but they fell flat, for his mind was with his two brave boys, Steenie and Baby Charles, in far away Madrid.

The success of Cambridge in 1615 had an amusing sequel. In 1619 the King published a Latin edition of his works and presented copies to both universities; and Oxford responded in noble fashion. James's gift was brought to the university by a special deputation, headed by the translators, Peter Young and Thomas Reid. The work was received with profound deference. A convocation was held, an oration delivered, a letter of thanks approved. Then in a solemn procession the book was carried by the Vice-Chancellor and twenty doctors in their scarlet robes to the Bodleian, where the librarian accepted it as a gift from heaven. Reverently it was placed *in archivis* 'with great solemnity as was fit for a relic and work of that worth'. Young, given money and other gifts, returned to James with a glowing account of the reception accorded to his writings. The King was delighted. It was not for naught, he declared, that he had always affected Oxford, his eldest daughter. He now preferred Oxford to Cambridge, for Cambridge had received his gift with no unusual demonstration, though its letter of thanks, written in elegant Latin by George Herbert, the university's public orator, deserves partial quotation. 'Now that we are sprinkled with the royal ink,' wrote Herbert, 'there is no subject too sublime for us. We can overcome all disputants. Would that some Jesuit might be given us, so that by mere friction against your Majesty's book we might pulverize the man forthwith.'[3]

Both universities received substantial benefits from James. He granted them the valuable right of returning members to Parliament, exempted them from taxation, and gave them advowsons confiscated from popish recusants. He added a substantial endowment to the chair of divinity at Oxford. He favoured both universities in their frequent differences with the town authorities.

But royal favour meant royal interference, and James meddled constantly with academic affairs. He not only recommended candidates for fellowships but permitted courtiers to use his name in recommending persons of whom he knew nothing. Cambridge complained bitterly in 1607 that its statutes were overthrown, that unworthy persons were obtaining fellowships, and that the morale of the tutors was undermined because their best students were passed over. The King was annoyed to discover that the statutes of the universities debarred Scots from fellowships, and a running fight on this score continued for many years. In 1609 James threatened a royal visitation. Occasionally he placed a Scot in a fellowship, but for the most part the universities stood their ground. The King interfered also in election of heads of houses. When Laud's election at St. John's, Oxford, caused a furore, James intervened, investigated and declared in Laud's favour. His tone may be gathered from a letter written, though apparently never sent, to Caius College, Cambridge, in 1619, commanding the election of Sir Thomas Wilson as Master, wherein, said the King, 'we will receive no denial, for that we know him to be a man, both for his learning, honesty and sufficiency and all other matters every way qualified for the same'.

He gave the universities a bad fright in 1604 when, in a glow of happiness at his accession, he declared he would relinquish all royal claims to impropriated tithes. He urged the universities to do the same. But Whitgift convinced him that the universities could not afford to abandon this source of revenue, and the King's Utopian suggestion faded into air.

Preaching at the universities must be to the royal taste. In 1622 a rash young Master of Arts, William Knight, in a sermon at St. Mary's, Oxford, expounded the view of Pareus, a German theologian, that resistance to tyrannical rulers was justifiable. The authorities at Oxford were horrified, and James boiled with rage. Knight's answers under examination showed him to be artless and naive rather than dangerous, yet he was imprisoned for two years in the Gate House whence he emerged only to die. The King took occasion to remind the universities that divinity students should read the Scriptures, the Fathers and the schoolmen, not 'those neoterics, both Jesuits and Puritans, who are known to be meddlers in matters of State and monarchy'. At both Oxford and Cambridge the doctrine of non-resistance was affirmed in plenary terms, the views of Pareus were condemned, and his books were hunted out and burned.

The universities were compelled to yield a rigid conformity to the established Church. James was determined that the rising generation of divines should be conformable; and he believed that this could be brought about only by thorough indoctrination in youth. In 1604 the universities were told there must be no laxness in wearing the surplice. All students, before they were admitted to their degrees, must take the oath of supremacy; an oath of unqualified acceptance of the Thirty-nine Articles; and a new oath of conformity to the Church of England, its liturgy and government. Oxford accepted the King's 'three darling articles' without demur, but Cambridge delayed until 1613, to James's great anger. In 1616 he issued new instructions. No clergyman who did not conform in every particular should be allowed to preach in the university towns. New seats erected for the proctors at St. Mary's, Cambridge, must be removed. All students must attend required sermons and must not attend elsewhere, they must not frequent houses in the town, they must adhere to academic costume, they must partake of the Communion in a kneeling position. Catechizing must be conducted in the colleges on Sundays and holy days. Divinity students must read only such works as conformed to the doctrine and discipline of the Church of England, and anything tending to Judaism, Popery, or Puritanism must be rigidly suppressed. The King demanded an annual report on these matters from the university authorities.[4]

Having thus taught the universities their duty, James determined to play the schoolmaster on a larger scale. In 1615 there appeared a little book in English and in Latin entitled *God and the King: or a Dialogue shewing that our Sovereign Lord King James, being immediate under God, within his dominions, doth rightfully claim whatsoever is required by the Oath of Allegiance.* This was a text-book for the instruction of children and young persons in the obedience and allegiance they owed the King. It has been ascribed to Dr. Richard Mocket, Warden of All Souls; and the suggestion has also been made that it came in part from the royal pen. We cannot be sure. Certainly it was inspired by the King who undoubtedly read it before publication, but it is dull and heavy and lacks his vigorous and pungent phrases. Never was the theory of divine right set forth in more lofty terms than in this booklet. Kings are declared to be so divine and so sacred that they are the angels of God and sons of the Most High. The allegiance of the people is inviolable, and cannot be dissolved by tyranny, nor falseness, nor heresy, nor apostasy. A subject must pay tribute to the king, must fight his battles, must esteem and honour him in heart and conscience as a god upon earth, and must refrain from criticism even in secret thought.

The King commanded that all schoolmasters and other teachers should instruct their students in the precepts of this book, and that 'every parson, vicar, or curate should see that every child be taught the same'. In Scotland James went further. He commanded that *God and the King* be taught not only in the schools but in the universities; that no university scholar be admitted to his degree until he had taken the oath of allegiance according to the doctrine of the book; and that every student in schools and universities, and every family containing a person who could read, must possess a copy. Yet very few copies of *God and the King* are now in existence, and one suspects that this project, so ample and ambitious, suffered a fate similar to many others set forth by the British Solomon.[5]

James wished to be considered the patron of institutions of learning. He talked as though he had founded the University of Edinburgh single-handed, though he had done very little. The beginning of the college that became the university resulted from the public spirit of the citizens; and the King's founding charter of 1582, as well as subsequent grants, were the result of pressure rather than of royal zeal. Indeed, when he visited Scotland in 1617, it was rumoured that he would have but two universities in that country, as in England; that he would retain St. Andrews and Glasgow but abolish Aberdeen and Edinburgh. If this was his purpose, his heart was softened by the performance of some of the masters from Edinburgh who, coming to him at Stirling, staged a series of those animated disputations of which he was so fond. The King listened, interrupted, applauded and 'spoke in good Latin and with much knowledge of the secrets of philosophy'. Proudly he pointed out to his English courtiers that there was sound learning in Scotland. 'These men', he said of the Scots, 'know Aristotle's mind as well as himself did while he lived.' In a jovial mood after supper he talked to them at length and thanked them in bad puns upon their names. 'I am so well satisfied with this day's exercise', he is said to have asserted, 'that I will be god-father to the college of Edinburgh and have it called the College of King James; for after the founding of it had been stopped for sundry years in my minority, so soon as I came to any knowledge, I zealously laid hand to it, and caused it to be established.' Further he promised that having given the college a name he would also give it 'a royal God-bairn gift for enlarging the patrimony thereof'. The gift never materialized; yet he did not wholly forget his promise, for an Act of 1621 confirmed the privileges of the college and placed it on an equal footing with the older universities of Scotland.

At the same time he showed that his will must be obeyed. In 1615 he had offered the principalship of the University of Glasgow to Robert Boyd, the son of the Archbishop. Boyd, who was living in France, came home to accept the post. But the King, discovering that Boyd was not conforming to the ecclesiastical rules laid down for Scotland, turned against him, and Boyd resigned. Subsequently, in 1622, he was appointed by the town council of Edinburgh to be Master of the college there. James demanded that the appointment be annulled. The town council demurred, at which the King wrote angrily: 'We think his biding there will do much evil; and therefore, as ye will answer to us on your obedience, we command you to put him not only from his office, but out of your town, at the sight hereof, unless he conform totally. And when ye have so done, think not this sufficient to satisfy our wrath for disobedience to our former letter.' Boyd then resigned once more.[6]

There are many other proofs of the King's interest in institutions of learning. Upon Trinity College, Dublin, he settled a pension payable from the Irish exchequer and endowed it with large estates in Ulster. He attempted to found a college of divinity in Chelsea. Prompted perhaps by a visit to England in 1617 of the Indian Princess Pocahontas, he conceived the idea of establishing a college in Virginia for the instruction of Indian children; for this purpose he urged the bishops to raise funds, and instructed the colony to set aside ten thousand acres for the support of the college. He also befriended the College of Heralds which contained at the time a body of learned men.

The fate of the Society of Antiquaries, however, must be cited against him. This famous society, founded in the reign of Elizabeth, had flourished for many years but had declined after 1603. There was hope that James would assist in its revival. 'Methinks that under so learned a King', wrote Richard Carew, the charming chronicler of his native Cornwall, 'this plant should rather grow to its full height than quail in the spring. It imports no little disgrace to our nation that others have so many academies and we none at all.' Camden, Cotton, Spelman and other learned antiquaries, attempting to revive the society in 1614, adopted new rules of government, among them a resolution not to meddle in their discussions with affairs of State or religion. 'But before our next meeting', wrote Spelman, 'we had notice that his Majesty took a little mislike of our society, not being informed that we had resolved to decline all matters of State. Yet hereupon we forbore to meet again.'

But though James frowned upon the Society of Antiquaries, he welcomed the idea of a national academy when it was presented to him in somewhat different form. The desire for an academy of eminent men to encourage the study of history, literature and 'heroic matter' continued in the minds of the former members of the Society of Antiquaries; and we learn of their thoughts from the writings of Edmund Bolton. In 1620 he besought the King 'to found an Academ Roial or college of honour where lectures and exercises of heroic matter and of the antiquities of Great Britain may be had and holden forever'. Bolton proposed that the academy be closely associated with the Order of the Garter, that it contain the flower of the nobility as well as other distinguished men, that it meet in Windsor Castle, keep a register of public events, and supervise the translation of foreign books into English. Buckingham mentioned the project in Parliament in 1621, coupling it with a plan of the late Prince Henry to found an academy for the instruction of the sons of the nobility. James welcomed the proposal in a letter written to Prince Charles in 1622. 'We have long had a desire to advance some public works,' he wrote, 'as creating an academy for breeding of youth and to encourage divers men of arts for the honour and profit of us and of our kingdom.' Lack of money, the King continued, had vetoed this project in the past, but he now had some funds available and promised more in the future. Yet for some reason there was delay; and plans for an Academ Roial ended with James's death, for Charles took no interest in the project.'

Though the King's interest in learning was sincere, his relations with some of the most learned men of his day were less cordial than one might suppose. Lacking the scholar's love of truth, he could not understand it in others. He occasionally consulted Sir Robert Bruce Cotton, whom he jestingly called 'cousin', but displayed little interest in Cotton's antiquarian lore. He did not compel William Camden, as an old story avers, to revise his *Annales* of Elizabeth's reign in order to paint a favourable picture of Mary Queen of Scots. But Camden, like other learned men, was to be used, and at James's command he defended Mary against the accusations of the French historian, de Thou. The King treated John Selden very badly. The secular tone of Selden's history of tithes, published in 1618, aroused a storm of protest from the clergy, who begged the King to come to their assistance. James talked with Selden on three occasions, learnedly, jestingly and sometimes in anger. He rambled from tithes to the number of beasts in the Apocalypse and to the date on which Christ's nativity should be celebrated. He feared that Selden leaned to the opinion of the obstinate Scots who refused to celebrate Christ's birth on any particular date. Denying this charge, Selden replied he was about to complete a pamphlet on the subject, and James asked at once that he be sent a copy. Hence Selden believed that his audiences with the King had gone fairly well. He was summoned, none the less, before the High Commission and compelled to express regret for publishing his history of tithes; his work was suppressed, and he was threatened with imprisonment if he answered his critics. Shortly thereafter, at the King's command, he wrote his *Mare Clausum* in answer to the doctrine of the freedom of the seas put forward by the Dutch. But as the work was about to be printed, James bethought himself that it might offend Christian of Denmark, to whom he owed a large sum of money, and hence the pamphlet was suppressed.

The King did not understand or appreciate Bacon's great plan for the advancement of science through more careful observation and sounder methods of inductive reasoning. This was not through lack of wooing. The *Advancement of Learning*, published in 1605, was written to catch the King's attention. It has been called an inaugural lecture in Bacon's vast design, and it dwelt upon the dignity and merit of learning as a proper work for kings. But James did not respond. Again in 1620 Bacon invited royal support. Having completed his *Novum Organum*, he sent it to the King, 'as no improper oblation to your Majesty, who, of men, is the greatest master of reason and author of beneficence'. Bacon asked James 'to set men on work for the collecting of a natural and experimental history; a thing which I assure myself will be an excellent recreation unto you; I say, to that admirable spirit of yours, that delighteth in light; and I hope well that even in your times many noble inventions may be discovered for man's use'. The King replied in a kindly letter, promising to read the book with care, though he stole some hours from his sleep, and to 'give a due commendation to such places as in my opinion shall deserve it'. Bacon, he added, could not have selected a subject more befitting his place or his universal and methodic knowledge. Yet James found the book hard reading; he remarked that it resembled the peace of God for it passed all understanding; and Bacon knew that his appeal had been in vain.

Magic, witchcraft and the monstrosities of nature caught James's imagination, but science did not. His patronage of Cornelis van Drebbel, the clever Dutch inventor who came to England in 1604, was nothing more than curiosity. Physicians he held in high disdain and never tired of making jibes at their expense, though in his didactic way he himself propounded medical opinions in which a great deal of nonsense was mingled with some common sense.

Happily that common sense prompted an act which was to have a profound effect upon the history of medicine in England. The apothecaries, at this time members of the Grocers' Company, were growing in knowledge, skill and importance; they visited patients, and administered the treatment that the doctors prescribed. Hence they grew restless under the grocers' control. Led probably by Gideon Delaune, a Frenchman who had grown rich in England by compounding a famous pill and who was Anne's apothecary, they sought separation from the grocers, first by Act of Parliament, and then in 1617 by petition to the King. They contended that their craft affected the health of the people and that they should not be governed by the grocers who knew nothing of their profession. James granted their petition and gave them a royal charter, thus inaugurating the Society of Apothecaries which came in time to be a great training school for the general practitioner.[8]

All commonwealths, wrote the King in his *Counterblaste to Tobacco*, are subject to infirmities and corruptions. In England, he continued, 'peace and wealth hath brought forth a general sluggishness, which makes us wallow in all sorts of idle delights and soft delicacies. Our clergy are become negligent and lazy, our nobility and gentry prodigal and sold to their private delights, our lawyers covetous, our common people prodigal and curious. For remedy whereof, it is the King's part (as the proper physician of his politic body) to purge it of all these diseases, and by the example of his own person and by the execution of good laws to reform and abolish these old and evil grounded abuses'. His ideal of kingship and his didactic nature prompted him to uplift the social customs of his people; and though his efforts were often ineffective and misguided, they deserve something better than the ridicule which has been heaped upon them, for he set his face against certain evils that were real, and his approach to social problems was frequently sane and sensible.

Tobacco was known and used in England probably as early as the 1560s, but smoking first became a general practice about 1586, when Drake captured a 'great store of tobacco' in the Indies and when Ralegh's unhappy settlers, returning from Roanoke Island, brought the habit with them. The English took to smoking with avidity, and a group of young gallants in London carried the habit to bizarre excess, supplying themselves with equipment of gold and silver, seeking instruction from 'professors of the art of whiffing', and smoking in public with foppish ostentation. It was perhaps the dissipations of these reeking gallants that first aroused the ire of King James. And he doubtless liked smoking the less because it had been made fashionable at court by Ralegh, whom he accused of first introducing tobacco into England. 'It was neither brought in by king, great emperor, nor learned doctor of physic, but by a father generally hated.'

Whatever the cause, James conceived a violent aversion to tobacco and began a campaign against it which lasted the rest of his life. His *Counterblaste to Tobacco*, one of the most famous of anti-tobacco pamphlets, appeared in 1604. He apologizes for dealing with so light a theme. His pamphlet, he says, is a mere toy. 'And since the subject is but of smoke, I think the fume of an idle brain may serve for a sufficient battery against so fumous and feeble an enemy.' His only care is that his dear countrymen may rightly conceive even by this smallest trifle his sincerity in promoting their welfare.

The habit of smoking tobacco, he continues, sprang from a base and barbarous origin, for it was begun by the Indians as a stinking and unsavoury antidote or suffumigation against a corrupt and execrable malady, the syphilis. Why, asks James, should we imitate the beastly manners of the godless and slavish Indians? Why should we take upon ourselves the imputation of that disease which the Indians sought to cure? Why should we adopt a vile and affected custom through an inconsiderate and childish love of novelty?

Tobacco was widely thought to possess rare medicinal power and to be a cure for all and sundry disorders; and the bulk of the *Counterblaste* is a scathing attack upon these claims. The King's notions of medicine and anatomy are, of course, absurd. He speaks of the body as composed of four complexions, analogous to the elements of earth, air, fire and water. He believes that the smoke of tobacco enters the brain, though he ridicules the notion that the brain, being wet and cold, derives benefit from the hot and dry smoke of tobacco. Smoking, he asserts, makes a kitchen in the inward parts of a man, soiling and infecting them with an unctuous and oily soot. Yet he is on solid ground in challenging the therapeutic powers claimed for tobacco. Smoke flies up into the head, he scoffs, yet is supposed to cure gout in the lower limbs. It is a remedy for diseases directly opposed to each other. It makes a drunken man sober and a sober man drunk, it induces sleep yet quickens and awakens the brain. It is used in America by the poor pocky Indians but in England it is refined and will cure only the diseases of gentlemen. O omnipotent power of tobacco! It can indeed chase out devils, as did the smoke of Tobias's fish, 'which I am sure could smell no stronglier'. James, moreover, is correct in asserting that tobacco is habit-forming, expensive — that precious stink, he calls it — and uncleanly. He exaggerates its sinfulness, for he compares it to excessive drinking, and he condemns with needless fury the social pressure that marked a man as peevish and ill-natured who would not take a pipe with his fellows. In a famous peroration he denounces smoking as 'a custom loathsome to the eye, hateful to the nose, harmful to the brain, dangerous to the lungs, and in the black stinking fumes thereof nearest resembling the horrible Stygian smoke of the pit that is bottomless'.

He continued to attack tobacco in his writings and conversation.

He would say, when a heavy fog descended, that the Devil was smoking. Were he to invite the foul Fiend for dinner, he would serve him with three dishes: a pig, a pole of ling with mustard and a pipe of tobacco. He denounced the 'tobacco-drunkards who cannot abstain from that filthy stinking smoke, because, forsooth, they are bewitched by it'. That witch tobacco, he wrote, 'hath quite blown away the smoke of hospitality and turned the chimneys of men's forefathers into the noses of their children'. He rebuked courtiers whom he saw smoking. Mountjoy, thus reproved, is said to have answered softly that when the King had lived longer in England he 'would find greater faults to pardon among us'. James told Sir John Harington that tobacco injured the brain, that no learned man should taste it, and he wished it forbidden. About to visit St. Paul's in 1619, he ordered the demolition of a tobacco shop that stood near the cathedral. And when he visited Cambridge in 1615, the university authorities, fearing some untoward incident, threatened to expel any student who smoked while the King remained at the university.

The royal blast against tobacco encouraged others to write in a similar vein, and a literature arose depicting in vivid colours the horrible effects of smoking. One of these diatribes contained the lines:

> Tobacco, that outlandish weed,
> It spends the brain and spoils the seed.
> It dulls the sprite, it dims the light,
> It robs a woman of her right.

In October 1604, the King imposed the exorbitant duty of six shillings and tenpence upon every pound of tobacco imported into England, an increase of some four thousand per cent. Tobacco, he declared, was smoked not only by the well-to-do but also by disorderly persons among the lower classes who thereby rendered themselves unfit for labour and consumed their time and wages in idle vanity. Since the better grades of tobacco came from the Spanish Indies, James also had sound mercantile reasons for depressing the traffic. He obviously hoped to deal it a devastating blow, to withhold tobacco from the common people, and to force the rich to pay dearly for their folly. But he shortly discovered that he had encouraged smuggling and that people would buy tobacco at high prices; and he was faced with the dilemma that the vile weed he so detested was the producer of greater revenue than he could afford to relinquish. In 1608 the duty was lowered, and there followed a bewildering number of tobacco farms, leases and patents. James's difficulties increased as Virginia became a tobacco colony. For some years the Virginia Company enjoyed the right to import its products into England duty free, but this privilege lapsed in 1619; and thereafter the government drove a series of hard bargains with the company in order to obtain as high a duty as possible. Clearly the King was compromising with his dislike of tobacco in order to augment his income. Yet he was not wholly inconsistent. He made strenuous efforts to induce the Virginia planters to turn to other crops. Tobacco culture in the colony, he often declared, was merely a temporary shift until such time as the Virginians could find another staple. He prohibited tobacco growing in England, not only to recompense the Virginia Company for the duties it must pay, but also to protect the soil of England from pollution by tobacco; and he obtained a dubious opinion from the College of Physicians that the domestic product was even more vile and poisonous than that grown in hotter climates.

But the witch tobacco proved stronger than King James. The habit of smoking steadily increased and the fume-sucking gallants continued their obnoxious intemperance. High Customs duties and restrictions (James prohibited the importation of Spanish tobacco in 1624) led to smuggling, adulteration and illegal planting in England. The frowns of royalty added an element of pleasurable naughtiness to smoking, increasing its allurements. The pamphlet war begun by the *Counterblaste* produced defenders of tobacco as well as critics, and smoking was given a publicity that tended to increase the habit. Indeed, it has been said that at James's death the custom lost its best advertiser and that only then did excessive smoking begin to subside. In Scotland the King had issued a lordly proclamation prohibiting in most absolute terms the importation and sale of tobacco; yet both were legal in the northern kingdom when he died. [9]

His contempt for women rendered him intolerant of feminine vanities in matters of dress and adornment. He often contrasted the natural beauty of the modest woman with the borrowed feathers of the courtesan, and talked as though paint, powder and frizzled hair were synonymous with loss of virtue. 'I wonder not so much that women paint themselves,' he declared pompously, 'as that when they are painted men can love them.' The ladies of the court went to great extremes, dressing in strange and exotic fashion and decking themselves with jewels and trinkets. Chamberlain spoke with scorn of a young lady whom he saw at Whitehall and of 'the multitude of jewels wherewith she was hung as it were all over'. The men were quite as bad, but the ladies had to bear the frowns of the King. In 1616 he talked of new sumptuary laws to moderate excess in apparel of both sexes. In 1620 he instructed the London clergy to preach 'against the insolency of our women and their wearing broad-brimmed hats, pointed doublets, their hair cut short or shorn, and some of them stilettoes and poniards, and other trinkets of like moment, adding withall that if pulpit admonitions did not reform them he would proceed by another course'. Chamberlain wrote a few weeks later: 'Our pulpits ring continually of the insolence and impudence of women, and to help the matter forward the players have likewise taken them to task, and so do the ballads and ballad-singers so that they can come nowhere but their ears tingle. And if all this will not serve, the King threatens to fall upon their husbands, parents, or friends that have or should have power over them and make them pay for it.' When, however, the Dean of Westminster refused to admit to his church ladies who wore yellow ruffs, the King relented, declaring he had meant 'other manlike and unseemly apparel'. Yet as he rode to open Parliament in 1621, seeing a window 'full of gentlemen and ladies all in yellow bands, he cried out aloud, "A pox take ye! Are ye there?" at which, being much ashamed, they all withdrew themselves suddenly from the window'.

He blamed the ladies also for the way in which nobility and gentry remained in London instead of living on their estates. Husbands and fathers must bring their wives and daughters to the capital, he said, because, forsooth, 'the new fashion is to be had nowhere but in London; and here, if they be unmarried, they mar their marriages, and if they be married, they lose their reputations and rob their husbands' purses' in following French and Italian fashions. 'Let us in God's name leave these idle foreign toys and keep the old fashion of England' that persons of quality should live in the country and dispense hospitality. In 1617 he issued a proclamation that nobility and gentry should repair to their estates and remain there in the future. A similar proclamation appeared in 1622, but neither appears to have been obeyed. The King threatened the gentlemen with the Star Chamber and addressed the ladies in verse:

> You women that do London love so well,
> Whom scarce a proclamation can expel,
> And to be kept in fashion fine and gay
> Care little what your honest husbands pay,
> Who dream on naught but visits, masques, and toys
> And thinks the country contributes no joys,
> Be not deceiv'd, the country's not so bare, . . .
> Your complete gallants and your proper men
> Are not confined to Fleet Street or the Strand . . .
> Therefore depart in peace and look not back,
> Remember Lot's wife ere you suffer wrack
> Of fame and fortune, which you may redeem
> And in the country live in good esteem . . .
> The country is your orb and proper sphere.
> There your revenues rise, bestow them there.
> Convert your coach-horse to the thrifty plow,
> Take knowledge of your sheep, your corn, your cow,
> And think it no disparagement or tax
> T'acquaint your fingers with your wool and flax . . .
> Your husbands will as kindly you embrace
> Without your jewels, or a painted face . . .
> And you, good man, its best you get you hence,
> Lest honest Adam pay for Eve's offence.

About the same time James issued a third proclamation. 'It is nothing pleasing to all,' wrote Chamberlain, 'but least of all to the women.'[10]

In more kingly and purposeful fashion James took a stand against the vicious custom of duelling. The brawls and bloody affrays of the later Middle Ages had given place to the duel, refined by rules and by a code of honour, but barbarous enough. Duelling was an evil before 1603 but it greatly increased in the decade that followed and was dangerously fashionable by 1613. In that year Chamberlain spoke of half a dozen quarrels that might result in duels, though most of them were prevented by the vigilance of the King and Council. James was alarmed at the number fought between Englishmen and Scots. In 1609 Sir George Wharton and Sir James Stewart, both of them young and brave and favourites of the King, killed each other in a savage duel. James ordered that they be buried in a single grave. He then hastily removed from the capital, taking with him the Scots who followed the court. In 1613 a duel was fought between Sir Edward Sackville, brother of the Earl of Dorset, and Lord Kinloss, son of the King's old friend and adviser. It was a horrible affair, fought near Antwerp in a meadow ankle-deep in water, and resulted in the death of Kinloss.

The King regarded duelling with horror and fierce hatred. It was wicked in the sight of God, for vengeance belonged to the Lord. The duellist, said James, was a wilful murderer, ready to lose his soul for all eternity rather than injure his worldly reputation; and passionately the King denounced the false code of honour that prompted men to take the field. Duelling was an affront to public justice, an injury to the challenged party, and an insult to the King's authority, for duellists snatched the sword of justice from his hands and submitted to no judgment save the sudden flashes of their own fury. Duelling slaughtered brave young men, thus opening a vein by which the commonwealth might bleed to death. The King, wrote Bacon, was touched by compassion as he saw himself attended by goodly lords and gentlemen, for he remembered 'that none of their lives were in certainty not for twenty-four hours from the duel; for it was but a heat or a mistaking, and then a lie, and then a challenge, and then life'.

James acted with unusual caution, consulting Coke as to the law and Bacon as to remedies. No Act of Parliament dealt with duelling. The common law took no cognizance of giving the lie or of issuing a challenge but merely punished the duellist after the fact for murder, manslaughter, or battery. Nor did the law extend to duels fought overseas. An intent to fight was punishable in the Star Chamber by fine and imprisonment, but the King wanted preventive measures of wider scope and welcomed the advice of Bacon that he issue a 'grave and severe proclamation'.

He began, however, with two minor measures, one a proclamation in January 1613, against small daggers and short pistols known as pocket dags that could be concealed in the clothes. Such weapons led easily to duels, and the King, always fearful of assassination, declared they could also be used 'to more execrable ends'. A second proclamation in October, written by the King, forbade private publications regarding duels. Sometimes a man intending to fight a duel, but finding his intention frustrated, issued a kind of open letter stating his desire to fight and explaining why the duel in question had not taken place. Such letters, James declared, were offensive to God and to the King, usurped his prerogative of issuing proclamations, and led to new quarrels. Persons who wrote them should henceforth be brought before the Star Chamber. At the same time James instructed Bacon to begin action in that court against all who attempted to fight duels. I will prosecute, said Bacon, if any man appoint the field, though no fight take place; if any man send a challenge; if any man carry a challenge, or accept one, or agree to be a second; if any man leave England in order to fight; if any man issue letters such as those forbidden by the late proclamation. And the King told Bacon that in prosecuting duellists he must not know a coronet from a hatband.

In February 1614, James issued a solemn proclamation, which he had written himself, forbidding challenges and duels. Annexed to the proclamation was a royal edict or treatise, a hundred and nineteen pages long, in which the King set forth the measures he proposed to employ against duelling. Commissioners for the office of Earl Marshal should adjudicate quarrels that arose at court, while Lords-lieutenant or their deputies should do the same for the rest of the country. The commissioners, upon hearing of a quarrel, were to summon the parties and effect a settlement. If one of the parties had insulted his adversary, he should be confined to his house or chamber until he made amends. If he had given his enemy the lie or had assaulted him, he should be imprisoned until he admitted his fault and renounced duelling as a means of redress. He should then be bound over to keep the peace and to absent himself from court for six months. So much for prevention. If a man fought a duel, he was left to the common law, which could inflict the death penalty, and the King declared in solemn terms that there would be no royal pardons or interference with the course of justice. He added the penalties of withdrawal of royal favour and of revocation of all royal grants. He was ready, he declared, to stretch his prerogative to punish those who fought beyond the seas.

The authorship of the edict is interesting. Chamberlain at first suspected that Bacon had written it, but quickly discovered that it came, as he said, from a higher hand. Its involved sentences and flowery conceits betrayed the pen of Northampton. James had employed a method with which we are familiar, had gathered the material he wished to set forth, and had entrusted Northampton to put his thoughts in writing.

These measures produced some good. In 1617 the King boasted in the Star Chamber, having come to preside in an action against two duellists, that there had been but three challenges in the last three years. Duelling, he continued, concerned the peace of the kingdom which the King, as a shepherd of his flock, must strive to conserve. He thought that the word shepherd fitted him well, especially since his name derived from that of Jacob who was a shepherd. And as Jacob had protected his sheep from being spoiled and devoured, so he would defend them against the quarrelsome ram, thus justifying his title of *Rex Pacificus*. Two years later, however, he had to confess that duelling had again increased, and his measures did not end the evil. Yet something was accomplished. He took a stand against a vicious practice. He defined the law and gave it better enforcement. He strove most earnestly to reconcile disputes, chided quarrelsome courtiers in no uncertain terms, and adopted extraordinary measures to prevent duels from taking place.[11]

Throughout his efforts at social reform there runs an honest indignation that men and women should stoop to crime and folly at the dictates of fashion; and though his own shortcomings were sadly apparent, it can at least be said that he did not do evil things merely because other people did them.

Much has been written upon the manner in which the author of the *Daemonologie* dealt with witchcraft in England. Some older writers depict his reign as a time of intense persecution, with the King in the van of the witch-hunters. A more moderate view assumes that he was no persecutor but that royal interest in witchcraft increased the tempo of the superstition, rendered magistrates more ready to try and punish witches, and encouraged Parliament to pass severer laws against them;[12] while a recent judgment exonerates the King at all points and declares he was far ahead of his time.[13] There is room for disagreement, but it is clear that James gradually modified his early views on witchcraft.

In Scotland his interest had been intensely personal. The machinations of the Scottish witches had been aimed at him directly and had been made more terrifying by the madcap Earl of Bothwell. But as James relaxed in the protected ease of his new kingdom, witchcraft ceased to be a haunting personal dread and receded into the realm of wonders, fascinating but innocuous. The King was well aware before he left Scotland that many of the charges against witches and sorcerers sprang from the malice of their enemies, and he grew suspicious of the weird seizures and wild talk of those who claimed to be bewitched. Time and again, as he examined such persons, he found them to be impostors seeking revenge or notoriety. He grew wary of their accusations. Indeed, he became suspicious of all supernatural events. The age of miracles, he said, was over. And we are faced with the fascinating possibility that the royal witch-hunter, by dint of his constant and skilful inquiries, gradually undermined his own belief in witchcraft.

We catch some early glimpses of his changing point of view. The *Daemonologie*, despite its faith in witches, warned the magistrate of his duty to protect the innocent as well as to punish the guilty. About the time of his accession James wrote to Prince Henry: 'I am glad of the discovery of your little counterfeit wench. I pray God ye may be my heir in such discoveries. Ye have oft heard me say that most miracles now a days prove but illusions, and ye may see by this how wary judges should be in trusting accusations without exact trial, and likewise how easily people are induced to trust to wonders.' There is also a letter of the King to a nobleman who had told him of a woman that lay in prolonged trances and claimed to subsist without food. 'Leave nothing untried to discover the imposture,' James wrote, 'trying by any deceits ye can devise to expose the cheat, as I am sure no mortal living could fast for so long a time. It becomes us to lose no opportunity of seeking after the real truth of pretended wonders, that if true we may bless the Creator who hath shown such marvels to men, and if false we may punish the impudent inventors of them.'

The King's investigations were sharp and constant. He 'was ever ready to search into secrets,' wrote Goodman, 'and I did know some who saw him run to see a man in a fit whom they said was bewitched'. 'He took delight to sound the depth of brutish impostures and he discovered many.' One of the first in England was that of a physician, Richard Haydock, who gained great notoriety by preaching excellent sermons in his sleep. James detected the fraud when he pretended to be highly incensed at something the sleeper said. Drawing a sword, the King shouted, 'God's wounds, I will cut off his head', at which Haydock leaped in terror from his couch. Another of the King's more blithe inquiries involved a young woman of Windsor, Ann Gunter, who 'gave out that she was possessed of a devil and was transported with strange ecstatic frenzies'. In her hysterical trances she vomited pins, at that time considered an infallible proof of witchcraft. But the King was sceptical. Summoning the young woman to court, he pretended great pity for her and promised to treat her kindly if she would confess the truth, whereupon she admitted that her hysteria and 'pin-pranks' were all a hoax. She also confessed that she was deeply in love. The King allowed her to marry and gave her a wedding portion, thus quickly curing her ills; and he wrote in triumph that she danced and leaped 'in our view' with great strength, comeliness and agility. We catch a glimpse of another woman who, in fits of hysterical anaesthesia, 'cast up at her mouth pins, and pins were taken by divers in her fits out of her breast'. In some way the King discovered that she was an impostor. There was also a certain Mary Glover, a poor wretch who honestly believed her convulsions were caused by witchcraft. At James's command she was examined by a competent physician who declared her illness due to natural causes; and the witch she had accused was set free.

In conducting his inquiries James 'applied remedies suitable to the distemper, wherein he made himself often very merry'. Some of his devices were innocent enough. Hearing of a woman who was seized with fits at a set hour each day, the King came to see her some hours before her appointed time, when she, thinking it unmannerly to keep royalty waiting, instantly ran through her whole zodiac of tricks. Another woman, who was strangely affected when she heard a certain verse from the Bible, displayed no symptoms when the King had the verse read to her in Greek, 'her English devil, belike, understanding no other language'. But James stooped low in asking a courtier to make love to a woman who claimed to be bewitched, when 'quickly Cupid's arrows drove out the pretended darts of the Devil'. And he stooped lower when he visited a woman who lay in bed in trances. Suddenly he plucked the bed-clothes from her, exposing her naked to the company, at which she started up, thus showing her trances to be fraudulent.

The King's most famous exposure of counterfeited bewitchment occurred in 1616. On a visit to Leicester during a progress James heard of a boy who suffered from fits in which he foamed at the mouth and displayed other strange symptoms. As a result of his accusations nine persons had been hanged for witchcraft and six others were in prison awaiting trial. 'The King,' wrote the essayist Francis Osborne, 'being gratified by nothing more than an opportunity to show his dexterity in discovering an imposture (at which I must confess him the promptest man living), convened the boy. Where, before him (possibly daunted at his presence or terrified by his words), the boy began to falter, so as the King discovered a fallacy.' The boy confessed all his tricks to be frauds; the witches in prison were released; and James gave the judges a sharp reprimand for their carelessness in hanging the other nine.

This admonition was of great importance, for the judges acted thereafter with the greatest caution, and more than once adopted extraordinary measures to prevent doubtful convictions for witchcraft. Only five witches are known to have been executed in the last nine years of James's reign.

Whether the King abandoned entirely his belief in witchcraft it is impossible to say. Fuller is quite explicit. 'The frequency of such forged possessions wrought such an alteration upon the judgment of King James, that he, receding from what he had written in his *Daemonologie*, grew first diffident of, and then flatly to deny, the workings of witches and devils, as but falsehoods and delusions.' Osborne says the same. The King's judgment of witchcraft, he writes, may be gathered from his admonitions to the judges; 'nor had he concluded his advice in a narrower circle (as I have heard) than the denial of any such operations, but out of reasons of State and to gratify the Church'. It is likely that these statements go too far. In all probability James never abandoned a theoretical belief in witchcraft, though he grew suspicious of each individual case. He gave many pardons to witches and sorcerers, he did not disturb some persons against whom he might have taken action, he mitigated the persecution in various ways. From a firm belief in witches he moved to a position of doubt if not of scepticism; and though he did not prohibit the trials, which was beyond his power, he taught his people to employ the utmost circumspection.[14]

CHAPTER XVII

THE GREAT SCHOOLMASTER OF THE REALM: SCOTLAND, IRELAND AND VIRGINIA

IN the *Basilikon Doron* James criticized sharply the faults of each estate in Scotland; 'but I protest before God', he added, 'I do it with the fatherly love that I owe to them all, only hating their vices, whereof there is a good number of honest men free in every estate'. His words were sincere, for he wished well to his native land. Yet as he played the schoolmaster towards his old kingdom, he dropped the moderation and urbanity of England and became harsh, revengeful and treacherous. His actions were more dictatorial, his insistence on obedience more rigid, his fury against opposition more savage and remorseless. The Scots had caused him many an awkward moment and he would show them who was master. Sincerely anxious to uplift and instruct, the great schoolmaster of the realm turned petulant, cruel and contemptuous at the backwardness of his Scottish pupils.

In the Tudor machinery of absolute government he found an armoury of weapons that could be used against the Scots, and quickly he established a despotism in Scotland such as that kingdom had never known. 'This I must say for Scotland,' he boasted in 1607, 'here I sit and govern it with my pen, I write and it is done, and by a clerk of the Council I govern Scotland now, which others could not do by the sword.' This was accomplished through the Scottish Privy Council. The number of Scottish councillors was reduced, and the work of government was done by a handful of devoted and obedient officials who, like their English counterparts, awaited instructions and followed them closely. James kept a sharp eye upon his Scottish councillors. 'We cannot but wonder at the inexcusable negligence of you, our councillors', he wrote. 'We have just cause to weary to continue thus still a tutor unto you to remember so often our directions, as tutors are accustomed to repeat their lessons to their children.' Yet in truth he had small reason to complain.

Steadily he increased his power over other Scottish institutions.

Parliament was easily controlled through the Lords of the Articles. This all-important committee, selected within the first few days of a Parliament to sift and prepare its legislation, came to be nominated largely at the King's direction; it was made the only channel through which new laws could come; and by an ingenious abuse of the prerogative James prevented Parliament from meeting while the committee was at work. Hence the full Parliament assembled only to elect the Lords of the Articles and again to receive their report, when the legislation they proposed was voted upon *en bloc*. That vote was tampered with. Since there were no divisions, members were called upon in turn to give their opinions orally, a practice that exposed them to royal pressure. In 1621, not only were they 'threatened and boasted with menacing eyes and looks by the Secretary', but their feeble murmurs of dissent were brazenly recorded as votes of approval. The Chancellor told them to speak audibly, but the Secretary remarked: 'Nay, my Lord, let them alone; those that will not speak out, let the clerk mark them as consenters.' The King interfered also with elections, and since he was gaining increased power over the Scottish burghs through nomination of their provosts, he could often control their election of members of Parliament. In meetings of the General Assembly of the Kirk he employed similar tactics, but here he was compelled to act openly and directly, and hence his methods appear even more crass, dishonest and tyrannical than was the case with Parliament. He was successful because the nobles, more sophisticated and more pliant than of old, normally supported the policy of the Crown.[1]

Exulting in his new-found strength, James determined to assimilate the Scottish Church to that of England by building episcopacy in Scotland. In 1600, as we know, he had appointed three diocesan bishops; and on his way to England, hearing of the death in France of James Beaton, the aged Catholic Archbishop of Glasgow, the King named John Spottiswoode to the vacant see and sent him back to Scotland. But the Scottish bishops had little power. They could be members of Parliament and of the Privy Council, but their control of their own dioceses was all but nil. That control still rested in the courts of the Kirk, the presbyteries and synods, while supreme authority remained in the General Assembly. James's policy, therefore, was to strike at these bodies, to force the ministers into line, and to transform his ghostlike bishops into bishops of flesh and blood. He succeeded surprisingly well. Later in the reign he began to meddle with the ritual of the Kirk, but in this he was far less successful.

For some years after 1603 the King forbade a meeting of the General Assembly. When the clergy protested in excited local gatherings, he issued a proclamation from Hampton Court. Despite his constant care for the advancement of true religion, he said, certain unquiet and turbulent spirits among the ministry, hoping to reduce the Kirk to anarchy, dared to assemble in extraordinary manner upon pretexts drawn from their own fantasies. Such assemblies were forbidden under harsh penalties; and James intimated in a letter to Salisbury that there would be no more General Assemblies in Scotland for some time. It was rumoured, however, that an Assembly would meet at Aberdeen in July 1605. A new proclamation at once declared that any minister who went to Aberdeen would be denounced as a rebel. Yet nineteen ministers assembled, and ten others, arriving late, associated themselves with their brethren. The King was furious at this act of insubordination. Wrathfully he wrote that the proceedings at Aberdeen savoured of sedition, treason and plain contempt of royal authority. The clergy had asserted that they would obey as far as their consciences permitted, which meant, said James, that they would not obey at all. They talked of their duty to God but made no mention of their duty to the King. Here was a case, he continued, in which his normal clemency would be misplaced, and he ordered that the ministers be punished with the utmost rigour, lest their gangrene affect all society. The Aberdeen Assembly was obviously to be used against the Kirk as had been the riot in Edinburgh in 1596. Reluctantly the Scottish councillors summoned the ministers, quickly dismissed sixteen who expressed regret, and proceeded to try the others. The ministers refused the jurisdiction of the Council. They were, however, found guilty of rebellion and were imprisoned to await the sentence of the King. But James was not satisfied. He ordered the astonished councillors to try the ministers again, this time for treason in declining the jurisdiction of the Council. Councillors found themselves 'in innumerable straits'. But they obeyed, and six of the clergymen were tried in a travesty of justice. Dunbar, coming from England, crowded Linlithgow, where the trial was held, with his friends, placed his kinsmen on the assize, threatened and bullied prisoners and jurymen, and carried the day 'by his dexterity in advising what was fittest to be done in everything'. The ministers, convicted of treason, were now in danger of their lives. But the shameless methods employed in the trial were patent to all, and councillors begged the King 'to put them to as few essays in the like causes as may possibly stand with the weal of your Majesty's service'.

Far from appeased, James commanded that the imprisoned ministers be treated as men condemned, except that they should not be put in irons, and that Balmerino, the Secretary, should prepare an account of the trial for the edification of the public. He need not discuss General Assemblies, to which the King was deeply attached; he need only describe 'the punishment of an insolent riot directly disobeying our commandments'. Furthermore, since only six of the ministers had been tried for treason, the others should now be brought to the bar upon that accusation. This command, however, struck terror into the hearts of councillors who gathered the courage to protest. They declared that the first conviction had been obtained only because they had shown themselves more partial than became the modesty of judges, and the outcry of the people had been very great. At this the King gave way, but was not to be balked of his vengeance. The ministers convicted of treason were exiled; they embarked at Leith on a stormy November day, amid the prayers and lamentations of their friends, and sailed for the Continent, never to return. The others, who had not been tried for treason, were banished to remote parts of the Western Isles.

Meanwhile the King was preparing another blow at the Scottish clergy. Saying that he wished to hold a conference for the pacification of the Kirk, as he had done for the English Church at Hampton Court, he summoned to London eight of the principal clergymen of Scotland, among them Andrew and James Melville. They arrived in August 1606. But James had no intention of holding a conference on any equitable terms. His purpose was to lure the Scots into England, to confront them with the English Church, and to entrap them into words or actions that could be used against them. Their first audience went well enough. The King was in a pleasant mood after dinner, joked with one of the ministers about his long beard, and dismissed them favourably. Three days later they were summoned to Hampton Court, where they found the King surrounded by Scottish bishops, councillors and nobles. James, of course, made a speech, then asked the ministers pointedly what they thought of the 'pretended' Assembly at Aberdeen, of which he spoke most bitterly, and how they proposed to pacify the Scottish Kirk. The Scots asked time to consider their answer, which was allowed.

Next day they appeared once more before the King who sat in state, surrounded by English as well as Scottish dignitaries. Bancroft, the old enemy of the Kirk, stood at his right hand, and Prince Henry at his left. The ministers were asked the same questions as before. They answered on their knees, 'but freely, to the admiration of the English'; they justified the Aberdeen Assembly; and Andrew Melville spoke 'all his mind in his own manner, roundly, soundly, fully, freely and fervently, almost the space of an hour'. He turned upon Thomas Hamilton, King's Advocate, who had acted as prosecutor in the trial at Linlithgow, calling him 'the accuser of the brethren'. The King, recalling a passage from the Book of Revelation, caught at these words. 'What?' said he with an oath, 'Methinks he makes him the Antichrist! By God, it is the Devil's name in the Revelation! He has made the Devil of him!' The King turned his back upon the Scottish ministers and departed. An ill-chosen word ended the second Hampton Court Conference as it had ended the first.

Meanwhile James forced upon the reluctant Scots a closer acquaintance with the doctrines and ceremonies of the Church of England. They attended sermons prepared for their enlightenment by leading Anglican divines, one of whom, John King, made 'a virulent invective against the Presbyterians, crying to the King, "Down, down with them!" ' They witnessed a solemn celebration, with music and high service, of the feast of St. Michael in the royal chapel at Windsor. They watched the ceremony of the royal touch. They were summoned to private interviews with English churchmen. Montagu, Master of the Chapel, spoke with James Melville on the question of the royal supremacy. Supremacy in the Church, said Melville, must go either to the Pope, or to the prince, or to the presbytery. 'The Pope should not have it, we say all. Mr. Calvin gives it to the presbytery, and so do we.' 'That is treason in England,' Montagu answered, 'for the prince has it by our laws.' 'Not by ours of Scotland', came the prompt retort. 'But ye must have it so', said Montagu, abruptly ending the conversation. Hoping that good company would improve bad manners or perhaps wishing to rub salt into the wounds he was inflicting, James proposed that the Scots be billeted upon the English bishops. But Scots and English united in opposition, and the suggestion was dropped.

Amid these trying ordeals Andrew Melville found relief in writing some caustic Latin verses defaming Bancroft and the Anglican Church. On November 30th he was summoned before the English Council. Bancroft, who was present, ordered him to kneel, but he refused; and though forced into a kneeling position by the Council's attendants, he sprang to his feet the moment he was released. He freely acknowledged that the verses were his. Warming to his discourse, he told Bancroft 'plainly to his face before the Council all that he thought', charging him with vanities, corruption and superstition, calling him the persecutor of the faithful and the upholder of popish ceremonies. Striding to the astonished prelate, Melville grasped his white lawn sleeves, shook them roundly, and called them popish rags. 'Often was he interrupted', but this proving no let to his invective, he was 'at last removed to a part by himself'. Such a scene — the ruffled primate, the astonished councillors, the rash and violent Scot — must have been long remembered. Within a few months Melville was sent to the Tower where, by an egregious tyranny, he was kept without trial for more than three years. In 1611 he was permitted to go to France, and there ended his days. Thus did James win his lifelong battle with that bold and ardent spirit.

Six of the ministers were at length permitted to return to Scotland. But James Melville was commanded not to go north of Newcastle, where he remained in exile. Some years later Dunbar, stopping at Newcastle on a journey to Scotland, offered Melville preferment in the Scottish Church if he would conform. But Melville refused. He accompanied Dunbar to Berwick, gazed across the Border, then turned his back upon his native land.

The Kirk was thus deprived of its leaders, and the King pressed forward with its assimilation to the Church of England. His method was to obtain concessions from Parliament and from informal and nominated conventions of the clergy, to enlarge these concessions by a vigorous use of the prerogative, to confront the General Assembly with what he had done, and to extract reluctant acquiescence. The foundation was laid by an Act of Parliament in 1606 which acknowledged 'his Majesty's supreme authority, princely power, royal prerogative and privilege of his Crown over all estates, persons and causes whatsoever'.

The powers of the Scottish bishops were steadily increased. The Act of 1587 — that vile Act of annexation, as James called it — which vested all ecclesiastical property in the Crown, was rescinded, and the bishops received once more, on paper though often not in fact, their ancient lands and revenues. A convention of ministers summoned to Linlithgow in December 1606, was persuaded to name perpetual Moderators for all the presbyteries of the kingdom. But when the official record of this convention was submitted to the King, he boldly inserted a clause providing perpetual Moderators for synods as well, and despite much opposition and some sacrilegious brawls, bishops were gradually installed as the permanent heads of the synods in their dioceses. Acts of Parliament in 1609 further augmented the bishops' powers. To them was restored their ancient jurisdiction in spiritual cases and they were permitted to set up consistory courts. In 1610 the King created two Courts of High Commission for Scotland, one in each archbishopric, modelled upon the High Commission in England, thus giving the bishops large powers of fine and imprisonment. A General Assembly at Glasgow in 1610 allow them to adjudicate upon presentations to livings and to exercise the right of visitation, while a Parliament in 1612 further increased their authority.

There were now eleven bishops and two archbishops in Scotland. They had, however, been appointed by the King without consecration by other bishops through the laying on of hands, and James determined to remedy this flaw. Three of the Scottish bishops were summoned to England where they were consecrated according to the Anglican form. They then returned to Scotland and performed similar rites for the other bishops of that kingdom. This was done, as Calderwood observes, without the consent of the General Assembly, and implied a further diminution of its authority.

Although by 1612 episcopacy was an accomplished fact in Scotland, the Presbyterian system was far from broken. The courts of the Kirk were active and vigorous and could fight the bishops successfully on many counts. Ritual remained unaltered. Congregations remained seated as they received the Communion, the observance of holy days was rare, the clergy preached in their black Genevan gowns and followed Knox's

Book of Common Order. To the mass of the people these forms of public worship were of greater importance than the resurgence of episcopacy.

After the lapse of some years, however, the King determined that ritual as well as ecclesiastical government in Scotland should conform to English practice, and he began the dangerous experiment of forcing Anglican ceremonies upon the Scots. It was for this purpose that he came to Scotland in 1617. The organs, choristers and surplices that then appeared at Holyrood and so scandalized the Presbyterians were there for the purpose of instruction. To a small informal convention of the clergy at St. Andrews in July the King proposed five innovations — that Communion be received in a kneeling position, that private Communion and private baptism be permitted in cases of necessity, that the festivals of the Church be properly observed, and that confirmation be administered by bishops. These were matters of high import, and the convention took refuge in the argument that only a General Assembly could deal with them. Thus James left Scotland without achieving his object. But a General Assembly at Perth in 1618, subjected to outrageous pressure, accepted the King's five articles, which were also confirmed by Parliament in 1621. James discovered, however, that the resentment against these alterations in ritual was deep and universal and that the people now supported the clergy against the Crown. The new rules were widely disobeyed; churches that observed them were deserted while those that defied them were eagerly attended; the High Commission could not cope with the task of enforcement. This was the situation at James's death.[2]

In other aspects of government he exercised a despotism benevolent in intent but often brutal and treacherous in method. Against lawlessness and feuds he continued to do battle, and fines and imprisonment were imposed upon offenders with a regularity that had been impossible in the past. The Highlands were beaten into something akin to order. The Clan Gregor, guilty of barbarous outrages against its neighbours, was condemned to utter extinction. Its chief, Alexander Macgregor, having been lured into England under a safe-conduct, was seized upon the pretext that his safe-conduct applied only in Scotland, and was promptly hanged. An edict of fire and sword proclaimed against the Macgregors was carried out in ruthless fashion by their neighbours.

The very name of the clan was abolished, yet such was the animosity of the King that years later he acted to prevent the miserable remnant of the Clan Gregor from assuming the name of its forefathers. The peninsula of Kintyre and the Southern Hebrides, where the Clan Donald in Islay was very troublesome, called also for pacification. The King's first efforts in Kintyre proving ineffective, he determined in 1608 upon a major blow. An expedition of considerable strength appeared that August in Mull, where the chieftains of the area, summoned to meet the King's Commissioners at the Castle of Aros, were welcomed by a scurvy trick. They were invited on board ship to hear a sermon by Andrew Knox, the Bishop of the Isles. Dutifully they attended and hearkened to the bishop's words. But suddenly the ship weighed anchor, and the chieftains soon found themselves in various dungeons on the mainland. A year later they agreed to the 'Band and Statutes of Icolmkill' by which James hoped to bring civility to the Southern Hebrides. Churches must be repaired, inns established, vagabonds, beggars and bards cleared from the islands; the importation of wine and whisky and the carrying of fire-arms were forbidden, and the chiefs were made responsible for the obedience of their people. The chieftains, moreover, must send their eldest sons to school in the Lowlands until they could speak English. These measures brought a gradual improvement, but two rebellions by the Macdonalds in Islay had to be subdued before order was established in that island. James also had to deal with his cousin Patrick Stewart, Earl of Orkney, commonly known as 'Earl Pate', who ruled in the Orkneys with such brutal oppression that he was imprisoned in Edinburgh Castle. Yet the Earl, though a prisoner, managed to intrigue with his brother and with his natural son, Robert, to raise rebellion in the islands, and the King was forced to take further measures. He annexed the Orkneys and Shetlands to the Crown in 1612. Two years later, having crushed a revolt by Robert Stewart, he brought that handsome young savage to Edinburgh and hanged him; and shortly thereafter he hanged the Earl himself, much against the wishes of many Scottish nobles. By such implacable severity James brought some order into the wilder portions of his northern kingdom.

His policy in Scotland sprang from his past experience and was entirely his own. Of Ireland he was more ignorant. He had to depend upon advice that was often bad. Yet he quickly made his own decisions, imposed them upon Ireland in hasty and peremptory fashion, and assumed that all would be well. It need not surprise us that he dwelt upon his benevolence, upon his piety and wisdom, and upon his desire to instruct and to uplift. He would bring peace and prosperity to a land ravaged by war, civilization to a barbarous people, true religion to replace Catholicism, and would at the same time establish the British interest in Ireland for ever. He was not ignorant, he wrote in 1612, that the English and Scottish plantation in Ulster deeply concerned the peace and security of Ireland. Yet even if that were not so, he would pursue it eagerly, 'merely for the goodness and morality of it, esteeming the settling of religion, the introducing civility, order and government amongst a barbarous and unsubjected people to be an act of piety and glory and worthy also a Christian prince to endeavour'. And no doubt he relished greatly Ben Jonson's *Irish Masque* in which an Irish bard declared to his countrymen:

> This is that James of which long since thou sungs't,
> Should end our country's most unnatural broils;
> And if her ear, then deafened with the drum,
> Would stoop but to the music of his peace,
> She need not with the spheres change harmony.

James had a great opportunity in Ireland. The long and terrible rebellion against Elizabeth had at last been crushed; and at the moment of the Queen's death Tyrone and other chieftains were coming in to make humble submission. Ireland, torn and bleeding, was a conquered country in which the new King, profiting by what Elizabeth had accomplished, would have far greater power than his predecessor. James talked as though peace had come to Ireland entirely through him, and boasted that now that he was King the English exchequer need be drained no longer to support the Irish wars. Such words were empty enough. But it was true that the change of dynasty brought hope of a brighter era. James's peace with Spain gave him tremendous advantage in Ireland, leaving him free to pacify the country without fear of Spanish intervention. His relations with Tyrone had been friendly; and English officials in Ireland could no longer intrigue with Edinburgh as Essex had done.

Yet his rule in Ireland forms but a sorry tale. In the southern portions of the country, where conditions were fairly settled and the people obedient, at least in the vicinity of the English army, he greatly embittered feeling by attempting to force the Roman Catholics into the English Church. Upon Ulster in the north he imposed a land settlement which was highly dangerous and grossly unjust. In both instances he was thinking primarily of his own security and profit.

Notions of English law and civilization had made little progress as yet in wild and barbaric Ulster. Authority remained in the hands of the tribal chiefs, of whom Tyrone and Tyrconnell were the most important, and they thought in terms of the days when English power was confined to the Irish Pale. They lived as of old, surrounded by bands of swordsmen, exercising a harsh and capricious tyranny over lesser chieftains and simple tribesmen. Yet the tribesmen, maltreated as they were, believed that the lands over which they followed their cattle belonged in common to the tribe and thus in part to them.

The King and Sir Arthur Chichester, the able soldier and administrator who became Lord Deputy in 1605, believed that advance could come in Ulster only by undermining the preponderance of the great chiefs. James sought to teach the Irish to look to him as their sovereign lord. He proclaimed that all Irishmen were his 'free, natural and immediate subjects', dependent upon him and not upon their chiefs. The great Irish lords, he added, had been placed in their present position by the English Crown. It became his policy that when land fell to him in Ireland it should be distributed as freeholds held by English tenure, for he hoped in this way to create a class of lesser lords, or gentry, as a counterpoise to the great chieftains. Meanwhile the courts were doing all in their power to obliterate the crude concepts of Irish law.

Small wonder that Tyrone and Tyrconnell became suspicious and malcontent. They had hoped to be let alone. At their submission in 1603 they had been taken to England where the King had received them with a cordiality that caused some astonishment. 'How I did labour after that knave's destruction', wrote Sir John Harington as he saw Tyrone at court. 'I adventured perils by land and sea, was near starving, ate horse-flesh in Munster, and all to quell that man that now smileth at peace at those that did hazard their lives to destroy him.' The King was paying his debts.

Then the lords returned to Ulster and to hard reality, to quarrels with lesser chieftains and to the steady advance of English influence. The ancient powers of The O'Neill and The O'Donnell were fading fast. Tyrone and Tyrconnell grumbled, talked rashly when they were drunk, which was very often, and probably plotted treason. Suddenly in 1607 Tyrone was summoned back to England. He believed he was to be imprisoned in the Tower. He understood that Sir Patrick Murray, a Scottish favourite, had said to the King that Tyrone was an honest man and that James had answered ominously: 'Patrick, I pray God he prove so.' Tyrone and Tyrconnell then took a fatal step. Gathering their kinsmen about them, they secretly embarked at Lough Swilly in September 1607, and sailed from their native land. They planned to go to Spain to beg for military assistance, but a storm drove them up the channel and they landed in Normandy whence Henry IV hurried them into the Spanish Netherlands. James's peace with Spain stood him in good stead, for though the Spanish made much of the Irish lords, they did not invite them to Madrid, and no aid was forthcoming. Early in 1608 the exiles made their way to Rome. Death hounded their company. Worn by travel and despair, by unaccustomed climates and habitual intemperance, the Irish lords died quickly. Tyrone survived his companions but, except for a visit to Naples, he never again left papal territory.[3]

First tidings of the departure of the Earls from Ireland caused the government great anxiety. Chichester, the Lord Deputy, prepared as best he could for an assault from Spain, and the King issued an angry proclamation against the base and godless monsters who had broken from the gentle yoke of their allegiance. He begged foreign princes to treat them as those princes would wish their own rebels to be treated abroad. But it soon became evident that the flight of the Irish lords placed Ulster at James's feet and opened the way for sweeping changes. Sir Geoffrey Fenton, the Secretary in Ireland, wrote that the King could now pull down the great houses in the north, settle the lands of Ulster in the Crown, increase royal revenues, bring in British settlers, and reward the English in Ireland without charge to the exchequer. 'His Majesty's happy government', wrote Sir John Davies, the sprightly Solicitor-General, 'will work a greater miracle in this kingdom than ever St. Patrick did, for St. Patrick only banished the poisonous worms, but suffered the men full of poison to inhabit the land still; but his Majesty's blessed genius will banish all those generations of vipers out of it and make it, ere it be long, a right fortunate island.' These prospects were brightened by the abortive rising of Sir Cahir O'Dogherty in Inishowen. He was slain red-handed in revolt, and his lands fell to the Crown.

James determined at once upon a plantation of Ulster on an unprecedented scale. Two plans were laid before him. The first came from Chichester, who proposed that the King should divide the bulk of the forfeited lands among its present inhabitants, giving to each man of substance as much as he could conveniently cultivate. The King might then grant what remained to English who had served in Ireland (the servitors) and to English and Scottish colonists. This statesmanlike proposal might have altered the course of Irish history. Unfortunately a series of commissions appointed by James in England evolved a different plan. Instead of providing first for the Irish and giving what was left to servitors and new settlers, the commissions provided first for the newcomers, secondly for the servitors, and lastly for the native Irish. The lesser chiefs, though innocent of the misdeeds of the great lords, would thus receive only a fraction of the lands to be divided, while the mass of the peasants would be given nothing at all.

With the two plans before him, the King deliberately chose the second. It would, he believed, civilize Ulster quickly, it would secure the British interest, and would provide a welcome means of rewarding importunate suitors without expense to the Crown. More than two-fifths of the forfeited lands were assigned in course of time to English and Scottish settlers, or undertakers, more than one-fifth was reserved for the Church and education, and little more than a fifth was divided between servitors and native Irish. The Irish, much more numerous than the servitors, received small allotments which amounted to scarcely a tenth of the lands distributed. Of the injustice of this arrangement, and especially of the great wrong done to the simple tribesmen, James appears to have taken no thought. He had no sympathy with the Ulster peasants. He had once said that the Scots in the Western Isles were wolves and wild boars who were to be rooted out to make room for colonies of civilized and dependable Lowlanders, and he appears to have thought of the Irish tribesmen in much the same way.

Their barbarism angered him as had the barbarism of the Western Isles. They might remain on the lands assigned to servitors or Irish freeholders, but they must be cleared from the estates of English and Scottish colonists who should bring labourers with them from Britain. The King was greatly enraged at a later time when he discovered that many colonists retained Irish on their estates, 'the avoiding of which was with us the fundamental reason of that plantation'. But the Irish were cheaper than imported labour and were found indispensable; and hence, despite explosions of royal wrath, they remained as landless labourers on the estates of the British undertakers, ready, when time served, to cut the throats of their employers.

The planting of Ulster was always close to James's heart. 'We intend nothing with greater earnestness', he wrote in 1609, 'than that the plantation of Ulster with civil men well affected in religion shall be accomplished with zeal and integrity. We might have converted those large territories to the great improvement of the revenues of our Crown. But we chose rather, for the safety of the country and the civilizing of the people, to depart with the inheritance of them at extreme undervalues and to make plantations of them.' So grandly did he think of his accomplishment. Yet in sad reality he had laid the ground not only for the Irish rebellion in 1641 but for the whole problem of modern Ulster.

With an equal lack of insight he attempted to force his Irish subjects into the Church of England. A number of reasons induced him to embark on such a policy. The news of his accession had been followed in southern Ireland by a remarkable resurgence of Catholicism. The country swarmed suddenly with 'priests, seminaries, friars and Roman bishops', the ceremonies of the Roman Church were openly performed, and the people appeared eager to flaunt their Catholicism in the face of the government. No doubt the deeper meaning of this outburst lay in the fact that Romanism was the symbol of Irish opposition to English rule. But there was another cause for which James was not blameless. It was widely rumoured in Ireland that he was, or might become, a Roman Catholic, and it was assumed that he would grant Catholics at least a toleration of their religion. These rumours and beliefs, told to the people by their priests as positive truth, must have originated partly in James's secret approach to the Catholic world before he became King of England. The impressions current in Ireland were exactly those he had hoped to create among the English Roman Catholics and thus his duplicity rose to plague him.

He was also led to a policy of persecution because Irish Catholicism implied disloyalty to the Crown. He cherished the hope that in England Catholicism and loyalty might not be incompatible, but no such hope was possible in Ireland where the priests taught the absolute supremacy of the Pope and urged the people to rebellion. 'The Pope is your father *in spiritualibus*,' said James to a deputation from the Irish Parliament, 'and I *in temporalibus* only, and so you have your bodies turned one way and your souls drawn another way. You send your children to the seminaries of treason. Your Irish priests teach you such ground of doctrine as ye cannot follow them with a safe conscience, but you must cast off your loyalty to your King.' Hence the enforcement of anti-Catholic laws would serve 'to rivet the State of Ireland, to plant religion and to kill rebellion'.

James discovered, however, that the legal powers at his disposal were small. Elizabeth's early church settlement, embodied in the Acts of Supremacy and Uniformity, had been passed by an Irish Parliament, but the harsher legislation of her later years had not. James could command officials, including the Irish judges, to take the oath of supremacy or forfeit their places; and he could exact a fine of one shilling a Sunday for non-attendance at church. That was all the law permitted. Hence his proclamation of July 4th, 1605, was less stringent than he would have wished. He declared in vigorous terms that he had no intention of granting toleration, and commanded that officials take the oath of supremacy, that the shilling fines be imposed, and that all Jesuits and Roman priests leave the country within five months. The Irish resisted fiercely at every turn. The priests remained in Ireland, and since they found sanctuary in every house and hamlet they were rarely apprehended. Some of the poor were dragooned by the shilling fine into attendance at the established Church, but the wealthy stayed away. The government issued mandates or royal letters, commanding rich men to come to church, but this device was fought with skill and determination, and Chichester became convinced that he was driving the Irish into new rebellion. On his advice, the King drew back and the persecution faded away. Yet James, intermittently throughout his reign, made efforts to begin it once more and by so doing united the whole of Ireland in solid opposition to his decrees.

The one Parliament summoned by the King in Ireland, that of 1613-15, revolved in large measure about religion. He had many new laws in mind, among them an Act increasing his powers to deal with Roman Catholics; and a bill was prepared that banished priests on pain of treason and inflicted heavy penalties on laymen who gave them shelter or support. No Catholic Parliament would pass such an Act. James was therefore faced with the necessity of turning a Catholic majority into a Protestant one. Catholic peers, he believed, could be counterbalanced by Anglican bishops; and by a monstrous abuse of the prerogative he created no less than thirty-nine new parliamentary boroughs, nineteen of them in Ulster, and gave two members to Trinity College in Dublin. He thus added eighty members to the Irish House of Commons and assured a Protestant majority. He also permitted a rumour to circulate in Ireland that members would be required to take the oath of supremacy. The rumour was false, but James hoped it might help elect Protestants.

Small wonder that the Catholics came to Parliament determined to fight anti-Catholic legislation. Before the session began, a group of peers petitioned the King, complaining that penal laws were about to be imposed on Catholics by the votes of Protestant members from wretched villages newly erected into parliamentary boroughs. The peers also petitioned Chichester against the new boroughs and against malpractices in the elections, audaciously expressing a fear that gunpowder was stored under the Parliament chamber in Dublin Castle. When Parliament opened in May 1613, an unseemly scuffle took place in the Commons over the election of a Speaker. Catholic members, knowing they were outnumbered, gathered 'in a plump' so they could not be counted, and placed their candidate in the chair while the Protestants were being counted in the lobby. The Protestants returned, picked up their candidate, Sir John Davies, not a small man, and dropped him in the lap of the Catholic nominee who was then removed — so gently, said the Protestants, that his hat remained upon his head throughout the operation. The Catholics stalked from the chamber and would not return, the Catholic peers refused to attend the House of Lords, and Chichester could only adjourn Parliament and await instructions.

Deputations of Catholic and Protestant members soon crossed to England to tell their stories to the King. After long delays caused partly by a royal progress, James summoned the Irish before him and gave his judgment in a speech that combined, as so often, shrewdness, wit and lack of dignity. He enlarged upon his patience in hearing complaints and in making inquiries and then soundly berated the Catholic members. Their petitions, he said, savoured of insolence and of disrespect for their sovereign. His prerogative to create parliamentary boroughs had been questioned. He had been troubled by foolish complaints of irregularities in the Irish elections, for members must not expect the kingdom of Ireland to resemble the kingdom of heaven. In Parliament their actions had been most reprehensible. Having refused to accept his nominee as Speaker, they were a body without a head, a headless body. 'You would be afraid to meet such a body in the streets — a very bugbear. My sentence is that you have carried yourselves tumultuously, and that your proceedings have been rude, disorderly, and worthy of severe punishment.'

Yet when members returned to Ireland to resume the Parliament, affairs proceeded with surprising smoothness. The reason was simple, for the King abandoned his anti-Catholic legislation, and thus the Parliament was a Catholic victory. James soon had enough of it, dissolved it in 1615, and fell back as in England upon prerogative government.[4]

The same lofty motives, he often asserted, that underlay his policy in Ireland, prompted him also to favour the great movement of planting British colonies beyond the seas. His noble aim was to bring civilization and Christianity to wild and heathen parts, to enhance his prestige and that of his kingdoms, and to solve social and economic problems by emigration and by the extension of commerce. No form of conquest, he said in a proclamation in Scotland, was so easy or so innocent as that of plantations, especially in areas commodious to live in yet inhabited only by infidels. Scotland, he added, was well adapted to plant colonies, for a colony required the exportation of men, women, cattle and victuals, but not of money. Colonial products could relieve Britain of buying from foreign countries. Colonies could drain away unwanted population, idle rogues and sturdy beggars, reprieved criminals, vagrant children and troublesome Borderers. Nor was he without a sense of responsibility for the welfare of the colonies after they had been established. He made an enormous number of colonial grants, in areas as widely scattered as New-foundland and the Amazon.

Yet on the whole his record was a sad one. After his glow of satisfaction in launching a noble project had subsided, he was apt to lose interest. His financial embarrassments led him to seek too keenly for profits, and he was ready to enrich his favourites at the expense of colonial and commercial ventures. The inconsistencies of his foreign policy played havoc with colonial enterprise. During his first years in England he took a firm tone with Spain, for which he should have credit, but later he yielded shamefully to Spanish pressure. Yet at the same time he allowed the Dutch to injure the English East India Company because he wished to retain Holland as an ally against Spain. His actions were so vacillating and his policy so unstable that commerce and colonies may be said to have advanced in spite of him rather than because of his assistance.

The planting of Virginia, fortunately, fell early in the reign. The peace with Spain in 1604, as we have seen, did not exclude Englishmen from the new world. When the Spanish protested against the settlement in Virginia, James answered that Spain had made great discoveries and he thought that his own people should be allowed to do the same. If they trespassed upon lands occupied by Spain, the Spanish could drive them out. He had never understood that the Spanish had a claim to Virginia. He did not look for any great return from the settlement at James-town; and if wealth was produced it would go to his subjects and not to him. Thus his reply to Spain, though rather non-committal, rejected Philip's claim to monopoly and implied that aggression against Virginia would be resisted.

The King's first patent to the Virginia Company and his first instructions for the government of the colony, both issued in 1606, gave every indication that he planned to control the settlement in strict and detailed fashion. But his interest in Virginia soon waned. Perhaps he knew he had set up an impractical form of government. More likely he foresaw that Virginia would bring loss and not profit for some time to come, and was glad to be rid of it. He abandoned royal control in the charters of 1609 and 1612 and left the Company to make its way as best it could.

About 1616 his interest revived because of the cultivation of tobacco in Virginia. Detesting tobacco, he commanded the colonists to plant hemp, fruits, vineyards and mulberry trees for use in raising silkworms. He sent instructions, prepared by his servant, John Bonœil, for the cultivation of vineyards and for the manufacture of silk. It is a rather surprising fact that for many years James toyed with the idea of introducing sericulture into England. He planted mulberry gardens at Whitehall and at some of his country houses where silkworms were raised under the care of special officers, and a groom of the Chamber once asked reimbursement for carrying about the King's silkworms 'whithersoever his Majesty went'. In 1609 a consignment of silkworms was sent to Virginia but was lost at sea, and when the King tried again in 1622 the worms expired *en route*. Meanwhile, to his disgust, tobacco culture grew apace.

The bitter disputes that arose in England among the managers of the Virginia Company caused the King anxiety, and in 1624 he dissolved the Company. He has been accused of yielding to Spanish pressure, of striking a blow at Sir Edwin Sandys, his old opponent in Parliament, who was one of the managers of the Company, of wishing to crush the nascent democracy that was appearing in Virginia. But quite apart from these conjectural motives, he could easily see that things were going badly in the colony and that Virginia was not progressing under Sandys's ambitious management. The dissolution of the Company may have been unjust to the investors, but it brought benefit to Virginia, though a commission appointed by the King to reorganize the colony under the Crown had made but little progress at the time of his death.

He was anxious that Scotland should share in the colonial movement, and he took a lively interest in the ambitious plans of Sir William Alexander, the courtier-poet who was helping him translate the Psalms. In 1621 he granted to Alexander, under the Scottish Crown, all the territories lying between New England and Newfoundland. This prodigious area was to be named New Scotland, but since Alexander was a scholar his charter was written in Latin and the name appeared as Nova Scotia. The Scots, however, proved most reluctant colonists, and two expeditions, in 1622 and 1623, both on a very small scale, failed to plant a settlement. Alexander lost £6000 which the King promised to repay from the Scottish exchequer though he never did. Yet he tried to revive the project. Declaring he would make it a work of his own, he created an order of baronets of Nova Scotia open to Scots who, in return for a barony in the new world, would come forward with funds to support a settlement. In his last days James is said to have declared that the colony in Nova Scotia was 'a good work, a royal work, and one for the good of the kingdom'. Charles at first supported it, but in a treaty with France in 1632 he resigned all claims to the area.[5]

The fortunes of the English East India Company form a striking example of James's instability. Having confirmed the Company's monopoly, he permitted Sir Edward Michaelbourne, a former associate of Essex, to sail as an interloper to the east. Michaelbourne did the Company great harm by plundering native shipping; and the English agent at Bantam spoke of the dangers that would follow 'if any more such as he be permitted to do as he did'. Having broken one promise to the Company James made it another in a charter of 1609. Yet eight years later he gave letters patent to a Scot, Sir James Cunningham, allowing him to trade in the east. Perhaps the King thought he was creating a Scottish East India Company. But Cunningham was no merchant, and merely blackmailed the English Company until he was bought out. In 1622 the King permitted a shameful episode. The Company had achieved a brilliant success by driving the Portuguese from Ormuz and by establishing an English factory at that strategic location. But though the royal navy had had no hand in this exploit, James forced the Company to pay £10,000 to Lord Admiral Buckingham as his share of the booty and demanded an equal sum for himself. This was sheer robbery. In 1624 news reached England of the horrible massacre at Amboyna where the Dutch tortured eighteen English factors and murdered ten of them in a criminal bid for commercial supremacy. James wept, but did nothing more.[6]

CHAPTER XVIII

THE EARL OF SOMERSET

DURING the first decade of James's reign in England, while Salisbury's solid judgment and steady nerve lent cohesion and purpose to government, the Elizabethan administration continued to function and was not without its successes. But then came a series of calamities. The deaths of Henry IV, of Salisbury, of Prince Henry were, each in its way, a grievous blow, while the quarrel with Parliament in 1610 and the angry dissolution of the Commons were repeated with increasing acrimony four years later. The weaknesses of the King grew more apparent, finances fell into chaos, foreign affairs became more difficult. James exalted a worthless favourite and increased the power of the Howards. As government relaxed and honour cheapened, we enter an era of decline and weakness, of intrigue, scandal, confusion and treachery.

So fully had Salisbury been the centre of the government that its normal activities narrowed to a trickle in the weeks of his illness, and after his death the whole administration required rebuilding. But instead of seeking for talent, the King resolved to assume a more direct and personal control of affairs. It is difficult to reconstruct his thinking. Perhaps he felt a pricking of conscience at his past neglect of business. Doubtless he nursed a secret resentment against Salisbury's preponderance, and wished to show the world he could play a more kingly role. He was a man to whom good resolutions came easily, ever new and undimmed by the failures of the past, and he now resolved to act as his own chief Minister of State.

Of the principal offices held by Salisbury, he filled but one, and that in a probationary way. Sir George Carew, a man of no great prominence, who became Master of the Wards, explained in his oration upon taking office that the King was making a temporary trial of his services. 'His Majesty meaneth to be as it were Master of the Wards himself, and those whom he useth are to be but his substitutes and move wholly by his impulsion and within the circle of his own motion.' The King, Carew continued, desired a reformation in the concept of the court. Since he was not only *pater patriae* but also *pater pupillorum*, he was resolved to play the part of a natural father in watching over his wards, and Carew spoke of reforms and new procedures suggested by the King. But alas! The new Master was given supplementary instructions of which the obvious purpose was to augment revenue, and James contented himself with pious resolves.

No Lord Treasurer was appointed. Remembering perhaps that he had once been well served in Scotland by a group of financial experts known as the Octavians, the King entrusted the treasury to commissioners, of whom Northampton was the most important. But the duties of the great office of Principal Secretary he would perform himself. 'The King makes no haste to nominate any,' wrote Chamberlain, 'but says he is pretty skilled in the craft himself and till he be thoroughly weary will execute it in person.' Dispatches from abroad were now addressed to him; and having read them and perhaps consulted with his favourite, Robert Carr, now Viscount Rochester, James employed a group of lesser secretaries to draft replies, while Sir Thomas Lake, who remained in attendance, wrote letters to the councillors in London about domestic affairs. But the experiment ended in failure. The King continued to live much of the time in the country and was too indolent to carry through the task he had undertaken. The Council was soon complaining of delays in business and was begging the King to appoint a Secretary, 'for though his Majesty at first took delight to show his readiness and ability in those causes, yet that vigour begins to relent, and he must daily more and more intend his own health and quiet'. Competition for the vacant office, meanwhile, became fast and furious, creating bitterness, intrigue and faction.

The Earl of Northampton, now the principal minister in London, laid the King's business before the Council and wrote to James of the results as Salisbury had done in the past. It is amusing to find that he was quickly in trouble, for within a few weeks he made some observation at which James took offence. Greatly disturbed he wrote to Rochester: 'God is my judge that I cannot for my life conceive what should displease the King, nor in what one point he should rest unsatisfied.' He begged for Rochester's assistance. 'Sweet Lord, let me beseech you to give me your advice what inconvenience to shun, for tomorrow next I may incur the like if I be not by your noble and friendly care premonished.' To Lake he made a similar request, asking for secret intelligence: 'If you were a good fellow you would sometimes refresh your friends with your occurrences.' His letters — so different from Salisbury's — show clearly the venomous and creeping nature of the man. Rochester he courts with the greatest assiduity. The favourite's skill in answering letters, he says, make all men think that Rochester should have the office of Secretary. There is scarcely a letter in which he does not cast some sneer or jibe at Salisbury. How he hated him! Any difficulty in business is traced to the little lord who kept all affairs to himself. When a letter cannot be found, it is because Salisbury 'made his own cabinet the treasury of the State's whole evidence and intelligence'. Northampton's own interests figure largely. He asks for many favours, reminding the King how he served him (more than any) in securing the English throne and how his very life was then in danger. It is astonishing that James could stomach such a councillor, much less trust him.[1]

About Northampton gathered the faction of the Howards — Lord Chamberlain Suffolk; his son-in-law, Lord Knollys; and Nottingham, the elderly Lord Admiral. They were joined by Worcester, a confessed, and Lord Wotton, a secret Catholic, and by Lake, in search of a patron after Salisbury's death. They were able to draw the favourite to their side, thus for a time becoming well-nigh impregnable. Here were the origins of the famous Spanish party and, though it stood for things inimical to the temper of the nation, it was the faction to which the King inclined. Yet, powerful as the Howards now became, there was a party aligned against them: Lord Chancellor Ellesmere, very Protestant and anti-Spanish; Archbishop Abbot; Pembroke, the richest peer in England, aristocratic, cultured and attractive, noble in resolve though weak in action, always the mortal enemy of Spain; Southampton, hot-headed and contentious, in touch with the parliamentary opposition. Sir Thomas Overbury, the favourite's favourite, belonged to this group, which was strengthened in 1614 when Sir Ralph Winwood, recalled from his ambassadorship in Holland, was named as Secretary. The bitter rivalry of these two factions was to dominate politics for many years.

Although these parties had not been created by the King, he had made them possible and indeed inevitable by his peace with

Spain and by his advancement of the Howards. Accustomed to faction in Scotland, he appears to have accepted it in England as a normal and not wholly undesirable thing. It is true that in foreign affairs it helped him to play his game of simultaneous friendship with Protestant and with Catholic powers. But at home it led to weakness and to divided counsels.

Occasionally the King was now troubled by ill health. Twice during the summer of 1613 he suffered from nephritis, or inflammation of the kidneys, a painful disease that was rendered more acute by alcohol. Yet to the strict programme of remedies prescribed by his physician, Mayerne, he paid small attention while he was ill and none at all after his health improved. Scarcely had he recovered from his first attack when he began a progress that took him as far as the New Forest and the Isle of Wight, with the result that he was ill again upon his return. Later in the year he was kept abed by arthritis. 'Pains invaded the King's right foot,' wrote Mayerne, 'which had an odd twist when he was walking and a position less correct than the other and which grew weaker as he grew older.' James also became subject to violent digestive disturbances sometimes occasioned by eating too much fruit but more often by nervous strain which could quickly affect his health. Following the dissolution of Parliament in 1611 and again after the death of his son the King was prostrated in this way, with diarrhoea, heartburn, palpitation, vomiting, and with great sighing and sadness, melancholy and dread. The vigour of youth was gone, and he was now in middle age.[2]

The great event of these years was the rise to power of Robert Carr whom James created Viscount Rochester in 1611. This handsome but shallow young Scot had come to England in 1603 as a page who ran beside the royal coach. English fashion, however, called for footmen, not running pages, and Carr, with £50 in his pocket and a new suit of clothes, had been dismissed. After a sojourn in France he returned to England in 1607 when he attracted the King's attention by the lucky mischance of falling from his horse during a tilt and breaking his leg. James recognized his former page, commanded that he receive medical attention, and often came to see him while he was ill. It was during these visits that Carr made his great conquest; for although, as Arthur Wilson wrote, the King could find in him no great depth of literature or experience, yet he discovered so smooth and calm an exterior 'as made him think there might be good anchorage for his most retired thoughts'. After Carr's recovery, which James awaited with some impatience, the King made him a Gentleman of the Bedchamber and 'laid a foundation by his daily discourses with him to improve him into a capacity of his most endeared affection'.

'The Prince leaneth on his arm,' wrote a courtier, 'pinches his cheek, smooths his ruffled garment, and, when he looketh at Carr, directeth discourse to divers others. This young man doth much study all art and device; he hath changed his tailors and tiremen many times, and all to please the Prince, who laugheth at the long grown fashion of our young courtiers and wisheth for change every day. Carr hath all favours; the King teacheth him Latin every morning, and I think someone should teach him English too, for as he is a Scottish lad he hath much need of better language. The King doth much covet his presence, the ladies too are not behindhand in their admiration; for I tell you this fellow is straight-limbed, well-favoured, strong-shouldered, and smooth-faced, with some sort of cunning and show of modesty; though, God wot, he well knoweth when to show his impudence.'

He is described as 'rather well compacted than tall, his features comely and handsome rather than beautiful; the hair of his head flaxen, that of his face tinctured with yellow'.[3] That his attraction for the King was physical there can be no doubt; and though one must suspect the scandalmongers of the court, there is something in Osborne's remark that when James pawed his favourites so fondly in public he was not likely to restrain himself in private. The vice was common to many rulers and we need not be too shocked. Yet the completeness of the King's surrender to it indicates a loosening of his moral fibre.

A royal illness provided the favourite with an opportunity to show by his solicitous care how great was his devotion; and James, to whom personal service was service of the highest order, swore that he saw how truly Rochester loved him.

As Salisbury's death opened the way for new appointments, Rochester's first thought was to secure great office. He considered Worcester's place of Master of the Horse. Quickly he showed hostility to Lake who had grown officious as though to insinuate a claim to the office of Secretary. He may have aimed at becoming Lord Treasurer. But none of these appointments was made, and it was thought that Rochester was slow in pushing his own interests. The truth was, however, that the King had something else in mind. Rochester was to combine the role of intimate friend and boon companion with that of a faithful, obedient and watchful servant. He was not to govern but to protect James's interests in the government. He was to be the King's remembrancer on a grand scale. Suits of all kinds were to pass through his hands and he was to sift them, always with an eye to the royal advantage. 'I must confess', wrote the King, 'you have deserved more trust and confidence of me than ever man did, in secrecy above all flesh, in feeling and impartial respect, as well to my honour in every degree as to my profit. And all this without respect either to kin or ally or your nearest and dearest friend whatsoever, nay, unmovable in one hair that might concern me against the whole world.' This was James's hope and not reality. But Rochester, though lacking in ability and judgment, was for a time discreet, shunning his Scottish compatriots and his own kindred. He discovered shortly that he enjoyed the benefits of great office though he held none, and that money flowed to him from the gifts of all who had to deal with the Crown. He boasted that he did not take bribes, by which he meant that he told the King of the presents offered to him; and James with easy acquiescence allowed him to accept them.[4]

Inevitably he was under pressure to join one of the two factions into which the court was divided. His friend Overbury sought to draw him to the side of the anti-Spanish party and of the 'parliamentary mutineers'; while Northampton offered him fawning blandishments from the opposite camp. For some time he held aloof, thinking it wiser to make no move 'save where the King had his interest'. So slow was he in taking sides, wrote Thomas Erskine, Lord Fenton, a lesser Scottish favourite, that he could hardly do so without some peril, at least if the English 'had a little of our Scots humour'. But Fenton did not know that a new force had emerged. For Rochester had fallen in love with Lady Frances Howard, the daughter of Suffolk and the wife of the young Earl of Essex, son of Elizabeth's unruly favourite. Irresistibly Lady Frances drew Rochester towards alliance with the Howards. He had good and affable qualities, wrote Arthur Wilson, till they were all swallowed up in this 'gulf of beauty'.

In James's last years in Scotland he had stilled the feuds of the

nobility by arranging marriages between rival houses, and he proposed to do the same in England. One such alliance was a
marriage between Salisbury's son and a daughter of the Earl of
Suffolk; while another of Suffolk's daughters, Lady Frances
Howard, was married in 1606 to the Earl of Essex. This young
Earl, who was only twelve in 1603, the King had greeted with
fatherly affection, taking him in his arms and kissing him, and
declaring that he was the son of the most noble knight that England had ever bred. It was James's hope that by these marriages
the houses of Cecil and Essex might become reconciled in friendly
alliance with the Howards. But Lady Frances and her husband
were mere children and they did not live together. The Earl went
abroad and Lady Frances grew up at court, where she received
but an evil education. She became proud, headstrong and violent,
capable of implacable hatred and of shameless immodesty.

Late in 1609 the Earl returned. But meanwhile Lady Frances
and Rochester had become interested in each other; and Lady
Frances saw her happiness extinguished by the arrival of a husband who did not attract her. She conceived the morbid resolve
of being his wife in name only and of saving herself in a physical
sense for Rochester. She administered drugs to her husband,
assuming so hostile an attitude towards him that she succeeded in
stopping his advances. Having lived after this fashion for three
years she thought of obtaining a divorce on the ground that her
husband was impotent. She secured the support of her father and
of Northampton, who knew that a divorce would be followed by a
marriage to Rochester. She doubtless thought that Essex, glad of
escape, would not challenge her story. But he would made no
admission reflecting on his physical condition. And Lady Frances
and her lawyers fell back on the dubious ground that Essex was
bewitched and was impotent only in regard to her.

James became deeply interested in this wretched affair,
swallowed the lies of Lady Frances, and used all his influence in
her behalf. He was always attracted by the morbid and the unnatural, he was shockingly inquisitive in matters of sex, and was
surrounded by men who favoured the divorce. To its moral
implications and to its evil as a precedent, he was singularly blind.
Doubtless he regretted his own part in furthering the childhood
marriage that had produced such tragic results, for at one point
in the trial he inveighed against early marriages. He saw the

advantage of an alliance between Rochester and the Howards. Above all, probably, he could not resist the pleadings of his favourite.

In May 1613, he appointed a commission to try the case. The commission consisted of four bishops, Abbot, Andrewes, King and Neile, two councillors, Parry and Caesar, and four doctors of the civil law, Sir Daniel Donne, Sir John Bennet and Drs. James and Edwardes. The King meddled constantly with their deliberations. Finding that a majority of them opposed the divorce, he spoke to them privately and allowed Suffolk to do the same. Neile found that his opposition displeased the King and soon altered his opinion. Andrewes also opposed the divorce 'until such time as the King spoke with him and then his judgment was reformed'. Thenceforth he sat almost silent among the commissioners. Parry came round after Suffolk talked to him, and other members of the commission were earnestly dealt with. Abbot, courageous in opposition, was put under terrible pressure. The King reasoned with him privately on several occasions; and Abbot found himself moving in an atmosphere of complaints, threats and trickery. James called the commissioners before him at Windsor and argued with them for three hours. When Abbot saw the King's earnestness he fell upon his knees and begged with tears to be removed from the commission. At the same time he spoke so strongly against the divorce that the King was shaken, though James's words imply that he was less disturbed by moral considerations than by fear the commissioners would not do his will.

'What a strange and fearful thing it was,' wrote Abbot, 'that his Majesty should be so far engaged in that business; that he should profess that himself had set the matter in that course of judgment; that the judges should be dealt with beforehand, and, in a sort, directed what they should determine.' He decided to write the King a letter. But his letter was disappointingly weak. He argued that neither the Scriptures nor the records of the primitive Church dealt with impotency induced through witchcraft. Such an evil, he believed, might have existed in the time of popish superstition but had probably disappeared after the Reformation. Prayer and medical attention were the proper remedies. Yet they had not been applied. James answered at great length. The Scriptures, the Fathers and the early councils, he argued, could not be expected to provide an exact answer;

Abbot should be satisfied if they said nothing to inhibit the divorce. Probably the Devil had not then discovered the device of impotency through witchcraft but invented it later in the time of papal darkness. 'Look my *Daemonologie*.' Nor was there any reason to believe that Satan had lost his power as a result of the Reformation; indeed he was particularly active in the matter under discussion. The King accused Abbot of prejudice against the Lady Frances, 'which prejudice is the most dangerous thing that can fall in a judge for misleading of his mind', and the Archbishop was piously reminded of Christ's admonition not to judge others. On the other hand, James wrote, he himself was totally impartial. He asked Abbot 'to have a kind of faith implicit in my judgment, as well in respect of some skill I have in divinity, as also that I hope no honest man doubts of the uprighteousness of my conscience; and the best thankfulness that you that are so far my creature can use towards me is to reverence and follow my judgment and not to contradict it, except when you can demonstrate unto me that I am mistaken or wrong informed'.[5]

Discovering that the vote of the commissioners would be a tie, the King added two more bishops, Bilson and Buckeridge, to the commission, with the result that on September 25th the divorce was granted by a vote of seven to five.

For months the divorce remained a topic of general conversation, casting in the minds of decent people the greatest odium upon the King and his bishops. Abbot and Bishop King had voted bravely in the negative, but four other bishops, including Andrewes and Bilson, had bowed to royal pressure, and the verdict had been obtained by votes of the episcopal members. Chamberlain, certainly no prude, spoke sadly of Andrewes's concurrence. How could the people believe, in view of these things, that episcopacy was of divine origin, or how could persecution of Puritanism carry moral conviction? As for James, his partiality, his improper meddling, his use of theology in such gross matters, his packing of the commission, were duly observed and remembered. His habit of employing discreditable methods had dragged him lower than he knew.

The divorce had a darker side of which the world was as yet unaware. On September 15th, ten days before it was granted, Sir Thomas Overbury, then a prisoner in the Tower, died of poison. His story is a tragic one. He was a young man of education and of some literary attainment, 'a very witty gentleman', wrote Goodman, 'but truly very insolent, and one who did much abuse the family of the Howards'. On a visit to Scotland about 1601 he had met Rochester and the two had become fast friends. The favourite's rapid rise in England appeared to open brilliant prospects for Overbury, especially since Rochester, conscious of his deficiencies, obtained help from his friend in writing dispatches and in composing love letters to Lady Frances Howard. But relations between the two friends became difficult. Overbury had some standing at court, but his position was nothing compared to that of the man he was assisting; while his arrogant boastings that he had laid the foundation for his friend's good fortune must have irritated Rochester. To an intrigue between his patron and Lady Frances, Overbury had no objection, but he was violently opposed to a marriage between them. He was associated in politics with the enemies of the Howards, and he foresaw that a marriage alliance between the Howards and Rochester would quickly result in his ruin. He tried to dissuade Rochester by blackening the character of Lady Frances; and this led to a coolness between the friends though not to an open break.

Meanwhile Overbury had the misfortune to incur the displeasure of the King, who, wrote Chamberlain, 'hath long had a desire to remove him from about the lord of Rochester, as thinking it a dishonour to him that the world should have an opinion that Rochester ruled him and Overbury ruled Rochester'. James determined to assert his independence. Without consulting Rochester he offered Overbury a diplomatic post on the Continent, which Overbury refused in so peremptory and insolent a manner that the King, deeply incensed, imprisoned him in the Tower. This action should not be construed as a diminution of Rochester's credit, said James, for he took more delight in Rochester's company and conversation than in those of any man alive. Thus the favourite had no hand in his friend's imprisonment. None the less, the temporary removal of Overbury from public life during the divorce proceedings must have come as a relief to Rochester, for Overbury knew enough to be dangerous. Rochester kept in touch with him and gave him the impression that he was working for his liberation. [6]

Overbury, however, was hated by a more dangerous person than the King. Lady Frances Howard was determined that he should die. She sent poison through one Richard Weston whom she had been able to have appointed as Overbury's keeper, but Weston's design was discovered and prevented by Sir Gervase Helwys, Lieutenant of the Tower. Helwys suspected the culprit but dared not accuse her, and so merely kept the matter quiet. Lady Frances, however, continued to send poison. She may have put some in food which Rochester sent to the prisoner. Finally she bribed an apothecary's boy to administer poison to Overbury of which he died the following day. For two years the secret of his death died with him.

On the day after Christmas, 1613, Rochester and Lady Frances were married with great magnificence. Despite a slight illness the King took a lively interest in preparing the festivities; and despite the stringency of his finances — so that 'the poor posts that trot up and down' were without their pay — he bore the cost of the marriage and sold Crown lands worth £10,000 to provide a gift of jewels for the bride. Rochester was created Earl of Somerset so that Lady Frances might remain a countess. The marriage was attended by the King, Queen and Prince Charles, by most of the nobility and by many of the bishops. Courtiers, officials and trading companies gave costly gifts, which James endeavoured to make as rich as possible. Masquing, feasting and revelry continued until Twelfth Night when the court celebrated another marriage, that of the Queen's favourite, Jane Drummond, to Robert Ker, Earl of Roxburgh. A few days later James left London. Surfeited with the court, he 'thought it long till he was gone; for he went through that night to Royston, and so to Newmarket'.

The year after Somerset's marriage marked the height of his fortunes. James's confidence in him appeared boundless. He was, wrote Fenton, 'more absolute than ever any that I have either heard of or did see myself'. Sarmiento, the new Spanish ambassador, reported: 'The Viscount Rochester at the Council table showeth much temper and modesty, without seeming to press and sway anything. But afterwards the King resolveth all business with him alone, both those that pass in Council and many others wherewith he never maketh them acquainted.' All things, wrote Chamberlain, were carried *in scrinio pectoris* between the King and the favourite. Yet Somerset's position had altered and his ruin was in the making. He was no longer the King's remembrancer, acting only in the interest of the Crown, but was now aligned with

one of the factions that divided the State. He permitted the
Howards to govern his policy, and he became as pro-Spanish as
they. Moreover, success was turning his head. He grew lofty,
arrogant and imperious; he was less than respectful even to the
King, whose foolish indulgence was spoiling the few good qualities
which the favourite possessed.

That indulgence had made Somerset a very rich man. In April
1613, when the commissioners of the Treasury were at their wits'
end for money, he had grandly offered to lend the King £22,000,
and at the time of his marriage he was said to have spent £90,000
within the last year. Yet James's finances were in a shocking
condition. The debt, which Salisbury had reduced to £160,000
at the beginning of 1610, had risen steadily since that time,
amounting to £500,000 in the spring of 1612 and to £680,000 in
the early months of 1614. Fortifications were in decay, officials
were unpaid, arrears in the spending departments ran to some
£488,000. £125,000 was due for money borrowed a year earlier;
£67,000 of the anticipated revenue of 1614 was already spent.
The decay in public finance had turned to dead rot.[7]

It was penury that turned the King's reluctant thoughts towards a Parliament. But since the quarrel in 1610 he had ceased
to regard Parliament as an accepted part of the Constitution, and
he now had to be coaxed into calling the Commons together; his
hesitation intensified the clash of Howard and anti-Howard factions. Northampton opposed a Parliament as far as he dared.
On one occasion he spoke boldly, telling James that in no case
should he call together his enemies, 'for such were those of the
Parliament, that would do nothing which he desired, as he had
seen by experience. The King heard him with much attention,
and afterwards, calling him aside, told him he had spoken with
much freedom but with as much truth'. Anti-Spanish councillors,
on the other hand, regarded Parliament as essential, not merely
to supply money but to heal the breach between Crown and
people.[8]

The King was urged in the same direction by two other persons
at court who proffered unsolicited advice. Bacon told him that
Salisbury's attempt to strike a bargain with the Commons had
been a gross and egregious blunder. James must deal with Parliament not as a merchant, offering his favours for sale, but as a
King; for subsidies were of small importance in comparison with

the good will of the Commons. 'Until your Majesty have tuned your instrument you will have no harmony. I, for my part, think it a thing inestimable to your Majesty's safety and service that you once part with your Parliament with love and reverence.' Sir Henry Neville also advised James to summon Parliament. A courtier and diplomat who had supported the popular cause in 1610, Neville held that reconciliation of King and Commons was not impossible. He drew up a list of concessions which he wished James to offer Parliament; and he ventured the bold prognostication that if these concessions were made the Commons would prove more tractable. Unfortunately his proposals were too slight to be highly valued, they did not pierce to the root of the difficulty, and his plan, offered with the best intentions, was to have unpleasant results.

The King's actions were a medley of these various advices. He summoned a Parliament which met in April 1614. Recognizing the need of a Secretary to represent him in the Commons, he selected Sir Ralph Winwood, his former ambassador in Holland, a zealous Protestant and an honest and energetic official. Winwood's appointment was a concession to the popular party. But though he had much to recommend him to the Commons, his manner was brusque and peremptory, with a kind of Hollander's austerity which rubbed members the wrong way. His appointment came very late, only a week before the session opened, he was totally inexperienced in Parliament, and he was hounded by the envy of disappointed competitors for his office. James followed Neville so far as to prepare bills embodying minor concessions, while Bacon's advice may be traced in two speeches with which the King opened Parliament.

If members looked upon him with unpolluted eyes, James began, they might see that his integrity resembled the whiteness of his robe, his purity the gold in his crown, his firmness and clearness the precious stones he wore, and his affection the redness of his heart. Three causes had moved him to summon Parliament. The first, he said, was the increase of Popery. The second was his wish to establish the succession in his infant grandson, Frederick Henry, the child of his daughter Elizabeth, should Prince Charles die without issue. Since Elizabeth had been young and a woman, both subject to frailty, he had selected her husband with great care. His third reason for summoning Parliament was financial.

He touched upon the many expenses he had had since his coming to the Crown. Yet he would not deal with the Commons like a merchant nor tell them how much they should give. This was to be a Parliament of love in which he and the Commons would aid each other in a spirit of mutual affection.

A few days later he spoke again. Bills containing his concessions were about to be introduced; and he trusted the Commons would respond by voting supply. He repeated much of his former speech. He hoped to be in love with Parliaments, to call them frequently, and to come eventually to a happy time when he need not ask them for money. The quarrels of 1610 he blamed on one who was gone (God forgive him!). He was not so tender of his prerogative as rumour pictured him. He wished for a golden mean, for though he would lose his life rather than yield the flowers of his Crown, yet he had no thought of extending his prerogatives beyond those of his predecessors. He then made a startling suggestion: that he propound to each House by bill the matters proper to it, that he speak to both Houses himself, and so receive their answers. And again he called for love and harmony.

How could such disingenuous words affect the Commons except to accentuate the gulf between King and people? When he spoke of his purity, members must have thought of the Essex divorce. When he mentioned the increase of Popery, they must have suspected his sincerity. When he hoped for a time in which he need not ask for money, they must have looked incredulously at the mounting debt. When he suggested that he propose bills to them, they must have reflected that he knew little of the nature of his Parliaments. James offered neither concessions nor hope of amendment; and members can hardly be blamed if they looked askance at the offer of his love.

This Parliament proved a difficult one. A furore arose at once over suspicions that the Crown had tampered with elections. Neville's plan had been distorted by rumour into a plot by a group of courtiers to influence elections on a wide scale in return for promises of office. James had probably added to the alarm. Hearing that the elections were going badly, he had implored councillors to use what influence they could; and letters of recommendation had flown about the country from great persons at court. The result was exactly the opposite of what the King had hoped. Hotheads and radicals increased among the Commons until, as a courtier complained, the House became more like a cockpit than a council.

The Commons began at once to investigate elections, and though they could find but little, their scrutiny prompted them to expel a councillor, Sir Thomas Parry, for corrupt practices and to question the eligibility of the Attorney-General, Bacon, to sit in the Commons. These things were done with a firmness and a gusto that boded ill for the Crown. It soon became evident, moreover, that grievances, including impositions, were to be dealt with before supply. On May 4th James addressed the Commons in defence of his right to impositions. He regarded them, he said, as a great flower of his prerogative, the judges had assured him of their legality, he would die a hundred deaths before he would curtail his rights. Debate on impositions continued and grew warmer. The Spaniards, a member said, had lost the Low Countries because they had levied impositions. Henry IV had died like a calf under the butcher's knife for the same reason. Kings who followed these examples might see their doom written before them. The Commons, asking the Lords for a conference on impositions, were refused, and Bishop Neile made a bitter attack upon the Lower House. Deeply incensed, the Commons determined to conduct no business until they had received satisfaction, and though they were told by the King that if they did not vote supply he would dissolve the Parliament, they held their ground. '*Rebus sic stantibus*,' said a member, 'we have nothing to give but are as it were slaves, and if anything be given now it is for fear of a dissolving of the Parliament.' The Parliament ended in June, having lasted but two months and having passed not a single measure.

To this grave decision the King was impelled by many reasons. He was passionately angry with the Commons. They had spurned his proffered love, refused him supply, assaulted his prerogative, and spoken irreverently of kings. Perhaps they sought his life. There had been an ugly intrigue, of which he was as yet unaware, by which Northampton had increased the turbulence of the Commons. Two of his dependants, Dr. Lionel Sharp and Sir Charles Cornwallis, though not members of Parliament, had secretly urged some of the Commons to make violent speeches and thus anger and intimidate the King. One member, promised the protection of Northampton and also, apparently, of Somerset, had been persuaded to hint at a new Sicilian Vespers against the Scots. This speech was at once reported to the King as a threat against his life and the lives of his favourites. In all probability he believed himself in danger of assassination.

Three days before the dissolution he visited Northampton, who was ill, and there can be no doubt of the advice he was given. Somerset's opinion must have been similar. The King also took the strange course of consulting Sarmiento, the Spanish ambassador, and of asking him whether, if he broke with the Commons, he could rely upon Philip as a friend. Sarmiento replied with comforting if vague assurances which, he boasted, 'helped greatly to induce the King to break with the Puritans, contrary to the advice which he received from many'. The anti-Howard faction had besought the King to prorogue Parliament instead of dissolving it and had urged the Commons to vote supply in return for a prorogation.

Shortly after the dissolution the King talked again with Sarmiento. Saying that he regarded Philip as his firmest friend, he asked that the story of the Parliament be reported to Spain as it actually was and not as it was told in the London streets. He complained that the House of Commons was a body with no head; its five hundred members voted without rule or order amid cries, shouts and confusion. He was astonished that his predecessors had tolerated such an assembly, but he had found it in England upon his arrival and had not been able to do without it. Here he looked annoyed as though he remembered what it had done to him, and Sarmiento came to his assistance by remarking tactfully that it lay in the King's power to call and dissolve Parliament at will. James brightened, said that that was so and that without his consent the Acts of the Commons were nothing.[9]

In these conversations with Sarmiento the King was childishly garrulous and confiding, but he should not be painted blacker than he was. Without a doubt he was thinking of the dowry that a Spanish bride, with the wealth of the Indies behind her, might bring to England. He regarded the break with Parliament as final. If he had had his way the Commons would never have met again, and a Spanish dowry was a most attractive alternative. His old habit of hoping to obtain advantage even from his enemies was leading him into deep water, for the dissolution of Parliament and the reopening of negotiations for a Spanish marriage went hand in hand.

Although Northampton had the satisfaction of seeing the Parliament ended, within a week of the dissolution he was dead. An operation on a tumour in his thigh was performed so unskilfully that the sore became very foul, gangrened and killed him. He was a bad man, his life was one long intrigue, as noisome and sinister as the ailment that carried him off.

His offices of Lord Privy Seal and of Warden of the Cinque Ports the King did not fill at once but entrusted their duties to Somerset, whose letters indicate gross ignorance of the functions he was called upon to perform. But Northampton had been so important in the Commission for the Treasury that James decided he must now appoint a Lord Treasurer. In a double ceremony in July that office was conferred upon Suffolk, while Somerset became Lord Chamberlain. The King declared that he had suffered much at the hands of earlier Treasurers, especially Salisbury, who had entertained him with epigrams and devices 'which yet he saw would pay no debts'. He was therefore selecting a plain honest gentleman who, if he committed a fault, would lack the rhetoric to excuse it. The office of Chamberlain, James continued, was a place of great nearness to his person and he had therefore chosen him 'who of all men living he most cherished, my lord of Somerset. To whom, addressing himself with the most amiable condescension that might be used, he said these words, "lo, here, friend Somerset"'. These appointments, with others later in the year, did little to strengthen a feeble government. Suffolk was honest enough as official honesty went in James's reign, but his lax and easy-going ways made no progress against the mounting debt, and he tolerated grave abuses. The poverty of the Crown became ever more abject. Not only officials but the tradesmen who supplied the court with food now went unpaid. If they were willing to extend credit to the King, he protected them against their own creditors; if not, they might find themselves in prison. In 1615 James began to sell titles of nobility, and in the next year he sold the Cautionary Towns to the Dutch.

His manner of life remained unchanged. In the summer of 1614 he made an extended progress, first to Audley End, Suffolk's magnificent estate, then to Bletsoe, Kirby, Apethorpe, Burley, Belvoir, Newark, Rufford and so to Nottingham and Sherwood Forest. The progress was interrupted by an unexpected visit of Christian of Denmark who landed incognito, as a kind of royal jest, and arrived in London before his identity was known. James hastened to the capital to embrace his fellow-monarch whom he entertained with a week of hunting, hawking, running at the ring, bear-baiting and fireworks, and with plays in the evenings. Knowing his taste, the King invited Christian to a drinking-feast at Whitehall in his private chamber where healths passed to and fro till late into the night. But Christian's visit was short; and James, after parting with him on August 5th, 'went to Theobalds that night, the next day to Huntingdon, and so to Sir Anthony Mildmay's [at Apethorpe] where he overtook his dogs that went the ordinary progress'. The royal visit to Apethorpe was a momentous occasion, for there for the first time the King saw a young newcomer to the court, George Villiers.[10]

It was during the later months of 1614 that James experienced a gradual disillusionment regarding Somerset. He had spoiled him completely. And the foolish favourite, dazzled by his success and by his high connections, no longer concealed the fact that he found the King a bore. He showed him neither respect nor consideration. When he did not have his way, he rushed to James, complaining like a fretful child and upbraiding him for things that were not his fault. High words passed between them; and the King, to his deep sorrow and chagrin, began to see his favourite for what he was. Somerset was having his crosses. He knew that his enemies sought his ruin; he resented James's attentions to Villiers. Yet these things might have been handled by a man of judgment. Fenton wrote in September that although a youth named Villiers 'begins to be in favour with his Majesty, yet all things are absolutely done by one man and he more absolute than ever he was. Neither his father-in-law, with whom he keeps good quarter, nor any man else dare touch him'. In November he was able to prevent Villiers's appointment as a Gentleman of the Bedchamber.

Early in 1615 the King wrote Somerset a letter in which wounded vanity, slighted affection and sincere sorrow combine to make strange reading. He calls God to witness that there is no truth in the idle complaints with which the favourite has been troubling him. What can Somerset desire that he does not have? 'Do not all courtesies and places come through your office as Chamberlain, and rewards through your father-in-law as Treasurer? Do not you two as it were hedge in all the court with a manner of necessity to depend upon you?' Does not Somerset have infinite privacy with the King and many offices? And should not these benefits answer false reports that he is losing his master's favour?

For a long time, the King continues, a wild frenzy has seized upon Somerset, with 'streams of unquietness, passion, fury and insolent pride, and a settled kind of induced obstinacy'; and the favourite's new art of railing has passed beyond the freedom permitted by his place. He has brought complaints at unseasonable hours, depriving the King of rest, as though of purpose to vex him. He has spoken as if he doubted the honesty of James's love, as though he held him by awe and not by favour. He has refused to sleep in the royal bedchamber. The court has observed their raised voices, the sadness of the King after their interviews, his inability to find repose. James has suffered Somerset's passions with an aching heart, hoping to correct them by gentle admonitions, 'yet shall I never pardon myself, but shall carry that cross to the grave with me, for raising a man so high as might make him presume to pierce my ears with such speeches'.

He writes 'from the infinite grief of a deeply wounded heart', and can bear this grief no longer. He cannot consume himself with remorse when the welfare of the kingdom, indeed of all Christendom, depends upon him. Somerset must not hasten the death of the man who made him and who prays sincerely for him. 'For the easing of my inward and consuming grief, all I crave is, that in all the words and actions of your life you make it appear that you never think to hold me but out of love, and not one hair by force. Consider that I am a freeman if I were not a King. Remember that all your being, except your breathing and soul, is from me. I told you twice or thrice you might lead me by the heart and not by the nose. If ever I find you think to retain me by one sparkle of fear, all the violence of my love will in that instant be changed into as violent a hatred. God is my judge, my love hath been infinite towards you; and only the strength of my affection towards you hath made me to bear these things and bridle my passion. Let me be met, then, with your entire heart but softened by humility. Let me never apprehend that you disdain my person and undervalue my qualities; and let it not appear that your former affection is cold towards me. Hold me thus by the heart; and you may build upon my favour as upon a rock.'

This kindly warning Somerset ignored, and his difficulties increased. In April 1615, his enemies made a move to lessen his position by pushing the fortunes of George Villiers. Abbot tells how he and other lords begged Queen Anne to recommend to the King that Villiers be named a Gentleman of the Bedchamber. Anne at first refused, saying with true foresight that Villiers, if advanced, would soon prove a plague to his backers, for the King would turn him against them. But Abbot persisted, and Anne agreed to urge the appointment. As a result, it was made, and the King knighted Villiers in the Queen's bedchamber while both Abbot and Somerset waited anxiously at the door.

Nor did this end Somerset's reverses. Having been entrusted at Northampton's death with the duties of the Lord Privy Seal and of the Warden of the Cinque Ports, he wished to retain the first of these offices for himself and to secure the second for Bishop Bilson. But neither appointment was made. The King sent him another warning. 'I have been needlessly troubled this day with your desperate letters', he wrote. 'You may take the right way if you list and neither grieve me nor yourself. No man's nor woman's credit is able to cross you at my hands if you pay me a part of that you owe me. But how you can give over that inward affection and yet be a dutiful servant, I cannot understand that distinction. Heaven and earth shall bear me witness that if you do but half your duty unto me you may be with me in the old manner, only by expressing that love to my person and respect to your master that God and man crave of you, with a hearty and feeling penitence of your bypast errors. God move your heart to take the right course, for the fault shall only be in yourself, and so farewell.' In July 1615, Somerset gave ample proof of his apprehensions by seeking a formal pardon broad enough to cover any and all offences he had committed in the past. The pardon was prepared, but Ellesmere refused to pass it under the Great Seal. In a debate in the Council the King supported Somerset, saying he should continue to enjoy royal favour as long as he deserved it. 'And so, my Lord Chancellor, seal the pardon immediately, for that is my will.' Ellesmere still demurred; and the King, angrily telling him to do as he was commanded, left the Council chamber. But besieged in private by those who backed the Chancellor, James escaped into the country. The pardon was never sealed.

Sarmiento reported that though Somerset remained an adviser of the Crown the King listened to tales against him, that courtiers cut the favourite ostentatiously, and that the situation was one of great embarrassment.

Somerset's ruin, however, came through sudden revelations from the Tower. In September 1615, the Lieutenant, Sir Gervase Helwys, came to Winwood and confessed that he had known of attempts to poison Overbury, but that these attempts had been prevented until an apothecary's boy had given the prisoner poison of which he died. Helwys's confession did not mention the Earl or Countess of Somerset but it pointed directly at them; and James was faced with the scandal that his favourite was suspected of murder. The King laid the confession before some of the Council, asking whether it appeared to be genuine. The councillors replied that the matter seemed very grave. James then appointed commissioners to conduct a thorough investigation. At the same time he 'made in the Council a great protestation before God of his desire to see justice done, and that neither his favourite, nor his son himself, nor anything else in the world should hinder him'. His resolve, he told the commissioners, was 'to use all lawful courses that the foulness of this fault be sounded to the depth, that for the discharge of our duty both to God and man, the innocent may be cleared, and the nocent may severely be punished'.[11]

To this resolve he adhered throughout the investigations and trials which followed. His motives were simple. He knew that the affair was dangerous for him, but he realized that thorough inquiry would be less harmful than any attempt at concealment. If, he later wrote Somerset: 'I should have stopped the course of justice against you in this case of Overbury, who was committed to the Tower and kept there a close prisoner by my commandment, and could not have been so murdered if he had not been kept close, I might have been thought to be the author of that murder and so be made odious to all posterity.' Having resolved that investigation was the safest course, James could allow his sense of duty as a kingly judge, appointed to sit upon God's throne, to come fully into play; and for this selfless love of justice he assumed the greatest credit. His interest in all the proceedings was intense, his interference was constant, he sifted evidence and counselled judges; but his meddling did not do injustice, or at least not very much, because his object was to discover the truth. Before the affair was over he resorted to some scurvy tricks. Yet, on the whole, his conduct was creditable.

His parting with Somerset, probably on October 15th, was affectionate. 'The King hung about his neck,' wrote Weldon, 'slabbering his cheeks, saying, "For God's sake, when shall I see thee again? On my soul, I shall neither eat nor sleep until you come again." The Earl told him on Monday. "For God's sake, let me," said the King, "Shall I, Shall I?" then lolled about his neck. In the same manner at the stair's head, at the middle of the stairs, and at the stair's foot.' Yet as the Earl entered his coach James said: 'I shall never see his face more.' The scandalmongers seized upon this scene as the classic example of the King's dissimulation. But it was not unnatural. James was a sentimental person. He was parting from a man whom he had loved, though he loved him no longer.

Somerset had good cause for alarm. Very probably he was innocent, but he knew that many things would count against him. Foolishly he now acted in a way to increase suspicion. He seized some letters in the possession of Mrs. Turner, the depraved woman from whom the Countess had obtained charms and poisons. He burned letters that had passed between himself and Northampton and affixed false dates to others. He wrote to the King complaining of ill usage. James, he said, had placed his enemy Ellesmere on the commission of inquiry. He threatened the King with the loss of the friendship of the house of Howard unless the affair was dropped. James reproached him for his 'scribbling and railing, covertly against me and avowedly against the Chancellor'. The King declared that his conscience and reputation were at stake. He could not alter the commission at the request of those under examination. Somerset, he said, was acting like a man who feared inquiry. 'I never had the occasion to show the uprightness and sincerity that is required by a supreme judge as I have in this. If the delation prove false, God so deal with my soul as no man among you shall so much rejoice at it as I; nor never shall spare, I vow to God, one grain of vigour against the conspirators. If otherwise, as God forbid, none of you shall more heartily sorrow for it; and never king used that clemency that I will do in such a case. But that I should suffer a murder (if it be so) to be suppressed and plastered over, to the destruction both of my soul and reputation, I am no Christian. I never mean wittingly and

354

willingly to bear any man's sins but my own; and if for serving my conscience in setting down a fair course of trial, I shall lose the hands of that family, I will never care to lose the hearts of any for justice sake. I have no respect in this turn but to please Him in whose throne I sit.'

Somerset begged the King for an interview, pretending he had State secrets to impart. But James told him that he was merely doing himself harm. The trials, set for May 1616, must take place. If Somerset and his wife were innocent, the trial would clear them. If they were guilty, they should confess and ask for mercy, 'I being to follow the example of Almighty God who does not forgive sins until they be confessed and sorrowed for, no more can I show mercy where innocency is stood upon and the offence not made known by confession unto me.'

The King was eager to obtain a confession from Somerset. He believed that the Earl was probably guilty; but as he and Bacon worked over the evidence they had to admit that while the case against the Countess was unchallengeable, that against Somerset rested largely on presumption. If Somerset could be induced to confess, his confession would relieve the government of the necessity of advancing evidence that was weak, it would remove suspicions against the King, it would silence the prisoner during the trial where it was feared he might burst forth with wild accusations, it would render more natural the pardon which James was ready to give. Again and again, Somerset was pressed to admit his guilt, 'to honour God and me', as James put it, by confessing the truth. Just before the trial the King stooped to low methods. Somerset was told that he was certain to be found guilty, that the judges were prejudiced against him, that his wife had said she would expose his guilt. James's boasted flair for solving criminal mysteries amounted to little more, after all, than breaking down the defences of the accused until a confession was obtained. In this case he failed. Somerset stood on his innocence.

Shaken by anxiety as the trial approached and badgered by the agents of the King, Somerset resorted to threats. He had some secret, he said, presumably to James's discredit, which would be revealed if the trial was not abandoned. Historians have speculated as to the nature of this secret. James had no doubt about it. 'It is clear to see', he wrote, 'that he would threaten me with laying an aspersion upon me of being in some sort accessory to his crime.'

James stood his ground, but he was nervous and apprehensive. While Somerset's trial was taking place, May 25th, the King, who remained at Greenwich, 'was so extreme sad and discontented, as he did retire himself from all company, and did forbear both dinner and supper until he had heard what answer the Earl had made. It seemed something was feared should in passion have broken from him; but when his Majesty had heard that nothing had escaped him more than what he was forced to answer to the business then in hand, his Majesty's countenance soon changed, and he hath ever since continued in a good disposition'. Weldon, as usual, adds a note of scorn: 'But who had seen the King's restless motion all that day, sending to every boat he saw landing at the bridge, cursing all that came without tidings, would have easily judged all was not right, and there had been some grounds for his fears of Somerset's boldness; but at last one bringing him word he was condemned, and the passages, all was quiet.'

Somerset and Lady Frances carried themselves worthily at the ordeal of their trials. The Countess's trial was short, lasting only two hours, for she pleaded guilty. She won pity by her sober and humble demeanour. The Italian Pallavicino was quite swept off his feet by her grace and sweetness and felt confident she had been led into crime by her wicked husband. But Chamberlain considered her behaviour too confident for a lady in such distress, 'yet she shed or made show of some tears divers times'. Somerset, on the other hand, had to face his judges and a world of spectators from ten in the morning till ten at night. Some of his replies were weak, but he maintained his innocence with constancy and undaunted courage. He and his wife were both found guilty and sentenced to death; and it was thought that the King had so fully committed himself to impartial justice that he would allow the sentences to be carried out. But he had no such intention. The prisoners remained in the Tower until 1622 when they were permitted to live in retirement in the country.[12]

Amid such dark shadows ended the career of Somerset. But the King had learned nothing. He was already in love with a new favourite, more dangerous, because more able, than the old.

CHAPTER XIX

RALEGH'S LAST VOYAGE

THE death of Salisbury marked a turning point in foreign as well as domestic affairs. Not only were his solidity and judgment sadly missed as policy fell into weaker hands, but ominous changes appeared in the international balance of power and in England's relations with foreign States. During the first decade of the reign, as we have seen, James had drawn closer to Protestant and to anti-Spanish Europe. The peaceful friendship he had offered Spain appeared by 1613 to be on the rocks and his course in foreign affairs appeared to be set. Then came a gradual shift. Unhappy and acrimonious quarrels estranged him from his old friends; Protestant Europe lost faith in its champion. At the same time, in dealing with Spain, James knew that his position had deteriorated. He had suffered a series of disasters while Spain had grown in strength abroad if not at home. Her relations with France were infinitely better; she was not fighting the Dutch though she might have to do so at any time; she had in England a most astute ambassador, Sarmiento, later Count Gondomar, whose cunning in diplomacy far surpassed that of the British Solomon.

As a result James grew more conciliatory. He could no longer continue his lofty tone of a great Protestant monarch whose primary alliance was with Protestant States but who was willing to accord to Spain the few crumbs of friendship that remained. He now treated with Spain as with an equal or even a superior power. The value of a friendly understanding with her was enhanced. He began to think of a Spanish dowry not as a convenience but as a necessity and he was far more anxious to conclude the Spanish marriage than were the Spaniards. Yet Spanish power must be held within reasonable bounds. Falling back upon his precept of a golden mean, James sought a balance between himself and his allies on one hand and Spain and her satellites on the other. He would be the friend of Spain, and at the same time would lead a coalition formed against her. But the impracticability of such a policy was soon made clear. His quick and nimble mind, though able to see both sides of an international question, lacked the solidarity and force to achieve the equilibrium he sought. He vacillated from side to side, floundering in contradictions, until he appeared to have no policy at all. Hence the benefits of Anglo-Spanish friendship went to Spain, as the stronger party, and not to England, while the King slipped into appeasement, ready to make concessions and to ask his allies to do the same. The first great milestone of this downward drift was the execution of Ralegh in 1618.

James's efforts to draw his friends together and to form an anti-Spanish front should not be overlooked. Having signed a treaty of mutual assistance with the German Protestant Union at the time of his daughter's marriage, he persuaded the Dutch to join the alliance. He employed his influence with Christian of Denmark to draw that country into the confederacy of States which, as he boasted, had been set up under his auspices. Denmark's relations with Holland were very bad, but James was able to lessen friction. He helped to make peace between Denmark and Sweden in 1613, improved Danish relations with the States of northern Germany, and urged Venice to send an ambassador to Denmark. He aided in reconciling a quarrel between Saxony and Brandenburg in 1613; and in the next few years sent missions to end disputes between Sweden, Poland and Russia. In southern Europe, having settled a quarrel between Venice and Savoy in 1614, he attempted to draw them both into closer relations with his friends in the north. At one time he proposed a league of the States of northern Italy — Venice, Savoy, Mantua, Parma, together with the Swiss and the Grisons — to block the advance of Spanish influence. 'The end and aim of the King is to obtain peace everywhere and a defensive union to secure all parts from attack by the Spaniards.'[1]

Yet these moves amounted to little beyond an occasional local success. James's error was to assume that leagues and alliances would spring into existence at his mere suggestion and that they would function without leadership, backed by military power, from England. He made sweeping promises and easy commitments. But he did almost nothing more. When the structure he erected was put under pressure he evaded his responsibilities, leaving his friends to shift for themselves. Hence they became disillusioned, and his enemies came to rely upon his inactivity.

His influence on the Continent, which might have been tremendous, was frittered away; while his numerous, stately and expensive
embassies inspired ridicule rather than respect.

The manner in which he exasperated his allies is illustrated by
the Treaty of Xanten in 1614. A new crisis had arisen over the
succession to Cleves and Julich when the two claimants, the
Elector of Brandenburg and Count Wolfgang Wilhelm of Neuburg,
drifted into hostilities. The Brandenburg party seized Julich and
summoned the Dutch to their aid; while the Neuburger, recently
turned Catholic, called upon the Spanish who responded eagerly
and seized Wesel. James's first thought was anger at the aggression of the Spaniards. He denounced them roundly and stormed
at Sarmiento in heated interviews. Working with the French and
the Dutch, he managed to arrange the Treaty of Xanten which
provided for a restitution of territories pending a settlement. But
he had been so eager to conclude the treaty that he had not considered carefully how it was to be fulfilled. He asked the Spanish
to evacuate first but they refused. He then turned to the Dutch,
but they declined to evacuate before the Spanish. James thought
the Dutch unreasonable and grew angry. His petulant and doc-
trinaire diplomacy placed him in the position of pressing the
Dutch to make concessions to Spain. The Dutch could not understand such conduct. The Elector of Brandenburg withdrew his
ambassador from London in disgust. The French, who had
guaranteed the treaty, saw James tinkering with its provisions
without consulting them. And while the King quarrelled with
his friends, the Spaniards gave their answer by fortifying Wesel.
Spanish and Dutch troops continued to hold Wesel and Julich in
the names of the rival candidates.

This episode was but the beginning of James's difficulties with
the Dutch. There was the hard fact of economic rivalry. All over
the world, wherever the English went to trade, or fish, or plant
colonies, they met the competition of the Dutch, aggressive, ruthless and tight-fisted. Dutch shipping increased enormously. The
new Sea-Herrs, wrote Ralegh, aimed 'to get the whole trade and
shipping of Christendom into their own hands', until they won the
mastery of the oceans. There were constant disputes over
fisheries. The King attempted to levy tolls upon the Dutch who
came to fish for herring off the east coasts of Britain, for he
believed that his right to these seas amounted to absolute owner-

ship, and he doubtless thought of the tolls laid upon shipping by Christian of Denmark. There followed angry diplomatic exchanges with the Dutch and angry clashes at sea. When a Dutch captain seized a Scottish official who attempted to collect the tolls and carried him prisoner to Holland, the King all but burst with indignation. He demanded that the offender be sent to England for punishment; and he would have carried his point had not the captain died during the negotiations.

English and Dutch clashed again in the whale fisheries around Spitzbergen. In 1613 English whalers annexed the islands under the name of King James's Newland, and thenceforth the King maintained his claim to exclusive possession with the utmost stubbornness. When Dutch whalers appeared near Spitzbergen he denounced them as interlopers in an area 'solely belonging to us and to our people'. In 1618 a pitched battle was fought between the rival fleets.

There was also a serious quarrel over the cloth trade. The Merchant Adventurers, now established at Middelburg in Zeeland, exported unfinished woollen cloth which was dressed and dyed in Holland. But the King listened to a plan advanced by Alderman Sir William Cockayne that the cloth be finished and dyed in England before it was sent abroad. This was sound mercantile doctrine and the King approved. He gave Cockayne a patent for the monopoly of selling dyed cloth in England; and in 1615 he prohibited the export of undyed cloth, called in the charter of the Merchant Adventurers, and allowed the formation of a new company with Cockayne at its head. The result was disastrous. The Dutch refused to purchase dyed cloth from England, and Cockayne, having lost the Dutch market, could not make a profit. The weaving industry in England was soon in chaos. Correspondence between James and the Council is filled with the difficulties that arose, and the King turned angrily upon the luckless promoter who had caused him so much trouble. The new company, having failed, surrendered its charter in 1617, while the Merchant Adventurers received their old charter anew.

Another quarrel was becoming acute. Both the Dutch and the English East India Companies, following the Portuguese, focused their attention on the little East Indian islands where the best spices were produced. But the Dutch company was determined that the East Indies should be a Dutch monopoly and was prepared to use any means, however bloody and dishonest, to oust its English rival. The relations of the two companies in the east were a state of war.

The plump Hollanders, moreover, whom the King had regarded with supercilious condescension, were proving stronger than the English. From every encounter they emerged victorious. They had formerly treated with James as subjects with their lord, wrote the Venetian ambassador in 1617, but now they negotiate as with an equal. The change was not lost upon the King, who resented it deeply. The Dutch presented a complex and baffling problem. Yet James might have observed that, whenever his policy hardened towards Spain, his relations with the Dutch improved.[2]

Nor was he on good terms with France. Negotiations for a marriage between Prince Charles and the little French Princess Christina had been begun in 1613 and for a time made excellent progress, but the King brought them to an end three years later and turned instead to Spain. He was repelled by the chaos in France where many nobles were in chronic revolt and the Huguenots were extremely restless. Both nobles and Huguenots begged him for assistance. But to the French nobles he replied that he could not sanction rebellion, and in a similar vein he reminded the Huguenots that prayers and tears were the arms of the Church. Thus he had no thought of intervention, yet his dealings with the rebels were sufficient to anger the French government.

There was degeneration also in his relations with Charles Emmanuel of Savoy who in 1613 became involved in a serious quarrel with the Spanish in Milan. Deeply interested, James declared loudly that there was nothing nearer his heart than assistance to Savoy. Perhaps even to his own astonishment, he found a small sum of money, though its transmission was so bungled that it did Charles Emmanuel little good. Beyond this the King did nothing except to urge others to come to Savoy's assistance, and, as the Venetian ambassador reported with a touch of scorn, he wrote 'in all directions in the service of the Duke'. But his object was peace, and after a maze of negotiations he obtained the Treaty of Asti in June 1615, which provided for simultaneous disarmament in Savoy and Milan. In his eagerness for a settlement, however, he urged Charles Emmanuel to set an example by disarming first; and thus, as after Xanten, he pressed an ally to make concessions to a Spanish power. The Duke agreed only when James gave solemn pledges of support should the Spanish violate the treaty.

Savoy disarmed but Milan did not, and war broke out in earnest in the autumn of 1616, soon involving Venice, in alliance with Savoy, and Naples and Sicily, in alliance with Milan. Charles Emmanuel called upon James to fulfil his commitments. But the King resorted to the most miserable shuffling. Scarnafissi, Savoy's ambassador in London, was put off with one excuse after another. At last in February 1617, after a futile mission of nearly two years, Scarnafissi lost patience and accused James of bad faith. He was told that the King's finances were such that nothing could be done.[3]

Yet for all his poverty James might have rendered some assistance, and he did so indirectly. The secret of Tudor naval strength lay in the sailing ship armed with heavy guns arranged to fire broadsides. Hence the introduction of northern fighting ships into the Mediterranean was dreaded greatly by Spain. In 1617, when Venice was in grave danger, she was able to charter a number of these ships in Holland and England and to bring them into the Adriatic. At the same time Ralegh was preparing his ill-fated voyage; and for a moment, tempted by Scarnafissi, James played with the idea of sending Ralegh against Genoa. There was also talk of an English expedition against the Barbary pirates. So alarmed was Spain at these developments that she decided to make peace with Savoy and Venice. Ironically enough, the great peacemaker helped to make peace, without taking part in the negotiations, through the silent pressure of a weapon which he did not know that he possessed.[4]

The dwindling cordiality between James and his old friends was further disturbed by his negotiations for a Spanish marriage alliance. These famous negotiations, continuing for more than a decade, were so closely connected with Sarmiento, who came to London late in 1613, that we must look at this remarkable man before we go further.

Sarmiento was the perfect diplomat, courtly, dignified, beautifully poised, in command of every situation. He possessed a wonderful gift of apt reply both in serious business and in the lighter art of social conversation; and the King, with his love for lively talk and for the give and take of argument, found him a delight though also something of a terror. For Sarmiento had deeper qualities: courage, audacity, strength of will and fixity of purpose. His complete confidence in himself and in his country gave strength to his diplomacy and majesty to his deportment. The most wily, artful and crafty of men, with a cunning that was diabolical, he could perpetrate his deceptions with an air of moral grandeur and could make the most insolent demands in a tone of imperial dignity which inspired deference and even awe. His manner was that of a man who moved the world. There was a great deal of bombast about him, but it was a bombast that carried conviction; and his boastings not only imposed upon James, but upon the ambassador himself, upon his government, and upon historians who have taken his dispatches at their face value.

He was a witty man who increased the impact of his arguments with a kind of barbed jocularity, and he entered fully into James's type of tumbling humour. 'The King took delight to talk with him,' wrote Arthur Wilson, 'for he was full of conceits and would speak false Latin on purpose in his merry fits to please the King; telling the King plainly that he [James] spoke Latin like a pedant, but I speak it like a gentleman.' Patiently he conformed to all James's fancies. 'Thus while hunting with the King,' said the Venetian ambassador, 'he vies with him in putting his hands in the blood of bucks and stags, doing cheerfully everything that his Majesty does and in this way chiefly he has acquired his favour.' He obtained the paramount advantage of negotiating in an atmosphere of informal and jesting familiarity, for with a folly bordering on madness James admitted to intimacy the most dangerous man with whom he ever had to deal.

Sarmiento studied him for many years. James's love of peace and hatred of aggression, his dislike of rebels and republicans, his prejudice against the Dutch, his devotion to the rights of kings, his fondness for mediation, his vanity, his apprehensions and his horror of assassination, his growing indolence — all his qualities, good and bad — were played upon by Sarmiento in the interests of Spain.

Sarmiento explained to his government the methods he employed in dealing with the King. One was to dwell upon the might and power of Spain. Philip, said Sarmiento, could afford to be disinterested in friendship, 'there being always a superfluity

of worlds and states' at his command; and James admitted that
Philip 'had many kingdoms and more subjects beyond comparison
than he had'. Great power was accompanied by great wealth.
In his grand Spanish way Sarmiento gave the impression that the
size of the dowry was a matter of indifference to his master. At the
same time he employed a most telling form of flattery. Despite his
wealth and power, it appeared, the King of Spain was deeply
interested in securing James's friendship. Philip was keenly
aware of James's wisdom and virtue; and no prince in Christendom possessed greater influence at Madrid than did the King of
England. Philip longed to lay aside old quarrels and to live with
the British Solomon as with a brother. At the same time, by some
subtle art, Sarmiento contrived to convey an impression of can-
dour and frankness and to convince the King of his personal
integrity. It is astonishing that James, an experienced and
sophisticated ruler, should have been deluded by such blandishments. And yet the Venetian ambassador said exactly the same
thing as Sarmiento. One wins the King's favour, the ambassador
wrote to the Doge, 'by praising and admiring him and by making
him believe that all those who have the honour to treat with him
learn a great deal from his extraordinary wisdom; by showing him
the frankness with which your Serenity negotiates, your affection
and esteem for him and by making him recognize one's truthful-
ness and straightforwardness in all things'.

Sarmiento also stressed the security that would come with
Spanish friendship. Once the King was allied with mighty Spain,
his enemies would yield in abashed submission or fade away with
little shrieks of despair. The English Roman Catholics would become his staunchest supporters. This was a telling argument, for
James regarded the fanaticism of English Catholics as the most
likely source of plots for his assassination, and he began to identify
the security of his person with the maintenance of peace with
Spain. This suggests a deeper reason for Sarmiento's success. He
was by far the stronger man of the two. He learned that he could
speak not only with frankness but with an audacity that passes
belief. James's weaker nature quailed before that of the fiery
Spaniard; and it was the King, not the ambassador, who yielded.
Thus Sarmiento became perhaps the most influential foreign
ambassador ever to reside in England, to the exasperation and
horror of its people. [5]

His first impression when he arrived in London in 1613 was that the French marriage could not be prevented. But he hinted in his insinuating way that the King could easily obtain better terms in Madrid than in Paris. Then came the dissolution of Parliament in 1614 which underscored James's poverty and drew him towards the Spanish party. He learned that Philip was contemplating a new approach to England; and hence, as he talked with Sarmiento of his troubles with the Commons, it was a simple matter for the ambassador to suggest a Spanish marriage. James listened. And thus began those endless negotiations that were to fill his thoughts for many years to come.

Sarmiento believed that he had won a tremendous triumph in turning James's mind from a French to a Spanish marriage alliance. He saw a crisis approaching in Europe between the old religion and the new. Should the King conclude the marriage with France, there might arise a great anti-Spanish block of States to spell the doom of Catholicism. But if the King could be drawn to the Spanish alliance, the entire process might be reversed, the Protestants might be crushed, and Christendom united in the one true faith. All depended upon England. Most earnestly, therefore, Sarmiento begged Philip to negotiate with moderation. He should not insist upon the immediate conversion of the Prince, a sweet and gentle child, open to instruction at a later date. Nor should Philip demand the instant repeal of the anti-Catholic laws. That, too, could come later. For if, by the non-enforcement of the penal laws, James would permit the English Catholics freedom of worship, the rest would follow in time. Little by little, concessions could be stretched and enlarged until all was conceded. If the penal laws were relaxed, the number of Catholics would quickly increase until they filled Parliament and repealed the anti-Catholic laws. Thus grossly did Sarmiento underrate the strength of Protestantism in England. He thought that if he won the King, he had won all. And meanwhile, he added, the marriage negotiations could be employed to draw James ever further from his continental allies.

The ambassador's enthusiasm for the marriage found little echo in Madrid; Philip consulted the Pope, who expressed strong disapproval. And yet the possibility of converting England opened dazzling vistas. Even if that were not achieved, the King's friendship was highly valuable, and negotiations would be well worth while if they merely kept him neutral in the quarrels of the Continent. The marriage was a propitiatory sacrifice that might have to be made; but the negotiations for it could be prolonged for years, and the opposition of the Papacy might offer means of final escape. It was in this spirit of qualified acquiescence that the Spanish government, accepting Sarmiento's advice, prepared articles to serve as a basis for negotiations. These articles arrived in England in May 1615.

The first thoughts of the King as he studied the Spanish articles were hostile. The Spanish began by saying that they found the marriage difficult but not impossible. Its success depended upon the treatment accorded to Roman Catholics in England, and it was stipulated that they should be allowed the exercise of their religion through non-enforcement of the penal laws. On this vital question the King unwisely postponed decision. 'No answer is to be given', he noted, 'till we have agreed upon the rest.' The Pope, ran the next article, must grant a dispensation for the marriage. 'Let the King of Spain procure what dispensations he pleases,' wrote James, 'it being a thing with which I have nothing to do.' But he was to discover that he should not have dismissed this point so lightly. The Infanta, ran other articles, must control the education of the children, they must choose their own religion, and must be baptized according to the Roman use. 'It is clear', wrote James, 'that I, too, shall be careful to instruct my children in my religion, since I am as confident of its goodness as the King of Spain is of the goodness of his; yet there shall be no compulsion on the one side or the other. The children are to be baptized after the use of England.' If the children should become Roman Catholics, said the next article, they should not thereby be barred from the succession. This touched a tender point. 'The laws of England', wrote James, 'teach and oblige subjects to obey their king of whatever religion he may be. It is only the Jesuits who teach the contrary.' The Infanta's household, said the Spaniards, should come with her from Spain and should be Catholic; the wet nurses of the children should be Catholic. To this James answered that members of the Infanta's household should have liberty of religion, but he thought that wet nurses should be selected on the basis of their health. The Spanish asked that the Infanta's chapel be large, free and public, and that if her oratory was private she should also have a public church for her household as well as a special burial ground. These articles demanded public exercise of the Roman Catholic faith, and James refused them. 'The Infanta', he wrote, 'is to have a large chapel or oratory. The household will not have any other church or chapel, but a decent place to bury their dead in.' The priests of the Infanta's household, said the Spaniards, should be permitted to wear their proper habits in public. 'It will cause scandal', James noted. Another article asked that the marriage be celebrated by proxy in Spain. To this the King agreed but added: 'Yet they will also have to be married personally by an English bishop.'

These comments of the King, jotted down as marginal notes, amounted to a rejection of the Spanish articles, yet after some hesitation James foolishly told Sarmiento that he would accept the articles as a basis for negotiation. His mind was then diverted to other events occasioned by Somerset's disgrace, and for six months the Spanish match dropped out of sight. Yet he was often reminded of the advantages that might accrue from a Spanish alliance. He was alarmed by the strength and recalcitrance of the Catholic recusants in Ireland and by the words of an obdurate English Catholic, John Owen, who declared that 'the King, being excommunicated by the Pope, might be lawfully deposed and killed by any whatsoever'. Here was Jesuit doctrine in most blatant form. Terrified and unnerved, the King slept for some nights behind a barricade of empty beds, and when he went abroad he drove at high speed, surrounded by a phalanx of running footmen. He must have pondered Sarmiento's argument that an alliance with Spain would quiet the English Catholics. He was also disturbed by the violent and rancorous hatred of all things Spanish that was springing up at court; for anti-Spanish councillors, led by Abbot, Pembroke and Winwood, terrified at what the King was doing, now boldly demanded war as the only means of stamping out the Spanish match for ever. Their advice to the King to summon Parliament occasioned a struggle of factions behind the scenes, of which we have only hints. But it is safe to guess that James balked at a Parliament, that a Spanish dowry loomed ever larger in his thoughts, that the martial spirit abroad in the nation was repugnant to him and turned him in the opposite direction.

Late in January 1616, he summoned Sarmiento. James had the gout and was seated with one foot on a stool, but he arose, ad-

vanced a few steps, and said he had been counting the days until
Sarmiento came to see him. For some time the conversation was
miscellaneous. James spoke of a rumour that the Spanish were
strengthening their fleet, but Sarmiento answered that this was idle
gossip. He told the King of an English spy who had offered his
services to Philip but whom Philip had repelled with scorn. At
this James arose, took off his hat, and called God to witness that
he knew full well the true friendship of the King of Spain. The
conversation turned to the Dutch, who were roundly abused.
James spoke of the Spanish bride of Louis XIII, declaring that the
Spanish knew well how to educate their women. At this point, so
wrote Sarmiento, 'he looked at me very attentively and asked me
whether, if he wished to court a lady in Spain, I would assist him
in it. I told him I was glad to find him in so good a disposition,
that I confessed that I was useless for anything except as a pimp,
but for that reason I would be the safer. At this he burst into loud
laughter. By God, he said, I am in the same state, and it is
therefore necessary for me to find a substitute if the love-making
is to come to anything; and I have found one in my son, who will,
I hope, content you'. In this strange fashion negotiations were
reopened.

James asked for some assurance that the Pope would grant the
dispensation required by Spain. He complained with justice that
he was asked to make commitments while Philip was under no
engagement, for the Spanish made everything contingent upon
the Pope's consent, which was yet to be obtained. Much evil
would have been avoided if James had stood his ground; but he
dropped the point when Sarmiento argued that the Pope could
hardly be asked to approve until the terms of the marriage were
arranged. As a matter of fact, Philip consulted the Pope once
more in 1616, only to find that papal disapproval had not diminished. Philip then turned to a junta of theologians in Spain, asking
them to consider all aspects of the marriage and to give him their
advice.[6]

These consultations imposed long delay, the negotiations
dragged, and James became irritated at the dilatory coyness of his
proposed ally. As he grew sullen and annoyed, a method of prod-
ding Spain into greater activity was unfolding itself before him.

For some time he had been under pressure from the anti-
Spanish faction to liberate Sir Walter Ralegh and to permit him

to make a voyage to the Orinoco River. The moment was auspicious for Ralegh: Northampton was dead, Somerset in difficulties, and the new favourite, George Villiers, was willing to be bribed. Winwood, Abbot and Pembroke saw in Ralegh's voyage a wonderful opportunity to force a break with Spain. Thus the King was confronted with strong sentiment in Ralegh's behalf and he yielded to it. In March 1616, the prisoner was released from the Tower and began preparations for his voyage. That James permitted this is astonishing. His reasons become clearer if we look at Ralegh's project more closely.

During his long years in the Tower Ralegh's mind had constantly turned to the region of the Orinoco which he had visited in 1595. He held that as a result of his voyage the territory was English; and he dreamed of an English empire in Guiana and in the Orinoco valley, an empire that would stretch westward to Santa Fé and the Pacific, divide Mexico from Peru, and at last destroy Spanish power in the Indies. He had also the more immediate object of finding gold. Indian legend told of El Dorado somewhere in the interior, with the golden city of Manoa and its golden king, a rival to the wealth of the Incas in Peru. This vision faded, but there remained a belief that valuable gold deposits existed along the banks of the Orinoco. In 1595 Ralegh had ascended the river some hundred and twenty miles to its junction with the Caroni, where he found a deposit of quartz which he believed to contain gold. He had also seen from a distance a mountain perhaps thirty miles to the south-east which the Indians said was auriferous. Thus he knew of two places where he thought that gold could be obtained. In 1596 he sent an expedition under Laurence Keymis, who reached the vicinity of these mines. Keymis, however, discovered to his chagrin that since Ralegh's visit the Spanish had established themselves at the confluence of the Orinoco and the Caroni and had built a hamlet, San Thomé. Hence Ralegh knew that he could not work the mines without collision with the Spaniards. That he believed in the mines there is no doubt. He hoped that their gold might open his prison doors. In 1607 and again in 1611 he had appealed to Salisbury and to other persons at court in the hope of obtaining royal permission for a voyage.

Salisbury was cautious and the project came to nothing, but it implanted the thought in the King's mind that gold might be obtained along the Orinoco and that the area was worth possessing. James longed for gold. What happy changes could be brought about by English treasure fleets from the Indies! And if Ralegh had established a royal claim, James was not the man to relinquish it.

The King permitted Ralegh to sail and to sail heavily armed, yet at the same time extracted from him the most solemn pledges that he would go only to the mines and would commit no spoils upon any Spanish subject. Ralegh was warned that if he broke his pledges he would pay with his life; and his commission omitted, at the King's command, the usual words 'trusty and well-beloved' which might imply a pardon from the death sentence of 1603. Ralegh sailed with the threat of death upon him. To Sarmiento's fiery protestations James replied with one of equal intensity — on his faith, his hand and his word — that he would send Ralegh to Spain bound hand and foot if he injured a single Spaniard. If he brought home shiploads of gold robbed from Spain, James would restore it to Philip and would send Ralegh to be hanged in Madrid. To appease Sarmiento further, the King gave him detailed information of Ralegh's plans.

The minds of kings are inscrutable, as James said. The usual explanation of his conduct has been that he decided to remain in studied ignorance of the geography of the Orinoco. If Ralegh spoke the truth when he said that the mines were not in Spanish territory, the expedition was justified. If he was lying and if he came into collision with the Spaniards, let him pay with his head. The responsibility was Ralegh's.

Recent research suggests some modification of this view. It is now thought that James could not have been ignorant of the geography of the Orinoco. With maps and charts available and with Sarmiento to point an accusing finger, he must have known the truth. Guiana, to be sure, was unoccupied, a no-man's-land between the Spanish Main and Portuguese Brazil. But the Orinoco was a different matter. The Spanish were established on the coast of modern Venezuela and at Trinidad. They had planted San Thomé at the very site of the mines. Had the King adhered to his principle that effective occupation conferred exclusive rights, he must have been aware that Spanish title to the Orinoco River was very strong.

Why, then, did he act as he did? A modern answer is that James considered the Orinoco a highly desirable possession and was prepared to take some risk in order to acquire it. He accepted Ralegh's contention that the voyage of 1595 had established some kind of English claim. He believed that if matters were managed skilfully Ralegh could avoid a direct attack on San Thomé. He knew that Ralegh hoped to enlist some Frenchmen in his venture; and if it could be arranged that Frenchmen, not Englishmen, assaulted San Thomé, or if the French could neutralize it while the English collected gold, the letter of Ralegh's pledges would be fulfilled. The same would be true if Ralegh stood strictly on the defensive, refusing to make an attack. Excuses and explanations to Spain would be rather thin, but they might do.

If James thought along these lines, his policy was bolder than has been imagined, and his treatment of Ralegh a little less dastardly. He was making a bid for treasure and for territory that might rightfully be his. He was giving Ralegh a chance, albeit that chance was small. Dishonest and heartless his policy was, but not so dishonest and not so heartless as has been supposed. In the summer of 1617, after several false starts, Ralegh sailed for the Indies.[7]

The attempt to prod Spain into action appeared for a moment to be successful, for the Spanish ministers, alarmed at English aggressiveness, hastened to give new life to the marriage negotiations. James was much pleased; and early in 1617 sent Digby to Spain to conclude the treaty and also spoke of the negotiations to the Privy Council. This, however, was little more than a gesture, for anti-Spanish councillors were excluded, the information offered was fragmentary, and the King's presentation was deceptive. He must, he said, make use of his son's marriage to obtain money for the payment of his debts, and hence he could do no less than test the validity of the generous and honourable overtures that had been coming from Spain. The Spanish 'did neither expect alteration in the religion of the Prince nor any liberty nor toleration for his Majesty's subjects, nor other course in religion which might be displeasing to his Majesty's subjects, nor any alteration in his affairs or correspondences with foreign princes, whereby he might lose or abandon them'. Some of this was true, some of it half-true, some deliberately false. Councillors were not asked whether they considered the marriage advisable, but whether, as things then stood, the King was justified in continuing negotiations. They could only answer cautiously that the King appeared to have 'as much assurance of good success as in such a case could be had', which meant little or nothing. But James was satisfied. The articles that had come from Spain in 1615 were drawn up in the form of a treaty and Digby was sent on his mission.

A rude surprise awaited both the ambassador and his master. Almost a year earlier Philip had laid the marriage project before a junta of theologians, and their answer was at length forthcoming. It greatly raised the Spanish terms. English penal laws must not be held in abeyance but must be repealed altogether, and until this was done, the Infanta was not to leave Spain nor a penny of the dowry be paid. The Prince must come to Spain for his bride, the implication being that his visit would result in his conversion. No attempt must be made by the English to convert the Infanta after the marriage, a large Catholic church in London must be open to all the world, and priests must appear in their ecclesiastical habits. These points, set forth by the zealous theologians, became the accepted policy of Spain.[8]

Confronted by such demands, Digby could only say that they exceeded his instructions. In England Sarmiento, now Count Gondomar, strove mightily to extract from the King a promise that he would repeal the penal laws. James made the most vehement protestations that he would go as far as he could. He was ready to relax the enforcement of the laws, but to repeal them he knew that he was powerless. Repeal could come only through Parliament, and such action by the Puritan Commons was unthinkable. Hence negotiations were deadlocked. Spain was asking the impossible, and the King could not give way if he would. Yet neither side was willing to terminate the prolonged negotiations. James hoped that by some lucky chance he might yet obtain a Spanish dowry, while Spain was glad to play out the game as long as the King would follow. James was most anxious to please the Spaniards in every way he could. It was at this unfortunate juncture that Ralegh returned to England, not only empty-handed but guilty of an assault upon a Spanish settlement in America.

The voyage was a tragic failure. The fleet was tormented by contrary winds, it was smitten by a hurricane, it lay in the doldrums in mid-ocean while fever raged among the men. Ralegh was so ill that when a landfall was made he could not come on deck. His captains, fearful of a Spanish fleet, insisted that Ralegh stand guard with the larger ships at the mouth of the Orinoco while smaller boats ascended the river, and thus in this great crisis Ralegh had to trust his fortunes to other hands. Command of the mission to the mines was given to Keymis, faithful but lacking in fortitude and judgment, and to George, Ralegh's nephew, brave but impetuous. No Frenchmen, who might have been used to attack San Thomé, had joined the voyage, but Ralegh hoped for an Indian uprising or for Spanish disaffection within San Thomé. He instructed Keymis to approach close to the town, to invest it by land and water, and thus to neutralize it without fighting while a search was made for gold. The plan miscarried. Keymis landed close to San Thomé, but during the first night his pickets were fired on by the Spaniards, a general mêlée ensued, young Walter Ralegh, the great adventurer's son, foolishly rushed forward in an attack that cost him his life, and the English surged towards the town, which was quickly in their hands. Ralegh's promise had been broken.

In possession of San Thomé, Keymis found that having traded places with the Spaniards he was now besieged by them as they lurked in the woods. He wasted his strength in fruitless sallies. His search for the mine nearby was so aimless and haphazard that his captains became convinced there was no mine at all. His men could not forage for food without being fired upon. They lived in constant dread of the arrival of Spanish reinforcements, and their one thought was escape. After twenty-nine days at San Thomé, Keymis admitted defeat and returned down the river, having made no search for the second mine some twenty miles inland. He rejoined Ralegh, poured out his ghastly tale, and committed suicide.

Ralegh was half-mad with grief and uncertainty. Broken-hearted he wrote his wife of young Walter's death: 'God knows, I never knew what sorrow meant till now.' Many wild notions raced through his mind. His first thought was to make a new attempt to reach the mines, but his hold upon his captains had slackened and they would not hear of it. He considered a raid upon the Spanish in the Caribbean or a search for the treasure fleet, alternatives that Winwood had urged upon him, but they would require hard fighting for which he now lacked strength since his fleet was breaking up and his captains deserting. He thought of a privateering venture only to reject it. There was nothing to do but to make his way homeward. We find him at Nevis, off the coast of Newfoundland, and finally again at Plymouth on June 21st, 1618, with one ship and a depleted crew. Quickly he was under arrest. He thought of escape to France, but one attempt was abandoned and a second betrayed. Lodged once more in the Tower, he was now with little hope.

James's anger and resentment against Ralegh, as the details of the voyage gradually reached England, amounted to cold and merciless fury. Shortly after Ralegh had sailed, one of his captains, John Bailey, deserted and returned home where he defended himself by declaring that Ralegh was about to turn pirate. Bailey's tales were given the lie by other reports. But James had been suspicious and had apologized to Gondomar for what he feared Ralegh had done. 'The King promises', Gondomar wrote to Spain, 'that he will do whatever we like to remedy and redress it'; and Lake wrote that 'his Majesty is very disposed and determined against Ralegh and will join the King of Spain in ruining him'. Then, shortly before Ralegh landed at Plymouth, another of his captains, Roger North, arrived in England and told the story of the attack on San Thomé, of Spaniards slain, of the burning of the town. Repeating what most of the captains believed, North discredited the existence of a mine. There had never been any mine at all; and Ralegh had planned to turn pirate and seek protection in France. [9]

One can imagine James's thoughts. If there was no mine, he had been deluded by a gigantic hoax, tricked into an anti-Spanish adventure by a restless and unpredictable rogue. As a result he was now in difficulties. If he punished Ralegh, he admitted his folly in allowing Ralegh to sail. If he did not punish him, Spanish friendship and the Spanish marriage were things of the past. And Ralegh had brought no gold. Gondomar was thirsting for vengeance, demanding in strident tones that James fulfil the letter of his promise that Ralegh, if guilty of attacking Spaniards, should be sent to Spain for punishment. It is small wonder that the King's old dislike and suspicion were fanned to white heat. Ralegh had always been troublesome. Now he was unbearable. James struck at him in hatred and exasperation. There was no shred of pity for his shattered fortunes, his broken dreams, his son dead by the lonely Orinoco.

On June 21st, James called his councillors together and

harangued them on Ralegh's misdeeds. He must punish Ralegh, he said, if he hoped to be considered a King of peace. Ralegh's friends could not contradict the King, but they complained of Gondomar's insolence in demanding that Ralegh be hanged in Madrid as though England was tributary to Spain. Somewhat taken aback, James said he was a peaceful man, but he knew how to defend his honour. Should he go to war with Spain in order to defend Ralegh? Should he not punish those traitors who had advised the voyage? Thus threatened, councillors conceded that Ralegh deserved punishment.[10]

Next day the King had a fateful interview with Gondomar. He had been examining witnesses all the morning and was in some doubt. Keymis, it would seem, not Ralegh, was responsible for the attack on San Thomé. But Gondomar, assuming a lofty and insolent tone, declared that the King could not act as judge because he had given Ralegh his commission and was surrounded by Ralegh's friends. If Gondomar had the power he would punish Ralegh himself. As matters stood he could only point out that the culprit was as yet unhanged and that his friends in the Council remained at liberty. One wonders how Elizabeth would have answered such audacity. Even James grew angry. He threw his hat on the floor, clutched his hair, and shouted that that might be justice in Spain but it was not justice in England. Till God forsook him, he would not punish a man unheard. Should an assassin strike down the Prince of Wales, he must be tried before he was punished. Gondomar sneered that there was indeed a difference between England and Spain in the punishment of piracy. He enlarged upon Ralegh's crimes. The King, cooling down, admitted that they were scarlet, forgot his principle that a man should be heard before he was punished, and gave a formal promise that Ralegh would be sent to Spain for execution unless Philip wished the punishment to take place in England. Thus did Gondomar win a resounding triumph while James yielded in dastardly fashion. In the Council there was open opposition when the King announced his resolve, but he declared that he was King and would take what course he pleased 'without following the advice of fools and badly disposed persons'.

Thus committed to punishment, he appointed a commission of councillors — Bacon, Abbot, Worcester, Caesar, Coke and Naunton — to examine Ralegh. It is not surprising that these men, on the basis of the evidence before them, came to conclusions that were erroneous. They found many contradictions in Ralegh's story. They thought he had been plotting with France. They believed that the mine was a hoax and that Ralegh sailed with the purpose of plundering the Spanish in America. They concluded that his offences were so gross as to deserve the death penalty.

Word came from Spain that Philip preferred that the punishment take place in England, and James asked the commissioners how it could be done. They offered two suggestions. Ralegh, they said, had been under sentence of death since 1603 and could be executed at any time. He could not be tried again. But if the King wished to give him a hearing, something approaching a trial might be arranged. Ralegh might be summoned before the Council afforced by the judges, and a selected group of nobles and gentlemen might be asked to attend the proceedings. The occasion would thus be semi-public, the procedure would simulate a trial, and councillors and judges could then advise the King whether, in their opinion, he was justified in carrying out the sentence of 1603. The commissioners would not have made this suggestion had they not felt sure of their ground.

But though James wished to give Ralegh some kind of hearing, he had no mind to allow him an opportunity to win the sympathy of his auditors or to voice the popular hatred of the Spanish match. 'It would make him too popular, as was found by experience at the arraignment at Winchester [in 1603], when by his wit he turned the hatred of men into compassion of him. We have therefore thought of a middle course.' Ralegh should be heard, but only before the six commissioners who had been examining his case. This was the procedure followed, and the commissioners reported that in their opinion the sentence of 1603 could justly be carried out. Ralegh was hurried to the block, despite the desperate pleading of his friends.

His death was perfect. 'He was the most fearless of death that ever was known; and the most resolute and confident, yet with reverence and conscience.' He was constant in his professions of loyalty. 'If I had not loved and honoured the King truly, and trusted in his goodness somewhat too much, I had not suffered death.' On the scaffold he asked to see the axe. Running his finger along the edge, he said: 'This is sharp medicine; but it is a

sure cure for all diseases.' At the moment of execution, the heads-
man hesitated. 'What dost thou fear?' asked Ralegh: 'Strike,
man, strike!' So ended his gallant spirit.

James was fully aware of the fierce indignation of the people.
When Sir 'Judas' Stukely complained of the abuse heaped upon
him for his betrayal of Ralegh's second attempt to escape, the
King remarked: 'On my soul, if I should hang all that speak ill of
thee, all the trees in the country would not suffice.' Bacon and
others were instructed to draft a statement defending the actions of
the government, and this *Declaration*, a very able document, was
carefully edited by the King. 'We have put the *Declaration* touching
Ralegh to the press,' wrote Bacon, 'with his Majesty's additions
which were material and fit to proceed from his Majesty.' But
the *Declaration* appeared after Ralegh's death. Once more James
had denied him a public hearing. The people looked upon his
execution as a national disgrace and as base appeasement of
Spain. They were not far wrong.[11]

CHAPTER XX

THE RISE OF BUCKINGHAM

B Y 1616, when the King had reached the age of fifty, he was already beginning to grow old. Henceforth there was a slow but steady deterioration not only in his physical powers but also in his strength of will and in his character. Business became more burdensome, decisions more difficult, fears more acute, emotions more overpowering, temptations more irresistible. Slowly the British Solomon sank into physical decay and into premature senility.

He was frequently ill. From nephritis he appears to have been free until a dangerous illness in 1619, but arthritis, combined with gout, became chronic in the damp and sunless winter months. He had suffered attacks for some years. 'At last in 1616', wrote Mayerne, 'this weakness continued for more than four months with swelling of both feet. In the years that followed, the pains went to other joints, to the great toe of the left foot and to both knees, and to the shoulders and hands, sometimes with redness, more often with swelling. For the first two or three days the pains are acute, raging by night, now worse, now milder, and are followed by weakness which does not disappear for a long time. In winter the arthritis is much worse, nor are the joints free from it until the return of the sun and of the warmth of summer restores health to his Majesty.' Illness depressed his spirits and rendered him irritable, morose and difficult. 'He is extremely sensitive,' wrote Mayerne, 'most impatient of pain; and while it tortures him with violent movements, his mind is tossed as well, thus augmenting the evil. He demands relief from pain without considering the causes of his illness.'

In eating he was temperate, being rather indifferent to food, but he ate what he pleased, roast meats with no bread, and great quantities of fruit of which he was inordinately fond. Goodman tells a story of a Mr. French of the spicery who would bring him the first strawberries and cherries in the spring and would attempt a little speech of presentation, 'but the King never had the patience to hear him one word, but his hand was in the basket'. Since he was losing his teeth he bolted his food without chewing it. And as he grew older he drank much more heavily. Not only did he indulge to excess at feasts and suppers, but allowed his lesser potations throughout the day to increase in size and number. 'He drinks frequently and immoderately between meals,' wrote an ambassador, 'to the sorrow of those who love him.' To water he had the strongest antipathy both as a drink and as a means to cleanliness. He never washed. 'His skin', wrote Weldon, 'was as soft as taffeta sarsnet, which felt so, because he never washed his hands, only rubbed his fingers' ends slightly with the wet end of a napkin.' As a result he itched insufferably. He was troubled with overheating and perspiration, especially at night, after exercise, and after hearty meals, and for this reason he had his clothes cut full and loose and made of pervious texture. When he was hot he threw off his outer garments, sat in a draught, and caught cold. He was always sneezing and blowing his nose. A light sleeper, he often awoke during the night and called one of his attendants to read to him until he fell asleep once more. His face was a convivial red, he was growing heavier, his hair was turning white.

In his diet, apparel and journeys he followed a constant routine dictated by long habit. 'By his good will', wrote Weldon, 'he would never change his clothes until worn out to very rags, his fashion never, insomuch as one bringing to him a hat of a Spanish block, he cast it from him, swearing he neither loved them nor their fashions.' And when he was brought roses for his shoes he asked his attendants whether they meant to make him a ruff-footed dove; a yard of sixpenny ribbon would serve that turn. Most of his wanderings, except the summer progress, were variations upon his continual journeys to Theobalds, Royston and Newmarket. He hunted with unabated ardour though with less violent exertion and followed his dogs more slowly, often without holding the reins in his hands but relying upon grooms to guide his horse as they ran by its side. Of Tom Badger, the master of his harriers, he wrote joyfully: 'Blessing, blessing, blessing on my sweet Tom Badger's heart-roots and all his for breeding me so fine a kennel of young hounds, so fair and well shaped, and some of them so fine pretty little ones as are worthy to lie on a bed, and all of them run together in a lump both at sight and view.' To the gentlemen of Bedfordshire he addressed a complaint that he no longer enjoyed hunting in that county because the game had grown scarce.

Unless they wished to banish him from those parts, thus proclaiming their indifference to his visits, they must restock their parks. A meditation on the Lord's Prayer, which he wrote in 1619, was filled with stories of the chase, and theology and stag-killing went hand in hand. As he grew older he enjoyed gentler rural pleasures: picnics, masquerades and light theatricals, often with dancing, since Villiers danced unusually well. For the cares involved in government he displayed increasing abhorrence. When he was ill he refused access to his secretaries. We find him dodging Winwood to escape unpleasant business and refusing to leave his sports when his ministers summoned him to London. One wonders whether he cared, whether ease and indulgence had not become the most important things in the world.[1]

The year 1616, which saw the release of Ralegh from the Tower and the trial of the Earl and Countess of Somerset, witnessed two other events of prime importance: the dismissal of Sir Edward Coke from the bench, and the rise of George Villiers to an eminent position in the State.

The battle over prohibitions proved to be merely the beginning of Coke's recalcitrance, and three new disputes rendered him wholly obnoxious to the King. Of these the first concerned a soured and broken clergyman, Edmund Peacham, who had vented his bitterness of spirit by writing notes for a sermon in which he made foul charges against the King and predicted his early death. It was not certain, however, whether Peacham could be convicted of treason, and James, intent on severity, decided to consult the judges before the trial. But he feared that Coke might prove difficult. He therefore hit upon the plan of consulting the judges one by one and not as a group. To this Coke objected, declaring that 'judges were not to give opinions by fractions, but entirely, and that this auricular taking of opinions, single and apart, was new and dangerous'.

Coke had just grounds for fear that the independence of the Bench was in danger, for the King's opinion of Peacham's case was well known. He had written savagely that Peacham had not spewed forth his venom in drunkenness or in sudden passion but after long premeditation. Peacham, he said, condemned him utterly, 'not to be a King, not to be a Christian, not to be a man or a reasonable creature, not worthy of breath here nor of salvation hereafter. This I say is plain proof that he intended to compass or imagine the King's death. If the judges care more for the safety of such a monster than for the preservation of a Crown in all ages following, whereupon depend the lives of many millions, happy then are all desperate and seditious knaves, but the fortune of this Crown is more than miserable'. The judges who went down into the country to try Peacham were well instructed in their duty and he was duly convicted, but the miserable man died in prison before the time set for his execution.

A crude attack by Coke upon the Court of Chancery further incensed the King. The idea of Chancery as the custodian of the King's conscience, tempering law with equity and justice with mercy, appealed strongly to James. 'Laws are ordained as rules of virtuous and social living,' he wrote, 'and not to be snares to trap good subjects; and therefore the law must be interpreted according to the meaning and not to the literal sense.' He thought of the Chancery as a court close to the Crown, under its protection, and independent of other courts. If complaints arose against it, they should be brought to him, for 'the King only is to correct it and none else'. Moreover, he had found in Lord Chancellor Ellesmere a stalwart royalist, a safe and faithful guardian of the prerogative, and he therefore branded Coke's actions as inept and presumptuous.

Finally there arose the famous case of *Commendams* which concerned a living that the King had given to Bishop Neile of Lichfield. This case led to debate of the prerogative before the courts, and James therefore asked the judges to halt proceedings until he had consulted with them. But Coke persuaded them to reply that they could not delay justice at the King's request. To this James answered in a long and angry letter. The judges, he said, need teach him no lessons in speeding justice nor in the principles of the law, 'for although we never studied the common law of England yet are we not ignorant of any points which belong to a king to know'. He would not tolerate debate of the prerogative by upstart lawyers, and he commanded the judges, 'out of our absolute power and authority royal, to forbear to meddle any further in this point until our coming to town'.

On June 8th, 1616, he called the judges before him and hotly accused them of disobedience. They fell upon their knees, begging forgiveness, and while they remained in that position they were

asked, each in turn, whether in cases involving the prerogative
they would in future delay action until they had consulted with
the King. All answered in the affirmative but Coke, who said that
when such a case arose he would do what was fitting for a judge to
do. James told him he was a knave who argued in sophistries. He
should go and study the common law, said the King, and he
would find how fully it upheld the prerogative.

So vastly was James pleased with this encounter that a few days
later he came to the Star Chamber, something he had never done
before, and made a long speech in which he reviewed his whole
case against the judges and against the courts of common law. It
was an excellent speech, forceful and vivid, with pungent phrases
and palpable hits. But it was marred by a vanity that defies
comprehension. James knew, he said, that his people had yearned
to hear him speak in the Star Chamber. But though an old and
experienced King, he had refrained. Now he had come, remembering Christ's words, 'My sheep hear my voice.' He would come
again, though not for any personal or partial end, for in matters of
justice he would remain unspotted all the days of his life. He
asked the judges to represent him to the people as he really was, to
tell of his zeal in religion, his desire to maintain the law, his wish
that all men should enjoy peace and justice under a just and
peaceful king. His speech gave him the greatest satisfaction; and
courtiers, catching the royal note of triumph and self-glorification,
received it rapturously. The King had spoken, said one listener,
not as a man but as an angel.[2]

His exaltation of spirit continued. Within a few days he resolved
that the time had come when all his prose writings and some of his
printed speeches should be brought together in one volume. The
task of editing was entrusted to Bishop Montagu, who supplied a
preface of which the tone may be gathered from its opening sentences. The King had set forth divers works in print, said the
Bishop, as divers works of God were set forth in the Bible. And
just as the first of James's writings, his paraphrase of the Book of
Revelation, revealed his understanding of the Kingdom of God,
so the King's last pearl, his speech in the Star Chamber, revealed
his power in the kingdoms he held on earth. Such was the vanity
of this King who could regard himself as the link between God and
the judges and who could tell Coke to study the common law!

James determined to be rid of Coke's perpetual turbulence.

Coke was sequestered from the Council, forbidden to ride the summer circuit, and ordered to revise his law reports 'wherein (as his Majesty was informed) there were many exorbitant and extravagant opinions'. In the following November he was dismissed from the Bench. By this drastic action James freed himself from the opposition of the judges, but he struck a heavy blow at the moral weight of their decisions. Coke's shortcomings were forgotten, and he became the martyr of the commonwealth, the symbol of the widely held conviction that the liberties provided by the common law should be left as they were.

Meanwhile the King turned easily to his pleasures. In June he was at Hatfield at the jovial christening of the Earl of Salisbury's young son, where in high good humour he gave many kisses to the child's grandmother, the Countess of Suffolk, and did honour to Lady Compton, the mother of George Villiers. Two weeks later he was entertained by another Cecil, the Earl of Exeter, at Wimbledon, and again he showed great interest in the ladies, especially in Lady Hatton, the Earl's daughter, whom he kissed over and over. A little later we find him at Woodstock amid the delights he loved. On one day he killed three great stags. On the next he was visited by a deputation from the university led by the Vice-Chancellor, who thanked him in a Latin oration for his past munificence to Oxford and begged him to do something more for the professors. Laud preached the Tuesday sermon. From the story of Miriam stricken with leprosy for murmuring against Moses, Laud drew an obvious lesson for those who spoke against the government of kings. On the same day James created Villiers Viscount Buckingham, 'performing the ceremonies of that action with the greatest alacrity and princely cheerfulness'; and as he was about to rise from supper, Buckingham and other courtiers crowded about him with glasses of wine in their hands, fell upon their knees, and drank his health. Right joyfully he pledged them in return.[3]

The central theme of these years was the rise of Buckingham, whom James loved with a passionate affection. The King, wrote Sir John Oglander, 'loved young men, his favourites, better than women, loving them beyond the love of men to women. I never yet saw any fond husband make so much or so great dalliance over his beautiful spouse as I have seen King James over his favourites, especially Buckingham'. Buckingham became his joy. When he was depressed or ill at ease the very sight of his favourite brought him quiet and repose. 'The King is not well without him, his company is his solace.' James made no secret of his enslavement. To the Council he declared in 1617: 'I, James, am neither a god nor an angel, but a man like any other. Therefore I act like a man, and confess to loving those dear to me more than other men. You may be sure that I love the Earl of Buckingham more than anyone else, and more than you who are here assembled. I wish to speak in my own behalf and not to have it thought to be a defect, for Jesus Christ did the same and therefore I cannot be blamed. Christ had his John, and I have my George.' It was a love that grew and deepened with the years until it became riveted in the King's nature. His letters to his favourite breathe a spirit of the closest intimacy, of overpowering emotion, utter lack of restraint, and ineffable tenderness. Buckingham is his 'Only sweet and dear child', 'Sweet heart', 'Sweet Steenie gossip', 'Sweet child and wife', while he signs himself 'Thy dear dad', 'Thy dear dad and steward', 'Thy dear dad and purveyor'. 'My only sweet and dear child,' begins one letter, 'I pray thee haste thee home to thy dear dad by sunsetting at the furtherest, and so Lord send me comfortable and happy with thee this night. James R.'

Buckingham was a seductive young man, with something of the allurements of both sexes. He was esteemed one of the handsomest men in the whole world. Tall, comely and beautifully proportioned, he had great physical vigour and skill in bodily sports. 'No one', wrote Arthur Wilson, 'dances better, no man runs or jumps better. Indeed he jumped higher than ever Englishman did in so short a time, from a private gentleman to a dukedom.' At a masque in 1618 the King became bored and cried out petulantly: 'Why don't they dance?' at which Buckingham leaped forward and excelled all present in the dexterity of his capers. James patted his face in approbation. The grace of his carriage was constantly admired. 'From the nails of his fingers, nay, from the sole of his foot to the crown of his head, there was no blemish in him. And yet his carriage and every stoop of his deportment more than his excellent form were the beauty of his beauty.' A contemporary wrote of the charm of his colouring and the grace of his carriage, and the antiquarian and diarist, D'Ewes, recorded: 'I saw everything in him full of delicacy and handsome features, yea, his hands and face seemed to me especially effeminate and curious.' His combination of masculine strength and feminine delicacy, his fine forehead and dark chestnut hair, his pointed beard of golden brown, his clear skin, finely formed features, and handsome dark blue eyes must have made him most alluring. Assuming, that is, that one was allured by these things.

He was very amorous. 'He affected beauty where he found it,' wrote Arthur Wilson, 'and if his eye cull'd out a wanton beauty he had his setter that could point a meeting.' Years later one finds a touching letter of gentle reproof from his sweet and loving wife.

He lent himself docilely to all James's foibles and became his constant companion, a role that Somerset had found intolerable. In parting from the King, he says, he parted from himself, 'all my perfect joys and pleasures chiefly, nay, solely, consisting in attending your person'. He allowed himself to be pawed and petted. He pleased the King by his diligent attendance at divine worship. When James wrote a meditation on certain verses in St. Matthew, Buckingham begged to be the King's amanuensis. A boring task for a spirited and ignorant young man!

Skilfully he pretended to return James's love. The King tells him to make his letters merry, and he replies: 'How can I but write merrily when he is so I love best and beyond all the world.' He thanks James for a gift: 'I am now going to give my Redeemer thanks for my maker.' But he cannot really thank the King properly, 'for if I speak I must be saucy and say thus, so short of what is due my purveyor, my good fellow, my physician, my maker, my friend, my father, my all, I heartily and humbly thank you for all you do and all I have'. Again he writes: 'I naturally so love your person, and adore all your other parts, which are more than ever one man had, that were not only all your people but all the world besides set together on one side and you alone on the other, I should to obey and please you displease, nay, despise them all.'

He possessed the wit to enter fully into the banter of James's familiar conversation, and developed a playful impudence which the King appeared to relish. He requires a coach, and James is to bestir himself to find one. The King is his purveyor to send him game and his steward to supply him with money. He sells a passport to a person whom the King wished to keep in England, and James asks the cause of his conduct. 'Because', comes the pert answer, 'you never give me any money yourself.' At this the King pulls Buckingham's hair, kisses him, and sends him from the

room. Such disrespect was certain to breed contempt, and we
doubtless reach the nadir of disdain in a letter ending with the
words: 'And so I kiss your dirty hands.' But this was in the future;
and for the moment Buckingham, with youthful affability, cap-
tivated the King and was not unpleasing to the court.

By January of 1617 he had become Master of the Horse, a
Knight of the Garter, Earl of Buckingham, and a member of the
Council, with gifts of land said to be worth £80,000. To some
extent James repeated the pleasure of instruction. He took daily
care, he said, to better Buckingham's understanding for the royal
service, resolving 'to make him a masterpiece and to mould him,
as it were Platonically to his own idea'. He did not plan to trust
him as he had trusted Somerset. Buckingham was to be first a
joyous companion and secondly a private secretary to write letters
and to arrange the business that came before the King. He was
not to be the King's remembrancer but merely the channel
through which suits and petitions were to come. Yet the old
situation soon repeated itself, and James quickly fell into the habit
of conferring office, honour and advantage only with the favourite's approval. Buckingham 'is now the man by whom all things
do and must pass and he far excels the former in favour and
affection'.[4]

He had what everyone craved: the ear of the King and the
patronage of the kingdom. Great men and small paid homage to
him, and the King was the foremost of his worshippers. It is small
wonder that his head was turned and that he became vain, wilful and arrogant. Furious at any cross, he grew quarrelsome and
easily offended. He cared little at first about shaping policy,
merely accepting that of the King; but he gloried in his control of
patronage. Infinitely proud of his influence with James, he
demanded that all aspirants to office make their terms with him.
In a shocking episode in 1617 he opposed the appointment of Sir
Henry Yelverton as Attorney merely because Yelverton had not
solicited his support. But he went further. The Ministers of
State must be his creatures, swelling the crowd of his hangers-on
and making the world aware of their subservience. Nor could
they depend upon his constancy. He was too ready, wrote Hacket,
to cast a sudden cloud upon his creatures, to root up those he had
planted, and to make trial of others. His path became strewn with
men whom he had helped to ruin.

His monopoly of patronage acquired other sinister aspects. His mother, Lady Compton, a rapacious and predatory old termagant, made it her business to trade upon her son's influence in order to advance her family and to provide wealthy husbands for her 'numerous and beautiful female kindred' who came in droves to London. Lady Compton became a power; and Gondomar is said to have jested that he did not despair of England's conversion when he saw more prayers and oblations offered to the mother than to the son. Buckingham and Lady Compton developed a vicious system of spoliation and blackmail. They exerted many kinds of pressure, they used promises of advancement and threats of ruin; and though their promises were illusory their threats were very real. The King to his shame entered into these machinations, thinking it no disgrace to employ the influence of the Crown to advance the family of his beloved. But though in his cups he could honour Lady Compton and kiss her fondly, he found her meddling all but intolerable. Buckingham was soon begging her to stay away from court, and when she failed to appear in London after her creation as Countess of Buckingham in 1619, it was thought that a bargain had been struck to be rid of her.

We cannot do justice to her many schemings. But a word may be said of her search for wealthy wives for Buckingham's two brothers, Sir John and Sir Christopher. John was a weakling in mind and body, Christopher dull and unattractive. But they could hope for great things, and one of the court wits prophesied that

> Above in the skies shall Gemini rise,
> And Twins the court shall pester,
> George shall call up his brother Jack
> And Jack his brother Kester.

In the spring of 1616 Sir John and his mother set their hearts upon the beautiful Frances Coke, daughter of Sir Edward and of Lady Hatton. At this time Coke had been suspended though not yet dismissed from his judgeship. He was offered a restoration to favour, which meant that the King knew what was afoot, if he would agree to the marriage, give a portion of £10,000 with his daughter, and settle land upon her worth £1000 a year. But he refused, saying churlishly that the King's favour was uncertain and could be bought too dearly. His dismissal from office followed.

Early in 1617 he changed his mind and accepted Lady Compton's high terms. But he encountered difficulties with his wife, who opposed the marriage, and a violent family quarrel took place that might have ended in strange tragedies. Coke had his way. Sir John Villiers and Frances Coke were married in September 1617, at Hampton Court. King, Queen and Prince were present, James gave the bride away and drank countless healths to her happiness, while the bridegroom stood in a place of honour behind the royal chair. 'The next morning the King visited them in bed, having first given order they should not rise before his coming.' But Coke obtained nothing beyond re-admission to the Council. He had been milked dry, and Buckingham and his mother now concentrated upon Lady Hatton, who was wealthy in her own right. They gave feasts in her honour, and she in return gave a feast at which 'his Majesty was never merrier nor more satisfied, who had not the patience to sit a quarter of an hour without drinking the health [of his hostess]. But the principal graces and favours lighted on the Lady Compton and her children, whom the King praised and kissed and blessed all those who wished them well'. As he was about to enter his coach he ran back into the house to give Lady Hatton half a dozen kisses. However, her fall from favour was to be as sudden as her rise. When it was discovered that she clung to her money with adamantine tenacity, the Villiers family had no further use for her.

Buckingham's other brother, Christopher, lent comedy to a sombre tale, for the ladies would not have him. Of three heiresses at whom he and his mother took aim, one rejected his proposals with ridicule, one was protected by her father, and one made a runaway match in order to escape. Some years later he married a distant kinswoman.

Lavish and extravagant feasts, some costing thousands of pounds, were now the fashion, a fashion led by Buckingham and by Hay, the wastrel Master of the Wardrobe. The court grew riotous and drunken. And so did James. He was frequently intoxicated, which he would remember next day and repent with tears, though he was ready enough for the next feast when it came. We find him at one in November 1617, when Hay was married to Lucy Percy, the charming daughter of the Earl of Northumberland. 'The King was exceeding merry all supper time', and countless healths went round. He then went into the bride's chamber where he praised the beauty of her handsome gentlewoman, a Mrs. Washington, and was very pleasant with all the company for nearly an hour. Probably he was not sober when a few weeks later he visited Montgomery and his wife at Enfield to comfort them after the death of their young son. He kissed Lady Montgomery many times, embraced Montgomery, protesting how he loved him, and at length fell upon his knees and drank the health of the lady and of the boy wherewith, as he hoped, she was pregnant. He had a strong interest in pregnancy as proof of fecundity and hope of future joy.[5]

Thus Buckingham's ascendancy brought favouritism, corruption and debauchery, while his system of plunder poisoned the atmosphere and pointed the path for all who had business at Westminster.

The easy laxness of the King was the less excusable because of his finances, for the deficit in 1616 was running at the rate of about £90,000 a year. There came a moment's relief from the sale of the Cautionary Towns to the Dutch, who offered about £210,000 to cancel loans of almost thrice that figure. James paid his most pressing debts, wasted much money, and employed his shored-up credit to obtain a loan of £140,000 from the city. But all the old projects for raising cash were soon being debated once more, the sale of peerages increased, and the spectre of mounting debt was as threatening as ever.[6]

The penury of the Crown was underscored by the progress to Scotland in 1617, a 'very costly voyage every way', and most unwelcome to both kingdoms. Yet it is of great interest. A breath of fresh Scots air revived in the King his former self, and we see the old James once more, tenacious, humorous, slippery, didactic, self-righteous, petulant, revengeful, yet anxious according to his lights to do well by his native land.

He wished to visit Scotland, he asserted, because of a salmon-like instinct to see once more the land of his birth, but his true motive was to impose Anglican ritual upon the Scottish Kirk. This was suspected in Scotland, and apprehension in the north was not allayed by a sanctimonious letter to the Scottish Council in which the King protested he would do nothing but what tended to the glory of God and to the welfare of the commonwealth. The Scots knew well the value of his pious protestations.

He achieved his purpose of revisiting Scotland through sheer will, for all his advisers opposed it. Their letters were wails of lamentation at the expense. Coming to the King in a body, they begged him on their knees to reconsider his resolve, and they obtained the support of Buckingham. But all was in vain. James swore that those who opposed the progress were traitors; he turned so viciously upon Buckingham that the favourite 'was glad to run away'. Most unreasonably the King placed the blame for his lack of funds upon his Treasurer, Suffolk, whose disgrace in 1618 stemmed in part from the financial difficulties of the Scottish progress. A new loan was at length obtained from London, though the Council was forced to collect it piecemeal from reluctant citizens, one of whom was ordered to follow the King on foot until he paid.

The progress began with a number of petty irritations. The King was furious at delay in the appearance of a proclamation commanding the nobility and gentry to leave London. The carts that were to carry the royal luggage proved to be defective; the park at Theobalds was not properly enclosed; his apothecary and surgeon lacked funds to go to Scotland; a riot of apprentices in London increased his anger. Melons and cherries must be sent north, and his favourite divines must come with him to celebrate Easter. 'I cannot well by letter tell you', wrote Lake, 'how much he is moved at these things.'

Yet the King enjoyed his journey northward. He hunted, hawked and feasted, warming the country as he went with the glories of the court. Delighted with the region about Lincoln, he declared that he would spend his winters there in future. As he was making his formal entry into the city, the mayor presented him with a sword which he pushed aside and asked if there was to be a speech of welcome. Twice he attended service at the Minster and touched many persons for the Evil. His stay was enlivened by horse races and by cocking — four cocks fighting in the pit simultaneously — which made his Majesty very merry. A similar programme awaited him at York where he stayed at the King's Manor, an ancient abbey which he had destined in 1603 as a half-way palace for his visits to Scotland. Thence he travelled to Berwick where he knighted Anthony Weldon, little dreaming of the slander that rascal was to pass upon the Scots. On May 13th he crossed the Border, and Latin and Hebrew orations of welcome now took the place of English ones.[7]

For more than a year the Scottish Council had been busy with preparations. Extensive repairs were undertaken at Edinburgh, Stirling and Falkland; roads were remade, the capital cleared of beggars, laws passed for the preservation of game. Tapestries, robes and silver vessels came by sea from London, while Scotland was ransacked for similar objects. At the King's command his Scottish royal robe was sent to England for inspection and he saw to this inspection himself.

The principal burden fell upon Edinburgh. There the provost and bailies must have winced when they were ordered to provide lodgings for five thousand people — far more than came — and provender for five thousand horses. The Scots nobility who had reserved their normal lodgings in the Canongate were told to find accommodation elsewhere. At the Nether Bow Port a statue of the King was erected. Alterations in the royal chapel at Holyrood excited great alarm and consternation. An organ arrived from England. The English craftsman who came with it declared he had been accorded better treatment when a captive of the Turks than he now received in Scotland. It appeared that gilded wooden figures of apostles and patriarchs were to be set up in the chapel. The Scottish bishops besought the King to omit these Romish toys. James yielded in a letter half-humorous, half-sneering, in which he deplored the ignorance of his Scottish clergy and said that his English doctors would give them instruction. Had he ordered figures of dragons and devils, he said, the Scots would have had no objection.

In Scotland the King stopped first at Castle Douglas and then at Seton, where he was entertained by the Earl of Winton, a nephew of his old friend Dunfermline, and was welcomed by verses from the pen of William Drummond of Hawthornden. The poem was a graceful and sprightly invitation by the Forth to other Scottish streams to join in the holiday of the King's return. The poet prayed that the King would remain in Scotland.

> Ah why should Isis only see thee shine?
> Is not the Forth as well as Isis thine?
> Though Isis vaunt she hath more wealth in store,
> Let it suffice thy Forth doth love thee more.

He entered Edinburgh, May 16th, on horseback to be seen by the people, and was royally received by provost, bailies and principal citizens. An oration of welcome declared him to be as upright as David, as wise as Solomon, as godly as Josias. The very hills and groves, so ran the address, had lost their verdure at his departure in 1603 but now blossomed with joy at his return. The King was presented with a basin of gold and a purse containing 10,000 marks. After a sermon in St. Giles, he went to Holyroodhouse where faculty and students of the college in Edinburgh offered him a volume of Greek and Latin verse. Next day, wrote Calderwood, the ritual of the Church of England was begun in the Chapel Royal with choristers, surplices and playing upon organs, and James commanded the Scottish councillors and bishops to kneel as they partook of the Communion.

Within a few days he travelled to Falkland and thence into Perthshire where he hunted and then journeyed on to make an entry into Dundee. He was back in Edinburgh for a meeting of Parliament which he addressed at length, stressing his life-long desire to settle the Kirk and the kingdom in unity and concord. Scotland, he continued, contained many barbarities, and he wished that the Scots would ape the English in good manners as readily as they did in drinking healths, in wearing fine clothes, and in smoking tobacco. These remarks did not aid him in obtaining the legislation he desired, and he met with further opposition from a clerical assembly at St. Andrews where he demanded those alterations in ritual that were to cause such trouble during the later years of his reign. When they were refused he turned in fury upon the Scottish bishops who, he said, had led him to believe that he would have his way. 'But now, finding himself disappointed, he called them dolts and deceivers.' The virile pungency of Scottish speech was returning to him rapidly, and it found full vent in a clash with the clergyman and historian, David Calderwood, who was summoned before the Scottish Court of High Commission and was banished from the kingdom.

That the progress had its lighter side was evident at Linlithgow where James was greeted by the schoolmaster of the town encased in the plaster figure of a lion:

> Thrice royal Sir, here I do you beseech,
> Who art a lion, to hear a lion's speech,
> A miracle, for since the days of Aesop,
> No lion till these times his voice dared raise up

To such a Majesty; then, King of men,
The King of beasts speaks to thee from his den;
Who, though he now enclosed be in plaster,
When he was free, was Lithgow's wise schoolmaster.

There is a tradition that during a visit to Dunfermline the King inspected a colliery where the works ran underground to a spot which at high tide was surrounded by water. Brought to the surface at this point, he suddenly found himself on an island, and in great alarm he shouted 'Treason!' but his faithful guides quickly dispelled his fears.[8]

Following a second visit to Stirling, July 19th, he journeyed to Glasgow, Hamilton, Dumfries and thence to Carlisle, having bid farewell to his native kingdom. The progress southward took him through Lancashire, Cheshire, Staffordshire, to Coventry, Warwick, Leicester, Woodstock and so to London. He reached the capital on September 15th, after an absence of seven months.

The King's home-coming was rather dismal. During the winter of 1617-18 he was ill much of the time with arthritis and gout, for which he gave the unlikely explanation that he had sprained his leg in bed. Christmas at Whitehall was dull and dreary, for Queen Anne was ill, also; and in January the King was worse. 'His toe hath been of late so sore that sometimes he could hardly endure the sheet to touch it. And now the pain is crept up into his knee, and later into his arm.' Depressed and irascible, he was not cheered by the birth of his second grandson in the Palatinate; his despondency vented itself in petty tantrums. Annoyed to hear that Montgomery had given a masque at Enfield, he declared that he wished no court in the vicinity but his own, and he took spiteful pleasure in a gift from the Czar of Russia because it was richer than any given to Queen Elizabeth. 'I am sorry to hear', wrote Chamberlain, 'that he grows every day more froward.'

The chronic problem of finance continued to harass him. It was reported by the Council in September 1617 that the ordinary revenue for the past year had almost equalled ordinary expenditure, but that extraordinary expenses — the Christmas revels of 1616, the Scottish progress, gifts, embassies, Theobalds Park — left a deficit of £137,000, while the total debt stood at £726,000. Much concerned, the King made one of his periodic resolves to reform. He told councillors that he was determined to retrench, that they must show him how to do it, that he wanted action not words. The Council was delighted. Committees, commissions and inquiries were set in motion, and a house-cleaning, long over-due, was begun. In this work of reform James took great interest, busying himself with retrenchments in various departments, issuing a directive to suitors in which he listed with some naivety the things that might be asked for and the things that might not, and planning a weekly audience with his Secretary to decide on suits. By his own standards he was doing great things; and Buckingham, following after, supported reform. In Sir Lionel Cranfield he found a man able and willing to undertake the solid work that was required.

This pushing man of business who had begun as a mere city apprentice had won rapid success as a cloth merchant and as a member of the Mercers' Company. Gradually he abandoned trade to become a farmer of various royal revenues. 'The first acquaintance I had with him', James said later, 'was by the lord of Northampton, who often brought him unto me as a private man before he was so much as my servant. He then made so many projects for my profit that Buckingham fell in liking with him and brought him into my service. He found him so studious for my profit that he backed him against great personages and mean. Buckingham laid the ground and bare the envy; he took the laborious and ministerial part upon him, and thus he came up to his preferment.' In the household, in the wardrobe, from which Hay was induced to resign, in the exchequer, in the navy, in the ordnance and in the administration of Ireland Cranfield was able to save money for the King.[9]

Courtiers sneered at the base fellow who was cutting down their incomes. They found him forward and saucy, and in truth he was rather insufferable. His portrait is that of a city man, highly pleased with his own success; and one reads in his face not only shrewdness and resolution, but also effrontery and arrogance. To Suffolk he was particularly objectionable, for the pride of the Howards could not co-operate with a London apprentice, especially when the Treasury was under suspicion.

From this movement for reform there developed a struggle for power between Buckingham and the Howards. The Howards owed nothing to Buckingham, nor could they forget that he was an upstart, his fortune founded upon Somerset's ruin. Opposing his appointments, they offered candidates of their own, until every vacancy produced a clash of factions. But it was Buckingham who triumphed, for the stream of fortune was running strongly in his favour. On New Year's Day, 1618, James made him a marquis, the first he had ever made in England, protesting he did it 'for the affection he bore him, more than ever he did to any man, and for the like affection, faith and modesty that he found in him'. 'My lords,' cried the King at a feast given by his favourite, 'I drink to you all, and I know we are all welcome to my George, and he that doth not pledge with all his heart, I would the Devil had him.'

Falling back upon an old device, the Howards brought to court a handsome young man, a son of Sir William Monson, in the hope that he would attract the King's fancy and displace the reigning beauty. They took great pains 'in tricking and pranking him up, besides washing his face every day with posset curd'. Poor fellow! The Howards produced several rosebuds of this kind until the mustering of minions, to use Chamberlain's phrase, occasioned subdued tittering at court. These young men fancied themselves the King's favourites, wrote an observer, because they exceedingly desired to be so and lost no opportunity to present themselves for inspection. James was at first unaware of what was going on. When he understood it, he asked the young men to depart, thus dealing 'a shrewd cross blow' to the Howards.

Suffolk 'was not so much caressed by the King as I think he would wish', wrote Fenton, and his fortunes were obviously waning. In June 1618, James heard that Lady Suffolk took bribes from persons doing business with her husband and he ordered her to leave London. But she soon returned. Flying into a rage, the King swore that if she did not leave at once he would have her removed in a cart like a common whore. In July, Suffolk was called upon to resign. Both he and his wife were tried for embezzlement of funds, were found guilty, and were forced to pay heavy fines. The charges, however, were grossly exaggerated, for Suffolk's error was laxness rather than dishonesty, though his wife certainly took bribes.

The fall of Suffolk was followed by that of Secretary Lake. In the clash of Buckingham and the Howards, Lake hoped to remain neutral, and he might well have survived had he not been dragged down by his wife and by his venomous daughter, Anne,

who had married Lord Roos, the grandson of the Earl of Exeter.
A brilliant match. But it was followed by family quarrels in which
the Lakes tried to bleed the young man of his money. Lady Roos
threatened him with divorce on the ground of impotency if he did
not yield, and he found life so intolerable that he fled abroad and
died shortly afterwards in Naples. Meanwhile Lady Roos turned
upon Frances, Countess of Exeter, the Earl's second wife and some
forty years his junior, 'a most comely, handsome lady', as Goodman wrote, 'of excellent carriage, very discreet, and full of charity'.
She had befriended young Roos in various ways. Lady Roos now
made the most outrageous charges against her, accusing her of
incest with Lord Roos and of a plot to poison the Lakes. Lady
Exeter appealed to the King for a trial which took place in the
Star Chamber in February 1619.

This was a case that fascinated the King, for it roused the spirit
of the detective and offered scope for the prurient. Summoning
Lady Roos, James asked her to swear upon the Bible to the truth
of her accusations, which she declined to do, to the King's great
suspicion. He determined to preside at the trial. But dreading
the tedious arguments of the lawyers, he instructed the judges to
delete extraneous matter and to conclude the trial in two half-
days. This proved impossible, however, and it lasted for almost a
week, yet James attended daily and manfully endured till noon,
though he constantly interrupted the lawyers with admonitions
to speak briefly and to the point. In his opening speech 'he compared himself to Solomon that was to judge between two women
and to find out the true mother of the child (that is, verity), for
which purpose he came furnished with all fit instructions, but
specially with equity and impartial affection'.

The case of the Lakes grew ever blacker, for they could not
prove their charges and were shown to have suborned their
witnesses. One of these, a maidservant of Lady Exeter, declared
she had stood behind some curtains at Wimbledon and overheard
the Countess confess her guilt, but the King, taking the maid to
Wimbledon and placing her behind the curtains, pointed out
triumphantly that they scarcely reached to her knees. Lake, his
wife, and Lady Roos were found guilty of false accusation and
were fined and imprisoned. In pronouncing the sentence James
'spoke long and excellently to every point, comparing this to the
first judgment, Sir Thomas Lake to Adam, his Lady to Eve, and

Lady Roos to the serpent'. A few days later when Sir George Calvert was sworn Secretary, the King questioned him sharply about his wife, and was relieved to hear that Lady Calvert was a good woman and the mother of ten children. During the trial he had warned officials not to reveal State secrets to their wives, which seemed to show, wrote Chamberlain, 'that the King is in a great vein of taking down high-handed women'.

The Howards now fell in rapid succession. Knollys lost the Mastership of the Wards, from which office James said he was sorry to remove him since he was guilty of no fault, but he, like his friends, 'was altogether guided and overruled by an arch-wife'. Suffolk's sons, Lord Howard de Walden and Sir Thomas Howard, temporarily lost their places at court. Nottingham was at last removed, though by negotiation without the scandal of a trial, and the post of Lord Admiral was given to Buckingham. There were courtiers who hoped that the favourite would resign the Mastership of the Horse, but the King would not hear of it. In some Latin verses he explained the close affinity of the two offices. Had not Neptune who ruled the waves been famous for his horses?

With the fall of the Howards Buckingham became supreme. Some few of the great personages at court were under no obligation to him, but the majority of officials, receiving their places through him, knew that they retained them at his pleasure. He brought reforms of a kind. Some of his appointments went to men like Cranfield, Naunton and Calvert, who were bureaucrats, industrious, devoted and efficient. The King, wrote Weldon, naturally loved honest men who were not over-active, and that was what he was getting. It is true that Buckingham developed skill in obtaining work from such officials. He was illiterate, wrote Wotton, 'yet had learned at court, first to sift and question well, and to supply his own defects by the drawing or flowing unto him of the best instruments of experience and knowledge, from whom he had a sweet and attractive manner to suck what might be for the public or his own proper purpose'.

The King rejoiced at the success of his favourite, not only because he loved him, but because Buckingham kept alive the royal sense of triumph and achievement. We find him at Deptford in 1619 inspecting two new warships, congratulating his youthful Lord Admiral, and christening the vessels *Buckingham's Entrance* and *Reformation*. When in January 1619 a sudden fire destroyed the banqueting hall which James had built in 1606, he at once erected at Whitehall a new and more beautiful building, the stately edifice which still exists, and laid plans to remodel the entire palace on a scale so magnificent as to rival the Temple of Solomon. How he proposed to pay for it we do not know, and it faded away like most of his vast designs.[10]

Neither Buckingham nor his master received credit from the nation for the reforms of this period. As long as Buckingham employed his influence to enrich his family, corruption and waste could not be quelled. The favourite was becoming the grievance of grievances, an impassable gulf between Crown and people.

CHAPTER XXI

THE CRISIS OF THE REIGN

Although the years between 1618 and 1622 were to be filled with high questions of politics, diplomacy and war, emerging from the clash of Catholics and Protestants, they opened upon a note of bitter division and controversy among Protestants alone. There had been in Holland for many years a mounting tension between the Calvinists, who accepted the doctrine of strict predestination, and the followers of the theologian Arminius, who modified that doctrine by asserting the free will of man and by speculating — often in a daring and sacrilegious manner — upon the essence of God and upon limitations on His power. It was a controversy that divided Holland in an astonishing way, producing at length a political revolution in 1617 and a great church council in the year that followed. King James was deeply interested in this quarrel, and we have a picture of him discussing it learnedly with his clergy. 'He was very pleasant at dinner and sat long, a divine reading to him all the time, and four bishops standing near about him, of which the Bishop of Llandaff [George Carleton] was one, with whom the King spake oft', comparing Arminianism with the heresies of the British monk Pelagius in the fourth and fifth centuries. James, however, allowed himself to be swept away by a furious and vindictive hatred of the Dutch Arminians. He had hounded Vorstius to ruin, and he acted in similar fashion against another Dutchman, Taurinus. When an English divine, Edward Simpson, dared advocate Arminian views in a sermon at court, the King exploded with anger and was unappeased until Simpson formally renounced his opinions.

Dutch statesmen hoped that Britain's king-theologian could help them quiet a dispute that distracted their country. But though James meddled and lectured insufferably, his advice was useless. His first suggestion to the Dutch in 1610 was merely that they silence discussion. He had never quite made up his mind, he said, about predestination, and though he had studied the subject exhaustively and regarded his own opinion as the best of any, he had concluded that nothing certain could be laid down in regard to it. 'My lords the States would therefore do well to order their doctors and teachers to be silent on this topic.' But after the revolution in Holland in 1617 James changed his mind. He now advised a synod, suggesting that Prince Maurice, who had supported the Calvinists, summon the Arminians before him in a kind of Hampton Court Conference. The King forgot that Hampton Court had been no great success, and he gave naive instructions to the delegates whom he sent to the Synod of Dort in 1618, for they were told to soften Calvinist asperity, though the very calling of the Synod rendered moderation impossible. The Arminians were punished with outrageous severity, and James heartily approved.

The Anglo-Catholic clergy in the Church of England, who opposed predestination and sympathized to some extent with other Arminian views, appeared to have suffered a heavy blow. They dared not object to what had been done. Bishop Carleton, returning from Dort, found some murmuring in corners, 'but his Majesty's judgment puts all adversaries to silence and nothing is heard but approbation of those things which his Majesty approves'. Yet Arminianism in the English Church recovered quickly. At least one of the English divines at Dort, Joseph Hall, returned with increased sympathy for Arminian doctrines. Among the upper clergy the number of anti-Calvinists tended to increase, and in 1621 Laud, who was to be the great leader of English Arminianism, at length became a bishop. James made the appointment with some reluctance. Hacket relates that when Buckingham recommended Laud for the bishopric of St. David's, the King remarked testily: 'I find he hath a restless spirit and cannot see when matters are well, but loves to toss and change and to bring things to a pitch of reformation floating in his own brain.' Then he yielded, saying to Buckingham: 'Take him to you, but on my soul you will repent it', and so he turned away with fierce and ominous words too tart to be repeated. It has been said that in the last years of his reign James grew more tolerant of Arminianism because it exalted the prerogative, but in truth there is no evidence that he altered his opinions.[1]

In 1618 there was a new clash between King and Puritans. Strict observance of the Sabbath day had long been a Puritan doctrine; but the common people, accustomed to sports on Sunday afternoons, resented Puritan efforts to end their pastimes. As

the King passed through Lancashire in 1617 he found a quarrel
of this kind, for though large numbers of the Lancashire gentry
were Roman Catholic, the magistrates were strictly Puritan, while
the people were devoted to their sports. They liked

> To throw the sledge,
> To jump, or leap over ditch or hedge;
> To wrestle, play at stool ball, or to run,
> To pitch the bar or to shoot of a gun,
> To play at loggets, nine holes, or ten pins,
> To try it out at football by the shins.

They therefore petitioned the King that they should not be disturbed in Sunday games, and he readily granted their request.
He discovered, however, that he had opened the way to licence,
for the people, gloating over their victory, laughed and shouted
outside the churches during divine service, annoying the worshippers within. The King consulted Morton, Bishop of Chester,
as he should have done in the first place; and together they drew
up a *Declaration of Sports* for Lancashire. No games were to be permitted until the people attended church, but after that they might
have their lawful sports, including May games, Whitsun ales and
morris-dances.

Here the controversy might have ended. But in May 1618
James re-issued the *Declaration* generally for all England, ordering
that it be read in all the churches. His reasons are not clear. Perhaps he acted from bravado. His own observance of the Sabbath
was far from puritanical and he thought of sports as a means of
amusing the people and of keeping them quiet. But the King's
'dancing book' was bitterly resented by the Puritans, and the
clergy objected so strongly to reading the *Declaration* in church
that James withdrew his command for them to do so.[2]

In 1619 the King composed a brief meditation upon the Lord's
Prayer, a trifling little piece which affords startling proof of
decline in his mental powers. He explains in a meandering
preface that having written on the mysteries of the Book of
Revelation, wherein an elephant may swim, he finds relief in
contemplation of the smooth and easy Lord's Prayer which every
old wife can mumble and every child expound. He is growing
old, he says, and old men are twice babes, and he is therefore
leaving solid meat to feed on milk. As Buckingham's oecumenical

father, he dedicates the meditation to his favourite. Buckingham's prayer must be short, for he is constantly occupied with the King's affairs; it must be simple, for he is no scholar; it must be practical, for he must not forget God's service in the King's. In prayer, James continues, man speaks with God and becomes half-angel; but the nation has turned from prayer to prattling, the Puritans long for sermons, and simple craftsmen presume to interpret Holy Writ. Extemporaneous prayer he denounces as that 'monstrous conceit of conceived prayers without premeditation'. The Church, he continues, is like a city built upon a hill; once a man leaves her protecting towers, he stumbles, falls, and ends in a lake of fire and brimstone. The churchman becomes a Puritan, then a Separatist, then a Brownist or Anabaptist, and finally a judaized Thrascist or profane Familist. And the Puritan is father of them all.[3]

Turning to the Lord's Prayer, the King interprets it phrase by phrase with homely common sense and with most pious observations. The words 'Our Father' denote reverence, infinite love, and greatness, contrasting with the practice of the Puritans who talk with God as with their equal and 'who love to sit Jack-fellowlike with Christ at the Lord's Table'. 'Hallowed be Thy Name' is our first petition, the reverse of swearing; it is our homage to God, for we can ask nothing of our King before we have paid our allegiance. Thus James rambles on. His thoughts wander to stories of the chase, to the wickedness of private vengeance, to smoking tobacco, to jibes at Arminians, at Papists and especially at Puritans.

In the following year he wrote a meditation upon the passage in the Gospel of St. Matthew in which the soldiers mock Christ and place a crown of thorns upon His head. The verses are wrenched from their context and are employed to warn Prince Charles that a king has many burdens. 'Look not to find the softness of a down pillow in a Crown but remember that it is a thorny piece of stuff and full of continual cares.' The meditation has a melancholy tone reflecting the difficulties that had arisen in Bohemia. But James is reminded of the theme of kingship; and Prince and melancholy are alike forgotten in rapturous contemplation of the institution of monarchy. The meditation concerns the King of Kings, it is written by a King, it is addressed to a King's son. It does not deal fully with its theme. But James promises at some future time 'if God shall spare me days and leisure, to set down at large as in the descant the whole principal points belonging to the office of a king. And if my leisure cannot permit, whereof I despair, I intend (God willing) to set some more nimble pen on work with my instructions'.[4]

Changes meanwhile were taking place in the royal family and among the persons with whom the King was intimate. Queen Anne, after constant ill health for several years, developed a dangerous form of dropsy and died on March 2nd, 1619. For some time she and her husband had not been on the best of terms. As her health declined she had fallen more completely under the influence of the priests whom she kept by her; and finally they refused her the sacraments unless she ceased to attend the Church of England. This had caused angry words between Anne and the King, but when she became seriously ill their relations grew more kindly and during the last few months of her life James visited her twice a week. In February, when she appeared to be mending, he went to Newmarket. Then suddenly she became very ill. Frivolous to the last, she refused to think that death was near until it was upon her. In her last hours she called for James but he was far away.

For a good many years the King and Queen had not seen much of each other. About 1606 or 1607 they ceased to live together, Anne spending most of her time at Denmark House or Greenwich, while James was constantly on the move. The King, wrote Weldon, 'was ever best when furthest from his Queen'; to which Bishop Goodman answered that James and Anne had lived together during their first years in England and had had children. 'It is true', the Bishop added, 'that some years after they did not keep much company together. The King of himself was a very chaste man, and there was little in the Queen to make him uxorious; yet they did love as well as man and wife could do, not conversing together.'[5]

The King 'took her death seemly'. He had not gone to her in her last hours nor did he attend her funeral. And in some verses which he composed to her memory he appears more concerned with the majesty of kings than with the death of his wife:

Thee to invite the great God sent His star,[6]
Whose friends and nearest kin good princes are,
Who, though they run the race of men and die,

Death serves but to refine their majesty.
So did my Queen from hence her court remove,
And left off earth to be enthroned above.
She's changed, not dead, for sure no good prince dies,
But, as the sun, sets, only for to rise.

James's horror of the presence of death is sufficient to explain his absence from his wife's death-bed. But it is only fair to add that he was ill at Newmarket and that after Anne's death he fell into a dangerous sickness brought on in part by melancholy. His illness began with 'a shrewd fit of the stone' coupled with arthritis. He travelled to Royston about the middle of March, arriving very weak and faint. Then all his old ailments came down upon him together, 'being at once troubled with the stone, the gout and a scouring vomit'. He could not eat or sleep. 'After the Queen's death,' wrote Mayerne, 'pain in joints and nephritis with thick sand, continued fever, bilious diarrhoea, hiccoughs for several days, bitter humours boiling from his mouth so as to cause ulcers on his lips and chin, fainting, sighing, dread, incredible sadness, intermittent pulse. The force of this, the most dangerous illness the King ever had, lasted for eight days.' At the height of his distress he voided three stones; and the violence of the pain distempered all his body and caused horrible vomiting, while the irregularity of his pulse was alarming. At one point the physicians despaired of his recovery. But then he began to mend; and though he was terribly weak, so that he had to be lifted from one bed to another, the doctors pronounced him out of danger.

His nature asserted itself even in this extremity. Summoning the Prince, Buckingham and the principal councillors who had come post-haste from London, he made what he thought to be a death-bed speech. Those present declared they had never heard words so wise, so religious, so divine. To Charles he recommended certain councillors by name; some, as Lennox, for their close kinship, some, as Buckingham, for their love, some, as Arundel, for their ancient nobility, but specially Hamilton and Buckingham. He had words of high praise for Pembroke.

His strength returned very slowly. About a month after his illness, he came to Theobalds, part of the way in a litter and part in a portable chair borne on men's shoulders. Upon his arrival, weak and weary as he was, he would not go indoors until his deer

had been driven past 'to make a muster before him'. He was soon
able to ride and was often out in his litter, but he could not walk.
In June he made a solemn entry into Whitehall to show himself
to the people. He was dressed gaily in pale blue satin with silver
lace and a blue and white feather, more like a wooer than a
mourner. The scene did not pass without a tantrum, for he was
irritated at being met by London's Recorder and not by its Lord
Mayor. Hunting was now resumed and with it the King's spirits
revived. 'On Saturday last the King killed a buck in Eltham
Park and so soon as it was opened stood in the belly of it and
bathed his bare feet and legs with the warm blood; since which
time he has been so nimble that he thinketh this the only remedy
for the gout. He hath been of late exceeding merry, though so
troubled with petitions that he saith surely England is the kingdom
of petitioners.' 'He is fallen to his old diet and will not be persuaded to forbear fruit nor sweet wines.'

The people were sincerely thankful for his recovery. Bishop
King preached a thanksgiving sermon at St. Paul's, dwelling upon
James's patience and piety during his illness; and John Rawlinson
preached another, constantly repeating the triumphant phrase,
Vivat Rex! The death of a king, even a poor one, was something
to cause consternation.[7]

James's illness aged him considerably, and, as he aged, his love
for Buckingham deepened. Their relations were not disturbed by
Buckingham's marriage in 1620 to Lady Catherine Manners, the
only daughter of the Earl of Rutland. The match was a brilliant
one even for the favourite. Yet Buckingham and his mother made
such exorbitant demands that for a time the marriage appeared
doubtful. There was another difficulty, for Rutland and his
daughter were Roman Catholics. Declaring that Buckingham's
wife must go to church and remarking that he would not be
cozened with a mere church-papist, the King put forth his theological powers to convert Lady Catherine to the Church of England. One of his chaplains, John Williams, a rising cleric and a
plausible man of the world, also talked with her; and since she
was deeply in love with Buckingham her resistance was like that
of Ovid's mistress who strove but as one that would be overcome.
Her conversion infuriated her father, who quarrelled violently
with his prospective son-in-law. Yet the marriage took place in
May. That it proved a happy match was due to the bride. Lady

Catherine was a tender and devoted wife who regarded her husband as the noblest of mankind in spite of his many infidelities. 'Dear Heart,' she wrote, 'I cannot express the infinite affection I bear you. There never was woman loved man as I do you.'

James took her to his heart, loving her as a daughter. 'My only sweet and dear child,' he wrote Buckingham shortly after the marriage, 'Thy dear dad sends thee his blessing this morning, and also to his daughter. The Lord of Heaven send you a sweet and blithe awakening, all kind of comfort in your sanctified bed, and bless the fruits thereof, that I may have sweet bedchamber boys to play with me (and this is my daily prayer). Sweet hearty, when thou riseth keep thee from importunity of people that may trouble thy mind, that at meeting I may see thy white teeth shine upon me, and so bear me comfortable company in my journey; and so God bless thee. James R.'[8]

Prince Charles, now emerging as a person of consequence, was also coming within the orbit of his father's love. The Venetian ambassador thus describes an audience in 1617: 'The Prince is a youth of about sixteen, very grave and polite, of good constitution so far as can be judged from his appearance. His hair is light and he closely resembles his royal mother. He was dressed in scarlet and gold lace, with a gilt sword and white boots, with gold spurs according to the fashion of the country.' Slowly Charles had developed from a delicate child into a healthy though not a robust young man, fond of theatricals and sports, an excellent horseman who delighted in hunting and in riding at the ring. It is well to recall his youthful tastes, for Charles in these years appears almost too virtuous. He was sober, religious, correct and frugal, he blushed at an indelicate word, he was most filial. 'His chief endeavour', wrote the Venetian ambassador, 'is to have no other aim than to second his father, to follow him and do his pleasure and not to move except as his father does. Before his father he always aims at suppressing his own feelings.' Doubtless the King's rapid conversation, quick intelligence and choleric temper overawed and silenced the son, who was so much slower in thought and speech. Charles's contacts with his father were really very harmful. His secretive nature was not encouraged to expand and to meet the world half way but was driven in upon itself, and he became accustomed to the arts of petty dissimulation. There was, of course, another factor, for Charles was rather dull. His silence, praised by the court as wise and judicious, sprang partly from the fact that the young Prince had nothing to say.

As Charles grew into a youth he resented the glamorous favourite whom all were called upon to adore; and the King with great folly made no effort to conceal the fact that he loved Buckingham more than he loved his son. In an episode in 1616 Charles admired a ring of Buckingham's, tried it on his finger, and forgot to return it. Next day the ring was not to be found. The spoiled favourite complained to the King who, sending for Charles, 'used such bitter language as caused his Highness to shed tears', and ordered him out of his presence until the ring was located. On another occasion Charles playfully turned the pin of a fountain so that water spouted into Buckingham's face. Buckingham was furious, and the King, seeing what had happened, lost his temper completely, spoke angrily to the Prince, and gave him two boxes on the ear. Courtiers spoke of these things as evidence of Buckingham's overweening presumption, but they reflected much more upon the King. A more serious quarrel between Charles and Buckingham occurred in 1618 over a game of tennis.

James now forced a reconciliation by calling the young men before him and commanding them on their allegiance to love each other. Buckingham, perhaps sensing that he had best mend his ways, made much of the reconciliation. To commemorate it he gave a feast at Wanstead in Essex, an estate he had recently acquired. The feast was held out of doors in a lovely setting under the trees from which hangings were draped in such a way as to form the walls of an imaginary palace. Buckingham spoke of the occasion as the friends' feast. The King was overjoyed. He drank a toast to each of Buckingham's relations in turn, then drank to the whole of that noble race, declaring his desire to advance it above all others. 'I live', he said, 'to that end.' And now, he added, he could promise that his posterity would do the same.

Such drunken folly was hardly a solid foundation for friendship between the Prince and the favourite. But both the King and Buckingham made so much of the reconciliation that Charles dutifully fitted into the picture. He and Buckingham became close friends. James spoke as though he had achieved a momentous pacification. 'I must confess to my comfort without flattery,' he wrote Charles, 'that in making your affections to follow and second thus your father's, you show what reverent love you carry towards me in your heart, besides the worthy example you give to all other kings' eldest sons for imitation.' Buckingham spoke of Charles's friendship as an added blessing that the King had bestowed upon him. He wrote to the King of 'Baby Charles, whom you by your good offices made my friend.' One wonders whether James suspected what he was doing, for he was destroying any chance his son might have of becoming a popular sovereign.

There were moments when James was jealous of his son. A play by Charles's comedians, in which a prince drove his royal father from the throne, unnerved the King completely. There was a misunderstanding in 1619 over some jewels of Queen Anne's which Charles, apparently by a slip of the pen, claimed to be his of right. James rebuked him angrily, and Buckingham was able to step forward as peacemaker. But the King's tempers were ephemeral. Charles and Buckingham were intimates, and James's love for his son increased. [9]

The King was now to face the crisis of his reign when foreign and domestic affairs merged into one great problem and when he was called upon to direct and lead the genius of his people as he had never been called upon before. It was his tragedy that the time of testing came upon him when he was past his prime, when the vigour of mind and body were ebbing away. Unable to solve the problems before him, he fell into timid uncertainty and hesitation. A passion for avoiding decision grew upon him, troublesome news filled him with impatience, escape became his great objective.

While James was enjoying his progress in 1618, for which he had obtained money by the creation of four earls, he learned that a revolution had taken place in far-away Bohemia. The aged and childless Emperor, Matthias, seeking to secure the succession to his dominions for his cousin, Ferdinand of Styria, had demanded in 1617 that the Bohemian estates accept Ferdinand as their future king. But the Bohemian nobles, who were largely Protestant, regarded Ferdinand as the arch-enemy of their religion. They rose in wild revolt. In May 1618, they broke into the palace at Prague, seized the Emperor's regents, and flung them out of the window. The rebels were soon in possession of Bohemia. Unless they could be crushed, the eastern Hapsburgs faced ruin; and the fighting was almost certain to broaden into the long-threatened war between Catholics and Protestants in Germany.

What would be the policy of other powers? The German Lutheran States were conservative. John George of Saxony, the leading Lutheran Prince, was attached to the Emperor as the symbol of law and order; his wish was merely to put out the fire. But the German Calvinists were more adventurous. Their hopes ran high that the Austrian Hapsburgs might now be destroyed for ever. Their leader was James's son-in-law, Frederick of the Palatinate, who was himself led by the tempestuous Christian of Anhalt. Instead of seeking a common policy with Saxony, Frederick ventured into reckless schemes to fan the flames in Bohemia.

Philip of Spain was bound to the Emperor by every tie of blood and interest. Yet it was far from certain that Spain would engage in a great war. Her treasury was empty and her people in misery. The Twelve Years' Truce with the Dutch was about to expire. If England came in on the Protestant side, Spain would have to fight both in Bohemia and in the Netherlands and face a naval struggle with Holland and England. The seas would swarm with privateers, the treasure fleets would be endangered. It is no wonder that there was hesitation in Madrid.

The Bohemians at once begged James for assistance and Frederick warned that hostilities would likely spread into Germany. But the King's mind was taking a turn of its own. In July 1618, a suggestion had come from Spain that James, as a virtuous Prince with great prestige in Europe, should mediate between the Emperor and the Bohemians. The suggestion was informal, a chance shot in the game of diplomacy, but the King grasped at it eagerly. Flattered to think that Philip trusted him, he saw a proof of Spanish friendship and promised that he would negotiate in a similar spirit of good faith. He had not answered the letter of the Bohemians, he said, because he guessed that he might be called upon to mediate and because he had heard only one side of the quarrel. Could the Spanish supply him with the Emperor's position?

James's mediation was not only an utter failure but placed his whole diplomacy upon a false foundation. The Spanish suggestion was, of course, a bit of trickery. But the King accepted it so quickly, without caution or reservation, that he all but invited the

Spaniards to cheat him. What wonder that they decided to keep him amused while they sent aid to the Emperor! With keen insight Gondomar analysed James's motives. They were, he said, his inclination to peace, his fear of Frederick's indiscretions, his lively sense of his own interests, above all his vanity. 'The vanity of the present King of England is so great that he will always think it of great importance that peace should be made by his means, so that his authority will be increased.' His mediation, said Gondomar, could do no harm and might make him ashamed of his own folly.

James knew almost nothing of the complicated situation in Bohemia, and his embassy of mediation, led by the luxurious Hay, now Viscount Doncaster, was dispatched with naive and unrealistic instructions. Doncaster speedily discovered that the King's mediation was regarded as inadmissible not only by Ferdinand, whose military position had improved, but also by the Bohemians, who declared that James should send them aid rather than arrange a settlement to their disadvantage. Doncaster's imposing company, one hundred and fifty strong, sent at a cost of some £30,000, crossed and re-crossed Europe, the laughing-stock of everybody. Meanwhile great events were taking place. Matthias had died in March. In August, partly as a result of Frederick's blundering, Ferdinand was elected Emperor, and at almost the same instant the Bohemians formally deposed him as their King and elected Frederick in his place. Frederick hesitated, then made the fateful decision to accept, and travelled to Prague in October.[10]

These events caused a surge of anti-Catholic and anti-Spanish sentiment in England. Council, court and nation were stirred by the roll of Protestant drums in Bohemia, nor was Ralegh's death forgotten. Abbot, with greater zeal than wisdom, declared that the prophecies of the Book of Revelation were about to be fulfilled in the destruction of Catholic power. The anti-Spanish faction in the Council was hot for war, and Buckingham, drawing Charles after him, joined the war party, while other councillors, though more cautious, were ready for a strong anti-Spanish policy. With the Howards out of office and Gondomar on a visit to Spain, the old Spanish party appeared to be dead; and the King thus found himself under heavy pressure to drop his friendship with Spain and to support his son-in-law. In a letter of Pembroke the noble and generous impulses of the nation found expression. 'It is true', he wrote, 'that the King will be very unwilling to be engaged in a war. And yet I am confident, when the necessity of the cause of religion, his son's preservation, and his own honour call upon him, that he will perform whatsoever belongs to the Defender of the Faith, a kind father-in-law, and one careful of that honour which I must confess by a kind of misfortune hath long lain in suspense.'

The King was in sad perplexity. Deeply vexed with Frederick, he spoke hotly of his rashness. When Baron Dohna, Frederick's ambassador in England, suggested that his master might be elected King of Bohemia, James answered at once that such action would be aggression against the Emperor and that he would have none of it. He believed that the Bohemians, in deposing Ferdinand, had committed an outrageous act of rebellion and that Frederick, in accepting the throne, became the abettor of rebels and the wicked usurper of a kingdom that belonged to someone else. James hated all war; but from a war in support of revolt and usurpation he shrank as from the plague. He loathed the trouble and vexation of action. He had no army; and his only hope of obtaining one lay in summoning Parliament, a most unattractive prospect. If he assisted Frederick, where was his reputation as the peacemaker of Christendom? What became of the Spanish match? The prize for which he had sacrificed so much would slip away. The Spanish would foster plots among the English Catholics and his life would be in danger. He believed, wrote the Venetian ambassador, that he could not keep at peace or even remain alive except by union with Spain.

And yet Frederick was his son-in-law and Frederick's wife was his daughter. Prince Frederick Henry, his little grandson, wrote him a letter in which the child was taught to ask for help, and James was deeply moved. Should he desert his own flesh and blood? There was a thrill in the thought that his son-in-law and daughter were now a King and Queen. Despite his irritation with Frederick, those about him easily saw his delight at this new royal title; and when the Venetians accorded the title of King to Frederick, James was infinitely pleased. Had Frederick been able, by some great coup, to obtain the Bohemian Crown without causing his father-in-law any trouble, the King would assuredly have given the deed his blessing. Nor was James blind to the danger of Spanish duplicity. Occasionally he broke into denunciations of the Spaniards, declaring that they were playing with him. If they were sincere, why did not Gondomar return to complete the marriage treaty?

Torn this way and that, James fell into sad irresolution. He seized upon every excuse to postpone decision; and month after month he followed a policy of drift. 'It seems to me', wrote Tillières, the French ambassador, 'that the intelligence of this King has diminished. Not that he cannot act firmly and well at times and particularly when the peace of the kingdom is involved. But such efforts are not so continual as they once were. His mind uses its powers only for a short time, but in the long run he is cowardly. His timidity increases day by day as old age carries him into apprehensions and vices diminish his intelligence.' James consulted his Council; but finding that councillors favoured aid to Frederick, he would not permit them to voice their opinion. Frederick, he said, had acted rashly without his consent. An excuse might be found in Frederick's youth, but he himself was an old King who could not enter such a great business unadvisedly. He would have to study the Bohemian constitution to determine the legality of Frederick's election. Sensing the irritation of councillors, he told them roundly that it was for him, not them, to decide questions of war and peace, and so dismissed the meeting.

The King took refuge in a quibbling study of the niceties of Bohemian public law. He had long conferences with Dohna and with Lafuente, the Spanish agent in England, and as a result he became more confused than ever. He told Lafuente plaintively that his only desire was to know the truth. He was, he said, 'in a great strait, being drawn to one side by his children and grandchildren, his own flesh and blood, and to the other side by the truth and by his friendship to Philip and to the House of Austria'. Lafuente noted with care that the King placed truth on the side of the Emperor. James suddenly became alarmed lest the Hapsburgs should imagine that, while posing as an impartial mediator, he had secretly prompted the Bohemians to elect Frederick as their King; and he protested loudly, on his word as a Christian Prince, that he was innocent of any such charge.

Meanwhile the Catholic powers planned their campaign. Maximilian of Bavaria, the ambitious leader of the Catholic League, offered to aid Ferdinand on condition that he be given Frederick's electoral dignity and a large portion of his possessions. Ferdinand assented in the most secret of compacts. The agreement was made known to Philip who was asked to provide a diversion by attacking the Palatinate from the Netherlands. Philip concurred, though only with great reluctance; and it seems certain that if James had been more forceful, Philip's decision would not have been what it was.

The possibility of a Spanish attack upon the Palatinate was in all men's minds in 1620. Here James should have made a stand. He was right in thinking the Bohemian adventure an act of aggression; and he was right in believing that English assistance could not salvage that hopeless enterprise. But the Palatinate was quite a different matter. It was Frederick's rightful possession, and an attack upon it was no less an outrage to public law than revolt in Bohemia, while a Catholic victory would dissolve the Union and threaten every Protestant interest in southern Germany. Yet James was not to be moved. When he was reminded of Spanish preparations he cried: 'What do you know? You are ignorant. I know quite well what I am about. All these troubles will settle themselves; you will see that very soon. I know what I am talking about.' He received Buwinckhausen, the ambassador from the Union, with harsh reproaches. Any danger to the Princes of the Union, James said, was due to their intrigues in Bohemia. His alliance with them was defensive; under present conditions he was not bound to assist them.[11]

James eagerly awaited the arrival of Gondomar, now returning from Spain, as though that sly fox would bring enlightenment. Their first audience took place on March 12. The King pleaded with the ambassador to be patient. He was, he complained, in a sad quandary. He had done all he could to avoid offending Spain. He was surrounded by three hundred Winwoods and he must not be squeezed. 'I give you my word', he declared, 'as a king, as a gentleman, as a Christian, and as an honest man, that I have no wish to marry my son to anyone except your master's daughter, and that I desire no alliance but that of Spain.' Here he took off his hat and wiped his forehead with his handkerchief. Gondomar replied that the King had it in his power to rectify these ills. 'All that is needed', James answered, 'is that we two should talk over these matters together.' He then approached the great question of the hour. Would the Emperor attack the Palatinate? 'What would you do,' answered Gondomar, 'if anyone had taken London from you?' The King said weakly that he hoped God would arrange matters for the best.[12]

Thus tamely did James allow himself to be thrown on the defensive, giving Gondomar every advantage. He permitted him to justify an attack upon the Palatinate in general terms and he negotiated with him in secret without the support of the English Secretaries of State. His vacillations were those of a man in an agony of indecision. At one time he boasted that he would send great armies to the Palatinate, and then he whimpered that since he could obtain no aid for himself he could not be expected to defend others. He wrote the Princes of the Union that he was sure they were safe from attack, and then he said he would not desert them in their danger. He permitted Dohna and Buwinckhausen to raise volunteers, but would not allow them to do so in his name. Hearing a rumour that Frederick was seeking the alliance of the Turks, James declared hotly that in that case he would himself fight his son-in-law. With utter indiscretion he said to Gondomar: 'The Palatine is a godless man and a usurper. I will give him no help. It is much more reasonable that he, young as he is, should listen to an old man like me, and do what is right by surrendering Bohemia, than that I should be involved in a bad cause. The Princes of the Union want my help; but I give you my word that they shall not have it.'[13] It is not surprising that Gondomar reported to Spain that the Palatinate could be invaded without fear of a war with England.

Moreover, James quarrelled with the Dutch at this most inopportune moment. The Dutch were offering to do more than their part for the defence of the Palatinate. But in May 1620 news arrived of outrages inflicted by the Dutch upon English merchants in the Spice Islands. The King had a right to be angry; but he had no right to take his complaints to Gondomar or to speak of the Dutch as his enemies. Unhappily, Buckingham followed him. Dutch attacks upon English sailors in the East offended the Lord Admiral of England, and Buckingham displayed the shoddy stuff of which he was made by plotting with Gondomar for an English attack upon Holland. The plan was imbecile; yet James listened to it, gave it his sanction, and permitted Gondomar to report it to Spain as a serious proposition.

The King's inaction grew more maddening every hour. He had to listen to open and angry accusations against Gondomar and

Spain, not only from his councillors, but from his household attendants who were with him at all hours. His one thought was escape, and he hurried away from London on his summer progress; but his cares followed him into the country. The Venetian ambassador, who saw him at Salisbury in August, has left a vivid picture. The King, he said, 'seemed utterly weary of the affairs that are taking place all over the world at this time, and he hates being obliged every day to spend time over unpleasant matters and to listen to nothing but requests and incitements to move in every direction and to meddle with everything. He remarked [and we can almost hear him]: "I am not God Almighty" '.

In August 1620, the blow fell. A Spanish army from the Netherlands threw itself upon the Palatinate, while the Emperor's forces moved against Prague.

The Spanish invasion of the Palatinate, which drove the English to fury, was for a moment too much for even James to swallow. In an audience with Gondomar at Hampton Court on September 24th, the King's anger blazed forth fiercely. Gondomar, he shouted, had deceived him. He would never trust a Spanish Minister again. He would not permit either his children or his religion to perish. He would go in person to defend the Palatinate. Gondomar answered loftily that he had never promised that the Palatinate would not be invaded. And James, knowing this was true, burst into angry tears.

While his wrath was still hot, he made a formal declaration in the Council that he would defend the Palatinate. This appeared to lift a great weight from his mind. All during the day he was unusually happy; and at night he gave a banquet, drinking many toasts to his children and distributing wine throughout the court as though the news of some great victory had arrived.

But his mood was ephemeral. The difficulties and dangers of war and the fear of offending Spain again loomed large before him. Playing his cards with great skill, Gondomar declared that the invasion of the Palatinate was the road to peace. Let Frederick renounce his claim to Bohemia and the Palatinate would be restored to him. Gondomar demanded that the King acknowledge there had been no Spanish promise regarding the Palatinate; and James weakly consented. Gondomar also complained of Secretary Naunton. This appeared to the English as the height of arrogance, 'as if all our councillors were petty companions in respect of him, the great ambassador (as he calls himself) of the great King of Spain', but James tamely suspended his Secretary from office. Gondomar's influence was reaching its height. 'He is not only an ambassador,' wrote Tillières, 'but one of the first councillors of State of this kingdom, being day and night at the palace of Whitehall, where the most secret counsels are confided to him and where they listen to his advices and follow them almost to the letter.' He had access to the court at all hours and obtained audience without appointment. His hold on the King was most extraordinary.

James's councillors told him that a Parliament was essential, but the King hesitated. He was annoyed and alarmed at the popular hatred of Spain and at the freedom with which it was expressed. A famous pamphlet, *Vox Populi*, castigated Spain, while preachers dwelt upon the plight of Frederick and the perfidy of the Spaniards. Wrathfully remarking that his people were becoming too republican, James issued a proclamation that forbade licentious speech on matters of State. Gondomar and Buckingham did all they could to prevent the calling of Parliament. 'The Puritans have rendered Buckingham Spanish,' wrote Tillières, 'for seeing that they mean to attack him, he knows no way of securing protection against them except by the Spanish match.' Thus the favourite was reviving the old Spanish party.

Yet Parliament was a necessity and James took the decision to call it. Before it met, the news arrived that Frederick had been completely defeated at Prague and was flying northward for his very life. The Bohemian adventure was over. The King, deeply grieved, abandoned his rabbit-hunting at Newmarket, of which, said the Venetian ambassador, he could never have enough even in bitter and windy weather, and shut himself up in his room in great sadness and dejection, forbidding the courtiers any kind of game or recreation.[14]

Although the Parliament of 1621 appears strangely devoted to domestic issues, it was none the less conditioned by events abroad. The Commons were in deadly earnest. Domestic abuses and a miserable foreign policy gave them a touch of that grim and terrible hardness that foreshadowed the civil wars. Nor was the King in a mood to be trifled with. Yet both King and Commons knew that a quarrel was the road to disaster and they both displayed self-restraint for many months.

At the opening of Parliament on January 30th, the King was suffering from arthritis and, though he rode to the Parliament cheerfully, he had to be carried in a chair into the House of Lords, 'being so weak in his legs and feet that it is doubted he will find little use in them hereafter'. His speech followed an old pattern. He commended brevity and spoke for over an hour. After reading Parliament a lecture on its proper place in the framework of monarchy, he asked for money, pointed to recent economies, and hoped that the Parliament would prove a happier one than its predecessors. Adding a word on the sad state of Christendom, he declared that peace remained his objective, but he wished to treat with a sword in his hand; and if by peaceful means he could not defend the Palatinate, he would spend his all, his blood, the blood of his son, to restore it to its rightful owners. These were good words, but they lacked detail and sincerity. The Commons were not told how the Palatinate would be defended. The King's protestation was belied by his dilatory policy and by the words he spoke in private to Gondomar.[15]

The first great question was that of finance, and here a gross error was committed, for which the Commons were not blameless, yet for which the King must bear the greater responsibility. Some months earlier he had appointed a council of war and he now had its report: that an army of 30,000 men was essential for the defence of the Palatinate, that the initial cost would be £250,000, and that subsequent expenditure would reach the annual figure of £900,000. Not daring to ask the Commons for such vast sums, James told them that an army of 30,000 men was necessary and that it would cost £500,000, a gross underestimate. Yet this figure was sufficient to alarm the Commons who cut it down to a mere £160,000, which they said was not for war but for the King's other necessities. The grant none the less was their answer to a request for war supplies, and they must have assumed that some of it would go for preliminary war expenditure. It was James's duty to tell them the truth, for if the country wanted war, it must learn what war would cost. But the King, overjoyed at the prospect of some money, accepted the grant with delight and thanked the Commons effusively. By so doing he blunted their zeal and betrayed their confidence. What would they do when he asked again?

Warned away from foreign affairs, the Commons turned to

domestic matters and soon focused their attention on patents and
monopolies in which they found gross abuses that pointed directly
at the favourite. Though Buckingham obtained but small advantage from the patents, he had supported them for the benefit of his
relations. Sir Giles Mompesson, one of the worst offenders, was
his kinsman; his half-brother, Sir Edward Villiers, and his brother
Christopher drew money from obnoxious monopolies. Greatly
alarmed, Buckingham rushed to the King and demanded the
dissolution of Parliament. But James refused; and Buckingham,
seeking the advice of Williams, the worldly Dean of Westminster,
decided to swim with the tide, to win applause by ending abuses,
and to throw over the monopolists although they were his kinsmen.

The King's problem, however, was more complex. The Commons were eager not only to expose the monopolists but also to
investigate the referees, those advisers of the Crown to whom
patents had been referred before they had been granted. The
principal referees were Lord Chancellor Bacon and Lord Treasurer
Mandeville and, if these men were prosecuted, the Commons
would revive in essence the medieval procedure of impeachment.
'Those who will strike at your Chancellor,' warned Bacon, 'it is
much to be feared will strike at your Crown.' James therefore told
the Commons in an angry speech that they were not omnipotent
and that they must respect the prerogative. But he soon altered
his tone, deciding that he, too, must swim with the tide. He was
heard to remark that he was but one King while the Commons
were above four hundred. He told them that he would assist them
in punishing offenders. The Commons took the hint, continued
to investigate monopolies, but dropped their charges against the
referees.

Yet hostility to the referees remained; and when dramatic
charges of bribery were brought against Bacon the Commons
listened eagerly. Bacon was not the ordinary taker of bribes.
'When the book of hearts shall be opened,' he said, 'I hope I shall
not be found to have the troubled fountain of a corrupt heart in a
depraved habit of taking rewards to pervert justice, however I
may be frail and partake of the abuses of the times.' Yet he did
things that an honest man would not have done. From this
episode the King emerges rather well. He wished to befriend
Bacon but he had no intention of shielding a guilty person.

Characteristically he suggested that the matter be settled by a commission outside of Parliament chosen by himself. When this was refused, he warned the Lords to be impartial and left the trial in their hands. He did what he could to keep the Commons in good humour. He recalled many patents, and when Parliament rose for the Easter holidays he made a gracious speech, thanking the Houses for showing him that his kingdom was an unweeded garden, cursing those advisers who in the past had dissuaded him from summoning Parliament, and promising to rule in future so that, were the Crown elective, he should be chosen king by general acclamation.

After the Easter holidays, however, James's relations with the Commons degenerated. There were quarrels over a number of things of which the most important was money, for when the King asked for additional supplies, the Commons refused. He had a difference with the Lords over Sir Henry Yelverton who had dared attack the favourite. Under pressure from Buckingham and Gondomar to dissolve the Parliament, James compromised by a sudden adjournment of the Houses in May, to the anger of the Commons, who considered their work but half done.

In foreign affairs, meanwhile, the King had continued to drift. He made no military preparations but allowed his policy to revert to what it had been in 1619: reliance upon Spanish friendship and upon efforts at mediation. He convinced himself that he had Philip's promise to restore the Palatinate once Frederick renounced all claims to Bohemia. He would, he said, offer the Emperor his son-in-law's renunciation of Bohemia, coupled with promises of good behaviour, and attempt to make peace on that basis. If the Emperor proved obdurate, James would call upon Spain to fulfil its pledge. If Spain refused, he would end the Spanish alliance and employ force. 'I am a King who loves peace. I do not delight in shedding blood and therefore I strain every nerve to avert it if possible. But if notwithstanding my great dexterity and his promises, the King of Spain will not do his duty and fulfil them, I shall then have every reason and justice to take up arms against him and his, hoping with God's help, in so righteous a cause, to make him repent of having roused a pacific lion.' Meanwhile the pacific lion deemed it wise to cultivate the goodwill of Spain and of its ambassador in the hope that Spanish pledges would some day be fulfilled.[16]

In May, James sent Digby to Vienna to lay his terms before the Emperor; but the chances of successful mediation were small. Frederick had no intention of abandoning the struggle. Refusing to believe that his defeat in Bohemia was irretrievable, he called for assistance from Protestants everywhere. His actions infuriated James, who declared they were undermining his diplomacy. Unfortunately, Frederick's general, Mansfeld, was proving a mere predatory adventurer. Driven from Bohemia into the Upper Palatinate, he increased the size of his army, lived upon the wretched peasants, and threatened friend and foe alike.

Digby managed to arrange a temporary truce, but it was soon broken on both sides. Frederick's cause collapsed. Maximilian invaded the Upper Palatinate from Bavaria, driving Mansfeld towards the Rhine, while in the Lower Palatinate the Spaniards threatened to carry all before them. Digby came home in October, discouraged and disillusioned. If Frederick was to regain his old dominions, it would have to be through assistance from England.

The new crisis roused James to a moment of activity. Military preparations, months overdue, were now begun. Money was sent to Frederick, and pressure was brought upon him to place himself at the head of his troops in the Palatinate and to renounce his claims to Bohemia. Above all, Parliament, prorogued to the following February, was called into sudden session on November 20th.

But having done this much, the King sank into inaction. With criminal folly he left London before Parliament opened and remained away during the entire meeting. 'His Majesty seems to hope', wrote the Venetian ambassador, 'that the Parliament will readily afford him every means of making war with little trouble on his part.' Delayed a few days at Royston by an illness of Buckingham, hopefully but falsely reported in London as the smallpox, James journeyed on to Newmarket. He took Buckingham with him and also some of the ladies of the Villiers tribe. He does not appear to have been ill. His absence from London was sheer indulgence, proof that he had sunk lower in his love of ease, of Buckingham, and of Bacchus. By loitering at Newmarket where Buckingham, for his own ends, urged him to remain, James placed his ministers at a terrible disadvantage in dealing with the Commons.[17]

The Commons, assembled on November 20th, were told to devote themselves solely to finance, and to reserve other matters for February when they would be called again. They should avoid long speeches and invectives which the King would not endure. A grant was needed at once to support Frederick's forces during the winter and a much larger grant would be needed in the spring.

If James hoped that the Commons would confine their debates within this narrow limit, he was hoping for the impossible. How could able and intelligent men, deeply perturbed by the dangers to their country and to their religion, be expected to vote money in the dark without discussion of the issues that were at stake? Had they trusted the King, they might have given him money and left decisions to him; but they did not trust him. And, perhaps before they knew what they were doing, they launched into a debate on foreign affairs that was certain to anger him greatly.

The gulf between James and the nation was now apparent. He was paying for having framed his policy without thought for the wishes and prejudices of the people, who could not follow the vagaries of his diplomacy. How could England fight Spain in the Palatinate and be friendly with her elsewhere? How could James oppose the designs of Philip and conclude a marriage alliance with him? Or how could the King defend Protestantism abroad and be kindly tolerant of Catholics at home? In this great debate on foreign policy member after member pointed to Spain as the great enemy abroad and to the Catholics as the great menace in England. Let the war be against Spain, not merely by pottering in the Palatinate but by attacking Spain and the Indies on land and sea in true Elizabethan fashion. Let measures be taken against the Roman Catholics at home. They must be punished, not because of their religion but because they were seditious enemies of the commonwealth. The debate reached its crescendo in a violent speech by Coke who, throwing all restraint aside, poured forth vituperation upon Spain and Catholicism. The Commons voted one subsidy to aid the Palatinate during the winter; but they also framed a petition embodying the essential points of their debate. They asked for the enforcement of the anti-Catholic laws; they asked for a war with Spain; they asked that the Prince be married to a Protestant.

When James first heard of the petition, he is said to have cried 'God give me patience.' His anger was sharpened by a letter from

Gondomar who wrote audaciously that he would leave the country if he was not sure that the King would punish the Commons, for if James did not do so he would cease to be King. Without waiting until the petition reached him, James dashed off an angry letter to the Speaker. His absence, he said, had emboldened some fiery and popular spirits to debate matters far above their reach and capacity, 'tending to our high dishonour and breach of prerogative royal'. He commanded that henceforth no member should meddle with his government nor with deep mysteries of State, nor 'deal with our dearest son's match with the daughter of Spain, nor touch the honour of that King'. He added 'that we think ourselves very free and able to punish any man's misdemeanours in Parliament as well during their sitting as after; which we mean not to spare henceforth'. Nor would he receive the petition unless the Commons modified it greatly.

This letter struck the Commons like a thunderbolt. It showed that when the King was angry the privileges of Parliament had no meaning for him. In one wild note he had denied them all. The Commons had no course but to stand firm. They drew up an explanatory petition, much milder in tone, in which they asked James not to listen to garbled reports of their debates, to receive their first petition, and to confirm their privileges.

This second petition was taken to Newmarket by twelve of the Commons. James received them graciously. Jestingly he called upon attendants to bring stools for the ambassadors. He was, he said, freest of any king alive from trusting to idle reports. 'We are an old and experienced King, needing no such lessons.' The Commons, he said, first usurped his prerogative and then declared they had not meant to do so. How could they presume to determine upon the Prince's marriage without committing high treason? 'What have you left unattempted in the highest point of sovereignty in that petition of yours?' He could not allow the Commons to call privilege their undoubted right and inheritance. He assured them that as long as they kept within the limits of their duty, he would protect their lawful liberties, but they must not trench upon the prerogative, for then he, or any king, would reduce the privilege of those who dared pluck the flowers of his Crown.

The Commons drew up a protestation. They would quarrel

with the King no longer but would set down a statement of their rights. This protestation declared that the privileges of the Commons were their ancient and undoubted birthright and inheritance, that weighty affairs of the kingdom ought to be debated in Parliament, and that every member had freedom of speech and freedom from arrest.

During the Christmas holidays James considered what he should do. He was in great perplexity. A dissolution would leave him without money and at the mercy of Spain. Councillors, almost to a man, begged him not to dissolve Parliament. But the protestation had driven him to fury. 'The plain truth is,' he wrote, 'we cannot with patience endure our subjects to use such anti-monarchical words to us concerning their liberties, except they had subjoined that they were granted unto them by the grace and favour of our predecessors.' Gondomar played upon this point with audacious skill. Spain could not negotiate while such a Parliament remained in existence; indeed dissolution was now necessary for the King to be well seated on the throne. Buckingham, and probably Prince Charles also, urged James to dissolve. Gondomar wrote that 'the King was being valiantly urged on by the Marquis of Buckingham and other good friends'; and Tillières said that Buckingham scarcely acted as if he were English. James made his decision about December 30th. He came to the Council chamber, declared his intention of dissolving Parliament, then called for the journal of the Commons and with his own hands tore out the page containing the protestation.[18]

The dissolution of Parliament marked the eclipse of James as a potent and respected ruler. Cut off from his people, he could not hope to send assistance to the Palatinate. If Frederick retained some part of his former dominions, it would not be due to England but to the goodwill of Spain. The King could now do nothing but ask Spain to be kind. The dissolution of Parliament, wrote Gondomar exultingly, was the best thing that had happened during the last hundred years. It left James contemptible alike at home and abroad.

He was deeply depressed, but he had one solace. Shortly after these events, wrote Tillières, the King returned to Newmarket, seemingly without a care. He took Buckingham with him, 'with whom he uses the word of friend and not of King, thinking to hide under the name of friendship his base actions, feasting his eyes on what cannot satisfy his nobler sentiments. And, to conclude, all things end with the goblet'.

There was always a touch of the ridiculous about James. Passing Theobalds on his way north, 'his horse stumbled and cast his Majesty into the New River, where the ice broke. He fell in so that nothing but his boots were seen. Sir Richard Young was next, who alighted, went into the water, and lifted him out. There came much water out of his mouth and body. His Majesty rode back to Theobalds, went into a warm bed, and, as we hear, is well, which God continue'.[19]

CHAPTER XXII

THE SETTING AND THE RISING SUN

THE King's portraits in his last years are those of a broken, debauched and repulsive old man. The eyes are sunken, the glance suspicious and fearful, the expression of the face at once perplexed and disillusioned. The portraits tell something also of the King's physical weakness — for he was now a semi-invalid except in the warm summer months — and of the feebleness of mind and will that came upon him in his dotage. He had grown heavy, wrote the Venetian ambassador, more and more irregular in his manner of life, and more fearful of death.

His timidity had turned to abject dread and terror. Upon hearing of the fall of Heidelberg, Frederick's capital in the Palatinate, James wept but protested that if he made war on Spain he would surely be assassinated. On another occasion, as he sat in his chamber dejected and deep in thought, he suddenly cried out: 'And so the King of Spain thinks he can use me in this fashion; does he think me dead? He will find me only too much alive and determined.' Then casting a furtive glance around the room as though fearful of having been overheard, he remarked: 'I have trusted and still trust the ambassador Gondomar more than any man living.' That the King yielded more to terror than to any other persuasion was the conviction of all foreign envoys. Gondomar jested that for every defeat of the Protestants on the Continent the King would surrender a point in religion. 'He now believes in two sacraments; if the Protestants are beaten in Germany, he will believe in three, if the Huguenots suffer defeat, in four, if the Dutch, in five.' The King was alarmed at trifles. When some roaring boys at Gray's Inn shot off a cannon in the dead of night, James started from his bed at Whitehall, shouting 'Treason!' The entire court was aroused, and Arundel, sword in hand, came running into the royal sleeping-apartment to defend the King.

James clung to Buckingham with the excessive fondness of an aged parent for a beloved child. His maudlin letters invoked blessings upon his favourite, expressed alarm at Buckingham's slightest ailment and sadness at his slightest cross, lamented his absence, and prayed God for a happy and comfortable meeting with his 'sweet dear child, scholar and friend'. Buckingham replied in a similar vein. When he was about to return to England from Spain in 1623 he wrote: 'Sir, my heart and very soul dances for joy; for the change will be no less than to leap from trouble to ease, from sadness to mirth, nay, from hell to heaven. I cannot now think of giving thanks for friend, wife, or child; my thoughts are only bent on having my dear dad and master's legs soon in my arms; which sweet Jesus grant me, and your Majesty all health and happiness.' But changes were taking place in their relationship. James was finding that this beautiful young man was becoming his master, not his servant. The King lacked the strength and courage to assert his authority; and Buckingham, strong in the affection of the Prince, grew impatient with the fumbling timidity of the old King and was ready to thrust him aside. James's love grew beclouded by suspicion. But it was now too late.[1]

The King had never cared for the company of women, but in his old age he became rather fond of some of the ladies of the Villiers family. He had always been attached to Lady Catherine, whom he thought of as his daughter, and he liked Susan, Lady Feilding, the favourite's sister, and also Frances Coke who had married John Villiers. These ladies coddled him, nursed him and kept him company, 'affording him much pleasure, accompanying him in his carriage, at table, and at hunting, in honourable fashion, making his days pass pleasantly'. When Lady Catherine's first child was born in March 1622, the King was wholly absorbed in the event. During her pregnancy he had written Buckingham: 'My only sweet and dear child, The Lord bless thee this morning and thy thing my daughter; I pray thee, as thou lovest me, make her precisely observe these rules: let her never go in a coach upon the streets, nor never go fast in it. Let your mother keep all hasty news from coming to her ears; let her not eat too much fruit and hasten her out of London after we are gone.' The King squeezed money from his Treasurer to meet the expenses of Catherine's lying-in. He lavished costly gifts upon her attendants. During her labour he prayed for her most earnestly and was at Wallingford House early and late both before and after she was delivered, no doubt making a great nuisance of himself. He was greatly interested in the baby, Mary, whom he called 'little Mall'; and there

KING JAMES, IN OLD AGE

are some charming passages in Lady Catherine's letters telling the King of his little god-daughter. James's blessings upon sweet Kate and little Mall were gushing and sentimental but none the less sincere.[2]

The ladies, however, presented a sudden difficulty. The King discovered that the old Countess, Buckingham's mother, was listening to the persuasions of a Jesuit, Father Fisher, and was contemplating a change of faith. James also became aware that Catherine's conversion to the Church of England was most superficial. He was annoyed that these ladies, to whom he had spoken so often, should disregard his precepts in such wayward fashion. But worse was behind; for Buckingham himself, surrounded by Catholic influences, toyed for a moment with the notion of turning Roman. The King was indignant. To appease him, Buckingham brought a great troop of his female kindred to the Bishop of London and had them confirmed *en masse*. He also arranged a series of colloquies between Fisher and two Anglican divines, Dr. Francis White, a royal chaplain, and Bishop Laud. These discussions were attended by Buckingham, by his wife and mother, and also by the King. James produced a long series of questions to which he demanded that the Jesuit reply. The King, sneered Tillières, 'assumed the functions of a preacher; and if souls are to be converted by screaming, swearing, and denying God and all the saints, the Countess has done very wrong not to follow his doctrine'. The one gainer by these debates was Laud. He defended the Church of England with much skill. He failed to move the Countess, Buckingham's mother, who announced her Catholicism and was banished from court amid universal satisfaction. But Buckingham declared himself convinced, and a close alliance arose between Laud and the favourite. The King was also pleased with Laud, asked him to draw up an account of the meetings, and set him writing in reply to Roman tracts. Laud's star was at last beginning to rise.[3]

Meanwhile, following the dissolution of Parliament in 1621, the King's finances fell once more into chaos. The debt stood at £900,000. 'The more I look into the King's finances', wrote Cranfield who had become Lord Treasurer, 'the greater cause I have to be troubled.' Yet Cranfield was not without hope. 'If God bless me,' he wrote Buckingham, 'and his Majesty, the Prince, and your lordship continue constant and will back me, I will perfect the work, and the King shall live with honour upon his own in spite of all the world.' Cranfield's great necessity was the support of the King, and he begged hard for it. He obtained a promise that grants should not be made without his approval; but James was incorrigible. He had once laid his hand upon Cranfield's head, saying sententiously: 'God's blessing and mine be upon thee.' But he never learned the rudiments of frugality or of loyalty to his financial officers. His gifts were endless, and he grew canny in extracting money from his own Treasurer. 'You cannot easily conceive', wrote Cranfield, 'into what straits I am daily driven for supply of money for his Majesty's occasions.'

Criticism of the King was naturally bitter. Tillières's dispatches dwelt constantly upon James's want of spirit, his licentiousness, and the dissolution of his intelligence. He was a King devoted to his own nothingness. A flask of wine was dearer to him than the welfare of his kingdom. He was hated and despised by his people. Tillières's language was rather overdrawn, but a more balanced observer, Valaresso, the Venetian ambassador, was severe enough. 'All good sentiments are clearly dead in the King', he wrote. 'He is too blinded in disordered self-love and in his wish for quiet and pleasure, too agitated by constant mistrust of everyone, tyrannized over by perpetual fear for his life, tenacious of his authority as against the Parliament and jealous of his son's obedience, all accidents and causes of his almost desperate infirmity of mind.' An anonymous pamphlet, *Tom Tell Truth*, accused the King of permitting Catholicism to sweep the Continent while he wasted his time in drunkenness and vice.

If such criticism reached James's ears, he cared little for it. He had Buckingham, he had Baby Charles, he had the ladies of Buckingham's family. The rest of the world was fading away.[4]

The King's foreign policy, controlled inexorably by the crippled state of his finances, followed an old pattern. He had but two avenues of action: first, to continue efforts at mediation between Frederick and the Emperor, and, secondly, to put the friendship of Spain to the touch and ask for her assistance. But he had to ask for a great deal: that Spain withdraw her forces from the Palatinate, that she persuade Ferdinand to do the same, and that, if Ferdinand refused, she assist England in driving him out by force. Spain was to set aside her heritage, to follow James's example by entangling herself in contradictory alliances, perhaps to make war upon the

Catholic Emperor in order to please the Protestant King of England. To expect this from Spain was fatuous. The Spanish led James on in order to keep him quiet, but their decision was against him, as he should have known it would be.

Late in 1621 the King obtained from Frederick a most unwilling promise to renounce all claims to the Crown of Bohemia, to make peace with his neighbours, to crave pardon of the Emperor and to render him all obedience and devotion. Laying these promises before Ferdinand, James asked him to restore Frederick to his titles and possessions, but such an easy solution proved impossible. Negotiations at Brussels between James and the Emperor came to nothing; Frederick abandoned Mansfeld's army in despair; Tilly, the great general of Maximilian of Bavaria, made steady progress in the Palatinate. By the end of 1622 Frederick held but one town, Frankenthal, in all his former possessions. The Palatinate was lost, and mediation collapsed. Ferdinand announced that he would assemble the Electors and Princes of the Empire at Ratisbon, which meant that he planned to transfer the electorate of the Palatinate from Frederick to Maximilian. In this move James should have seen new evidence of Ferdinand's strength and Frederick's weakness; but he saw merely an insult to himself. Ferdinand had been negotiating with him at Brussels and was now taking the negotiations elsewhere. James raved at the Emperor. He declared he would never rest until he made war against him and to do so he would move hell itself.

Actually he could only turn to Spain. There he believed that the road to success lay in the marriage alliance, and he pushed it hard in 1622. But the match was not going well. About a year earlier, the articles of the proposed treaty had been sent by Spain to the Pope who had not yet granted a dispensation for the marriage; and a group of Cardinals, appointed to study the articles, concluded that further concessions must be made in England. The King must repeal the penal laws and allow English Catholics full liberty of worship. The Infanta's church must be open to the public, her priests must be headed by a bishop and must be exempt from English law, she must control the education of her children until the girls were twelve and the boys fourteen.

These terms, which reached England in August 1622, went far beyond what James had promised or what he could possibly perform. His sad thoughts found expression in a letter from

Buckingham to Gondomar, who had just returned to Spain. The King, wrote Buckingham, had done everything he could to please the Spaniards, but all the news from abroad was most discouraging. Buckingham therefore besought Gondomar to obtain what concessions he could, for the King could do no more. Remembering a phrase from his prayers, Buckingham concluded: 'Only in thee is my trust.' To such pitiful supplications had James been reduced.

Within a few days news came to England that Heidelberg had fallen. Sir Richard Weston, ambassador in the recent negotiations at Brussels, loudly declared he had been tricked by Spain and Austria. A firmer tone was now taken in England. There was talk of war for the recovery of the Palatinate; and the Privy Council advised the King to make a formal demand upon Philip for assistance. James hesitated, but the Prince and Buckingham were against him. The King's demand was therefore sent to Spain by a special ambassador, Endymion Porter. Yet Porter also carried a secret note from Charles to Gondomar suggesting that the Prince come to Madrid to conclude the negotiations, a proposal which Charles had discussed with Gondomar while the ambassador was still in England. It appears the height of folly that Charles and Buckingham should thus have balanced the alternatives of war and of close alliance. But their dilemma was one to which the King's diplomacy quite naturally led.

It is not easy to gauge the policy of the Spaniards. Olivares, Philip's principal minister, though able and resolute, was narrow, bigoted and unversed in the internal affairs of foreign States. He therefore hoped for the impossible. He thought that Frederick could be deprived of the Palatinate and that yet in some way the Spanish could retain James's friendship. Olivares opposed the marriage, but he believed that Spain could avoid it by placing the blame for failure upon the Pope. And again the King of England was expected to acquiesce.

For a time in 1622 Philip believed that the marriage would have to take place. But Olivares found an unexpected ally in the Infanta, a pious and gentle Princess who none the less possessed great strength of will. She told her brother that rather than marry a heretic she would enter a convent. Philip thereupon concluded that he could not go on with the marriage and joined Olivares in opposing it. Other Spanish councillors, however, held a different view. Gondomar believed in the marriage and worked honestly for it; and many councillors, thinking that something would have to be done to satisfy England, regarded the marriage as inevitable.

Amid these diverse opinions, Olivares and Philip adopted the course of appearing to approve the marriage which they secretly opposed. They told the English King that they would give some aid in the Palatinate, though their promise was in the future tense and was very vague, and they gave the impression that Spain would be reasonable and helpful. James gladly accepted their assurances at face-value, he made further concessions in the marriage treaty, and he was happy and merry as he listened to Endymion Porter, who came home early in 1623. That he sincerely desired a general pacification of Europe is attested by his letter to the Pope, September 1622, in which he besought the Pope to work for peace. [5]

Negotiations for the Spanish match reached their climax in the journey of Charles and Buckingham to Spain in 1623. It is probable that the King first heard of the plan in the preceding autumn when Buckingham proposed that after negotiations were complete he as Lord Admiral should bring the bride to England and that Charles should embark secretly with him. Then, in February 1623, Charles and Buckingham approached the King with a new proposal. They wished to go at once, though negotiations were far from complete. They would ride across France incognito without a pass from Paris, conclude the treaty quickly, and 'bring back that angel' as Charles's wife. We may perhaps excuse Charles's boyish enthusiasm for a bold and romantic adventure. But for Buckingham to advocate such folly, to expose the Prince to such needless risks, and to place such advantage in the hands of Spain, was irresponsible to the point of wickedness.

The King was ill with arthritis. Without considering just what he was doing, he gave his sweet boys the permission they asked. Night brought more sober reflections, and on the following morning he begged Charles and Buckingham to abandon their plan. Vividly he pointed out the dangers, and then burst into tears. The two young men rudely brushed aside his objections and spoke to him with such vehemence that he was intimidated. Hoping for an ally he summoned Cottington, a diplomat with long experience in Spain. 'Cottington,' said the King, 'here are Baby Charles and Steenie who have a great mind to go by post to Spain to fetch home the Infanta, and will have but two more in their company, and have chosen you for one. What think you of the journey?' Cottington was aghast. Such a step, he said, would undo all that had been accomplished. The Spanish would certainly raise their terms. The King threw himself upon a bed. 'I told you this before,' he screamed, 'I am undone. I shall lose Baby Charles.' Yet in the end he yielded. On February 17th, Charles and Buckingham, under the names of Jack and Tom Smith, rode in disguise to Dover, took ship, and landed at Boulogne; they went to Paris, where they remained two days, and reached Madrid safely on March 7th. Gondomar had the news at once. He went to Olivares though it was late at night. 'What brings you here so late?' asked Olivares. 'One would think you had got the King of England in Madrid.' 'If I have not got the King,' said Gondomar, 'at least I have got the Prince.' His trump card could now be turned face upward. [6]

Meanwhile the King at Newmarket had to face the angry consternation of the court and people. Thrusting dark thoughts aside, he forced himself to think in terms of a swift journey, a successful mission, and a happy return by 'his sweet boys and dear venturous knights worthy to be put in a new romanso'. When the councillors who happened to be with him begged to know the truth, he answered at once that the Prince, weary of long delays, had gone to Spain to speed a settlement. A general pacification in Europe, said the King, would undoubtedly follow. He reminded councillors that he himself, his father, Darnley, and his grandfather, James V, had all journeyed to distant lands to fetch home their brides. He wrote some verses addressed to his son,

> Thy grandsire, godsire, father too,
> Were thine examples so to do;
> Their brave attempts in heat of love,
> France, Scotland, Denmark, did approve.
> So Jack and Tom do nothing new,
> When love and fortune they pursue.
>
> Kind shepherds that have loved them long,
> Be not too rash in censuring wrong;
> Correct your fears, leave off to mourn,
> The heavens shall favour their return!
> Commit the care to royal Pan,
> Of Jack his son, and Tom his man.

Thus the King forced upon the court a tone of confidence and optimism. He was angry at anyone who raised awkward questions. When Valaresso hypocritically praised the journey, the King was delighted, gloried in what he had done, and said that everything would be settled in a month.

Others did not treat the matter so lightly. Councillors, with Arundel as spokesman, expressed their consternation, pointed out the evils that were certain to follow, and hinted their astonishment that the journey had been permitted. When James was pressed in this way he faltered and threw blame upon Charles and Buckingham. He had yielded, he said, to the passionate pleadings of his son. But though the King was sharply criticized, hatred and resentment ran far deeper against the favourite. 'Detestation of the Marquis', wrote Valaresso, 'has increased beyond all measure.' Williams wrote to Buckingham that 'all the court and rabble of the people lay the voyage upon your lordship. The King would seem sometimes, as I hear, to take it upon himself (as we have advised him to do by proclamation); yet he sticks at it and many times casts it upon you both'. In solemn words Williams warned Buckingham and the Prince of the dangers with which they would be surrounded. Above all, he conjured them to do nothing prejudicial to their religion. Thus the nation was aghast, fearful alike for the Prince's safety and for his religion; and wise men, as Dudley Carleton wrote, betook themselves to prayer rather than to inquiry.

The King's letters to his sweet boys were written with ineffable tenderness that rose at times to an ecstasy of passionate emotion. He was far more concerned with their welfare than with matters of State. 'Alas! sweethearts,' he wrote, 'as long as I want the sweet comfort of my boys' conversation, I am forced, yea, and delight to converse with them by long letters. God bless you both, my sweet boys, and send you, after a successful journey, a joyful happy return in the arms of your dear dad.' 'I wear Steenie's picture in a blue ribbon under my wash-coat next my heart.'

He was fearful of harm to Baby Charles. Negotiations must be concluded before the heat of the Spanish summer. He begged Charles not to tilt in hot weather, 'for I fear my Baby may take fever by it. My sweet Baby, for God's sake, and your dad's, put not yourself in hazard by any violent exercise long as ye are there'. 'I pray you, my Baby, take heed of being hurt if ye run at tilt.'

He suggested that Charles and Buckingham keep themselves fit by private dancing, 'though ye should whistle and sing to one another, like Jack and Tom, for fault of better music'. He had written, he said, all with his own hand, consoling letters to Buckingham's wife and mother. We catch a pretty picture of him playing with little Mall, calling her pet names, and showing her his watch. He tried to keep her with him as long as possible, saying playfully how remarkable it was that so ugly a father could have so sweet a child.

He discovered that the journey created more difficulties than he had anticipated. Two ships were prepared at once to take Charles's servants to Spain. Courtiers were eager to go, and the King wrote plaintively that 'every man runs upon me for his friends so as I am torn in pieces amongst them'. He sent Charles and Buckingham their robes and insignia of the Garter, 'which ye must not forget to wear on St. George's Day and dine together in them, for it will be a goodly sight for the Spaniards to see my boys dine in them'. He also sent jewels which he selected with great care and described at length with loving and garrulous fondness. Other preparations were begun. Eight great ships and two pinnaces were to sail a little later to bring home Charles and his bride, for whom a magnificent cabin was provided, fit to receive a goddess. A wing of St. James's was enlarged for the Infanta's apartments, an oratory built, and the whole palace refurnished. All of this was very expensive. 'God knows how my coffers are already drained', sighed the poor King. 'In earnest, my Baby, ye must be as sparing as ye can in your spending there.' James could not be certain when the fleet would sail, and he begged to know as soon as possible, 'for the charge and trouble will be infinite if their equipage stay long aboard, consuming victuals and making the ships to stink'.

Meanwhile he had fallen ill. 'Your poor old dad is lamer than ever he was, both of his right knee and foot, and writes all this out of his naked bed.'

Unfortunately things went badly in Spain. Charles was accorded a magnificent reception, but the Spaniards were far from happy at his sudden appearance. He was debarred from making the acquaintance of the Infanta. Every device of a rigidly formal court was employed to keep them apart. When at last Charles was accorded an audience, he was told what he must wear and what he must say; and when he disobeyed by speaking to the Infanta of his affection, he was stopped by a frown from the Queen. He never spoke to the Infanta alone. His attempt to do so by leaping over the wall of a garden ended in fiasco. Even after the marriage appeared to be arranged, he was only permitted to see her at court theatricals where she sat impenetrably guarded by members of her family. But Charles had come with romantic notions that he was in love with her, and at the theatre he sat gazing upon her for half an hour at a time. Though he was deeply chagrined at the treatment he received, he did not awake from his delusion until the end of his visit.

The Spanish supposed that some great secret had brought him to Madrid, and they imagined that he had come to embrace Catholicism. He was invited to Catholic ceremonies and to theological discussions setting forth the allurements of the Roman faith. Had he told the Spaniards plainly that his conversion was unthinkable, he would have saved himself much trouble. But he and Buckingham thought it good policy to allow the Spaniards to hope for a conversion. James had no part in this foolish deception. He wrote his son not to be ashamed of his religion; if the English service was not permitted in Philip's palace, the Prince should attend it at the English embassy. 'I am sure', wrote the perplexed father, 'ye would not have me renounce my religion for all the world.' The King sent two chaplains to his son 'with all the stuff and ornaments for the service of God. I have fully instructed them so as all their behaviour and service shall, I hope, prove decent and agreeable to the purity of the primitive Church, and yet as near the Roman form as lawfully can be done'. But the chaplains were not permitted to enter the palace at Madrid. Charles had merely caused misunderstanding and irritation all round.

It was now two years since the Pope had been asked to grant a dispensation permitting the marriage. His decision was expected shortly but had not yet been given; and Olivares told Buckingham that in order to obtain it the King of England should grant full liberty of worship to Roman Catholics. Buckingham replied that that was impossible. Philip and Olivares, therefore, secretly urged the Pope to refuse the dispensation. It was not desired in Madrid, they said, unless the Prince was converted.

The Pope, however, saw no reason to act as the scapegoat of

Spanish policy. His objective was the advancement of Catholicism, and he therefore issued the dispensation but added new and stringent conditions and made Philip responsible for their fulfilment. The Infanta must control the education of her children until they were twelve, her church must be open to the public, and English Catholics instead of taking the oath of allegiance might substitute an oath drawn up by the Pope for the servants of the Infanta. James must not only agree to this gross violation of his sovereignty but must obtain the consent of both Council and Parliament. And Philip must take an oath that all the terms of the treaty would be observed in England as well as in Spain. Such were the terms of this monstrous document.

Buckingham, now thoroughly disillusioned, quarrelled with Olivares, and would gladly have ended the marriage negotiations altogether. But Charles wished to temporize. He had obtained his father's pledge to accept 'whatsoever you our son shall promise in our name', and he seemed to think that he could make promises in Spain and later escape their fulfilment in England. He therefore accepted the articles as amended in Rome. He promised that he, his father, and all the English councillors would swear that the penal laws should be suspended and that every effort would be made to obtain Parliament's approval. Later he went further and gave a pledge that the penal laws would be repealed within three years. And he gave a private engagement that he would never speak a word to his wife prejudicial to her religion yet would gladly listen to arguments from the Catholic side whenever they were offered.

His concessions merely produced new Spanish demands. A junta of theologians had been appointed to determine what security Philip must have before he took the oath required by Rome. The junta declared that James must issue a proclamation suspending the penal laws, and that King, Prince and councillors must swear that they would never be reimposed. The consent of Parliament must be obtained. And finally, until these things were done, the Infanta must remain in Spain for at least a year after the marriage. When this heart-breaking decision was known, Buckingham lost his temper completely, and stormed at Olivares in unmeasured terms. Charles was angry, silent, sullen and undecided. Yet he agreed that the new Spanish proposals should be placed before his father.

These negotiations imposed delay, dispatches to England grew infrequent, and the King grew alarmed. 'I begin now to long sore to hear more news from you,' he wrote, 'for this is the eleventh day since your last packet came to my hands.' Yet he was cheerful enough to write that Buckingham's bay Spanish mare 'hath an exceeding fair and fine horse-foal. God send my sweet Baby the like luck with his Spanish breed before this time twelve month'.

Early in May the King began to hear of the conditions with which the dispensation was clogged. He concealed his anxiety in the deepest secrecy. The packets from Spain were brought directly to him, he opened and read them alone and wrote the replies with his own hand. He confided in no one. We catch a glimpse of him reproving Hamilton who, peering eagerly over his shoulder, offered to decipher a difficult word. Valaresso noted that the King was melancholy, upset by trifles, incapable alike of consolation and counsel. He said to one of his intimates that he was desperate and damned. 'It is most probable', wrote the ambassador, 'that the King would not survive any calamitous event.'

After four weeks of complete silence from Spain in May and June, during which the King became more and more agitated, Cottington arrived in England, and James knew that things in Spain were very bad indeed.

He was quite crushed. Spain's new and exorbitant demands, the year's delay in sending the Infanta, and the horrible fear that his son was a prisoner were altogether shattering. His imagination conjured up terrible visions. 'My sweet boys,' he wrote, 'your letter by Cottington hath stricken me dead; I fear it shall much shorten my days, and I am the more perplexed that I know not how to satisfy the people's expectation here. The fleet that stayed for a wind this fortnight must now be stayed, and I know not what reason I shall pretend for the doing of it. But as for my advice and directions that ye crave, in case they will not alter their decree, it is, in a word, to come speedily away, and if ye can get leave, give over all treaty. And this I speak without respect of any security they can offer you, except ye never look to see your old dad again, whom I fear ye shall never see if you see him not before winter. Alas, I now repent me sore that ever I suffered you to go away. I care for match, nor nothing, so I may once have you in my arms again. God grant it, God grant it, God grant it, amen, amen,

amen! I protest ye shall be as heartily welcome as if ye had done all things ye went for; and God bless you both, my only sweet son, and my only best sweet servant, and let me hear from you quickly, with all speed, as ye love my life; and so God send you a happy and joyful meeting in the arms of your dear dad.' Thus the King's one thought was the return of his son and favourite. He told them that he would accept the demands of Spain. Charles might then marry the Infanta and return to England, leaving her to follow. If she never came, the English Church could quickly make him a free man.

The King announced that the negotiations were progressing favourably, but few were deceived. Valaresso wrote that the King could hardly conceal his agitation and that he spent some nights in unbroken fury. In the privacy of his chamber he wept and asked his intimates sadly whether they thought he would ever see the Prince again. When Holderness, presuming upon long service, reproved him for allowing himself to be duped by Spain, the King turned away in dull despair and asked to be let alone.

When James's offer of capitulation arrived in Spain, Charles and Buckingham attempted to obtain better terms. But the Spanish were adamant. Charles first declared he would return to England; then in an audience on July 7th, which Philip sincerely hoped would be their last, he suddenly accepted the Spanish terms. The treaty was signed on July 25th. Charles signed it without a definite agreement about the dowry, about the Palatinate, or about the exact time of the marriage. He spoke as though he would marry the Infanta and remain in Spain during the winter. If he had done so and if the Infanta had become pregnant, her departure might have been postponed indefinitely. Charles's folly was truly incredible.

Meanwhile the King received the text of the amended articles and of the required oaths. They made sad reading. He was indignant to think that his oath should have to be fortified by that of his Council. In the promise never to reimpose the penal laws he foresaw a perpetual immunity that would cause the Catholics to increase and grow insolent until his sovereignty was in danger. In the pledge to obtain parliamentary repeal of the anti-Catholic laws he saw an utter impossibility. Then he reflected helplessly that he was not a free agent, for the Spanish held hostages that were dearer to him than all the world. Terrified, he sought an excuse to yield; and this was supplied by the subtle Williams who told him that he could take the oaths with a good conscience since they did not require an alteration of religion but merely a toleration of English Catholics. The Prince, said Williams, was a good Protestant who would not prejudice his religion, to which the King assented with tears. He then summoned his Council. He wept as he admitted that the Spanish were doing him grievous wrong. But if their terms were not accepted and if councillors refused the oaths, the Prince would remain a prisoner. He asked the councillors to speak freely yet all but commanded them to yield; he silenced Abbot who raised objections, and declared that he himself was satisfied in conscience. His authority carried the day. The oaths were taken on July 20th. This King, wrote Valaresso, had a peculiar genius for doing himself harm, and the Council had lost its last opportunity to speak its mind.

Having taken the oaths, the King felt relief. All the devils in hell and all the Puritans in England, he said, could not now stop the match. 'Since it can be no better,' he wrote his sweet boys, 'I must be content.' His longing to see them was ever present in his mind. 'If you hasten not home, I apprehend I shall never see you, for my extreme longing will kill me; but God bless you both, my sweet boys, upon this good day [August 5th]; and He that delivered me from so great danger upon it, preserve you, and grant you a speedy, happy and comfortable return in the arms of your dear dad. Amen! Amen! Amen!'

Nothing now appeared to stand in the way of the marriage. And yet it never took place. For Charles was at last awakening from his delusion. Love began to wane and resentment against the Spanish began to dominate his thoughts. His position was most unpleasant. Buckingham was furious at the treatment he had received; the little group of English courtiers in Madrid was violently anti-Spanish; there were some awkward clashes between the two courts. Charles was told that if he remained in Madrid over the winter he would have to dismiss his Protestant servants. He also made the belated discovery that Spanish aid in the Palatinate was highly doubtful. And as he gazed upon the Infanta at the theatre he may have reflected that perhaps she was not as beautiful as he had at first imagined. Yet in his weak and purposeless way he might have lingered on indefinitely. But when in September he once more threatened to leave, the Spanish took him at his word and fairly hustled him out of Madrid half against his will. He left a proxy for his marriage, but secretly instructed Digby that it was not to be used until further instructions came from England.

Charles and Buckingham landed at Portsmouth on October 5th and hastened to the King at Royston. James had the gout. Forgetting all about it, he clambered down the steps to receive the returned travellers. 'They met on the stairs where the Prince and Duke being on their knees the King fell on their necks and they all wept.' James led them into a private room where the happy ecstasy of meeting could be decently hidden from the world. Charles and Buckingham poured forth their adventures and impressions in a breath. 'They that attended at the door sometimes heard a still voice and then a loud; sometimes they laughed and sometimes they chafed.' At length they came joyfully forth to supper. The ladies of the Villiers family were summoned in all haste. England was mad with joy; and an anthem was sung at St. Paul's from the 114th Psalm: 'When Israel came out of Egypt, and the house of Jacob from amongst the barbarous people.'[7]

The King's happiness continued for some days. 'The Prince and my lord of Buckingham', wrote Conway, 'spend most of their hours with his Majesty, with the same freedom, liberty and kindness as they were wont.' Embraces and familiarities continued between them, and 'welcome home' was the sole business for several weeks.

But James's delight was shortly over-clouded by new and startling developments. Buckingham was now as violently opposed to the Spanish match as he had formerly been in favour of it; he bombarded the King with abuse of all things Spanish, urging that the marriage treaty be denounced and that war be made on Spain. Charles was at first silent but soon joined forces with the favourite. Determined to have their way, they were ready to force their policy upon the King, to ruin councillors who opposed them, and to seek support from the popular party in Parliament.

James was horrified. Despite all that had passed, he clung to Spain as an ally and to diplomacy as the sole means of dealing with foreign States. The thought of war appalled him; and when he saw the Prince and Buckingham attacking pro-Spanish Ministers and allying with the popular lords in Parliament, he told them plainly that they were fools. But his mind was so muddled and his will so sadly impaired that he could not resist the vigorous handling which they were ready to employ. They had lost all sympathy with his tremulous hesitations and they showed small respect for his person. They spoke to him with unbecoming sharpness, silenced or ignored his objections, and hustled him into policies which he regarded with abhorrence. He was so frequently ill and so constantly away from London that they were able to assume the management of business. 'The Prince', wrote a courtier, 'is now entering into command of affairs by reason of the King's absence and sickness, and all men address themselves unto him.' James was half-excluded from government not only by ill health but by the deliberate policy of Charles and Buckingham. They kept him in a state of siege, debarring from his presence persons who sympathized with Spain; for, as the Venetian ambassador remarked, the King was as desirous of being deceived by the Spaniards as they were of deceiving him. Buckingham stayed with him at Newmarket like a sentinel, while Charles watched matters in London; the ladies of the Villiers family were pressed into service when Buckingham was away; and the King was almost a semi-prisoner in his own country houses.

He was well aware that the sceptre was being wrested from his grasp. His maudlin love for his son and favourite continued, and he oscillated between suspicion and forgiveness; but affection was mingled with jealousy and resentment. He had a sickening sense of being deserted by those he loved. Whining, suspicious, helpless and unhappy, he lamented that he was a poor old man who had once known how to rule but who now had lost his skill. On one occasion he told the Prince, perhaps to sound him, that he would leave the government entirely in his hands, while he, the King, would devote his energies merely to living on. He occupied himself with inconsequential matters, such as the importation of some Spanish asses from the Netherlands, 'making great estimation of those asses, since he finds himself so well served with the mules to his litter'.

'The King', wrote the Venetian ambassador, 'seems practically lost; he comes to various decisions and inclines to his usual negotiations; he does not care to fall in with the wishes of his son-in-law and the favourite. He now protests, now weeps, but finally gives in.' Tillières wrote more vividly: 'the King descends deeper and deeper into folly every day, sometimes swearing and calling upon God, heaven and the angels, at other times weeping, then laughing, and finally pretending illness in order to play upon the pity of those who urge him to generous actions and to show them that sickness renders him incapable of deciding anything, demanding only repose and, indeed, the tomb'.[8]

The first step of Charles and Buckingham was to urge that the marriage by proxy should be postponed until there was an understanding with Spain regarding the restitution of the Palatinate. Such a stipulation should have been made much earlier. To make it now was to dynamite the delicate settlement arranged by the Prince in Spain. The King perhaps did not realize what he was doing. It was easy for him to declare that he would not marry his son with a portion of his daughter's tears. He had pressed Spain on this point before and he was merely doing so again. But his demand for 'a punctual answer' from the Spanish was more of an ultimatum than he realized. Preparations in Spain for the marriage by proxy came to an end, and though negotiations continued, the marriage was given a shattering blow.

The Prince and Buckingham then pressed for a meeting of Parliament, which was certain to be violently anti-Spanish. The King's objections were overcome, opposition in the Council was silenced, and Parliament met in February 1624.

James's actions during his last Parliament were a series of contradictions, of feeble attempts to assert his authority, and of capitulations when he was placed under pressure. His opening speech, though highly praised by Hacket,[9] was weak and aimless. It began with a long passage of self-justification. He had always attempted to rule well and he deserved the love of his people. Now he had come to ask Parliament's advice. How should the Spanish treaties be handled so as to advance religion and the common good and to restore the Palatinate to his children? There were rumours that in recent negotiations he had sacrificed religion to expediency. 'But, as God shall judge me, I never thought or meant it, nor ever in a word expressed anything that savoured of it.' These words were sheer hypocrisy. He ended by saying that he thirsted for the success of the Parliament as a wanderer in a burning desert might thirst for water.

Thus invited, the Lords and Commons at once debated the Spanish treaties. They sent a petition to the King begging that the treaties be ended, and they presented him with an address promising assistance if war broke out with Spain. What else could James have expected? Yet he was greatly angered, declared that Parliament was meddling with matters beyond its comprehension, and sent some sharp rejoinders. The Prince and Buckingham, however, boldly explained away the King's words, entirely altering their meaning. No clearer proof was possible that James's reign was over. He understood the situation fully. Cursing and swearing, he had himself driven to Theobalds and would listen to neither Prince nor Parliament.

During the course of the session he made a number of attempts to assert his authority. He recalled a dispatch on its way to Spain to announce the ending of the marriage treaty. He sent secret instructions to the councillors in the House of Commons. He attempted to save Cranfield whom the Commons were impeaching at the instigation of Charles and Buckingham; and, finding that Buckingham would not abandon the impeachment, he said in great choler: 'By God, Steenie, you are a fool and will shortly repent this folly and will find that in this fit of popularity you are making a rod with which you will be scourged yourself.' Turning to the Prince he told him angrily 'that he would live to have his bellyful of Parliaments'.[10] On the last day of the session he stormed at the Commons and refused assent to a number of bills. He went so far as to say that he would alter the preamble of the subsidy bill since it did not mention the Palatinate. Forgetting decorum, the Commons gave open signs of discontent. But the King's efforts were all failures. The Spanish treaties were dissolved, Cranfield was impeached, the subsidy bill was unaltered, and a good deal of domestic legislation was enacted.[11]

The King was soon to have further proof of his loss of control over his son and his favourite. Through the spring and summer of 1624 Buckingham and the Prince were making warlike preparations and pursuing a warlike diplomacy. They hoped to build a grand alliance against Spain, and they made large commitments though they lacked the money to carry them out. They entertained great hopes of an alliance with France, a policy in which the King supported them, for if he broke with Spain he was eager for the alliance of other Catholic powers. Negotiations were begun for a marriage between Charles and the French Princess Henrietta Maria.

The negotiations, however, encountered difficulties. The French were not ready for an open break with Spain. And a more serious difficulty arose over the treatment to be accorded to English Roman Catholics. The King had promised the House of Commons that no future marriage treaty would include concessions to English Catholics, and though he assured the French that their alliance would incline him favourably towards his Catholic subjects, he believed that the promise to Parliament must be kept. Unfortunately the French, largely from a sense of pride, demanded an agreement no less favourable to English Catholics than had been offered in the treaty with Spain. James therefore concluded that the French marriage was impossible; but Buckingham thought otherwise. In his mind the French alliance was essential and the concessions demanded by France must be granted. He threw all his influence against the King; he made a confidant of the French ambassador, the Marquis of Effiat, as he had formerly made a confidant of Gondomar; he won over the Prince; and James was isolated. For three days in September the King resisted the pressure of his favourite. Then he capitulated. The public treaty with France was innocuous, but in a private letter James accepted the French formula and promised to fulfil it. The pledge to the Commons was thrown to the winds, and the King dared not assemble Parliament in the autumn of 1624.

It was obvious that since the return of Charles and Buckingham from Madrid events had placed a heavy strain upon James's relations with his favourite; but though the King was unhappy and suspicious, his love, rooted in long habit, was stronger than any other emotion. In 1624, while Spanish ambassadors were still in England, they had attempted to poison his mind against the favourite. They told him that Buckingham kept him a prisoner, undermined his authority by alliance with the popular party in Parliament, and was dragging him into war. They further charged that Buckingham planned to marry his little daughter to the son of the Electress Palatine, so that if Charles remained unmarried, the throne might some day be occupied by Buckingham's descendants. The King was quite unnerved. With terror and distress gnawing at his heart, he determined in his nervous way to seek repose at Windsor in the quiet of the country. As his carriage passed St. James's, the Prince and Buckingham came from the palace to speak to him. Upon sight of them the King's emotions

overpowered him and he burst into tears, blubbering that he was
the unhappiest man alive and was deserted by those who were
dearest to him. Yet that very night at Windsor, as the tears
trickled down his cheeks, he wrote his favourite a letter of forgiveness, begging him to come to Windsor quickly and to bring his
family with him. 'The Lord of heaven and earth bless thee,' concluded the King, 'and my sweet daughter, and my sweet little
grandchild, and all thy blessed family, and send thee a happier
turn, both now and thou knowest when, to thy dear dad and
Christian gossip, James R.' One of his last letters to Buckingham,
written in December 1624, ended with these words: 'I pray God
that I may have a joyful and comfortable meeting with you, and
that we may make at this Christenmass a new marriage, ever to be
kept hereafter; for, God so love me, as I desire only to live in this
world for your sake, and that I had rather live banished in any
part of the world with you, than live a sorrowful widow-life without you. And so God bless you, my sweet child and wife, and
grant that ye may ever be a comfort to your dear dad and husband.'[12]

The summer of 1624 was unusually warm and dry and the King
was free from arthritis. But in the autumn he had very severe
attacks, and his hands became so crippled that he could not sign
his name. He came to Whitehall for Christmas but kept his
chamber. Early in 1625 he went to Theobalds, Royston and
Newmarket, and was at Theobalds about the first of March. A
few days later he became ill with a tertian ague, an acute fever
that waxed and waned with convulsions every two or three days.
At first it caused no great alarm; but the King, as always, was a
bad patient. His irregularities, impatience and tantrums augmented his illness. When his fever abated, he refused to obey his
physicians and asked them petulantly where they thought his
ague had gone. Impatient with pain and hot with fever, he held
his hands in cold water and drank great quantities of small beer.
As a result he grew worse and his convulsions became more
alarming. He fell into profound melancholy. The recent death of
his Scottish favourite Hamilton preyed upon his mind and he
remarked sadly: 'I shall never see London again.'

After the King had been ill about a week, Buckingham and his
mother recalled that the favourite during a recent illness had
found relief in the remedies of a certain country practitioner, one

John Remington. His medicines were sent for and administered without the knowledge of the royal physicians. As a result the King grew worse; and his physicians protested violently. One of them, the Scottish John Craig, was dismissed, while another, George Englishman, also a Scot, published at Frankfort in 1626 a Latin tract in which he asserted that Buckingham had given the King a white powder that made him very ill, that the physicians declared he had been poisoned, that Buckingham in fury drove them from the sick-room, offering to draw his sword, and that his mother knelt before James and craved justice against accusations that she and her son had poisoned him. ' "Poisoned me?" said he; and with that, turning himself, swooned.'[13]

On March 24th the King's condition was very serious. He had a terrible convulsion, accompanied by fainting, 'which exercised much violence upon a weak body and struck fear into the hearts of his servants'. He called for Andrewes, but Andrewes was ill, and his place was taken by Williams and Abbot. Williams at first encouraged the King by cheerful conversation, but James did not respond; and Williams, perceiving the truth, knelt beside the bed of his master and told him that the end was near. The King asked to partake of the Communion. He repeated the Creed, declared himself in love and charity with his neighbours, and received the Sacrament 'with that zeal and devotion as if he had not been a frail man but a cherubim clothed with flesh and blood'. He called the Prince and attempted to speak, 'but nature being exhausted he had no strength to express his intention'.

Thereafter he sank rapidly. Williams prayed with him and read him short devotional phrases which the King attempted to repeat. 'But his soul began to retreat more inward and so by degrees he took less notice of external things.' On the morning of Sunday, March 27th, a little before noon, 'his lords and servants kneeling on one side, his archbishops, bishops and other of his chaplains on the other side of his bed, without pangs or convulsions at all, Solomon slept'.

Such was the pious picture left by the King's divines; and there is no doubt that James made a devout and godly end. But in fact his death was a horrible one. A day or so before he died he appears to have suffered a stroke which loosened the muscles of his face and caused his jaw to drop. This, with his swollen tongue and with great quantities of phlegm, almost killed him through suffocation. In the end a terrible dysentery carried him away and he died in filth and misery.

His obsequies were prolonged, ceremonious and extremely expensive. The body was embalmed, placed in a sumptuous coffin, and brought on April 4th in a solemn and stately procession from Theobalds to Denmark House, where it lay in state for a month's time. 'The great funeral was on the 7th of May,' wrote Chamberlain, 'the greatest indeed that ever was known in England. All was performed with great magnificence, but the order was very confused and disorderly. The whole charge is said to have arisen to about £50,000.'[14]

Poets, pamphleteers and clergymen poured forth a flood of lamentations and praise of which the deceased would have highly approved. Britain, that 'James-blessed isle', was darkened and made horrid by the death of 'nature's darling, earth's triumph, God's minion, man's delight'. Some years later Charles employed Rubens to execute a magnificent series of paintings on the ceiling of the banqueting-hall depicting the apotheosis of King James. A circle of paintings portray symbolically the glories of his reign. Royal bounty pours plenty from a cornucopia while avarice is trampled under foot. Bacchus rides a ram and draws a chariot laden with fruit, again expressing plenty. An angel appears riding upon a lion. The angel tickles the lion's ear while another draws his teeth, symbolic of harmony. Government with a bridle treads down rebellion; virtue demolishes envy; chastity destroys lust; Minerva instructs Scotland; peace and wisdom drive rebellion into hell. In a great central painting the King ascends to heaven. He tramples the globe and flies aloft upon the wings of an eagle. Justice, attended by religion, lifts him on high, while zeal, honour and victory place a crown upon his head. James's expression is one of alarm. Apprehensive, as so often in life, he appears unconvinced as to his destination.

NOTES

Books are published in London unless otherwise noted.

CHAPTER I

[1] Robert Pitcairn (ed.), Lord Herries, *Historical Memoirs of the Reign of Mary, Queen of Scots, and of King James the Sixth* (Abbotsford Club, no. 6. Edinburgh, 1836), 79.
[2] Thomas Thomson (ed.), Sir James Melville of Halhill, *Memoirs of his Own Life* (Bannatyne Club, no. 18. Edinburgh, 1827), 134. Thomas Thomson (ed.), *The Historie and Life of King James the Sext* (Bannatyne Club, no. 13. Edinburgh, 1825), 5.
[3] Herries, 78-85. *Historie of King James the Sext*, 3-5. *Cal. St. P. Scottish, 1563-1569*, 290, 322-6. M. Russell and Mark Napier (eds.), John Spottiswoode, *History of the Church of Scotland* (Spottiswoode Soc. Edinburgh, 1847-51. 3 vols.), II, 40-3, 55.
[4] Sir James Melville, *Memoirs* (Bannatyne Club), 261-2. P. Hume Brown, *George Buchanan* (Edinburgh, 1890), 254-60. Sir Alexander Grant, *The Story of the University of Edinburgh* (1884. 2 vols.), I, 171-3. *D.N.B.*, under Buchanan.
[5] George F. Warner, 'The Library of James VI', *Misc. of the Scottish History Soc.* (Edinburgh, 1893), I, ix-lxxv. *Misc. of the Maitland Club* (Edinburgh, 1840), I, 1-23. Allan F. Westcott, *New Poems by James I of England* (N.Y., 1911), xvii-xxiv.
[6] Dedicatory letter in Buchanan, *Rerum Scoticarum Historia* (Edinburgh, 1582). Robert Pitcairn (ed.), *The Autobiography and Diary of Mr. James Melvill* (Wodrow Soc. Edinburgh, 1842), 48. *Cal. St. P. Scottish, 1574-1581*, 13, 243. *Cal. St. P. Spanish, 1587-1603*, 260.
[7] Warner, 'The Library of James VI', *Misc. of the Scottish History Soc.*, I, xxvii-xxix, xx-lxxv. T. F. Henderson, *James I and VI* (Paris, 1904), 8-9.

CHAPTER II

[1] *Cal. St. P. Scottish, 1569-1571*, 670, 678. *Historie of King James the Sext*, 88-93.
[2] Sir James Melville, *Memoirs* (Bannatyne Club), 260. *Misc. of the Scottish History Soc.*, I, lxxiv. *Cal. St. P. Scottish, 1574-1581*, 337.
[3] Spottiswoode, II, 205-29. James Dennistoun (ed.), David Moysie, *Memoirs of the Affairs of Scotland* (Maitland Club, no. 3. Edinburgh, 1830), 2-15. Sir James Melville, *Memoirs* (Bannatyne Club), 262-5. *Correspondence of Robert Bowes* (Surtees Soc., vol. 14. 1842), 6-7, 11. A. Labanoff (ed.), *Lettres, Instructions et Mémoires de Marie Stuart* (Paris, 1844. 7 vols.), V, 52-67.
[4] Moysie, 22-7. Thomas Thomson (ed.), David Calderwood, *History of the Kirk of Scotland* (Wodrow Soc. Edinburgh, 1842-49. 8 vols.), III, 457-9. Bowes, 17. *Cal. St. P. Scottish, 1574-1581*, 370.
[5] Moysie, 25. Bowes, 15-127, *passim*, 142-53. *Cal. St. P. Scottish, 1574-1581*, 312-13, 355-6, 370-4, 388-97, 615-18, 632-3, 641, 675, 693. Calderwood, III, 559.
[6] *Diary of James Melvill* (Wodrow Soc.), 76-77. *Cal. St. P. Scottish, 1574-1581*, 388-95, 431, 611; *1581-1583*, 52, 120, 149. Moysie, 26. John Hacket, *Scrinia Reserata: a Memorial of John Williams* (1693. 2 parts in one vol.), I, 39. Calderwood, III, 468-9, 480, 648-58, 698, 774-5. Bowes, 16-17, 58.
[7] Bowes, 45, 139. James Craigie (ed.), *The Basilikon Doron of King James VI* (Scottish Text Soc. 3rd series, nos. 16, 18. Edinburgh, 1944, 1950. 2 vols.), I, 75. *Diary of James Melvill* (Wodrow Soc.), 119-20.
[8] *Cal. St. P. Scottish, 1581-1583*, 26, 35. *Cal. St. P. Spanish, 1580-1586*, 207-8.
[9] *Basilikon Doron*, I, 65-7, 75-77, 133, 149-51. *Cal. St. P. Scottish, 1581-1583*, 9, 48-9, 63-72, 125, 167, 595. *Cal. St. P. Spanish, 1580-1586*, *passim*. T. G. Law, 'English Jesuits and Scottish Intrigues, 1581-1582', *Edinburgh Review*, 187 : 319-42.
[10] Spottiswoode, II, 282-91. Calderwood, III, 595-643. P. F. Tytler, *History of Scotland* (Edinburgh, 1842. 9 vols.), VIII, 98, 383. *Diary of James Melvill* (Wodrow Soc.), 133.

NOTES

[1] Sir James Melville, *Memoirs* (Bannatyne Club), 283-5. Calderwood, III, 642-9, 674.

[2] Spottiswoode, II, 292. Bowes, 189, 425-31. *Cal. St. P. Scottish, 1581-1583*, 169-70, 246, 451, 477.

[3] Sir James Melville, *Memoirs* (Bannatyne Club), 285-95. *Cal. St. P. Scottish, 1581-1583*, 462, 522-4, 529, 558-68. Calderwood, III, 722; IV, 47. *Cal. Hatfield House MSS.*, III, 49, 51, 61. Spottiswoode, II, 323.

[4] Tytler, VIII, 151. Calderwood, III, 717-18, 762-4; IV, 2, 37-8, 62-5, 122-4, 197-9. Spottiswoode, II, 308-9. *Diary of James Melvill* (Wodrow Soc.), 53, 141-5. *Cal. St. P. Scottish, 1584-1585*, 33, 163, 171, 176. W. L. Mathieson, *Politics and Religion in Scotland, 1550-1695* (Glasgow, 1902. 2 vols.), I, 230-7. Gordon Donaldson, 'The Relations between the English and Scottish Presbyterian Movements to 1604', unpublished thesis, Univ. of London. Thomas Thomson (ed.), *Letters and Papers of Patrick, Master of Gray* (Bannatyne Club, no. 48. 1835), 15-16.

[5] Conyers Read, *Mr. Secretary Walsingham and the Policy of Queen Elizabeth* (Cambridge, Mass., 1925. 3 vols.), II, 202-25. *Cal. St. P. Spanish, 1580-1586*, 502-3, 517-19. *Cal. St. P. Scottish, 1581-1583*, 669-70.

[6] *Cal. Hatfield House MSS.*, III, 46-62, 117-20, 206-7.

[7] Labanoff, *Lettres de Marie Stuart*, VI, 16-32, 70-3, 85, 122-7. *Cal. St. P. Scottish, 1584-1585*, 405-6, 483-5. *Letters of Gray* (Bannatyne Club), 30-7.

[8] *Letters of Gray* (Bannatyne Club), 5-7, 54, 58-61. *Cal. St. P. Scottish, 1584-1585*, 121, 184, 204, 263, 652-82; *1585-1586*, 2-120, *passim*. T. F. Henderson, *James I and VI*, 80-1. Spottiswoode, II, 330-4. Sir James Melville, *Memoirs* (Bannatyne Club), 350-2. Calderwood, IV, 389-93.

[1] *The Historie of Judith in forme of a Poem: Penned in French by the noble poet, G. Sallust, Lord of Bartas: Englished by Tho. Hudson* (Edinburgh, 1584).

[2] Allan F. Westcott (ed.), *New Poems by James I of England* (N.Y., 1911). R. S. Rait (ed.), *Lusus Regius, being Poems and Other Pieces by King James I* (Westminster, 1901). A new edition is promised by the Scottish Text Soc.

[3] Calderwood, III, 784-5.

[4] Lily B. Campbell, 'The Christian Muse', *Huntington Library Bulletin*, 8 : 38-54.

[5] *Ibid.*, 8 : 48-55, from which the quotation is taken.

[1] *Cal. St. P. Scottish, 1585-1586*, 156-7, 172, 179, 188, 216, 225-6. D. Laing (ed.), *Original Letters of Mr. John Colville* (Bannatyne Club, no. 104. Edinburgh, 1858), 316-19. *Diary of James Melvill* (Wodrow Soc.), 228-49. Calderwood, IV, 448-94, 583-4.

[2] Read, *Walsingham*, II, 254. *Cal. St. P. Scottish, 1585-1586*, 151-415, *passim*. John Bruce (ed.), *Letters of Queen Elizabeth and King James VI* (Camden Soc. 1849), 20-34.

[3] Colville, 313-17. Randolph wrote that 'the King's judgment is equal to that of any councillor he has'. *Cal. St. P. Scottish, 1585-1586*, 157, 239, 340.

[4] Robert Bell (ed.), *Despatches of M. Courcelles, French Ambassador at the Court of Scotland* (Bannatyne Club, no. 22. Edinburgh, 1828), 4-10. Robert S. Rait and Annie I. Cameron, *King James's Secret: Negotiations between Elizabeth and James VI Relating to the Execution of Mary Queen of Scots* (1927). My account of Mary's death depends on this work, where references will be found.

[5] Rait and Cameron, 190-1, 205. Moysie, 60.

[6] *Despatches of M. Courcelles*, 29. *Letters of Elizabeth and James VI* (Camden Soc.), 46. Read, *Walsingham*, III, 186-93. Rait and Cameron, 200-2. *Cal. Border Papers*, I, 282. *Cal. St. P. Spanish, 1587-1603*, 215. *Letters of Gray* (Bannatyne Club), 149. Spottiswoode, II, 373. Helen G. Stafford, *James VI of Scotland and the Throne of England* (N.Y., 1940), 18.

NOTES

[7] Spottiswoode, II, 387. J. D. Mackie, 'Scotland and the Spanish Armada', *S.H.R.*, 12 : 1-23. J. D. Mackie, 'The Will of Mary Stuart', *Ibid.*, 11 : 338-44.

[8] *A Fruitful Meditation, Containing a Plaine and Easie Exposition, or Laying Open of the 7. 8. 9. and 10. Verses of the 20 Chapter of the Revelation, in Form and Maner of a Sermon.* Republished in 1603 in Robert Abbot's *Antichristi Demonstratio*, as a royal compliment to Abbot.

[9] *Cal. St. P. Scottish, 1586-1588*, 491. *Cal. St. P. Spanish, 1587-1603*, 260.

[10] *Letters of Elizabeth and James VI* (Camden Soc.), 47-55. Stafford, 24-5.

[11] *S.H.R.*, 12 : 21-22.

CHAPTER VI

[1] *Cal. St. P. Scottish, 1586-1588*, 655; *1589-1593*, 122. J. T. Gibson Craig (ed.), *Papers Relative to the Marriage of King James the Sixth* (Bannatyne Club, no. 26. Edinburgh, 1828), 4, 12-13. Sir James Melville, *Memoirs* (Bannatyne Club), 365.

[2] Annie I. Cameron and R. S. Rait (eds.), *The Warrender Papers* (Scottish Hist. Soc. 3rd series. Vols. 18, 19. Edinburgh, 1931-32), II, introduction and pp. 68-108. Helen G. Stafford, *James VI of Scotland and the Throne of England*, 50-55.

[3] *Cal. St. P. Scottish, 1589-1593*, 19, 73-137, 154-66. *Warrender Papers*, II, 34-46, 105n, 109-10. Henry Ellis (ed.), *Original Letters Illustrative of English History* (1825. 1st series. 3 vols.), III, 28-9.

[4] Westcott, *New Poems by James I*, 1-10, 22-4.

[5] *Reg. P. C. Scotland, 1585-1592*, xlvi-l, 423-31.

[6] P. A. Munch, 'Samtidig Beretning om Prindseese Annas, Christian den 4des Systers, Giftermaal med Kong Jacob d. 6te af Skotland og hendes paafölgende Kroning', *Norske Samlinger, udgivne af et Historisk Samfund* (Christiania, 1852), I, 450-512. A brief summary is found in *Scottish Rev.*, 21 : 142-61. *Cal. St. P. Scottish, 1589-1593*, 180-8. Calderwood, V, 67. Moysie, 81.

[7] Calderwood, V, 69, 82, 94-9. *Papers Relative to the Marriage of King James the Sixth. Cal. St. P. Scottish, 1589-1593*, 293-6, 305.

[8] Calderwood, V, 409, 459.

CHAPTER VII

[1] *Historie of King James the Sext*, 180, 299. Calderwood, IV, 613-14. *Cal. St. P. Scottish, 1589-1593*, 11, 523. *Basilikon Doron*, I, 83-9.

[2] Helen G. Stafford, *James VI of Scotland and the Throne of England*, 124-31. *Cal. St. P. Scottish, 1589-1593*, 257, 281-308, 315, 325, 330, 456-7.

[3] *Cal. St. P. Scottish, 1586-1588*, 699-702; *1589-1593*, 2-12, 17; *1593-1595*, 91, 165. Tytler, IX, 252-3.

[4] *Cal. Border Papers*, I, 481-4. *Cal. St. P. Scottish, 1586-1588*, 655. Calderwood, III, 759.

[5] Calderwood, V, 7-37, 54-9. *Cal. St. P. Scottish, 1586-1588*, 677, 699-709; *1589-1593*, 4-54, 83-4. *Warrender Papers*, II, 103. *Letters of Gray* (Bannatyne Club), 151-4. Stafford, 41-8.

[6] *Cal. St. P. Scottish, 1589-1593*, 294-5, 307, 311, 359, 420, 453, 522-5. *News from Scotland, declaring the Damnable Life and Death of Doctor Fian, a notable Sorcerer* (Edinburgh, 1591). M. A. Murray, 'The "Devil" of North Berwick', *S.H.R.*, 15 : 310-21. This article does not prove that Bothwell was the Devil of North Berwick but advances evidence suggesting the possibility. *Daemonologie* (Edinburgh, 1597).

[7] *Cal. St. P. Scottish, 1589-1593*, 504-18, 531-50, 573-5, 609-48. *Warrender Papers*, II, 121-3, 154-64, 203. Calderwood, V, 140-9. *Historie of King James the Sext*, 246.

[8] Calderwood, V, 100-6, 132-66. *Diary of James Melvill* (Wodrow Soc.), 281. *Letters of Elizabeth and James VI* (Camden Soc.), 63-4. Gordon Donaldson, 'The Attitude of Whitgift and Bancroft to the Scottish Church', *Royal Hist. Soc. Trans.*, 4th series, 24 : 95-115. W. L. Mathieson, *Politics and Religion*, I, 250-1.

[9] *Cal. St. P. Scottish, 1589-1593*, 707-29, 750-4. Spottiswoode, II, 421-2. Calderwood, V, 171.

[10] Calderwood, V, 215-17, 231, 251. Stafford, 87-9, 118-23. T. G. Law, 'The

NOTES

Spanish Blanks and the Catholic Earls', *Scottish Rev.*, 22 : 1-32. *Cal. St. P. Scottish, 1593-1595*, 66, 127.

[11] Calderwood, V, 250-99. *Cal. St. P. Scottish, 1593-1595*, 24-5, 130-80, 222, 236, 304-306. *Warrender Papers*, II, 191. Stafford, 81. *Diary of James Melvill* (Wodrow Soc.), 312-13. *Letters of Elizabeth and James VI* (Camden Soc.), 98-100.

CHAPTER VIII

[1] Tytler, IX, 130, 138-41. Moysie, 113. *Cal. St. P. Scottish, 1593-1595*, 386-424 615-82; *1595-1597*, 46-8, 88.

[2] *Cal. St. P. Scottish, 1595-1597*, 3-251, *passim. Basilikon Doron*, I, 70-1, 117. *Reg. P. C. Scotland, 1592-1599*, xxxvii-lii, lxxvi-cxii, 245-57. D. L. Tough, *The Last Years of a Frontier* (Oxford, 1928), 264-77. R. S. Brydon, 'The Finances of James VI, 1567-1603', unpublished thesis, University of Edinburgh.

[3] W. W. Seton, 'The Early Years of Henry Frederick, Prince of Wales, and Charles, Duke of Albany', *S.H.R.*, 13 : 366-79. A third son, Robert, was born in January 1602, but died in May. Two other daughters were born in England but also died in infancy.

[4] 'Take heed therefore, my son, to such Puritans, very pests in the church and commonweal, whom no deserts can oblige, neither oaths nor promises bind; breathing nothing but sedition and calumnies, aspiring without measure, railing without reason, and making their own imaginations the square of their conscience. I protest before the great God that ye shall never find with any Highland or Border thieves greater ingratitude and more lies and vile perjuries than with these fanatic spirits. And suffer not the principals of them to brook your land if ye like to sit at rest, except ye would keep them for trying your patience, as Socrates did an evil wife.'

[5] Calderwood, V, 394-625. *Cal. St. P. Scottish, 1593-1595*, 679; *1595-1597*, 174-80, 352-82. W. L. Mathieson, *Politics and Religion*, I, 254-83. *Diary of James Melvill* (Wodrow Soc.), 368-71, 403-43.

[6] St. P. Scottish, 52/66 : 64, quoted in L. A. Barbé, *The Tragedy of Gowrie House* (Paisley, 1887), 124-5. It is not impossible that the King retired with the Master for an immoral purpose. This is pure guess-work for which there is no proof.

[7] Their younger brothers, William and Patrick, were smuggled into England. Upon his accession to the English throne James at once issued a proclamation against them. William escaped to the Continent, but Patrick was imprisoned in the Tower where he remained for nineteen years without trial.

[8] Tytler, IX, 281-2. Calderwood, VI, 28-99. *Diary of James Melvill* (Wodrow Soc.), 489. Nicolson to Cecil, August 14th, 21st, 1600, Register House Trans. Barbé, 118-25.

[9] The recent edition by James Craigie in the *Scottish Text Society* (3d series, nos. 16, 18), to which I owe much information, is elaborate and definitive.

[10] I follow the edition of 1603. The edition of 1599 opens with two sonnets.

[11] James wrote the work in Scots, but both the edition of 1599 and that of 1603 are in English with many Scots words eliminated.

[12] *Basilikon Doron*, II, 39-62. *Huntington Library Quarterly*, 4 : 40.

[13] L. Pearsall Smith, *Life and Letters of Sir Henry Wotton* (Oxford, 1907. 2 vols.), I, 314-15.

CHAPTER IX

[1] Helen G. Stafford, *James VI of Scotland and the Throne of England*, 26-40, 193-5. To this excellent book I am much indebted, as the notes to this chapter will make clear. John Bruce (ed.), *Correspondence of King James VI of Scotland with Sir Robert Cecil and Others in England* (Camden Soc., 1861), 31-2, 55. *Statutes of the Realm*, IV, 704-5. *Basilikon Doron*, II, 208. F. L. Carpenter, *A Reference Guide to Edmund Spenser* (Chicago, 1923), 41-7. *Cal. St. P. Scottish, 1595-1597*, 354-60. Nicolson to Cecil, July 8th, 1598. Register House Trans.

[2] Parsons wrote under the name of R. Doleman, *A Conference about the Next Succession to the Crown of England. Cal. St. P. Scottish, 1595-1597*, 93, 100, 126, 140, 148.

[3] *Cal. St. P. Scottish, 1593-1595*, 430-31; *1595-1597*, 79-86, 120, 134. Roger Aston to Cecil, May 22nd, June 12th, Nicolson to Cecil, July 1st, 1598, September 22nd,

NOTES

November 21st, 1599, January 12th, 1600. Register House Trans. Tytler, IX, 247.
Colville, 204. *E.H.R.*, 51 : 300-1. Spottiswoode, III, 80.

[4] Stafford, 131-9, 158. *Warrender Papers*, II, 286-8, 358-80.

[5] J. D. Mackie, 'The Secret Diplomacy of King James VI in Italy prior to his Accession to the English Throne', *S.H.R.*, 21 : 267-82. T. G. Law, 'Documents Illustrating Catholic Policy in the Reign of James VI', *Misc. of the Scottish Hist. Soc.*, I, 1-70. Stafford, 139-52, 225-43. J. R. Elder, *Spanish Influences in Scottish History* (Glasgow, 1920), Appendix. *Correspondence of James VI with Sir Robert Cecil* (Camden Soc.), 39-40. J. D. Mackie, 'A Secret Agent of James VI', *S.H.R.*, 9 : 376-86.

[6] Nicolson to Cecil, October 3rd, 1598. Register House Trans. *Cal. Hatfield House MSS.*, XV, 301. A. O. Meyer, 'Clemens VIII. und Jakob I. von England', *Quellen und Forschungen aus italienischen Archiven und Bibliotheken*, VII (1904), 273-82, 301-6. *S.H.R.*, 2 : 249-52; 21 : 270-77. Calderwood, V, 740-4. *E.H.R.*, 20 : 124-7.

[7] *S.H.R.*, 21 : 277-8. *Cal. St. P. Venetian, 1603-1607*, 47. J. D. Mackie, *Negotiations between King James VI and I and Ferdinand I, Grand Duke of Tuscany* (Oxford, 1927). In 1601 Ferdinand, thinking he had discovered a Spanish plot to assassinate the King, dispatched Sir Henry Wotton to Scotland with a warning and with antidotes for poison. Wotton came disguised as an Italian under the name of Octavio Baldi, remained in Scotland for some time, and greatly pleased the King by his interest in letters. Later in England James 'took him in his arms and bade him welcome by the name of Octavio Baldi, saying he was the most honest and therefore the best dissembler that ever he met with'. L. P. Smith, *Sir Henry Wotton*, I, 40-5.

[8] Thomas Birch (ed.), *Memoirs of the Reign of Queen Elizabeth* (1754. 2 vols.), II, 506-7.

[9] *Correspondence of James VI with Sir Robert Cecil* (Camden Soc.), 53-76. M. A. Tierney (ed.), C. Dodd, *The Church History of England from . . . 1500 to . . . 1688* (1839-43. 5 vols.), IV, Appendix 1. W. Forbes-Leith, *Narratives of Scottish Catholics under Mary Stuart and James VI* (Edinburgh, 1885), 270.

[10] Stafford, 287. Calderwood, VI, 220-1. Gordon Donaldson, 'The Relations between the English and Scottish Presbyterian Movements to 1604', unpublished thesis, University of London.

[11] Birch, I, 176, 183. J. D. Mackie, *Negotiations between James VI and Ferdinand I*, ix-xi. Nicolson to Cecil, December 15th, Aston to Cecil, December 16th, 1599. Register House Trans. Nicolson to Cecil, June 29th, July 9th, 1600, St. P. Scottish, 52/66 : 37, 41. Colville, 297-8. James Spedding, *The Letters and Life of Francis Bacon* (1861-74. 7 vols.), II, 330-59. *Correspondence of James VI with Sir Robert Cecil* (Camden Soc.), 81-109. Stafford, 214-24.

[12] Nicolson to Cecil, February 15th, March 5th, 8th, 14th, 1601, St. P. Scottish, 52/67 : 17, 25, 27, 28. Birch, II, 510-13.

[13] *Correspondence of James VI with Sir Robert Cecil* (Camden Soc.), xlvi-xlvii, 1-24, 36, 45-76. Sir David Dalrymple, Lord Hailes (ed.), *The Secret Correspondence of Sir Robert Cecil with James VI* (Edinburgh, 1766); re-edited by Edmund Goldsmid in *Collectanea Adamantaea*, XIX (Edinburgh, 1887. 3 vols. in one), I, 16-47; II, 5-7, 19, 27-41; III, 5-22, 39, 51, 60. *Letters of Elizabeth and James VI* (Camden Soc.), 140-8. Stafford, 254-88. *Cal. St. P. Domestic, 1603-1610*, 1.

CHAPTER X

[1] *Cal. Hatfield House MSS.*, XV, 9-10, 138. Spottiswoode, III, 133-9. Calderwood, VI, 206-16. *Basilikon Doron*, I, 97. *Letters to King James the Sixth from the Queen, Prince Henry, Prince Charles* . . . (Maitland Club, no. 35. Edinburgh, 1835), xxviii-xxxiii.

[2] N. E. McClure (ed.), *The Letters of John Chamberlain* (Philadelphia, 1939. 2 vols.), I, 189. Spedding, III, 74. H. S. Scott (ed.), *The Journal of Sir Roger Wilbraham* (Camden Misc., X. 1902), 54-60.

[3] C. H. Firth (ed.), *Stuart Tracts* (Westminster, 1903), 11-82. Ellis, *Original Letters*, 1st series, III, 64-71. J. O. Halliwell (ed.), *Letters of the Kings of England* (1846. 2 vols.), II, 103-4. *Cal. Hatfield House MSS.*, XV, 30-58.

[4] John Nichols, *The Progresses . . . of King James the First* (1828. 4 vols.), I, 188, 272-3. V. Sackville-West (ed.), *The Diary of Lady Anne Clifford* (1923), 4-9. R. S. Rait, *Five Stuart Princesses* (N.Y., 1908), 53-4, 162-4.

NOTES

[5] See tracts by Thomas Dekker, Henry Petowe, Stephen Harrison and John Fenton. The first two are printed in Nichols, *Progresses*, though the editing is very bad.

[6] Ellis, *Original Letters* (1827. 2nd series. 4 vols.), III, 201. Arthur Wilson, *The History of Great Britain, being the Life and Reign of King James the First* (1653), 12-13. Francis Bamford (ed.), *A Royalist's Notebook. The Commonplace Book of Sir John Oglander, Kt., of Nunwell* (1936), 196-7.

[7] Spedding, III, 77. *Journal of Sir Roger Wilbraham*, 54, 60. *Cal. Hatfield House MSS.*, XV, 11, 31. John Fenton, *King James His Welcome to London* (1603). *Basilikon Doron*, II, 18. W. P. Baildon (ed.), John Hawarde, *Les Reportes del Cases in Camera Stellata* (1894), 179-80. S. R. Gardiner, *History of England* (1883-84. 10 vols.), I, 87. Arthur Wilson, 289-90. *Cal. St. P. Venetian, 1603-1607*, 8-9, 39, 510-11.

[8] *Sir Thomas Smithes Voiage and Entertainment in Russia* (1605). Roger Coke, *Detection of the Court and State of England* (1719. 3 vols.), I, 78. Thomas Park (ed.), Sir John Harington, *Nugae Antiquae* (1804. 2 vols.), I, 390-7. *Cal. St. P. Venetian, 1603-1607*, 25, 46.

[9] *Letters of John Chamberlain*, I, 192. Henry Petowe, *England's Caesar* (1603). Samuel Rowlands, *Ave Caesar* (1603). Anthony Nixon, *Elizaes Memoriall; King James his Arrivall; and Romes Downefall* (1603).

[10] James Montagu (ed.), *The Workes of the Most High and Mighty Prince, James* . . . (1616). In Nichols, *Progresses*, IV, 976, the King is compared to the Roman Emperors Constantine, Theodosius and Alexius I.

[11] M. A. Tierney (ed.), C. Dodd, *The Church History of England* (1839-43. 5 vols.), IV, 141. *S.H.R.*, 8 : 366-76. *Cal. St. P. Venetian, 1603-1607*, 44; *1623-1625*, 424. *Letters to King James the Sixth* . . . (Maitland Club, no. 35), xlix-l. Sir Anthony Weldon, *The Court and Character of King James* in Sir Walter Scott (ed.), *Secret History of the Court of James the First* (Edinburgh, 1811. 2 vols.), II, 9. Arthur Wilson, 12, 289. Raymond Crawfurd, *The King's Evil* (Oxford, 1911), 82-90.

CHAPTER XI

[1] *Cal. Hatfield House MSS.*, XV, 31, 87-8; XVI, 255, 383, 394-8. *Journal of Sir Roger Wilbraham*, 106. E. Sawyer (ed.), Sir Ralph Winwood, *Memorials of Affairs of State* (1725. 3 vols.), II, 57; III, 235. *A.H.R.*, 36 : 293-4. Sir John Harington, *Nugae Antiquae*, I, 344-6.

[2] *Cal. Hatfield House MSS.*, XVI, 210-20, 364; XVII, Introduction. *Cal. St. P. Venetian, 1603-1607*, 179. Ellis, *Original Letters*, 2nd series, III, 210-14. Nichols, *Progresses*, I, 466-589. E. K. Chambers, *Elizabethan Stage* (Oxford, 1923. 4 vols.), IV, 116-30.

[3] *Cal. St. P. Venetian, 1603-1607*, 70, 81, 90; *1617-1619*, 257-60. *Ambassades de M. de la Boderie en Angleterre depuis les années 1606 jusqu'en 1611* (Paris, 1750. 5 vols.), I, 399. *Commonplace Book of Sir John Oglander*, 196. Halliwell, *Letters*, II, 115. *Basilikon Doron*, I, 189; II, 268. P. P. Laffleur de Kermaingant (ed.), *Mission de Comte de Beaumont* (Paris, 1895. 2 vols.), I, 130. W. B. Rye (ed.), *England as Seen by Foreigners* (1865), 152-4. *Cal. Hatfield House MSS.*, XVII, 286-300. E. Lodge (ed.), *Illustrations of British History* (1838. 3 vols.), III, 137-8. *Letters of John Chamberlain*, I, 212; II, 265. *Diary of Lady Anne Clifford*, 60, 70. Nichols, *Progresses*, I, 577; II, 259. *Cal. St. P. Domestic, 1611-1618*, 189; *1623-1625*, 9, 13, 24, 52-65.

[4] Winwood, II, 57; III, 182. *Cal. Hatfield House MSS.*, XVII, 122, 349. Lake to Salisbury, January 22nd, the King to Salisbury, January 23rd, 1607, Hatfield House MSS. St. P. Domestic, 14 / 68 : 3. David Mathew, *The Jacobean Age* (1938), 19. E. K. Chambers, *Elizabethan Stage*, I, 12-13.

[5] Hacket, *Williams*, I, 227. *Buccleuch MSS., Winwood Papers, H.M.C.*, I, 111-12. Dunbar to Salisbury, August 8th, 1607, Hatfield House MSS. Lodge, III, 19, 108, 110.

[6] In the secret correspondence before 1603 Salisbury had been designated by the number 10, Northampton by 3.

[7] *Cal. Hatfield House MSS.*, XVI, 326-7, 394-8; XVII, 75, 80-1, 120-9, 450-7. St. P. Domestic, 14 / 15 : 105. Ellis, *Original Letters* (1846. 3rd series. 4 vols.), IV, 161-2. *Letters to King James the Sixth* . . . (Maitland Club, no. 35), xlix-l. Lake to Salisbury, December 5th, 6th, 1607, Hatfield House MSS.

[8] *Cal. Hatfield House MSS.*, XVI, 188. *Cal. St. P. Venetian, 1603-1607*, 27, 46, 60. *Diary*

NOTES

of Lady Anne Clifford, 4. Sir Nicholas L'Estrange, 'Merry Passages and Jests', Harl. MSS., 6395, f. 56v.
⁹ Arthur Wilson, 53-4. *Journal of Sir Roger Wilbraham*, 66. Winwood, II, 43-4. Nichols, *Progresses*, II, 52-94. Sir John Harington, *Nugae Antiquae*, I, 348-54. Scott, *Secret History*, II, 386-90. *Diary of Lady Anne Clifford*, 16-17. E. K. Chambers, *Elizabethan Stage*, I, 23.
¹⁰ A. Weldon in Scott, *Secret History*, II, 3. Roger Coke, *Detection of the Court*, I, 70-1. N. Moore, *History of the Study of Medicine in the British Isles* (Oxford, 1908), 98-9.
¹¹ *Journal of Sir Roger Wilbraham*, 56, 60. Archy Armstrong, *A Banquet of Jests* (1889, a reprint of the edition of 1640), 29, 35, 201. Archy was the court fool.
¹² *Salvetti Correspondence*, *Skrine MSS.*, *H.M.C.*, 6-7. Tobie Matthew to Buckingham, 1623, Harl. MSS., 1581, ff. 78-78v. *Cal. Hatfield House MSS.*, XVI, 396-7. F. L. G. von Raumer, *History of the Sixteenth and Seventeenth Centuries* (1835. 2 vols.), II, 196.

CHAPTER XII

¹ Hacket, *Williams*, I, 225. *Letters of John Chamberlain*, II, 152, 286, 299, 309, 362, 424, 451, 464, 470. Spedding, VI, 167. Thomas Fuller, *The Church History of Britain* (1842. 3 vols.), III, 294, 348.
² Isaac Walton, *Life of Richard Hooker* ('World's Classics', 1927), 221-2.
³ *Basilikon Doron*, I, 16-17, 38. *Letters of John Chamberlain*, I, 206. St. P. Domestic, 14/8 : 93.
⁴ Peter Heylyn, *Examen Historicum* (1659), 165-6, cited by G. Davies, *Huntington Library Bulletin*, 5 : 158.
⁵ Calderwood, VI, 222. Roland G. Usher, *The Reconstruction of the English Church* (N.Y., 1910. 2 vols.), I, 292-309, 316. Gardiner, I, 150-1. St. P. Domestic, 14/4 : 33; 14/6 : 21. D. Wilkins (ed.), *Concilia Magnae Britanniae et Hiberniae* (1731. 4 vols.), IV, 371.
⁶ William Barlow, *The Summe and Substance of the Conference . . . at Hampton Court* (1604), reprinted, with other material on the conference, in Edward Cardwell, *History of Conferences* (Oxford, 1840). See also Usher, *Reconstruction*, I, 317-18; II, 331-54.
⁷ Predestination was a battle ground of Puritan and Arminian and hence the King's views are important, but his remarks are puzzling and he appears to be evading the doctrinal dilemma. Perhaps he could not free himself from a Scottish belief in strict predestination and yet saw the difficulties to which that doctrine led. Arthur P. Kautz, 'The Jacobean Episcopate and its Legacy', unpublished thesis, University of Minnesota.
⁸ Sir John Harington, *Nugae Antiquae*, I, 181-2. Ellis, *Original Letters*, 3rd series, IV, 161-2.
⁹ St. P. Domestic, 14/6 : 89; 14/12 : 87. Wilkins, *Concilia Magnae Britanniae*, IV, 369, 406-14. *Bulletin of the Institute of Historical Research*, 19 : 155. Ellis, *Original Letters*, 2nd series, III, 216. *Cal. Hatfield House MSS.*, XVI, 363; XVII, 15, 28-9, 65, 75, 85, 165-6, 200. Gardiner, I, 199. *Letters of John Chamberlain*, I, 201. Winwood, II, 48.
¹⁰ G. Davies, *The Early Stuarts* (Oxford, 1937), 67. J. S. Brewer (ed.), Dr. Godfrey Goodman, *The Court of King James the First* (1839. 2 vols.), I, 328-9, 356. Fuller, *Church History*, III, 289-90. *Journal of Sir Roger Wilbraham*, 69. Nichols, *Progresses*, IV, 593-602. *Letters of John Chamberlain*, II, 299. St. P. Domestic, 14/90 : 95.
¹¹ St. P. Domestic, 14/8 : 41; 14/81 : 46; 14/88 : 136. *Cal. St. P. Venetian, 1603-1607*, 188; *1610-1613*, 183. Fuller, *Church History*, III, 268. Arthur P. Kautz, 'The Jacobean Episcopate and its Legacy', unpublished thesis, University of Minnesota. R. F. Williams (ed.), Thomas Birch, *Court and Times of James I* (1849. 2 vols.), I, 110.
¹² *Basilikon Doron*, I, 37; II, 93. Spottiswoode, III, 98. Wilkins, *Concilia Magnae Britanniae*, IV, 407-8, 432-3. David Daiches, *The King James Version of the English Bible* (Chicago, 1941), 63-72, 155-71.
¹³ *Huntington Library Quarterly*, 8 : 56-7 and references there. *S.H.R.*, 29 : 134. Rev. Charles Rogers, *Memorials of the Earl of Stirling and of the House of Alexander* (Edinburgh, 1877. 2 vols.), I, 53-4, 80-2, 142-4, 167-71. *D.N.B.*, under Sir William Alexander, Earl of Stirling.

NOTES

[1] *Correspondence of James VI with Sir Robert Cecil* (Camden Soc.), 36-7. C. H. McIlwain (ed.), *The Political Works of James I* (Cambridge, Mass., 1918), 122-9, 274-6. Gardiner, I, 115-16, 221. Halliwell, *Letters*, II, 187. *Cal. St. P. Venetian, 1603-1607*, 21-2, 360. Boderie, IV, 387. George Marcelline, *The Triumphs of King James* (1610).

[2] It was placed on the Index probably in January 1606, after Paul V had succeeded Clement VIII. A French translation in 1603 softened a number of references to Catholics. This was done, however, not by the author, but by the translator. *Basilikon Doron*, II, 26-38.

[3] *Cal. Hatfield House MSS.*, XV, 5, 119, 216, 283, 300-2. Gardiner, I, 141-3, 225-6. *The Copie of a Letter Written from Master T. M. neere Salisbury to Master H. A. At London* (1603). *Cal. St. P. Venetian, 1603-1607*, 68, 81, 86, 227. St. P. Domestic, 14 / 13 : 16. Winwood, II, 40. Ellis, *Original Letters*, 2nd series, III, 216-17.

[4] Gardiner, I, 265-72. St. P. Domestic, 14 / 19 : 94. Sir John Harington, *Nugae Antiquae*, I, 371-5. McIlwain, *Political Works of James I*, 281-9. *Cal. St. P. Venetian, 1603-1607*, 293-7, 308.

[5] References for most of the material in the remainder of this chapter will be found in my article, 'James I and His Literary Assistants', *Huntington Library Quarterly*, 8 : 35-57.

[6] The full titles are: (1) *Triplici nodo, triplex cuneus. Or An Apologie for the Oath of Allegiance* (1608); (2) *A Premonition to All Most Mightie Monarches, Kings, Free Princes, and States of Christendome* (1609); (3) *A Declaration Concerning the Proceedings with the States Generall, of the United Provinces of the Low Countreys, in the Cause of D. Conradus Vorstius* (1612); (4) *Declaration du sérénissime Roy Jacques Ier, Roy de la Grand' Bretagne et Irlande, défenseur de la Foy, pour le droit des Rois et indépendance de leurs couronnes, contre la harangue de l'illustrissime Cardinal du Perron, prononcée en la Chambre des Trois-Estats* (1615). This was anglicized under the title, *A Remonstrance for the Right of Kings, and the Independance of their Crownes.*

[7] The King to the Council, October 17th, the King to Salisbury (two letters), October 1608, Dunbar to Salisbury, March 12th, 1609, Hatfield House MSS.

[8] Andrewes had his difficulties. His work, said Boderie, was a web of Penelope, for as soon as he had completed a portion, the King found much that had to be rewritten. Boderie, IV, 271.

[9] Boderie, III, 131; IV, 302, 344, 374-7. *Cal. St. P. Venetian, 1607-1610*, 283. Winwood, III, 66-7. S. R. Gardiner (ed.), *The Fortescue Papers* (Camden Soc., 1871), 3-6. L. Pearsall Smith, *Life and Letters of Sir Henry Wotton*, I, 99-104, 463-8; II, 92.

[10] Fuller, *Church History*, III, 235-43.

[11] *Ibid.*, III, 252-6. *State Trials*, II, 731-2.

[1] Nichols, *Progresses*, III, 342. McIlwain, *Political Works of James I*, 62, 287-9, 302-16. *Basilikon Doron*, I, 61.

[2] St. P. Domestic, 14 / 8 : 93. James to the Council, December 7th, 1610, Hatfield House MSS.

[3] St. P. Domestic, 14 / 7 : 1, 27; 14 / 8 : 93. *Commons' Journals*, I, 156-71, 230. Winwood, II, 18-19.

[4] The chapel also contains Lady Margaret Douglas, the King's grandmother; Arabella Stuart; Mary Queen of Scots; Queen Anne; James's infant daughter Mary (1605-7); another daughter, Sophia (1607), who is buried in a tiny tomb shaped like a cradle, the sweetest and saddest of tombs; Prince Henry; Ludovick Stuart, Duke of Lennox, and his wife; George Villiers, Duke of Buckingham; and the King's daughter Elizabeth who died in 1662.

[5] *Letters to King James the Sixth* . . . (Maitland Club, no. 35), lv. St. P. Domestic, 14 / 7 : 38, 85; 14 / 8 : 2, 93; 14 / 9^A : 82. *Ibid.*, Gunpowder Plot Book, no. 17. Spedding, III, 77. *Commons' Journals*, I, 172-94. *Lords' Journals*, II, 287-8. McIlwain, *Political Works of James I*, 271-3, 291. *Cal. St. P. Venetian, 1603-1607*, 5, 201. S. T. Bindoff, 'The Stuarts and their Style', *E.H.R.*, 60 : 192-216.

NOTES

[6] See pamphlets by Sir William Cornwallis, John Thornborough, Bishop of Bristol, Sir John Hayward, David Home and Francis Bacon.

[7] Gardiner, I, 325-8. St. P. Domestic, 14 / 9ᴬ : 35; 14 / 10 : 40; 14 / 68 : 60. *Cal. Hatfield House MSS.*, XVI, 363. D. H. Willson (ed.), *Parliamentary Diary of Robert Bowyer* (Minneapolis, 1931), 203-82. McIlwain, *Political Works of James I*, 290-8. *Basilikon Doron*, I, 71.

[8] McIlwain, *Political Works of James I*, 310-12, 327-33. *E.H.R.*, 18 : 673. *Basilikon Doron*, I, 147.

[9] *State Trials*, II, 131-59. Wilbraham to the Council, October 11th, James to Salisbury, October 19th, Lake to Salisbury, November 24th, 25th, 27th, 30th, 1607, Hatfield House MSS.

[10] Spedding, IV, 127. St. P. Domestic, 14 / 61 : 99; 14 / 76 : 53. Usher, *Reconstruction*, II, 206-45. *E.H.R.*, 18 : 664-75. Coke, *Twelfth Report* (edition of 1777). Lake to Salisbury, October 13th, 18th, 1609, Hatfield House MSS.

[11] S. R. Gardiner (ed.), *Parliamentary Debates in 1610* (Camden Soc., 1862), x-xx. F. C. Dietz, *English Public Finance, 1558-1641* (N.Y., 1932), 100-26. McIlwain, *Political Works of James I*, 295. Gardiner, *History*, II, 64-5.

[12] *Cal. Hatfield House MSS.*, XV, 99; XVI, 394-7; XVII, 456-7. The King to the Council, October 19th, 1607, the Council to the King, 1609, Hatfield House MSS. St. P. Domestic, 14 / 48 : 102.

[13] McIlwain, *Political Works of James I*, 306-25. *Buccleuch MSS., Winwood Papers, H.M.C.*, I, 98. Winwood, III, 137.

[14] St. P. Domestic, 14 / 56 : 42. *Parliamentary Debates in 1610*, 34-6. *Letters of John Chamberlain*, I, 301. Further references will be found in D. H. Willson, *The Privy Councillors in the House of Commons* (Minneapolis, 1940), 125-9 and in *A.H.R.*, 45 : 281-4.

[15] Goodman, I, 39-45. St. P. Domestic, 14 / 65 : 79, 84, 86, 91; 14 / 66 : 54; 14 / 67 : 5, 35, 58, 90, 98, 100; 14 / 68 : 59, 60; 14 / 69 : 56, 59. *Journal of Sir Roger Wilbraham*, 105-6. Winwood, III, 235. A. Cecil, *A Life of Robert Cecil, First Earl of Salisbury* (1915), 333-45. *Letters of John Chamberlain*, I, 351.

CHAPTER XV

[1] Robert Aylett, *Peace and Her Foure Gardens* (1622). L'Himne de la Paix, Royal MSS., 19. A. 1. McIlwain, *Political Works of James I*, 270. King James, *Meditation upon the Lord's Prayer* (1619). John Hall, *The True Peace-Maker* (1624). John Dennison, *Beati Pacifici* (1620). Sir John Stradling, *Beati Pacifici: A Divine Poem* (1623). Phineas Hobson, *The Last Sermon Preached Before His Majesties Funerals* (1625). *Cal. St. P. Venetian, 1603-1607*, 21, 45. St. P. Domestic, 14 / 90 : 136.

[2] Francis Osborne, *A Miscellany of Sundry Essayes* (1659), 142-3. *Commonplace Book of Sir John Oglander*, 193. Anthony Weldon says the same thing in very similar words.

[3] *Cal. St. P. Venetian, 1603-1607*, 100. St. P. Domestic, 14 / 90 : 136.

[4] *Cal. St. P. Venetian, 1603-1607*, lxix-lxxvi, 20, 34, 40-1, 189-90, 359-61, 463-70. G. Edmundson, *Anglo-Dutch Rivalry during the First Half of the Seventeenth Century* (Oxford, 1911), 17, 32. Wilkins, *Concilia Magnae Britanniae*, IV, 405. Gardiner, I, 204-19, 340-354; II, 134-5. Winwood, II, 330. *Cal. Hatfield House MSS.*, XVIII, 61-3. L. Pearsall Smith, *Life and Letters of Sir Henry Wotton*, I, 77-85.

[5] Winwood, II, 329-35. Gardiner, II, 21-30, 88-101. Edmundson, 17-19. E. Lavisse, *Histoire de France* (Paris, 1911), VI, Pt. II, 119-22. *Cal. St. P. Venetian, 1607-1610*, 500.

[6] Sir Charles Cornwallis, *The life and death of Henry prince of Wales* (1641). Thomas Birch, *The Life of Henry Prince of Wales* (1760). Francis Bacon, 'Memorial of Henry, Prince of Wales', in *Collected Works* (1857-74. 14 vols.), VI, 327-9. Goodman, I, 250-1. *Cal. St. P. Venetian, 1610-1613*, 142, 450-4.

[7] R. S. Rait, *Five Stuart Princesses*, 49-69. S. C. Lomas (ed.), M. A. Everett-Green, *Elizabeth Electress Palatine and Queen of Bohemia* (1909). *Letters of John Chamberlain*, I, 380-2. Winwood, III, 403-4.

[8] S. R. Gardiner (ed.), F. Francisco de Jesus, *Narrative of the Spanish Marriage Treaty* (Camden Soc., 1869), 103-8. Gardiner, *History*, I, 220, 342-3; II, 22-4, 137-41, 152. Winwood, III, 291-2. St. P. Domestic, 14 / 70 : 11. R. F. Williams (ed.), Thomas Birch, *Court and Times of James I*, I, 191-2.

NOTES

[9] J. D. Mackie, *Cavalier and Puritan* (1930), 102. J. D. Mackie, *Negotiations between King James VI and I and Ferdinand I, Grand Duke of Tuscany*, 71-4. L. Pearsall Smith, *Life and Letters of Sir Henry Wotton*, I, 113-25. Gardiner, II, 137-57. St. P. Domestic, 14 / 71 : 1.

[10] St. P. Domestic, 14 / 71 : 31, 68. N. Moore, *History of the Study of Medicine in the British Isles*, 101. *Letters of John Chamberlain*, I, 390-4.

[11] Nichols, *Progresses*, II, 522-607. Dietz, 156. *Letters of John Chamberlain*, I, 392, 416-29. St. P. Domestic, 14 / 72 : 46.

[12] Halliwell, *Letters*, II, 118. St. P. Domestic, 14 / 71 : 5, 16.

CHAPTER XVI

[1] Sir John Harington, *Nugae Antiquae*, I, 366-71.

[2] Sir Isaac Wake, *Rex Platonicus* (Oxford, 1607). Anthony Nixon, *Oxford's Triumph: in the Royall Entertainement of his Majestie* (1605). C. E. Mallet, *A History of the University of Oxford* (N.Y., 1924-27. 3 vols.), II, 219-34. W. D. Macray, *Annals of the Bodleian Library* (Oxford, 1890), 31-4.

[3] J. B. Mullinger, *The University of Cambridge* (Cambridge, 1873-1911. 3 vols.), II, 515-53; III, 6-7. *Letters of John Chamberlain*, I, 440, 586-9; II, 308. Hacket, *Williams*, I, 21. Ellis, *Original Letters*, 1st series, III, 132. Macray, *Annals of the Bodleian*, 47n, 58-62. P. R. Lyall, *King James I and the Bodleian Library Catalogue of 1620* (Oxford, 1933). Mallet, II, 227-8.

[4] Vice-Chancellor and heads of colleges at Cambridge to Salisbury, July 13th, Fellows of Christ's College to Salisbury, August 10th, 1607, Hatfield House MSS. Mullinger, II, 455-8, 562-8, 635-6. Mallet, II, 246-7. St. P. Domestic, 14 / 10 : 68; 14 / 13 : 63; 14 / 66 : 25; 14 / 89 : 60, 61; 14 / 105 : 70.

[5] Goodman, I, 267-73. Grant dated March 3rd, 1615, Sign Manual, IV, no. 74, St. P. 39 / 4. Proclamation dated November 8th, 1615. *Reg. P.C. Scotland, 1613-1616*, cvii-cix, 521-2, 530-8, 599-600n.

[6] Alexander Morgan, *University of Edinburgh* (Edinburgh, 1937), 2-52. Sir Alexander Grant, *The Story of the University of Edinburgh*, I, 171-6.

[7] Sir Henry Ellis (ed.), *Original Letters of Eminent Literary Men* (Camden Soc., 1843), 99. Spelman's letter is quoted from a life of Camden in Edmund Gibson (ed.), William Camden, *Britannia* (1695). Ethel M. Portal, 'The Academ Roial of King James I', *Proceedings of the British Academy, 1915-16*, 189-208. St. P. Domestic, 14 / 131 : 70.

[8] D. Wilkins (ed.), John Selden, *Opera Omnia* (1726. 3 vols.), II, 1422-5. Gardiner, III, 253-7. Spedding, III, 88; VII, 120-2, 130. *Letters of John Chamberlain*, II, 339. Cecil Wall, *The London Apothecaries* (1932).

[9] *Witty Apophthegms by King James . . . Collected by Thomas Bayly* (1658). *Meditation upon the Lord's Prayer. The Peace-Maker.* L. Pearsall Smith, *Life and Letters of Sir Henry Wotton*, II, 497. *A.P.C., 1619-1621*, 165. Nichols, *Progresses*, III, 44. *King James, His Apophthegmes . . . By A. B., Gent.* (1643). Jerome E. Brooks, *Tobacco: Its History Illustrated by the Books . . . in the Library of George Arents, Jr.* (N.Y., 1937. 3 vols.), I, 56-63, 82-107, 401-543. *Cal. St. P. Domestic, 1619-1623*, 107, 158. *Reg. P.C. Scotland, 1613-1616*, 516-17; *1622-1625*, 28-30, 102-4.

[10] *Regales Aphorismi. Or a Royal Chain of Golden Sentences . . . delivered by King James* (1650). *Letters of John Chamberlain*, I, 470; II, 128, 286-94, 487. McIlwain, *Political Works of James I*, 290, 343-4. St. P. Domestic, 14 / 89 : 55; 14 / 90 : 150; 14 / 91 : 10. J. O. Halliwell (ed.), *Autobiography of Sir Simonds D'Ewes* (1845. 2 vols.), I, 170. *S.H.R.*, 29 : 140-2.

[11] *Letters of John Chamberlain*, I, 474, 509. *Cal. St. P. Venetian, 1607-1610*, 390. *The Peace-Maker.* Spedding, IV, 397-416; VI, 107-14. *Collectanea Curiosa* (Oxford, 1781. 2 vols.), I, 9-12. *A Publication of his Majesties Edict, and severe Censure against Private Combats and Combatants* (February 4th, 1614). St. P. Domestic, 14 / 75 : 13; 14 / 90 : 65, 81; 14 / 105 : 8.

[12] Wallace Notestein, *A History of Witchcraft in England from 1558 to 1718* (Washington, 1911).

[13] G. L. Kittredge, *Witchcraft in Old and New England* (Cambridge, Mass., 1929).

NOTES

[14] Halliwell, *Letters*, II, 102, 124-5. Goodman, I, 3. Arthur Wilson, 111-12. Lodge, *Illustrations of British History*, III, 154-5. *Cal. Hatfield House MSS.*, XVII, 136, 450-1. Kittredge, 300, 320-8. *Journal of Sir Roger Wilbraham*, 70. Notestein, 355. Fuller, *Church History*, III, 268-70. Francis Osborne, *A Miscellany of Sundry Essayes*, 4-9. *Letters of John Chamberlain*, II, 26.

CHAPTER XVII

[1] McIlwain, *Political Works of James I*, 301. *Reg. P. C. Scotland, 1604-1607*, xxv-xxvi. R. S. Rait, *The Parliaments of Scotland* (Glasgow, 1924). Parliament made at least a brave show, for the King decreed that Scottish peers wear robes of crimson cloth. He had at first prescribed crimson velvet, but altered his command upon discovery that in England velvet was reserved for peers of royal blood.

[2] *Reg. P. C. Scotland, 1604-1607*, lv, 13-14, 62, 471, 474, 480-6; *1607-1610*, 466n. D. Laing (ed.), *Original Letters Relating to the Ecclesiastical Affairs of Scotland* (Bannatyne Club, 1851. 2 vols.), I, 33. Calderwood, VI, 257, 264-91, 567-660; VII, 4, 37-62, 92-116, 150, 204-10. *Cal. Hatfield House MSS.*, XVII, 98. *Diary of James Melvill* (Wodrow Soc.), 653-83. P. Hume Brown, *History of Scotland* (Cambridge, 1900-9. 3 vols.), II, 240-72. R. S. Rait, *The Making of Scotland* (1911), 166-82. For an attempt by King James to reform the liturgy of the Kirk, see Gordon Donaldson, *The Making of the Scottish Prayer Book of 1637* (Edinburgh, 1954), 27-40.

[3] D. A. Chart (ed.), Sir Thomas Philips, *Londonderry and the London Companies, 1609-1629* (Belfast, 1928), 39. R. Bagwell, *Ireland under the Stuarts* (1909. 2 vols.), I, 146. Gardiner, I, 385-6. Cyril Falls, *The Birth of Ulster* (1936).

[4] *Cal. St. P. Ireland, 1603-1606*, 66, 218, 513, 574, 622, 749; *1606-1608*, lvii-lxxxix, 133, 268-77, 463; *1608-1610*, introduction. Gardiner, I, 388-401, 432-3; II, 284-303. Bagwell, I, 1-29, 78-138. D. A. Chart (ed.), Sir Thomas Philips, *Londonderry and the London Companies*, 16-17, 39-50. *Cal. Carew MSS., 1603-1624*, 42, 68-9, 265-7, 288-92.

[5] Charles Rogers, *Memorials of the Earl of Stirling*, I, 60-80. Alexander Brown, *Genesis of the United States* (1890. 2 vols.), I, 120-1. *His Majesties gracious Letter to the Earle of Southampton, . . . commanding the present setting up of Silke works and planting of Vines in Virginia* (1622). G. P. Insh, *Scottish Colonial Schemes, 1620-1686* (Glasgow, 1922), 40-112.

[6] J. A. Williamson, *The Ocean in English History* (Oxford, 1941), 43, 48, 105-6, 124-8. J. A. Williamson, *A Short History of British Expansion* (N.Y., 1931. 2 vols. in one), I, 163-83, 208-9.

CHAPTER XVIII

[1] *Letters of John Chamberlain*, I, 354-9, 402-9. Lake to Carleton, June 4th, 1612, St. P. Venetian Correspondence, 99 / 10. St. P. Domestic, 14 / 69 : 69, 70; 14 / 70 : 29, 34, 35, 36, 46, 54, 55, 60, 61; 14 / 75 : 40, 45.

[2] N. Moore, *History of the Study of Medicine in the British Isles*, 97-106, 162-76. St. P. Domestic, 14 / 74 : 52, 54, 55. Wake to Carleton, December 24th, 1612 / January 3rd, 1613, St. P. Venetian Correspondence, 99 / 11.

[3] Arthur Wilson, 54-5, 83. Sir John Harington, *Nugae Antiquae*, I, 390-7.

[4] *Mar and Kellie MSS., H.M.C.*, II, 41. Wake to Carleton, December 17th/27th, 1612, St. P. Venetian Correspondence, 99 / 11. St. P. Domestic, 14 / 71 : 6. *Letters of John Chamberlain*, I, 401-4. Halliwell, *Letters*, II, 126-7.

[5] *State Trials*, II, 794-820, 860-2.

[6] *Letters of John Chamberlain*, I, 443-9, 466, 469. Goodman, I, 215-16. St. P. Domestic, 14 / 72 : 146; 14 / 82 : 47. *Mar and Kellie MSS., H.M.C.*, II, 51-2. Nichols, *Progresses*, II, 672.

[7] *Letters of John Chamberlain*, I, 480-500, 515. Nichols, *Progresses*, II, 704-54. *Mar and Kellie MSS., H.M.C.*, II, 56. Account of the English Court, 1613, St. P. Spanish, 94 / 20. Gardiner, II, 199-201, 227-8. Dietz, 149-58.

[8] References will be found in *A.H.R.*, 45 : 284-90 and in D. H. Willson, *Privy Councillors in the House of Commons*, 130-46.

[9] Francisco de Jesus, *Narrative of the Spanish Marriage Treaty* (Camden Soc.), 286-8.

NOTES

[10] *Letters of John Chamberlain*, I, 541, 548, 553, 559, 583, 590. R. F. Williams (ed.), Thomas Birch, *Court and Times of James I*, I, 335-6. St. P. Domestic, 14 / 74 : 50; 14 / 77 : 59, 70; 14 / 78 : 58. Nichols, *Progresses*, III, 10-26.

[11] Halliwell, *Letters*, II, 126-33. John Rushworth (ed.), *Historical Collections* (1721-22. 8 vols.), I, 456-7. St. P. Domestic, 14 / 81 : 86; 14 / 82 : 75, 80, 91. *Archaeologia*, XLI, 168-9.

[12] A. Weldon in Scott, *Secret History*, I, 411-12, 424. *Archaeologia*, XLI, 75-92, 106. Halliwell, *Letters*, II, 134-7. St. P. Domestic, 14 / 87 : 29, 34, 40. *Letters of John Chamberlain*, II, 4-5.

CHAPTER XIX

[1] *Cal. St. P. Venetian, 1613-1615*, 15, 88, 172-3, 200.

[2] G. Edmundson, *Anglo-Dutch Rivalry during the First Half of the Seventeenth Century*, 34-57.

[3] James suggested a league of Venice, Savoy, the Princes of Germany, Holland and himself. *Cal. St. P. Venetian, 1615-1617*, 398-9.

[4] Julian S. Corbett, *England in the Mediterranean* (1904. 2 vols.), I, 1-43.

[5] Arthur Wilson, 145. Thomas Fuller, *Church History*, III, 328. *Cal. St. P. Venetian, 1617-1619*, 398-9; *1619-1621*, 145, 150. Francisco de Jesus, *Narrative of the Spanish Marriage Treaty* (Camden Soc.), 287-8, 293, 306.

[6] *Ibid.*, 15, 111-31, 286-93, 307-10. Gardiner, II, 252-5, 325-7. *Archaeologia*, XLI, 154-65. *A.H.R.*, 45 : 290-2.

[7] V. T. Harlow, *Ralegh's Last Voyage* (1932). Gardiner, II, 370-82; III, 39-58, 112n. William Stebbing, *Sir Walter Ralegh* (Oxford, 1899). Spedding, VI, 384-413.

[8] Spedding, VI, 146-9. The Spanish government rejected other points raised by the theologians: that Charles promise to be converted, that the English Catholics have complete freedom of worship, that Catholic professors teach at the universities. Francisco de Jesus, *Narrative of the Spanish Marriage Treaty* (Camden Soc.), 138-49, 298-313. Gardiner, III, 38-9, 102-3.

[9] Harlow, 54-5, 86-7.

[10] Gondomar to Philip III, July 15th, 1618, Spanish Trans., 12 / 39.

[11] Spedding, VI, 363-413. Gardiner. Stebbing. Harlow, 42-99.

CHAPTER XX

[1] N. Moore, *History of the Study of Medicine in the British Isles*, 97-106, 162-76. *Letters of John Chamberlain*, II, 22, 133, 146, 149, 155, 187. St. P. Domestic, 14 / 86 : 129; 14 / 87 : 55; 14 / 88 : 43, 89; 14 / 93 : 25; 14 / 97 : 10. Halliwell, *Letters*, II, 152-3. Goodman, I, 409-10. *Cal. St. P. Venetian, 1617-1619*, 47, 72, 79, 260, 314-15, 389-90, 406, 420. A. Weldon in Scott, *Secret History*, II, 1-5. Lodge, *Illustrations of British History*, III, 137-8.

[2] Spedding, V, 105-7, 236, 357-69. *State Trials*, II, 869-80. *Basilikon Doron*, I, 139-41, 147-9. Halliwell, *Letters*, II, 135. St. P. Domestic, 14 / 89 : 15; 14 / 90 : 24. McIlwain, *Political Works of James I*, 326-45. *Letters of John Chamberlain*, II, 6-7.

[3] Nichols, *Progresses*, III, 176-80. *Letters of John Chamberlain*, II, 10, 14, 33. St. P. Domestic, 14 / 87 : 74; 14 / 88 : 61.

[4] *Commonplace Book of Sir John Oglander*, 41. Gardiner, III, 98, 350. Arthur Wilson, 105. *Cal. St. P. Venetian, 1617-1619*, 113. Hacket, *Williams*, I, 39-40, 120. J. O. Halliwell (ed.), *Autobiography of Sir Simonds D'Ewes* (1845. 2 vols.), I, 166. Sir Henry Wotton, *Reliquiae Wottonianiae* (1654), 77-8. St. P. Domestic, 14 / 86 : 132; 14 / 88 : 57; 14 / 90 : 11, 16, 81, 135. *Letters of the Duke and Duchess of Buckingham, chiefly Addressed to King James I of England* (Edinburgh, 1834), 2-37. P. Yorke, Earl of Hardwicke (ed.), *Misc. State Papers* (1778. 2 vols.), I, 433, 451.

[5] St. P. Domestic, 14 / 93 : 114, 123; 14 / 94 : 11, 13, 15, 29. *Letters of John Chamberlain*, II, 52-8, 64, 88-118. Spedding, VI, 236-53.

[6] Dietz, 162-8. St. P. Domestic, 14 / 88 : 9, 14, 101; 14 / 89 : 33.

[7] *Mar and Kellie MSS.*, *H.M.C.*, II, 75. St. P. Domestic, 14 / 89 : 68; 14 / 90 : 20,

NOTES

36, 55, 135, 149, 150; 14 / 91 : 10, 35, 43, 46, 47; 14 / 93 : 25, 69. Nichols, *Progresses*, III, 255-300.

[8] Hon. G. A. Sinclair, 'The Scottish Progress of James VI', *S.H.R.*, 10 : 21-8. David Masson, *Drummond of Hawthornden* (1873), 53-60. Nichols, *Progresses*, III, 300-6, 326. *Book of the Old Edinburgh Club*, I, 100-1; II, 235. Calderwood, VII, 244-76. Spottiswoode, III, 240. John Adamson, *The Muses Welcome to the High and Mighty Prince James at His Majesties Happy Returne to his Olde and Native Kingdome of Scotland* (Edinburgh, 1618).

[9] St. P. Domestic, 14 / 93 : 99; 14 / 96 : 91, 93. Halliwell, *Letters*, II, 146-8. *D.N.B.* under Cranfield. Dietz, 168-81. Goodman, I, 310. *Letters of John Chamberlain*, II, 121, 149-50.

[10] St. P. Domestic, 14 / 95 : 3, 6; 14 / 96 : 7, 24, 38; 14 / 105 : 40, 60, 84. Goodman, I, 194, 280-90; II, 180-1. Richard Wingfield to Carleton, November 12th, 1619, St. P. Holland, 84 / 93. Halliwell, *Letters*, II, 149. Gardiner, III, 207. Sir Henry Wotton, *Reliquiae Wottonianiae*, 21.

CHAPTER XXI

[1] St. P. Domestic, 14 / 109 : 46, 60, 144, 157. *Letters of John Chamberlain*, II, 121, 140. A. W. Harrison, *The Beginnings of Arminianism to the Synod of Dort* (1926), 178-202 and *passim*. Hacket, *Williams*, I, 63-4.

[2] L. A. Govett, *The King's Book of Sports* (1890). *Basilikon Doron*, I, 93-5. *Cal. St. P. Domestic, 1623-1625*, 260.

[3] *A Meditation upon the Lord's Prayer, Written by the King's Majestie, For the Benefit of All his Subjects, Especially of Such as Follow the Court* (1619). *Basilikon Doron*, I, 39-41. 'Here is now a new sect called Thrascists, so named from their leader, Thrasco, who is now in prison here in London. Their opinions made his Majesty exceeding merry on Sunday at dinner and were almost the sole subject of his discourse. Amongst other things which they foolishly maintain, they hold it absolutely unlawful to eat any swine's flesh or black puddings.' St. P. Domestic, 14 / 96 : 38.

[4] *A Meditation upon the 27, 28, 29 Verses of Chapter 27 of St. Mathew, or a Paterne for a King's Inauguration* (1620).

[5] St. P. Domestic, 14 / 105 : 1, 8; 14 / 107 : 7, 9, 37, 38. *Letters of John Chamberlain*, II, 170, 219-20. A. Weldon in Scott, *Secret History*, II, 5-6. Goodman, I, 168.

[6] A comet was visible at the time.

[7] John Williams, *Great Britain's Salamon* (1625). *Letters of John Chamberlain*, II, 220-49. N. Moore, *History of the Study of Medicine in the British Isles*, 101. St. P. Domestic, 14 / 107 : 55, 60; 14 / 108 : 15, 16, 50, 70, 72; 14 / 109 : 19, 41, 76, 92. *Diary of Lady Anne Clifford*, 92.

[8] Hacket, *Williams*, I, 41-4. Halliwell, *Letters*, II, 156.

[9] *Cal. St. P. Venetian, 1617-1619*, 80, 250-1; *1619-1621*, 111, 151, 238, 524. Wake to Carleton, December 2nd, 1612, St. P. Venetian Correspondence, 99 / 11. St. P. Domestic, 14 / 80 : 27; 14 / 86 : 95; 14 / 87 : 40; 14 / 89 : 15; 14 / 91 : 48. R. F. Williams (ed.), Thomas Birch, *Court and Times of James I*, II, 78-9. Gardiner, III, 187. King James, *Meditation upon . . . St. Mathew. Letters of Buckingham* (Edinburgh, 1834), 12-13. Ellis, *Original Letters*, 1st series, III, 102-4.

[10] Edward McCabe, 'England's Foreign Policy in 1619', *Mitteilunger des Instituts für Österreichische Geschichtsforschung*, 58 : 457-77. S. R. Gardiner (ed.), *Letters and Other Documents Illustrating the Relations between England and Germany* (Camden Soc., 1865), I, 1-31. Gardiner, *History*, III, 284-307.

[11] *Cabala, Mysteries of State* (1654), 169-70. St. P. Domestic, 14 / 110 : 59, 81, 83; 14 / 112 : 10, 35, 93. Gardiner, *Letters and Documents*, I, 23-40; II, 23-6, 41, 58, 157-60, 188. *Cal. St. P. Venetian, 1619-1621*, 53, 148-9, 201, 377, 554. Tillières to Puisieux, July 3rd, 1620, January 6th, 1622, Paris Trans., 3 / 54; 3 / 56. R. F. Williams (ed.), Thomas Birch, *Court and Times of James I*, II, 188-92.

[12] Quoted in Gardiner, III, 336-8.

[13] The Turks were 'naturally detested by this King' who always considered war against them justifiable. *Cal. St. P. Venetian, 1619-1621*, 239, 308. Tillières to Puisieux, June 5th, 1620, Paris Trans., 3 / 54. Gardiner, III, 350.

[14] *Letters of John Chamberlain*, II, 317-18. Gardiner, III, 363-73. *Cal. St. P. Venetian, 1619-1621*, 327, 363, 429-40, 496. Tillières to Puisieux, March 9th, 1621, Paris Trans., 3 / 54. *A.H.R.*, 45 : 292-4.

[15] St. P. Domestic, 14 / 119 : 47. *Letters of John Chamberlain*, II, 334, 338.

[16] *Cal. St. P. Venetian, 1621-1623*, 68. 'The extravagance and general irresolution of this country and especially of the King give me a very great pain.' Tillières to Puisieux, June 24th, 1621, Paris Trans., 3 / 55.

[17] *Cal. St. P. Venetian, 1621-1623*, 171. *Letters of John Chamberlain*, II, 406-13. St. P. Domestic, 14 / 123 : 135.

[18] *A.H.R.*, 45 : 292-97. Gardiner, IV, 265-8. *Mar and Kellie MSS., H.M.C.*, II, 111. St. P. Domestic, 14 / 124 : 83.

[19] Ellis, *Original Letters*, 1st series, III, 116-17. St. P. Domestic, 14 / 127 : 26. 'If he had not been rescued promptly he would have drowned. All ill effect that he has had of it has been to put much water into his wine.' Tillières to Puisieux, January 24th, 1622, Paris Trans., 3 / 56.

Cal. St. P. Venetian, 1621-1623, 295, 444, 449, 460. Ellis, *Original Letters*, 1st series, III, 119. *Letters of Buckingham* (Edinburgh, 1834). *Hardwicke State Papers*, I, 451, 457.

[2] A second daughter, Jacobina, was born in 1623 but died in infancy. Occasionally the King took a fancy to other ladies at court. One was Cecilia, the handsome daughter of Sir John Croft. James made much of her in a playful way as his valentine. He also liked Mademoiselle St. Luc, a niece of Tillières. When she returned to France in 1623, the King shed tears and asserted that if she would marry and stay in England he would make her husband an earl. *Cal. St. P. Venetian, 1621-1623*, 442. Halliwell, *Letters*, II, 150-7. St. P. Domestic, 14 / 128 : 59, 97. *Letters of John Chamberlain*, II, 429, 477.

[3] Gardiner, IV, 279-82. Peter Heylyn, *Cyprianus Anglicus* (1671), 95-6. Tillières to Puisieux, June 5th, 1622, Paris Trans., 3 / 56.

[4] Dietz, 191-201. Goodman, I, 307-29; II, 202-18. *Cal. St. P. Venetian, 1621-1623*, 572. In February 1623, the King wrote some verses enlarging upon the glory of kings and upon the folly of those who criticized them. *S.H.R.*, 29 : 134-40.

[5] Gardiner, IV, 299-411, *passim. Cabala*, 376.

[6] Gardiner, V, 3-10.

[7] Halliwell, *Letters*, II, 157-222. Goodman, II, 290-96. *Letters of John Chamberlain*, II, 484-6, 516. *Cal. St. P. Domestic, 1619-1623*, 502-3, 529-30, 552. *Cal. St. P. Venetian, 1621-1623*, 581-4, 635; *1623-1625*, 22-7, 50-6, 78. Tillières to Puisieux, March 5th, 1623, Paris Trans., 3 / 57. Hacket, *Williams*, I, 116-17, 141-3, 165. Gardiner, V, 20-114. Ellis, *Original Letters*, 1st series, III, 154-7. Nichols, *Progresses*, IV, 907-31.

[8] St. P. Domestic, 14 / 149 : 67; 14 / 153 : 21, 22, 31, 81; 14 / 154: 10, 71; 14 / 159 : 7. Conway to Carleton, October 10th, 1623, St. P. Holland, 84 / 114. *Cal. St. P. Venetian, 1623-1625*, 174, 201, 208-10, 216, 308. Tillières to Puisieux, December 29th, 1623, Paris Trans., 3 / 57.

[9] Hacket asserts that George Herbert, who held the chair of rhetoric at Cambridge, ignored the orations of the ancients but dwelt upon the speeches of King James. Hacket, *Williams*, I, 175. Mullinger, II, 553. Fuller, *Church History*, III, 328.

[10] W. D. Macray (ed.), Clarendon, *History of the Rebellion* (Oxford, 1888. 6 vols.), I, 28.

[11] On the day the Parliament was prorogued the King sat at dinner attended by Bishops Andrewes and Neile. He asked them whether he could take his subjects' money without parliamentary sanction. Neile assented at once, but Andrewes replied, 'Sir, I think it is lawful for you to take my brother Neile's money, for he offers it.' The company was pleased but the King was not. Shortly after, a certain lord entered the apartment, and James called out, 'My lord, they say you lie with my Lady ———.' 'No, Sir,' said his lordship in confusion, 'but I like her company because she has so much wit.' 'Why, then,' said the King pointedly, 'do you not lie with my lord of Winchester [Andrewes] there?' Nichols, *Progresses*, IV, 977.

NOTES

[12] Gardiner, V, 206-8. *Cabala*, 90-3, 217-22. Hacket, *Williams*, I, 195-8. Halliwell, *Letters*, II, 232-6.

[13] George Englishman's tract was translated and printed in London in 1642 under the title, *The Fore-runner of Revenge*.

[14] *Letters of John Chamberlain*, II, 606-9, 616. Lettre d'un anonyme sur la mort du Roi d'Angleterre, Paris Trans., 3 / 61. *Cal. St. P. Venetian, 1623-1625*, 625-7. *Commonplace Book of Sir John Oglander*, 197. Nichols, *Progresses*, IV, 1028-52. John Williams, *Great Britain's Salamon*. Hacket, *Williams*, I, 222-23. R. F. Williams (ed.), Thomas Birch, *Court and Times of Charles I* (1848. 2 vols.), I, 1-5.

INDEX

INDEX

INDEX

Camden, William, 297-8
Campbell, Archibald, seventh Earl of Argyll, defeated at Glenlivet, 114
Campbell, Colin, sixth Earl of Argyll, seizes James, 29-31; joins Lennox, 33
Campbell (b. Stewart), Janet, Countess of Argyll, 17
Canongate, 31, 106, 124, 391
Canterbury, Dean of, 161; Chapter at, 211; prebend at, 241; Archbishops of, 176; *see* Whitgift, John; Bancroft, Richard; Abbot, George
Carberry Hill, 19
Carew, Sir George, 333-4
Carew, Richard, antiquarian, 296-7
Carey, Henry, first Lord Hunsdon, 159
Carey, Sir Robert, 159-60, 162
Carleton, Sir Dudley, 192, 433
Carleton, George, Bishop of Llandaff and Chichester, 199, 212, 399-400
Carlisle, 119-20, 393
Caroni River, 369
Carr (b. Howard), Frances, Countess of Somerset, divorce from Essex, 198, 213, 338-41; poisons Overbury, 342-3; marries Somerset, 343; trial of, 353, 356
Carr, Robert, Viscount Rochester, Earl of Somerset, 281, 369, 380; appearance and character, 336-7; rise of, 268, 334-8; marriage of, 338-44; Parliament, 267, 347-8; Lord Chamberlain, 349; fall of, 350-6
Cartwright, Thomas, Puritan, 109
Casaubon, Isaac, scholar, 230-1, 239-40
Castiglione, Baldassare, 22
Castile, 179-80
Castle Douglas, 391
Caterina, Infanta of Tuscany, 284
Catesby, Robert, plotter, 223
Catherine de Bourbon, Princess of Navarre, 85-6
Catherine de Medici, 14, 80
Catholic League, 412
Catholics, Roman, and Catholicism,
  Scotland: 14, 18, 24, 30, 55, 122; plottings by Catholic nobles, 41, 81, 98-103, 106-8, 110-17, 122-3, 125;
  England: James woos prior to 1603, 148-9, 197; opinion of Church of England, 198-9; attitude of James in 1603, 217-18; Watson Plot, 218-19; increase in numbers, 222; oath of allegiance, 227-8; pamphlet war, 228-42; James denounces, 402; James fears, 364, 367, 411; Parliament demands severity towards, 421; terms of Spanish marriage treaty regarding, 365-6, 372, 429, 435-6, 438-9, 460; terms of other marriage

treaties, 284-5, 444; *see* Gunpowder Plot; Jesuits; Papacy; Popes; Spain; *Ireland*: 326-9, 367; Catholic League, 412
Cautionary Towns, 275-6, 349, 389
Cecil (b. Lake), Anne, Lady Roos, 395-7
Cecil, Sir Edward, 279
Cecil (b. Drury), Frances, Countess of Exeter, 396-7
Cecil, John, priest, 144
Cecil, Robert, Earl of Salisbury, Secretary, Master of the Wards, Lord Treasurer, 164, 180-1, 184-5, 190, 193, 195, 209, 222, 233-4, 240, 254, 257, 259, 278, 283, 315; rivalry with Essex, 149-50; secret correspondence, 153-8; position in 1603, 159, 162-3, 168, 175-8; 'little beagle' letters, 186-9; Gunpowder Plot, 224-5; Ralegh appeals to, 369; reproved by James, 235; Lord Treasurer, 261-3; Parliament, 247-8, 264-7, 344; James turns against, 267-9, 346, 349; death of, 269-70, 333, 357; hated by Northampton, 178, 335
Cecil, Thomas, Lord Burghley, Earl of Exeter, 163, 175, 383, 396
Cecil, William, second Earl of Salisbury, 339, 383
Cecil, William, Lord Roos, 395-6
Cecils, the, 140, 287
Chamberlain, John, news writer, quoted *passim*
Chancery, 247; Court of, 381
Charles Emmanuel, Duke of Savoy, 182, 284, 361-2
Charles, Duke of York, Prince of Wales, 122, 176-7, 192, 224, 227, 290, 292, 297, 343, 361, 372, 427, 447, 460; warned that the Crown brings cares, 402; councillors recommended to, 404; character and appearance, 365, 406-7; early relations with James, 406-8; for war in Bohemia, 410; advises dissolution of Parliament, 423; journey to Madrid, 430-40; old age and death of James, 440-4, 446; King, 195, 216
Charterhouse, 164
Chatham, shipyards at, 280
Chelsea, college proposed in, 239, 296
Cheshire, 393
Chester, Dean of, 198, 214; Bishop of, 401
Chichester, Bishops of, 198-9
Chichester, Sir Arthur, Lord Deputy in Ireland, 323-8
Chisholm, William, Bishop of Dunblane and Vaison, 80, 146
Christ Church, Oxford, 289

INDEX

INDEX

473

INDEX

474

INDEX

Oslo, 88, 90-1
Ostend, 275
Overbury, Sir Thomas, 335, 338, 341-3, 353
Owen, John, 367
Oxford, city, 179; University, 214-15, 383; Millenary Petition, 202; relations of James with, 172, 289-90, 292-4; colleges in, 204, 238, 289-94

PADDY, DR. WILLIAM, 289
Palatinate, 393, 413-21, 428-39, 442-3; *see* Frederick V
Pallavicino, Edward, 356
Pale, the English, 323
Papacy, James offers a compromise to, 219-21; pamphlet war, 228-42; quarrel with Venice, 277
Paraeus, David, 293
Paris Garden, 182
Parker, William, Lord Monteagle, 224, 226
Parliament, England, 139, 165-6, 170, 176, 178, 183, 189, 223-7, 271, 273, 297, 299, 304, 308, 333, 336, 367, 372, 411, 428, 436, 438, 440; background of quarrel with King James, 243-6, 261; (1604-11), 247-57, 263-7; (1614), 344-7, 365; (1621), 416-23; (1624), 442-4, 462; Scotland, 50, 108-9, 125-7, 139, 243, 253, 313-14, 318-20, 392, 459; Ireland, 327-9
Parma, 358
Parry, Sir Thomas, 340-1, 347
Parsons, Robert, Jesuit, 140, 221, 233-4, 236
Patents, 418
Paul V, Pope, 228, 231, 233, 277; refuses sanction to marriage treaties, 284, 365-6, 368; places *Basilikon Doron* on Index, 456
Paul, Seigneur, envoy from Guise to Scotland, 42
Paulus, Dr., 92
Peace-Maker, The, 271
Peacham, Edmund, 380-1
Pelagius, British monk, 399
Pembroke, Earl of, *see* Herbert, William
Penry, John, Puritan, 109
Percy, Henry, Earl of Northumberland, 148, 155, 157, 175, 388
Percy, Lucy, afterwards Viscountess Doncaster, 388-9
Percy, Thomas, plotter, 223-4
Perron, Cardinal du, 240-1
Perth, 42, 102; General Assemblies at, 124-5, 320; Gowrie Plot, 126-30, 172
Perthshire, 392
Peru, 369

Peterborough, 268, 287
Petowe, Henry, poet, 169, 454
Pett, Phineas, shipwright, 280, 286
Philip II, King of Spain, 76, 111, 143; policy and plots in Scotland, 30, 40-1, 80-1, 98-9, 101-3, 110-12, 114; James appeals to, 51; James fears, 52, 80-1; the enterprise against England, 52, 80-3; claims English throne, 80, 140; James's diplomacy with, 143-4, 148; Spain cannot prevent James's accession, 157
Philip III, King of Spain, 238, 278, 283-4, 348, 363-5, 368, 370, 372, 374, 409, 413, 415; *see* Spain
Philip IV, King of Spain, 182; *see* Spain
Physicians, 299; College of, 303
Pigott, Sir Christopher, 255
Pirates, 274, 362
Plague, 164
Plymouth, 374
Pocahontas, American Indian Princess, 296
Poland, 191, 358
Pont, Robert, 254
Popes, *see* Gregory XIII, Sixtus V, Clement VIII, Paul V, Gregory XV
Porter, Endymion, 430-1
Portsmouth, 440
Portugal, 278, 332, 360
Prague, 408, 410, 416
Psalms, 49, 62-3, 215-16
Puritans, 172, 174, 178-9, 183, 188-9, 341, 348, 439, 455; James's dislike of, 135, 200, 219, 223, 402, 452; James offers hopes to, 109, 135-6, 149-50, 197, 203; Millenary Petition, 199-202; James equates with Presbyterians, 202-3; Hampton Court Conference, 202-9; forced to conform, 209-10, 249; at Cambridge University, 290-1; *Declaration of Sports*, 400-1; said to render Buckingham Spanish, 416
Purveyance, 249, 264
Puteanus, Erycius, 239

QUIN, WALTER, poet, 141

RAINOLDS, JOHN, Puritan, Hampton Court Conference, 204-8; King James Version, 213, 215
Ralegh, George, 373
Ralegh, Sir Walter, 300, 359, 362, 380; James warned against, 157; hated by Northampton, 178; trial of, 222; Prince Henry admires, 280; voyage to Orinoco, 368-74; execution of, 358, 374-7, 410
Ralegh, Walter, 373

INDEX

Rammekens, 275

Ramsey, John, Earl of Holderness, 183, 438; Gowrie Plot, 128-9; profits greatly in England, 176

Randolph, Thomas, diplomat, 34-5, 71-3, 450

Ratisbon, 429

Rawlinson, John, royal chaplain, sermon by, 405

Reformation, 340-1; in Scotland, 14-15; James's opinion of, 37-8, 209

Reid, Thomas, 292

Remington, John, physician, 446

Revelation, Book of, 317, 410; James's interest in, 81-2, 298, 382, 401

Rhine, 278, 420

Richmond, 179, 184

Rizzio, David, 16, 50

Roanoke Island, 300

Robert, Prince, son of James, 452

Rochester, city, 286; Bishop of, 341; Viscount, see Carr, Robert

Rome, 41, 85, 198, 220, 222, 227, 324

Roos, Lord, see Cecil, William

Ross, James appoints a bishop of, 126

Rowlands, Samuel, 169

Roxburgh, Earl of, see Ker, Robert

Royston, 179, 184-5, 209, 232, 234, 266, 343, 379, 404, 420, 440, 445

Rubens, Peter Paul, 447

Rudolph II, Emperor, 238, 279

Rufford, 349

Ruggle, George, 291

Russell, Francis, Earl of Bedford, 17-18, 56

Russell, Sir Francis, 56

Russia, 168, 358, 393

Ruthven, Alexander, Master of, in Gowrie Plot, 126-30, 452

Ruthven, Beatrix, 127, 130

Ruthven Castle, 42

Ruthven, John, third Earl of Gowrie, in Gowrie Plot, 126-30

Ruthven, Patrick, Lord, murders Rizzio, 16, 127

Ruthven, Patrick, brother of third Earl of Gowrie, 452

Ruthven Raid, 44-8

Ruthven, William, first Earl of Gowrie, 127-9; in Ruthven Raid, 42; executed, 48; widow of, 48

Ruthven, William, brother of third Earl of Gowrie, 452

Rutland, Earls of, see Manners

SACKVILLE, SIR EDWARD, 306

Sackville, Thomas, first Earl of Dorset, Lord Treasurer, 175, 289; financial policy of, 261-2; widow of, 189

St. Andrews, 46, 56, 71, 120, 123, 320, 392; Archbishops of, 17, 38, 46, 49-50; Castle, 46; University, 295

St. Augustine, 220

St. Bernard, 220

St. David's, Bishop of, 400

St. James's Palace, 281, 434, 444; Park, 183

St. John of Bletsoe, Lord Oliver, 172

St. John's College, Oxford, 293

St. Luc, Mademoiselle, 462

St. Mary's Church, Cambridge, 294; Oxford, 293

St. Matthew, James's meditation upon a passage in, 385, 402-3, 461

St. Patrick, 324

Salisbury, 415; Bishop of, 199, 212; Dean of, 200, 253; Earl of, see Cecil, Robert

Sampson, Agnes, witch, 103

Sandys, Sir Edwin, 255, 331

Santa Fé, 369

San Thomé, 369-75

Sarmiento de Acuña, Diego, Count Gondomar, 357, 359, 367, 387, 425; comments on Somerset, 343, 353; character and policy of, 362-5; interviews with James, 368, 413-14; Ralegh, 370, 374-5; analysis of James's motives, 410; plot against the Dutch, 414; great influence of, 415-16; works against Parliament, 348, 416, 419, 422-3; journey of Charles to Madrid, 430-2

Savile, Sir Henry, 237-8

Savoy, 13, 182, 358, 361-2, 460; marriage negotiations with, 283-4

Saxe-Weimar, Duke of, 181, 184

Saxony, 358, 409

Scarnafissi, Antonio, Count of, ambassador, 362

Scioppius, G., attacks James, 238-9

Scotland, problem of the nobles in, 96-115, 134, 321; government of after 1603, 313-21; Roman law, 257, 264; God and the King, 295; tobacco, 303; colonial schemes, 331-2; Scots in England, 175-6, 211, 255, 293; Prayer Book of 1637, 216

Scott of Buccleuch, Sir Walter, first Lord Scott of Buccleuch, 116, 119-20

Second Book of Discipline, 38

Selden, John, 298

Semple, Col., Catholic agent, 81, 84

Semple, Robert, Lord, 144

Session, Court of, 98, 121, 124

Seton, 391

Seton, Alexander, Lord Urquhart, Earl of Dunfermline, Lord Chancellor of Scotland, 121, 391

Seton, George, Earl of Winton, 391

INDEX

INDEX

Date Due